P9-DWT-043

The Iran-Iraq War

THE IRAN-IRAQ WAR

PIERRE RAZOUX

Translated by Nicholas Elliott

The Belknap Press of Harvard University Press
Cambridge, Massachusetts
London, England
2015

Originally published as *La Guerre Iran-Irak, 1980–1988: Première guerre du Golfe*
Copyright © Perrin, un département d'Edi8, 2013

Library of Congress Cataloging-in-Publication Data
Razoux, Pierre.
 [Guerre Iran-Irak, 1980–1988. English]
 The Iran-Iraq war / Pierre Razoux ; translated by Nicholas Elliott.
  pages cm
 Originally published: La Guerre Iran-Irak, 1980–1988: Première guerre du Golfe.
Perrin, un departement d'Edi8, 2013.
 Includes bibliographical references and index.
 ISBN 978-0-674-08863-4 (alk. paper)
 1. Iran-Iraq War, 1980–1988. 2. Geopolitics—Middle East. 3. Geopolitics—
Persian Gulf Region. I. Elliott, Nicholas, translator. II. Title.
 DS318.85.R38613 2015
 955.05'42—dc23

                                                          2015016051

Book design by Dean Bornstein

For André Martel and Jacques Frémeaux,
who know how much I owe them
~

Every war is easily begun but ended with extreme difficulty.
—Sallust

. . .

War is a godsend.
—Ayatollah Khomeini

CONTENTS

MAPS

Map Key

Size of military units:
XXX: Corps
XX: Division
X: Brigade
III: Regiment
II: Battalion

Type of Military Units:

AD: Armored Division
Airb. B: Airborne Brigade
Airb. D: Airborne Division
Art. D: Artillery Division
ED: Engineer Division
IB: Infantry Brigade
ID: Infantry Division
INF: Infantry troops
IRGC: Iranian Revolutionary Guards Corps
MB: Mechanized Brigade
MD: Mechanized Division
Pasd: Pasdaran = IRGC
RG: (Iraqi) Republican Guard
SF: Special Forces
SFB: Special Forces Brigade
SFD: Special Forces Division

PREFACE

On May 1, 2003, George W. Bush gave his "Mission accomplished" speech on board the aircraft carrier *Abraham Lincoln*. Was he aware that he had just offered the Iranian Islamic regime, one of his fiercest enemies, the victory over Iraq that it had dreamed of since 1980? By pulverizing the Iraqi army in a few weeks and dismantling Saddam Hussein's Ba'athist regime, the forty-third president of the United States had just accomplished what the mullahs had failed to do over the course of a brutal war against Baghdad (September 1980–August 1988). By doing so, George W. Bush created a profound upheaval in the Gulf region's geopolitical balance, a balance his father had striven to maintain as vice president, then president of the United States. The elder Bush had not hesitated to forge ties with Saddam Hussein, judging that the Iraqi dictator was the best shield against the radical Shiite revolutionary expansionism preached by the Ayatollah Khomeini. His decision to spare Saddam Hussein following his invasion of Kuwait was made in pursuit of the strategy to contain Iran. Neoconservative ideology would later replace realpolitik in an attempt to create a new Middle East.

By pulling out of Iraq in December 2011 after more than eight years of military occupation, the United States allowed Iran to reap all the desired benefits from the new geopolitical order. Ali Khamenei, Akbar Hashemi Rafsanjani, Mohammad Khatami, and Hassan Rouhani must have enjoyed a moment of profound satisfaction when they realized that the American administration had done their work for them: it had put in place an Iraqi state that was weak, divided, and dominated by the Shiite community, three major objectives that the Iranian regime had vainly attempted to accomplish. Twenty-three years after its defeat, the Islamic Republic of Iran could now celebrate its victory.

The Iran-Iraq War was a turning point in the history of the Middle East. One cannot understand the contemporary situation in the Gulf, ranging from Iran's nuclear ambitions to the Iraqi and Iranian political crises, without a firm grasp of the complex mechanisms, age-old hatreds, relentless power struggles, and persistent frustrations and fears directly stemming from this merciless war, which has left a lasting impression on the collective imaginations of people in the Gulf and in the West. Can anyone forget those disturbing images of child soldiers thrown into the chaos of battle, of bloody trenches, cities in ruins, burning oil refineries, gassed corpses, tanks stuck in the mud, and oil tankers in flames?

Yet the war between Iran and Iraq was far more than that. The last major conflict of the Cold War era demonstrated the importance of the concept of energy security and forced several Western states to become lastingly involved in the Gulf. By allowing the Iranian regime to survive and solidify, the war led to new political and military power dynamics in the region and increased terrorism in the Middle East and Europe. From a military perspective, it served as a lab for the development of innovative tactics and a testing ground for the most sophisticated weapons.

The longest war of the twentieth century, the Iran-Iraq War remains relevant. Its consequences are still perceptible: Iraq has been marginalized, Iran radicalized, and the Iranian nuclear program has been accelerated. Given these two ancient nations' political development, they could feasibly clash again to reestablish their respective national unities and reinforce the legitimacy of the governments in place, once again using nationalism, religious sectarianism, and xenophobia to achieve political means. Though dominated by Shiites, the Iraqi press regularly unearths the question of the Shatt al-Arab's status. Whoever succeeds Nouri al-Maliki may be tempted to play the nationalism card again to save Iraq from disintegration. Should al-Maliki's successor choose this path, his choice will be limited to the three options that have always mobilized Iraqi Arabs: bringing the Kurds to heel, reclaiming Kuwait, and raising the Shatt al-Arab question. He will be forbidden to use the first by Turkey and the United States, which have key interests—notably in energy—in the current autonomous region of Iraqi Kurdistan. The second will be put aside because the United States has established itself as Kuwait's protector and is prepared to fight to save it. That leaves the third option, whose risks could appear acceptable should the country remain an outcast in the international community for much longer. From the Iraqi perspective, the last option could also offer the advantage of a rapprochement with the Gulf monarchies, which would be delighted to have Iraq resume its role as a shield from the Iranian mullahs' revolutionary regime.

A certain number of questions about the war remain unanswered. Why did Saddam Hussein embark on this expensive, long, and useless conflict? Why did it last eight years when it could have been brought to an end in three months? How were the great powers and France involved? What was the impact of the oil factor? How were front-page issues such as Iran-Contra, terrorist attacks in France, and kidnappings in Lebanon connected to the war? Who were the conflict's true winners? These are the many questions I have attempted to answer in this book, the fruit of ten years of research that led me from Paris to the Gulf capitals via Washington, London, Rome, Istanbul, Beirut, Cairo, Jerusalem, and Amman. I have drawn on the rare reference works on the subject, invaluable unpublished military archives, and extraordinary, previously unexploited oral sources: interviews with significant players in the war's history (notably Iranian ones), Iraqi generals who left Iraq after the fall of the Ba'athist regime, and analysts who studied the progress of hostilities.

Over the course of my research, I had access to the well-known "Saddam audiotapes" seized by the American army in Baghdad in 2003. The Iraqi dictator knew that he was an orator, not a writer. Knowing that he would not leave any writings to posterity and wanting to be remembered by his people, Saddam systematically had all seats of power and meeting rooms wiretapped so that his speeches and public statements could be recorded. The goal was to leave a record allowing Iraqi historians to glorify his major decisions after his death, but also to keep his deputies and ministers under surveillance. Naturally, these recordings follow the military high command discussions between Saddam Hussein and his generals, notably during the war's crucial phases. Studying transcriptions of the tapes was a fascinating experience that allowed me to sit in on these conversations from afar. These discussions were often, but not always, controlled by the Iraqi president—for Saddam had an astonishing ability to listen.

This treasure trove is now carefully preserved in Washington by the National Defense University and can be consulted on site, under specific conditions, or by contacting the Conflict Records Research Center at CRRC@ndu.edu.

This patiently accumulated and cross-checked information has informed my narrative, which is far different from the story told by Western press and historians, as well as the Iraqi and Iranian authorities over the last thirty years. My data also allowed me to make a precise assessment of the forces on the field, a reasonable estimation of the losses, and the real volume of military aid provided to the belligerents, notably by the five permanent members of the United Nations Security Council. In this regard, France stood out for its delicate position, having sided with Iraq while continuing to negotiate with Iran.

This story is also a reflection on power. In the cases of Saddam Hussein and Ayatollah Khomeini, the war was used to hold onto or reinforce personal power. In the cases of Akbar Hashemi Rafsanjani and Ali Khamenei, the current Supreme Leader of the Islamic Revolution, it was used to take power. A quarter of a century later, the rivalry between the latter two men still drives power struggles in Tehran, influencing essential decisions. President Hassan Rouhani's recent election is the latest development in this situation. The Iranian Islamists' method of seizing power by successively marginalizing their rivals also has much to teach us about the revolutions currently underway in the Arab world.

Finally, I must remind the reader that I am writing on my personal behalf, and that my remarks do not represent the positions of the French Ministry of Defense or the Institut de recherche stratégique de l'Ecole militaire (IRSEM; Strategic Research Institute of the French War College). Most importantly, I did not attempt to impose a specific reading of history, only to move it forward by taking apart a number of myths and opening new paths for reflection.

ABBREVIATIONS

AFP	Agence France-Presse
AKP	Justice and Development Party
AWACS	Airborne Warning and Control System
CEA	French Atomic Energy Commission
CIEEMG	Commission interministérielle pour l'étude des exportations de matériel de guerre (Interministerial Commission for Scrutiny of War Material Exports)
CNRS	Centre National de la recherche scientifique
CSPPA	Comité de solidarité avec les prisonniers politiques arabes et du Moyen-Orient (Committee of Solidarity with Arab and Middle East Political Prisoners)
DGSE	Direction générale de la sécurité extérieure (General Directorate for External Security)
DPSD	Direction de la Protection de la Sécurité et de la Défense (Directorate of Protection, Security and Defense)
DST	Direction de la surveillance du territoire (Directorate of Territorial Intelligence)
GCC	Gulf Cooperation Council
GRU	Main Intelligence Directorate (Russia)
IAEA	International Atomic Energy Agency
ICJ	International Court of Justice
ICRC	International Committee of the Red Crescent
IRGC	Islamic Revolutionary Guards Corps
IRP	Islamic Republican Party
KDP	Kurdistan Democratic Party
KDSP	Kurdistan Democratic Socialist Party
LNG	Liquefied Natural Gas
METF	(Middle East Task Force)
NLAI	National Liberation Army of Iran
NPT	Treaty on the Non-Proliferation of Nuclear Weapons (Non-Proliferation Treaty)

OIC	Organization of Islamic Cooperation
PDKI	Democratic Party of Iranian Kurdistan
PKK	Kurdistan Workers' Party
PLO	Palestinian Liberation Organization
PUK	Patriotic Union of Kurdistan
RCC	Revolutionary Command Council
RG	Direction centrale des renseignements généraux (General Intelligence Directorate)
RPR	Rassemblement pour la République (Rally for the Republic)
SEAL	Sea, Air, and Land
SNIAS	Aérospatiale
SNPE	Société nationale des poudres et explosifs (National Company for Gunpowder and Explosives)
UAE	United Arab Emirates
UN	United Nations

The Iran-Iraq War

Chapter 1

Escalation

After many years of apparent calm, relations between Iran and Iraq suddenly took a turn for the worse during the winter of 1979–1980. Violent demonstrations in front of the Iraqi embassy in Tehran called for the removal of Saddam Hussein's Ba'athist regime. Iraqi flags and effigies of the Iraqi president were burned before representatives of the international press. In the border province of Khuzestan (literally, "the land of towers"), long claimed by Baghdad and primarily populated by Arabic speakers, the Iraqi consulate in Khorramshahr was pillaged and its consul expelled. Numerous schools teaching Arabic were vandalized and their teachers assaulted. Alleging that mujahidin hostile to the Islamic Revolution were present in Iraq, the Iranian regime sent its air force into Iraqi air space and simulated attacks on Iraqi barracks. Baghdad retaliated by bombing several border villages, ordering the closing of the Iranian consulates in Basra and Karbala, and reaffirming its rights over the Shatt al-Arab River, which flows 155 miles (250 kilometers) from the convergence of the Tigris and Euphrates to its mouth in the Persian Gulf. Its last sixty-two miles (one hundred kilometers) form the border between Iraq and Iran. With a width varying from 1,300 to 4,920 feet (400 to 1,500 meters), the river feeds a vast marsh-covered delta on the banks of which Iraq and Iran built two of the largest oil refineries in the world: Basra and Abadan.

The Media War

On February 8, 1980, Saddam Hussein appeared on television wearing his traditional olive green uniform to call on the solidarity of all Arab nations to help him oppose Iranian provocations by any means required. Everyone in the Arab world understood that the Iraqi president now only had one goal in mind: to block Iran's maneuvers, if necessary by force.

In Iran, the repression initiated by the revolutionaries who had overthrown the Shah in February 1979 continued savagely and relentlessly. Fierce battles raged between guardians of the Revolution and the Shah's former supporters. The situation remained chaotic. Shapour Bakhtiar, the imperial regime's last prime minister, now exiled in France, added fuel to the fire by emphatically declaring that, "Khomeini will soon be done with, it will last seven or eight months at most! Less than a year in any case. That is certain."[1] In Baghdad, these statements were taken as proof that the Iranian army was weakening. Members of the Iranian opposition who had sought shelter in Baghdad reinforced this impression by describing the apocalyptic situation in their homeland. They were echoed by Iraqi intelligence reports.[2] The émigrés attempted to convince the Ba'athist regime to help them overthrow the provisional government, emphasizing the prevailing anarchy, the administration's collapse, and the purges and desertions that had rendered the army inoperative. The Iraqi authorities prudently gave the opposition lip service, doubting their actual ability to topple the revolutionary regime. The Iraqis preferred to act surreptitiously by arming the independence movements trying to emancipate themselves from central Iranian power in Kurdistan, Baluchistan, or oil-rich Khuzestan Province.

Meanwhile, verbal jousting between Tehran and Baghdad escalated. On March 15, 1980, Ayatollah Khomeini called on Iraqi public opinion: "O Iraqi people, beware your leaders and make revolution until victory." Six days later, his son Ahmad made an even more threatening declaration: "We must deploy all the necessary efforts in order to export the revolution to other countries and reject the idea of containing it within our borders."[3] For its part, the Iraqi government demanded the repeal of the Algiers Accord of March 6, 1975, which had allowed Saddam Hussein and the Shah of Iran to announce to the world press that they had made an agreement to put an end to their divergences. By its terms, the two parties had accepted to definitively demarcate their terrestrial and fluvial borders, which had been contested for centuries.[4] The river border would now run through the middle of the Shatt al-Arab rather than along the Persian bank that had served as its past demarcation.

On April 1, 1980, Tariq Aziz, one of Saddam Hussein's closest collaborators and a figurehead of the Iraqi Christian community, was attacked while giving a speech at Baghdad University. A grenade exploded several feet (a few meters) from Aziz, lightly injuring him. A dozen students were killed. A Shiite activist was immediately arrested. The Iraqi secret service accused the activist of being an undercover agent for the Iranian SAVAMA, the new secret service agency that had replaced the fearsome SAVAK. The next day, the Iraqi president made a sensational announcement declaring that the blood spilled would not be forgotten. Three days later, another bombing rocked the capital during the funeral for the first assault's victims: a homemade bomb was thrown from an Iranian school along the funeral cortege's path, killing and wounding dozens of people. The Iraqi regime protested vehemently, blaming Tehran. Iranian president Abol Hassan Bani-Sadr promptly responded, accusing Baghdad of gross provocation and denouncing Ba'athist ideology as "no more than an amalgamation of Nazi, Fascist, and Marxist doctrines."[5]

The situation was becoming increasingly heated. In Tehran, Ayatollah Beheshti told the international press that, "Saddam, the butcher of Baghdad, the accomplice of Menachem Begin, is just a puppet in the hands of the United States."[6] This provocation hit the bull's-eye: the Iraqi dictator was driven by a pathological hatred of Jews and saw himself as a leader in the fight against Israel. He could not tolerate for his credentials in this area to be called into question. Since the ayatollahs seemed determined to unearth the hatchet, they would get as good as they gave. Saddam Hussein addressed an extremely firm warning to Ayatollah Khomeini and called upon the United Nations Security Council, demanding a vote for a resolution condemning Iran's illegal occupation of the small Emirati islands Tomb and Abu Musa (located near the Strait of Hormuz). To make his resolve clear to Ayatollah Khomeini, Saddam ordered the immediate execution of Ayatollah Mohammad al-Sadr, who had been the Supreme Leader of the Iranian Revolution's companion in exile.[7] He also ordered the expulsion to Iran of 40,000 Iraqis of Iranian origin. Khomeini reacted by openly calling for the overthrow of Saddam Hussein and viciously criticizing the "monstrous and perverted regime of Iraq's Ba'ath Party, a veritable Little Satan which has put itself at the service of the Great Satan [the United States]." No longer hiding his intentions, he went so far as to declare: "We want to found an Islamic State gathering the Arab, the Persian, the Turk, and the other nationalities under the banner of Islam."[8] Upon hearing this, the Gulf monarchies braced for war, knowing that they would have to unite one way or another, but also that they would be forced to support Saddam's regime to contain Iranian Shiite expansionism.

Occasional clashes continued on the field. In mid-April, an Iranian patrol machine-gunned a border post in retaliation for an Iraqi helicopter attack on an Iranian position. Psychological warfare intensified. On April 27, 1980, Radio Tehran announced the assassination of Saddam Hussein, spreading disinformation to destabilize the Iraqi regime. Three days later, the Iranian embassy in London was attacked by a commando claiming to belong to the previously unknown Democratic Revolutionary Front for the Liberation of Arabistan. The British Special Air Service was called to the rescue and intervened five days later to free the Iranian diplomats held hostage.

To make the situation even more complicated, Iran granted asylum to the Barzani brothers, two leaders of the historic Kurdish rebellion that had raged in northern Iraq from 1974 to 1975. The brothers Idris and Masoud Barzani took the opportunity to resurrect their networks of *peshmergas* (literally, "freedom fighters"). The Iraqi government, seeking to avoid the resumption of war on the Kurdish front, multiplied concessions to the Barzanis' major rival, Jalal Talabani, while launching a series of deadly raids against the peshmergas rallied behind the Barzani brothers. Jalal Talabani seized the chance to establish his control over the cities of Iraqi Kurdistan, notably in the oil region of Kirkuk, leaving his rivals to control the mountainous border area. He negotiated an agreement with Saddam Hussein by which his partisans would stop militarily harassing the regime in exchange for greater regional autonomy. This suited the Iraqi president in that it divided the Kurdish guerillas and prevented a united front from forming against him.

Meanwhile, the situation in Iran remained as chaotic as ever. President Bani-Sadr intensified operations against the new regime's opponents and kept the armed forces under close surveillance, fearing a coup d'état. His precautions were not in vain: on July 4, 1980, General Oveisi asserted that he could take control of Tehran by the end of the summer. On the night of July 9 to 10, a vast military plot was foiled a few hours before it was to be set in motion. The coup d'état had been orchestrated from Paris by General Oveisi and Shapour Bakhtiar and was to be triggered on the Nojeh air base near Hamadan by General Said Mehdiyoun and General Ayat Mohagheghi. The mutineers had chosen this base, home to several powerful Phantom fighter squadrons, due to its proximity to the Iranian capital. The plan was for some thirty heavily armed planes to set out at dawn and bomb Ayatollah Khomeini's residence, the presidential palace, the seat of government, and several Revolutionary Guards barracks. Detachments of soldiers faithful to the Shah would then have been transported into the capital by helicopter to take control of the symbols of power, with reinforcement from several ground force battalions.

The revolutionary regime reacted fiercely. More than 600 commissioned and noncommissioned officers were arrested, including some fifty pilots. Most were executed following a summary trial supervised by the Revolutionary Guards, who had now surrounded the principal air bases. The air force, which already suffered from personnel purges,[9] insufficient crew training, and a lack of spare parts, was now in complete disarray. Most fighter planes and helicopters were grounded for several weeks. As for General Oveisi and Shapour Bakhtiar, their active participation in the conspiracy signed their death warrant. The Iranian regime would mercilessly hunt them down over the course of the next several years.[10]

Did Saddam Hussein back the attempted coup d'état? There is no evidence to support such a theory. Admittedly, several Iraqi fighter planes crossed the Iranian border to attack a radar station located near the Nojeh air base at the exact moment when the coup was to be launched. Those who believe that the conspirators and the Iraqi regime were in collusion claim that this air attack would have served as a pretext for the Iranian Phantoms to take off and lull the suspicions of military personnel faithful to the revolutionary government. But in that case, why wasn't the Iraqi army on alert? And why weren't the Iranian mujahidin in exile in Iraq standing ready to cross the border and go reinforce the mutineers? It seems unlikely that Saddam Hussein played a major role in this plot, particularly since he hated Iranians and did not give their opponents much credit. There is every indication that he was playing a waiting game, though he was certainly aware that a significant attempt at overthrowing the Islamic regime was imminent, probably thanks to King Hussein of Jordan and

King Khalid of Saudi Arabia, who had both been warned by the CIA, which was in turn discreetly supporting the military networks faithful to the Shah.

Saddam Chooses War

The conspiracy's failure solidified Saddam's convictions. First, the Iraqi president realized it was illusory to hope for a military coup d'état to wipe out the Islamic Revolution. He understood that despite the CIA's active support, the Iranian opposition no longer stood a chance. The Kurds, the Azeri, and the Baloch were fighting for their autonomy, potentially their independence, but not to overthrow the regime in Tehran. Saddam also grasped that it would be a mistake to hope for military intervention from the United States or the Soviet Union, which had been mired in Afghanistan for the last ten months. And relying on the oil monarchies would be a joke. He therefore came to the conclusion that, short of being able to overthrow the Iranian regime, he needed to act quickly to durably weaken it. The two regimes were now on a collision course. Invective and provocation had gone too far to be forgiven. The Iraqi dictator was firmly convinced that Ayatollah Khomeini would no longer compromise and that he would stop at nothing to bring Saddam down. Saddam Hussein came to the logical conclusion that in order to preserve his power, he needed to preemptively attack Iran. He hoped this would weaken Khomeini and possibly precipitate his downfall. Most importantly, he would be able to reestablish Iraqi sovereignty over the entire Shatt al-Arab and erase the affront of the Algiers Accord, which had been a personal humiliation. All the better if he could take control of some bordering oil-rich Iranian territory while he was at it.

The timing seemed perfect, given that the Iranian army, in disarray following the Revolution and the Western embargo, was no more than a shadow of its former self.[11] What remained of the army was scattered across several fronts to battle Kurd, Azeri, Arab, and Baloch separatists with the assistance of the Revolutionary Guards. The Iraqi secret services' reports also specified that the Iranian air force, once the Imperial Army's spearhead, had been grounded since the failure of the Nojeh plot. The Iraqi dictator believed a quick war with Iran would allow him to occupy his soldiers and increase his prestige. He seemed all the more confident given that his nuclear program was moving in the right direction, while Iran's had been called to an abrupt halt by the revolutionaries. According to his experts, the "Osirak" nuclear power station, built with France's help at al-Tawita (on the banks of the Tigris, some twenty miles [thirty kilometers] southeast of Baghdad), would be operational within about fifteen months, allowing Iraq to upgrade its category and play with the big boys.

Saddam Hussein was also persuaded that by attacking Iran he would establish himself as the leader of the Arab world, thus marginalizing his greatest rival, the Syrian Hafez al-Assad. He was convinced that once faced with the fait accompli, the Gulf monarchies, notably Saudi Arabia and Kuwait, would have no choice but to support him and back him financially. According to him, the United States would hold back and simply wait and see what happened. Saddam believed the Europeans would follow him because they were worried about the risks of the Islamic Revolution spreading throughout the region. They also relied on selling him weapons. In fact, his only concern was with the Kremlin, whose reaction he had trouble predicting. His intuition told him that the Soviets, having lost all influence in Egypt, would respect the friendship and assistance agreement tying them to Iraq and would not risk losing a weighty ally in the Middle East.

In mid-July Saddam Hussein summoned his chiefs of staff to ask them to prepare to go to war with Iran, yet did not mention a date or a specific military objective. However, he gave his generals a single month to prepare the army and provide him with a coherent battle plan, ignoring the fact that such an enterprise generally requires considerably more time. Most of the generals took the news with worry and skepticism, but none had the courage to openly question the decision, not even Adnan Khairallah, who enjoyed significant prestige in the military institution as first cousin to the president and holder of the coveted position of minister of defense. All those involved knew that Saddam was impervious to advice that did not adhere to his ideas and that he ruthlessly eliminated anyone who stood in the way of his projects. Ra'ad Majid Rashid al-Hamdani, one of his officers, would later confess: "[Saddam] looked you straight in the eye, as if to

control you. Not knowing what was on his mind was scary. . . . Saddam had
a number of personality traits. . . . One moment he would be extremely
affectionate, the next moment he would be extremely hostile and cruel. . . .
One minute he could be overly generous, the next he could be extremely
stingy. . . . He could take ideas from every one and create a new idea. At
a political level, he was an excellent tactical player; however at the strategic level, 99 percent of his concepts were wrong. His problem was that
he imposed tribal standards on the administration of a country."[12] No one
dared to expose himself to the dictator's wrath by warning him that he
was running the risk of straying into an uncontrollable venture.

Having muzzled his generals, Saddam could no longer count on them
to tell him the truth and prevent him from making a mistake. For the
army was not truly ready for war. Though its equipment was being modernized, it generally remained inferior to that of the Iranian army. Training
left a lot to be desired. Logistics were not coordinated. Motivation remained weak. The Iraqi military would have been prepared to do battle
to protect their country, to fight the Kurds, or to invade Kuwait, which
they considered a part of Iraq, but attacking Iran was an entirely different
proposition. The Iraqi military high command began to prepare for a
large-scale military operation in utter secrecy, without the slightest enthusiasm. The generals all knew that their leader would not tolerate the
slightest leak and that a dreadful fate awaited anyone responsible for the
slightest indiscretion. A self-confident Saddam spoke to the press, praising
"the Iranian peoples' struggle against the ayatollahs' reactionary and des-
potic behavior and the retrograde principles hidden behind the mask of
religion" and singling out the people of Arabistan (the Arabic name for
the Iranian province of Khuzestan) for standing up to "the racist clique
in Tehran."[13]

Meanwhile, the power struggle raged on in Tehran. Ayatollah Khomeini relentlessly pursued his three priorities: consolidating the Islamic
Revolution, preparing the clergy's rise to power, and keeping Iran from
falling under a foreign power's influence again. Led by Ayatollah Beheshti
and Ayatollah Montazeri, the clergy took advantage of ideological divisions weakening the secular camp to reinforce their positions and openly
criticize President Bani-Sadr. Though he enjoyed the Supreme Leader's

support, Bani-Sadr was reproached for his inability to put down the revolts destabilizing the provinces of Khuzestan and Kurdistan. In an attempt to regain control, Bani-Sadr, who had reestablished the compulsory
military service suspended following the Revolution, decided to send
major reinforcements to both provinces. To the south, he dispatched the
92nd Armored Division, whose officers had proven their loyalty to the regime, as well as two tank battalions and three infantry battalions belonging to brigades guarding the eastern borders with Afghanistan and
Pakistan. By doing so, he hoped to deal a mortal blow to the independence fighters of the Arab Front for the Liberation of Al-Ahwaz led by
Mohammad Taher Khanqani. Bani-Sadr's large contingent was backed by
local Revolutionary Guards units. To the north, the Iranian president deployed the 28th Mechanized Division to assist the 64th Infantry Division
with hunting down the peshmergas of the Democratic Party of Iranian
Kurdistan (PDKI). In the center, near Kermanshah, Bani-Sadr put the 81st
Armored Brigade, the 84th Mechanized Division, and the 1st Army Aviation Brigade on alert to reinforce the northern or southern front as needed.
All of these units now close to the Iraqi border would absorb the impact
of the Iraqi invasion a few weeks later.

The poisonous mood in Tehran was exacerbated by the fact that the
Iranian government seemed incapable of righting the economy, which had
collapsed following the evacuation of Western technicians eight months
earlier. No one seemed to imagine that Iran was on the brink of war with
Iraq, despite the fact that skirmishes had continued throughout the
summer, taking on a routine character that lulled the Iranian leadership's
suspicions. The secular camp attempted to make strategic headway and
limit the clergy's growing influence, without any concern for what was
taking place outside the country. On July 27, 1980, the news of the ousted
Shah Mohammad Reza Pahlavi's death in Cairo was met with indiffer-
ence. President Anwar al-Sadat gave him a grandiose funeral, further
provoking the Iranian regime's ire and leading it to vilify Egypt. While
Ayatollah Khomeini was aware of the growing risks of armed conflict
between Iran and Iraq, he did nothing to avoid them, convinced that, in
case of war, Iraq's Shiite population would rise against Saddam and precipitate his downfall.

Final Preparations

On August 16, 1980, Saddam Hussein summoned his chiefs of staff again. He informed his generals of his irrevocable decision to attack Iran, though he had not yet determined a specific schedule. The day to trigger hostilities would be chosen at the last moment, based on circumstances. Instinctively, the Iraqi president was still hesitant to attack, particularly since his army did not seem ready. While he did not know much about military affairs, he was fully aware that he could not launch a total war against Iran with the aim of wiping out the Iranian army and taking Tehran. Iran was far too vast a country, too mountainous and heavily populated for such an objective to be feasible. Instead, Saddam simply aimed for a limited war that would allow him to make territorial gains and renegotiate the location of the border and the status of the Shatt al-Arab to his advantage by preying on the Iranians' momentary weakness. He imagined a kind of blitzkrieg, limited in space and time—a few weeks at most—intended to durably enfeeble the Iranian regime and institute a new power dynamic favorable to Iraq. He hoped that a rapid victory would shake Khomeini's power and force him to rein in his hegemonic ambitions. Infuriated by his chiefs of staff's prudence, Saddam reprimanded his generals: "What prevents you from advancing in Iran and encircling and capturing the enemy armies? No one said there would be no resistance! No one said there would be no losses and no deaths! We must now penetrate Iran and show that we can strike our adversary."[14]

The objectives to be reached remained as unclear as the timing of the war's onset, but appeared to be limited to the conquest of the coastal plains of Khuzestan and the securing of both banks of the Shatt al-Arab River. The chiefs of staff did not intend to assault the Zagros Mountains, particularly given the perspective of autumn or, worse, winter. From this mountain range, which rises to over 13,100 feet (4,000 meters), the Iranians dominated the Iraqis in the plains. To avoid an Iranian counterattack from the mountains, the Iraqi generals planned to take control of a few strategic high-altitude points that would enable them to better guard access to Iraqi cities. Khuzestan Province was chosen as the offensive's principal target. The Iraqi generals hoped that Khuzestan's flat terrain would allow their tanks to move freely, despite the presence of many

marshlands. The area's road network was quite dense, allowing for encirclement and diversion maneuvers. Additionally, two-thirds of Iran's oil
production was concentrated in the province. Capturing or destroying
Iran's oil infrastructure would further weaken the Iranian regime by considerably reducing its oil revenue. Saddam Hussein was also convinced
that Khuzestan's Arabic-speaking population would rise up with the arrival of the first Iraqi tanks, welcoming his soldiers as liberators. He saw
himself as the heir to the Abbasid caliphs endowed with a mission to bring
down the Persian enemy, who was always prompt to oppress the Arab
people. One could also conceive that Saddam's thuggish disposition instinctively led him to attempt to rob Iran's oil reserves, though he knew
that it would be very difficult to exploit them due to the extensive time
and extreme cost it would require to connect Khuzestan's oil deposits to
Iraqi pipelines. With this in mind, he ordered his generals to mobilize numerous tanker trucks to bring as much refined product back to Iraq as
possible.

On August 26, 1980, three days after Saddam Hussein's visit to the
Khanaqin border garrison located near the Iranian city of Qasr-e-Shirin,
the situation along the Iraqi-Iranian border abruptly became tenser. Shots
were fired from both sides of the border, including by heavy weaponry,
without any clear sign of which side had instigated hostilities.[15] But one
thing was certain: crime paid for Iraqi power, which could thus increase tension to justify a casus belli. These skirmishes also allowed Saddam to justify
sending significant reinforcements to border areas. Iranian soldiers readily
retaliated, sometimes disproportionately, thus playing right into Saddam's
hands. They had received clear orders from President Bani-Sadr, who encouraged them to deal with their Iraqi neighbor as firmly as possible. And
in order to avoid inconvenient witnesses, the Iranian government forbade
foreign journalists access to conflict zones, thereby reinforcing the international community's distrust of Tehran.

On September 4, the artillery was called in and the situation began
to degenerate. Iranian guns pounded the Iraqi towns of Khanaqin and
Mandali, located in the center of the Iraqi layout at the foot of the Zagros
Mountains, a little over sixty miles (one hundred kilometers) from Baghdad.
Saddam Hussein breezily accused the Iranians of instigating hostilities,
sparing no effort to bring foreign journalists to see bombed villages.

Seizing the opportunity, he ordered his army to reoccupy several parcels of Iranian territory claimed by Iraq. In a few days, Iraqi troops backed by artillery and tanks took control of a few rocky islets on the Shatt al-Arab River, as well as two contested zones covering a total area of 201 square miles (324 square kilometers). The Iranians lost two patrol boats on the Shatt al-Arab, five tanks, and about fifty soldiers. The Iraqis lost about one hundred combatants during the operation.

Air skirmishes also picked up. On September 7, five Iraqi helicopters crossed the Iranian border. They were immediately intercepted by an Iranian Tomcat, which shot one helicopter down and let the others turn back. This was a bitter surprise for the Iraqi pilots, who thought that Iran's F-14 air-superiority fighters were grounded. The next day, the first air battle between fighter planes took place. Two Iraqi MiG-21s shot down an Iranian Phantom firing at tanks deployed along the border. Two days later, an Iranian F-5 fighter was blown apart by another MiG-21. On September 10, the Iranians took their revenge. For the first time since the Tomcat had been put into service, one of these formidable air-superiority fighters succeeded in destroying an Iraqi Su-22, demonstrating the power of its long-range Phoenix missiles. Four days later, President Bani-Sadr himself had a close brush with death. While he was carrying out a helicopter inspection of the border to personally assess the situation on the ground, his aircraft was intercepted by a roaming MiG-23. The Iraqi pilot fired his two air-to-air missiles without any idea who was on board his target. The Iranian pilot immediately released decoy flares and dove toward the ground, following a sequence of evasive maneuvers, while his escort attempted to fight off the Iraqi fighter. A Phantom cruising nearby came to the rescue and scared the troublemaker away. The Iranian president got off with a bad fright. The next day, an Iranian Tomcat brought down an Iraqi MiG near the border and the Iranians moved back into the lead.

On September 16, Saddam Hussein gathered his closest advisers for a final consultation and told them he had decided to go to war with Iran in the following days. Only Ali Hassan al-Majid, his other first cousin and the head of the fearsome Mukhabarat (secret services), was brave enough to point out the risks of such an endeavor and list the reasons for which he thought war was premature. Having politely listened to him, the dictator refuted his arguments one by one and asked him, "Ali, why do you always bring me the bad news, never the good news?"[16] The marginalized Ali Hassan al-Majid spoke no more. The Iraqi president continued by summoning his generals and ordering them to immediately go on the offensive. He would not tolerate the slightest delay on their part. They were free to determine the ideal date and time, so long as the confrontation took place.

On the next day, September 17, 1980, Saddam Hussein denounced the Algiers Accord, declaring it null and void. He announced to the world that "the legal status of the Shatt al-Arab must return to what it has always been historically, and what it should never have stopped being, that is to say an Arab river that allows Iraq to enjoy all the rights ensuing from full sovereignty."[17] Accordingly, the Shatt al-Arab border would no longer run through the middle of the river, but back along its eastern bank. With this statement, the Iraqi dictator crossed the final line separating him from war with Iran. In an ultimate gesture of provocation, he invited the Iranian government to engage in negotiations to ratify the river's new status. He may secretly have hoped that the Iranian regime, conscious of its army's weakness, would agree to the negotiations, give in, and accept to be subjected to an iniquitous agreement that would be the Iraqi revenge for the Algiers Accord.

The Iranian minister of foreign affairs dispelled any such illusion the next day. He bluntly stated that his country rejected both the Iraqi government's offer to negotiate and the unilateral abrogation of the Algiers Accord. Conscious that he no longer had any choice but war, Saddam Hussein sent Tariq Aziz as a pedagogical envoy to the principal Arab leaders. The message was clear: the Iranians were responsible for the situation's deterioration and it was the duty of those Arab countries that could afford to do so to finance the crusade Saddam was preparing to lead to contain the Persian aggressor. This message was also relayed to the West, which began worrying about the turn of events. The United Nations Security Council, which was locked in a Cold War logic that prevented its members from agreeing on a resolution, could only stand by and watch the danger grow. On the field, combat intensified along the Shatt al-Arab. The city of Abadan was targeted by Iraqi artillery. In the air, two Iranian F-5 fighters were shot down by anti-aircraft defense while attacking Iraqi tanks deployed along the border. One of the two pilots was killed, but the other was able to eject. Sub-Lieutenant Hossein Lashgari was immediately captured by the Iraqis, who would not free him until 1996, making him the Iranian combatant who spent the longest time in Iraqi hands.

On September 18, 1980, the generals put the final touches on their battle plans. The favorable weather forecast for September 22 led them to decide to attack that day, leaving them only three days to alert their units. The ticking time bomb was set. Nothing could stop it now.

The Forces on the Field

In normal circumstances, the Iraqi regime could not have reasonably started a war with Iran. Iran was four times the size of Iraq and had three times its population. Its oil revenue was twice that of Iraq's. The principal Iranian cities, located a safe distance from the border, were protected by the towering Zagros Mountains. Iran's capital was also 460 miles (740 kilometers) from the front, deep on a plateau backed against high mountains overlooking the Caspian Sea. It had a younger population, providing it with a larger reserve of troops. Finally, its military budget was 60 percent greater than Iraq's, but was a smaller drain on GDP (4 percent versus 6.5 percent). The Iranian government had more room to maneuver financially than the Iraqi government. Iran's sole weakness was in its network of oil pipelines centered on the coastal plain of Khuzestan, home to its principal oil fields, its principal hydrocarbon deposit (Ahwaz), its principal river port (Khorramshahr), its principal refinery (Abadan), but especially its two principal oil terminals (Kharg and Bandar Khomeini).

With the exception of its rivers and marshes, Iraq had no natural defenses. Its largest cities were close to the front, with Baghdad only 100 miles (160 kilometers) from the border by road—six minutes by air. Basra, the country's second largest city, was within cannon range of Iran. The Iraqi generals had to hold firm to the ground while their Iranian counterparts could count on an elastic defense in depth. The Iraqi oil network was particularly vulnerable in that it was divided between two unconnected production centers (in the areas of Kirkuk in the north and Basra in the south).

To compensate for its structural weaknesses, Iraq had overequipped itself and built an imposing army of 250,000 men, four-fifths of whom served in the ground forces.[18] These included three army corps, twelve divisions (five armored, two mechanized, and five infantry) and six independent brigades comprising 1,750 tanks, 2,350 other armored vehicles, and 1,350 artillery pieces. The Popular Army, which accounted for one-quarter of ground forces, reinforced the regular army and made up the majority of the infantry divisions. It was also deployed throughout the nation to protect the regime. The air force consisted of 295 fighter planes divided among eighteen squadrons scattered across eleven air force bases; another sixty old fighter planes were warehoused to compensate for potential losses while waiting for new aircraft to be delivered. Army aviation, though part of the air force, was principally used to support ground forces and included 300 helicopters, fifty-eight of which were equipped for antitank combat. Anti-aircraft defense relied on a dense network of surveillance radars and nine brigades equipped with surface-to-air missiles and rapid-firing cannons. These units, which were assigned to the most sensitive sites as well as the protection of armored divisions, had an instant firing capacity of over 400 surface-to-air missiles. Theoretically, they formed a powerful anti-aircraft umbrella over Iraqi territory. Lastly, the navy, the armed forces' poor relative, had only fourteen missile boats, three amphibious assault ships, and twenty-eight light patrol boats, including ten torpedo boats. These meager resources were divided among the naval bases at Basra, Umm Qasr, and al-Faw, at the mouth of the Shatt al-Arab, which were in turn defended by four naval infantry battalions.

The Iraqi armed forces were structured according to a hybrid model inspired by both the British and Soviet systems. Armored and mechanized units based their organization on that of the Russian army, while infantry divisions remained close to the British model. Anti-aircraft defense faithfully reproduced the Soviet blueprint, while the air force was organized in independent squadrons like the Royal Air Force. For the most part, these forces were outfitted with Soviet equipment, much of it dated.[19] Though coarsely crafted, this equipment had the advantage of being robust and easy to maintain. The Iraqi army's truly modern equipment was limited to fifty-four MiG-23 fighters (though these were only export versions and were less reliable than those operated by the Soviet air force), eighteen Mi-24 combat helicopters, barely one hundred T-72 tanks, two hundred BMP-1 infantry fighting vehicles, and sixty SAM-6 and SAM-9 surface-to-air missile launchers. The limited amount of non-Soviet equipment was Brazilian (Cascavel vehicles) and French (Panhard M-3 and AML-60/90 light-armored vehicles; Alouette III, Gazelle, Super Frelon, and Puma helicopters). Large quantities of weapons were also on order from France, notably Mirage F-1s, but had not yet been delivered at the time Iraq prepared to go to war.

Overall, the Iraqi army's efficiency was mediocre, particularly since the government had done everything possible to politicize the institution and discourage the military's sense of initiative. The only officers and soldiers able to boast of real combat experience versus a heavily mechanized adversary were those who had fought on the Golan front in the Yom Kippur War seven years earlier. Many of them had since fallen victim to successive army purges. The pool of battle-hardened fighters exposed to tank combat was therefore extremely limited. On the other hand, Iraq's infantrymen had acquired crucial battle experience in the first half of the 1970s during the war against the Kurds. Unfortunately for them, the tendency was toward mechanizing the army—drawing inspiration from the Soviet model, Iraqi generals were turning a growing number of classic infantry battalions into dismounted infantry units able to follow and protect tanks aboard their own armored vehicles. These infantrymen were no longer trained to storm enemy trenches, and their motivation left something to be desired. The only elite corps Saddam could rely on were the Republican Guard's Armored Brigade, the special forces, and the engineering corps.[20] The air force served as the regime's ultimate shield. Its commanders and pilots were pampered and enjoyed many privileges.

Iran had an army (*artesh* in Farsi) of 290,000 men, three-quarters of whom belonged to the ground forces. These were divided into one army corps, seven divisions (three armored, three mechanized, and one infantry), and seven independent brigades gathering 1,710 tanks, 1,900 other armored vehicles, and 1,100 artillery pieces. At the time, the Army of the Guardians of the Islamic Revolution (*sepah* in Farsi), consisting of the Pasdaran and the Basij, accounted for only one-sixth of ground troops, but the ratio was quickly shifting in its favor. The revolutionary regime intended to privilege this corps, which was entirely devoted to the regime, unlike the regular army, of which it remained suspicious. The Army of the Guardians was composed of independent units that had gradually replaced the military police[21] and were only accountable to the Supreme Leader. The government had committed to creating large units of Pasdaran (brigades and divisions) to absorb the spectacular growth in their ranks.

The air force, long considered the Imperial Army's elite corps, had 421 planes divided into twenty-three squadrons garrisoned on nine air force bases. Only half of the planes were operational, due to lack of maintenance, pilots, and spare parts. Paradoxically, the air force had significant stocks of munitions and spare parts, but these were scattered across numerous far-flung locations managed by a complex computer program, which had been left uncompleted by American engineers when they were called back to the United States. Iranian technicians now found themselves responsible for warehousing a vast stock of equipment for which they did not have plans or nomenclature. They were faced with the challenge of identifying spare parts for a Phantom fighter stored unlabeled next to those for Tomcat interceptors and Cobra helicopters. To make matters worse, many technicians had deserted. Those who remained had devoted themselves to the endlessly daunting task of recreating a coherent management system, but their work was far from finished when hostilities began. The air force's major asset remained four Boeing 747s converted into flying command posts and a dozen Boeing refueling aircraft, which allowed Iranian fighters to remain in the air far longer than their adversaries and to strike deep within Iraqi territory if required.

The air force and the ground forces' light aircraft included 800 helicopters, of which only a third were operational. Anti-aircraft defense consisted of sixteen battalions equipped with surface-to-air missiles and rapid-firing cannons. While very modern, the aerial detection network suffered from the same maintenance problems as the air force. Organized so as to cover the country's principal cities and air bases, as well as the border with the Soviet Union, the network had many gaps that would have allowed any determined Iraqi pilot to get away with flying over part of Iranian territory.

On the other hand, the Iranian navy was still the most important naval force in the Gulf. It had three destroyers, four frigates, four corvettes, nine missile boats (with three more on order from France), five amphibious assault ships, ten auxiliary ships, thirty-five helicopters, as well as twenty-six light patrol boats, including fourteen hydroplanes able to carry out devastating raids on enemy oil platforms. These ships were primarily docked at the naval bases of Bandar Abbas, on the Sea of Oman, and Bushehr, on the Gulf.

The Iranian armed forces' structure was inspired by both the British and American systems. The ground forces' divisional composition was strikingly similar to the U.S. Army's: a limited number of very large divisions, heavily staffed and equipped, able to act independently from each other thanks to powerful back-up, but not particularly flexible, and highly dependent on logistics. On the other hand, brigades and battalions were organized on the British model, which favored versatility and reactivity. The air force reproduced the U.S. Air Force model: wings specialized in a particular type of mission, each consisting of two or three squadrons of some twenty aircraft. The composition of the army air force was also reminiscent of the American model: mixed brigades consisting of several reconnaissance, transport, and antitank helicopter battalions. The navy's organization was directly inspired by that of the British Royal Navy.

Ironically, while the Iranians rejected all references to the West, they applied its structures to their military. As a further reflection of this ambivalence, the Iranian army had primarily equipped itself with American and British apparatus, thereby complicating its logisticians' task. Aside from the air force, which remained entirely equipped with American-made weapons systems, the rest of the army had equipment of disparate origins, without the same standards or even operating modes. A tank driver would therefore have to readjust all his reflexes depending whether he was fighting aboard an American Patton tank or a British Chieftain tank. The same was true for an artilleryman, who could find himself firing the American Hawk surface-to-air missile system or the British Rapier system. To make matters more complicated, the ground forces had 1,000 Soviet-made armored personnel carriers (BTR-50 and BTR-60), delivered by the USSR in the early 1960s, at a time when the Shah was determined to maintain a cordial relationship with Moscow.

Though disparate, all this equipment had the advantage of being very modern, giving the Iranian army a considerable edge. Most of these weapons systems (Phantom and Tomcat fighters, Chieftain and M-60 tanks, M-107 and M-109 self-propelled guns, Hawk surface-to-air missiles, Vosper Mk-5 missile frigates) outclassed those of the Iraqi army.[22] In practice, however, many of these weapons were no longer operational, due to lack of maintenance or qualified personnel to use them. Consequently numerous airplanes, tanks, and helicopters were "cannibalized" to allow the Iranians to keep other equipment running. Additionally, units were scattered across the entire country to hold ground against the insurgents, protect the regime, and cover all the borders. Thus, only half of the Iranian army was in a position to face the Iraqi army from the beginning of hostilities.

Aside from the quantitative aspect, the postrevolutionary Iranian army's qualitative weaknesses should be noted: excessive politicization of the executive, the crippling presence of political commissars inhibiting officers' spirit of initiative, growing rivalry between the regular army and the Revolutionary Guards, poor coordination between the armed forces' various branches, and lack of training. The latter issue was particularly troublesome given that the Iranian army had no real experience with high-intensity mechanized combat. As far back as its officers could remember, their only adversaries had been the guerilla fighters of the Popular Front for the Liberation of the Occupied Arabian Gulf, when the Imperial Army assisted the Omani army in the early 1970s, and more recently, the PDKI's Kurd peshmergas, the Popular Front for the Liberation of Ahwaz's fedayeen, and Baloch and Azeri freedom fighters. None of these opponents had been equipped with heavy weaponry, helicopters, fighter planes, and tanks.

While Iranian soldiers had once been prepped to face Soviet armored divisions, most of this know-how had been lost since the Islamic Revolution. The situation was not much better at the top of the hierarchy. The rotation of appointments did not favor efforts undertaken to improve the army. Three ministers of defense and three army chiefs of staff had succeeded each other in less than fifteen months.[23] As for the military high command, it was made up of individuals with perfect revolutionary credentials, but highly limited operational experience and command abilities. Worse, no general or colonel could claim to be a true strategist. The Pasdaran corps was no better off. Ayatollah Ali Khameini, its commander, was a cleric well versed in dialectics and intrigue, but not in the realities on the ground. The Revolutionary Guards needed a commander able to lead them into combat, not a censor checking the religious orthodoxy of their behavior.

While the Iranian army appeared more powerful than the Iraqi army on paper, the force ratio was actually in the Iraqis' favor, notably regarding the number of planes and armored vehicles. On the front line, stretching more than 560 miles (900 kilometers) from the depths of Kurdistan to the mouth of the Shatt al-Arab, the Iraqis outnumbered the Iranians two to one, and in some sectors of the front, their superiority reached four to one. Granted, this advantage was not supposed to last. But it could have proved sufficient in the case of the blitzkrieg Baghdad wanted. Knowing this, one can better understand Saddam Hussein's decision to risk going to war with Iran.

[Chapter 2]

Saddam's Qadisiyyah

The Iranian leadership in Tehran had become conscious of the danger of war. Ayatollah Khomeini received the principal commanders of the armed forces, who had just participated in a closed session of Parliament under the high authority of its speaker Akbar Hashemi Rafsanjani. On September 20, 1980, the national security council met for over six hours under President Abol Hassan Bani-Sadr. Prime Minister Mohammad-Ali Rajai and Defense Minister Mustafa Chamran listened to the alarmist opinions of the military's leaders, who were all aware that the army was unprepared. Tension at the meeting was aggravated by the fact that the president and prime minister were clearly in opposing camps. Prime Minister Ali Rajai, who was extremely close to the clergy, seemed ready to stop at nothing, including denying the risks of war, to weaken the position of Bani-Sadr, whom the ayatollahs considered too progressive. After interminable haggling, the Iranian president was able to impose the calling up of 120,000 reservists, in the hope that their presence would dampen Iraq's hunger for war.

Meanwhile, in Baghdad, the generals were putting the finishing touches on their preparations. Saddam Hussein pompously named the offensive "Echo of Qadisiyyah," in reference to the Battle of al-Qadisiyyah (636 CE), at which the conquering Arab armies had crushed the Persian army to the south of Najaf, on the western bank of the Euphrates. The battle had since become a symbol of Arab victory over the Persians.

The Iraqi operation began classically, with an attack of its adversary's air force bases. The generals were not particularly keen to risk their precious aircraft deep over enemy territory, but Saddam Hussein insisted. The Iraqi dictator was convinced that "his" air force was capable of reproducing the exploits of the Israeli pilots who had destroyed the Arab air forces on the ground in a few hours on June 5, 1967. No doubt the desire to erase this unhappy memory had combined with his ambition to strike a big blow that would establish his prestige in the Arab world to convince him of the necessity of such an aerial attack. Once again, his objectives were political, not military. A good apparatchik, General Mohamed Jessam al-Jeboury, commander of the air force, followed the dictator's wishes. He swept aside the rare objections of those subordinates courageous enough to point out the efficiency of the Iranian surface-to-air defense system and Iraq's lack of effective weapons to destroy their adversary's concrete hangars. Due to the difficulty of destroying Iranian fighter planes inside their reinforced hangars, Iraqi pilots would focus on neutralizing runways and logistics depots to prevent the Iranian air force from taking off and winning air superiority over the front. Fighter planes stationed on the edge of the runways would be strafed, but would not be the primary targets of these preemptive strikes. Military strategists reasoned that Iraqi pilots should prioritize striking the adversary's radar and anti-aircraft systems, despite the fact that they did not have any missiles specially conceived for such a mission. This is but one of many examples of incompetence illustrating the lack of professionalism of the overly politicized Iraqi military institution, which had only reluctantly planned the war.

Saddam's Falcons Kick Off the War

On September 20 and 21, 1980, General Salim, chief of air force operations, discreetly inspected the six air force bases from which the fighter-bombers were to take off and passed on his orders and objectives. Contrary to usual practice, the attack would not take place at dawn, but at midday, in order to allow Iraqi pilots to avoid detection by enemy radar by flying nap-of-the-earth through the heart of the mountains. The Iraqi air force's Soviet planes were not equipped with terrain navigation systems, nor were its pilots trained for night flights. In order to carry out a coordinated strike on all the targets at daybreak, the pilots would have had to take off by night and fly most of the distance in total darkness, which was beyond their abilities. The operation's planners evaluated that a noon attack would give the Iraqi pilots the best chance of escaping the enemy.

Throughout the day, pilots and mechanics worked frenetically to prepare the planes. In the late evening, the planes' tanks were filled and runway denial missiles were attached to the bottom of the MiGs and Sukhois. Given the distance to some of the targets, the military load was reduced to allow for the maximum amount of external fuel tanks. On average, each aircraft only carried two parachute drag bombs, which was not much to neutralize the sprawling air bases that the Shah had built on the American model. However, the Tupolev bombers' bays were fully loaded with iron bombs, which were ideal to pound the target.

Action stations were taken on September 22, 1980. After a final briefing, the tense but confident pilots boarded the 192 planes assigned to the first assault wave in the late morning. At noon, the air bases were rumbling with the sound of jet engines being started in quick succession. Each squadron then gradually moved to the runway according to a rigorously established order and timing, then lined up and took off for Iran. The assailants flew nap-of-the-earth in formations of four to six planes, maintaining total radio silence. They guided themselves using aeronautical charts and what landmarks they could briefly make out. They were not escorted, for speed and the element of surprise were considered their best protection. Iraqi fighter planes were on call to assist them in case they were intercepted while returning from the mission.

The first planes to reach their target were Su-20s from Kirkuk. They bombed the Nojeh air base in Hamadan at 1:45 p.m., causing some damage to the runways. Strictly following their orders, the pilots did a single firing run and immediately turned back, limiting the chances of being shot down. Further north, the Su-22s that had taken off from Mosul struck the Tabriz air base. The Iraqis lightly damaged the base and were able to strafe an Iran-Air Boeing 727 that had just landed. But this was meager prey for Saddam's Falcons. They were flying too fast and did not have enough training to line up the few Tiger fighters scattered around the base's perimeter in their crosshairs. The other planes were safely tucked away in their concrete hangars. In the meantime, fighters flying from Basra bombed the Dezful and Bushehr air bases. The former was the most heavily affected. Its runways and infrastructure were severely damaged, but once again no fighter planes were destroyed. Further south, an early warning patrol shot down two attackers. The Sukhois were powerless against the Phantoms.

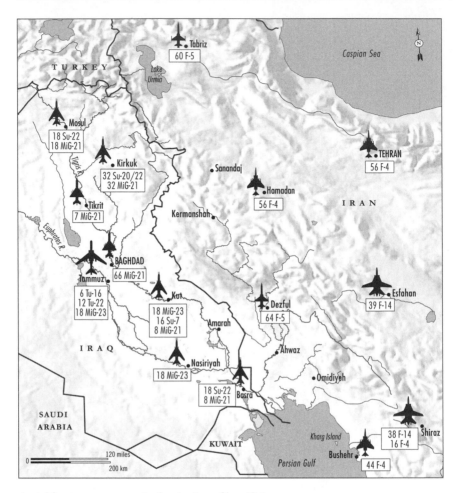

Aerial forces present at the beginning of hostilities

The MiG-23s from Nasiriyah, which were optimized for ground attack, bombed the sprawling Kermanshah military base, where numerous Iranian helicopters were assembled. MiG-23s and Su-7s based in Kut bombed the civilian airports in Ahwaz and Sanandaj, which served as dispersal fields for Iranian airmen.

The most spectacular attack took place at 2:20 p.m., when five Tu-22 bombers from the Tammuz base (known as Habbaniyah when it was under British control) flew over Tehran at very low altitude and split into two formations. The first attacked Mehrabad International Airport, which was base to a Phantom squadron. Its 1,100-pound (500-kilogram) bombs missed the runways, but destroyed a C-130 Hercules transport plane and Boeing 707 flight-refueling plane and severely damaged two other civilian planes. Through a lucky twist of fate, as the bombers banked steeply to return to their home base, one of the rear gunners noticed a row of Phantoms passing through his sights as if lined up on parade. He frenetically pulled the trigger of his 23 mm gun, literally tearing one of the fighters in half. This would be the only Iranian combat aircraft destroyed over the course of the day. Meanwhile, the second formation bombed the air force command's barracks, hoping to wipe out its leadership. But once again, the Iraqi pilots missed their target, and Iranian surface-to-air defense retaliated and shot down one Iraqi plane.

At 2:30 p.m., four Tu-16 heavy bombers, also based in Tammuz, majestically burst into view over the Esfahan airfield, which served as a base for half of Iran's F-14s. The Iraqi pilots scattered their bombs around the base's perimeter, without succeeding in destroying the runways. Their sighting system was not designed for low-altitude bombing. Iranian surface-to-air defense jolted into action, forcing the assailants to execute abrupt evasive action. Taken by surprise, the formation leader crashed into a nearby mountain, his four-reactor plane bursting into a ball of fire upon impact. Images of its shell would be seen around the world, bearing witness to the failure of the Iraqi offensive.

At 2:40 p.m., the last four Tu-22s reached the Shiraz air base, the most distant of the day's targets. It was an important attack, for the other half of Iran's F-14s were based in Shiraz. The Iraqi pilots landed a few bombs on the runways and blew up an arms depot, but failed to destroy any of the precious interceptors. The Bandar Abbas and Kangan air bases, both located close to the Strait of Ormuz, were too distant to be attacked.

Once on the ground, the MiGs and Sukhois were quickly resupplied. Late in the afternoon, they took off again to attack the four closest air bases: Tabriz, Hamadan, Dezful, and Bushehr. These strikes were no more accurate than the previous ones. The Iraqi pilots' major concern was to avoid Iranian fighters, a task made considerably easier by the fact that those in the air had been assigned to protect Tehran and the Shiraz and Esfahan air bases, which were no longer targeted that day. The Iraqi air force put an end to the assault with this second wave and ordered most of its aircraft to be scattered among secondary airfields. It sent some of its heavy bombers to Jordan and North Yemen to protect them from an Iranian counterattack. At day's end, the results of the 250 missions flown were slim: only four enemy planes were destroyed (including three transport planes), versus five planes lost (one Mig-21, one Tu-16, one Tu-22, and two Su-22s). The Iranian air force came out of this operation, which was designed to permanently ground it, unharmed. It would have taken more appropriate weaponry and five times the number of sorties to durably neutralize it. Most of the craters left by Iraqi bombs were filled during the night. By morning, the principal Iranian air bases were operational again.

The Iranian Eagles Strike Back

Taken by surprise by the Iraqi attack and lacking proper contact with their chiefs of staff, who were overwhelmed with calls, the Iranian air base commanders were left to their own devices for the conflict's first twenty-four hours. They could only fall back on general directives, which were of no use in these circumstances. Their priorities were to protect the airplanes, rally all the pilots available, arm the aircraft, repair the runways, and select targets. In the absence of recent instructions, the commanders dug up an operations plan conceived under the Shah. It called for the simultaneous attack of Iraqi air bases. Meanwhile, Commander of the Air Force Colonel Javad Fakouri traveled to Mehrabad to try and get a clearer understanding of the situation. He successfully made contact with the other base commanders, evaluating the damage incurred and coordinating the broad outlines of the counterattack, relying on his subordinates for the details. The essential plan was to strike the enemy as soon as possible, to affect its morale, and to show that the Persian lion would not let itself be assaulted without consequences. But it was also crucial to convince the civil authorities that the air force was loyal and able to react quickly. Looking out the window while working the phone, Colonel Fakouri could see the Elburz Mountains looming over Tehran in the distance. He decided to borrow their name for his operation.

Working through the night, mechanics meticulously prepared those airplanes in flying condition, and pilots studied the freshly exhumed operations plan. The principle was simple: each base would attack the target(s) closest to it. Boeing 707s and 747s would position themselves in Iranian airspace to in-flight refuel the Phantoms flying out of Tehran and any combat aircraft low on fuel. The few operational Tomcats would ensure air defense of Tehran, Esfahan, and Shiraz. Unfortunately, Iraqi radar and surface-to-air missile batteries could not be attacked because the few crews qualified for this kind of mission had been thrown in jail following the Revolution.[1]

At 4:00 a.m. on September 23, the Mehrabad, Hamadan, Bushehr, and Tabriz bases were ready to launch 120 Phantoms and 40 Tigers, all armed to the teeth. This was an impressive feat, given the supposedly disorganized state of the Iranian air force. The pilots made the last checks, started the jet engines, then rolled out of their hangars in a well-coordinated pattern. The first planes took off at 5:00 a.m. and immediately headed west to Iraq in formations of eight aircraft. A Phantom crashed at takeoff following a mechanical failure, killing the entire crew, but the incident did not disrupt the operation. At the break of dawn, the fighters were flying over Iran at low altitude, in total radio and radar silence, using the terrain's relief to mask their approach. Each Phantom carried two external fuel tanks and six bombs, as well as a 20 mm Gatling gun with a very high rate of fire and six air-to-air missiles to ensure its own defense in case of interception by Iraqi fighters. The small Tiger fighters made do with a single external fuel tank, two bombs, and their 20 mm guns.

Once they had crossed the Zagros Mountains, the pilots descended to extremely low altitude and accelerated to maximum speed. Flying at more than 560 miles/hour (900 kilometers/hour), 65 feet (20 meters) from the ground, they were theoretically close to undetectable. At 6:00 a.m., the Phantoms from Hamadan were the first to reach their target: the Baghdad military airport, where three MiG-21 squadrons were deployed. Caught by surprise, the Iraqis did not have time to fire their surface-to-air missiles. As they approached the base, the Iranian pilots nosed up to an altitude of 3,280 feet (1,000 meters) to visualize their target, then guided their planes into a slight dive to attack the airport from several different angles and create confusion among the defense crews, a tactic they had learned from the Israelis.[2] Like the Iraqis, the Iranian planes only did one firing run, dropping their bombs and strafing available targets. They turned back without any losses, just as the anti-aircraft defense was coming alive. They were followed a few minutes later by two Phantom formations from Tehran and Bushehr. Due to a lack of coordination, these two formations appeared above Baghdad at the same time, though they had been intended to arrive ten minutes apart. As a result, the Iranian pilots spent more time avoiding colliding with their comrades and steering clear of projectiles fired by anti-aircraft defense than precisely aiming bombs. Iraqi surface-to-air defense fired a long succession of SAM-2 and SAM-3 missiles, many of which fell back on the city and its surroundings, killing numerous civilians. In the confusion, pilots shot down one of their own transport planes, an Il-76 on the verge of landing. By the time the sixteen Phantoms turned back to Iran, the base had only been lightly damaged. With the exception of an Antonov-26 transport plane, no Iraqi planes were destroyed on the ground, with most fighter planes parked in protected shelters.

The Tammuz air base west of Baghdad was hit hard. The Iranians had hoped to catch the Iraqi bomber fleet here. To ensure their success, they had committed sixteen Phantoms based in Tehran and Hamadan. Here, the two formations arrived at the correct interval, but found an empty nest. All operational bombers had been moved to shelter outside Iraq. Though the MiG-23 squadron responsible for defending the base did not have time to take off, the Iranian pilots did have to contend with the base's surface-to-air defense. One pilot's aircraft was severely damaged by the explosion of a SAM-3. Another pilot, struck by 23 mm cannon rounds, struggled to maintain control of his plane. The Phantoms turned back after having riddled the two runways and the overrun with hits, but were immediately intercepted by four MiG-21s that had taken off from another base. The Iraqi pilots proved tenacious, severely damaging two Phantoms before the Iranian aircraft were able to get away.

Meanwhile, several Phantoms struck the Iraqi capital again, concentrating their attacks on the international airport, where they destroyed a few civilian aircraft, and the Daura refinery, which supplied fuel to the Baghdad area. Other Phantoms, flying from Bushehr, bombed the Kut and Nasiriyah airfields. One was shot down by Iraqi anti-aircraft defense. The Basra air force base suffered two consecutive and rather successful air strikes, with the assailants managing to destroy two Su-20s in their protective bays and to damage several others. They also scored several direct hits on the runway. All the planes in this raid returned to base unscathed.

Four other Phantoms attempted to destroy the strategic bridge over the Tigris at Amarah. This was the only bridge over the Tigris on the main Baghdad-Basra road. Destroying it would disrupt the entire logistics network between the capital and the south of the country. To strike at this particularly important target, the fighter-bombers were armed with one-ton bombs (GBU-10) guided by ground laser location designators. The Iranians only had a small number of systems of this type and would only use them to bomb engineering works and bunkers. In this case, the Iranian planes came face-to-face with a MiG-21 patrol, which shot down one Phantom and pushed back the other three.

To the north, Tigers flying from Tabriz attacked the Mosul base. Two were shot down by MiG-21s, and two others were severely damaged by anti-aircraft defense. The others landed several bombs on target. One plane made a wrong maneuver and crashed down in a terrible firestorm.

By mid-morning, the planes had returned to their bases to be rearmed. However, Iranian logistics were reaching their limits: in the early afternoon, only fifty planes were ready to fly out to assault the Iraqi bases again. These included some twenty Tigers, which were able to take off from the Dezful airfield after one of its runways was put back in service following twenty-four hours of uninterrupted work. This second wave focused on the Basra and Kirkuk airfields. The former base was heavily defended; one of the assailants was disintegrated by a SAM-2 missile. As in Baghdad, most of the volleys of surface-to-air rockets fell back on inhabited areas, proving more dangerous for the local population than the enemy air force. The other fighters destroyed an Antonov-24 and damaged several MiG-21s.

The Iraqi air force attempted a few sporadic raids against the Tabriz and Bushehr air bases, without any significant results. It even lost two MiG-23s shot down by Iranian fighters. It also bombed the Kermanshah camp, destroying a few helicopters. Iraqi air-superiority fighters multiplied patrols over their airfields; three MiG-21s were accidentally shot down by Iraqi anti-aircraft defense, due to a malfunction in their transponders (which were supposed to identify them as "friendly"). At dusk, several Phantoms equipped with sophisticated photographic equipment flew over the Iraqi bases to evaluate the damages inflicted on the enemy. It would be an understatement to say the results were unimpressive. The Iranian air force had succeeded in neutralizing only some ten aircraft, while losing five Phantoms and three Tigers.

In the night of September 23 to 24, Iranian leaders met with air force commanders to plan the continuation of operations. The airmen prepared an operations plan called "Kaman" ("Crossbow"), which would serve as their guide for the next few days.[3] The plan was to try and devastate the Iraqi fighters in flight, since they were unable to destroy them on the ground.

On September 24, 1980, some sixty bomber-fighters attacked the Basra, Nasiriyah, Kut, Baghdad, Kirkuk, and Mosul bases again. This time they were escorted by planes charged with engaging the MiGs that intercepted them. The Iraqis did not fall into the trap, relying instead on their anti-aircraft defense to repel their assailants. The tactic paid off, with two Tigers shot down by anti-aircraft defense over Mosul and Basra, while a third was severely damaged by the explosion of a surface-to-air missile and barely made it back to base, missing one tail fin. Another Tiger flew so low while trying to avoid Iraqi missiles that it collided with a hill. Yet another Tiger was shot down by its own anti-aircraft defense while preparing to land. The tense Iranian artillerymen had mistaken the outline of the F-5 for that of a MiG-21. The Phantoms also paid their due: two were seriously hit and forced to land on their bellies upon returning from their missions, and a third plane had crashed upon takeoff. Two other Phantoms were shot down by MiGs. Nonetheless, the Iranian pilots' bombs made numerous direct hits. In Kirkuk, they strafed an Antonov-24 transport plane, two MiG-21s, and a venerable Hunter fighter that had just been put back in service to participate in fire support missions. They destroyed one Su-22 in Basra and two Su-7s in Kut.

Over these two days, Iranian pilots also targeted Iraqi oil infrastructure. They bombed refineries in Baghdad and Basra, as well as several fuel depots. They even damaged the oil pipeline connecting Iraq to Turkey, but it was soon repaired and the flow of black gold returned to its regular rate a few days later. The Iraqis struck back by launching raids against the Bandar Khomeini petrochemical complex and Ahwaz fuel depots. Colonel Fakouri seized the opportunity to engage in combat with the Iraqi air force. He ordered his Tomcat early warning patrols to stop covering the three major Iranian cities and engage the enemy near the border. Thanks to Boeing refueling planes circling over Iran, the crews did not need to land. Several pairs of Phantoms previously held in reserve were given orders to take off and fly to the combat zone. The maneuver paid off. Using their sophisticated radar, the Iranian pilots could detect their adversaries long before they themselves were spotted. They could therefore position themselves at the best angle to fire their long-range missiles; five MiG-21s, five MiG-23s, and two Su-20s were shot down without ever seeing the Sparrow missiles that tore them out of the sky.

After four days of intensive operations, the air combat score was sixteen to five in favor of the Iranians, but was more balanced when all air losses were taken into account.[4] If we include severely damaged fighter planes, the Iraqis lost forty planes and the Iranians twenty-four. At this rate, air operations could not last for long. In fact, Iraqi General al-Jeboury prudently ordered an end to the raids, placing his air force on the defensive. He limited its missions to protection of the Iraqi territory and backing the ground forces, which had just invaded Iranian territory. He also ordered the bombers scattered around the Arabian Peninsula to return to their base in Tammuz, where the runways had just been repaired.

Despite the losses incurred, his Iranian counterpart Colonel Fakouri had scored two points: he had humiliated the Iraqi regime—which now had to explain to its citizens why Iranian planes had been able to fly over the major Iraqi cities—and given proof of his devotion and loyalty to the Iranian regime. President Bani-Sadr was grateful to him and hastened to convince his government, the Supreme Leader, and a few of the most influential mullahs that it was necessary to free the pilots and mechanics rotting in Iranian jails since the purge that had followed the Revolution. Those implicated in the attempted Nojeh putsch the previous July remained in their cells, but the others were able to rejoin their unit after a week of self-criticism sessions. To guarantee their loyalty and avoid defections, the regime put the airmen's families' fate in their hands. Those who deserted or acted cowardly would have their parents ruthlessly arrested and tried. This unexpected pardon allowed Iran's two Tomcat squadrons to reclaim two-thirds of their navigation personnel. Ultimately, Colonel Fakouri had lost twenty pilots, but their sacrifice had allowed him to free many more.

The Ground Offensive

Disappointed by his pilots' poor performance, Saddam Hussein put all his hopes in the ground offensive, which was calculated to reach his objectives. The Iraqi generals had gone digging through their archives to plan the offensive. They found preparatory documents for a general staff exercise conceived in 1941 by the British instructors at the Baghdad military school. The objective for the Iraqi students of the time was to take the cities of Kermanshah, Dezful, Ahwaz, and Abadan with four motorized infantry divisions in less than ten days. The Iraqi generals took the British maneuver plan, merely dusting it off to fit the current situation. With ten divisions at their disposal, half of them armored, they estimated they could easily reach the same objectives, particularly since they could rely on significant artillery support, which the British did not. As agreed, the units of the 2nd Army Corps (two armored divisions and three infantry divisions) would have to take control of several strategic points at the foot of the Zagros Mountains, in the center of the layout, in order to improve the defense of Baghdad by making the city less vulnerable to an Iranian counterattack. The principal thrust, entrusted to the 3rd Army Corps, would take place in the south, in the direction of the vast coastal plain of the province of Khuzestan, in order to take control of the cities of Dezful, Ahwaz, and Khorramshahr, isolating the Abadan oil complex, which should then fall into Iraqi hands like a ripe fruit. If everything went as planned, these troops would then continue toward the port of Bandar Khomeini. The city of Ahwaz was the offensive's center of gravity. The Iraqi military high command had concentrated three armored divisions and two mechanized divisions on this part of the front.

No operations were concurrently planned in Kurdistan, where the 1st Army Corps' two divisions were struggling to combat the Barzani brothers' peshmergas and prevent Kurdish reinforcements from infiltrating Iraq from Iran. The Iranian troops deployed on the other side of the border did not represent an immediate threat to Iraq, for they were busy fighting their own peshmergas: those of the Democratic Party of Iranian Kurdistan (PDKI), supported by Baghdad.

On September 20 and 21, Adnan Khairallah, minister of defense and cousin to the president, undertook a marathon border inspection to meet the commanders of each of the ten divisions involved in the assault on Iraq. He was accompanied by Chief of Staff of the Armed Forces Jabar Khalil Shamshal, Inspector General of the Armed Forces Mohammed Salim, and Abdel Jabar Assadi, head of operations in charge of coordinating ground forces. The four men gave each of the division heads the relevant sealed orders, wished them luck, and reminded them it would be unwise to disappoint Saddam. The circumspect Iraqi generals took these last instructions to be a signal to be cautious and advance slowly, scrupulously following the manual and limiting risks, rather than throwing themselves into a stampede that could expose them to deadly counter-attacks. When dealing with an individual like Saddam, the quest for glory was a dangerous luxury.

Late in the morning of September 22, 1980, the camouflage netting was removed from tanks, artillery batteries were armed, and the tanks' engines were started. After a light meal, infantrymen boarded the vehicles in which they would cross the border. The sun was shining, the temperature was still high after a sweltering summer, and an ocher heat haze veiled the horizon, hiding the Iranian outposts. The attack was not only scheduled for dawn so that it could be coordinated with the air offensive, but also to ensure the assailants did not have the sun in their eyes as they attacked the Iranian positions to the east, which faced the rising sun. After the first wave of fighter-bombers had flown over, 1,600 tanks, 2,000 armored vehicles, and 4,000 trucks set into motion in a whirlwind of dust at noon, headed for the Zagros Mountains and the arid plains of Khuzestan. The first assault wave numbered some 100,000 men. In the opposite camp, the 25,000 Iranians deployed along the front had 800 tanks and 600 other armored vehicles, half of which were unmovable. The force ratio was close to four to one in favor of the Iraqis.

Northeast of Baghdad, the 6th Armored Division and the 8th Infantry Division left their quarters at Khanaqin headed for Qasr-e-Shirin, a strategic crossroads on the road connecting Baghdad to Kermanshah. These two units crossed the border without the slightest opposition, then deployed to cut off Qasr-e-Shirin. In the late afternoon, the Iraqi advance guard entered the encircled city, which was defended by a detachment of military police, a few regular police forces, and a Revolutionary Guards company. In all, these were no more than 200 men equipped with light weapons, hardly a match for the Iraqi tanks and cannons. But with all escape routes blocked by the Iraqis, the Iranian fighters were determined to inflict the maximum number of losses. The Pasdaran succeeded in destroying the Iraqis' lead vehicles with RPG-7 rocket-propelled grenade launchers, sending the Iraqi troops into disarray and forcing them to change tactics. The Iraqis put their artillery in batteries and pounded the Iranian town for more than two hours. They called in the air force to increase their chances of success.

With every single MiG and Sukhoi mobilized to attack enemy bases, the general staff could only send them four venerable Hunter fighters, which had just been put back into service after years in the hangars. Lacking information, the Hunter pilots fired their rockets haphazardly over Qasr-e-Shirin, merely adding to the chaos. One was shot down by the single anti-aircraft defense battery in the city. At nightfall, the Iraqi dismounted infantrymen companies attacked again, backed by tanks. Advancing under deadly sniper fire, they cleaned out the neighborhoods one by one. Throughout the night, the battle raged on around the deserted houses.[5] The Iraqis took advantage of the first light of day to silence the last pockets of resistance. This first victory had cost them over 100 dead and close to 300 wounded. On the opposing side, a few Iranians had surrendered, but most chose to sacrifice their lives, giving their enemies a foretaste of their compatriots' determination. The Iraqis spent the rest of the day regrouping and evacuating prisoners and the wounded.

On September 24, the 6th Armored Division kept advancing to the Zagros Mountains, supported by the 8th Infantry Division's infantrymen. For the time being, there was no question of rushing to Kermanshah, the regional capital. This kind of offensive along easily blocked narrow mountain roads would only be conceivable if the Iranians collapsed. For now, the appropriate move was to neutralize Sarmast and Eslam Abad-e-Gharb in order to prevent a potential counterattack from the Iranian 81st Armored Division. To do so, the Iraqis first had to take control of the villages of Sar-e-Pol-e-Zahab and Geilan Zarb. While they easily captured the

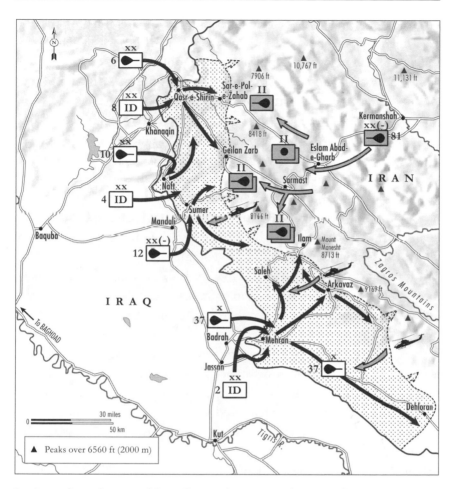

Iraqi assault on the central front (September 22–October 1, 1980)

latter village, the former gave them a harder time. Their tanks advanced at the pace of the dismounted infantrymen, who had disembarked from armored personnel carriers deemed too vulnerable. It took three days to cover the roughly thirty miles (fifty kilometers) between Qasr-e-Shirin and their objective. When the Iraqi soldiers came within sight of Geilan Zarb, they were greeted by heavy gunfire from a group of indefatigable Pasdaran who had rushed out of Kermanshah by bus two days earlier to get to the still fluctuant frontline. Rather than risking useless losses, the Iraqis settled out of range and patiently awaited their artillery's arrival, which cost them an additional day. On September 29, after intense bombing devastated Geilan Zarb, the Iraqis assaulted and forced the village's defenders to withdraw to the mountains, but not until they had inflicted significant losses upon the assailant. The Iraqis then continued toward the crossroads leading to Sarmast.

Further to the south, the 4th Infantry Division, which had left from Baquba and was reinforced by the Republican Guard's 10th Armored Brigade, took control of Naft. After having left a brigade of infantrymen garrisoned in the village, its commander continued his slow advance along the border road to join the other divisions that had invaded the sector. A few days later, he linked up with the 8th and 12th divisions, while the Republican Guard's armored brigade returned to the Baghdad area to serve as a mobile reserve unit for the general staff.

Meanwhile, the 12th Armored Division had left Mandali and crossed the border toward the ancient region of Sumer. It encountered unexpected resistance from a detachment of military police and Pasdaran who had entrenched themselves on site. After thirty-six hours of intense preparation, the two brigades overran the defenders, penetrated the city, and successively neutralized isolated areas of resistance. The 12th Division's commander could boast of having limited casualties, but he had lost precious time, which allowed the Iranians to react and send a tank battalion against him, slowing his advance toward Sarmast and inflicting significant losses. The terrain gave the Iranian Chieftains an advantage. Well sheltered behind the hills, they harried the assailant, backed by a squadron of Cobra helicopters, which scored numerous direct hits on Iraqi tanks.

Even further to the south, the 2nd Infantry Division crossed the border to the east of Jassan and Badrah to encircle Mehran, where a mechanized infantry battalion had been dug in for several weeks. Lacking detailed information on his adversary's assets, the Iraqi division chief took a cautious approach and opted for steamroller tactics. After having sounded the cannon for several hours, he took advantage of the sun setting in the Iranians' eyes to order his brigades to assault. The battle lasted thirty-six hours; the Iraqis took control of Mehran, but lost the equivalent of two battalions of men. On September 25, they continued moving forward. Two infantry brigades headed for Ilam, a small town nestled halfway up the slopes of Mount Manesht and overlooking one of the roads leading to Kermanshah. Ilam was strategically significant because it controlled access to an important radar station. This station, located at the peak of a neighboring mountain, enabled the Iranians to detect any air activity from the bases in Kut and Baghdad. Because control of Ilam was crucial to the Iranians, they had dispatched their 81st Armored Division's reconnaissance battalion to defend the town before Iraqi troops arrived. It was joined by a hastily assembled mechanized infantry battalion, while two tank battalions from the same division backed by two battalions of 155 mm self-propelled Howitzers took position in Sarmast and Eslam Abad-e-Gharb to repel the armored brigades coming from Sar-e-Pol-e-Zahab and Geilan Zarb. Combat helicopters patrolled the sector to evaluate the advance of Iraqi troops. Flying nap-of-the-earth in pairs, they made the most of the terrain's relief to hide their presence and set up deadly ambushes. The rest of the 81st Armored Division remained in Kermanshah for the time being, long enough to fill out its ranks, repair as many tanks as possible, and wait for orders from military high command. The Iranian senior officers had studied tank combat with the Israelis and learned from Tzahal's mistakes during the Yom Kippur War's first phase, seven years earlier, when the Israeli tank commanders had charged the Egyptians in small groups, without any infantry or artillery support, and were decimated by antitank missiles.

The arrival of these reinforcements went undetected by the 2nd Infantry Division's command, which had no efficient means of collecting intelligence. The Iraqi division chief therefore calmly went about following his operation plan. While one of his brigades firmly held onto Mehran, two others took control of Saleh and Arkavaz, then continued toward Ilam. The infantrymen progressed slowly, striding across one barren rocky hill after another, beneath a blazing sun and the running fire of their own mortars systematically hammering any position potentially hiding a sniper. Cobra helicopters occasionally burst into view overhead, firing at them, then taking shelter behind the mountains. Once they came within range of their objective, they were beaten back by the accurate fire of Scorpion tanks and Iranian dismounted infantrymen entrenched on the city's outskirts. For forty-eight hours the two brigade commanders sent their scouts to survey enemy defenses. Convinced that they were solid, they asked their division chief for tank and artillery backup, but he refused, ordering them instead to establish a defensive position. The 2nd Infantry Division's commander had just committed his tanks along the border road leading to Dehloran to assume control of this strategic byway and link up with the 3rd Corps, thereby uniting the Iraqi layout. The tank column was led by the 37th Armored Brigade dispatched from the 12th Division. Its advance was slowed by relentless Iranian Cobra attacks. In a few days, the Iraqis lost some forty T-55 tanks. On September 30 they seized Dehloran and took control of the scattered surrounding oil fields.

Meanwhile, the 2nd and 4th Infantry Divisions' commanders followed Baghdad's orders and instructed their engineers to destroy the water reservoirs on the mountain's flanks, as well as the irrigation system supplying the arid plain along the Iraqi border between Naft and Dehloran. By drying out this arable land 125 miles (200 kilometers) long and 15 miles (25 kilometers) wide, the Iraqi leaders intended to discourage the rural population from trying to return to this crucial sector of the front. It hoped to annex it and shift the border some 12 miles (20 kilometers) east, to the foot of the Zagros Mountains, in order to confine the Iranians to their peaks.

Attacking Khuzestan

On September 22, 1980, three Iraqi armored divisions and two mechanized divisions entered Khuzestan, each in a specifically assigned sector. To the north, the 10th Armored Division crossed the border near the village of Kuwait, headed for Musiyan and reaching the small town thirty-six hours later. Once they had taken control, the Iraqi tanks turned due east, continuing their itinerary toward the Karkheh River. This roughly sixty-mile (hundred-kilometer) journey proved much longer and more difficult than expected. A single winding and plunging road connected Musiyan to the village of Naderi, on the banks of the Karkheh, cutting across a uniformly ochre, folded, and cracked arid landscape of high rocky plateaus with scattered dried-out wadis forming natural obstacles and sharp ridges, giving it a lunar aspect. The division chief had no choice but to put his brigades in single file along the road, led by a reconnaissance regiment charged with detecting obstacles and traps. In this configuration, the Iraqi tanks were particularly vulnerable to Cobra helicopter ambushes. The Cobras had occupied the zone separating the Karkheh River from the Iraqi border and turned it into a vast hunting ground. The Iranian pilots were masters of tactical flight, coming in low through the canyons, appearing out of the blue, striking, then vanishing into the shelter of the chaotic relief. In a few days, the Cobras put some sixty tanks and close to one hundred trucks and other armored vehicles out of commission. Yet several Cobras were brought down by Iraqi anti-aircraft defense, which let loose the moment it heard the thrum of the helicopters. The tracked ZSU-23x4s proved to be formidable adversaries for the Cobra pilots. In these conditions, the 10th Armored Division only advanced about ten miles (sixteen kilometers) a day. Paradoxically, it did not en counter any enemy ground troops. In order to try and limit its losses and accelerate its progress, the division's commander called in Iraqi combat helicopters, including heavily armed and well-protected Mi-24s and Gazelles equipped with 20 mm guns. These helicopters escorted his division and scouted as it progressed, regularly engaging in combat with the Iranian Cobras.

On September 28, the 10th Armored Division reached the Karkheh River and crossed it on the Naderi Bridge, sweeping aside the 138th Infantry Battalion guarding the bridge. It immediately established a bridgehead and waited to be joined by the 1st Mechanized Division, which had crossed the border by Faris, easily taken control of the village of Fakkeh, then split in two to advance along two distinct axes. One of the two mechanized brigades skirted the border to the south in the direction of Bostan, left a detachment to occupy this important crossroads, then turned northeast through a vast network of dunes toward the village of Alvan.

As elsewhere, the Iraqi tanks came up against Iranian helicopters, which harried them relentlessly, destroying several Panhard armored cars as well as some fifteen OT-64 troop carriers. The rest of the division had continued east, headed for Shush. Once it was near the Karkheh River, the general commanding the 1st Division ordered an outflanking maneuver. While his mechanized brigade took control of the bridge leading to Shush, his armored brigade moved a few miles to the south to ford the river. The environment they found on the other bank was totally different. A vast agricultural plain with scattered farms, embankments, and thickets stretched from the Karkheh to the Dez River, providing a significant

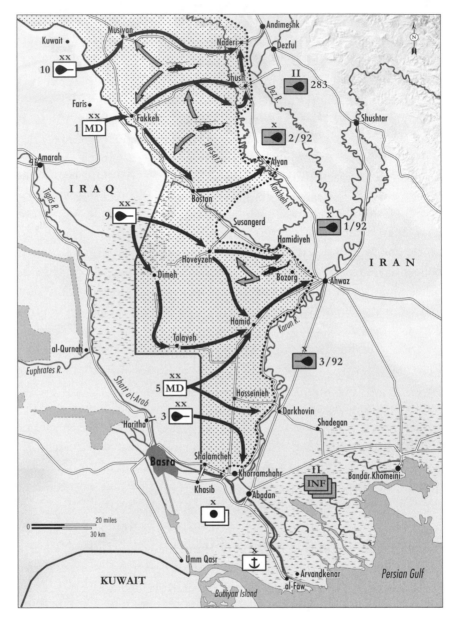

Iraqi assault on Khuzestan (September 22–October 1, 1980)

improvement to the rocky arid hills that the Iraqi tank operators had nearly gotten used to. This flat fertile terrain facilitated the tanks' progress and they soon encircled Shush, attacking its defenders from the rear and rapidly linking up with the 10th Armored Division's tanks. For two days, Iraqi troops supported by the divisional artillery and a few combat helicopters attacked the city of Shush, which was defended by the 141st Infantry Battalion backed by several Pasdaran companies. Encircled, the Iranian survivors eventually surrendered. Yet the Iraqis barely had a chance to catch their breath before the bridgehead was counterattacked by the 283rd Reconnaissance Battalion's Scorpions and the 92nd Armored Division's 2nd Chieftain Brigade. These two units were supported by the accurate fire of a battalion of self-propelled Howitzers. About thirty tanks were destroyed on the Iraqi side and twenty on the Iranian side before the Iraqi artillery was unleashed and pushed back the Iranian tanks.

A little further south, the 9th Armored Division had also reached its provisional objectives. Initially deployed to the southeast of Amarah, it had to cross a marshy area, which was passable at the end of the dry season, before hurtling into an arid rocky plain to take control of Dimch and Hoveyzeh. From there, it split into three columns. The first followed the longest itinerary to reach Ahwaz from the south, initially skirting the Iraqi border to Talayeh, then turning toward Hamid. After having overcome the few troops entrenched in the former village, this first column continued toward Ahwaz, following the western bank of the Karun River. Since there were no bridges across the river in the area, the Iraqis were able to progress without any risk of being attacked on their right flank. A second column rushed to Susangerd, which it crossed without encountering any resistance, the city having apparently been left defenseless. The column continued in the direction of Hamidiyeh. It came into contact with the 92nd Armored Division's reconnaissance regiment, which met it with effective in-depth defense. Yet the Iranians eventually had to yield in the face of Iraqi pressure. Their Scorpions' 90 mm guns did not hold their weight against the T-62 tanks' 115 mm guns. The Iraqis thus took control of Hamidiyeh, then Bozorg. The third column left Hoveyzeh by following the road through the desert to the Karun River. It ran into the 92nd Division's 1st Brigade, which succeeded in slowing it down with backup from a few Cobras. The Iranian tank commanders avoided a full-on confrontation, choosing instead to hold their adversaries at a distance. To advance, the Iraqis had to rely on their artillery, and Gazelles armed with HOT anti-tank missiles. Several of the Gazelles were shot down.

At the end of the first week of operations, the 9th Armored Division arrived within sight of Ahwaz, but no longer had enough troops, munitions, fuel, or water to launch an assault on the capital of Khuzestan, home to 300,000 inhabitants and numerous depots, as well as an important railway and road junction. The division's lines of communication were stretched to the limit and its logistics had fallen behind. An immediate attack would have been suicidal, given that this city, which sprawled along the Karun River's eastern bank, was solidly defended by the rest of the 92nd Armored Division, significant artillery, and sizeable contingents of the Revolutionary Guards. Its six bridges were carefully guarded, and their surroundings meticulously swept by combined artillery and tank fire.

The Iraqis Grind to a Halt outside Khorramshahr

While the ground offensive took place more or less according to plan in the other sectors of the front, it immediately ground to a halt in the area of Basra. On the first day of the war, the 3rd Armored Division, reinforced by the 5th Mechanized Division's 26th Tank Brigade, took control of the Shalamcheh border post, allowing Iraqi engineers to start building a pontoon bridge across the Shatt al-Arab River. A brigade of SAM-6 surface-to-air missiles was deployed nearby to protect their path. Once finished, this bridge connecting Khasib to Shalamcheh would facilitate the delivery of supplies and reinforcements. Simultaneously, the Iraqi artillery took aim at Abadan's oil refinery and fuel depots. The bludgeoning fire would last for several weeks and amount to a tremendous waste of ammunition. The Iraqi leadership's goal was twofold: to destroy the biggest refinery in the world in order to weaken the Iranian economy and to raze the partially deserted city in order to punish Tehran. Since the oil facilities were immediately next to the city, the bombing transformed it into a vast field of ruins, which only served to make its defenders' task easier. The Iranian artillery struck back by pounding the Iraqi port of al-Faw, which had also been evacuated.

Without further ado, the 3rd Division launched a concentric attack on Khorramshahr to try to divide the city, reach the two bridges over the Karun River, and establish a bridgehead toward Abadan. Defying all logic, Iraqi command sent its tanks on the assault rather than the infantry. The tank columns did not hold out for more than a few hours in the heart of this city, which was defended by 1,500 fighters from the 151st Fortification Battalion, a naval infantry detachment, and several Pasdaran companies. The Iranians fought doggedly, repelling the assailant with RPG-7 fire, magnetic antitank mines, and Molotov cocktails. The Iraqi tanks came up against improvised barricades made of buses, public work vehicles, and knocked-over trucks, which funneled them into a dead-end labyrinth. Rooftop snipers took advantage of the situation to fire at the dismounted Iraqi infantrymen and eliminate the tank commanders who dared to cast an eye outside their turret. Pinned inside their tanks, the Iraqis finally retreated after having lost the equivalent of one tank battalion and one mechanized battalion. The general commanding the division immediately decided to change tactics and lay siege to Khorramshahr while waiting for infantry reinforcements, subjecting the city to intense artillery shelling.

About eighteen miles (thirty kilometers) to the north, the 5th Mechanized Division occupied the arid plain stretching from the border to the Karun River, easily taking Hosseinieh, then Hamid. Controlling Hamid was particularly important because it locked in the logistics chain supplying the 3rd Corps.

On September 28, 1980, Saddam Hussein realized that his army's rate of progress was slower than planned and that if the Iranians were prepared to negotiate it might be preferable to stop the offensive. He considered he had made enough of a show of strength to propose a ceasefire and to expect that negotiations would give him the upper hand. He serenely declared to the international press that, "Iraq is prepared to negotiate directly with the Iranian party, or through a third party or any international organization, for a just and honorable solution that guarantees our rights."[6] In essence, the Iraqi president wanted Iran to renounce the Algiers Accord and recognize Iraqi sovereignty over the entire Shatt al-Arab, as well as a certain number of enclaves that his army had recently seized, notably around Qasr-e-Shirin, Sumer, and Mehran. To convince the Iranian party to accept his offer, he ordered a unilateral truce for the first week of

October. Iran's biting response was not long in coming. On September 30, the Iranian government listed a set of unacceptable conditions for talks to be held: Saddam Hussein was to step down; the Iraqi regime was to recognize that it was the aggressor and agree to compensate Iran for the damages incurred; Basra was to come under Iranian control until Iraq paid off its war debt; a referendum was to be held in Iraqi Kurdistan to allow the Kurds to choose between autonomy and being integrated to Iran. Any negotiation was thus impossible. The decision would have to be won on the battlefield. Though it did not come to pass, the truce announced by Saddam cooled the ardor of the Iraqi soldiers, who did not understand why their president sent them to battle while announcing that he was prepared to negotiate with the enemy.

[Chapter 3]

How Did It Come to This?

The Iran-Iraq War resulted first and foremost from the desire for confrontation of two men with conflicting ambitions, Saddam Hussein and Ayatollah Ruhollah Khomeini. Each leader believed the survival of the regime he had forged relied on the destruction or, at the very least, the weakening of the other. But the ruthless confrontation between these two tyrants would never have degenerated into a total war if Iraqis and Iranians on both sides had not been convinced that they were fighting for their legitimate rights in the name of an ancestral rivalry. Indeed, Arabs and Persians had long fought over the Middle East's Fertile Crescent, once known as Mesopotamia, and which now included most of Iraqi territory and a small part of Iranian territory.

Old Border Disputes

In the early sixteenth century, the Ottoman and Persian empires faced off along a fault line that followed the natural border of the Zagros Mountains, long the division between the Arab and Persian civilizations. This power struggle between the Ottomans and Persians soon took on a religious connotation. While the former considered themselves heirs to the caliphs and defenders of Sunni Islam, the latter saw themselves as the champions of Shia Islam. Ismail I, founder of the Safavid Dynasty, declared Shia Islam the official religion of the Persian Empire in 1503. While waiting to seize the holy sites of Najaf and Karbala, which were inaccessible because they were under Ottoman control, he sanctified the city of Qom, home to the religious school responsible for training the Shiite community's clergy, but also the city of Mashhad, home to the mausoleum of Imam Reza, who was assassinated by the Sunni caliph Al-Mam'un, a native of Baghdad.

45

Qom and Mashhad soon became pilgrimage sites for Iranian Shiites, and Persia established itself as the guardian of Twelver Shia Islam.

In 1534 Sultan Suleiman the Magnificent conquered Baghdad and signed the Treaty of Amasia (1555), by which Persia renounced all claim to Mesopotamia and the Shatt al-Arab (literally, "the shore of the Arabs"), which were integrated into the Ottoman Empire in the vilayets of Mosul, Baghdad, and Basra. The Treaty of Qasr-e-Shirin (1639) confirmed its predecessor's terms. The border between the Persian and Ottoman empires was stabilized, with the exception of the coastal plain of Khuzestan, which extends from the Shatt al-Arab to the Zagros Mountains. The Persians claimed this marshy area, arguing that it had always been their natural opening to the waters of the Gulf. Several tribes native to the Arabian Peninsula contested Persian sovereignty over the coastal region where they had settled. Seeing his chance in the decline of the Safavid Dynasty, the Banu Kaab's tribal chief felt powerful enough to defy the Shah and rename the area "Arabistan." This was unacceptable to the Persian authorities, who launched a series of punitive expeditions, creating more friction with the Ottoman Empire. Yet the power dynamic remained favorable to the Sublime Porte, which imposed Amir Ashraf's treaty (1727) by which Persia committed to no longer interfering in Arabistan's affairs. From this point on, Iraq replaced Mesopotamia in official nomenclature.

European powers took an interest in the region following the Congress of Vienna (1815). The English and Russians demanded that the Persians and Ottomans come to an agreement about a permanent border in order to stabilize the region and protect their interests. In 1843 a mixed Anglo-Russian commission delimited the Persian-Ottoman border from Mount Ararat to the Arab-Persian Gulf. This new border was sanctioned by the Treaty of Erzurum (1847). The Ottomans kept Iraq and the entire Shatt al-Arab, but had to surrender the mountainous foothills between Mehran and Qasr-e-Shirin. The Persians reclaimed Khuzestan and were given the right to navigate the Shatt al-Arab, but had to abandon their claim to the province of Sulaymaniyah, which was primarily populated by Kurds.

In the late nineteenth century the situation was complicated by the arrival of a significant number of Shiite tribes fleeing the proselytism of

Wahabis established in the Kingdom of Nadj. These tribes settled in the south of Iraq, notably in the area of Basra, but also and especially near Najaf and Karbala, thus returning to their religion's holy places. Their dynamism led to a massive wave of conversions, which would gradually shift the balance between Sunni and Shia Muslims in Iraq.

In 1911, the Persians and Ottomans called the Treaty of Erzurum into question. The British and Russians pressured them to accept new mediation. Teams of cartographers traveled to the area and established an extremely precise border delineation, which was formalized through the Constantinople Protocol of November 4, 1913. The land border was fixed, and Ottoman sovereignty over the Shatt al-Arab reaffirmed, with the exception of a dozen small islands located between Muhammara and the mouth of the Gulf, which would no longer be under Turkish control. This protocol was accompanied by reports meticulously describing the border's delineation. The British admiralty maps appended to these documents would serve as references to Iraqis and Iranians until the end of the twentieth century and the appearance of satellite maps.

The First World War turned this careful political construction upside down. As soon as the Sultan entered the war on the Germans' side, the British occupied Basra, then advanced toward Baghdad. The Russians reinforced their grip on the northern part of Persia. By the end of the war, the British were the masters of Iraq. The Russian Revolution and the fall of the Ottoman Empire allowed them to consolidate their position by establishing themselves in Qatar and obtaining a League of Nations mandate in Iraq through the Sykes-Picot Agreement, which divided the Middle East into British, French, and Russian spheres of influence. London was particularly pleased to control Baghdad, given that significant oil deposits had been discovered in the areas of Kirkuk and Mosul.

From the advent of Iraqi independence on June 30, 1930, King Faisal reaffirmed Iraqi sovereignty over the Shatt al-Arab, while the Shah of Iran, Reza Pahlavi, demanded shared sovereignty over the river and denounced the 1913 Constantinople Protocol. Following negotiations moderated by the British, the Iranians and Iraqis agreed on a new treaty in Tehran on July 18, 1937. The agreement recognized the overall validity of the Constantinople Protocol, but established that for a narrow stretch of the Shatt al-Arab extending between the river ports of Khorramshahr and Abadan the border would now be along the thalweg—the river's median line. In exchange, Iraq conserved a monopoly on piloting along the river.

The Second World War modified the geopolitical landscape. The Americans replaced the British as Iran's "sponsors," while the Soviets were forced to evacuate the country's northern part. Beginning in the mid-fifties, the new Shah of Iran, Mohammad Reza Pahlavi, asserted a pro-Western line and imposed himself as one of the most influential leaders in the Middle East. Meanwhile, the situation in Iraq became volatile. A series of bloody revolutions brutally deposed the monarchy (July 14, 1958), then the juntas of generals Qasim (February 8, 1963) and Arif (July 17, 1968). The Shah of Iran, who was canny about winning American and British backing, took the opportunity to return to the question of the Shatt al-Arab. But he had failed to consider the Soviets' committed support of the Iraqis. The Russians blocked the renegotiation of the agreements. The Cold War had invited itself into the Middle East, and the Kremlin multi-plied overtures and arms deliveries to Baghdad, where the Ba'ath Party (literally, "renewal" party) had taken power. Founded in Damascus by two Syrian intellectuals in the 1940s, this secular socialist party intended to resurrect the feeling of brotherhood and unity among Arabs. This doc-trine seduced the Sunni Muslim-dominated Iraqi intelligentsia worried by the Shiite community's growing power. These intellectuals saw Ba'athist ideology as a way to get rid of religious rivalries. For similar reasons, the Ba'ath Party attracted large numbers of Iraqi Christians. On July 17, 1968, the Revolutionary Command Council (RCC) was founded and appointed General al-Bakr president of the Republic, giving this fifty-four-year-old former educator, who had devoted his life to the military and the Ba'ath Party, the ultimate recognition.

Iraq's new strong man brought along his nephew by marriage, a man called Saddam Hussein, who had gradually imposed himself as one of the pillars of Ba'athism. Like al-Bakr, Saddam was a native of the town of Tikrit, about sixty miles (one hundred kilometers) from Baghdad. Al-Bakr felt he did not have much to fear from this thirty-one-year-old with an arrogant mustache: while he was an undoubtedly ambitious man, he lacked military experience and did not have connections to rival al-Bakr's own.

Enter Saddam Hussein

Born on April 28, 1937, to a modest peasant family, Saddam Hussein was left to his own devices at an early age. To escape his brutal stepfather's stick, he became a shepherd, then went to live with his maternal uncle Talfah Khairallah. This nationalist teacher and former military man would educate Saddam, send him to school, and introduce him to revolutionary culture. The young man had unlimited admiration for his mentor, who initiated him to Iraqi history and the revolutionary writers and taught him how to handle a weapon. He became close with Sajida, Khairallah's daughter and his first cousin, whom he would marry a few years later, as well as Adnan, the first cousin whom he thought of as a brother and who would later become his closest advisor. After following the Khairallah family to settle in Baghdad, Saddam struggled to finish his high school education and failed the entrance exam to the military academy. Disappointed, he took on a variety of small jobs that allowed him to learn the harsh realities of the street and establish himself as a gang leader. He now discovered the power of intimidation and violence.

In the mid-fifties he joined a clandestine cell of the Ba'ath Party through the intervention of his uncle Talfah, who had become a member a few years earlier. Here, Saddam proved determined, ruthless, and, when necessary, brutal. These three traits would characterize the rest of his career. Ready to serve as a gunman, he was imprisoned for the murder of a royal police informer, then freed after the 1958 revolution. Saddam tried to keep a low profile for a while but was soon drawn back to clandestine action when the new regime decided to hunt down Ba'ath Party members. On October 7, 1959, he was part of the group that tried and failed to assassinate President Kassem. Wounded, he fled to Damascus. Here, he met Michel Aflaq, the Ba'ath Party icon, who predicted he would have a brilliant future and advised him to study law in Cairo. Saddam proved a barely passable student. Academia did not suit the man of power and action. The 1963 revolution gave him an opportunity to return to Baghdad. With the support of Michel Aflaq, he became an intermediary between the Syrian and Iraqi branches of the Ba'ath Party, which allowed him to rekindle his ties with General al-Bakr, his uncle by marriage, and gradually win his trust.

In 1964, shortly after the birth of his first son, Uday, Saddam Hussein was arrested during a sweep to eliminate the party's leaders. Prison time served to deepen his revolutionary knowledge. He became fascinated with the writings of Stalin, whose thought now served as his intellectual model. In 1966, he escaped during a prison transfer and went underground again, taking various positions in the secret services of the party's clandestine leadership. On July 30, 1968, Hassan al-Bakr appointed Saddam Hussein deputy secretary general of the Ba'ath Party, in essence making him the regime's number two man. Now that he had acceded to power, Saddam intended never to let go. From then on, he strived relentlessly for absolute power, knowing he would have to carefully handle his mentor long enough to solidify his position and seize control of the party. To reach his goal, he had himself appointed head of the regime's security services. With the support of his clan, his immediate family, and those in his debt, Saddam Hussein eliminated his rivals and took control of Baghdad. Aside from his uncle Talfah and his cousin Adnan Khairallah, he knew he could count on his half-brother Barzan al-Tikriti, his cousin Ali Hassan al-Majid, and two comrades from the years of underground struggle: the Christian Tariq Aziz and the Kurd Taha Yassin Ramadan.

Tariq Aziz belonged to Iraq's Chaldean Christian community and was an intellectual steeped in Anglophone culture. He was of the same generation as Saddam Hussein, whom he had met in 1957 when he joined the Ba'ath Party. Captivated by Saddam's personality, he staked his career on Saddam's, using his talents as a polyglot and a journalist to advocate for his mentor abroad, particularly in Europe. Taha Yassin Ramadan had been a mere eighteen-year-old bank clerk when he joined the Ba'ath Party in 1956. As a Kurd, he knew he needed an Arab protector to have a career within the party. Fascinated by Saddam, he trusted him completely and became one of his most fervent supporters. He quickly made his way up the echelons to become head of the People's Army, the militia in charge of protecting the Ba'athist regime.

Mindful of the previous coups d'état, Saddam Hussein decided to bridle the army, putting it under the political control of the Ba'ath Party to quell any insurrectionary leanings. The most brilliant officers were dismissed, and large-scale exercises were cancelled. Munitions reserves were reduced to the absolute minimum. Major units were reorganized and assigned political commissars. Leadership positions in the military high command were frequently reshuffled. Soviet advisors were sidelined. Meanwhile, the police and national security forces were reinforced and given special treatment. The security services, which were under Saddam's direct control, became all powerful. Every effort was made to defend the regime, even at the cost of weakening the border and reducing the army's credibility. General al-Bakr was distressed by the situation, but knew he was powerless to act if he wanted to hold onto the presidency. These developments did not go unnoticed by the Shah of Iran, who saw an opportunity to take action. On April 19, 1969, he denounced the 1937 Treaty of Tehran and decreed that the Iran-Iraq river border would now run down the middle of the Shatt al-Arab, as opposed to its eastern bank. Baghdad refuted this claim and reaffirmed Iraqi sovereignty over the entire river. To increase pressure on the Iraqi regime, the Shah armed the Kurdish guerilla fighters struggling for independence from Baghdad.

In the late 1960s, twenty million Kurds lived in Turkey, Iran, Iraq, and Syria. Most came from mountain tribes divided by clan rivalries that were largely responsible for the failure of their attempts at emancipation. At the time, there were three million Kurds in Iraq, who made up close to 20 percent of the population and were concentrated in the mountainous provinces in the north of the country, around the cities of Sulaymaniah, Kirkuk, and Mosul. They occupied a highly strategic area, home to the principal oil fields responsible for the country's wealth. The oil pipeline connecting the Kirkuk oil fields to the Dortyol oil terminal in Turkey ran next to the Kurdish bastions controlled by the *peshmergas*. This key area also held the passes leading to Turkey and northern Iran, allowing the peshmergas to move between countries and find shelter in either one depending on the turn of events. Those in control of Iraqi Kurdistan therefore controlled both Iraq's economy and the northern gateway to the nation, which explains why the central Iraqi government desperately attempted to control this area by artificially dividing it into three distinct provinces (Erbil, Sulaymaniah, and Duhok). Its strategy was to divide and conquer, alternating its alliances among the principal clans fighting for effective control of Iraqi Kurdistan. The most powerful clan was headed by Mustafa Barzani, founder of the Kurdistan Democratic Party (KDP), the Iraqi Kurdish community's official showcase since 1960.

As soon as he came to power, General al-Bakr launched a military campaign against the peshmergas. He ran into dogged resistance from Kurdish fighters entrenched in their mountains, who successfully harried the regular troops and threatened the Iraqi oil infrastructure. Barzani's troops owed part of their tenacity to the fact that they were armed by Iran. Saddam Hussein saw the benefits of this situation, which allowed him to keep the army busy, giving him free rein to reinforce his personal power and undertake the economic and social reforms the country needed. Saddam knew he had to obtain Kurdish neutrality to implement his reforms and modernize Iraq. He decided to negotiate with Mustafa Barzani. Doing so allowed him to win on all fronts. He stabilized the country, weakened his mentor, took on the part of the strong man who managed to make an agreement with the Kurdish resistance, and pulled the rug from under the Shah's feet by preventing him from using the Kurdish insurgency to his own ends. On March 11, 1970, Saddam granted the Kurds autonomous status, which recognized their cultural and linguistic identity, gave them significant power on the local administrative level, and brought five Kurdish ministers into his government. Saddam Hussein and Mustafa Barzani gave themselves four years to apply this autonomous status. This bought both men precious time to reinforce their positions.

The Rivalry for Regional Supremacy

In December 1971, in an effort to save money, the British government withdrew from the Gulf region after having guided the emancipation of the emirates previously subject to its protectorate. In becoming independent, Oman, the United Arab Emirates, Qatar, and Bahrain joined Saudi Arabia, Kuwait, and Iraq on the front lines in attempting to contain Iran's regional ambitions. For, by leaving the area, the British had handed the Iranians the responsibility for being the Gulf's policemen. Iran, which had signed major arms contracts with the United Kingdom, took advantage of the opportunity to seize three small islands (Abu Musa and the Greater and Lesser Tunbs). These islands controlled access to the Strait of Hormuz, whose strategic value had consistently risen since two-thirds of the Middle East's oil production had begun passing through it. The islands belonged to the United Arab Emirates but had been claimed by Iran since the eighteenth century. Their occupation was the result of bargaining between Tehran and London. The British government, conscious that the United Arab Emirates would be unable to defend the islands, preferred to see them come into the hands of Iran, a reliable ally to the West. In exchange, the Shah had committed to giving up any claim on the island of Bahrain. This tiny emirate, nestled between Qatar and Saudi Arabia, thus remained the British Crown's principal vector of influence in the Gulf.

Bogged down in the Vietnam War, the American government openly banked on the Shah and promised him significant military assistance. Richard Nixon and Henry Kissinger considered the Iranian monarch to be the West's best rampart against Soviet activism in the Middle East. The United States shipped him vast quantities of weapons, turning the country into a true regional power able to cast its influence far beyond its borders. This avalanche of equipment was financed by oil riches. The White House had such confidence in the Shah that it agreed to ship him eighty Tomcat interceptors equipped with the formidable Phoenix missile—which could destroy a target more than 90 miles (150 kilometers) away—despite its previous refusal to export this ultrasophisticated fighter for fear of having the technology fall into Soviet hands. Several thousand Iranian military students (including all the country's young pilots) were trained in the United States every year. Better yet, Washington embarked on a civil nuclear cooperation program with Tehran and promised to deliver the Shah several fully operational weapon factories. This technical assistance was accompanied by close cooperation in the intelligence sector. Since the mid-fifties, the CIA had been working closely with the SAVAK, Iran's secret police. Its famous U-2 and SR-71 Blackbird spy planes regularly operated from Iranian soil. Some flew over Iraq, informing the Shah about his boisterous neighbor's military disposition.

In Iraq, Saddam Hussein was determined to get his country out of its diplomatic isolation in order to play a part up to his standards in the Arab world and more effectively counter the two states he saw as his fiercest adversaries: Iran and Israel.[1] He conceived a three-step maneuver to attain his goal and had it endorsed by General al-Bakr. First, he reconciled with the Soviet Union, acting not on an ideological decision, but out of pure realpolitik. Baghdad needed modern weapons and the guaranteed support of the United Nations Security Council to block Iranian, Israeli, and American attempts to isolate the Ba'athist regime. For its part, the Kremlin sought to improve its position in the region. Though they had no illusions regarding the Iraqi regime's genuine commitment to their cause, Soviet leaders were eager to divide the pro-Western camp and contain the American push into the Gulf. Saddam Hussein eagerly agreed to travel to Moscow to move discussions along, leading to the signature of a friendship and cooperation pact between Iraq and the Soviet Union in Baghdad on April 9, 1972. In exchange, the Ba'athist regime committed to accepting the Iraqi Communist Party and to stop hunting down its members. Iraq also received large quantities of weapons, which allowed it to come close to reestablishing parity with its powerful Iranian neighbor. The equipment was not particularly reliable, but it was enough to dissuade Iran from recklessly attacking Iraq.

After drawing closer to the Russians, Saddam Hussein decided to reinforce his relationships with Europe in order to stay out of East-West antagonism and avoid both American hostility and overdependence on the Soviets. The Ba'ath Party was nationalistic first and foremost and refused to come under the control of any kind of protector. This is why the Soviets were not given access to Iraqi bases. With the Germans considered too close to the Israelis, the British out of favor, and the Italians not credible, the Iraqis naturally turned to the French, who seemed to be the only ones who could provide Iraq with everything it needed: close cooperation in the oil sector, large-scale assistance with civil nuclear power, and modern weapons to dissuade their Iranian neighbor. France quickly established itself as a precious source of weapons for the regime in Baghdad.

Saddam Hussein put the final touches on his diplomatic maneuver by turning on the charm in the principal Arab capitals. In the Gulf, he presented himself as the Arabs' natural shield from Iranian imperialism. In the Near East, he claimed to be a champion of Palestinian liberation and the struggle against the Israeli occupier. He sent part of his army to fight the Israelis on the Golan Heights during the October 1973 Yom Kippur War, his participation in the war allowing him to momentarily appease his rivalry with the Syrian Ba'athist regime. Since General Hafez al-Assad had seized power in Damascus in November 1970, tensions between Iraq and Syria were exacerbated and the two nations increasingly came to seem like rival brothers. Though Hafez al-Assad was a tried-and-true Ba'athist, he did not share the Iraqi Ba'athists' vision. He courted Cairo and Moscow, haughtily ignoring Baghdad. Most significantly, the Syrian leader represented Ba'athism's militarist line, while Saddam saw himself as the champion of a "civil" line that aimed to subject the military institution to the party's diktats. Tensions eventually drove the Ba'ath Party's general leadership to splinter. Michel Aflaq fled Damascus to seek shelter in Baghdad. From then on, the Iraqi regime prided itself on being the only representative of the party's historic line. Buoyed by this legitimacy, Saddam Hussein reorganized Iraqi political life around Ba'athism and gagged the opposition once and for all.

While pulling Iraq out of diplomatic isolation, Saddam Hussein devoted himself to his other priority: nationalizing the oil industry. On June 1, 1972, the Iraqi government nationalized the Iraq Petroleum Company and all the oil companies operating on Iraqi territory. This was a terrible blow to Anglo-Saxon companies, which had done everything possible to oppose the decision. Thanks to an energy partnership with France, the Iraqi leadership put two offshore oil terminals (Mina al-Bakr and Khor al-Amaya) in service. Oil production increased, growing from 2 to 3.5 million barrels per day in a few years, and making Iraq both a major player within the Organization of the Petroleum Exporting Countries (OPEC) and a serious rival to Iran on the energy front.

The Algiers Accord

While Iraq's situation had improved regionally, it had deteriorated domestically. Saddam Hussein had not lived up to his word: he had not implemented the autonomous status promised to the Kurds, provoking the fury of the Barzani clan. Worse, the Iraqi regime had embarked on a vast program to transfer the populations of the country's two principal Kurdish cities, Mosul and Kirkuk, and force their Arabization.

In the spring of 1974, Mustafa Barzani mobilized his troops and called for the creation of an independent Kurdistan with Kirkuk as a capital. More than 50,000 peshmergas went underground, threatening to put a stranglehold on Mosul and Kirkuk. This time Mustafa Barzani could count not only on the active support of Iran, which saw an opportunity to weaken Iraq and force it to renegotiate the Shatt al-Arab's status, but also the backing of the United States and Israel, which sought any means to destabilize the Iraqi regime—the Americans because they considered Iraq to be in the Soviets' pocket, and the Israelis because they saw it as their most dangerous enemy. The CIA, Mossad, and SAVAK were highly active in financing, arming, and training Kurdish guerilla fighters, greatly displeasing Baghdad, which mobilized 100,000 soldiers and most of its tanks, artillery, and air force to attempt to crush this new revolt. General al-Bakr took matters in hand, seeing this as an unhoped-for chance to boost his prestige and restore the army's influence within his party. Aside from a few local successes, the peshmergas could hardly stand up to the now well-equipped Iraqi steamroller. They were inexorably driven back to the Turkish and Iranian borders. Battles were fierce and crackdowns brutal. Yet late in 1974, the Iraqi army started to show signs of weariness. The Shah leapt on the occasion to send several thousand Iranian soldiers as reinforcements in disguise as peshmergas. Backed by armored vehicles and artillery, these soldiers directly participated in hostilities. Mohammad Reza Pahlavi was determined to make Baghdad yield.

Early in 1975, the Iraqi offensive was running out of steam and the front was stabilizing, encouraging the Shah to increase his assistance to Mustafa Barzani's KDP. The Iraqi government realized this civil war was costing it a great deal and preventing it from pursuing the country's modernization, which had just started to bear fruit. The fighting had left close to 20,000 dead, and the Iraqi army had lost some 100 tanks and about 20 aircraft; 200,000 Iraqi Kurds had taken refuge in Iran. General al-Bakr and Saddam Hussein, thoroughly aware that the force ratio was not in their favor, understood that they could no longer afford to directly confront the Iranian army and that they had no choice but to deal with the Shah. The United States feared that persistent tension between Iran and Iraq would play into the Kremlin's hands and was therefore favorable to a negotiated conclusion, even if it meant abandoning its Kurdish auxiliaries. The Soviet Union remained silent, divided between its natural empathy for the Kurdish movement and its contractual obligations to the Iraqi government. Only Israel wanted the fighting to continue, for it had the distinct advantage of simultaneously occupying and weakening the Iraqi army.

The Iraqis and Iranians agreed to take up negotiations under the authority of Algerian president Houari Boumediene, the sitting president of the group of nonaligned states, who maintained excellent relations both with Baghdad and Tehran. Boumediene invited the Iraqi and Iranian leaders to meet in Algiers on the occasion of the OPEC summit, of which Algeria was holding the rotating presidency. On March 6, 1975, Saddam Hussein and Mohammad Reza Pahlavi found common ground and agreed to proceed to the definitive delineation of their terrestrial border on the basis of the 1913 Constantinople Protocol and to delineate their fluvial border based on the thalweg line. The border would be drawn down the middle of the Shatt al Arab. The Shah had won. In exchange, he immediately withdrew all support to the Kurdish rebellion. The Iraqi leadership had given in on the question of the Shatt al-Arab to ensure it could rapidly crush the Kurdish rebellion beneath its steamroller. Mustafa Barzani was left no choice but to flee with his sons Idris and Masoud and wait for better days. General al-Bakr magnanimously decreed an amnesty for those peshmergas who agreed to put down their weapons.

But Saddam Hussein felt humiliated. The Ba'ath Party's most nationalist fringe reproached him for having cheaply yielded the Iraqi people's interests in the face of the Iranian despot. With his pride hurt, Saddam would now do everything possible to reverse the power dynamic and create the conditions for a repeal of the Algiers Accord, which was perceived as his only political failure. Determined to come out on top, he turned to the interior and used the nation's oil wealth to launch a policy of major public works and accelerate economic and social reforms allowing the middle class, the Ba'ath Party's most solid base, to improve its living conditions. Saddam understood that for Iraqi society to accept the regime's authoritative nature, it needed to be able to increase its wealth and attain a certain standard of living. By doing so, the strong man of Baghdad hoped to pull the rug from under the feet of Shiites who had joined forces in the Dawa Party and had recently been displaying their growing influence through a growing number of demonstrations.[2]

While tightening his hold on Iraqi society, Saddam Hussein did his utmost to rein in the army. Now that it was no longer busy on the Kurdish front, he had to ensure its docility and wipe out any seditious leanings, all the while treading softly with General al-Bakr. Al-Bakr was part of his family, but he maintained ultimate control over the military. To achieve his ends, Saddam Hussein had the RCC appoint himself as a general, despite the fact that he had no experience in the army and had not even done his military service. To reinforce his position, he entrusted the Ministry of Defense to his first cousin Adnan Khairallah, who had made a career in the military and distinguished himself in the war against the peshmergas. With Khairallah's support, Saddam Hussein could increase his control over the military, while bolstering its arsenal to impress foreign observers and shift the force ratio with Iran in his favor. He founded a corps of young commissioned and noncommissioned officers devoted to the regime. He instilled a general climate of terror by purging the army of individuals perceived as rebellious. In early 1978, a "plot" was brought to light within the army: twenty officers were arrested and executed following a parody of a trial. Meanwhile, major arms deals were signed with the Soviet Union and France to provide Iraq with modern weapons, notably Scud ballistic missiles capable of hitting Iran.

Saddam Hussein was also active on the regional level. While General al-Bakr attempted to negotiate the terms of an institutional union between Iraq and Syria based on the principle of Ba'athist solidarity that supposedly united the two countries, Saddam sought a rapprochement with the Gulf oil monarchies. He regularly consulted with King Khalid of Saudi Arabia, using flattery if necessary. He worked hardest at improving relations with Turkey, for Baghdad depended on Ankara for its freshwater supply (the sources of the Tigris and Euphrates are both in Turkey) and for selling its oil. Fate dealt Saddam Hussein a lucky hand. Anwar al-Sadat's visit to Jerusalem, followed by Israel and Egypt's signing of the Camp David Accords, discredited the Egyptian president in the eyes of the Arab world. The Iraqi vice president jumped on the opportunity to position himself as the new champion of Pan-Arabism and the mediator of the various movements hostile to Israel. His ambition was nothing less than to become a new Nasser, though he had only ever spoken of Egypt's late president in the most disparaging terms. In November 1978 he hosted the Eighth Arab Summit in Baghdad, which allowed him to marginalize Egypt and put himself in the race for regional leadership against Syrian president Hafez al-Assad. To top it all off, he created the illusion of a peaceful relationship with the Shah of Iran. Relations between Baghdad and Tehran had indeed been cordial since the signing of the Algiers Accord, apparently guided by the principles of realpolitik. Each government seemed ready to accept coexistence with the other. Prince Gholam, the Shah's brother, even made an official visit to Iraq, underscoring the two countries' apparent reconciliation. Mohammad Reza Pahlavi was all the more cordial in his dealings with the Iraqi authorities given that he was facing an increasingly delicate situation on the home front. Protest was gaining ground in Iran, and the Shah's days were numbered.

Ayatollah Khomeini's Arrival in Tehran Changes the Game

On January 8, 1979, a massive crowd rushed into the streets of Tehran demanding the Shah's ouster. The situation degenerated into violent clashes. The army stood by with arms at the ready, leaving the SAVAK to try and hold back an apparently unstoppable flood of people. Knowing that he had been abandoned by American president Jimmy Carter, the aging and sick Shah decided to take his family and leave the country to prevent the situation from escalating into a real civil war. On January 16, 1979, the imperial couple embarked on a pathetic exile that would lead them from Egypt to Morocco and from the Bahamas to Mexico, the United States having refused to offer them shelter. Over the following two weeks, Prime Minister Shapour Bakhtiar tried everything possible to regain control of the situation, ordering the dissolution of the SAVAK and freeing numerous political prisoners. But it was not enough to calm a fiery mob that wanted a real change of regime and was calling for opposition forces to unite. Ayatollah Khomeini, who enjoyed widespread popular support to take the Revolution's moral leadership, realized that the time had come for him to take action. On February 1, 1979, he left his French exile and triumphantly returned to Tehran. A teeming crowd was at the airport to cheer him on.

A grandson and son of ayatollahs, Ruhollah Khomeini (born in 1902) was orphaned at an early age. He was taken in by his paternal aunt, who taught him the values of justice and the principles of rigorist Shia Islam. Having spent his childhood between Koranic school and his family home, he continued his theological studies at the University of Qom. He earned his degree at age twenty-five, became a professor at the same prestigious university, married, and was later given the title of ayatollah, which allowed him to take responsibilities in the clergy. He quickly became one of the most renowned professors on the theology faculty. Leading an ascetic life, he pursued intensive spiritual activity, never separating religion and politics. His mysticism, life story, and even his first name (literally, "spirit of God") convinced him that he was to have a unique destiny. In the late fifties, he became involved in the opposition to the Shah's regime, vigorously criticizing its fervent Westernization policy. He called for the monarchy to be overthrown, Sharia law to be adopted, and the Americans to be expelled. His political commitment put him at loggerheads with the government. In 1964, after being briefly imprisoned, he was forced into exile. He was sent to Turkey, from which he traveled to Iraq. He spent the next fourteen years in Najaf, then in Karbala, Shia Islam's holiest sites, among Iraqi Shiites who welcomed him as one of their own. He took advantage of this forced exile to denounce the Shah's regime in increasingly virulent terms,[3] but also to facilitate a rapprochement between the Iraqi Shiites and the Iranian clergy, with whom he remained in close contact. He fraternized with Mohammad al-Sadr, the founder of the Dawa Party.

Ayatollah Khomeini's proselytism deeply bothered the Iraqi authorities, and particularly Saddam Hussein, who finally asked the French authorities to give him political exile and expelled him in October 1978. In France he was kept under surveillance in a house in Neauphle-le-Château, outside Paris. He openly continued his policy of destabilizing the regime, notably through his preaching and by mailing audiocassettes, which were widely distributed in Iran and further contributed to weakening the Shah. His attacks were also aimed at the Iraqi government, which he reproached for having forced him into a dishonorable exile in the land of the infidels. Meanwhile his portrait spread throughout the streets of major Iranian cities. His intransigence, patriarchal appearance, graying beard, and black turban, a sign of his line of descent from the prophet, contributed to making him the most visible opponent to the Shah's regime. Numerous Iranian intellectuals were won over by his imposing bearing and charisma.

Though seventy-seven years old, Ayatollah Khomeini still had a razor-sharp mind and steely determination. Intent on having his world vision prevail, he called for the foundation of an Islamic republic, hoping it would hasten the return of the Hidden Imam. This theological rhetoric did not please the progressive opposition in Iran, but it was ready to accept any alliance, including with the Islamic fundamentalists, to get rid of the Shah and his regime. The "land of the rose and the dove," to paraphrase the legendary Persian poet Omar Khayyám, had just turned an important page in its history.

On February 5, 1979, Ayatollah Khomeini proclaimed himself the "Supreme Leader of the Revolution" and dismissed Shapour Bakhtiar, who fled to France. Though it favored the monarchy, the army wanted to preserve its cohesion and save whatever could still be saved: it declared its neutrality and committed to serving the new regime. The Imperial Guard was dissolved. Numerous colonels and generals were fired. Some paid for their participation in state repression with their lives. They were replaced by commissioned officers close to the new regime, sometimes by mere noncommissioned officers. Revolutionary committees appeared in army units. Numerous conscripts put down their guns and went home. The situation became so anarchic that the military authorities were forced to stop conscription. Like the administration and the oil industry, the army descended into chaos. The possibility of the collapse of Iranian oil production and fears of regional destabilization sparked a second oil crisis, which would have a lasting impact on the economies of industrialized nations. The price of oil rose by 65 percent in a few months, its greatest leap since the first oil crisis in 1973.

In late February Ayatollah Khomeini appointed Mehdi Bazargan as prime minister. This seventy-three-year-old engineer belonged to the liberal movement and had spent several years in the Shah's prisons. He sought to reconcile religion and modernity. Highly reputed for his piety and integrity, he wanted to integrate democratic and liberal principles in a moderate Islamic framework. His closeness with Western intellectual circles was intended to reassure Washington regarding the Iranian Revolution's agenda. In order to try and rapidly gain the support of the disinherited, Mehdi Bazargan adopted an egalitarian social policy and massively subsidized agricultural revenue. Yet his lack of charisma did not serve him well. He had tremendous difficulty establishing himself in the shadow of Ayatollah Khomeini, who enjoyed a real cult of personality.

On April 2, 1979, following a popular referendum, Ayatollah Khomeini proclaimed the Islamic Republic of Iran and charged a commission of jurists with writing a new Constitution. The purges accelerated. People's courts were set up in large cities. Several thousand people were arrested. At least 200 of them were summarily executed, including some 50 generals and senior officers belonging to the former Imperial Guard. Many imperial laws were repealed, notably those protecting women's rights. These restrictions on individual rights led to massive emigration among the wealthier layers of society. Many military professionals chose to desert and go into exile in the West. Most of the pilots and sailors in training in the United States, tagged as "pro-Western," preferred to stay abroad, fearing for their lives if they returned to Iran. Their absence severely undermined the armed forces' operational availability, particularly in the case of the air force and navy. But the new regime was so driven to de-Westernize the country that it paid no heed. Meanwhile insurgent forces took advantage of the chaos to try and grapple certain provinces' autonomy from the central authorities. The Azeris, Kurds, Arabic-speakers, and Balochs[4] became dissidents and battled the revolutionary committees. The most violent clashes took place in Kurdistan and Khuzestan.

To reestablish order, but mostly to keep an eye on the regular army (of which he was extremely suspicious), Ayatollah Khomeini decided to create a parallel army entirely devoted to the regime. On May 5, 1979, he passed a decree establishing the *Pasdaran e-Enqelab* (literally, "the Guardians of the Revolution," also referred to in English as the Revolutionary Guards). This corps, under the direct supervision of the Supreme Leader, was divided into three principal commands charged with protecting Tehran, defending the major provincial cities, and guarding the borders. The authorities wanted to ensure that the regular army would not let counterrevolutionary forces infiltrate the country from abroad. A fourth command was devoted to training young Pasdaran. Initially, the entire force comprised only 15,000 men, divided into small units the size of a company or battalion and exclusively equipped with small weapons. Their numbers would later swell rapidly. Ayatollah Khomeini chose to put the corps under the leadership of the young Ali Khamenei, a rising star of the Islamic Party in whom he had complete trust. Khamenei was backed by a general staff that had total power to requisition materials, gas, equipment, and food. In order to preserve the balance between secular and religious soldiers and ensure a heterogeneous recruitment that guaranteed accurate representation of Iranian society, the authorities decided to let young people who wanted to serve their country choose between the regular army or the Pasdaran corps—for the first months of the Revolution had divided Iranian society in two camps.

The first camp consisted of those who considered that revolutionary issues and republican principles should outweigh the religious dimension, though religion was not denied—most political leaders considered themselves good Muslims. This side included the liberals, the sociodemocrats, the intellectuals, and the middle classes. It was notably backed by the People's Mujahidin (Mujahidin e-Khalq), which called for a modern and secular Islamic society, and the urban extreme left, which consisted of the Tudeh Communist Party, the People's Fedayeen (Fedayan-e Khalq),[5] and the Revolutionary Workers' Organization of Iranian Kurdistan, better known as Komala. Though it was in the majority, this progressive camp remained deeply divided. No authority figure, not even the elegant Massoud Rajavi, head of the People's Mujahidin, could claim its leadership.

The opposing minority camp consisted of the clergy and the Islamic fundamentalists. This side put primary emphasis on the Islamic dimension and considered the revolutionary phase as a transitional stage toward establishing a real theocracy. They had every intention of using the progressive side as a steppingstone to power. Their strategy was simple: to take root in political life, then successively push aside every one of their adversaries. But who were they and what did they stand for? The clergy, though divided into a multitude of schools of thought, agreed on recognizing the key importance of Ayatollah Ali Montazeri, who had been at the center of religious opposition to the Shah throughout Khomeini's years of exile. This fifty-seven-year-old cleric had studied philosophy under Khomeini before becoming one of the most respected theologians at the University of Qom. His peasant roots, great sincerity, and years spent in the Shah's jails established his popular legitimacy. Everyone knew he was sensitive to human suffering and that he privileged ethics and justice over politics. Ali Montazeri had been one of the first to adhere to the principle of Islamic Revolution and had become its ideologist, which did not prevent him from criticizing the new regime when he deemed it necessary.

He quickly became the Iranian "Trotsky," arguing that the new regime's top priority should be to export the Revolution to other countries. To many, he appeared to be Ayatollah Khomeini's legitimate successor.

The Islamic fundamentalist movement, which was very influential in rural areas and among the lower classes, had coalesced around the Islamic Republican Party (IRP), headed by Ayatollah Mohammad Beheshti, a faithful supporter of Ayatollah Khomeini. Fifty years old, ambitious, attentive to international relations, he had headed the Islamic Center in Hamburg, an institution charged with indoctrinating Iranian students staying in Europe, for several years. He planned on using his numerous connections to impose himself as Ayatollah Khomeini's successor. To do so, he intended to marginalize his rivals, notably Grand Ayatollah Kazem Shariatmadari, who opposed Ayatollah Khomeini on questions of dogma. Beheshti also did his utmost to hold back much younger clerics eager to climb to the top of the clergy. Two of them were already honing their arguments, if not their knives: Akbar Hashemi Rafsanjani and Ali Khamenei.

Saddam Takes Power

Meanwhile, the situation in Iraq changed. In the spring of 1979, Saddam Hussein marginalized the Communist Party and declared the Shiite Dawa Party illegal. Its leaders, who constantly railed against the Ba'athist regime, were arrested. Saddam's forceful actions were partially driven by his concern over the Iranian Islamic Revolution's potential impact on the Ba'athist regime. Nonetheless, in an effort to handle its new interlocutors with care, the Iraqi government sent a circumspect congratulatory telegram to Mehdi Bazargan, the head of the Iranian Republic's provisional government. The gesture was intended to display Baghdad's support to the secular revolutionary faction in order to avoid the victory of the religious fundamentalists who called for the foundation of an Islamic state that included the holy cities of Najaf and Karbala. Yet this telegram, meant as an appeal for sustained cordial relations between the two countries, led to acute tension between their capitals. Ayatollah Khomeini, offended that he had not been the telegram's addressee, poured out acerbic criticisms of the Ba'athist regime and openly called for the Iraqi Shiite population to rise up.

Saddam Hussein was convinced he now had to be as firm as possible with the new Iranian regime. He considered that General al-Bakr lacked the necessary determination to dissuade the Iranian government from executing its strategy of destabilizing the Iraqi regime. But most significantly, he believed that his aging mentor had had his day. Now forty-two and champing at the bit, he felt strong enough to openly lead the country, which for all practical purposes he had been doing for many years. On July 16, 1979, with the support of the members of his clan, Saddam Hussein deposed his former mentor and took power in Baghdad. General al-Bakr was discreetly placed under house arrest. It was officially announced that he had stepped down for health reasons. Worn down, al-Bakr chose to avoid a confrontation with Saddam and agreed to a golden retirement in a sumptuous villa in the capital's chic suburbs in exchange for his permanent withdrawal from political activity.[6]

Saddam Hussein was intent on eliminating any collegiality and firmly establishing his own power, even if it required bloodshed. He concurrently held the positions of president and prime minister, appointed his cousin Ali Hassan al-Majid to the strategic position of head of intelligence, and confirmed his half-brother Barzan Ibrahim al-Tikriti as head of the secret police. He promoted his friend Tariq Aziz to the rank of vice prime minister and entrusted him with the Ministry of Foreign Affairs, where his primary mission would be to maintain the regime's positive image in the West. With this inner circle's support, Saddam eliminated all his potential rivals within the party. He put an end to his predecessor's attempt at a rapprochement with Syria, judging that the potential union between the two nations, which aimed to create a new Arab state stretching from the Gulf to the Mediterranean, would diminish his own power and increase Hafez al-Assad's. Saddam had not fought for power all these years to share it with the man he considered his greatest rival. On July 28, 1979, he denounced an alleged Syrian-devised plot to overthrow him during an exceptional assembly of the RCC.

Several dozen delegates were arrested in the midst of the meeting, accused of treason, and taken outside to be executed on the spot. Saddam even shot several men himself, using the pistol he always carried, after having ordered his clan's closest members to do the same in order to permanently compromise them and ensure their loyalty. These executions were filmed and distributed to leaders throughout the Gulf and Middle East to intimidate them and convince them of Saddam's extreme determination. The Iraqi president was resolved to establish himself as the new strong man in the region. The methods of intimidation he now used with his peers were the same ones that ensured his success when he had had to impose himself on the streets. With his falsely debonair appearance, he sought to create the image of a leader both paternalistic and pitiless, combining the personalities of Stalin and Al Capone. It was no accident that Saddam allowed himself to be photographed wearing a fedora, smoking a cigar, and brandishing the Thompson machine gun that had established the Chicago gangs' notoriety. The photo was seen around the world and played its part in forging the myth of an implacable dictator.

Saddam also shared more traits with Stalin than one might expect. Both men came from modest backgrounds and were exposed to paternal violence in childhood. They both struggled with their education and were always suspicious of intellectuals and doctors, fearing criticism and poisoning. Both were imprisoned and imposed themselves as gang leaders operating outside the law. They were always fascinated by state might and violence, considering fear the best way to establish their power.[7] They both established themselves by taking control of their respective parties' bureaucratic apparatus. Finally, they were both always able to be shrewd, cynical, falsely jovial, and cruel when it was necessary, and ready to compromise when the balance of power was not in their favor. Yet Saddam Hussein differed from Stalin in several ways. Unlike his model, he never displayed military talent or a strategist's abilities. Most significantly, he always placed tremendous importance on his family and clan, always ready to forgive the weaknesses of his inner circle at the risk of making serious mistakes. In this he revealed a personality closer to that of a mafia godfather than an ideological dictator. Lastly his actions did not stem from a long-term strategic vision—Saddam Hussein was not a visionary.

Having reined in the party, the Iraqi president ordered his cousin Adnan Khairallah to purge the military of officers faithful to General al-Bakr, knowing full well this would reduce the efficiency of an army he might need to face the Iranian regime. But his obsessive fear of a military coup d'état outweighed reason. Saddam forced every lieutenant who graduated from the academy to pledge his allegiance to him and insisted

on meeting every senior officer to evaluate his loyalty before he was promoted. Promotions were now only made on a political basis. General
Jabbah al-Shemshah, a servile member of the Ba'ath Party, was appointed
to the key position of chief of staff of the armed forces. Taha Yassin
Ramadan, a longtime companion of the president's, was entrusted with
the leadership of the People's Army. Conscious that a praetorian guard
would be useful, Saddam Hussein turned one of his armored brigades into
a "Republican Guard." This elite unit, identified by the orange triangle
painted on each of its vehicles, was directly under the command of Adnan
Khairallah. Fitted out with the most modern equipment, it was deployed
in the Iraqi capital so that it could immediately intervene in case of an
attempt to overthrow the regime.

To further establish his power, the new president developed a cult of
personality. Flattering portraits displaying his carnivorous smile quickly
spread all over the country. Whether wearing a uniform, a three-piece
suit, or a djellaba, Saddam Hussein seemed to look out from these posters
to keep a close eye on the population. He knew no limits in his quest for
recognition, comparing himself to Nebuchadnezzar or Saladin. Frescoes
appeared across the walls of Baghdad depicting Saddam riding an Arabian thoroughbred, sword in hand as he battled the Persian lion. For good
measure, the dictator commissioned the production of a film called *Al-
Qadisiyyah*, which vaunted the bravery of Arab fighters against Persian
troops. This rather interesting historical epic gathered the greatest Arab
actors of the time in what remains the most expensive film ever produced
by the Arab film industry. Naturally the reference to this symbolic battle
aimed to condition Iraqi minds and remind them who remained their
natural enemies: the Iranians, descendants of the Persians. As a wild beast
of the political arena, Saddam Hussein intuitively sensed menaces. In late
1979 he foresaw that in one way or another he would soon have to confront Ayatollah Khomeini, whose vindictive speeches did not leave much
ambiguity regarding his desire to bring down the Iraqi government. The
two regimes' goals were too contradictory. Saddam Hussein could coexist
with the Shah, but he could not do so with Ayatollah Khomeini.

Chapter 4

Did the United States
Push Saddam to Attack?

Shortly after the outbreak of the Iran-Iraq War, a rumor snowballed that the U.S. government had incited Saddam Hussein to attack Iran, dangling the prospect of Washington's political backing and significant material assistance to allow him to finance the war. The allegation was that the U.S. government had acted to avoid the spread of Islamic Revolution to the Gulf monarchies, but especially to punish the Iranian regime implicated in the hostage crisis. The rumor stemmed from statements made by Abol Hassan Bani-Sadr a few months after he was ousted from power, openly accusing the United States of having incited Iraq to attack Iran and claiming that the Iraqi regime would have been unable to go on the offensive without Washington's support. The former Iranian president, who was probably using these charges to justify the Iranian army's lack of preparation but especially his own difficulties at the head of the armed forces, maintained the same line in the autobiography he published after the war.[1] Perhaps this was also a way for Bani-Sadr to take revenge on the Americans who had never believed in him, considering him a leftist devoted to European social theories.

In 1985, as they were attempting a rapprochement with Iran, the Saudi Arabian authorities leaked statements backing Bani-Sadr's claims to the British press: Jimmy Carter's government was said to have incited Saddam Hussein to action, and even to have pressured King Khalid to encourage Saddam to launch the crusade against Khomeini and promise him the oil monarchies' financial backing. The Iraqi president was alleged to have traveled to Riyadh on August 5, 1980, at the king's request, to be told he could count on American support. Using these various statements as evidence, the journalist Dilip Hiro propagated the rumor in a successful book.[2] It was immediately picked up by certain European and Arab intellectual circles that are always eager for conspiracy theories and to fall into step with anti-American assumptions. The rumor subsists to this day, particularly in Iran—for obvious reasons of anti-Western propaganda—as evidenced by Ayatollah Khamenei's 2009 speech in reaction to President Barack Obama's outstretched hand policy: "The United States gave Saddam the green light. This was another play by the US government to attack Iran. If Saddam did not have the green light from the United States, he would not have attacked our borders."[3]

However seductive the theory may appear, it does not bear scrutiny. As early as 1988, Paul Balta, Le Monde's correspondent in the Middle East and a journalist who could hardly be suspected of leniency toward American foreign policy, wrote: "There is no real evidence to support the theory that Washington pushed Baghdad to open hostilities."[4] Since then, a meticulous analysis of the events, context, and statements by contemporary authorities, combined with more recent sources and interviews granted by certain key participants, has left no doubt that the American government did not push Saddam Hussein to criminal behavior.

Iraq had broken all diplomatic ties with the United States after June 1967, following the Six-Day War, accusing Washington of having backed Israel in this preventive war against its Arab neighbors. Iraq then fought the Israeli army in 1973. As Israel's main protector, the United States was far from appreciated in Baghdad, particularly since they had supported Iran and always opposed Iraq's claim on the Shatt al-Arab. Driven by his visceral hatred of Jews, Saddam Hussein constantly vilified American leaders and considered that a rapprochement with Washington was simply impossible. The audiotapes seized in 2003 bear witness to this. The Iraqi dictator was persuaded that the United States wanted to eliminate all the "progressive" regimes in the Arab world, including his own, to replace them with Islamic regimes considered more apt to resist Communist subversion. He was deeply suspicious of American politicians and had no direct contact with them. His only intermediaries were King Hussein of Jordan and King Khalid of Saudi Arabia, both of whom were in close contact with the American government. Saddam did not trust either of them. He may not have been entirely wrong, for in this case the Saudis were double-dealing, putting the responsibility for their actions on the American government.[5]

While many accounts verify Saddam Hussein's trip to Riyadh on August 5, 1980, all agree that it was not to receive the American administration's green light but, on the contrary, to inform King Khalid of his plans to invade Iran and obtain financial support.[6] The Saudi monarch ostensibly shared his reservations with the Iraqi president. He is said to have feared that a confrontation with Iran could have pushed Tehran to openly destabilize the oil monarchies, as a then-recent terrorist attack in Mecca led him to believe. He is also said to have emphasized his own army's weakness in case of a direct confrontation with Iran and the danger of a Soviet military intervention in the region, which would have been disastrous both for the Gulf states and the United States. But he was allegedly most emphatic on drawing Saddam Hussein's attention to the risks a major war between Iran and Iraq would entail for the entire oil industry, the principal source of revenue for the kingdoms from which Saddam was requesting assistance. Such a war would have forced Saudi Arabia to adopt a policy of hiking oil prices, contrary to its energy strategy of maintaining low oil prices. Unable to change Saddam's mind, King Khalid allegedly gave him his tacit agreement on condition that the Iraqi army abstain from attacking the Iranian oil industry, to avoid setting off a retaliatory cycle aimed at oil infrastructures throughout the region. The Saudi monarch is said to have privately told his advisors: "If Saddam wins, it will be 'his' war and 'his' victory; if he loses, it will be 'our' fault!"[7]

The American administration, which analyzed world affairs through the prism of the Cold War, considered Iraq an ally of the Soviet Union and therefore a potential adversary. Hadn't Baghdad and Moscow signed a friendship, cooperation, and military assistance treaty eight years earlier? Wasn't the Iraqi army equipped with Soviet weapons? Wouldn't inciting Iraq to launch a blitzkrieg on Iran risk creating a showcase for Soviet arms, when U.S. foreign policy aimed to demonstrate the superiority of American-made weapons? The U.S. administration certainly did not see the Ba'athist regime as a partner with whom to remodel geostrategic balances in the Gulf. It clearly identified three threats to security in the Gulf: the USSR, Iran, and Iraq. Ba'athist socialist theories were considered contrary to the principles that American diplomats were doing their utmost to promote, particularly in the Middle East. Saddam Hussein was deemed "a Mafioso dictator who was impossible to manipulate and nobody trusted."[8] His hostility toward Israel and his nuclear program (suspected to be a cover for the clandestine acquisition of the atomic bomb) totally discredited him in the eyes of Congress, the White House, and the powerful go-betweens Israel strategically kept in Washington. The Israeli government, led by Menachem Begin—to whom the American president had been beholden since Begin had made peace with Egypt—maintained constant pressure to avoid any rapprochement between Washington and Baghdad. The State Department, the Pentagon, and the CIA had been clearly warned that a rapprochement with Iraq would be an unacceptable violation of the alliance binding Israel and the United States, at least so long as the Iraqi nuclear program was not somehow neutralized. Finally, more prosaically, the American administration was relatively disinterested in Iraq because it remained obsessed with Iran.

The Islamic Revolution Muddies the Waters

In the months that followed the Islamic Revolution, everyone in Washington tried to absolve themselves of failing to anticipate the Shah's downfall. The establishment was divided between those who wanted to leap on the opportunity to rebuild a partnership with Tehran and those who criticized the administration for its disastrous handling of the Iranian crisis—notably Republicans eager to oust Jimmy Carter. Those who had been in business with the former regime echoed the large Iranian community demanding an uncompromising attitude toward the Revolution. The general mood was rendered more poisonous by the fact that many believed the KGB had played a decisive role in sparking the Iranian Revolution as a first step to a major Soviet offensive in the Gulf region. More significantly, the Carter administration had lost nearly all its contacts and lacked reliable information to follow the Iranian political maelstrom. The report of the American chargé d'affaires in Tehran was bleak: "We simply do not have the bios, inventory of political groups or current picture of daily life as it evolves at various levels in Iran."[9] Worse, most experts chose to leave their positions or were forced to step down. The CIA and State Department sorely lacked confirmed analysts able to interpret the situation's developments. In order to reestablish their contact list, the American authorities naturally turned to the most Westernized, liberal Iranian political figures, including Prime Minister Mehdi Bazargan, his Minister of Foreign Affairs Ibrahim Yazdi, his Defense Minister Mustafa Chamran, and his Minister of Information Sadeq Ghotbzadeh.

The CIA also attempted to rekindle its ties with the Iranian leadership. Several of its experts traveled to Tehran in August 1979 to inform the local authorities of American positions and warn them about risks of Soviet destabilization in the region.[10] Ambassador Sullivan tried to open a dialogue with Ayatollah Beheshti, but the meeting yielded no further discussions. Zbigniew Brzezinski, President Carter's national security advisor, tried to approach Ayatollah Khomeini, but word of his initiative got out. Under the influence of lobbyists close to the former regime, Congress forced Brzezinski to stop short. Khomeini, who had been flattered at the prospect of this meeting, would hold a fierce grudge for its being called off. Yet no one in Washington worried about it or understood that the situation could move forward without direct dialogue between the Supreme Leader and the top American decision makers. In fact American bureaucrats only had one major concern: to maintain the weapons contracts and flow of oil connecting Iran to the United States.

All this changed in August, when Iran cancelled its arms contracts with the United States. Mehdi Bazargan had to make drastic cutbacks to compensate for the disastrous drop in oil revenue caused by disarray in this key sector of the Iranian economy. According to Bazargan's advisors, the Shah's colossal spending had left the army with enough modern equipment. With this decision, more than ten billion dollars in arms contracts went up in smoke, leaving American industrialists furious. Congress responded by putting an embargo on the delivery of spare parts promised to the Iranian army. The White House no longer had any reason to go easy on the new Iranian leaders.

In late October Zbigniew Brzezinski met Mehdi Bazargan in Algiers. He informed him of President Carter's decision to authorize the severely ill Shah to travel to the United States to receive an emergency operation in a New York hospital. By granting Mohammad Reza Pahlavi the right of asylum, Washington torpedoed the Iranian liberals' efforts to maintain a dialogue with the United States. Sensibilities were still raw, and anti-

American rhetoric was constantly growing. The Iranians could not forget that they had been manipulated by outside powers for close to two centuries. The population reacted with furor when it learned that the Shah had arrived on American soil, accompanied by rumors—cannily spread by Mehdi Bazargan's enemies—that a secret meeting had occurred between their prime minister and a high-ranking American emissary. The Iranians interpreted this news as proof that the American government sought to restore the former regime. From his residence in Qom, where he supervised the activities of the revolutionary committees—modern-day versions of the French Revolution's Committees of Public Safety—Ayatollah Khomeini immediately saw the opportunity to deal a fatal blow to the American presence in Iran while ousting the liberals, whom he considered too close to the West.

On November 4, 1979, a crowd of demonstrators paraded through the streets of Tehran, a now customary sight. As they passed the American embassy, a group of enraged students climbed over the legation's wall, spread through the compound, and took the chargé d'affaires and American diplomatic staff hostage. Overwhelmed, the guards were unable to respond. The Iranian "students" involved in this coup de force made only vague demands, calling for the United States to change its policy in the Middle East. Ayatollah Khomeini publicly expressed his support to the hostage-takers, stating that he understood their grievances. He followed by dissolving Mehdi Bazargan's government, dismissing Bazargan, and replacing him with Mohammad-Ali Rajai, an academic who had ties to radical Islamic circles and had contributed to purging the academy of any Western influence. He also instituted the Basij (literally, "mobilization"), a corps of the Revolutionary Guards comprising young students devoted to the Islamic cause—and, by extension, adolescents still in middle school or high school but potentially eager to serve the revolutionary ideal. This movement, which was entrusted to Hassan Rahmani, the Supreme Leader's faithful ally, would serve as a reserve force for the Pasdaran.

The United States was thrown into a panic. Some fifty American citizens were being held hostage in Tehran. In a matter of days, the administration had lost its remaining few contacts in the Iranian government. The distraught administration imagined the wildest scenarios to rescue its citizens, as shown in Ben Affleck's remarkable film *Argo,* which relates the CIA rescue operation of six American diplomats who took shelter in the Canadian embassy at the last minute. Outraged, President Carter froze Iranian assets in American banks and decreed an embargo on weapons shipments to Iran. He ordered American technicians living in Iran and maintaining American equipment there to return to the United States.[11] But he refused to break off diplomatic ties with Tehran. Immediately ruling out the use of force, Carter trusted the State Department to resolve the hostage crisis peacefully. But the situation quickly became more complicated as events in Iran started to create ripples throughout the region. On November 20, 1979, a group of fundamentalist pilgrims held several hundred worshippers hostage inside the great mosque in Mecca. They called to fight the corruption of the Saudi state and denounced its compromises with the American government. Following a siege of several days, Saudi forces finally attacked. The hostage taking ended in a bloodbath, leaving 135 dead. This tragedy sounded the alarm for the Gulf monarchies. Feeling under attack, they revived their old anti-Shiite demons, which only served to attract Ayatollah Khomeini's vituperations.

To further strain the situation, the Soviet army staged a surprise invasion of Afghanistan on December 26, 1979, to return former Marxist president Babrak Karmal to power. It was immediately clear that the Kremlin was prepared to take advantage of the United States' apparent weakness to make a power play in the region. The Gulf monarchs were concerned to see the Soviets come dangerously closer to their precious oil wells. Even the Iranian revolutionaries were nervous: the reinforcement of Soviet military presence was visible along their borders. With the troops deployed in the Soviet Republic of Armenia and Afghanistan, the Soviets now had significantly more strength on the field than the Iranian army. Moreover, Tehran could no longer dispatch the majority of its forces to counter the USSR, as it could have under the Shah, because it had to quell internal revolts and prepare itself to respond to the Iraqi regime's threats. Saddam Hussein was also worried, fearing that his Soviet allies might be tempted to repeat the Afghanistan scenario in Iraq. He knew that Moscow saw him as a difficult partner: hard to negotiate with, often unpredictable, and, to top it off, hostile to the Communist Party. The Kremlin's elders could have been disposed to overthrow him. Determined to reaffirm his power, he openly criticized the USSR's imperialist attitude, dismaying its leaders, who upbraided him with a reminder that their military assistance would not last forever.

The Carter Doctrine

President Carter continued to hesitate to use force to liberate the American hostages, fearing that a military intervention would push Iran into the Soviets' arms. On January 12, 1980, he sent a memorandum to Tehran in which he proposed the establishment of a joint commission to examine the concrete measures required to resolve the crisis. Yet Washington made the same mistake as Baghdad. The White House tried to negotiate with the Iranian government without bothering to address the person who actually held power: Ayatollah Khomeini. The Supreme Leader may have been a holy man, but he remained fundamentally arrogant. He could not tolerate that his interlocutors acted as if he did not exist. And so the American administration came up against a flat refusal.

Offended by the Iranian attitude and worried by Soviet activity, President Carter sent some thirty naval vessels—including the aircraft carriers *Nimitz* and *Coral Sea*—into the Gulf of Oman, the largest American naval concentration ever gathered in the region. This Middle East Task Force was headquartered in Manama, on the small island of Bahrain, to protect it from any attempt at Iranian or Soviet destabilization. The Kremlin retaliated by ordering the deployment of a dozen cruisers and destroyers, backed by five attack submarines, in the Indian Ocean. On January 23, 1980, Jimmy Carter formulated a new containment doctrine that would take his name, by which he declared in the clearest terms that any attempt by an outside power to take over the Gulf region would be considered an attack on the vital interests of the United States of America and be repelled by whatever means necessary, including recourse to military action. To show his determination, Jimmy Carter announced the creation of a Rapid Deployment Force tasked with defending American interests in the region.

The Carter Doctrine did not much impress those in power in Iran, who were far more concerned with the internal struggles dividing the regime. The progressive camp, seriously weakened after Mehdi Bazargan's dismissal, could now only count on the socialists and left-wing Muslims to stop the Islamic Republican Party (IRP) steamroller behind Ayatollah Beheshti. Beheshti then appeared more powerful than ever since his two principal rivals had been recently—and opportunely—assassinated.[12] The Communists of the Tudeh Party had been marginalized. The People's Mujahidin lived in semi-obscurity, constantly expecting to be stalked down by the Pasdaran, who were only waiting for word from the Supreme Leader to embark on a relentless hunt. As was his wont, Ayatollah Khomeini remained above the fray, moving his pawns and playing people off each other in order to secure his function as an arbiter, which was contested by the clergy's ultraconservative members. These clerics objected to the establishment of the Islamic Republic, considering that it was improper for man to take God's place in deciding upon the arrival of the true Islamic Revolution, that is, the one that would lead to the return of the Hidden Imam. On the opposite pole of the political spectrum, the urban extreme Left contested the regime's religious character and demanded the founding of a Marxist republic. In this merciless power struggle, the clergy could count on the Supreme Leader, the Assembly of Experts, and the Council of Guardians of the Revolution, while the secular camp relied on the president of the Republic and the parliament.

This was the tense context in which the Iranians elected Abol Hassan Bani-Sadr president of the Republic on January 25, 1980. This forty-six-year-old intellectual had trained as an economist and studied and lived in France for many years before joining Ayatollah Khomeini's exile in Neauphle-le-Château. He returned to Iran with the ayatollah, thereby earning the position of minister of finance. A dedicated patriot, good Muslim, and son of a mullah, he championed socialist ideas and resolutely positioned himself in the camp of progressives who sought to find a balance between their religious beliefs and republican principles. In the Western political model, he would be the archetypal left-wing Christian. His peers questioned his practical competence and underlined his lack of charisma, but recognized that he had a sharp intelligence and irreproachable integrity. He personally saw himself as a pure intellect rather than a man of action. In fact, his election to the presidency was the result of a compromise. Ayatollah Khomeini, who appreciated him and was grateful for his loyalty, remained opposed to the idea that members of the clergy occupy government positions; Bani-Sadr appeared the perfect compromise candidate to allow him to play to the progressives, whom he still needed to consolidate revolutionary gains. To ensure that Bani-Sadr would not overstep his role, Khomeini imposed that he retain Mohammad-Ali Rajai as prime minister. Rajai was clearly in the religious camp, though not a member of the clergy. The two men agreed on a government of technocrats without any real political weight. To lock this system in place, Khomeini appointed Ayatollah Beheshti, the secretary general of the IRP, as head of the Council of Guardians of the Revolution.

With their hands full with these political maneuvers, the Iranian leaders did not have the time or desire to establish functional relations with an American administration perceived as moribund. Negotiations between Washington and Tehran collapsed due to lack of drive on the Iranian side and lack of consistency on the American. Torn between Zbigniew Brzezinski, who argued for firmness in dealing with Iran, and Secretary of State Cyrus Vance, who was in favor of appeasement, Jimmy Carter was unable to commit to one or the other. It would be his tragedy. Merely able to take stock of the fact that attempts at discussion had led nowhere, he finally broke off diplomatic relations with Iran on April 7, 1980.[13] Carter declared a blanket embargo on Iran and decided to use force to rescue the hostages. The Pentagon was champing at the bit: it brought out plans for a vast military operation calling for air strikes, naval blockades of Iranian ports, and parachuting the 82nd Airborne Division over Tehran. The White House immediately cooled the generals' enthusiasm, opting for a clandestine operation carried out by Army Special Forces and the CIA. No one was in a rush to start the Third World War, after all.

On April 24, 1980, President Carter launched Operation Eagle Claw: the plan was for eight Sea Stallion helicopters to take off in the middle of the night from the aircraft carrier *Nimitz*, which was cruising off the coast of Iran in the Gulf of Oman. These helicopters, fully loaded with fuel, were to fly to an ad hoc landing strip known as Desert One, located 375 miles (600 kilometers) southeast of Tehran in the heart of the desert. Here they would find four C-130 Hercules transport planes, which would have arrived a few minutes earlier from Oman carrying fuel and, most importantly, the Delta Force commandos assigned to the operation. After refueling the helicopters were to leave for a second meeting point, fifty miles (eighty kilometers) south of the Iranian capital. Here, the Delta Force troops would board trucks gathered on site by CIA agents, which would take them to the heart of Tehran to attack the three locations where American hostages were being held. The element of surprise was supposed to guarantee the mission's success. The helicopters would then take the hostages and their saviors back to an assault ship cruising in the Gulf.

On paper, the operation read like a James Bond movie. In reality, it was a complex coordination nightmare. And, in practice, the carefully laid plan came apart very quickly. While flying over the desert, the helicopters were caught in a fierce sandstorm that created hellish flight conditions. Two aircraft were forced to turn back. The others barely made it to Desert One. There, a third helicopter had a mechanical malfunction, while a fourth crashed into one of the Hercules planes, killing both aircraft's crews. The Delta Force no longer had enough helicopters to continue the mission. It was aborted, and the hostages left to their fate. The fiasco was total. Most humiliating of all, the American soldiers were forced to abandon the wreckage of their aircraft, leaving a signature on their misdeed.[14] Panic ensued in Washington. Jimmy Carter nobly took responsibility for this failure, while his secretary of state, who had opposed the principle of a military operation from the beginning, loudly resigned. Military options to resolve the Iranian crisis were now off the table.

In Tehran, the Iranian government rejoiced. President Bani-Sadr understood that the American debacle would offer him an unhoped-for respite. No longer fearing U.S. military intervention, he could score points against the radical clergy that were set on doing everything possible to undermine his authority. He sent his defense minister Admiral Ahmad Madani to Khuzestan as governor, vested with full powers to eradicate the rebels of the Arab Front for the Liberation of Al-Ahwaz. He also adopted a more aggressive, unyielding rhetoric toward the Iraqi regime with full support from Ayatollah Khomeini. They both recognized the need to revive an exterior threat to strengthen the national cohesion damaged by the Islamic Revolution. What better distraction than the Iraqi scarecrow?

For its part, the American administration remained obsessed with the hostage crisis. Following the failed liberation attempt, the White House was certainly not prepared to make the slightest move that could endanger the hostages' lives. From its perspective, a war between Iran and Iraq could only slow their liberation. Every account by former diplomats, CIA heads, and members of the National Security Council attest to this. As for Jimmy Carter, he was absorbed in the presidential campaign. It is simply not plausible that a few weeks short of the election of November 4, 1980, Carter would have risked provoking a major crisis that could destabilize the Gulf and send oil prices skyrocketing while his country was already in the throes of a second oil crisis. Military intelligence services feared that a war between Iran and Iraq would serve as a pretext for the Kremlin to launch a military intervention in Iran, thereby giving Moscow a decisive advantage.

From Washington's perspective, an Iraqi victory over Iran would be catastrophic because it would reinforce the Soviet Bloc's influence in the region. The White House clearly preferred the status quo between Baghdad and Tehran over a war that could have a boomerang effect. The State Department and National Security Council had not given up hope of rekindling diplomatic ties with Tehran. In his memoirs, former Secretary of State Warren Christopher relates that an American emissary met Sadegh Tabatabai, the brother-in-law of Khomeini's son, in Germany to discuss conditions for the hostages' release one week before the outbreak of war between Iran and Iraq.[15] What the American administration did not know was that emissaries of Republican presidential candidate Ronald Reagan had raised the stakes by simultaneously making contact with Tehran, demanding that no agreement be concluded before the November election.[16] In the American elite's eyes, the natural partner of the United States clearly had to remain Iran; Iraq could only serve as a foil. Given that, how could the president's advisors risk creating havoc?

Meanwhile, the CIA and Pentagon were involved in discreet negotiations with the Iranian authorities to trade the hostages' freedom for the delivery of spare parts, despite the embargo decreed by Congress. George Cave, one of the CIA's best experts on Iran, had opened the way a few months earlier by traveling to Tehran to inform the Iranian authorities of the Iraqi military disposition. The CIA and Pentagon also kept banking on the Iranian opposition to destabilize the regime. Iraq simply did not figure in their considerations. Ultimately, can anyone really believe that the well-intentioned, occasionally stunningly naïve Jimmy Carter would have been able to promote such a Machiavellian scheme as to encourage Saddam to invade Iran? Ultimately, only Carter could have authorized such a maneuver. Certain influential bureaucrats probably did consider exploiting Iraq, but it is simply impossible that they would have launched such a risky operation without the president's permission. Yet the most obvious argument against this conspiracy theory is that Saddam Hussein needed no encouragement: he was already determined to take action.

Not only did the American government not push Saddam Hussein to declare war but it worried about renewed tension between Iran and Iraq. Since the fall of the Shah, American intelligence services had kept a close watch on Iran and its periphery. Aside from their U-2 and SR-71 spy planes regularly flying over the region, they had two reconnaissance satellites (Key Hole type) regularly transmitting images of the area. They quickly came to the conclusion that the Iraqi army had sufficient resources to launch a large-scale attack on Iran.[17] On June 18, 1980, the CIA wrote a warning memorandum indicating that the intensification of border incidents between Iran and Iraq had reached such a point that the prospect of conflict between the two warranted serious examination.[18] The intelligence community concluded that Iraq was preparing to launch a vast operation in retaliation for the Iranian bombings, but did not imagine that a real war could be in the offing. General Oveisi sent the CIA warnings that it could be a real war, but these were not taken seriously. The former general had lost his credibility since the failure of the Nojeh plot. Nonetheless, the State Department recommended that American employees working in Iraq evacuate the country as a cautionary measure and gather in Kuwait. Some members of Carter's entourage suggested that the United States should warn the Iranians in order to get in their good graces and speed a potential resolution to the hostage crisis. Opting for caution, the White House finally rejected this proposal. Moribund, traumatized by the failure of its military intervention in Iran, torn between its fear of the Soviet Union and its mistrust of Iraq, the Carter administration displayed a fatal wait-and-see attitude.

Washington Announces Its Neutrality

The onset of hostilities between Iraq and Iran upset the agendas of President Carter and his advisors, who were fixated on two priorities in late September: winning the presidential election and resolving the hostage crisis. Polls predicted Republican candidate Ronald Reagan would win by a wide margin. In a briefing to reporters at the White House, Carter declared: "There should be absolutely no interference by any other nation in this conflict . . . we have not been and we will not become involved in the conflict between Iran and Iraq."[19] The next day, he announced that he was sending the missile cruiser *Leahy* to the Gulf and that four AWACS aerial surveillance planes, whose radomes were designed to detect anything that flew or sailed within a radius of several hundred miles, were being deployed to Saudi Arabia. These reinforcements would serve to protect Saudi coasts from attacks by either of the belligerents. In Washington's view, the danger posed by Baghdad was as significant as that posed by Tehran.

In the first days of October, the Carter administration went for broke and resumed contact with the Iranian regime, offering to deliver spare parts, restitute the Shah's belongings, and lift the freeze on Iranian assets in exchange for the liberation of the hostages before the presidential election.[20] The Iranian authorities rejected the American offer, but carefully left the door open to negotiation, counting on Ronald Reagan to win the election. It would have been foolish to make a deal with the loser; better to negotiate with the Oval Office's future occupant from the get-go.

On November 4, 1980, Ronald Reagan won the election by a landslide. The following January 20, as Reagan was being sworn in, Tehran liberated the fifty-two American hostages after 444 days of captivity. Jimmy Carter's humiliation was complete. Officially, the Iranian regime claimed to be showing its goodwill and displaying its intention to rebuild its relations with Washington. In reality, the freeing of the hostages was the fruit of wheeling and dealing between the Iranian government and the new American administration, conducted through the intercession of Algerian diplomats. Fierce negotiations had been held between Akbar Hashemi Rafsanjani and William Casey, a secret advisor to Ronald Reagan who would soon become head of the CIA. Late in December, Tehran had threatened President Reagan's emissaries with putting the hostages on trial as spies. In mid-January, the Iranians and Americans concurred on an agreement in principle, which was signed on January 19, 1981, in Algiers, the day before the new president was sworn in.[21]

In exchange for the hostages' liberation, Washington returned eight billion dollars of Iranian assets frozen in the United States and committed to delivering 480 million dollars' worth of spare parts for the Iranians' tanks and aircraft, despite the congressional embargo.[22] To keep up appearances, Washington carried out these deliveries via beholden allies. Beginning the following month, South Korea, Taiwan, Greece, and Turkey discreetly provided Iran with the equipment it had been promised. The Pentagon then restocked these accommodating countries' military supplies at its own expense. The first deliveries included tires for the heavy twin-engine Phantom fighter, which constantly needed replacements. Alexander Haig, the new secretary of state, reminded the belligerents that the United States would not allow either of them to endanger the Gulf monarchies' security. As for Henry Kissinger, who would serve as an advisor to the new American administration, he quickly understood that this war held potential benefits in that it neutralized Israel's two fiercest enemies, better allowing Israel to engage with Syria, an ally of the Soviet Union. He even allowed that it was "a shame there can only be one loser!"[23]

Moscow Punishes Baghdad and Courts Tehran

Despite the barrage of observation satellites it had launched to keep track of developments, the Kremlin was also surprised by the outbreak of war.[24] Faced with the fait accompli, Soviet leaders were furious not to have been consulted by Saddam Hussein. They were particularly stunned, given that they considered him one of their best allies in the area and that he had assured Anatoli Barkovski, the Soviet ambassador to Baghdad, that he did not intend to carry out any wide-scale operations against Iran a few days earlier.

The general feeling in the Politburo was that the Iraqi dictator's arrogance had gone too far. He needed to be punished, particularly since he had dared to fiercely criticize the Soviet intervention in Afghanistan and that he continued to persecute Iraqi Communist Party members, despite his promise to go easy on them. Even more serious, his war on Iran threatened to help Americans reinforce their position in the region, which was exactly what Moscow was trying to avoid. Like their American and Chinese counterparts, the Soviet leaders analyzed this war through the prism of the Cold War. They feared being drawn into a war that went against their interests. If everything went wrong, the Iraqi president would probably ask them for military intervention. They had no idea this was exactly the kind of intervention the Iraqi dictator sought to avoid, convinced that its objective would be to remove him from power. Instead, they worried they had been duped by Saddam Hussein, whom they suspected of wanting to change alliances like Anwar al-Sadat, who had armed himself with Soviet weapons to launch a war against Israel, a war which had ultimately allowed him to make peace with the Israelis and ally himself with the Americans. The members of the Politburo had no desire to look like they had been taken for a ride planned in Baghdad and Washington. Using the Moscow-Washington hotline, they agreed with the White House to contain the conflict within its regional dimension.

While they agreed on their analysis of the situation, the Kremlin's elders were divided on the policy to adopt. After Egypt's turn to the Western camp, the Iranian Islamic Revolution, and the Soviet intervention in Afghanistan, they knew that they were unpopular in the Middle East. Minister of Foreign Affairs Andrei Gromyko and Chairman of the KGB Yuri Andropov considered this war an opportunity to shift their alliance. They proposed to distance themselves from Iraq and draw closer to Iran, which had imposed itself as a first-rank strategic objective, far more important than Iraq. They underlined the Iranian regime's anti-American rhetoric, which led them to believe there could be potential points of agreement between Moscow and Tehran. They noted the importance of the Iranian Communist Party. Finally, they insisted on the necessity for the Soviet Union to make ties with political Islam in order to weaken the mujahidins' resistance in Afghanistan and cool the Soviet Muslim republics' ardor for independence.

For his part, party ideologue Mikhail Suslov was torn between the desire to support the Iraqi Ba'ath Party's secular and progressive theories and his empathy for the Kurdish people mistreated by the very same party.[25] He uncomfortably noted that an ally of the USSR had attacked a Third World country that had just escaped from the grips of the West—not a good scenario for Soviet propaganda! He therefore argued for a rapid end to hostilities. Alexei Kosygin, the chairman of the Council, was too sick to take an active part in debates. He would die a month later. Marshal

Dimitry Ustinov defended the Iraqi alliance tooth and nail, emphasizing that it would be disastrous to support Iran and drop Iraq, since Moscow armed Baghdad. An Iraqi defeat would inevitably be seen as a defeat of Soviet weaponry. The old marshal also freely reminded his colleagues of the importance of the arms contracts signed with Iraq, while underlining the risk of seeing Baghdad turn to other supply sources if abandoned by Moscow.

Leonid Brezhnev, the Party's secretary general, finally decided for a median position. Worn down and sick, he knew he had to count on the military's support for this difficult end of reign characterized by an increase in tension between the two blocs. He could not disavow his minister of defense. He therefore chose to preserve diplomatic relations with Baghdad and maintain the 1200 advisors assisting the Iraqi army. However, he ordered an immediate end to all weapon deliveries to Iraq and the freezing of any contracts under negotiation, notably those relating to the delivery of the powerful MiG-25s. Three freighters brimming with military supplies instantly received orders to turn back, while two of them were already within reach of the Iraqi port of Umm Qasr. The Iraqis thus saw a precious supply of T-72 and BMP-1 tanks disappear before their very eyes. At the same time, Brezhnev asked Gromyko and Andropov to sound out the Iranians to see if they would accept the Soviet Union's assistance. To keep up appearances, he told the press: "The USSR considers itself a friend to Iraq and Iran and hopes that these two countries are able to solve their problem through negotiation, as quickly as possible, in order to put an end to their fratricidal battle."[26] The Secretary General of the Communist Party accompanied this statement with a letter to the Iraqi president, in which he called for him to put an end to this war that played into the West's hands. Saddam Hussein was not surprised. He was expecting a visceral reaction from the Soviets but felt that he could get by without their support for a few weeks, long enough to conclude a blitzkrieg on Iran. He considered that the Kremlin would not be able to shut him out indefinitely, particularly once Iraq had joined the exclusive club of nuclear states.

Meanwhile, Vladimir Vinogradov, the Soviet ambassador to Tehran, met the Iranian prime minister to inform him of the Kremlin's offer to provide assistance as a means to cement new relations between the two nations.[27] After having relayed the offer to Ayatollah Khomeini,

Mohammad-Ali Rajai came back to the Soviet ambassador to tell him the Supreme Leader had said no. Through their desire for freedom, the Iranian people had managed to emancipate themselves from the guardianship of Western powers; they were not now going to come under the influence of another power, one that was both atheistic and anticlerical and shamelessly mistreated Afghan Muslims. Yet the Iranian authorities left the door open to a quietly continued dialogue. Early in 1981, they made contact with Moscow again to say that they were ready to accept Soviet military assistance, so long as it remained secret and did not require any political compensation. The Kremlin cautiously acquiesced, knowing that Iran's internal situation was changing. For months, KGB analysts had been predicting the clergy's rise to power. The Iranian authorities' change of tone allowed Moscow to move ahead with their strategy. Soviet assistance was particularly logical in that the Iranian army had been capturing large quantities of Soviet-made equipment. It needed spare parts and munitions to put it to use in its own units.[28]

Over the course of 1981, Iran received 150 BTR-60, T-55, and T-62 tanks, as well as large quantities of light weapons and munitions from Bulgaria. Via the port of Bandar Anzali on the Caspian Sea, the USSR directly delivered to Iran several hundred trucks, large quantities of spare parts, as well as portable SAM-7 surface-to-air missiles, which would allow Iranian infantrymen to shoot down several Iraqi jet fighters. Better yet, the Soviets sent Iran 300 military advisors to help them repair and maintain the tanks they had captured from the Iraqi army. Naturally, the Soviet authorities charged top dollar for this assistance, drawing on Iran's still significant reserves of petrodollars. In reciprocation, Iran gave the Soviet Union one of its precious Tomcat fighters, the jewel in the crown of American technology, to allow Russian engineers to study it and Russian pilots to test it.[29]

To maintain a balance between the two belligerents and avoid having the Iraqi assault turn into a routing, Moscow decided to discreetly help Iraq through the intervention of other socialist countries. In this case, they did not provide ultramodern armaments but hardy weapons taken from the abundant stockpiles of the Warsaw Pact. Iraq thus received 500 T-55 and T-62 tanks, 850 armored vehicles (BMP-1, OT-62, OT-64, and BRDM-1), and several tens of thousands of light weapons from Romania,

Poland, Czechoslovakia, and Hungary. However, Iraq did not directly receive any weapons from the Soviet Union during this period: not a single fighter plane, combat helicopter, or ultramodern artillery piece. By withholding its direct support, Moscow was putting pressure on Saddam Hussein to withdraw his forces to the international border and hasten the conflict's resolution, for the Kremlin had come to understand that the Iranians would not accept a ceasefire so long as they had not reclaimed the territory invaded by the Iraqi army. Tariq Aziz traveled to Moscow in March 1981 to attempt to sway the Soviet leaders, but his requests fell on deaf ears.[30]

Beijing Banks on Baghdad

The People's Republic of China was also unnerved by the outbreak of the Iran-Iraq War. Chinese leaders feared that the conflict would allow Washington and Moscow to improve their positions in the region. Beijing was primarily worried about Moscow's next moves, given that the United States seemed to be losing traction in this part of the world following the fall of the Shah and the failure of the hostage rescue operation. Chinese leaders, who had maintained excellent relations with the Shah due to shared geopolitical interests,[31] feared that the Iranian regime's hardening toward Washington would inevitably lead to a rapprochement between Iran and the USSR. While China was obsessively suspicious of the Kremlin, it was also concerned about Tehran's proselytism, worrying that the exporting of the Islamic Revolution could destabilize the Chinese province of Xinjiang, home to an Islamic Uyghur population. This had driven Beijing to criticize the change of regime in Tehran.

President Deng Xiaoping thought China should do everything possible to counter the Soviets' plans. Since the Kremlin seemed to be turning away from Baghdad to privilege opening up toward Tehran, it seemed clear to him that China had to support Iraq to weaken the Soviet position in the area. Thinking pragmatically, Deng Xiaoping was ready to discreetly arm Baghdad in order to wrestle Iraq from the Soviet sphere of influence. This military assistance would also allow Beijing to collect some precious currency, of which the regime was in desperate need. However, it could not precipitate the fall of the Iranian regime, which would be in

Moscow's interest. The Chinese government's position could thus be summed up by three priorities: containing the Soviet Union, conquering new markets, and maintaining the balance between the belligerents. Huang Hua, the Chinese minister of foreign affairs, made his government's position official by declaring: "We are deeply concerned about the recent conflict between Iraq and Iran. We sincerely hope that the two parties will promptly put an end to hostilities and put an end to their differences through negotiation, in order to prevent themselves from being exploited by those pursuing shameful objectives."[32]

Meanwhile, a Chinese military mission traveled to Baghdad to evaluate the Iraqi army's needs. Given that the Iraqis were furious about the Soviet stance, the Chinese were offered a particularly warm reception. As inferior copies of Soviet equipment, Chinese weapons were not of the highest quality, but they had the advantage of being available quickly and in large quantities. Discussions largely centered on ground equipment, Iraq having turned to France to reinforce their air force. The deal was struck quickly, for the Iraqi generals were prepared to pay top dollar. The first arms and munitions freighters left China in late fall 1980 and arrived in Iraq in the beginning of 1981. After this, the Iraqis regularly received shipments of T-59s and T-69s (copies of T-55s and T-62s), type-59 towed field guns (copies of the 130 mm M-46), type 56 assault rifles (copies of the famous Kalashnikov), and millions of shells and various types of ammunition. Throughout the conflict, China would be Iraq's third biggest arms provider, behind the USSR and France.

[Chapter 5]

France Sides with Iraq

The outbreak of war put the French government in a delicate position. It was faced with the dilemma of trying to preserve its arms trade and industrial cooperation with Iraq without breaking with Iran. Paris had no intention of dropping Baghdad, for its economic and industrial interests in Iraq were too important to lose. Yet the French authorities worried that overly clear support to Iraq would provoke violent reactions in Iran. The Ministry of Foreign Affairs' spokesperson prudently declared: "France is nobody's enemy; its commercial links with Iraq do not imply hostility toward the Islamic revolution."[1] The French government's pusillanimity did not reassure Tehran. Several Iranian representatives traveled to Paris and warned the French authorities that the continued delivery of weapons to Iraq could lead to a severe deterioration of relations between Paris and Tehran. The French military high command responded by reinforcing its naval presence in the Gulf, deploying the guided-missile frigate *Suffren* and the replenishment oiler *Isère* to join the avisos *Schoelcher* and *Bouvet*. Tariq Aziz also traveled to France for news. Valéry Giscard d'Estaing assured him that Iraq could count on France's indefectible support. To understand Paris's commitment to Baghdad, we need to look back to the decades before the war.

Iraq, the New Eldorado for French Industrialists

Following General de Gaulle's publicly stated neutrality in the Arab-Israeli Six-Day War of June 1967, France's popularity was at a peak in the Middle East. The French government felt free to acknowledge the pro-Arab policy discreetly implemented since the end of the Algerian War. By doing so, France hoped to regain some of the influence it had lost in the Middle East after the end of the Second World War. It also sought to win captive markets in several Arab states that had become rich on their oil revenues. On February 7, 1968, General de Gaulle welcomed his Iraqi counterpart in Paris, reminding him of the ancestral connection between Charlemagne and the Abbasid Caliph Harun al-Rashid. He flattered him and dangled the benefits of a potential cooperation with France. It was a difficult task, for Iraq was closely tied to the USSR and thus ostracized by many Western nations. Yet these initial contacts were fruitful. Panhard, a company with deep ties to the French government, sold a first lot of 106 AML-60 light armored cars to the Iraqi army, while Berliet and Saviem were awarded a contract to deliver 687 military trucks.

As soon as the nationalization of the Iraqi oil industry was announced in spring 1972, Baghdad informed Paris that every provision would be taken to safeguard French interests. The Iraqi government stated that it was prepared to sign an agreement for close cooperation with the Compagnie française des pétroles (CFP), the Total group (which owned 23.75 percent of shares in the Iraq Petroleum Company [IPC]), and Entreprise de Recherches et d'Activités Pétrolières (Elf-ERAP). Negotiations proceeded smoothly thanks to the mediation of Jean Duroc-Danner, a CFP executive who had unparalleled connections in Baghdad and had established himself over the previous fifteen years as the leading figure in French-Iraqi relations. On June 11, 1972, Saddam Hussein made his first official visit to Europe to travel to France and finalize the conditions of petroleum cooperation between France and Iraq. He reassured potential partners by promising that French companies would be the last to be nationalized. He also seized the opportunity to make a strategic move and declare that he was prepared to purchase weapons. He gave the French authorities a list of equipment that Iraq was eager to acquire as soon as possible: Mirage fighter planes, helicopters, radar, and various ground weapons.

The French oil industry, anxious to preserve its interests in Iraq, launched a press campaign supporting the Iraqi regime and pressured the authorities to accept Saddam's request in the name of defending French industrial interests. The issue was hotly debated within the government. Prime Minister Jacques Chaban-Delmas and Minister of Defense Michel Debré were very much in favor. Valéry Giscard d'Estaing, then minister of finances, was far more cautious, questioning the Iraqi state's solvency.

Minister of Foreign Affairs Maurice Schumann was fiercely hostile to the proposal. He was against bolstering an enemy of Israel and emphasized the Iraqi regime's authoritarian nature. Ultimately President Georges Pompidou, wanting to expand his predecessor's policy of opening France to the Arab world, decided to approve the Iraqi request, but forbade the sale of Mirages and tanks.

On June 18, 1972, the French and Iraqi governments signed an agreement ensuring the preservation of French oil interests in Iraq for ten years. The CFP was entitled to buy as much oil as it wanted at extremely advantageous prices. This agreement swept aside the French authorities' remaining reservations. The Société nationale d'industrie aérospatiale (SNIAS, "the National Company for Aerospace Industry") committed to delivering to Iraq 102 helicopters (forty-seven Alouette IIIs, forty Gazelles, twelve Super Frelons, and three Pumas). Though it could not provide Iraq with its Mirage, Dassault delivered three ultramodern Mystère 20 liaison planes, while Panhard sent a new lot of 194 light-armored vehicles. Brandt sold Iraq 580 mortars with 420,000 shells. Thomson-CSF was charged with modernizing Iraq's anti-aircraft defense network with six highly reliable radars. Paris was particularly well disposed toward Iraq after it served as France's advocate within OPEC and refused to subject it to the embargo decreed by the other Arab nations during the first oil crisis. Cooperation between the two countries reached new heights with the election of President Valéry Giscard d'Estaing and the nomination of Prime Minister Jacques Chirac. Chirac, a close friend to the Dassault family,[2] was in Baghdad from November 30 to December 2, 1974, to deliver some good news: France had agreed to supply Iraq the Mirage F-1s it had hoped for. The French prime minister was lavishly received in the Iraqi capital. He was won over by Saddam Hussein's personality and brought home more than three billon dollars' worth of contracts. An initial contract covering the sale of forty Mirage F-1s was signed, calling for delivery in late 1980.

Jacques Chirac also returned with interesting news: the Iraqi government wanted to cooperate with France in the field of civil nuclear energy, which would be a bonanza for French companies Saint-Gobain and Framatome. Saddam Hussein had proven a shrewd negotiator by enticing the French authorities with lucrative contracts in the petroleum

and weapons fields. This was a winning strategy, given that French industrialists in both sectors were now increasing press campaigns to convince the
government to accept Saddam's request, arguing for the defense of their
interests in Iraq.

French and Iraqi delegations met several times over the course of 1975
to negotiate the terms of nuclear cooperation. Paris offered to deliver
enriched uranium to Baghdad and build an 800-kilowatt research reactor,
as well as a 70-megawatt nuclear power station called "Osirak." From September 5 to September 8, 1975, Saddam Hussein was in France to finalize
negotiations. Jacques Chirac received him with the following words: "You
are my personal friend. Please be assured of my esteem, my consideration,
and all my affection."[3] Better yet, the prime minister spent a weekend with
Hussein in a farmhouse in Provence before treating him to a luxurious
time in the French capital.

The Franco-Iraqi cooperation agreement was signed with great pomp
in Baghdad on November 18, 1975. The United States, which still saw Iraq
as a henchman to the USSR, and Israel, which considered Iraq its principal enemy, openly criticized the French attitude and threatened to do
whatever it could to make their cooperation fail. During the night of
April 6 to 7, 1979, an Israeli commando penetrated the boatyards of La
Seyne-sur-Mer in France and sabotaged the dome built to hold the Iraqi
nuclear reactor's core, slowing the entire program. A few months later
(June 14, 1980), Mossad assassinated Yahya El Mashad, an Egyptian physi-
cist involved in the Iraqi nuclear program.

In France, the agreement on civil nuclear power removed the last restrictions preventing the sale of the most sensitive materials to Iraq. From
1976 to 1979, French weapon manufacturers had a field day selling Iraq
everything its army needed and could not get from the Soviets: 11,000 missiles (Milan, HOT, AS-12, Magic, Exocet), 255 HOT and Milan antitank
missile launch units, electronic war equipment, and a third lot of 150 Panhard light-armored vehicles. Military cooperation accelerated with the
signing of several bilateral agreements covering the training of student
pilots and technicians responsible for putting the Mirages and helicopters in service. This training policy extended to enrolling Iraqi students
in the French Military Academy. Every year, close to one hundred Iraqis
were trained in France, including a dozen pilots. Meanwhile, despite the

fact that Iraq only had narrow access to the Gulf, the Direction des Con-
structions Navales (Direction of Naval Construction) offered the Iraqi
military high command the opportunity for a real blue-water navy by
proposing to sell them several escort vessels, frigates, and submarines. As
Admiral Pierre Lacoste, former head of Raymond Barre's military cabinet,
told the author, this project was deemed illogical by Prime Minister Raymond Barre's cabinet and would not come to fruition. All in all, France
earned five billion dollars from weapons sales to Iraq during the 1970s.

This cooperation with Iraq also extended to the fields of construction
and public works. The Bouygues group paved the country, expanded its
airports, and built numerous underground shelters for the Iraqi army. By
the end of the 1970s, more than sixty-five French companies were operating in Iraq, and 10,000 French technicians were living on site to implement the multiple industrial projects between the two countries. Iraq had
become France's primary commercial partner in the Middle East and its
second biggest oil supplier. It may also have become a significant source
of financing for the Gaullist Party,[4] which had heaped praise on the Iraqi
regime, echoing certain intellectuals who readily described it as true "Arab
Gaullism." In fact, Paris and Baghdad had become so close that they now
held each other hostage.

Eurodif at the Heart of the Franco-Iranian Dispute

At first glance, relations between France and Iran were simpler and more
wholesome in that they primarily rested on cultural exchanges. The Shah
Reza Pahlavi was recognized as a friend to France, though many denounced his regime's authoritarian nature. The Franco-Iranian relationship seemed all the more clear given that Paris knew it could not sell
Tehran weapons—with the exception of a few missile boats—because Iran
was American and British turf. The French government therefore focused
on commercial ties, reaping more than seven billion dollars' worth of contracts for rail, automobile, audiovisual, and especially nuclear equipment.
Since France was a leader in the nuclear field, its experts did not have
much trouble convincing the Shah to massively invest his petrodollars.
The royal welcome he was given in Paris in June 1974 by Valéry Giscard
d'Estaing, who had recently been elected president, accelerated negotia-

tions. The president and his prime minister had divided their charges: the former, who had an excellent relationship with the Shah,[5] kept cooperation projects with Iran for himself, while the latter supervised commercial ties with Iraq.

On June 27, 1974, the French government committed to selling Iran several civil nuclear power stations. It suggested that the French company Technicatome build three research reactors in Tehran and that a Franco-Iranian company exploit any natural uranium deposits discovered in Iran and share the benefits with both countries. Most importantly, Paris proposed that Tehran invest in the construction of the Eurodif uranium enrichment plant in order for Iran to acquire the fuel required to run its future civil nuclear power stations. The Eurodif plant was run on the basis of a multinational agreement supervised by the International Atomic Energy Agency (IAEA). On November 18, the French minister of industry authorized the sale of two Westinghouse nuclear power plants to Iran, to be built under license by Framatome.

In December 1974 the Shah granted France a one billion dollar loan in exchange for Iran's 10 percent share in Eurodif's capital (at the time, the company's capital was 27.8 percent French, and also included Belgian, Italian, and Spanish funds). It was agreed that this investment would allow Iran to buy 10 percent of the enriched uranium produced by the Tricastin plant once it began operating in 1981. The French Atomic Energy Commission (CEA) and its Iranian counterpart promptly founded Sofidif (Société franco-iranienne pour l'enrichissement de l'uranium par diffusion gazeuse [Franco-Iranian Company for the Enrichment of Uranium through Gaseous Diffusion]) to manage nuclear cooperation between the two nations. To hasten the process, the Shah paid France an additional 180 million dollars. Nonetheless, the cooperation process dragged on. Meanwhile, Framatome broke ground on the first nuclear power plant in Iran at Bushehr.

On October 5, 1978, Valéry Giscard d'Estaing granted political asylum to the Ayatollah Khomeini, who had been expelled from Iran, after receiving the Shah's discreet approval.[6] The French government, which was focused on the recognition of the Palestinian people's legitimate rights, did not do much to oppose its cumbersome guest's proselytism, not realizing how quickly the situation in Iran was deteriorating. Caught short by unfolding events, the French made an agreement with their American and German allies to back Khomeini at the Guadeloupe Summit (January 5, 1979). In fact the Ayatollah Khomeini would board an Air France plane to make a triumphant return to Tehran on February 1, 1979, and take power.

On April 9, 1979, the new Islamic government denounced the nuclear cooperation contract with France, suspending current payments and demanding reimbursement of the one billion dollar Eurodif loan granted by the Shah. Yet, it confirmed that Iran was a shareholder in Eurodif. Paris categorically refused to reimburse the loan and opposed Iran's prerogative to exercise its rights as a Eurodif shareholder. Tehran accused Paris of extortion. Paris retorted that Iran was not a reliable commercial partner. This was the beginning of a long dispute that would poison Franco-Iranian relations for a decade and have severe repercussions on the security of France and its citizens. Bilateral relations were further complicated when an Iranian commando unit headed by Anis Naccache was captured on July 18, 1980, following a failed assassination attempt on Shapour Bakhtiar, then in exile in Neuilly. Before being arrested, the five panicked Iranians had killed one bystander and a police officer. They were sentenced to twenty years in prison, throughout which Tehran would relentlessly demand their release.

Mitterrand Backs Saddam

The situation did not change with the election of a socialist government in France in May 1981. While he had constantly criticized French backing of Iraq, newly elected President François Mitterrand sent Saddam Hussein a message on May 25, assuring him of French support. He publicly declared that he did not want Iraq to be defeated and that it was essential to maintain equilibrium between Persians and Arabs. Faced with the facts, the socialist government recognized the power of the industrial lobby, which was fiercely defending the alliance with Baghdad. This alliance would in fact satisfy a significant part of the Socialist Party, which saw Iraq as a model of modernism, progressiveness, and secularism in the face of the oil monarchies' conservatism and the Iranian Islamic Revolution's obscurantism. Minister of State Jean-Pierre Chevènement became head of the France-Iraq parliamentary group. Pierre Joxe, the chair of the National Assembly's socialist group, made numerous public statements in favor of the Iraqi regime. Minister of Foreign Affairs Claude Cheysson stated that "Iraq is the only barrier to an Islamic onslaught that would destabilize the entire region and topple the moderate Arab regimes."[7] The French government emphasized the necessity of protecting its energy supply sources and the moral obligation to support the only progressive state in the area that could contain the Islamic Revolution's dangerous proselytism. Such discourse could only stoke the mullahs' anger. The situation became even worse when the Iranian government took advantage of the Tricastin nuclear power plant's opening to claim its right to 10 percent of the enriched uranium produced and to once again demand the reimbursement of the Eurodif loan. Tehran was turned down flat.

Scattered Europeans

In Brussels, capital of the European Economic Community (EEC), the news from the Gulf in late September 1980 was greeted with the same cacophony set off by every crisis in the Middle East. European security and defense policies were not yet on the agenda, and the principal European powers, unable to agree on a common strategy, fought for their own political and commercial interests—which were often contradictory. The EEC only managed to eke out an insipid declaration expressing its serious concern regarding the situation and reiterating that it was crucially important for Europe to enjoy freedom of navigation in the Gulf. The Europeans were admittedly far more dependent on oil from the Arabian Peninsula than the Americans. They were thus more vulnerable to destabilization in the area, and the potential closing of the Strait of Hormuz remained one of their worst nightmares. Still reeling from the second oil crisis, they felt unable to endure another abrupt rise in fuel prices. Their priority was therefore to secure their energy supplies and protect their commercial relations with the oil monarchies. To do so, they had to tread softly both with the belligerents and the Gulf sovereigns. European leaders thus vehemently opposed a United Nations' embargo on arms sales to countries in the region, fearing that these countries would retaliate by decreeing an oil embargo on Europe, as they had during the Yom Kippur War. The

Europeans were also keenly aware that the continued sale of military equipment to the Gulf countries would largely benefit their weapons industries.

In these economically hard times, European leaders kept their eye on macroeconomic indicators. British prime minister Margaret Thatcher, for instance, was facing a major social crisis that made it impossible for her to sacrifice the market shares England had struggled to acquire in Iran over the last decade, though she deeply loathed the regime born of the Islamic Revolution. She adopted a position of strict neutrality, refusing to take sides. Her priorities in terms of foreign policy were elsewhere, primarily aimed at containing the Soviet Union. So long as the USSR did not intervene in the Gulf, and British interests there were not directly threatened, London had no reason to interfere in the conflict. Margaret Thatcher could also rest more easily in that she could count on oil from the North Sea to reduce England's energy dependency on the Middle East. This pragmatic attitude allowed the British to sell both belligerents pharmaceutical products, automobile equipment, and machine tools.

Regarding military matters, the British government imposed two strict rules: contracts signed before the war would be honored, but the sale of equipment likely to significantly increase either side's military capacities was banned.[8] Interpreting these regulations loosely, the British government delivered both the Iranians and the Iraqis motors and spare parts for Chieftain and Scorpion tanks, which would allow the former to maintain tanks acquired under the Shah and the latter to repair tanks captured from the Iranian army. London also supplied Tehran with components for Rapier surface-to-air missiles and electronic countermeasure systems and would maintain and modernize the local aerial detection system. Ultimately, the Islamic Republic would become the United Kingdom's biggest customer in the Middle East after Saudi Arabia. To maintain a balance, the British delivered artillery radar guidance systems and 300 Land Rovers to Baghdad. They enrolled many Iraqi students in their military academies and provided basic training for some of Saddam's pilots. They also offered to supply the Iraqi government with a turnkey factory to assemble 200 Hawk training planes in Iraq. But negotiations dragged on, and the Iraqis eventually bought Czech, Swiss, and Brazilian training planes.

German Chancellor Helmut Schmidt also adopted a posture of strict neutrality, referring to the German Constitution, which prevented him from involving his country in armed conflict. In reality, his arguments were as mercantile as those of the British. Over the years Iran had become Germany's primary commercial partner in the Middle East, and the two countries were bound by major contracts, which had survived the Islamic Revolution. Masses of German-made vehicles continued to move through Iranian cities, outside of which factories were often run with machine tools imported from Germany. Striking evidence of these shared interests was Iran's 25 percent share in the famous Krupp industrial conglomerate's capital. Chancellor Schmidt was determined to do anything to avoid sacrificing this privileged relationship, including discreetly supplying Tehran with military equipment such as Mercedes trucks, tank transport trailers, or small-arms munitions manufactured by the Werner Company. To ease the German political class's qualms, this equipment was modestly qualified as "nonoffensive." The German government had more trouble justifying the negotiations over the sale of ultramodern type 209 submarines. Washington, Paris, and Riyadh applied so much pressure that the negotiations did not go through. Their failure was partially responsible for the kidnapping of two Germans in Lebanon (Rudolph Cordes and Alfred Schmidt). Cordes and Schmidt were used as bargaining chips to attempt to convince Bonn to reopen the negotiations, but also to free a Shiite terrorist of Iranian origin held in Germany. The minister of foreign affairs even traveled to Iran on an official visit to attempt to resolve the situation, publicly describing Western attempts to isolate the Islamic Republic as "monumental errors."[9] The election of Helmut Kohl did not modify the German position, which remained unchanged until the end of the war.

The German authorities hedged their bets with mastery and much sweet-talking, managing to maintain cordial relations with Baghdad. This was quite an exploit, given the hostility the Ba'athist regime unleashed toward those who supported its adversaries. While the Iraqis were hardly fooled by the German ambassador to Baghdad's kind words, they took everything his government was ready to sell them: Mercedes for the regime's elite, machine tools and chemical components for the engineers responsible for developing weapons of mass destruction, tank recovery vehicles and heavy-tonnage trucks for the army. To ease its conscience, Bonn trained Iraqi military doctors and delivered several army hospitals to Baghdad. German industrialists also sold Baghdad some sixty BO-105 attack helicopters equipped with devastating HOT antitank missiles. These were quietly delivered to Iraq via Spain, which assembled part of the helicopters in order to allow Germany to coolly display its neutrality vis-à-vis the two belligerents. The German government maintained this façade to avoid a violent reaction from the Israelis, who were fiercely opposed to the sale of sophisticated weapons to Iraq and with whom German leaders had complex relations, a fruit of the tragic history that compelled them to avoid doing anything that could compromise Israel's security.

Like Germany, Italy tried to preserve its commercial ties both with Iraq and Iran. The president of the Italian Council of State, the Christian-Democrat Francesco Cossiga, declared he was neutral and wanted to maintain cordial relations with Baghdad and Tehran. He forcefully emphasized that contracts signed before the war would be honored. He ordered that Iran be shipped twenty-four Chinook transport helicopters with their lots of motors and spare parts, several dozen electronic warfare systems, and thirteen coastal surveillance radars. His government also authorized the delivery of several million shells and several hundred thousand mines, some of which were shipped via Singapore. Unfortunately for Cossiga, the governmental instability that plagued Italian politics led to his rapid downfall. Coalitions further to the left on the political spectrum forced his successors to ban all weapons sales to the belligerents. Contracts under negotiation were frozen. This was particularly bad news for the Fincantieri firm, which had just agreed on the sale of eleven warships to Iraq (four frigates, six corvettes, and one oil tanker tender) and seven patrol boats to Iran. In a few months the Italian authorities managed to fall out with both belligerents, who clamored for the delivery of the ships they had been promised. These two thorny deals would poison relations between Rome, Baghdad, and Tehran, making life difficult for Italian diplomats for years to come. The embargo was even more problematic in that the Italian government ordered that the Iraqi warships be built in order to maintain employment in their naval yards. Once completed, the ships rotted in the dock, waiting for their unlikely delivery to the Gulf. The Italian government finally transferred the ships' right of ownership to the Iraqi navy, which christened them with their war names and sent reduced crews to take charge of them. However, the ships were not authorized to leave the Mediterranean and therefore did not participate in the hostilities. To cool the Iraqis' and Iranians' anger, the Italian authorities looked the other way and allowed Italian companies to involve themselves in a great deal of trafficking in light weapons, mines, and ammunition intended for both sides. The Italian government was eventually forced to arrest the heads of the Valsella Company (a subsidiary of the Fiat group that specialized in assembling mines) after they went too far, outrageously violating the embargo decreed by Rome.

Spain and Greece, both totally dependent on Middle Eastern oil, also refused to take sides with either of the belligerents, but let them know they were standing by to discreetly provide them with arms and ammunition in order to collect revenue. Both countries needed the money to lift themselves out of the depths of the economic crisis. Since their own pilots flew Phantoms, the Spanish and Greek governments delivered Phantom spare parts to Iran, ignoring the potential repercussions for their own air forces. Determined to make the most of the opportunity the war provided to replenish its coffers, Spain also sold Iraq light weapons, recoilless antitank guns, and Santana Land Rovers, as well as handling the sale of BO-105 helicopters contracted with Germany.

The Scandinavian countries, like the Benelux nations, proved more independent in their attitudes. They condemned Iraq and Iran for having mutually drawn each other into a stupid and criminal conflict. Far less dependent on Middle Eastern oil due to their access to North Sea oil and with no business interests in the region, the Scandinavians could allow themselves to speak freely without fear of the consequences. Nonetheless, they too got their hands dirty by signing a few lucrative contracts with one or the other of the belligerents, and sometimes even both. Overall, European countries delivered twenty-seven billion dollars' worth of military equipment to Iraq and Iran, making up a quarter of their weapon purchases.[10]

[Chapter 6]

The Arabs Divided

As soon as war broke out Arab leaders understood they needed to take a position. But this was rendered particularly difficult by the fact that it was impossible to base the position on any of the three dividing issues then determining international relations. To begin with, the conflict had nothing to do with the face-off between East and West. It also bore no relation to the Israeli-Arab conflict, which would have allowed the Arabs to gather under one banner. It had nothing in common with the decolonization wars, for the Iraqi and Iranian regimes both claimed to be anticolonial, nationalist, and Third World. And, this war pitted two Muslim nations against each other. Hence the difficulty in defining an ideological stance that would guide the Arab leaders' choice, one that was particularly delicate in that the Arab world was profoundly divided along several fault lines: "conservative" monarchies versus "progressive" republics; secular regimes versus Islamic regimes; pro-Western states versus pro-Soviet states; states willing to hold discussions with Israel versus those belonging to the refusal front; rich countries versus poor. These sometimes radical divergences were apparent in the four major issues that divided the Arab League: the Palestinian question; the Yemenite conflict (between the Marxist South and the pro-Saudi North); the Western Sahara conflict (between Morocco and the Polisario Front backed by Algeria); and OPEC's definition of a concerted price policy. Faced with the Iran-Iraq War, which transcended these dividing lines, Arab leaders took positions based on their own interests, the nature of their bilateral relations with Baghdad and Tehran, but especially their rivalries—for several of them harbored ambitions to impose their leadership on the Arab-speaking world. Yet all agreed on one thing: everything had to be done to avoid letting the conflict develop into a regionwide war that could potentially degenerate into a military conflict between the Americans and the Soviets, with the Arabs left to bear the devastating consequences. In this respect, pragmatism overcame any historical, ethnic, or religious considerations.

King Hussein of Jordan, Herald of the Pro-Iraqi Camp

On September 23, 1980, King Hussein of Jordan became the first to react and to unreservedly side with Saddam Hussein. While he evoked the principle of Arab solidarity, his position was also shaped by realpolitik. Iraq's defeat would leave Jordan in a highly uncomfortable situation, without strategic depth to face Israel and squeezed between Syria and Saudi Arabia, both of which wanted to extend their influence over the Hashemite Kingdom. King Hussein also suspected the Iranian mullahs of wanting to destabilize his kingdom and turn it into a fundamentalist republic governed by the Palestinians. The Jordanian monarch thus drew closer to Baghdad, which provided him with priceless guarantees of safety and cheap oil in exchange for permanent access to the Jordanian port of Aqaba. The road between Aqaba and Baghdad, which was expensively modernized by Saddam Hussein, became a major Iraqi supply route.

While Jordan was a poor country, and King Hussein could not do much to help Iraq financially, he provided it with all his diplomatic support. He notably made himself the American envoy to Saddam, with whom the United States did not communicate directly. To provide military assistance to Baghdad, Hussein authorized the Iraqi air force to scatter its planes on his H-5 air base near the Iranian border and to use it to refuel. He encouraged Iraqi fighter pilots to train in his air space by facing off against Jordanian F-5s similar to those used by the Iranian army. He also let Iraqi engineers examine his Hawk air defense missiles, which were identical to Iran's, in order to allow the Iraqis to develop the best evasive tactics. He looked the other way when weapons were delivered to Iraq via Jordan. When Baghdad received its first Mirage F-1s from France, King Hussein made part of his own F-1 fleet available to the Iraqis. About ten of them would do battle under Iraqi colors, while some fifteen Jordanian pilots would fly Iraqi Mirages throughout the entire war. Finally, from the moment Iran penetrated Iraqi territory, King Hussein dispatched his "Al-Yarmouk" Mechanized Brigade to help Saddam hold the front lines. He authorized several thousand Jordanian volunteers to enroll in the Iraqi army for the duration of the hostilities. King Hussein's unstinting commitment to Iraq allowed him to reap extensive economic benefits for his country. Aqaba was transformed into a prosperous harbor zone, which would become the kingdom's economic heart. The road network was significantly improved, leading to the development of numerous transportation companies. Kickbacks from trafficking to Iraq allowed for the embellishment of the Jordanian capital of Amman.

In the Maghreb, King Hassan II of Morocco and President Habib Bourguiba of Tunisia promptly followed in their Jordanian counterpart's footsteps, but each leader declared his support for Saddam Hussein for different reasons. The Moroccan king's primary concern remained the conflict in the Western Sahara. He had launched into the conquest of this vast desert area, rich in minerals, to reinforce his reign and ensure it would be lasting. Since 1976 he had been fighting the local Polisario Front, which demanded the former Spanish colony's independence. The Iraqi regime had always been one of the most fervent advocates for Morocco's claim to Western Sahara. It opposed any separatist movement on principle, knowing such movements could indirectly reinforce its own Kurdish minority. King Hassan II was grateful to Baghdad and returned the favor by supporting it with all his religious and political might. He was also encouraged to support Baghdad by the fact that Algeria, his rival in the Maghreb, was unquestionably sympathetic to Iran. Lacking the means to provide Iraq with any material or financial assistance, Hassan II provided it with a contingent of "volunteers" from the regular army.

President Bourguiba saw Ba'athist Iraq both as a model for a secular Arab society of the kind he had been struggling to establish in Tunisia and a barrier against Iran's religious fanaticism, which he feared more than anything. Saddam's authoritarian character did not particularly bother him, for he was convinced that only an enlightened autocrat could lead the Arab people out of poverty and obscurantism. Like Hassan II, Habib Bourguiba was only too happy to support the Iraqi president who stood up to the Algerian authorities, whom the Tunisians suspected of conspiring against them. President Bourguiba's political support was particularly crucial to Saddam because Tunisia had been the seat of the Arab League since Egypt had been blacklisted.

Though King Khalid of Saudi Arabia also took Saddam's side, he did so with a little less enthusiasm. He obviously had to back Iraq, which he saw as a natural barrier to the Iranian regime's aggressive proselytism. Saddam had informed him of his plans, and Khalid had been left with no choice but to reluctantly support him. The Saudi monarch was wary of the Iraqi dictator, whom he suspected of being excessively ambitious, which could eventually pose a threat to the Gulf monarchies' sovereignty. In his view, it would have been problematic for Saddam to come out of his crusade against Iran overly strengthened. The right approach was to back him enough so that he would not lose, but not give him the means to win resoundingly. In fact, King Khalid's ideal solution would have been a permanent status quo between the two belligerents. His own priorities were to reinforce his financial base and his dominant position in OPEC, to prevent an overly visible presence of foreign troops on his soil in order to honor his role as guardian of the holy places, and, finally, to implement a regional security structure centered around Saudi Arabia, which could allow him to resolve the thorny Yemenite conflict to his advantage. Khalid knew he had to handle Iraq with kid gloves to attain these ambitious objectives. He therefore assured Saddam Hussein of his support and promised him important loans, which would allow him to finance his war against Iran (from 1981 to 1988, Saudi Arabia paid Iraq sixty billion dollars). He guaranteed Iraq right of transit to bring in weapons purchased throughout the world. He also provided delivery of merchandise to Iraq. Finally, he agreed to extract oil from the neutral zone on Iraq's behalf and sell 300,000 barrels of oil per day to partially compensate Baghdad's loss of revenue. The neutral zone was a small area covering 2,700 square miles (7,000 square kilometers) between Iraq and Saudi Arabia, a result of the Uqair Protocol agreed to by the Kingdom of Nejd and the British Mandate Authority in 1922. This agreement, carried forward by Iraq and Saudi Arabia, authorized each of the two parties to freely exploit the zone on the condition that they did not build any military installations there. This relic of a bygone era would be eliminated following the second Gulf War in 1991.

The other oil monarchies were divided regarding the position to adopt. They nervously observed the triangular struggle between Iraq, Iran, and

Saudi Arabia for control of the Gulf, and hoped not to be too adversely affected. Emir Jaber III of Kuwait and Emir Isa of Bahrain were the most reticent to openly support Baghdad and thus openly provoke Tehran, because they knew how vulnerable they were. The former was conscious that the Iranian border was only a stone's throw from his own, but was also deeply aware that Iraq had always dreamed of reclaiming Kuwait and considered it its nineteenth province. He worried Saddam would take advantage of the confusion of battle to extend his hold on the emirate. The latter had to handle a primarily Shiite population secretly supported by Iran. The indubitable risk of destabilization was heightened by the memory of the previous year's bloodshed in Mecca, which had shaken all of the Gulf leaders.

The two heads of state adopted different stances. Emir Jaber forcefully reaffirmed his opposition to the presence of foreign troops on his soil, including Arab troops. He made a wide variety of contacts to demonstrate his faith in the international community and avoid falling under the heel of either belligerent. His strategy consisted of bringing as many players into the Gulf as possible. Nonetheless, Jaber remained realistic and knew he had to handle Saddam carefully. He discreetly ensured him of his financial and logistical support. Kuwait thus became Iraq's biggest sponsor after Saudi Arabia: from 1981 to 1988, it paid Baghdad fifteen billion dollars. For his part, Emir Isa placed himself under the double military protection of Saudi Arabia and the United States, calling for greater Western military presence in the region.

Sheikh Khalifa Al Thani of Qatar was close to King Khalid and aligned himself with the Saudi position. He openly supported Saddam Hussein, but only provided him with nominal financial backing. Sheikh Zayed, the sovereign of Abu Dhabi and thus the president of the Federation of the United Arab Emirates (UAE), took a nuanced position. He sided with Baghdad out of Arab solidarity, but stated his desire to maintain cordial relations with Tehran, despite Iran's occupation of the Tunb and Abu Musa islands. Naturally, the new port of Jebel Ali and the city of Dubai had recently become trading hubs with Iran, generating vast revenue for the UAE. Nonetheless, Sheikh Zayed contributed five billion dollars to the Iraqi war effort.

Oman, Egypt, and Algeria's Leaders Refuse to Align Themselves

Sultan Qaboos of Oman took the most reserved position in the Gulf by refusing to take sides with either of the belligerents and offering his services as a mediator ready to facilitate any attempt at reconciliation. His choice was informed by geography. The sultan controlled the Strait of Hormuz. He was responsible for serving as its guardian and ensuring freedom of passage through this strategic corridor. Additionally, Sultan Qaboos was economically dependent on Iran, had to take into account the influence of his population's significant Shiite minority, and could not forget that it was the Iranian authorities who had helped him to quash the Dhofar rebellion a few years earlier. He could not afford to indispose Tehran. He did not provide any financial or material assistance to Baghdad and refused to have his air bases host the Iraqi bombers that Saddam Hussein wanted to deploy there to have better access to Iranian maritime traffic. To guarantee his own security, Oman's sovereign counted on the presence of American and British bases, which allowed Washington and London to closely monitor aerial and naval activity around the Strait of Hormuz.

Egypt's President Anwar al-Sadat was in a difficult situation. He had no choice but to verbally support Iraq, not out of Arab solidarity, but out of hatred for the Iranian regime, which he considered the greatest threat to the Arab world's stability. He feared that Iran's victory could reinforce the Muslim Brotherhood movement in his own country and destabilize his regime. Yet he was not prepared to assist Saddam Hussein, whom he had publicly scorned since Saddam had fiercely criticized the Egyptian Rais for concluding a separate peace with Israel. Sadat had since been ostracized by his peers and banned from the Arab League and the Organization of Islamic Cooperation. He had no reason to accommodate the Iraqi dictator. Yet after his assassination by the Tanzim al-Jihad on October 6, 1981, a combination of pan-Arabism and realpolitik led his successor Hosni Mubarak to draw closer to Baghdad.

Early in 1982 President Mubarak started providing significant material support to Saddam Hussein: spare parts for his numerous Soviet-made weapons, a wide variety of munitions and missiles, T-55 tanks, and even some thirty Su-7 fighter-bombers. The Iraqis considered the latter obsolete and too poorly maintained for flight and used them as decoys on their air bases. To make up for this, Mubarak sent one of his Mirage V fighter squadrons to help defend the Iraqi front. He also authorized the deployment to Iraq of roughly one hundred pilots and several hundred technicians, who would contribute to making Saddam's MiG fleet operational. Finally, he agreed that several tens of thousands of the one million Egyptians residing in Iraq join the Iraqi army for the duration of the hostilities in return for a good salary. Hosni Mubarak's assistance made it possible to implement a Baghdad-Amman-Cairo axis to counterbalance the Tehran-Damascus-Tripoli axis. His efforts were rewarded: thanks to the combined efforts of Saddam Hussein and Tariq Aziz, Egypt rejoined the Organization of Islamic Cooperation in 1984 and later returned to the head of the Arab League.

Algerian President Houari Boumediene also found himself in a delicate position in that he had good reasons to support both Iran and Iraq. Like Algeria, both countries had resolutely affirmed their desire for independence and modernity and turned their back on the West. They were also important players in the oil business. The Algerian authorities did not want to enter into conflict with either side. Boumediene also aspired to recognition as a credible mediator, capable of bringing greater stability to the Middle East. It was therefore consistent for him to claim a neutral position, offering his services to both belligerents. In fact, he was determined to secretly help Iran due to several grudges he was nursing against Saddam Hussein. Saddam supported Morocco, Algeria's greatest rival, and refuted the Sahrawi people's right to independence. Worse yet, he had committed the capital offence of denouncing the Algiers Accord, of which the Algerian president had been a major architect. Houari Boumediene did not go so far as to financially or materially support Iran, whose downward spiral into theocratic authoritarianism he criticized, and made do with discreet diplomatic backing, which he hoped would allow him to count on Tehran's support in OPEC.

Hafez Al-Assad, Leader of the Pro-Iranian Camp

Syrian president Hafez al-Assad immediately rallied behind Tehran, respecting the alliance he had made with the Iranian regime a year earlier. Until that point, Syria had openly been in the Arab camp, both out of solidarity and self-interest. In a state of permanent confrontation with Israel, Syria needed material assistance from Arab countries as well as their political support to maintain pressure on the Jewish state and continue to supply the Palestinian resistance. Maintaining an impressive military arsenal was a very costly proposition, and Syria, which could only rely on meager agriculture and a little oil, constantly struggled to balance the books. Unable to count on the oil monarchies, which rejected its republican regime and socialist orientation, the Syrian government had long since turned to Egypt and Iraq, the other two Arab republics that shared its values and its animosity toward Israel. Following Sadat's about-face and the signing of a peace treaty between Egypt and Israel, Damascus had little choice but to bank on a closer relationship with Baghdad, despite the old quarrels dividing the Ba'athist rivals. At the time, Hafez al-Assad thought he could eclipse President al-Bakr and impose himself as the Middle East's strong man, taking advantage of his position as the Front of Refusal's leader.

The situation altered when Saddam Hussein came to power in the summer of 1979. The slap in the face Saddam gave Assad just as the two countries were about to sign a unity agreement forced the Syrian president to radically change his position. Suddenly finding himself isolated in the heart of the Arab world, Hafez al-Assad reinforced his ties with the USSR and turned to Iran, which appeared to him to be the only regional power able to put sufficient pressure on the three countries most threatening to his security: Israel, Turkey, and Iraq. Syria had considered itself at war with Israel since 1948. It also wanted to reclaim the Sanjak of Alexandretta arbitrarily attached to Turkey by the French Mandate authorities in 1939. It also knew that Turkey, which controlled the sources of the Tigris and the Euphrates, could considerably reduce both rivers' flow and dry up Syrian agriculture. As for Iraq, Damascus feared that Baghdad would seize the few Syrian oil fields near the Iraqi border.

Iran shared a border with Turkey and could threaten it if necessary, though the border had not been contested since the mid-seventeenth century. Revolutionary Iran was also capable of exerting significant pressure on Israel via the large Shiite community in South Lebanon, which had recognized the authority of the Ayatollah Khomeini since the June 24, 1975, Saïda Agreement between the Iranian clergy and the Lebanese Shiites. Iran also had numerous ways of pressuring Iraq. Finally, petroleum-rich Iran was prepared to deliver large quantities of oil to Syria. It was therefore perfectly logical for President Hafez al-Assad to follow a Bismarckian geopolitical approach and open discussions with the Iranian regime in the fall of 1979 to create an informal alliance with Tehran. The Iranians were particularly receptive to this proposal, given that they knew that the Alawite minority—to which the Assad clan belonged—claimed to be part of the Shiite community, though it did not identify with the Twelver Shia Islam advocated by the Iranian clergy.

This unexpected turnaround offered the Iranian leaders an un-hoped-for opportunity to fragment the Arab camp and weaken Iraq, which would no longer be able to count on reinforcement from Syrian troops in case of war. Iraq's oil exports were also threatened, for part of its oil flowed through Syria via a pipeline from Kirkuk to the port of Baniyas. This rear alliance seemed particularly sound in that Iran and Syria did not share a border, thus limiting potential sources of friction. Most importantly, it convinced the Iranian clergy, which wanted to export the Islamic Revolution, that its destabilizing action had to primarily be aimed at Iraq in order to constitute a new Shiite axis made up of Iran, Iraq, Syria, and Lebanon.

For his part, Hafez al-Assad saw Saddam Hussein as an even more ruthless rival now that he supported the Syrian Muslim Brotherhood. The moment hostilities broke out between Iran and Iraq, Assad decided to provide military assistance to Tehran. He ordered the delivery of vast quantities of missiles, munitions, and other Soviet-made light equipment to complement what the Iranians captured from the Iraqis. All these weapons were billed at top dollar. Syria also provided Iran with numerous pharmaceutical and food products and allowed it to deploy several hundred Pasdaran in Lebanon. This gave Iran a foothold in the land of the Cedar, allowing it access to the Mediterranean and an opportunity to tighten its grip on the Lebanese Shiite community. These Pasdaran would form the core of Hezbollah and the Islamic Jihad. In return, they helped the Syrian dictator rout militias hostile to Damascus. Now that his Iraqi neighbor was busy fighting Iran, Hafez al-Assad no longer had to guard himself on that front and was free to do as he pleased in Lebanon and to savagely put down the Muslim Brotherhood in Syria. In February 1982, he launched his army against the Muslim Brotherhood fighters entrenched in the city of Hama. The clampdown left 30,000 dead and destroyed a third of the city. To weaken Baghdad and please Tehran, Assad opened his borders to Iraqi Kurd leaders trying to escape Saddam's secret police. He even went so far as to order terrorist attacks on Iraqi interests in Lebanon. For instance, Syrian agents were implicated in the destruction of the Iraqi embassy in Beirut in December 1981.[1]

Hafez al-Assad was not the only one to take Iran's side. Muammar Gaddafi, the leader of the Libyan revolution, had long been waiting for his chance to take revenge on Saddam Hussein, who had always treated him contemptuously and considered him a lunatic. Colonel Gaddafi reproached Saddam Hussein for reinforcing Israel by adopting a hostile attitude toward Syria. He also reproached him for supporting Yasser Arafat when several Arab capitals had dropped the PLO leader, accusing him of destabilizing Lebanon. But Gaddafi's position was primarily determined by his rivalry with the Iraqi dictator. Gaddafi liked to see himself as a challenger to Saddam and Assad in the race for leadership of the Arab world. Since he had understood that the Iraqi was the favorite, he chose to ally himself with the Syrian. On September 1, 1980, three weeks before the beginning of hostilities, he offered the Syrian president a merger between the Libyan Jamahiriya and the Syrian Republic, declaring that he was ready to financially support Syria and align himself with its foreign policy. Thus when war broke out between Iraq and Iran, Colonel Gaddafi found himself stuck, forced to support Tehran with Assad. Nonetheless, this position offered him the possibility to redeem himself in the eyes of the Iranian clergy and put the murky assassination of Imam Musa al-Sadr behind him.

Two years earlier, this Lebanese imam, who was close to the Ayatollah Khomeini, had mysteriously disappeared during an official visit to Libya. The Libyan authorities claimed he had left the country, but no one had ever seen him since. Very popular in the Lebanese Shiite community, and known for his moderate positions and his commitment to interdenominational dialogue, he had made numerous enemies, notably among the Palestinian leaders, whom he accused of wanting to weaken Lebanon. His activism had profoundly irritated the Syrian regime. Shortly after his disappearance, the Iranian clergy had accused Colonel Gaddafi of organizing the holy man's elimination, probably at the behest of the Palestinians or Syrians. In 2011, the Libyan ambassador to the Arab League took advantage of the popular uprising against Gaddafi to declare that Imam Musa al-Sadr had indeed been assassinated and buried in Libya. In 1980, Colonel Gaddafi was eager to be forgiven for the imam's disappearance and promised the Iranian government large quantities of military equipment. It was easy for him to make good on this promise, given that his vast stock of weapons, paid for in cash thanks to oil riches, was collecting dust in warehouses. Starting in 1981, cargo ships and airplanes shuttled back and forth between Libya and Iran delivering T-55, T-62, and T-72 tanks, BTR-60 and BMP-1 armored vehicles, antitank and anti-air weapons, and several million shells and various munitions.

Ali Nasir Muhammad, who ran South Yemen's Marxist regime with an iron fist, took up the cause of Iran to punish Saddam Hussein for supporting North Yemen. Six months earlier, the Iraqi president had committed to supporting North Yemen to be in the Saudi king's good graces. South Yemen was poor and could not provide Iran with material assistance, but its geostrategic position at the mouth of the Red Sea was precious to Tehran, which wanted to carry out attacks in the Bab el-Mandeb Strait and harry maritime traffic in the Red Sea. Most weapons acquired by Iraq passed through the Bab el-Mandeb, as well as a significant part of the oil extracted in Saudi Arabia. South Yemen thus became a pawn in the regional exchequer, allowing Iran to increase pressure on Saudi Arabia. Symmetrically, North Yemen's government allied itself with Iraq, and its president Ali Abdullah Saleh committed to sending several thousand "volunteers" to fight on the Iraqi front.

The ultimate symptom of all these regional divisions was the Arab League's inability to react. Its only initiative was to call a summit at the end of which the participants agreed on a highly conservative statement asking Iran to accept a ceasefire. Every one of its following initiatives would be torpedoed by one of the factions supporting or opposing one or the other belligerent.

The Gulf Cooperation Council Steps In

On May 25, 1981, after several months of intense debate, the sovereigns of Saudi Arabia, the United Arab Emirates, Kuwait, Bahrain, Qatar, and Oman signed the Gulf Cooperation Council (GCC) into being. This council did not constitute a military alliance, but—more modestly—a tool for economic integration to benefit its six member states. Its objective was to promote a regional common market that would eventually have a shared currency. The six oil monarchies' leaders were convinced that military power alone would not suffice to guarantee their security if it did not rest on a solid financial base. They felt it necessary to coordinate their economic policies to more effectively counter Iran (notably within OPEC) and display their unity to the belligerents. Despite border disputes and tribal antagonisms, these six monarchies appeared to be six natural partners sharing a common cultural heritage, similar political systems, and the same dangerous strategic environment.

The war served as a goad to convince the monarchs to put aside their rivalries in favor of their common interests (thirty years later, the GCC remains active and has allowed its members to progress toward greater regional integration). This was a political victory for King Khalid, who had gone all out to convince his peers to support his initiative. It was indeed the first time that the six Gulf monarchies united on a political project that would allow them to reinforce their positions on Iran and Iraq, but also vis-à-vis the Western nations coveting their oil riches in an increasingly open manner. To flatter each player's sensitivities and avoid giving the impression that the council was dominated by Saudi Arabia, the position of secretary general was given to Abdullah Bishara, a seasoned Kuwaiti diplomat. In actuality, the Saudi monarch and the president of the UAE pulled the strings of this organization, which would establish itself as the instrument for coordinating financial assistance to Iraq (which explains why Iran always opposed the GCC's attempts at mediation).

To express its dismay and wariness, Tehran multiplied provocations aimed at Kuwait, which was considered the GCC's weak link. On June 13,

1981, four Phantoms took off from Bushehr and conspicuously flew over the emirate. They avoided the local anti-aircraft defense, but did not fire at any targets. The message was intended to be clear: the emirate was to remain neutral and not openly side with Baghdad, or risk incurring Tehran's wrath. These violations of Kuwaiti air space would continue until October 1981, when a pair of Phantoms was intercepted by Mirage F-1s that had been delivered in haste to the emirate by France.

Chapter 7

Israel Banks on Iran and Turkey Benefits from the War

From the first days of the war, Israel supported Iran, despite the fact that Ayatollah Khomeini pilloried the Israeli "Little Satan" and called for Muslims the world over to launch a Jihad to liberate Jerusalem from the Zionist occupation. While apparently paradoxical, the Israeli stance was in fact perfectly rational. Since it was founded, Israel had maintained excellent ties with Iran under the Pahlavis, sharing their interest in containing the Arab camp. Iran had always been the perfect rear ally for Israel, and vice versa. All the principal Israeli political leaders had visited Iran at one time or another and most of the heads of the Imperial Army had traveled to Israel to study Tzahal's victories over the Arabs. Iranian Phantom pilots regularly trained in the Negev to improve their aerial combat skills with ace Israeli pilots. This alliance had relieved Arab military pressure on Israel in the 1967 and 1973 wars. It had also allowed numerous Iraqi Jews to flee their country and reach Israel via Iran. For twenty-five years, Israel had purchased its oil supplies from Iran. Mossad and the SAVAK had closely collaborated. Israel and Iran were both favored allies of the United States.

Six months before the Shah's fall, his deputy minister of war, General Hassan Toufanian, had met with the highest Israeli authorities in Jerusalem to reinforce military relations between the two nations, going so far as to consider a joint raid on the future Iraqi nuclear power plant, Osirak. Even after the Revolution, many thought the Islamic Republic would not last and that, once free of this avatar, the Iranians would revive their strong ties with Israel to once again put up a common front against the Arabs. Yitzhak Rabin would later describe the Jews' natural empathy for the Iranians: "For 28 of 37 years, Iran was a friend of Israel.

If it could work for 28 years . . . why couldn't it [again] once this crazy idea of Shiite fundamentalism is gone?"[1] The Israeli government considered it was in its best interest to keep the channels between Jerusalem and Tehran open while it waited for the mullahs' regime to collapse.

A Pragmatic Strategy

Israel's position was largely shaped by its desire to undermine the Iraqi regime. At the time, Iraq appeared to be Israel's most dangerous enemy—moreover, an enemy that was trying to acquire the atomic bomb. The Iranian Islamic regime was perceived as a far more distant threat. From Israel's perspective, every effort had to be made to block Saddam and weaken his army. General Amnon Shahak, head of military intelligence, had an alarmist interpretation: "An Iraqi victory would be a nightmare for us!"[2] Faced with two evils, Menachem Begin chose the lesser of the two. After a restricted defense meeting, he decided to support Tehran and supply the Iranians with discreet military assistance. He immediately understood all that Israel had to gain from a war that had the tremendous advantage of immobilizing and weakening two of its enemies—so long as it lasted long enough to exhaust them. By supporting Iran, which initially seemed weaker than Iraq, the Israeli prime minister hoped to prolong the conflict. He famously stated: "I wish both belligerents good luck and much success!" The thundering Ariel Sharon was more explicit, plainly stating that "Israel has a vital interest in the continuation of the war in the Persian Gulf."[3]

A third factor sheds light on the Israeli attitude toward the war. Since the beginning of the Islamic Revolution, Jerusalem had believed the Iranian Jews were in danger and wanted to bring as many as possible home to Israel. The Israeli government was reassured neither by the traditional protection enjoyed by the Iranian Jewish community (estimated at 75,000 at the time) nor the Ayatollah Khomeini's statements guaranteeing its safety. It encouraged Iranian Jews to leave the country. But to persuade Tehran to let them go, Jerusalem had to find a bargaining chip. What could be more convincing than a promise of military assistance during war? From winter 1980 to summer 1988, 55,000 Iranian Jews were authorized to leave Iran and did so without fearing for their lives (20,000 others remain in Iran). Each time negotiations between the two capitals stalled, the flow of refugees dried up and Israel had no choice but to resume weapon shipments to unblock the situation.

These arms sales allowed the Israelis to do a favor to the Americans, who were looking for intermediaries to deliver the spare parts they had promised Iran, but also allowed Israel to find new outlets for its own weapons industry. Times were difficult, and indicators were in the red. Israel, hit hard by the financial crisis, needed to sell its products to save jobs. By selling off some of its relatively antiquated stock, Israel could replace outdated equipment with its own weapons. Over six years (1980–1986), Israel made between one and two billion dollars from weapon and spare-part shipments to Iran, becoming the fourth biggest weapon supplier to Tehran. In 1986 alone, these sales allegedly reached the record figure of 750 million dollars.[4]

Beyond the fact that the war allowed Israel to get along with Iran at Iraq's expense, negotiate the repatriation of Iranian Jews, and collect revenue, it also left Israel free to take a hardline position toward Syria and the Palestinians. It was thus utterly logical for the Israeli government to open discussions with the Iranian military authorities only a few days after the beginning of the war and offer them Israel's help. Since the break in diplomatic relations, the Israelis no longer had access to Iranian decision makers. Jacob Nimrodi, the former Israeli military attaché to Tehran (1975–1979), attempted to reestablish contact. Born in Baghdad to a Jewish Iraqi family and with a background in the secret intelligence services, Nimrodi had had a privileged relationship with the Imperial Army's military high command. He would be one of the few Israelis to regularly travel to Iran after the foundation of the Islamic Republic. According to several sources, he sent a fax to one of his former contacts in the Iranian air force asking, "What can we do to help you?" The answer is said to have come several days later in the form of a long list of varied materials and weapons, requesting the immediate delivery of motors and spare parts for Phantom fighters, Cobra helicopters, and Patton tanks. Israel immediately set up a channel through which to supply Iran. The network depended on several intermediaries. In Israel, this operation, called "Shellfish," was supervised by Prime Minister Menachem Begin. Jacob Nimrodi remained its linchpin, given that he had all the necessary contacts in Iran. He was also responsible for suggesting what Israel could and could not deliver to Tehran to avoid creating a threat to its own security. Yitzhak Hofi, the director of Mossad, Zvi Reuter, export director at the Ministry of Defense, and Al Schwimmer, CEO of Israeli Aircraft Industries, were also closely involved. Even Shimon Peres and Yitzhak Rabin, the leaders of the Labor opposition, were informed of the operation and supported it. The Iranian liaison between Iran's authorities and Jacob Nimrodi were military officers who were used to working with the Israelis and had since sworn allegiance to the Islamic regime. They could rely on the moral backing of Ibrahim Yazdi, a close ally of the Ayatollah Khomeini.

One of the Iranians met his Israeli counterpart in Zurich to determine how the operation would function. Farouk Azizi, an Iranian arms trafficker well known to Israel's secret services, was put in charge of organizing delivery to Iran via the Argentine charter company Transporte Aereo Rioplatense. The company's cargo planes were loaded with crates of military equipment in Israel, stopped in Cyprus, then flew over Turkey and the high plateaus of Anatolia before unloading their cargo in the area of Tabriz, in Iran. More cumbersome equipment was delivered by boat, via maritime brokers serving as front companies. Iran remunerated Israel in oil delivered at advantageous prices. Everyone got what they wanted. As a sign of goodwill, the Iranians even sent the Israelis photos of the Iraqi nuclear power plant. They allegedly received the following message in reply: "Do not worry about this target, we are taking care of it."[5]

The Israelis provided the Iranians not only with spare parts but growing quantities of weapons and ammunition. These supplies would include several hundred Hawk, Sidewinder, and Sparrow missiles, 1,250 TOW antimissile tanks, jammer pods for improving Iranian fighter planes' penetration capacity, radar equipment, 1,000 field telephones, several hundred jeeps, fifty Soltam M-71 155-mm towed howitzers, 150 M-40 antitank guns, several thousand light weapons with millions of cartridges, and several hundred 105-, 130-, 155-, 175-, and 203-mm shells.[6] These clandestine shipments would probably have remained completely undisclosed if a CL-44 four-engine cargo plane shuttling between Cyprus and Tabriz had not been brought down by Soviet fighters on July 18, 1981. Following a navigation error, the aircraft strayed into Soviet airspace near the Turkish border. The squadron of Su-15s sent to intercept it opened fire. The plane crashed in Armenia, leaving no survivors. The case drew tremendous attention, but was quickly covered up by the Israeli authorities and the American government, who did not want the international press to take too much interest in the affair.

Turkey, the Silent Victor

Like Israel, Turkey took advantage of the Iran-Iraq War to benefit both on the economic and political fronts. The outbreak of hostilities came barely ten days after the September 12, 1980, coup d'état that put the Turkish military in power. General Kenan Evren, head of the new junta, could not have asked for a better diversion to attenuate the criticism that the international community aimed at his country as it stood on the brink of implosion. For several years Turkey had been struggling with a major economic crisis and catastrophic debt that had left the nation on the verge of bankruptcy and prevented it from receiving a single loan. This disastrous situation had resulted in the fragmentation of the political class, significant governmental instability, and a state of near civil war. Rightly or wrongly, the military had decided to take control of the situation. General Evren dissolved the National Assembly, banned political parties, and formed a government of liberal technocrats whose priority was to put the Turkish economy back on track.[7] The war between Iran and Iraq would be a significant help in reaching this objective.

At the outbreak of war both belligerents saw Turkey as a country to be courted and with which it would be dangerous to have an antagonistic relationship. From Baghdad's point of view Turkey was a regional power that controlled one of the principal oil pipelines exporting Iraqi oil to the West, but which also regulated the flow of the Tigris and Euphrates, the two rivers vital to Iraqi industry and agriculture. It was seen as an essential axis of communication to allow Iraq to expand from the Gulf region and open up to the Mediterranean. The Iraqi generals were also mindful that the Turkish army was one of the most powerful in the Middle East. The Iraqi regime had two additional reasons to closely collaborate with Turkey. First, Ankara purchased a significant part of Iraq's oil production without challenging its conditions. Second, the two capitals were equally determined to fight the Kurdish independence movement. They had every interest in getting along to prevent the Kurdish community in either country taking shelter on the other's territory and reinforcing itself there. The relationship with Turkey seemed important enough for Saddam Hussein to appoint his minister of commerce as his special representative to the junta. He would shuttle between Baghdad and Ankara throughout the entire war.

The Iranian perspective also crystallized based on mutual interests. Iran and Turkey share a mountainous border, which had been stable for three and a half centuries, to the benefit of local populations. Neither protagonist wanted to return to a confrontational mindset by which both Iranians and Turks stood only to lose. Iran and Turkey were comparably powerful nations (in size, population, and wealth), which would merely wear each other down in an endless conflict if pitted against each other. On the contrary, each nation had excellent reasons to cooperate with the other. Turkey needed to conquer new markets to escape the economic crisis it had struggled against for several years. Iran was attempting to break its isolation and secure a line of communication toward the West. Turkey was undergoing rapid industrialization and needed affordable energy. Iran was a major oil producer and could deliver to Turkey at advantageous terms.

The Iranian regime knew it had no choice but to deal with Turkey, since its only alternative to bringing foreign-bought goods into Iran would be through the port of Bandar Abbas or Pakistan. Either itinerary would be much longer, more expensive, and risky. And, using Soviet territory had far more drawbacks than advantages. Thus, over the next several years, the two roads connecting Tabriz to the Turkish cities of Erzerum and Van served as strategic supply routes for Tehran. The Iranian authorities also remembered that the Persians and Turks had fought the Arabs throughout history. They knew that Turkey could potentially influence the large Turkish-speaking Azerbaijani community that formed a quarter of Iran's population. They were especially aware that Iran and Turkey would be well advised to agree on the Kurdish question, for the same reasons that Ankara was pushed to collaborate with Baghdad regarding the Kurds.

The Turkish government knew all this. It chose to take advantage of the situation to deal with both belligerents, while displaying a façade of neutrality that fooled no one, but allowed it to keep up appearances. On

October 2, 1980, after having upped the ante by leaving the Iraqis and Iranians hanging for nearly ten days, General Evren officially committed his country to a path of "active neutrality." In practice, this meant maintaining excellent relations with both belligerents, without privileging either one. As with the Israelis, it was in the Turks' interest for the war to drag on and on.

In mid-October, Ankara doubled its volume of oil purchases from Iraq (via the Kirkuk-Dortyol pipeline) and Iran (via the Kharg terminal), having first negotiated a significant discount. The Turkish government concurrently set up a constant shuttle of trucks supplying Iran and Iraq with a wide variety of goods, which had the added benefit of resurrecting the Turkish road transport system. Turkey looked the other way regarding arms shipments passing through its territory, whether headed for Baghdad or Tehran. Naturally, it claimed its transit levy.

On May 5, 1981, Turkey and Iran signed an agreement to increase their commercial exchanges and connect their telecommunication networks. Roughly one hundred Turkish military doctors traveled to the front with large quantities of medical supplies to assist the Iranian health services, which were overwhelmed by the number of wounded. In Tehran, Akbar Hashemi Rafsanjani exerted himself to convince his peers to play the Turkish card to the hilt. He did not hesitate to refer to Turkey as a functional ally. Minister of Foreign Affairs Velayati also sought to win over Ankara, multiplying contracts between the two countries (to the great satisfaction of Turkish industrialists). Better yet, the Iranian regime hired Turkish labor to replace Iranians who had left for the front. Over five years, the volume of Turkish exports to Iran grew twelve-fold, increasing from eighty-five million dollars in 1980 to a little over one billion in 1985. By then, Turkey was Iran's leading commercial partner, with Iran absorbing a quarter of Turkey's exports. Ankara and Tehran even planned to build an oil pipeline from Iran to the Mediterranean via Turkey, but significant technical difficulties and insufficient funds led the Iranian authorities to bury the project. Yet the Turkish junta retained free rein: despite Tehran's repeated and insistent requests, Turkey refused to expel Iranian soldiers who had sought shelter there after the rise of the mullahs, notably Colonel Javad Hussein, who fled to Turkey on March 16, 1981, after seizing an Iranian air force C-130 cargo plane.

The increase in commercial exchanges was equally spectacular between Turkey and Iraq, growing from 135 million dollars in 1980 to 960
million dollars in 1985. The collapse of oil prices beginning in 1985 only
increased the belligerents' dependency on Turkey. Having lost part of their
oil revenue, Iraqis and Iranians would have to make do with low-quality
consumer goods produced in Turkey. The reversal of the trade balance in
Ankara's favor, both in relation to Baghdad and Tehran, would allow
Turkey to claim the title of "silent victor" of the Iran-Iraq War.

[Chapter 8]

The "Valmy" Effect

Contrary to Saddam Hussein's expectations, when Iraq invaded in September 1980, the province of Khuzestan's population did not welcome the Iraqis as liberators; there were no garlands of flowers or cheering crowds waiting at the entrance of its towns and villages. In the best of cases, the invading troops were considered with suspicion. Most of the time, they were fought with rage and determination. The ethnic factor—many inhabitants of Khuzestan had distant Arab roots—was minimized because border towns had been emptied of their populations. The militants of the Arab Front for the Liberation of Al-Ahwaz, who suffered violent repression by Tehran, were marginalized and unable to create the conditions for a popular uprising. Nationalist feelings largely prevailed, reinforced by acts of violence against Arabic-speaking tribes committed by some Iraqi generals during the first days of the war. For instance, General Tala al-Duri, commander of the 9th Armored Division, coldly had fifty-six Arabic-speaking Iranians executed for "treason of the Arab cause." In less than a week, the entire local population had turned against him. General Hisham Fakhri and General Taha Shakarji allegedly committed similar crimes in their respective sectors.

The spirit of resistance proved particularly strong in that it was based on a genuine revolutionary consciousness that rekindled national pride and demonized any foreign intervention. The Islamic regime could play on the Iranians' exacerbated patriotism, but also on the themes of the "endangered nation" and the "threatened revolution," which the French revolutionaries had used in 1792 during the Battle of Valmy, thus driving back the coalition armies and saving the republic.

As soon as the news of the Iraqi invasion spread through the country, tens of thousands of volunteers rushed to the recruitment offices to sign up with the Revolutionary Guards. Many boarded buses the moment they joined up and headed to the front, armed only with their good will, courage, and the light weapons the Pasdaran were willing to give them. Their epic story is told in the Iranian director Iraj Ghaderi's film *Barzakhiha* ("The Imperiled"), which recounts the extraordinary adventures of young fighters who escaped the Shah's prison cells and nearly accidentally wound up on the front lines. In many cases, these volunteers partnered in duos or trios, so that the only available weapon could be passed on when one partner died. Those who left from major cities near the border (Kermanshah, Khorramabad, Dezful, Ahwaz) reached the front quickly. Those from Tehran, Shiraz, and Esfahan faced a longer journey. Many young people left university to fight the Iraqis. They learned to use weapons in the field, where natural selection was brutal. The vast majority of them were rapidly killed. Those blessed with real charisma, tenacious character, undeniable military talent, and a good deal of luck rose over their comrades and became true war chiefs.

Several notable figures emerged and made a name for themselves in the Revolutionary Guards pantheon. Twenty-six-year-old Mohsen Rezaee was the first to rise to prominence. A technology student and bodyguard for Khomeini, he proved a formidable leader of men—blunt, feared, and respected. A year later he would take command of the Pasdaran. Twenty-three-year-old Hossein Kharrazi, a regular soldier who had deserted under the Shah, followed in his footsteps. After a few weeks, he took command of the Darkhovin sector between Ahwaz and Abadan. A few months later, he was made the general responsible for a new Pasdaran division, which would later lead him to oversee the organization of large-scale offensives entrusted to the Revolutionary Guards. Hossein Kharrazi played a decisive role in the battle that ended the siege of Abadan. He was also one of the first to cross back over the Karun River and chase the Iraqis to Khorramshahr. After having lost an arm in the Aurora 4 offensive, he led his division in the assault on the al-Faw Peninsula and was eventually killed by a mortar shell during the Karbala 5 operation in 1986. Twenty-two-year-old Rahim Safavi followed a similar course. Though he was of noble lineage as a descendant of the Safavid Dynasty, he was put in charge of a division. He would be one the few heroes of the first days of battle to survive the war. He became commander of the Pasdaran in 1997, then joined President Ahmadinejad's inner circle.

Mohammad Bagher Ghalibaf was only nineteen when he left university to go to the front in the sector of Ahwaz, then Abadan. He quickly showed that valor does not wait for age, carrying out numerous acts of bravery and taking command of a Pasdaran division at the head of which he would play a crucial role during the second battle of Khorramshahr. Though too young to be made a general, he took on all the rank's responsibilities, happily imagining himself as an Iranian Bonaparte. He was later appointed head of the Nasser Division, then took on important responsibilities with the Basij Corps. After learning to fly, he was made commander of the Pasdaran air force, then appointed chief of police under President Khatami in 1999. He unsuccessfully ran for president in 2005, but was elected mayor of Tehran the same year and kept his sights on the presidency. Defeated again in 2013, he is waiting for his time.

These combatants were all driven by what could be called the "spirit of Valmy." They were convinced that it was necessary to march against the invader to save their nation. While they were practicing Muslims, they considered themselves lay combatants engaged in a crusade to save their country and their institutions. They did not understand the clergy's tepidness and the lack of commitment of clerics whom they considered belonged among them rather than on the benches of Koran schools. This resentment would fuel many political conflicts in the heart of Iranian power during and after the war.

Prioritizing the Internal Front

Not only did the Iraqi assault fail to lead to the downfall of the Islamic Republic, as Saddam Hussein had hoped it would, but it reinforced and consolidated it, sealing the bond between the population and the regime in the blood of the martyrs. The Iranian authorities were quick to grasp that this confrontation with a despised enemy would allow them to unite the population behind them. In fact, the regime was fighting three wars at once. The first key battle was against the radical opposition movements that had taken up arms and were fighting the government in the major cities. These included Massoud Rajavi's People's Mujahidin, Hossein Ruhani's Peykar, and former supporters of the Shah led from abroad by Shapour Bakhtiar and General Oveisi. The second and no less important conflict was that against a wide range of independence movements in the provinces of Kurdistan, Azerbaijan, and Baluchistan. The most active of these were in Kurdistan, where the army and the Pasdaran were currently holding back the peshmergas of the PDKI, the Komala, and the People's Fedayeen.

The third war was the one between Iran and Iraq. It was currently of secondary importance to the Supreme Leader and was seen as a mere border dispute for control of the frontiers of the former empire. Naturally, there was no question of letting the invader spread out over the holy land of eternal Persia. But a large-scale counteroffensive was not immediately necessary, given that the Iraqi offensive was only aimed at limited targets. The Ayatollah Khomeini's priority was to defend the regime where it was truly threatened: on the internal front. A tacit agreement was quickly reached at the highest echelons of power. President Bani-Sadr and the army would conduct the war against Iraq with the help of the Pasdaran, while Prime Minister Mohammad-Ali Rajai would fight internal enemies with the support of the clergy and the most devoted members of the Revolutionary Guards and security services. This division of labor illustrated the terrible power struggle in Tehran, which continued to pit the clergy against the proponents of secularism. Gathered behind Abol Hassan Bani-Sadr, the secularists were facing increasing difficulty in maintaining a balance between the regime's two poles.

On October 1, 1980, having announced general mobilization and extended the length of conscription from eighteen to twenty-four months, the Iranian president took his quarters in the underground command center beneath Dezful air base along with chief of staff of the Armed Forces, General Hussein Shakari. The location was central, well protected, and allowed for rapid inspection of various sectors of the front using the base's numerous helicopters. But it was also chosen to send a powerful message: Dezful could not fall into Iraqi hands. Its fall would open the road to Esfahan and Tehran and split the front in two, making it very difficult to shift from one part to the other. The Iranian military high command used the few days of the unilateral truce decreed by Saddam Hussein to reorganize its military layout. Since the 81st Armored Division seemed to be holding the central sector for the time being, the priority was to reinforce the three sectors considered most vulnerable: most importantly, the cities of Andimeshk and Dezful, then the resistance area around Ahwaz, and finally the ports of Khorramshahr and Abadan.

The 55th Parachute Brigade was airlifted from its base in Shiraz to Dezful. Over three nights, transport planes flew numerous turnarounds in perilous conditions. The 84th Mechanized Brigade was deployed to Andimeshk. In Khorramshahr, it was replaced by the 3rd Brigade, 16th Armored Division, whose other units were moved to Dezful. The 16th's M-60 tanks took position outside the city, hidden behind the embankments dividing the cereal fields stretching from the Dez River to the Karkheh River. The mechanized infantry protected the tanks, while the self-propelled artillery held back close to the city. Military high command considered that these four brigades could hold off the Iraqi 1st and 10th Divisions, particularly since the city of Dezful had been reinforced by independent artillery and several Pasdaran companies.

Further south, the Karkheh's eastern bank was guarded by what remained of the 92nd Division's 2nd brigade. The rest of the division was deployed at the edge of Ahwaz to push back the Iraqi 5th and 9th divisions. The Iranian tank units were backed by the 21st Mechanized Division, which had left Tehran for the sector between Ahwaz and Abadan. Another brigade from the same division managed to sneak through to Khorramshahr and reinforce the besieged city along with several thousand Pasdaran who flocked in from all over the country in buses, cars, and even cattle trucks to prevent the Iraqis from taking this symbolic city. Abadan was also bolstered by the arrival of Revolutionary Guards, a marine infantry battalion, and the 37th Armored Brigade, which was normally based in Shiraz. Two other units were ordered to the front, but took several weeks to reach the battle lines due to the distances they had to travel: the 88th Armored Brigade, stationed at the Pakistani border, and the 77th Mechanized Division, deployed near the Afghan and Soviet borders in the area of Mashhad.

Military high command decided to leave several units in place to defend the internal front. The 28th and 64th Divisions remained in Kurdistan. The 15th Mountain Infantry Brigade guarded the passes controlling access to Tehran. The 23rd Special Forces Brigade remained in the capital to serve as the regime's final shield. The 30th Motorized Brigade continued to stand guard on the Soviet border—just in case.

Iraqi military command also took advantage of this brief interlude to reinforce its layout in the Basra sector. General Khairallah and General Shamshal ordered the 33rd Special Forces Brigade to Basra to prepare for an attack on Khorramshahr. These commandos would serve as a useful reserve of shock troops for taking the city. Meanwhile the dismounted infantrymen received accelerated training in urban combat from a few Soviet advisors and former army cadres urgently called back to service. Once inside the city, they would have to abandon the shelter of their armored vehicles to fight on foot, a prospect they did not find enchanting. Military high command also decreed that several sections of reservists be called up to increase the People's Army. Lastly, it ordered the 4th Infantry Division to leave the sector of Naft, which was now cordoned off, to join the 7th and 11th Infantry Divisions stationed in Kurdistan and help dissuade the peshmergas from reviving hostilities against the regime.

Combat Starts Again

The Iraqi generals made a big mistake that would cost them dearly: they forgot to occupy the city of Susangerd, which they had seized in the first days of the war. After crossing the city, their tanks immediately continued toward Ahwaz, leaving this strategic crossroads without a garrison. Early in October, the city rose up, and its authorities managed to gather several hundred combatants reinforced by a multitude of Pasdaran. The Susangerd salient became a thorn in the Iraqis' side. Luckily for them, the city was cut off from the rest of Iran by the dunes on the opposite bank of the Karkheh, preventing the insurgents from receiving heavy equipment. However, helicopters brought them reinforcements and munitions by night. Meanwhile, aerial operations had picked up again.

On September 30, 1980, the Iranian government displayed its determination by striking the Osirak nuclear power plant some twenty miles (thirty kilometers) southeast of Baghdad (Operation Incandescent Sword). Tehran, which was highly concerned about advances in the Iraqi nuclear program, wanted to neutralize this power plant before it became operational. Yet its intelligence services lacked reliable information to ascertain whether or not there was nuclear fuel in the main reactor. To avoid potential radioactive fallout, Tehran decided to limit the attack to the two research and reactor control buildings: four Phantoms took off from Hamadan, the pair in the lead conducting the mission, the pair in the rear standing by to replace them in case of a problem. If everything went as planned, the latter two would turn off at the last minute to bomb one of the two electric power plants that supplied the Iraqi capital. Meanwhile, other Phantoms would carry out diversion strikes to attract Baghdad-based fighter planes and distract the SAM-6 brigade responsible for the sector's protection. To accomplish this crucial mission, each Phantom was armed with six 500-pound (225-kilo) bombs and one ALQ-101 electronic countermeasure pod designed to jam enemy radar. After having taken off and refueled in flight, the four Phantoms flew at extremely low altitude, following a route that would allow them to penetrate Iraqi air space with minimal risk of being detected. Once close to the target, the two reserve Phantoms turned off toward Baghdad as planned, while the lead and his wingman slightly nosed up their planes to visualize the target, then dove toward it, carefully adjusting their aim and dropping their bombs in a single flyover. They immediately turned back to base, without knowing if the raid had been successful. In fact, the damage was relatively insignificant. French engineers on site at the time report that work on completing the plant soon resumed. The twelve bombs had scattered, only destroying a storage area for chemical products.

The next day, sixteen Phantoms returned to Baghdad. After a low-altitude approach that allowed them to evade anti-aircraft defense, they bombed the government's offices, Ba'ath Party headquarters, military headquarters, several Republican Guard barracks, and the Mukhabarat headquarters. The hits were imprecise and the damage light, for the pilots were more concerned with leapfrogging over the capital's roofs to avoid anti-aircraft fire.

The Iraqi counterattack was not long in coming. The very next day, twelve Su-20s took off from Kirkuk and strafed the Hamadan base with bombs, destroying three Phantoms and damaging several others. They made it home without suffering any losses. Beginning on October 3, the Iraqi air force launched a series of raids on the Iranian capital. Supersonic Tu-22 bombers infiltrated enemy territory and attacked the Tehran International Airport, the refinery that supplied the city, the aviation factories responsible for assembling Italian and American helicopters under license, as well as the government headquarters and the Parliament building. These flyovers proved highly imprecise, the Tupolevs' sights having been conceived for high-altitude strikes. Nonetheless, they were a shock to Tehran's inhabitants, who were stunned to see Iraqi planes overhead. Beginning on October 6, Esfahan and Qom were also targeted. These regular raids never involved more than four Tupolevs and were repeated until October 29, when Iranian anti-aircraft defense shot down two Tu-22s with Hawk missiles. After this, Iraqi bombers stopped all incursions deep into enemy territory.

The Iranians reacted by launching daily harassment raids against the Iraqi capital. These missions, known as the "Baghdad Express," were peculiar in that they only involved a single Phantom charged with breaking the sound barrier over the city, ideally at low altitude and around noon, after having flown over the symbols of the regime, notably the numerous presidential palaces. The Iranian pilots excelled in this game of hide-and-seek with the Iraqi interceptors, severely testing the Iraqi pilots' nerves. Nevertheless, two Iranian Phantoms were shot down, one by anti-aircraft defense and the other after being chased down by a MiG-23. These missions stopped when Iraqi raids on Baghdad came to an end in late October.

On October 8, 1980, Saddam Hussein ordered three Frog ballistic missiles to be fired at the Dezful air base, thereby signaling the launch of the terrestrial attack's second wave. This type of missile, which preceded the notorious Scud by a generation, has a range of only forty-five miles (seventy kilometers). However, these were the first Frog missiles to be fired since the beginning of hostilities. They would not be the last. Lacking accuracy, the missiles landed in the airfield's periphery, but the operation's primary goal was to show the Iranian president, then stationed at the base, that the Iraqi regime meant business. Simultaneously, three Iraqi armored brigades pressed toward the Dezful base. The Iraqi tanks charged across fields in battle formation. They were soon brought to a halt by salvos of TOW and Dragon missiles fired by Iranian infantrymen hidden behind the embankments. They retreated long enough for their artillery to wipe out the defenders, then returned to be confronted with the more accurate fire of M-60 tanks. The Iranians yielded some ground, but reestablished their defenses a little further along. At this pace, the Iraqis took only a few miles in three days, but used up nearly all their fuel and munitions. With supplies running dangerously low, they were forced to put an end to a game that had cost them some thirty tanks and won them very little. Yet one of their battalions had succeeded in reaching the Dez River, across from Shush. Lacking specific orders, its commander chose to retreat and rejoin his lines rather than fording the river and launching into a risky stampede on the other side. For the time being, the Iraqis' major concern was to maintain their supply chain.

Further north, General Latif, commander of the 2nd Army Corps, also tried to increase his gains, moving in the direction of Kermanshah, with his 6th, 8th, and 12th Divisions staggered between Qasr-e-Shirin and Sumer. His 2nd Division, heavily tested by the previous battles, was not in condition to participate in this new offensive, while his 4th Division had redeployed to Kurdistan to reinforce the 1st Army Corps; two armored brigades left Sar-e-Pol-e-Zahab, each moving along one of the two parallel roads leading to the strategic crossroads in Sarmast and Eslam Abad-e-Gharb. Meanwhile, a mechanized brigade climbed the steep road supposed to lead it to Sarmast, where it hoped to link up with one of the armored brigades having left Sumer. Through this maneuver, the Iraqis planned to isolate the Iranian garrison deployed in Ilam and seize the city, thereby gaining a foothold in the heart of the Zagros Mountains and getting closer to Kermanshah.

Initially, everything went off without a hitch. The columns of T-55s and T-62s advanced nearly twenty miles (about thirty kilometers) through the mountainous foothills. But they soon came face to face with the 81st Armored Division's tank battalions, which had carefully been deployed in ambush. Since the outbreak of hostilities, the Iranian tank crews had had time to gather, then deploy to well-prepared positions. The Iranian tanks were looking down on their enemy, backed by their self-propelled artillery, which was judiciously positioned to cover the principal lines of approach. The clash was fierce. The Iraqi brigades tried to overrun the Iranian tank squadrons, which engaged combat in rapid succession, but were forced to fall back under the precise fire of Iraqi Gazelles armed with HOT missiles. For the next forty-eight hours, Iranian Chieftains carried out effective delaying operations, yielding ground to wear down their adversary. Nonetheless, their numbers dwindled rapidly and they were forced to call in the air force and helicopters to beat back the enemy. The

Tigers and Cobras' intervention chased the Gazelles away, leaving the tanks unprotected. The arrival of more 81st Division battalions shifted the balance of power. Now it was the Iranian tanks pushing back the Iraqi armored vehicles. Yet they were unable to exploit their advantage because they were stopped short by salvos of Milan missiles fired by infantrymen dug in along the mountain roads. With neither side having enough troops to mount another assault, both returned to their initial positions. While the situation along this part of the front seemed to be at a standstill, it was very different around Basra, where Iraqis and Iranians fought a crucial battle for control of Khorramshahr and Abadan.

The Fall of Khorramshahr and the Siege of Abadan

At nightfall on October 10, 1980, the Iraqi 5th Division's sappers crossed the Karun River near Darkhovin aboard inflatable dinghies. With the support of the 3rd Army Corps' bridge-building battalion, they assembled a pontoon bridge in a few hours. By dawn, the 26th Armored Brigade had crossed the bridge and taken a defensive position to guard the bridgehead. Bridge-crossing operations ended at sunrise—the Iraqis feared Iranian air force strikes—and began again at nightfall. By the next morning, the 20th Mechanized Brigade had crossed the river. While it took control of Darkhovin, the 26th Armored Brigade cautiously followed the road heading north to intercept potential Iranian reinforcements. In the morning, its commander noticed a cloud of dust rising from a column of roughly forty tanks advancing on the road in his direction. This was a 92nd Armored Division battalion coming from Ahwaz. Having been alerted by phone by Darkhovin police forces entrenched in the city's police station, the Iranian tank crews rushed south, determined to repel the Iraqis. Meanwhile, the Iraqis had taken ambush positions. When the Chieftains came within range, the T-55s fired at them from less than 1,650 feet (500 meters) away, in ideal firing conditions. In less than a minute, ten Iranian tanks had been neutralized. The remaining vehicles had no choice but to flee toward the Karun. Most sank into the river's muddy banks. Chased by the Iraqi tanks, their crews abandoned their vehicles in the mud and escaped by climbing on the hulls of the fifteen tanks that pathetically turned back to Ahwaz. The Iraqis captured about twenty Chieftains, which they towed to the rear and proudly displayed for war correspondents to photograph.

Meanwhile, further south, General Aburi, commander of the 3rd Army Corps, launched the assault on Khorramshahr. Saddam's orders were clear: take control of the city at any cost, then continue in the direction of Abadan. On October 11, while the 3rd Armored Division got in gear to tighten the noose around Khorramshahr, its reconnaissance regiment sneaked across the bridge over the Karun five miles (eight kilometers) upriver from the city. Aside from the two bridges in the actual city of Khorramshahr, this was the only road structure over the Karun to the city of Ahwaz. Control of the bridge was therefore crucial. The Iraqi reconnaissance troops ventured to the Arvand River, a tributary of the Karun that flowed parallel to the Shatt al-Arab and into the Gulf. They occupied the only bridge over the Arvand, cutting off the road to Ahwaz. The port of Abadan, wedged along a narrow marshy peninsula formed by the Shatt al-Arab, the Karun, and the Arvand, was now totally isolated. Three days later, the 5th Mechanized Division took control of the Abadan-Ahwaz road on the Karun's eastern bank. It broadened the Iraqi bridgehead to the edge of the marshy area bordering the Gulf. No vehicle could travel beyond there without following the road leading to Bandar Khomeini, which had been laid with mines.

Along the same road, the Iraqi troops were unable to take control of Shadegan because the small town had just been occupied by a detachment of the Iranian 21st Division. On October 14, Abadan was besieged, but its garrison of about 6,000 men and sixty tanks held off the Iraqis, who had not yet gathered in large enough numbers to launch an attack on the city. On October 18, the 5th Division's commander ordered his 23rd Brigade to cross the Arvand on a pontoon bridge put in place by his division's sappers and attack the Abadan garrison from the rear. This attempt resulted in a stinging failure. The Iraqis were brutally repelled by M-48 tanks and intersecting bursts of machine-gun fire. After a few hours, they were forced to give up and retreat to their positions on the Arvand's eastern bank.

The situation was acutely different in Khorramshahr, where for two days 5,000 entrenched Iranians had been facing the unwavering attack of 12,000 Iraqis who knew Saddam had his eye on them. After heavy

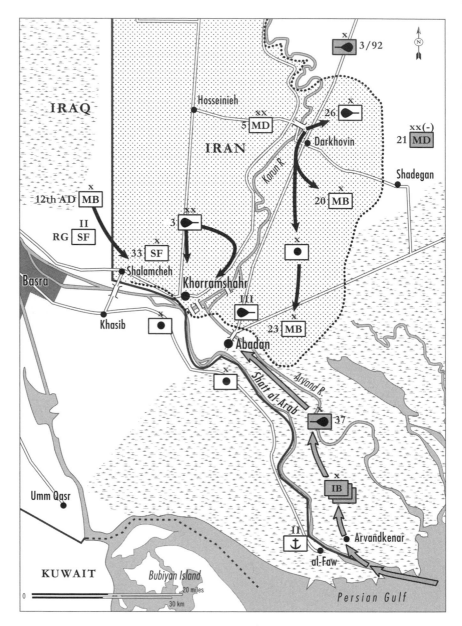

Fall of Khorramshahr and siege of Abadan (October 10–28, 1980)

saturation fire from over 300 cannons, the 3rd Armored Division's dismounted infantrymen and the 33rd Special Forces Brigade's commandos
entered Khorramshahr, backed by 200 T-55 and T-62 tanks, which now
accompanied the infantrymen rather than preceding them. The Iraqi soldiers proceeded slowly and methodically, one neighborhood after another. Fighting was fierce and often ended in hand-to-hand combat.

The Iranians clung to each block, each building, harassing the assailant
with antitank rockets and Molotov cocktails. Snipers prevented access to
an avenue for days at a time. To flush the snipers out, the Iraqis were often
forced to call on tanks and artillery to pound the city, turning it into a
vast field of ruins, which made their progress even more difficult. The
Iranians were driven to heights of fanatical devotion by the Ayatollah
Khomeini's solemn call for them to turn Khorramshahr into a "Persian
Stalingrad" that would be the enemy's grave. Both countries' air forces in-
tervened to attempt to support or slow the advance of Iraqi troops. A
Phantom and a Tiger were shot down by the SAM-6 brigade protecting the
Iraqi layout. On the ground, mines and booby traps took their terrible toll.
The number of casualties among the invaders was growing worrisomely
high. After ten days, the Iraqis had suffered 1,500 dead and 4,500 wounded.
Every night Iraqi commandos infiltrated enemy lines to sow terror and
capture a handful of soldiers from whom to extract information.

Meanwhile the Iranians received meager reinforcements from Abadan.
They yielded ground and retreated toward the two bridges over the Karun,
leaving a few pockets of resistance. Sensing victory was within reach, the
3rd Army Corps' commander asked Baghdad to allocate him more infantrymen to deal the deathblow. Having obtained Saddam's agreement, Iraqi
military high command urgently dispatched him a battalion of special
forces from the Republican Guard, as well as the 12th Armored Division's
Mechanized Brigade, which traveled from Sumner to Khorramshahr in
three days. These reinforcements allowed the Iraqis to take control of the
bridges and chase the Iranians fleeing on the other bank. On October 24,
General Jabouri announced the taking of Khorramshahr. After another
four days, he had wiped out the last pockets of resistance. It was an undeniable success, but one that had come at a price: 2,000 Iraqis were dead
and another 6,000 wounded. On the other side, 1,500 Iranians had been
killed. Two-thirds of the forces engaged in the battle had been put out of

commission. The fall of Khorramshahr spelled the end for General Hussein Shakari, who was replaced as the head of the Iranian armed forces by General Fallahi. General Qasim Ali Zahir Nejad replaced Fallahi as head of the army ground forces.

Given what it had cost them to seize Khorramshahr, the Iraqi military high command understood that it would be illusory to continue the assault in the direction of Abadan, particularly since they were out of infantry reserves and the Iranian garrison was receiving reinforcements brought in at night by helicopters and hydroplanes from Bandar Khomeini to the small port of Arvandkenar (located at the mouth of the Shatt al-Arab). The Iraqi generals thus decided to tighten the noose around Abadan.

Chapter 9

Stalemate

By late October 1980 the Iraqi troops' lack of progress on every front and failure to take control of Kermanshah, Dezful, Ahwaz, and Abadan raised the specter of a stalemate. From October 15 to 18, the Iraqis had even been violently counterattacked near Andimeshk and forced to retreat to the bridge at Naderi. The air force had had to intervene to allow the Iraqis to repel the Iranian tanks and reestablish their defensive line. Conscious of this stalemate, the Iraqi authorities attempted an overture to Iran. Taha Yassin Ramadan, commander of the Popular Army, publicly stated that "Arabistan's oil will be Iraqi as long as Tehran will not negotiate. Iraq has the means to support a war for over a year without any impact on its population; for two years and even more by imposing a few restrictions which our people are ready to accept."[1] His statements were clearly dictated by Saddam Hussein, who thought they would be better received if they came from someone other than him. The Iranian government imperturbably repeated its own conditions: the departure of Saddam Hussein, the fall of the regime, the recognition of Iraq's full responsibility for the war, and payment of significant war reparations.

The Southern Front Prioritized

In Tehran the Ayatollah Khomeini declared Khorramshahr a "martyred city," emphasizing that its example should serve as an inspiration to Iranian combatants. He asked the government to take social measures to privilege the families of the heroes that fell for the city. This led to the creation of the Martyrs Foundation a few months later, an organization dedicated to assisting the families of Revolutionary Guards killed on the front. Under pressure from the clergy—and particularly from Ayatollah Beheshti—the Supreme Leader ordered the establishment of the Supreme

Defense Council, which was to more strictly control the armed forces' actions and reinforce the Pasdaran's power. Along with Bani-Sadr, the council was composed of Akbar Hashemi Rafsanjani, acting as the Supreme Leader's representative; General Fallahi (chief of staff of the armed forces); the minister of defense; the commander of ground forces; the commander in chief of the Pasdaran; the prime minister; and the head of propaganda. The council had authority over the Pasdaran and the regular army and was charged with deciding on all matters relating to the conduct of the war. In case of a tied vote, the Supreme Leader's representative would cast the tie-breaking vote, which was another step in the marginalization of Bani-Sadr and the secular camp.

Though it stoked the rivalry between the Pasdaran and the regular army, the council's creation allowed for better operational coordination by establishing a division of responsibilities. The army was now in charge of combat in the open countryside, while the Revolutionary Guards supervised operations in urban areas, which allowed them to increase their prestige and recruit more fighters. As a result, close to a thousand volunteers per day joined the Pasdaran in Tehran alone. Throughout the country, 100,000 young recruits would join this parallel army over the last three months of 1980.

Meanwhile, Saddam Hussein intensified bombing of the cities of Khuzestan to punish the Iranian people and force Tehran to negotiate. Ahwaz and Abadan were daily targets of the Iraqi artillery. Since Dezful was out of cannon range, the Iraqi regime decided to fire a salvo of seven Frog missiles on the city on October 26 in order to strike at the population and sap its morale. Naturally, it obtained the opposite effect. Realizing that the objectives set had not been reached and that the situation was slipping into a dangerous quagmire, Saddam Hussein launched another trial balloon by publicly stating that, "Iraq is ready to withdraw its troops if Iran recognizes its legitimate rights."[2] The Iranian authorities flatly refused, choosing instead to mobilize two new age classes.

On November 13, the Iraqi military command launched a new offensive on Khuzestan on Saddam's orders. The 1st and 10th Divisions prepared to assault Dezful again. After advancing a few miles (a few kilometers), they were met with deadly barrage fire. The Iranian 16th Armored Division powerfully counterattacked. Their M-60s charged the T-55s and T-62s, engaging them in a chaotic free-for-all from which they came out on top. Having lost some sixty tanks, the Iraqi units were forced to retreat and seek shelter on the western bank of the Karkheh River. The Iraqi troops had suffered from poor coordination and weak air support. The Iranians lost some forty tanks, but recaptured Alvan, Shush, and Naderi. This was a success for General Fallahi and President Bani-Sadr, who held their heads up high and took the opportunity to silence the clergy's criticism.

Further south, the 9th Armored Division left its advance position in Hamidiyeh to make speed toward Ahwaz. The Iranians had been awaiting this offensive for several weeks, anticipating it by flooding the vast plain between the Karun and Karkheh rivers. By breaking the dykes, they turned the agricultural plain into a sprawling swamp. The Iraqi armored columns sank into the mire. To add to their misery, it began to rain, announcing the arrival of the wet season. Heavy showers turned the terrain into a horrific bog that brought tanks, reconnaissance vehicles, and armored vehicles to a dead halt. Under fire from the Iranian air force and artillery, the crews sank into mud up to their knees and struggled to extricate their vehicles. Many had to be abandoned. Lacking enough troops to maintain control of Hamidiyeh, the Iraqis were forced to evacuate the village and yield ground to reestablish better lines of communication. This bitter defeat was doubled by terrible humiliation when the Iranians brought countless dumbfounded war correspondents to discover the spectacle of 150 bogged-down Iraqi tanks, their guns pointed at Ahwaz. This picture seen around the world would come to symbolize the failure of the Iraqi offensive. The vehicles were then recovered by the Iranians, cleaned, repaired, and returned to working order, and incorporated to Iranian units. This episode did not improve the reputation of the 9th Armored Division, which was seen as the worst unit in the Iraqi army. But contrary to expectations, its commander, General Tala al-Duri, did not suffer the wrath of the Iraqi dictator, who appreciated and protected him. Though inept and violent, al-Duri was the kind of loyal and courageous officer Saddam liked.

The Iraqis also failed to reduce the Susangerd salient, though it was crucial to reestablish better lines of communication. Both their attempts came up against fanatical Pasdaran, who systematically repelled their assaults. Every night, Iranian helicopters brought reinforcements to Susangerd to replace the casualties. Tired, demoralized, and short on ammunition, the Iraqis stopped attacking and fell back on their artillery to harass the town. As in other battles, logistics had not really followed through. The episode led to the arrest of some ten officers, who were sentenced for defeatism and executed as an example.

No miracles took place outside Abadan either. The city's defenses did not crumble at the mere sight of the Iraqi combatants nor at the roar of their guns. Here again, the assaulting troops were pushed back. They did not insist and prudently retreated to the shelter of their positions. For reasons beyond understanding, Iraqi command did nothing to fully encircle Abadan. Its naval infantry battalion, which was entrenched in al-Faw, could easily have crossed the Shatt al-Arab and taken control of Arvandkenar or simply cut off the road leading to Abadan. The commandos could also easily have been carried by helicopter along this road to seal off the besieged city. Once again, lack of initiative seriously handicapped the Iraqi camp.

Air Duels over Khuzestan

Iranian pilots took advantage of the battle in Khuzestan to impose their supremacy. From October to December, they shot down roughly forty Iraqi fighters, while suffering only nine losses. Their Phantom pilots singlehandedly destroyed twelve planes, while only four Phantoms were shot down by MiGs. A fifth Phantom pilot was accidentally killed by his own anti-aircraft defense. The Tomcat pilots took the lion's share, bringing down twenty-three enemy planes (including ten MiG-23s) without suffering a single loss. There were three reasons for this impressive score. The first was the sophistication of the Tomcat's weapons system, which combined a highly precise radar with Sparrow and Phoenix long-range missiles, effective electronic countermeasures, and a "Combat Tree" Enemy IFF Interrogator for notifying flight crews of approaching enemy interceptors. The second was the skill of pilots used to whirling air combat and evasive actions. Many months of training in the United States under the Shah's rule, notably during the famous "Top Gun" exercises, had borne fruit and allowed the first pilots released from prison to quickly regain their operational qualification. The final reason was the motivation of crews burning to fight to the finish to prove their worth and show the regime's top dogs that they remained far superior to the Pasdaran, whom they generally considered to be a gang of fanatical vagrants.

Though three F-14s were severely damaged during these engagements, all were able to get back to base. One of their pilots, Squadron Leader Abbas Hazin, was awarded one of the highest Iranian distinctions and became a popular hero. While it continued to be wary of its pilots, the regime needed icons to stoke patriotism. On October 26 Hazin had safely flown his Tomcat back to base after his plane had been turned into a flying wreck by colliding with the debris of a MiG-21 he had just shot down. He was quickly promoted to colonel and would become one of the primary heads of the Iranian air force after the war.

Captain Mohammad Masbough also distinguished himself by using a single Phoenix missile to bring down three MiG-23s over Kharg Island. His missile was trained on the enemy formation's lead, but it blew up that plane as well as two wingmen flying too close to it. This exploit, enabled by the Phoenix's explosive charge (designed to destroy a bomber), was verified by the Iranian army, which found the wreckage of the three MiGs near the oil terminal. On October 29, Captain Seghi, another F-14 pilot in the 81st Squadron, became the first Iranian "ace" by shooting down his fifth victim over Abadan. A few days earlier, he had disintegrated four MiGs in quick succession. The Tiger pilots were not to be outdone, though their scores were more modest. One was able to destroy a MiG-23 without firing a single projectile, but by forcing his adversary into a series of abrupt maneuvers at very low altitude. The disoriented Iraqi pilot crashed into the ground. Cobra helicopter pilots also distinguished themselves by gunning down one Gazelle and two Mi-24s.

On the Iraqi side, the 7th Squadron's Captain Samir Abdul Razak saved face by bringing down four Tigers with his MiG-21. To boost public morale, the Iraqis exhibited the wreckage of Iranian fighter planes along the paths of al-Zawra Park in the heart of Baghdad. Iranians followed suit by lining up the remains of Iraqi aircraft in the squares of their major cities.

In late December, after three months of nearly daily air combat, the score was sixty kills to fifteen, in favor of the Iranians. The Shah's former pilots had won air supremacy over the battlefield. The Iraqi pilots, tired and discouraged from their losses, would now keep to very brief incursions over Iraqi bridgeheads, refusing to engage combat the moment they saw enemy fighters. It was now time for the navy to enter the fray.

Air and Sea Battle at the Mouth of the Shatt Al-Arab

So far, the Iraqi navy had not participated in Saddam's crusade. Granted, as the Iraqi army's poor relation, it had a highly limited supply of offensive equipment. It was not even headed by an admiral, but a servile general, Aladdin Hammad al-Janabi, an utter vassal of the regime whose only naval experience consisted in commanding a naval infantry battalion. The Iraqi navy knew it would be suicidal to send its patrol boats to fight the Iranian navy's corvettes, destroyers, and frigates, all of which were equipped with far better weapons and radar than its own.

For their part, the Iranians had devoted all their attention to defending the front and conducting aerial operations, knowing they would easily achieve naval superiority when the time came. Beginning on September 23, their air force had attacked the port of al-Faw, sinking one minesweeper and five light patrol boats. Two days later, several Phantoms had unsuccessfully attempted to assault the Umm Qasr naval base and were forced to retreat by dense anti-aircraft fire. The Iraqis counterattacked by striking at the Bushehr naval base, sinking three light patrol boats and one PF-103-class corvette. They also bombed several of the sixty-two oil tankers trapped along the Shatt al-Arab by the outbreak of hostilities. Several tankers were sunk, as well as a few minesweepers docked in Abadan.

On October 1, 1980, President Bani-Sadr promised the international community that he would not obstruct the Strait of Hormuz in order to avoid the intervention of Western powers. However, he decreed the blockading of the Iraqi ports of Basra and al-Faw. His naval aviation's Sea King helicopters mined the entrance to the Shatt al-Arab, while the artillery held back any ship that may have been tempted to escape the river into the Gulf. On October 6 and 7, the Iranian air force sank several cargo ships stuck along the Shatt al-Arab in order to more securely block the waterway. Since the river was no longer of any use to them now that the ports of Abadan and Khorramshahr were in ruins, the Iranians naturally intended to prevent the Iraqis from using it.

During the first weeks of the war, the Iranian navy limited itself to patrolling the area of the Strait of Hormuz in order to dissuade the Arabs and the West from carrying out any unwelcome action in the direction of the Tunb and Abu Musa islands.³ The few hydroplanes deployed in Bandar Khomeini were used to resupply the Iranian troops isolated in Abadan. The admiralty abstained from dispatching its warships too close to the mouth of the Shatt al-Arab for fear of exposing them to Iraqi air force strikes. On October 28 and 31, it tested the enemy's defenses by sending a flotilla of three patrol boats (the *Joshan, Paykan,* and *Garduneh*) to harass the oil facilities in al-Faw with their 76 mm guns. During both operations, the Iranian ships were escorted by a Sea King helicopter charged with radar detecting enemy ships. On the second attempt, the Iraqis reacted by sending three Osa II missile boats. The engagement was not conclusive. The Iraqi sailors more or less randomly fired their Styx missiles within the limits of their range, then retreated at full speed. The Iranian patrol boats easily avoided the salvo of missiles, but by the time they could retaliate, their adversaries were already safely in the estuary leading them back to their base in Umm Qasr.

In late November, the Iranians decided to hit hard in response to the Iraqi artillery's destruction of the Abadan refinery, which had halved their fuel production and forced Tehran to import gas. They resolved to neutralize the Kohr al-Amaya and Mina al-Bakr offshore oil terminals, through which two-thirds of Iraq's oil exports passed. By doing so, they planned to draw Iraq's navy out into the open sea and allow Iran's air force and navy to tear it apart. Tehran's hope was to suffocate the Iraqi economy and force Baghdad to withdraw. For the first time in the war, the Iranian chiefs of staff launched an interarmy operation, which was called Morvarid ("Pearl"), and relied on navy, ground force, and air force resources. The first phase of the operation was entrusted to Ship Captain Bahram Afzali, who had commanded the navy since Admiral Madani had been sidelined a few months earlier.

At nightfall on November 27, 1980, marine commandos carried by Iranian ground force Chinook helicopters burst into view above the Kohr al-Amaya and Mina al-Bakr oil terminals. An EC-130 electronic warfare plane was patrolling nearby to jam Iraqi communications. The navy's elite fighters slid down ropes onto their target, engaging combat with the few soldiers in charge of defending it. They were backed by fire from Cobra helicopters circling the oil terminals, made deadly accurate by night-vision goggles worn both by the pilots and gunners. The attack ended in hand-to-hand combat. The Iranians rapidly took control of both terminals. Less than an hour later, three hydroplanes left from Kharg Island, escorted by the *Joshan* and *Paykan* patrol boats forming Task Force 421 and backed by three other hydroplanes from Bandar Khomeini. The hydroplanes landed on the two terminals to deliver reinforcements and explosives. The Iranian commandos placed explosives all over the oil terminals; boarded the hydroplanes with their dead, their wounded, and their prisoners; and blew the whole thing up in a tremendous ball of fire. In just a few hours, the Iraqis had lost the ability to export oil extracted in the Basra area, a terrible blow to their war effort.

While the commandos returned to the port of Bandar Khomeini, the *Joshan* and *Paykan* patrol boats approached the mouth of the Shatt al-Arab to defy the Iraqi navy. A third missile boat, the *Zubin*, was on standby some fifteen nautical miles west of Kharg to replace either of the boats if it were sunk; two PF-103 corvettes and two other Combattante II-class patrol boats were on standby to leave their base in Bushehr to assist them.

The news of the attack was met with utter dismay at Iraqi admiralty headquarters in Basra. No one had ever thought the Iranians would pull such an audacious move. The assumption had been that they would limit themselves to firing their cannons at Kohr al-Amaya and Mina al-Bakr, but that they would never risk staging a landing. General al-Janabi, woken in the middle of the night, tried to take stock with the fragmentary information at his disposal. The al-Faw radar station reported two isolated Iranian patrol boats at the mouth of the Shatt al-Arab. The opportunity was too good to pass up. General al-Janabi ordered the immediate recall of all available crews and for all seaworthy ships to deploy. Shortly before dawn, four P-6 torpedo boats cast off from al-Faw, while five Osa I and II missile boats left their base in Umm Qasr, skirting Bubiyan Island in an attempt to attack the Iranian patrol boats from the rear.

The Iranian boats baited the Iraqis perfectly, making as if to escape toward Kohr al-Amaya and Mina al-Bakr. The Iraqi sailors, excited by this unexpected chase, sped up and fired a first salvo of Styx missiles. The Iranian patrol boats dropped decoys and engaged in a succession of evasive actions, easily avoiding this initial salvo. As soon as he passed Kohr al-Amaya, the *Joshan*'s commander made a U-turn and sheltered his boat inside the tangled metal, mixing his radar signature with that of the oil terminal destroyed earlier in the night. He occasionally pulled away from the terminal long enough to detect an adversary and fire at it with Harpoon missiles, which were reputed to be more reliable and accurate than the heavy Styx missiles with which the Iraqis were equipped. He succeeded in sinking a P-6 boat chasing him and in holding off two Osa missile boats. Once through its firing sequence, the *Joshan* returned to the protection of the massive metallic structure, which reflected the Iraqis' radar waves. Further south, the *Paykan*'s commander followed the same tactic, taking shelter behind the burned-out remains of the Mina al-Bakr terminal.

The two Iranian patrol boats carried on this game of hide-and-seek for several hours, holding back their adversaries and managing to sink two Osa boats with their Harpoon missiles. On the Iraqi side, caution prevailed. The other gunboats' commanders fired at random, trying to keep their adversary in place while waiting for the air force to intervene. The *Paykan* was eventually damaged by the nearby explosion of a Styx missile. A pair of Su-22s twice flew over the patrol boats, but failed to strafe them because the Iraqi pilots had not been trained to attack naval targets. Instead, the explosion of a shell fired by the *Paykan*'s 76-mm gun turret destroyed one of the Su-22s. Meanwhile, in Basra, General al-Janabi ordered one of his LSM assault ships to cast off for Kohr al-Amaya and Mina al-Bakr to regain control of the two terminals and evaluate the damage. This Polnocny-class landing ship transported the Iraqi navy's group of combat swimmers, as well as a hastily gathered naval infantry company. It was escorted by two Osa II missile boats, which had been able to cast off early in the day after haphazardly assembling a reduced crew.

By this point, the two Iranian patrol boats were running short of ammunition and asked for authorization to withdraw. The request was refused because Operation Morvarid was entering its aerial phase and air force chief Colonel Javad Fakouri needed the two boats to keep the enemy in place and scout the area. In mid-morning, several Phantoms from the Bushehr and Shiraz bases suddenly appeared over the water, guided by the *Joshan* and the *Paykan* as well as a Tomcat interceptor serving as an airborne radar station. The lead plane was piloted by Squad Leader Abbas Doran, the officer who had planned Operation Crossbow a few weeks earlier and participated in all delicate missions.

Doran carefully selected his target and fired a Maverick guided missile, pulverizing a P-6 torpedo boat. His wingmen sank the last two torpedo boats without encountering any opposition. The commanders of the three Osa missile boats on site, realizing the situation had just radically shifted, risked it all and charged the *Paykan* at maximum speed in an attempt to finish it off. They fired four missiles at it, hoping to saturate its defenses. The Iranian patrol boat, which could no longer retaliate and was already dangerously listing, managed to slalom and avoid the first Styx missile, but the following three made direct hits and disintegrated it. The three Osa boats then turned to the *Joshan,* which had just received authorization to disrupt combat and take shelter in Bandar Khomeini harbor. The Iraqi boats fired their last missiles, but missed. A section of four MiG-23s appeared above the combat zone and attempted to sink the *Joshan*. It was immediately intercepted by the Tomcats providing air cover, which shot down one of the fighters and routed the others. Meanwhile, another wave of Phantoms armed with Maverick missiles arrived on site, engaged with the remaining three Osa torpedo boats, and sank them. However, their crews had had time to fire several SAM-7 portable surface-to-air missiles at the Iranian fighters. One Phantom was shot down, while another was severely damaged and only made it back to base due to a particularly skillful pilot. Around noon, the Iranian air force attacked the Iraqi ships that had left Umm Qasr a few hours earlier headed for the Gulf. The Phantoms sank the amphibious assault ship, leading its two escorting patrol boats to panic and turn back to base at full speed. During the afternoon and into the evening, the Iranian air force pounded the al-Faw port facilities, destroying several light patrol boats as well as an Iraqi navy Super Frelon helicopter. Having learned from their previous defeats, the Iranian pilots carefully avoided the heavily protected Umm Qasr base. In any case, the nine remaining Osa torpedo boats deployed there were in extremely resistant concrete shelters.

By the evening of November 28, 1980, the outcome was indisputable. Having only lost the patrol boat *Paykan,* one Phantom, and a dozen navy

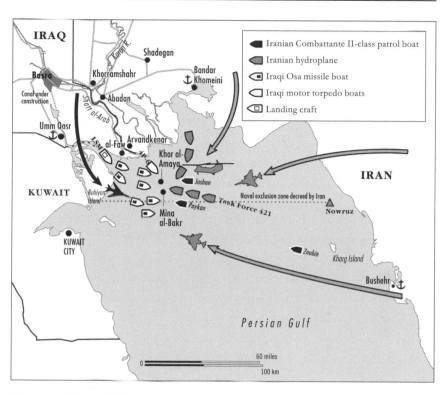

Operation Morvarid (November 27–28, 1980)

commandos, the Iranian sailors and aviators had destroyed two strategic oil terminals, killed more than one hundred enemy combatants, and shot down two aircraft. They had also sunk five missile boats, four torpedo boats, three light patrol boats, and an 800-ton amphibious assault ship. The Iranian navy glowed with its achievement, despite the fact that it owed most of its success to its comrades in the air force (November 28 would become Navy Day in Iran). The navy then maintained a dissuasive presence around the Kharg terminal composed of three missile boats and two corvettes. The naval blockade of Iraq was now firmly in place.

The Iraqi defeat was severe. The navy understood that any further sortie would be extremely risky. It drew the logical conclusion that it could now only operate at night, in order to avoid aerial strikes. With the exception of the occasional sortie, the Iraqi navy would spend most of the war in the safety of its base at Umm Qasr, while the naval infantry units would reinforce the defenses of Basra and al-Faw. The Iraqi admiralty eventually regained control of the two destroyed oil terminals, keeping a garrison of marine commandos on site. It reinstalled radar on Kohr al-Amaya, which allowed it to increase its detection capacity in the direction of the Gulf. General al-Janabi saved himself—for the time being—by admitting his failure to the Iraqi dictator. In fact, Saddam Hussein had never had the slightest illusion that his navy could break the Iranian blockade.

This defeat placed the entire responsibility for attacking Iranian maritime traffic on the Iraqi air force's shoulders. It also led to the acceleration of construction work on the canal connecting the Umm Qasr estuary to Basra. Since naval circulation on the Shatt al-Arab was now entirely impossible, the canal was needed to allow the Iraqis to evacuate the six torpedo boats, six minesweepers, and six patrol boats trapped in Basra to the Umm Qasr base, but also to resupply the port with low-tonnage ships.

A Highly Disappointing Initial Assessment for Baghdad

Early in December, the first freezing fogs of an early and rainy winter sounded the death knell for Saddam Hussein's ambitions and marked the end of the war's first phase. The Iraqis had missed the boat on victory and were now on the defensive. The Iranians had significantly reinforced their front lines, rendering any breakthrough for Iraq illusory. Facing Iraq's twelve divisions on the front, Iran now had the equivalent of eight regular army divisions and three Pasdaran divisions. In any case, most of the roads were no longer passable. The Iranians had gained the upper hand on the seas and in the air. On December 10, they even dared to launch an initial counteroffensive in the area of Darkhovin to attempt to break the siege of Abadan. The offensive failed due to poor coordination but succeeded in reducing the span of the Iraqi bridgehead along the Karun's eastern bank.

Three months after the beginning of hostilities, the Iraqi army controlled only 4,130 square miles (10,700 square kilometers) of Iranian territory (less than 1 percent). It had penetrated into Iran by under twenty miles (about thirty kilometers), though the tip of its layout had reached forty-five miles (seventy kilometers) in the direction of Dezful and fifty miles (eighty kilometers) in the direction of Ahwaz. Nonetheless, with the exception of Khorramshahr, Iraq had failed to seize any of the major cities originally targeted: Abadan, Ahwaz, Dezful, and Kermanshah. Saddam Hussein had come to understand that he could no longer win unless he had the atomic bomb: the audiotapes seized in Baghdad in 2003 attest to this. He now had to do whatever it took not to lose, even if that meant accepting a draw that preserved his image and his status as a recognized leader of the Arab world. The Iraqi dictator understood that the war would now be a drawn-out affair. In order for it to remain acceptable to the Iraqi middle classes who made up the majority of the Ba'ath Party's rank and file, the war's visible effects had to be limited. Saddam dedicated himself to keeping a semblance of normalcy in Iraqi daily life. He maintained the soldiers currently in the service, but for the time being refused to decree a general mobilization. He continued to inject oil money into society, pursued his public works policy, and ordered the acceleration of the Osirak nuclear power plant's completion. At the same time, he convinced the Gulf monarchies to finance his war effort, for his oil revenue had collapsed and keeping the army on the front was tremendously expensive.

After extensive discussions with his minister of defense about how to keep Iraqi losses within acceptable limits, Saddam Hussein decided to hold on to what they had won without trying to obtain additional gains. The number of casualties remained acceptable for the time being (4,000 dead, 10,000 wounded, and a few hundred prisoners), but it could not be allowed to spike. On the other hand, material losses were far heavier: 450 tanks, 350 armored vehicles, eighty airplanes (thirty-one MiG-21s, twenty MiG-23s, eleven Su-20s, nine Su-22s, three Su-7s, three Tu-22s, two Hunters, and one Tu-16), and forty helicopters (seventeen Gazelles, ten Mi-24s, eight Mi-8s, two Mi-4s, two Alouette IIIs, and one Super Frelon).

Some thirty other Iraqi fighters were too damaged to fly. With 110 planes destroyed or neutralized, the Iraqis had lost more than a third of their aerial potential. They now only had 180 fighter planes, a third of which were grounded for regular upkeep. The navy was decimated. Nonetheless, these material losses could potentially be compensated for by new arms shipments and war captures (the Iraqis had captured about one hundred Iranian tanks, for instance).

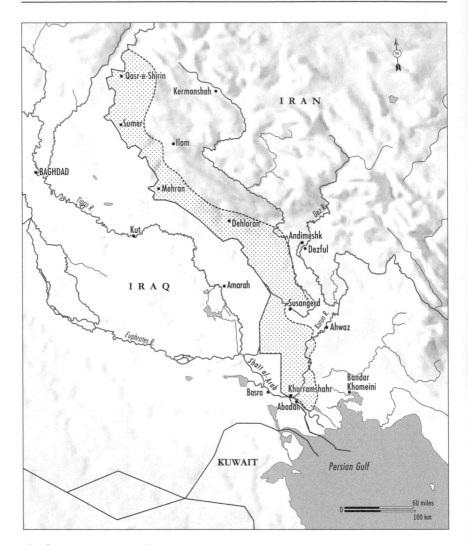

The front in late December 1980

Since he could no longer obtain a decision by force, the Iraqi dictator was determined to coerce Iran into negotiating by bombing its population and oil infrastructure. On December 24, 1980, the Iraqi air force launched its first raid on the Kharg oil terminal, which was responsible for 80 percent of Iranian oil exports. The Iranians responded by bombing the Basra refinery. The resulting loss of income was significant on both sides: four billion dollars for the Iraqis, six billion dollars for the Iranians (in 1980 alone).

In Iran, the regime considered it had withstood the worst. It had somehow contained the impact of the Iraqi invasion, despite the fact that it had had to yield some ground. Outside of Khorramshahr and Abadan, the Iranian soldiers were able to avoid the trap of a static confrontation, adopting a dynamic operational mode that allowed them to slow Iraqi progress and limit their own losses. As a result, losses were lower than what the military had expected: 4,500 dead, 12,000 wounded, and a few hundred prisoners—just a little more than their enemy's. On the other hand, material losses were lower than the Iraqis': 250 tanks, 150 armored vehicles, sixty helicopters (thirty-two Cobras, twenty-seven AB-205/212s, and one CH-47), thirty fighter planes (eighteen F-4 Phantoms and twelve F-5 Tigers), some twenty other severely damaged fighters, including three F-14 Tomcats, and a handful of transport planes. The Iranians hoped to make up for these losses by repairing the damaged aircraft and reconditioning equipment stocked deep in their hangars. They also planned to fix up the 120 Iraqi tanks they had seized.

Nonetheless, the Iranian government was faced with numerous challenges. It had to fight all those who wanted its downfall and those struggling for their independence. It had to maintain a balance between its two poles—the religious and secular camps—and find a solution to the power struggle between the radical members of the clergy and President Bani-Sadr. It had to manage the growing rivalries between the Pasdaran and the regular army and take charge of the million refugees who had left the combat zone and had been cramming into the outskirts of major cities for months, living in squalid conditions. Finally, it needed to deal with the growing difficulties of daily life, for the war was promising to be long and expensive and the Islamic Republic's financial resources were even more strapped now that oil production had collapsed. Unlike the Iraqi regime, which intended to conduct its war effort on credit by relying on the financial assistance and generous payment plans agreed to by the countries supporting it, the Iranian government could only count on itself, since no wealthy nation was prepared to help it. It would have to patch financing together, to save, and to invest and carefully manage its oil revenue in order to conduct the war as a "good provider"—at least on the financial front. Luckily for Tehran, the price of oil remained high and guaranteed it a substantial income, despite the fact that its oil income was half that of Iraq's. The following year, part of Iran's oil facilities were put back in service, and the trend was reversed in the Iranians' favor. Meanwhile Akbar Hashemi Rafsanjani, the Supreme Leader's representative in the Supreme Defense Council and the regime's leading money man (due to his position as speaker of parliament), parsimoniously allocated the necessary funds to acquire military equipment, focusing on what the armed forces most sorely needed: ammunition and spare parts.

[Chapter 10]

The Initiative Changes Sides

Early in January 1981 the Iranian authorities began planning the gradual recapture of the territories annexed by the Iraqi army. According to the chief of staff of the armed forces, the operation could not be launched before the spring, in order to allow the armed forces to reorganize, bolster their troops, repair damaged and captured equipment, improve coordination between regular troops and the Revolutionary Guard, and, most importantly, to wait for the dry season and the return of good weather. The clergy in Tehran did not share his opinion. They needed a quick first success—even merely symbolic—to silence popular discontent stoked by the revolts brewing in Kurdistan and Iranian Azerbaijan. The clergy could not afford to wait for spring. Ayatollah Beheshti, head of the Council of the Guardians of the Revolution, backed by Akbar Hashemi Rafsanjani, speaker of the Parliament and commander of the Pasdaran, asked the Supreme Leader to settle the question in their favor. They leaned on reports of the Iraqi army's extreme fatigue. But in a cynical fashion, they were convinced that they would win either way. If the first counteroffensive succeeded, they could claim responsibility for the victory. If it failed, it would be the fault of the regular army and its secular supporters. Ayatollah Khomeini did not take long to be persuaded. He pressured President Bani-Sadr to prepare to launch a large-scale military operation as soon as possible.

The Failure of the First Iranian Counteroffensive

Military high command urgently planned Operation Hoveyzeh, named after the small town targeted by the counteroffensive, located on the edge of the marshlands forming Iran and Iraq's border in Khuzestan. It hastily assembled the forces necessary for the assault, which would be launched

151

from Hamidiyeh. To ensure he had enough tanks, General Fallahi ordered the 88th Brigade to be turned into an armored division in its own right. This new 88th Armored Division absorbed the scattered battalions of the 92nd Division, which had been seriously diminished by the combat in the fall, to line up a total of 280 Chieftain tanks. However, the division lacked reconnaissance troops, mechanized battalions, or artillery. It was assigned to lead the assault in the direction of Hoveyzeh. It would be backed by the 55th Parachute Brigade, which would provide infantry support, while the 16th Armored Division held back, ready to follow up. Once Hoveyzeh was recaptured, the Iranians would need as many tanks as possible to press south toward the Karun to encircle the Iraqi units spread along the river and isolate the 5th Mechanized Division currently cordoning off the city of Abadan. By doing so, they hoped to force the 5th Division to retreat across the river, allowing them to regain control of the Ahwaz-Abadan road. Meanwhile, the Iranian paratroopers would stage a rear attack on the Iraqis still laying siege to Susangerd. The 21st and 77th Mechanized Divisions would only enter the fray once the road along the Karun had been cleared, helping to break the siege of Abadan. On the fringes of this central initiative, Iranian command was planning two more restricted operations on the central front intended to wear down Iraqi defenses and recapture part of their lost territory.

On January 5, 1981, Iranian military high command took advantage of a spell of good weather to launch Operation Hoveyzeh. The operation went awry from the very beginning. The Iranians were forced to move slowly, sticking to the roads to limit the chances of getting bogged down in the swamps they themselves had created two months earlier by flooding the arable land between the Karun and Karkheh Rivers. This time the cold and the mud were against them. The 88th Armored Division's three brigades had to advance in single file, followed by the 55th Parachute Brigade. This huge column, stretching nearly ten miles (roughly fifteen kilometers), was escorted by sixteen Cobra helicopters. This was all the air support available to the Iranians on this portion of the front. Facing them, the Iraqis had their 9th Armored Division, which had just been reinforced by a brigade of T-62 tanks detached from the 3rd Division positioned close to Khorramshahr. They had 240 tanks and about sixty other armored vehicles at their disposal.

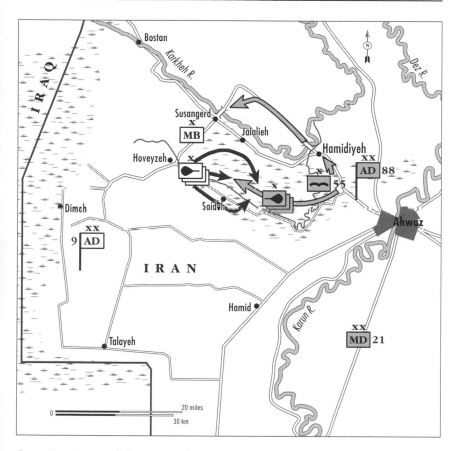

Operation Hoveyzeh (January 5–8, 1981)

The Iraqis were alerted by the presence of Iranian helicopters, and the armored column was immediately detected. General al-Duri, commander of the 9th Division, was ordered to stop it. He promptly dispatched his first tank brigade to hold the enemy along a line stretching from Jalalieh to Saideh, forcing the Iranians to maneuver on muddy terrain that would put them at a disadvantage. Early in the afternoon of January 6, the opposing forces made contact. The biggest tank battle since the Yom Kippur War was off to a start. As soon as they saw the Iranian advance guard, Iraqi tank crews feigned retreat, firing off a few gunshots to slow the enemy and indicate their positions. Applying the orders received, they yielded approximately half a mile (one kilometer), then reestablished their positions on a new line of defense held by most of their brigade, in the shelter of an embankment the sappers had built in a few hours. Believing he was only dealing with a reconnaissance column, the Iranian Armored Division's commander ordered his lead brigade to chase the Iraqi tanks. It fell right into the trap, its crews coming under a barrage of fire from the Iraqi tanks carefully arrayed behind the embankment. Trying to circumvent the Iraqis, several Iranian vehicles got bogged down and turned into easy targets. The others were picked off by tanks from the other two Iraqi brigades, which had now reached the battlefield. These reinforcements positioned themselves perpendicularly to the Iranians' line of attack, in order to take them from the rear.

Without any artillery or infantry support, facing attack from the front and their flank, the Iranian tanks were mercilessly decimated in rapid succession. The few survivors escaped under the cover of night. In a few hours, the 88th Division had lost the equivalent of an entire tank brigade. Determined to break through the enemy layout, its commander threw his second tank brigade into the battle. On the dawn of October 7, the brigade launched a fiery assault at the enemy positions. The Iranian brigade was immediately targeted by the artillery, which rained fire down on the area in an attempt to funnel the Iranian tanks into the net trap formed by the three Iraqi armored brigades. Nonetheless, the overwrought Chieftain crews managed to maneuver to engage the T-55s and T-62 in combat that often ended at point blank range. Throughout the day, Iraqi and Iranian tanks chased each other in a hellish scramble, slaloming between bogged-down tank wrecks, stopping abruptly to fire off a volley of shells at a tank on the lookout, indiscriminately mowing down crews desperately trying to get back to their lines after abandoning their damaged or wrecked vehicles, sinking knee-deep into the mud in bitter cold.

To add to the general chaos, Iranians Cobras and Iraqi Gazelles revved their turbines over the battlefield, haphazardly firing their missiles. The engagement ceased at nightfall, after each side had lost the equivalent of three tank battalions. But rather than cautiously withdrawing to gather his forces and save what could still be saved, the 88th Brigade's commander persisted. Persuaded that the Iraqis were on the verge of giving up, he decided to commit his last brigade. On the morning of January 8 the Iranian tank crews launched a third assault, without any more success than the previous day, though they managed to limit their losses by learning from their previous misfortunes. In the afternoon the remainder of the 88th Armored Division had no choice but to retreat. The defeat was severe for the Iranians, who lost 214 Chieftains and eight Cobra helicopters, versus about one hundred T-55s and T-62s on the Iraqi side. Naturally the Iraqis had to show off. They brought war reporters to the field to show them the shells of bogged down Chieftains and the burned-out wrecks of downed Cobras.

Meanwhile the 55th Brigade's parachutists had changed their tactics. Unable to attack the Susangerd garrison from the rear, they turned back to reinforce the Pasdaran under siege in the city by heading north along a secondary road starting in Hamidiyeh. The poorly maintained road followed the dunes on the opposite bank of the Karkheh River, providing an ideal shooting range for Iraqi pilots. Accordingly, the truck convoy carrying the brigade traveled by night. On January 10 the paratroopers were on the front lines to defend Susangerd, relieving the Revolutionary Guards who had been under relentless siege for three months. The paratroopers' antitank missiles, SAM-7 missiles, and mortars would help keep the Iraqis at bay.

The Iranians were more successful in the central part of the front. On the night of January 5 to January 6, 1981, the 15th Mountain Infantry Brigade's elite troops infiltrated Iraqi lines around Geilan Zarb in the Qasr-e-Shirin sector. They used the element of surprise to take control of several hills, encircled the village, and overran the defenses charged with cordoning it off. A few hours later, the 450 Iraqi infantrymen entrenched in Geilan Zarb surrendered. They were immediately sent to Tehran to be presented to the media for propaganda purposes. Meanwhile, the Iraqis counterattacked. On January 7 two 8th Infantry Division brigades backed by a tank brigade attacked Geilan Zarb again and recaptured it, following violent combat that left 400 dead in both camps. The Iranians abandoned the position but took shelter on the neighboring heights, partially isolating Geilan Zarb. A little further south, in the Mehran sector, the 81st Armored Division's dismounted infantrymen had seized Arkavaz. The Iraqi soldiers, poorly equipped to face the harshness of winter at high altitudes, had only met them with nominal resistance, choosing instead to take to their heels. Their commander would be brought before a council of war and executed.

These local successes could not obscure the fact that Operation Hoveyzeh was a dismal failure. Ahwaz remained under Iraqi artillery fire, and Abadan was still under siege. This initial counteroffensive's failure had two consequences: one political, the other military. The clergy saw it as an opportunity to rid itself of the president, who was openly accused of incompetence, and of the secular authorities, who continued to oppose the implementation of a true theocratic regime in Iran. Bani-Sadr's many critics paradoxically spared the military high command, which the clergy feared might still make a grab for power. Despite the Pasdaran's increasing strength, they were not yet on a scale to oppose the regular army.

On a military level, Operation Hoveyzeh's failure led to the postponement of the spring offensive. Most of the equipment that would have been used in the offensive had been lost in this botched operation. The Iranian general staff was no longer materially able to mount a major offensive before summer. It took advantage of the respite to reorganize its battle corps. Those Chieftains still able to see combat were divided between the 81st and 92nd Divisions. The 16th Armored Division gathered all of Iran's M-60 tanks. The 88th Armored Division, which had virtually been wiped out in the January counteroffensive, was reassembled with T-55 tanks shipped by Libya and Bulgaria. The 84th Brigade was turned into a Mechanized Division equipped with all the Soviet-made supplies captured from the Iraqi army. The 37th Armored Brigade, which had been decimated in the battles of Khorramshahr and Abadan, was not revived and vanished from the Iranian order of battle.

For their part, the Revolutionary Guards, who at that time had 140,000 men in their ranks, kept their structure of autonomous battalions. They simultaneously created three large Infantry Divisions—including the elite "Rasulullah" ("Messenger of God") Division—which formed their own field forces. From this point on, the Revolutionary Guards' field forces would systematically participate in every offensive with the regular army; following the regular army's humiliating setback, the clergy-dominated Supreme Defense Council had decreed that the Pasdaran would be involved in every military operation planned by military high command. Neither President Bani-Sadr nor his minister of defense was able to oppose this decision. The Revolutionary Guards' command also set up several infantry brigades that were later turned into divisions, based on need and available troops, and which would form a reserve of shock troops for the regime.

A New Front Opens in Kurdistan

In mid-January the Iraqi authorities schemed to take back operational initiative. Knowing they would not be able to break through in Khuzestan or advance in the Qasr-e-Shirin/Mehran sector, they decided to open a new front in Kurdistan to force Iran to send reinforcements there and relieve pressure on other fronts.

Baghdad anticipated a possible offensive in Kurdistan. In late 1980 the Iraqi regime had ordered General Amin, the 1st Corps' commander, to make arrangements to cordon off the region and secure the passes through which the Iranian 64th and 28th divisions, respectively garrisoned in Sanandaj and Mahabad, could potentially infiltrate their lines. On December 24, 1980, the 4th Infantry Division had crossed the border and seized a pocket of ground, allowing it to control the Rashah Pass and block any Iranian action in the direction of Sulaymaniah. It had not continued to Marivan because the city was defended by a large garrison. Meanwhile, the 11th Mountain Infantry Division, which was spread along the border, had dispatched one of its brigades to Halabja in order to protect the Darbandikhan Dam, which supplied electricity to Baghdad. Another of its battalions had deployed in the Mawat sector to secure the Dukan Dam, which supplied electricity to the oil city of Kirkuk. One of its brigades had occupied the Rayat Pass to prevent the Iranians from accessing it. Meanwhile, the 7th Infantry Division had focused on defending the Kirkuk sector.

On January 15, 1981, the infantry brigade that was deployed near Halabja crossed the snowy pass marking the border with Iran and took control of the plunging Nosud Valley in a few days. The Iraqis now had two bridgeheads in Iranian Kurdistan. Here again, the goal was not to launch a large-scale offensive to seize Iranian cities but to secure positions that would better enable them to defend their territory. Their task was made easier by the fact that the craggy relief of the Gharbi Mountains extending along the border was to the defender's advantage. The Iraqis also counted on another asset to prevent the Iranians from penetrating their territory:

Abdul Rahman Ghassemlou's Democratic Party of Iranian Kurdistan (PDKI) controlled this inaccessible mountainous area and was deeply beholden to the Iraqi regime, which supported it financially and supplied it with weapons. Baghdad was more concerned about the Kurdistan Democratic Party (KDP), which was supported by Tehran and remained very active in the north of Kurdistan despite the fact that the Barzani brothers were currently taking refuge in Iran, waiting for the appropriate chance to return to Iraq. But the Iraqi government considered itself in a better position in the Kirkuk area, which was dominated by Jalal Talabani's Patriotic Union of Kurdistan (PUK). Its agreement with Talabani appeared to remain solid. Saddam Hussein took the opportunity to invite Abdul Rahman Ghassemlou to set up his headquarters in Nosud, in the Iranian enclave controlled by the Iraqi army. This valley, which was connected to Baghdad by secure roads, would become the PDKI's bastion.

The rigors of winter prevented the Iranian regime from counterattacking. The area was snow-covered, and the extremely harsh weather conditions were unsuitable for military operations. The PDKI's peshmergas made the most of the opportunity to reinforce themselves thanks to Iraqi weapon deliveries. They extended their control in the direction of the Kurdish cities then held by governmental authorities, then patiently waited for the snows to melt and spring to arrive to move into action. Meanwhile, the army and Revolutionary Guards had their hands full quelling another uprising in the province of Azerbaijan. In February, the Peykar and People's Mujahidin led a popular uprising in Tabriz and surrounding cities, threatening the air base where the 2nd Fighter Wing was stationed. The Supreme Defense Council was forced to send major reinforcements, including two brigades of the 28th Mechanized Division, which was left with a single brigade to control the area around Mahabad, considered the "capital" of Iranian Kurdistan. This was a godsend for the peshmergas, who prepared their weapons for the upcoming operations.

As the last snows were melting in the first week of April 1981, the Kurdish resistance, headed by Abdul Rahman Ghassemlou, launched a general insurrection. Including every faction's troops, the insurrection had close to 40,000 combatants. Facing them, the Iranian authorities only had four regular army brigades (one from the 28th Division and three from the 64th Division) and a dozen Pasdaran battalions, totaling 20,000

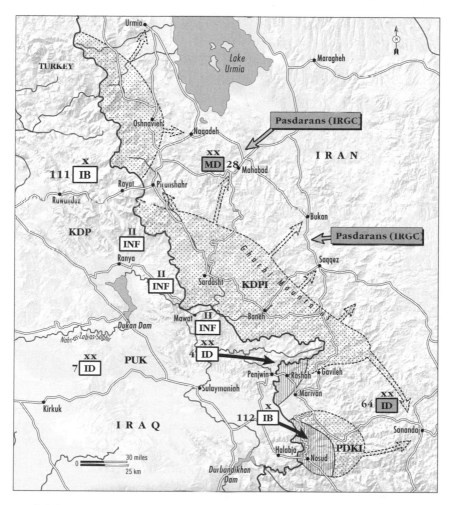

Kurdish front in the spring of 1981

men. In alliance with Komala activists, the People's Fedayeen descended on the principal cities. They disarmed a number of Pasdaran, who had enrolled to fight the Iraqis rather than their Iranian brothers. This was the case in Piranshahr, a strategic town that controlled access to one of the few roads leading to Iranian Kurdistan. Meanwhile the PDKI's pesh-mergas seized the main roads and rushed to the cities to assist their comrades engaged in fierce combat with those troops that had remained faithful to the regime. The Iraqi army did not directly participate in the insurrection, but continued to supply the combatants with munitions.

Over six weeks, the Kurds took control of Urmia, Naqadeh, Mahabad, Bukan, and Saqqez, also reinforcing their arsenal with captured tanks, artillery pieces, and heavy weaponry. Only the cities of Marivan and Sanandaj resisted their assault. In late May Abdul Rahman Ghassemlou decided to focus his efforts on Sanandaj, hoping that its fall would convince the Marivan garrison to surrender. Having surrounded the city, his troops launched a series of deadly assaults, slowly advancing from one neighborhood to the next. Its Iranian defenders displayed the same tenacity seen in Khorramshahr, resisting for a month before being forced to surrender due to a lack of munitions. In the battle of Sanandaj government troops lost 1,000 men, and Kurdish rebels lost nearly 2,000. By late June 1981 Abdul Rahman Ghassemlou could boast of having liberated nearly all of Iranian Kurdistan with the exception of Marivan, which refused to surrender despite its isolation. The exhausted peshmergas no longer had the means to capture the city.

The Iranian authorities were no longer able to regain control of this insurgent region. In Tehran President Bani-Sadr was now totally marginalized and desperately trying to keep his ship from sinking. He had to simultaneously fight the revolts in Azerbaijan and Kurdistan provinces, hold off the Iraqis along the front, and justify himself in the face of increasingly harsh criticism from all those who wanted his downfall. He no longer had enough troops available to put down the Kurdish rebellion. His two immediate priorities were to regain control of the province of Azerbaijan (for a quarter of Iran's population was of Azeri ethnicity) and to prevent the big cities that backed him politically from turning to armed protest. Even the Iraqi front became secondary. Pressured by the Supreme Leader to regain control, Abol Hassan Bani-Sadr reinforced his ties with Massoud Rajavi, who was the charismatic leader of the People's Mujahidin and had tremendous influence among the urban middle classes. Bani-Sadr's adversaries seized the opportunity to stigmatize this unnatural alliance and criticize the president, secretly hoping that the situation's deterioration would precipitate his downfall.

The Iraqis took advantage of the Iranians' temporary weakness to try once again to reduce the Susangerd salient. Their attempts were all unceremoniously repelled. Drawing a lesson from their defeat, the Iraqi command returned to its harassment strategy and restructured its military organization. It created the 4th Army Corps, which was responsible for securing the sector between Dehloran and Susangerd and was headquartered in Amarah. Its command was entrusted to General Fakhri, who had distinguished himself during the war's first phase. In the north, the 1st Army Corps remained responsible for Kurdistan, while the 2nd Army Corps focused on defending the sector between Qasr-e-Shirin and Mehran. It had the heavy responsibility of protecting Baghdad. In the south, the 3rd Army Corps continued to occupy southern Khuzestan. Military high command concurrently ordered the creation of three new Infantry Divisions (the 14th, 15th, and 16th—the superstitious Iraqis did not want a 13th division) and three training brigades in charge of rapidly training new recruits, which would then be dispatched to the new units. It also established twenty border guard brigades to keep watch over the Turkish, Syrian, Jordanian, Saudi, and Kuwaiti borders, now that the regular units had all been sent to the front. Iraq now had fifteen divisions to face the twelve mobilized by Iran (nine regular army, three Pasdaran).

The Iraqis also reorganized their anti-aircraft defense. They assembled batteries of Crotale and Roland surface-to-air missiles, freshly received from France, around Baghdad, as well as the SAM-9 mobile units that had previously protected their armored divisions. These reliable and highly complementary resources allowed them to create a far more effective defensive umbrella over the Iraqi capital. Saddam Hussein had decreed that not a single bomber could further disrupt Baghdadis' daily life. The SAM-6s were gathered around strategic sites, bridges, and airfields. Considered obsolete, the SAM-2s and SAM-3s were now mostly for show. The Iraqis did not really count on them to repel the Iranian air force. To defend ground units deployed along the front, the Iraqi general staff relied on its ZSU-23x4 Shilka self-propelled systems (which had proven their worth during the war's first phase), portable SAM-7 missiles provided by the Communist bloc, and the radar-guided S-60 57 mm anti-aircraft guns, which they acquired in Hungary. But they were primarily depending on their fighter planes: Iraq had finally received its first Mirage F-1EQs in February 1981, six years after purchasing them from France. These aircraft were assigned to the 79th Squadron and deployed on the sprawling Saddam Base recently completed by French technicians in the north of the country, near Mosul. The arrival of this modern air-superiority fighter, armed with Super-530 air-to-air missiles, was a technological leap forward that would change the operational order. Thanks to the aircraft's radar-guided missile, Iraqi Mirage pilots could engage the adversary face-on or from the flank, from above or below, and could avoid approaching combatants from the rear, as had been necessary with the previous generation's infrared missiles. The Iraqi pilots were now playing on an even field with the Iranian Phantoms. Only the best of them were authorized to fly the Mirage, after a conversion training course in France. They would later describe how happy they were to fly this comfortable, well-equipped plane, which was much easier to pilot than the antiquated Soviet fighters with which the other squadrons were equipped.

Raid on H-3

By early spring Iranian military high command was eager to regain the upper hand and erase the memory of its recent failures. The ground forces were still in shock and were not ready to launch another large-scale operation. However, the air force pilots were aware that their credibility remained fragile in the authorities' eyes, and they were prepared to take risks to prove their loyalty to the regime. They proposed a spectacular raid intended to show the Iraqis that the Iranian Air Force was able to strike their territory anywhere it wanted. Squad Leader Abbas Doran, a brilliant planner, suggested attacking the H-3 military airfield, located some thirty miles (fifty kilometers) from the Jordanian border. The base had previously not been a bombing target because it was considered a mere support airfield located much too far from the front to base fighter-bombers. In any case, it was out of the Iranian Phantoms' range. Yet the Iraqis had reactivated the base in the previous few months and were using it as an air depot to protect their Tupolev bombers (which they no longer dared to send over Iranian air space), to store military aircraft requiring heavy maintenance, and to serve as a relay base for the Mirage F-1s shipped from France via Jordan.

Believed to be safe, the airfield was also where most of the Egyptian and Jordanian technicians who maintained Mirages, MiGs, and Sukhois were stationed. Thanks to aerial photographs sent to them by the Israelis, the Iranians realized the H-3 airfield was a prime target: more than fifty aircraft of all types were scattered across the base in the open, without any protection save for anti-aircraft guns and a few obsolete surface-to-air missiles. The opportunity was too good to pass up. For the Iranian strategists, the challenge was to preserve the element of surprise. To do so, they selected an itinerary through Turkey and Syria, which would allow them to attack the Iraqis from the rear. Top Iranian authorities asked Hafez al-Assad to look the other way for a few hours. The Syrian president was only too happy to do the Iranian government this favor, knowing that it would harm his Iraqi rival.

Shortly before dawn on April 4, 1981, ten Phantoms took off from the base in Hamadan, heading northwest for the Turkish border. Each plane carried a mix of retarded bombs and fragmentation bombs, a single Sparrow air-to-air missile, one of the precious electronic countermeasure pods delivered by the Israelis, as well as three external fuel tanks. The distance to the target was 745 miles (1,200 kilometers), requiring several in-flight refuelings. The Iranians had never carried out such a long-distance strike. The last two Phantoms only flew as backup to replace potentially defective planes. The mission was coordinated from a Boeing 747 serving as a flying command post. Once aloft the pilots were initially refueled close to the Turkish border by two Boeing 707s flying from Tehran. This phase of the operation having gone smoothly, the two backup planes returned to their base, while the front formation, led by Major Farajollah Baratpour, headed west and followed the Iraqi-Turkish border at low altitude to escape radar detection.[1]

Two pairs of Tomcats took position over Iranian Kurdistan, ready to intercept any Iraqi fighter that came too close to the refueling planes in flight near the Turkish border. Meanwhile, further south, two Tiger formations penetrated Iraq and conspicuously headed in the direction of Kirkuk in order to distract Iraqi air defense's attention. For their part, the eight Phantoms flew nap-of the-earth over the Turkish mountains, keeping total radio silence, then turned southwest to enter Syria. There, they flew at very low altitude over the desert plain separating Syria from Iraq to the rendezvous point with two other refueling planes, which had left earlier from Istanbul and were registered as commercial flights between Istanbul and Tehran. After having arrived above the Anatolian plateaus, these two Boeing 707s turned off from their route and flew at low altitude to the rendezvous point in Syria, which was located about sixty miles (one hundred kilometers) northeast of Deir ez Zor. At the appointed time, the Phantom pilots linked up with the two Boeings above the desert and refueled near to the ground, in order to remain as discreet as possible. The refueling planes then flew back to a holding zone situated a little further north, also in Syrian air space.

Meanwhile the Phantoms accelerated to maximum speed and continued southwest. They crossed the Iraqi border some 200 feet (60 meters) above ground and headed for H-3. As they approached the target, they divided into three sections to appear from three opposite directions and disorient anti-aircraft defense. At 8:15 a.m. they burst into view over H-3, taking the base's defenses by total surprise. The first bombs were aimed at the runways in order to ground the pair of MiG-23s on alert. The next bombs fell on the anti-aircraft guns, most of which remained silent because the gunners were not at their stations. The remaining bombs mercilessly pounded the aircraft scattered around the base. Contrary to their usual tactic, the Phantom pilots did not limit themselves to a single run. They flew four bombing runs, creating total chaos and destroying eight MiG-23s, five Su-20s, four MiG-21s, two Mirage F-1s, one Tu-16 bomber, three transport An-12s, and four Mi-8 helicopters. About fifteen other planes were severely damaged, including two Tu-16 bombers and three Tu-22s. Approximately thirty technicians were killed, including four Egyptians and two Jordanians. At 8:30 a.m. the Phantoms abruptly ended the attack and turned back to base, keeping to the itinerary they had followed on the way. They refueled twice, in northern Syria and Iranian air space. At 10:30 a.m. the emotionally and physically exhausted Iranian pilots landed on the base in Hamadan, four hours and forty minutes after the mission had started. In a single strike, they had succeeded in putting more than forty Iraqi aircraft out of commission, including half of Iraq's bomber fleet, without suffering a single loss. The Ayatollah Khomeini personally congratulated them for this success, unprecedented since the beginning of the war. The same day two F-14s brought down two MiG-23s over Khuzestan, providing the icing on the cake.

The mood in Baghdad could not have been more different. Saddam Hussein demanded explanations and culprits. Six senior officers, including Colonel Fakhri Hussein Jaber, who was responsible for air defense of H-3's sector, were arrested and executed. Some twenty others were fired and imprisoned. Ten days later, the Iraqis took meager revenge when a pair of MiG-23s succeeded in shooting down the first Tomcat of the war over Kharg Island. Though the Iranians recognized the loss of this F-14, piloted by Captain Jafar Mardani, they attributed it to friendly fire from their own air defense. A week later a whirling air battle worthy of the film *Top Gun* resulted in the destruction of another MiG-23 and the grounding of a Tomcat, which had to make an emergency landing with its engines on fire. The Phantom pilots scored two MiG-21s and one MiG-23 without suffering a single loss. A Cobra helicopter pilot also distinguished himself by bringing down a Mi-24 helicopter with TOW antitank missiles. Meanwhile the troops on the ground were still waiting.

Osirak Out of Commission

On June 3, 1981, after hemming and hawing for several months, the Israeli government ordered the destruction of the Osirak nuclear power plant, which was scheduled to begin operating the following November. The Israelis considered it vital to put a halt to the Iraqi nuclear power program. Thanks to information from French technicians on site, they knew that the nuclear fuel had not yet been placed in the reactor. There was therefore no threat of radioactive fallout in case of an explosion. In agreement with Prime Minister Menachem Begin, the Israeli army's command launched Operation Opera. For six months Israeli aviators had been refining their plan, making the best possible use of the data they had received from French engineers involved in the plant's construction, but also from the Iranian authorities, who had sent them some information following the raid on the same target six months earlier.

To lead this crucial mission, Israeli high command called on its finest pilots and gave them the best planes at its disposal: eight F-16s and six F-15s recently delivered by Washington. The attack formation would be commanded by Lieutenant Colonel Ze'ev Raz, the most experienced F-16 pilot. Colonel Iftach Spector, a flying ace with fourteen kills and one of the most seasoned pilots in Tzahal, was given the most high-risk position of flying at the tail of the formation. The youngest member of the team, Lieutenant Ilan Ramon, was an exceptional pilot who would later become

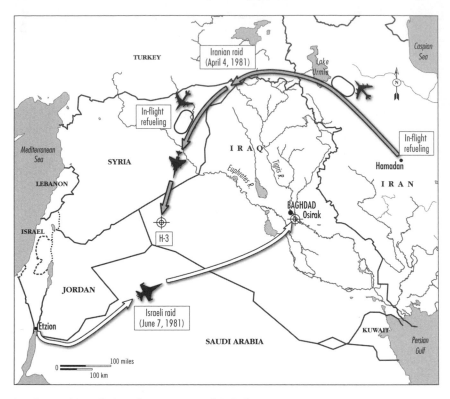

Iranian and Israeli air strikes on H-3 and Osirak

Israel's first astronaut (he died in the explosion of space shuttle *Columbia* in 2003). The Israeli pilots all knew the mission would be difficult: the target was defended by several SAM-6 batteries, abundant anti-aircraft artillery, and a MiG-23 squadron, not to mention the hazards of flying at extremely low altitude over the desert. Nonetheless, they hoped that the Iraqis would be caught up with the Iranian front. Their major asset was the element of surprise. Israeli military command had implemented an exceptional system to retrieve pilots forced to eject from their planes. A C-130 transport plane and two CH-53 helicopters full of commandos had discreetly landed in the heart of the desert on Jordanian and Saudi soil, at the ready to intervene immediately in case it was necessary to rescue pilots whose planes were downed.

At 4 p.m. on June 7, 1981, eight F-16 fighter-bombers escorted by six F-15s took off from Etzion air base, located in the Sinai near Eilat.[2] Each F-16 was equipped with two additional fuel tanks, two Sidewinder air-to-air missiles, its entire battery of electronic countermeasures, and two American 2000-pound (907-kilo) Mk-84 bombs. Rather than opting for a sophisticated guided projectile, the mission commander had chosen to use iron bombs to limit the risk of malfunction and to keep this delicate operation as simple as possible. He had confidence in his pilots' skills. The mission required a round trip of slightly over 1,240 miles (2,000 kilometers) with no in-flight refueling. Here again, the air force commander had opted for simplicity, choosing to avoid a complex refueling operation over enemy soil. The fourteen combat planes crossed the Gulf of Aqaba, quickly skirted the Jordanian border, then entered Saudi air space headed for Iraq, sticking close to the Jordanian border in order to deceive Saudi radars. The formation flew in total radio silence, about 330 feet (100 meters) above ground. Once they had crossed the Iraqi border, the pilots jettisoned their external fuel tanks and accelerated to the maximum speed allowed by their heavy cargo. Close to forty miles (sixty kilometers) from the target, the formation split in two. The F-16s continued at very low altitude on a curving trajectory directly aimed at their target, while the F-15s climbed to 26,250 feet (8,000 meters) in a few seconds to protect the F-16s. At this altitude, they could intercept any hostile aircraft threatening the Israeli fighter-bombers.

Once they crossed the Euphrates, the F-16 pilots knew the target was only a few minutes away. They armed their bombs and climbed to 5,000 feet (1,500 meters) to have better visibility of their target. At this point, they were detected, but it was too late. The Iraqi nuclear power plant appeared in the leader's sights, and he dove for his target. It was 5:30 p.m.; the sun was setting in the Iraqis' eyes when they looked in the direction of the attack. Lieutenant Colonel Raz released his two 2,000-pound (907-kilo) bombs on the plant's containment dome, abruptly tipped his plane to the left, climbed up, and flew straight west toward Israel. He was followed in single file by the remaining seven F-16s, each of which released both its bombs; fourteen bombs made direct hits, totally destroying the plant's main reactor, containment dome, and underground research lab.[3] The attack did not last more than two minutes. The surface-to-air missile batteries did not have time to be activated. By the time anti-aircraft fire was unleashed, the Israeli planes were long gone.

The return trip was simple: straight west at full speed, straight to Israel through Jordanian air space. The Israeli pilots separated into seven pairs randomly composed of F-15s and F-16s. Each pair chose a slightly different altitude and course in order to throw off potential pursuers. This was an unnecessary precaution, for the Iraqi fighters had been taken by surprise and did not have time to react. Meanwhile, several Israeli F-15s took off and conspicuously patrolled the length of the Jordan River to intercept any Jordanian fighter planes potentially tempted to get involved. This measure also proved superfluous: King Hussein of Jordan had meanwhile been notified that his air space had been crossed by "lost" Israeli fighters, but had ordered his fighter planes not to leave the ground. Soon after 6:45 p.m., the fourteen Israeli fighter planes all returned to Etzion air base safe and sound.

The next morning, the Israeli government released a communiqué claiming the destruction of the Iraqi nuclear power plant. When he learned of the extent of the damage, Saddam Hussein went into a fury and threatened to execute all the officers responsible for the disaster. Head of air defense General Oussama Yawer and the commander of the SAM-6 brigade in charge of protecting the nuclear plant were immediately dismissed. General Shaker Mahmoud, deputy director of air defense, was arrested and sent to the firing squad. The pilots were severely upbraided. After the slap in the face the Iranians had inflicted upon Iraq with the H-3 raid, the heads of the Iraqi air force were profoundly humiliated by this new defeat. For several weeks priority would be placed on air superiority missions to the detriment of fire support missions.

For the Iraqi dictator Osirak's destruction was a real catastrophe—without even mentioning the loss of the billions of dollars invested in its construction. It denied him the nuclear power status that would have allowed him to dissuade Iran from continuing the war and to impose himself as a natural leader in the Arab world. No one would have dared to attack the Iraqi regime if it had succeeded in providing itself with nuclear power, followed by the atomic bomb—not even Israel. Without the prospect of acquiring the ultimate weapon in the short or medium term, Saddam Hussein realized he no longer had any way to force the Iranian regime to put an end to the war. He intuited that the war would be long. Consequently, he accelerated his population's mobilization effort and ordered the nuclear program to be continued, with its facilities now scattered.[4] Unfortunately for him, none of his partners would support this project, not even France or the Soviet Union. Proving lucid, the Iraqi president did not order any retaliatory raids against Israel, knowing that he could not afford the luxury of opening a new front and that he had to concentrate all his resources against Iran. But he did increase his support to the Palestinian independence movement and all those preparing terrorist attacks on Israeli interests around the world.

Paradoxically, the destruction of the Osirak plant served the Iraqi regime, though it may not have been aware of it. It was only once Iraq lost any hope of having nuclear power—thereby limiting the risks of proliferation in the region—that Washington and Moscow considered reestablishing their ties with Baghdad. The United States and the Soviet Union had always agreed to avoid military nuclear proliferation in order to maintain their supremacy in the realm of atomic weapons. Via King Hussein of Jordan, the White House let the Iraqi president know that the United States would be willing to form closer ties with Iraq. As for the Kremlin, it made a goodwill gesture by accepting to deliver the first of the forty MiG-25s the Iraqis had ordered two years earlier but which had since been placed under embargo. This exceptional aircraft, which could fly at very high speed (Mach 3) and great altitude (82,000 feet/25,000 meters), was the only one able to carry out reconnaissance missions deep in enemy territory and effectively intercept Iranian Tomcats. The first MiG-25s delivered to Iraq would be put in service with the 87th Squadron in the fall of 1981.

The Iraqi nuclear program's interruptions also reassured European governments, which would no longer have any scruples about delivering weapons to Iraq. For its part, the Iranian government did not have much chance to rejoice over the destruction of the Osirak plant or to launch new military operations, for it was deeply entrenched in an inner battle over the future of the Islamic Revolution.

Chapter 11

The Mullahs Take Power

By June 1981 Iranian president Bani-Sadr had been struggling for political survival for several weeks. The most radical members of the clergy, particularly Ayatollah Beheshti, were determined to end his tenure. Early in June they openly accused him of treason, referring to his alleged ties with CIA executives. Javad Mansouri, an Islamic Republican Party (IRP) dignitary, unearthed a document written in September 1979 by Vernon Cassin, a CIA agent stationed in Tehran, that had been discovered during the sacking of the embassy. The document in question stated that the American intelligence services had attempted to recruit Abol Hassan Bani-Sadr. While the American spy had referred to him by the code name "SD/Lure1," the report's details made Bani-Sadr easily identifiable to the Iranian authorities. The president did not deny having been approached by an individual who offered him $5,000 a month in exchange for regular information, but insisted that he immediately rejected the offer.[1] Confident in the Supreme Leader's good faith, Bani-Sadr decided to rely on Khomeini's decision to determine his fate. The Supreme Leader realized that it was time to let go of his protégé, who was no longer an effective leader. On June 11, 1981, the Ayatollah Khomeini withdrew his confidence in Bani-Sadr and stripped him of his position as commander in chief of the army. On June 20, following a particularly tense session of Parliament, Bani-Sadr was dismissed from the presidency and the Supreme Leader ordered that he be placed in temporary custody.

The Elimination of the Secularists

Abol Hassan Bani-Sadr realized what was happening. Fearing he would be assassinated, he immediately went into hiding. He escaped from his home only a few minutes before the regime's henchmen arrived to arrest him, joining trusted friends who would hide him for several weeks. The next day his minister of defense, Mustafa Chamran, still one of his closest allies, died in the mysterious explosion of his military utility plane while he was inspecting the front. The prime minister, the head of Parliament, and the secretary general of the IRP agreed to form a triumvirate until presidential elections could be held. They took the opportunity to attempt to eliminate Massoud Rajavi, who joined Bani-Sadr in hiding. However, his People's Mujahidin were determined to retaliate. They rose up and launched a campaign of bloody terrorist attacks in the country's big cities.

On June 28, 1981, a deafening explosion destroyed the IRP's headquarters. The attack was attributed to the People's Mujahidin.[2] Ayatollah Beheshti, secretary general of the movement, head of the Council of Guardians of the Revolution, and the regime's number 2, was among the seventy-four victims. He had barely had time to enjoy his victory over Abol Hassan Bani-Sadr. His government had just been decapitated: fourteen ministers and secretaries of state were in attendance at the meeting over which he was presiding. Ayatollah Beheshti's death opened the way to two younger mullahs who had been scheming for two years to put themselves in the race for supreme power: Akbar Hashemi Rafsanjani, the older of the two, and Ali Khamenei.

The forty-six-year-old Akbar Hashemi Rafsanjani was a product of a privileged upbringing among the commercial class, jovial, pragmatic, epicurean, but above all formidably ambitious. He had been elected to Parliament in the first election after the Islamic Revolution. Born to an extremely wealthy trading family, he knew that real power lies in the hands of those who control the finances. This knowledge guided his decision to shrewdly maneuver to become speaker of Parliament, which would allow him to close the state budget and to attribute slush funds to the new regime's back rooms as it suited him. Despite his roly-poly, sincere appearance, Akbar Hashemi Rafsanjani was an insurgent at heart. He had lived underground in the last months of the Shah's regime to avoid the humiliation of being imprisoned. He was also a fighter and a strategist who took an interest in military questions and had not hesitated to spend several weeks at the front as the Supreme Leader's representative to the Supreme Defense Council. He aspired to establish a theocracy that preserved revolutionary gains side by side with a market economy.

This ambition fuelled his hostility to Marxist-aligned splinter groups such as the People's Mujahidin. His deepest wish was to reach the highest level of power to rebuild and modernize Iran in a manner compatible with the precepts of Shia Islam, while putting his name in the history books. He was ready to make any alliance to achieve his goal, including with outside forces, so long as they did not call into question the Islamic Republic's independence or sovereignty. Unlike many of the mullahs, who had never left Iran and were wary of the outside world, he was not frightened by other countries. He knew the Western nations and was aware that he could manipulate their leaders to reach his ends. The networks and alliances he had built at every level of society as the speaker of Parliament put him in a central position by which he became not only a worthy representative of the local bourgeoisie, but a key player in Iranian politics. In many respects, his personality was reminiscent of Danton's.

Ali Khamenei was much more like Robespierre. At forty-one, this blunt, frugal, elegant, uncompromising, and dogmatic intellectual represented the regime's most Jacobin faction. As the son and grandson of ayatollahs, Ali Khamenei had been immersed in the most rigorist doctrine of Shia Islam from an early age. He venerated the Supreme Leader as a holy man and was convinced that the advent of the Islamic Republic would hasten the return of the Hidden Imam. This intelligent, ideological, and wily tactician's ambition was to succeed the Ayatollah Khomeini and to preserve his revolutionary legacy and vision of political Islam, which avoided any foreign influence. He resolutely fell within the isolationist camp, which attracted those who refuted the need for Iran to open up to the outside world and posited that the country could develop on an autarkic model merely by relying on its human, natural, and spiritual resources. Like his mentor, Ali Kamenei was proud and inflexible on matters of principle. However, he was not a man of action. While he officially commanded the Pasdaran, his authority was moral and religious before anything else, and he functioned more as a political commissar than a war chief. To head the troops, he relied on a handful of young officers who had come up through the ranks.

Akbar Hashemi Rafsanjani and Ali Khamenei knew that the future belonged to them so long as they backed each other and intelligently shared power. While waiting for the seventy-nine-year-old Supreme Leader's death, they agreed to display a façade of unity intended to silence their detractors in the fundamentalist clergy. Despite their rivalry, a certain camaraderie developed between these two men; they had survived the hardships of the Revolution side by side and decided to work together to remove all potential rivals, beginning with Ayatollah Montazeri, whom the Supreme Leader had appointed as his legitimate heir apparent following the death of Ayatollah Beheshti. None of the other prominent clerics had the charisma, abilities, or ambition to succeed the Supreme Leader. Secluded in Qom, they preferred to concentrate on the clergy's affairs. Nonetheless, Rafsanjani and Khamenei were wary of Mehdi Karroubi (forty-three years old) and Mohammad Khatami (thirty-eight years old), two mullahs of their own generation whose careers and ambitions they would attempt to steer. Younger clerics such as Hassan Rouhani would have to bide their time.

In early July a vicious crackdown was launched on the People's Mujahidin and Peykar activists. The mullahs were determined to avenge their dead and assert their authority. In the summer of 1981 Iran underwent the radical second phase of its Islamic Revolution. In a few weeks more than 2,000 resistance fighters were arrested, given a summary trial, and executed. The provisional government hardly had time to concern itself with the Iraqi front, focusing all its attention on the internal front. Without a central guideline or specific target, military high command was unable to mount the major summer offensive everyone was expecting. Combat with Iraqis was limited to artillery duels and a few harassment operations, which did not lead to any notable gains. Sticking to his line of conduct, the Ayatollah Khomeini refused another truce proposed by Saddam Hussein.

Resurgence of Tension between Paris and Tehran

With the support of the Ayatollah Khomeini, Ali Rajai was elected to replace Bani-Sadr as president of the Republic on July 28, 1981. The Supreme Leader insisted that Mohammad-Javad Bahonar be appointed prime minister to maintain the fiction that power was shared between the different spheres of society. Bahonar was a forty-seven-year-old cleric who was highly erudite but lacked political ambition; his primary quality was that he represented the clergy's interests. A new government was formed in which the few laypeople, including Minister of Defense Colonel Namjoo and Minister of Foreign Affairs Mir-Hossein Mousavi, were all close to religious circles. Meanwhile, after the execution of several of their fellow travelers, Abol Hassan Bani-Sadr and Massoud Rajavi understood it was preferable to go into exile and continue the struggle from abroad. Having once released many pilots from prison, the former president could count on a reliable escape network thanks to his many connections in the air force.

On July 29 the two men entered the Mehrabad air base in Tehran's suburbs disguised as regular soldiers and carrying fake IDs. They boarded an aerial refueling Boeing 707 scheduled to conduct a training flight. Once in the air, the pilot claimed a mechanical failure as a pretext to escape to Turkey at low altitude. Ankara refused to offer Bani-Sadr political asylum, so the plane continued to France, where the former president had a solid network of friends in the Socialist government. The French authorities granted both men political asylum on condition that they renounce any political activism contrary to their status as refugees. Though very different, the two men were bonded by adversity and formed a friendship. In fact, Massoud Rajavi would marry Bani-Sadr's eldest daughter a few months later.

Bani-Sadr and Rajavi's asylum in France caused a sudden degradation in the strained relations between Paris and Tehran. The Ayatollah Khomeini furiously referred to France as a "little Satan." The warm feelings he had harbored for France following his stay in Neauphle-le-Château were now a thing of the past. Pierre Mauroy's government invited French citizens residing in Iran to return to France. Tehran responded by holding sixty-two French nationals in Iran, letting the threat of a hostage crisis similar to the one involving American diplomats two years earlier hover for over a week. To attempt to appease the Iranian government's anger, Paris shipped it the remaining three Combattante-class missile boats that France had embargoed since the fall of the Shah. But a particularly friendly meeting between François Mitterrand and Tariq Aziz at this time was given heavy media coverage and did not go unnoticed by Iranian intelligence.

On September 4, 1981, Louis Delamare, the French ambassador to Lebanon, was assassinated in Beirut. The killing was claimed by the Amal Shiite militia, but the French authorities were convinced that the militia had acted on instructions from Tehran.[3] The connections between the Lebanese Shiite factions and the Iranian clergy were notorious, and the mullahs' regime was constantly threatening France. Guy Cavallot, a Direction Générale de la Sécurité Extérieure (General Directorate for External Security; DGSE) agent whose investigations into Iranian networks in Lebanon got a little too close for comfort, was assassinated in Beirut with his wife.

Paris immediately radicalized its line against Tehran and increased its arms shipments to Iraq, signing the "Vulcain" contract with Baghdad, which called for France to deliver eighty-one ultra-modern GCT 155 mm AUF1 self-propelled guns capable of raining fire down on Iranian attack waves. This was a bonanza for GIAT Industries, from whom the Iraqi army also ordered one hundred AMX-10P tracked infantry fighting vehicles and ten AMX-30 battle tanks. The tank order was supposed to precede a larger order, but the Iraqi general staff did not follow through due to the stalemate, opting instead to buy artillery pieces and missiles. The French company SNIAS sold the Iraqis ten Pumas and forty new Gazelles equipped with HOT antitank missiles. Paris also committed to supplying Iraq with fourteen Roland anti-aircraft systems to allow it to better fight off Iranian air force incursions. French military advisors employed by service companies were sent to assist the Iraqi military on site. To show its gratitude, Baghdad renewed its special oil cooperation agreement with France.

Rafsanjani and Khamenei Share Power

In early August the Iranian government used air force personnel's involvement in Bani-Sadr and Rajavi's escape to justify another purge of the air force. All of Colonel Fakouri's efforts to win the authorities' trust had been for naught. Most missions were cancelled. Pilots were grounded and subjected to lengthy interrogations. Those who were authorized to fly only carried the minimum amount of fuel required, in order to ensure they resist the temptation to escape to a neighboring country. From this point on every mission had to be approved by a political commissar. The amount of arms carried were limited to prevent pilots from attacking the symbols of the regime. Naturally these drastic measures affected the air force's operational capacities, nearly entirely keeping it away from the front for several months. The Iraqis took advantage of the opportunity to increase their bombing missions against Iranian troops and oil facilities. Meanwhile terrorist attacks continued in Tehran, Tabriz, Shiraz, and Esfahan.

On August 30, 1981, an explosion rocked government headquarters as the Council of Ministers, presided over by Ali Rajai, was coming to a close. The president of the Republic was killed, as were his prime minister and several other ministers. The attack was claimed by the People's Mujahidin, acting in retaliation for the slaughter of their comrades. After a mere two months, the Iranian executive branch had been decimated again. The Ayatollah Khomeini decided the time was right to put power entirely in the clergy's hands. The progressive opposition had been gagged, the Shah's former partisans wiped out. The independence fighters and Mujahidin were certainly still around, but had been fiercely repressed. In agreement with those affected, the Supreme Leader divided responsibilities: while Akbar Hashemi Rafsanjani remained speaker of Parliament and in charge of finances, Ali Khamenei was elected president of the Republic. Ayatollah Montazeri was forced to accept this agreement because he had recently defied the Supreme Leader by severely criticizing his attitude toward the People's Mujahidin. Montazeri had opined that these men, whom he had known in the Shah's prisons, may have been hostile to the regime, but that they remained authentic Shiite Muslims who deserved to be treated more humanely. Ali Montazeri considered himself a free man—he was not a schemer and was not afraid to speak his mind.

Akbar Hashemi Rafsanjani and Ali Khamenei were jubilant. They had just acceded to the two highest government positions, and all their serious rivals were dead or marginalized. They formed a government composed of technocrats devoted to the clergy. Among the young men promoted was Ali Larijani, a twenty-four-year-old engineer and son of an ayatollah, who would hold the position of deputy minister for social affairs throughout the war and later be appointed minister of information, secretary of the National Security Council, then chief nuclear negotiator. He ran unsuccessfully in the 2005 presidential election, then became speaker of Parliament. He would establish himself as one of the key players of Iranian political life.

Conscious that it was in their best interest to avoid friction with each other to preserve their credibility and power, Rafsanjani and Khamenei agreed to appoint a colorless, hardworking, and devoted prime minister who would serve as a buffer for their antagonistic personalities. They chose Mir-Hossein Mousavi. The forty-year-old former minister of foreign affairs was of Azeri background and had the distinct advantage of not belonging to a particular clan or school of thought. He was the son of an ayatollah, an architect by training, an artist in his free time, both a socialist and a good Muslim, and lacked any major ambition. The Ayatollah Khomeini appreciated him for his selflessness, idealism, integrity, and modesty. As such, he was a perfect compromise candidate, responsible for administering everyday business and managing the general lack of financial resources. His first two tasks were to revive oil production in order to increase state revenues and to implement an effective ration-card system. Mir-Hossein Mousavi imposed himself as a good manager, close to the people, appreciated by his masters and his fellow citizens.

Akbar Hashemi Rafsanjani insisted that his protégé, the pediatrician Ali Akbar Velayati, only thirty-six years old, be appointed minister of foreign affairs. He hoped this appointment would allow him to keep control of international issues. Colonel Namjoo, forty-two years old, was confirmed as minister of defense. His role remained secondary, as he was only the manager of the armed forces and did not have a say in decisions regarding the conduct of the war. Ali Khamenei and Akbar Hashemi Rafsanjani also agreed to keep an eye on Mohammad Khatami by appointing him minister of information and culture. This affable, ambitious young cleric was a philosopher who had edited the IRP's newspaper since the proclamation of the Islamic Republic. He was now charged with heading the regime's war propaganda cell. Mohammad Khatami would be elected president of the Republic in 1997 on a reformist platform promising to improve women's status and to broaden young people's rights. Reelected in 2001, he was forced to withdraw at the end of his second term—as dictated by the Iranian Constitution—to make way for Mahmoud Ahmadinejad. He has since been active in the reformist camp, which calls for Iran to open up to the outside world while retaining the advances of the Islamic Revolution.

Mehdi Karroubi was made head of the Martyrs' Foundation, which had recently been founded by the Ayatollah Khomeini to assist the families of dead or wounded soldiers. Karroubi would remain the regime's leading social worker and the mediator between the government and the people throughout the war. He would be the one to directly receive the population's grievances, requests, and demands for help. This was a responsibility well suited to this appealing cleric, a lawyer by training, who was eager for recognition and embodied the traditional alliance between the clergy and the commercial world of the bazaar. After moving up the ladder within the Expediency Discernment Council, Mehdi Karroubi would become speaker of Parliament from 1989 to 1992, then from 2000 to 2004. He took up the reformist cause in 2005, immediately opposing President Mahmoud Ahmadinejad's conservative policies.

Beginning in the late summer of 1981, a generation of men in their forties—with the exception of the Supreme Leader—held power in Tehran. The most influential institutions were in the hands of the clergy, including the presidency of the Republic, the Parliament, the Assembly of Experts, the Discernment Council, and the Council of Guardians of the Revolution.

New Leader, New Doctrine

To put the finishing touches on this transformation of power, the Ayatollah Khomeini appointed Akbar Hashemi Rafsanjani to be the new commander of the armed forces. Rafsanjani was now concurrently responsible for chairing Parliament, managing the regime's finances, and leading the war effort. The Supreme Leader had learned from Bani-Sadr's failure to efficiently direct operations. He also wanted to spare the president and preserve his aura in case of military defeats. He may have been trying to protect Ali Khamenei, having understood that this was not the right man for the difficult task of heading the armies, a task which required charisma, real practical sense, and a pronounced taste for action and commanding. Akbar Hashemi Rafsanjani seemed to have all these qualities, though the Supreme Leader did not like his ambiguous relationship with the business world and his distinct taste for money.

The speaker of Parliament immediately understood that his first task would be to win the war against Iraq. This was how he intended to establish himself as a future president and possibly even a Supreme Leader. Calling on his gifts as a strategist, he completely invested himself in running the war. He would not hesitate to spend several weeks on the front to motivate the troops and follow unfolding operations as closely as possible. His priority was to rein in the chiefs of staff and give the Pasdaran more power. He found that the high command included too many individuals favorable to former President Bani-Sadr. On September 29, 1981, the C-130 carrying the chiefs of staff back from an inspection of the front went down in the middle of Iran. The four-engine transport plane had exploded in flight and crashed. The thirty-eight victims included General Valliolah Fallahi, chief of staff of the armed forces, Colonel Namjoo, minister of defense, and Colonel Fakouri, commander of the air force. The circumstances of this strange accident were never elucidated. Many saw it as the work of the regime's secret services.[4] In any case, the chiefs of staff had been eliminated. Akbar Hashemi Rafsanjani took advantage of the opportunity to promote new officers closer to the clergy. General Qasim Ali Zahir Nejad replaced General Fallahi as head of the armed forces, while his former position as commander of ground forces was entrusted to General Ali Shirazi. Colonel Hasan Mojunpur, a notorious religious bigot, became head of the air force, and Colonel Mohammad Salimi was appointed minister of defense. New generals were promoted to head several divisions. Meanwhile, the Iranian Revolutionary Guards Corps gained visibility. Its command was given to Mohsen Rezaee, a twenty-seven-year-old protégé of the Ayatollah Khomeini who had distinguished himself on the front in the first phase of the war against the Iraqis. Though he was somewhat unsophisticated, his charisma worked wonders in the field. He was seconded by Ali Shamkhani, a twenty-six-year-old agricultural engineer very popular among the peasants who made up the large battalions of Pasdaran units. Shamkhani had proven to be an exceptional leader during combat in Khuzestan. These two men, entrusted with tremendous power, reported exclusively to Rafsanjani, bypassing the entire traditional military hierarchy.

To increase their grip on the armed forces, the mullahs appointed a "political ideological director" to each general staff to serve as political commissar. Akbar Hashemi Rafsanjani retained the Supreme Defense Council, but implemented an unofficial parallel chain of command that was more flexible and reactive. It gave him authority over both the Pasdaran and the chief of staff of the armed forces, who could now impose Rafsanjani's views on all unit commanders. In agreement with the chief of staff of the armed forces, the all-powerful speaker of Parliament popularized the concept of the jihad (holy war), which was supposed to guide every Iranian combatant now that recapturing the lost territories had been assimilated into a religious crusade. To galvanize fighters, he asked the chiefs of staff to name all subsequent operations after events in the history of Shia Islam.

Stated in military terms, the concept was based on three principles. The first referred to the *velayat-e faqih:* since the Ayatollah Khomeini interpreted divine law, his orders were to be followed to the letter, without any discussion. The second was based on self-sufficiency: the army could no longer be as dependent on foreign nations for equipment and munitions as it had been in the past; every effort had to be made to allow a local arms industry to emerge and, until that happened, to develop alternative supply sources. The third banked on simplicity: to increase the chances of success and minimize the risks of friction between the regular army and the Pasdaran, officers in charge of operations had to prioritize simply executed plans, which limited imponderables. This new military doctrine implicitly favored resorting to the only inexpensive resource the republic had in large quantities: its troops. The mullahs were prepared to sacrifice untold numbers of their soldiers to compensate for their material inferiority and punish their adversaries. Having won the first war—for the conquest of power—they now had to win the next two—against their internal enemies and against the Iraqis.

[Chapter 12]

First Victories

Early in September 1981 the Iranian leadership mounted two offensives to recapture part of the territories they had lost a year earlier. In Khuzestan several Pasdaran brigades, supported by the 84th Mechanized Division, forded the Karkheh River near Shush and launched a series of attacks against Iraqi outposts. Their objective was not to breach enemy lines but to wear down their adversaries, make them yield ground, and mislead them as to the location of the principal offensive. For three weeks 30,000 infantrymen gnawed away at the terrain and pushed the Iraqis back roughly six miles (ten kilometers), which allowed them to establish a solid bridgehead west of the Karkheh and also to enlarge the Susangerd salient. The Iraqis expected armored battalions to burst into view, not hordes of combatants. Their tanks were dug in on the front line behind mere embankments and did not have infantry support capable of stopping the battalions of infantrymen washing over their positions. They were forced to pull back to avoid being overrun.

Meanwhile, the Iranians were rearranging their layout and discreetly moved reinforcements to the south of Ahwaz. Their 21st Mechanized Division deployed along the marshland between Shadegan and Abadan. A Pasdaran division quietly made its way through the marshes to the bridgehead held by the 5th Iraqi Division. For the first time the Iranian military high command established mixed units composed of regular troops and Revolutionary Guards.

The Rescue of Abadan

In the night of September 26 to 27, 1981, the Iranians launched the Samen-ol-A'emeh ("Eighth Imam") offensive, aimed to break the siege of Abadan and liberate the eastern bank of the Karun River. The element of surprise was total. The Iraqi 5th Division's chiefs of staff, headquartered in Dark-hovin, were pounded by Iranian artillery. Disoriented, the officers were unable to organize a counterattack. Yelling "Allahu Akbar," Iranian commandos carrying TOW antitank missiles infiltrated enemy lines as far as possible. They set deadly ambushes for Iraqi tanks, which attempted to react in utter disarray. Meanwhile, the Pasdaran advanced under the artillery's rolling fire, flanked by the regular army's tanks, which successively hammered each and every nest of resistance. The Iranians had learned from their past mistakes and rediscovered the virtues of the steamroller. No more tank stampedes! Two Pasdaran brigades that had left from Abadan joined the offensive. This time the force ratio was in their favor. Intent on galvanizing his troops, the Ayatollah Khomeini declared: "The encirclement of Abadan must be broken."[1] Confusion on the field was exacerbated by the fact that the 88th Brigade was equipped with T-55 tanks identical to those used by the Iraqis. In a panic, the Iraqis chaotically beat back to Darkhovin to try and cross the Karun on the pontoon bridge repeatedly targeted by Iranian air force strikes. The Iraqis abandoned some fifty T-55s, 200 other armored vehicles, and their entire heavy artillery on the eastern bank.

By September 29 the Iranians controlled the Karun's eastern bank and reopened the road from Ahwaz to Abadan. The 15,000 fighters who had been under siege in the city for close to a year broke through the vise holding them and pushed the Iraqi vanguard back to the other side of the river. The Iraqis reestablished themselves in Khorramshahr. Thousands of them wandered around, looking wild and distressed, trying to find a way to regain their lines. They were rapidly captured by the Pasdaran and exhibited for the international press to photograph. The message was intended to be crystal clear: the Iranians had taken back the initiative and were determined to recapture their territory by force. Though victorious, the Eighth Imam offensive had exhausted the Iranians: 2,000 of their combatants had fallen to break the siege of Abadan and more than 5,000 had been wounded. In Baghdad Saddam Hussein fumed and dismissed the 5th Division's commander, leaving the 3rd and 9th Armored Divisions to defend the Karun's western bank. Iraqi military high command took reinforcements from Kurdistan to hold the sector of Bostan, across from the Susangerd salient. The 14th Infantry Division was dispatched to the area to form a second line of defense along the border, in case the enemy broke through Iraqi positions.

Meanwhile, the Iranian authorities concentrated their attention on Kurdistan. They had mobilized 60,000 combatants, half of them Pasdaran, to regain control of the rebel province. Abdul Rahman Ghassemlou was down to 15,000 peshmergas to repel them. The Iranians' objective was to capture Sanandaj, where the PDKI had concentrated its best troops. Seizing the city would allow them to get supplies to their 64th Division besieged in Marivan.

Early in October the military high command launched the offensive against Sanandaj. Brought from Dezful, the 16th Armored Division's tanks overran the Kurdish outposts, encircled the city, and reestablished contact with the 64th Division. They were backed by the Zulfiqar Division's Pasdaran. With the support of the artillery, they recaptured the city after three weeks of particularly fierce combat. The deceptive calm that had prevailed in the region for the previous few months had dulled the peshmergas' vigilance. Now they were the isolated ones. Once Sanandaj had been recaptured, the Iranian authorities established their headquarters on site and continued their offensive to the north. In six weeks Iranian forces captured Saqqez, Bukan, Mahabad, Piranshahr, Naqadeh, and Urmia, after linking up with the 28th Division. Their advance was accompanied by brutal repression.

Captain Ahmad Kazemi, a twenty-three-year-old officer who had joined the Revolutionary Guards, distinguished himself at the head of an irregular unit of about fifty men charged with spreading terror in the enemy's rear lines. He established himself as an impressive manipulator and merciless killer, formed through his experience in the Lebanese civil war, where he had fought with the Amal Shiite militia straight through from 1975 to 1979 before returning to Iran on the eve of the Revolution. This elite soldier would distinguish himself in numerous battles. Wounded several times, he was made a general and commanded the Ashraf Division until the end of the war, then became a military advisor to President Rafsanjani and finally the commander of the Pasdaran ground forces. He rallied behind President Ahmadinejad in 2005, but died in the suspicious explosion of his military utility plane on January 9, 2006. In discussing his death, many experts mentioned President Ahmadinejad's jealousy and fear of this charismatic but prickly general.

Faced with the governmental forces' steamroller, the peshmergas were forced to retreat. They hurriedly launched a counterattack in the direction of Piranshahr to reopen the road by which they could get supplies from Iraq, but the operation failed. Late in November, with the area now covered in snow, governmental authorities were once again in control of the main road from Sanandaj to Urmia. The peshmergas had taken refuge in their mountain stronghold and now only controlled the small towns of Oshnavieh, Sardasht, Gavileh, and Nosud, as well as the city of Baneh, which was an important rear base. Abdul Rahman Ghassemlou was a realist: he knew he would have to bide his time through the winter and wait for combat to begin again in spring. In Tehran the new chief of staff decided the time was right to shift his efforts to Khuzestan, where the climate was less severe.

On the Way to Jerusalem

On November 29, 1981, General Nejad launched Operation Tariq al-Qods ("Jerusalem Way") in the Susangerd sector. He had mobilized his 55th Parachute Brigade, a Pasdaran division, and two tank brigades from the 92nd Armored Division. In all, 20,000 soldiers and sixty tanks headed for Bostan, moving at the infantrymen's pace under a driving rain. The Iranian objective was to take control of the town, then continue in the direction of the nearby Iraqi border so they could claim a symbolic victory before year's end. Akbar Hashemi Rafsanjani had promised Iran's parliamentarians that he would drive the invader back to the borders as soon as possible. The Pasdaran advanced in two columns, each following a bank of the Karkheh River. The artillery was hampered by the mud covering the area. Chieftain tanks were deployed along the flanks to engage enemy troops that attempted to skirt the two columns.

Given the poor weather conditions, the Iraqis had not been expecting an offensive. They yielded ground. In three days the Iranians had arrived outside Bostan. During the night of December 2 to 3 the Pasdaran tried to take the city in the pouring rain. They were eager to prove their valor

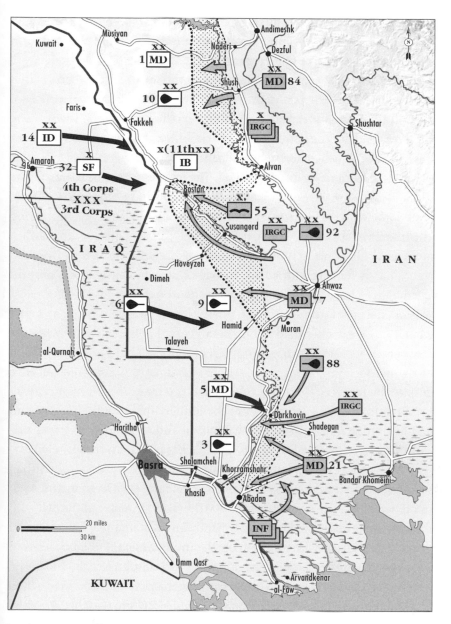

Iranian counteroffensives in Khuzestan in the fall of 1981

to their leaders, but also to their comrades in the regular army, who thought of them as cowards. It was a misguided attempt: the Pasdaran were violently pushed back after sustaining severe losses. The Iraqis were determined to hold this position to prevent the Iranians from setting foot on Iraqi soil. Over three days the Iraqi infantrymen entrenched in Bostan held off the Iranians' repeated assaults. For the first time in the war the Iranians tried out the new tactic of overwhelming the enemy with human wave attacks, which ended in brutal hand-to-hand combat. On December 6 the Iranians' tenacity finally paid off. The Pasdaran and the paratroopers seized Bostan, while the Iraqis withdrew to a position a few miles away (a few kilometers away) under freezing rain. Losses were heavy on both sides. The Iraqis had suffered 1,500 dead. They also lost about one hundred tanks, nineteen artillery pieces, and large stocks of ammunition. A little over 400 Iraqi soldiers had been captured. Nearly 1,000 wounded soldiers were alleged to have been killed on site by the enemy.[2]

For their part, the Iranians reported 2,500 dead and twice as many wounded. One dismounted infantryman battalion immediately made the most of the victory, entering Iraqi territory to be photographed in front of the border marker. Rafsanjani could boast of this symbolic success, despite the fact that the detachment had to retreat under pressure from Iraqi reinforcements dispatched to the border. The Iraqi high command had just ordered its 14th Infantry Division and 32nd Special Forces Brigade to deploy outside Bostan to hold back the Iranian troops. Concurrently it withdrew the 6th Armored Division from the Qasr-e-Shirin sector, sending it to the area of Hamid to help the 9th Division and what remained of the 5th to hold this part of the front. It replaced the 6th with the 17th Armored Division, which had been created a few weeks earlier by gathering all the Chieftain, Scorpion, and Patton tanks captured from the Iranian army in a single unit.

On December 12, 1981, Iranian military high command launched a new offensive called Operation Matla ul-Fajr ("Sunrise" or "Break of Dawn") in the Qasr-e-Shirin sector. In terrible weather conditions the Iranian 15th Mountain Infantry Brigade, backed by three Pasdaran brigades and four tank brigades detached from the 16th and 81st Divisions, attacked Geilan Zarb and Sar-e-Pol-e-Zahab by night. Taken by surprise, the Iraqis retreated and abandoned the two towns, though they were essential to maintain control of the front. Rain and extremely poor road conditions prevented the Iraqi 12th and 17th Armored Divisions from counterattacking. The 4th and 8th Infantry Divisions' infantrymen were left to vainly try and recapture the two towns over the next five days. The weather also prevented the Iraqi air force from intervening, easing the Iranians' work. Having sustained severe losses, the Iraqi troops were forced to retreat.

Meanwhile, the Iranians had gained a little ground in Khuzestan. Their 77th Mechanized Division, backed by the 92nd Armored Division's last brigade, advanced about a dozen miles (about twenty kilometers) in the direction of Hamid and Hoveyzeh. The mud was so deep that they could go no further without running the risk of getting bogged down. On December 16 they stopped their advance outside Hamid and took defensive positions to wait out the rainy season under the cover of their tanks and artillery. The next day the Iraqis launched a failed counterattack in the Shush sector.

By the end of 1981, after four months of constant offensives and fifteen months of war, the Iranians had managed to reclaim close to 40 percent of the territory captured by the Iraqis.

The Iraqi Sappers Hard at Work

The Iraqi army took advantage of the winter truce to reinforce and consolidate its positions. In the cold and humidity the engineer troops busied themselves creating defensive obstacles, improving the road infrastructure, opening new routes through marshy areas, and repairing damaged pontoon bridges and building new ones where they seemed indispensable, notably near Khorramshahr. The Iraqi sappers systematically raised and asphalted those roads in Khuzestan used to transport supplies and reinforcements to prevent them from becoming flooded and impassable during the rainy season. They began widening the road that runs along the Euphrates from Baghdad to Basra to relieve traffic congestion on the main road that follows the Tigris, which remained vulnerable to a potential Iranian breakthrough. They drained many marshy areas that could be needed to deploy tanks. They built numerous bunkers and buried an unbelievable number of antitank and antipersonnel mines. Their bulldozers dug trenches for infantrymen and prepared countless firing positions for tanks and artillery. Since the engineer corps' military resources were not sufficient for the scope of the task, the general staff requisitioned bulldozers and other dirt movers to conduct the work. Many civilian companies contributed to the war effort, sometimes under Iranian artillery fire.

During the winter of 1981–1982 the engineer corps' most spectacular accomplishment was the erection of a veritable "Persian Wall," as the Ba'athist regime referred to it, to protect Khorramshahr. The Iraqis were rightly convinced that the Iranians would try hard to liberate this symbol of Arab presence on Persian soil. The Iraqis spared no effort in reinforcing the city's defenses and turning it into an unassailable urban fortress. The sappers built a ten-foot (three-meter) tall and thirty-foot (ten-meter) wide compacted soil and sand rampart curving over six miles (ten kilometers) along the city's northeast edge. This fortified embankment was reinforced by a defensive complex composed of minefields, barbwire, a wide variety of traps, and an antitank ditch intended to stop the Iranian attack waves. The carefully dug-in tanks deployed at the top of the embankment covered the desert plain that extended from the city's edges. They were protected by machine gun and mortar nests ready to push back anyone who tried to climb or skirt the rampart.

Companies of dismounted infantrymen stayed further back, ready to counterattack any infantrymen who succeeded in getting through the defensive layout. Open spaces were filled with metal stakes to dissuade the adversary from launching an airborne assault on the city. Bulldozers razed buildings and groves that blocked sightlines, clearing as many lines of fire as possible. Bunkers were built at strategic hubs. The three bridges running over the Karun River in the direction of Abadan were barricaded and mined. Heavy artillery was assembled on the Shatt al-Arab's western bank, sheltered by another earthen rampart, which the engineer corps built at a perfect distance to cover the approaches to Khorramshahr. Cannons were carefully set to erect veritable walls of firepower outside the city.

The engineering troops were also involved in a gigantic project to protect the area of Basra. Acting as a shrewd minister of defense, Adnan Khairallah considered all the options and realized that the balance of power had shifted in the Iranians' favor. He understood that they could eventually attempt a major operation targeted at Basra. He knew the

Ba'athist regime could not afford to lose this position, which was both strategic and symbolic, since this port city, populated by a Shiite majority, was one of Iraq's two financial hubs and its only access to the Gulf. He asked the engineers' commander to suggest the best possible way to cordon off the city. The latter closely studied the terrain and consulted with his experts. He proposed to dig a thirteen-foot (four-meter) deep canal outside Basra on the Shatt al-Arab's eastern bank, running eighteen miles (thirty kilometers) long and 1.2 miles (two kilometers) wide. Supplied with water from a large lake known as the "Fish Lake" and three perpendicular canals running from the Shatt al-Arab, the defensive canal would become an impassable antitank ditch. Behind this artificial body of water, a fortified embankment modeled after the Persian Wall and spanning nearly forty miles (some sixty kilometers) would serve as Basra's advanced defenses. This titanic project occupied a large number of civil engineering firms day and night for three years.

Baghdad also took advantage of the winter truce to increase its ground troops, which soon grew to 450,000 men (300,000 in the regular army, 150,000 in the Popular Army)—the same size as Iran's troops. Military high command established three new infantry divisions (the 18th, 19th, and 20th), which would be divided along the border to form the basis of a second line of defense.

During a military parade on January 6, 1982, Saddam Hussein is reported to have declared that although certain units had suffered in the war, Iraq would not be in difficulty even if the war lasted another two or three years, and added that the country could mobilize nearly two million soldiers if necessary.[3] The optimism of the early days was no more than a distant memory. In private the Iraqi dictator openly considered using chemical weapons to contain the Iranian troops' advances, asking his generals to accelerate the manufacture of these "special munitions." Here again, the audio tapes seized in 2003 bear witness to Saddam's intentions.

Despite the early February mud and rain, the Iraqis launched a series of failed counterattacks to attempt to recapture Bostan. To cut their losses they reinforced the sector with the 11th Division, which had been brought back from Kurdistan, and sent several Popular Army brigades to reinforce the garrison in Khorramshahr as a precautionary measure.

Tehran also strengthened its military organization. To absorb the large volume of new recruits, military command created two new infantry divisions and a mechanized division (40th). The latter was supplied with tanks delivered by Libya and equipment captured from the Iraqi army. The 30th Motorized Brigade was turned into another armored division, equipped with T-59 tanks provided by China. These four divisions were put under the command of the Pasdaran, which significantly increased their striking power, much to the dismay of the regular army's generals.

A Hard Blow for Baghdad

To increase pressure on Baghdad, Tehran decided to radically reduce Iraq's oil-export capacity. Its occasional attacks on Iraq's oil infrastructure were not enough to deal a decisive blow to the Iraqi economy, which was already heavily affected by the destruction of the Mina al-Bakr and Khor al-Amaya offshore terminals. Bombing the Kirkuk-Dortyol oil pipeline, through which Saddam sent some of his oil to the West, was out of the question because it would be seen as a casus belli by Turkey, which Iran had no choice but to handle with kid gloves. This left the Syrian option. Beginning in the first weeks of 1982, the Iranian authorities repeatedly made overtures to President Assad to convince him to close the Kirkuk-Baniyas pipeline, which allowed Iraq to transport up to 550,000 barrels of oil per day—half the oil extracted in the north of Iraq—via Syria. The Syrian president immediately pointed out the revenue he would lose by closing the pipeline, since Syria took part of the oil for its own needs and received royalties on the rest. Undeterred, the Iranians assured him they were prepared to compensate him for this shortfall by signing a generous oil supply agreement with Syria.

Negotiations quickly commenced. In mid-March, the two parties found common ground. Iran committed to annually delivering close to nine million tons of oil to Syria, of which 80 percent would be at a highly advantageous price and the other 20 percent would be free. Tehran also committed to buying a significant amount of Syrian products, which Damascus had trouble moving. The agreement would provide Syria with a net income of roughly one billion dollars per year, as much as it was annually given by Saudi Arabia for the struggle against Israel. Recognizing a good deal, President Assad promptly agreed to it. To justify his decision Assad sparked some incidents at the Syrian-Iraqi border. Syrian fighter planes violated Iraqi air space on several occasions. One was shot down by an Iraqi MiG-23. Irritated by these provocations, Saddam Hussein took an aggressive tone.

On April 8, 1982, Hafez al-Assad made good on his promise to Iran and closed the Kirkuk-Baniyas pipeline. He also locked down the border with Iraq to prevent road traffic between the two countries. It was a terrible blow to the Iraqi regime, which had suddenly lost a crucial outlet for its oil and therefore a significant part of its revenue. Luckily oil prices were still high, which ensured Iraq substantial revenue (ten billion dollars in 1982, versus twenty-six in 1980)—but not enough to cover its war effort. So long as its finances were not reestablished, there would be no hope of launching a large-scale offensive. Furious, Saddam Hussein registered a complaint with OPEC's court of appeals on April 9 and ordered a series of measures to limit the damage. Contact was immediately made with Turkey to increase the Kirkuk-Dortyol pipeline's capacity and to begin the construction of a new parallel pipeline with a 400,000 barrel per day capacity. The Turkish government responded favorably, seeing this as a good opportunity to improve its finances and feeble economy. Construction work began in early summer and ended two years later. In the meantime the original pipeline was exploited to its maximal capacity of 650,000 barrels per day, and tanker trucks constantly shuttled between Kirkuk and the Turkish terminal of Dortyol, allowing for an additional 25,000 barrels per day to be transported via Turkey. But Iraqi military command had to assign an additional 30,000 men to protect this vital axis, and those men would be sorely missed on the rest of the front.

Meanwhile, the Iraqis also played the Jordanian card. They doubled the number of tanker trucks traveling between Kirkuk, Baghdad, and the port of Aqaba on the Red Sea, which allowed them to move 25,000 barrels per day, bringing their total export capacity to 700,000 barrels per day. But this was still hardly enough compared to the five million barrels Iraq could export before the war. The Iraqi authorities approached the Jordanian government about building a pipeline between Kirkuk and

Aqaba, which would be solely financed by Baghdad. King Hussein found the offer attractive, but had to consult with his allies before answering. The Saudis were not enchanted, but could not in good conscience oppose it. The Americans, initially in favor of a project that would reinforce their Jordanian ally and ease a potential rapprochement with the Iraqi regime, were forced to veto it once the Israelis learned of the project, declared they were hostile to it, and threatened to attack the pipeline if it were built.[4] The Israeli authorities were determined to oppose anything that could contribute to strengthening Iraq. The Jordanian option was out.

As a last resort, Saddam Hussein was forced to solicit Saudi Arabia's assistance again. This proved to be an exceptional way of getting in the good graces of King Fahd, who had recently succeeded his prematurely deceased brother Khalid. The new Saudi sovereign, far more open than his predecessor, saw this as an opportunity to reinforce his influence on Iraq. He was particularly glad to offer Saddam help now that the military situation had shifted in Iran's favor, creating concerns of a greater threat to the Gulf's security. He was also encouraged by the change of attitude in the United States, which no longer seemed hostile to Iraq. King Fahd proposed to rapidly build an oil pipeline section connecting the oil fields in southern Iraq to the gigantic Saudi Petroline, which could transport vast quantities of oil to the Dhahran terminal on the Gulf, but most importantly to the port of Yanbu on the Red Sea. Ground was broken a few months later. The initial part inaugurated in fall 1985 would allow 500,000 barrels of Iraqi oil to be transported per day. Meanwhile, the "Guardian of the Two Holy Mosques," as King Fahd liked to be called, continued to exploit the 300,000 barrels extracted per day from the oil wells in the neutral zone to the sole profit of Iraq. He also organized the maritime transport of the few tens of thousands of barrels that the Iraqi industry was able to send to Saudi and Kuwaiti ports by road. Lastly, he increased the volume of bank loans granted to Baghdad.

Until the Turkish and Saudi pipelines were put in service, the Iraqi regime could now theoretically export a little more than one million barrels per day. Yet it was unable to achieve this export level because its production was in freefall and a growing portion of it was absorbed by the war. Meanwhile, Iran managed to extract a little more than two million barrels per day—twice Iraq's production—and export four-fifths of them. Its

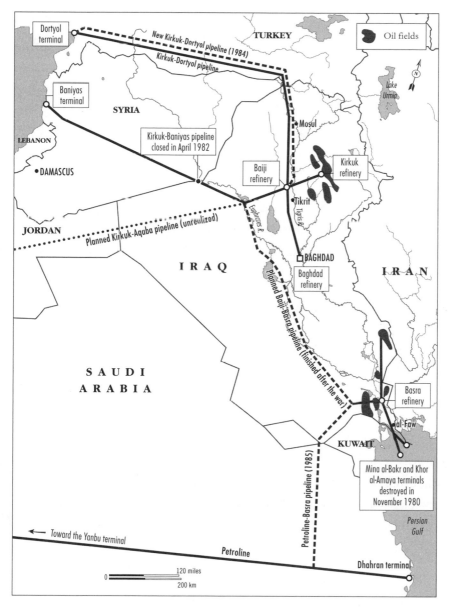

Iraqi oil network

coffers were filling up, which allowed Tehran to accelerate the pace of its military operations: since the coming of spring, its armed forces had returned to combat to liberate those territories still occupied by the enemy.

An Encouraging Victory

Iranian Chief of Staff of the Armed Forces General Nejad and General Shirazi, the commander of the ground army, had been studying the best strategy to adopt since late winter. Apart from the small pockets of Rashah and Nosud in Kurdistan, three border sectors remained under Iraqi control. The first extended from Qasr-e-Shirin to Mehran, at the north of the military disposition; the second centered around Fakkeh, facing Shush and Dezful; and the third included all of South Khuzestan, from Hoveyzeh to Khorramshahr. The first did not stand out as a priority, for the Iraqis were not threatening any essential objective in this mountainous region defended by troops solidly entrenched around the mountain passes. The third was the most important symbolically, but not the most urgent to recapture from a military perspective. The Iranian strategists therefore decided to focus their efforts on the sector of Shush. Their choice seemed logical in numerous regards. By attacking the center of the enemy layout, the Iranians were positioning themselves to strike its center of gravity in Amara, on the main Baghdad-Basra road. By doing so, they would divide the Iraqi army into several sections. If they anchored themselves in the center of the layout, they could easily swing their troops to one flank of the front or the other, based on necessity. It would be far more difficult for the Iraqis to execute similar maneuvers. The Iranian authorities also wanted to quickly regain control of oil facilities in the sector. For over a year the Iraqis had been pumping the oil gushing from the Dehloran, Musiyan, and Fakkeh oil fields, using the proceeds to fill Baghdad's coffers.

The Iranian chiefs of staff named the large offensive Fath ("Victory") and mobilized 120,000 men serving in four regular army divisions (the 21st, 77th, 84th, and 92nd), three Pasdaran divisions, two artillery brigades, one helicopter brigade, and the 55th Parachute Brigade. They gathered significant anti-aircraft resources as close as possible to the front line in order to repel the Iraqi air force.

Facing them, the Iraqi generals only had 40,000 men, but several hundred tanks. They were still counting on their tanks to stop the infantrymen. Their 1st Mechanized Division and 10th Armored Division were firmly dug in on the front line, ready to bear the attack's impact. The 11th, 14th, and 16th Infantry Divisions formed a second line of defense, close to the border. The 32nd Commando Brigade was entrenched outside Bostan. But Baghdad was primarily relying on its air force to hold back a potential Iranian breakthrough in this sector held by the 4th Corps.

On March 17, 1982, the Iranians launched Operation Fatimah in the direction of Hoveyzeh and Hamid. This was a diversionary attack intended to deceive their adversary regarding their actual intentions. The stratagem succeeded, for the Iraqi military command ordered the 14th Division to leave the Amarah-Fakkeh axis and make haste to Hoveyzeh. During the night of March 21 to 22 General Nejad and General Shirazi mounted their general offensive in the direction of Fakkeh. Chinook helicopters transported part of the 55th Parachute Brigade to the enemy's rear. Several paratrooper detachments sneak-attacked artillery positions about six miles (about ten kilometers) behind the front line. The Iraqi gunners, stunned to see heavily armed Iranian combatants appear behind them, were unable to react. The paratroopers destroyed roughly forty 130 mm howitzers, captured six officers, and boarded their helicopters to return to their lines. Concurrently, a 55th Parachute Brigade battalion was carried by helicopter to the surroundings of Ein Khosh and took control of the town without encountering any opposition. Since Ein Khosh was at the entrance of the gorges controlling the northern part of the battlefield, the Iranian victory isolated the Iraqi 1st Mechanized Division.

Meanwhile, two Pasdaran divisions deployed outside Shush and Naderi launched an attack on the Iraqi front lines to pin down their adversaries and prevent them from maneuvering. The waves of assault succeeded each other at a frenetic pace. The Iranian infantrymen got closer to the embankments and cut further into Iraqi defenses with every attack. Between two onslaughts, the Iranian artillery pounded the defense line. Partially muzzled, the Iraqi artillery was unable to effectively retaliate. For forty-eight hours human waves broke at the foot of Iraqi defenses, which began to waver and lack ammunition. For the first time in the war several thousand Basijis fought alongside the Pasdaran. Akbar Hashemi Rafsan-jani had traveled from Tehran to galvanize them, preemptively absolving them of all their sins, promising those who would die a martyr's death that they would immediately go to heaven. On the front he read the troops a message from the Ayatollah Khomeini, exhorting them to fight to their last breath for the glory of God, the Islamic Revolution, and the nation. Roused to fanaticism, the Iranian infantrymen tirelessly returned to the attack, undeterred by their losses. Several tank battalions from the 92nd Division were sent to support the Pasdaran and force the Iraqi tanks to hold their positions.

During the night of March 23 to 24 the Iranian generals launched the second phase of their offensive. Their 21st and 84th Mechanized Divisions infiltrated enemy lines, following stony, ploughed-up paths hard on the tanks' running gear and axles. The Iraqis had mined the area but left it unoccupied, thinking their enemy would be unable to advance on such rough terrain. While close to one hundred Iranian vehicles broke down, enough tanks succeeded in enveloping the Iraqi 1st and 10th divisions through a classic flanking maneuver. Meanwhile, two Revolutionary Guards brigades that were deployed to the north of the Iraqi positions struggled to advance on foot across a moonlike landscape alternating dunes and impassable rocky ridges, which were supposed to protect the 1st Mechanized Division's left flank. At dawn the Pasdaran came hurtling from the division's rear, taking its defenders from the back.

The situation further south was developing rapidly. As soon as the huge dust clouds kicked up by the Iranian mechanized divisions came into view, the 10th Armored Division's tank crews called the air force to the rescue—they had their own hands full repelling the Pasdaran's frontal attacks. About twenty Sukhois and MiGs quickly appeared over the bat-tlefield and strafed the Iranian columns. While they made direct hits, the Iraqis were severely challenged by the HAWK missile batteries deployed nearby; two Phantom and Tomcat patrols held as reinforcements were immediately sent to the spot. In a few minutes six Iraqi fighter planes were downed, and six others were damaged. For their part, the Mirage F-1 pilots brought down three Phantoms.

On March 25 the Iranians circumvented the Iraqi entrenchments. Bat-talions of dismounted infantrymen counterattacked in an attempt to push

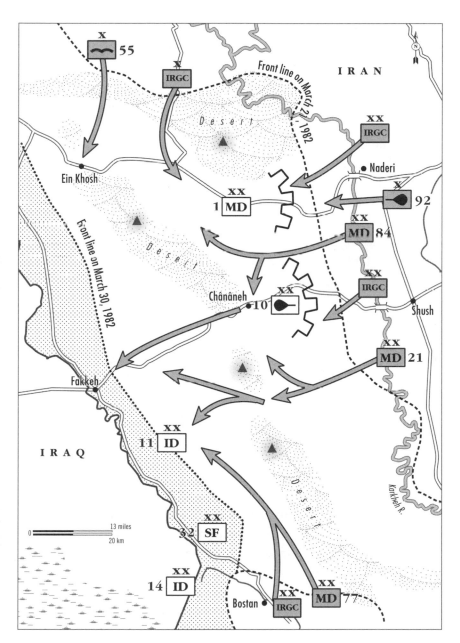

Iranian Undeniable Victory offensive (March 21–30, 1982)

back the assailant. They were rapidly overrun. At risk of being encircled, the two Iraqi divisions' commanders asked for authorization to retreat. Authorization was delayed to give the chiefs of staff time to get to Amarah and personally assess the situation's gravity. The Iranians took the opportunity to encircle and split the enemy layout. The 84th Division's lead brigade linked up with one of the two Pasdaran brigades that had positioned itself behind the Iraqi 1st Division. Meanwhile, the other two Iranian brigades converged near Chânâneh, taking this strategic crossroads in a pincer movement.

At dawn on March 26 both Iraqi divisions' commanders sounded the retreat. Their decision came at the very moment that the two Iranian mechanized divisions launched into combat. Throughout the day an apocalyptic tank battle developed around Chânâneh. Iranian Chieftains and T-59s chased the Iraqi T-55s and T-62s attempting to clear a passage for themselves toward the gorge controlling the road to Fakkeh, crushing any infantrymen who tried to stop them. A few mechanized battalions managed to clear a path through the Iranian layout. All the others were mercilessly wiped out. By nightfall the 1st Mechanized Division had been destroyed. General Dakhil Ali Hilali chose to surrender rather than face Saddam's wrath. The 10th Armored Division had lost all its artillery and two-thirds of its tanks, but was able to save one brigade, which would arduously make its way to Fakkeh by the next day.

On March 27 Iranian high command took advantage of the confusion in the Iraqi ranks to launch the third phase of its offensive, which it had since renamed Fath ol-Mobeen ("Undeniable Victory") in a surge of enthusiasm. The 77th Mechanized Division left the sector of Bostan supported by a heavy contingent of Pasdaran, skirted the 32nd Brigade, and pressed on to Fakkeh. It hoped to take control of this strategic crossroads, which commanded the road to Amarah, along the Tigris, thereby intercepting the retreat of units chaotically flooding back from Chânâneh along the same road. It quickly encountered two 11th Infantry Division brigades, which desperately tried to slow its progress. The Iraqi infantrymen bravely fought to hold it back, allowing the 10th Armored Division's survivors to reach Fakkeh and take refuge there. But they paid a heavy price and had to yield ground after losing two of their brigades.

Faced with this turn of events, the Iraqi president authorized the 4th Corps' units to retreat in order to save what could still be saved. As General Makki, then the commander of the neighboring 3rd Corps, would later point out: "Saddam may have been arrogant; he may have been strong-willed, but he was not a fool."[5] On March 29 Iraqi troops reestablished themselves about six miles (about ten kilometers) from the border, using the terrain as best they could to reconstitute a cohesive defense line. For their part the Iranians were intent on making the most of their advantage and had assembled several armored brigades in Chezareh to send them to assault Fakkeh. But they let themselves get carried away and committed a serious mistake. Their tanks hurtled down the rocky arid plain gently sloping to the Iraqi border without noticing that they had left the protected zone covered by the HAWK missile batteries deployed near Shush. Iraqi military command seized its chance and immediately launched an air attack on the armored columns. For thirty-six hours Iraqi fighters swept over the vast plain in rapid succession to stop the Iranian breakthrough. They destroyed close to one hundred tanks, forcing the Iranians to retreat. Saddam Hussein learned an essential lesson from this incident: when used wisely, the air force could stop an enemy breakthrough. It should therefore be used sparingly. He ordered that, henceforth, fire support missions should be given to attack helicopters in order to keep as many fighter planes as possible in reserve for extremely urgent strikes or missions considered relatively safe.

Meanwhile, the Iranian military high command reorganized its military disposition, supplemented its stock of ammunition, and moved the artillery closer to the new front line. Its troops regained control of Musiyan on their way. Despite the losses inflicted by the Iraqi air force, the Iranian generals knew that they had won their first major victory. In one week, they had advanced nearly forty miles (about sixty kilometers), reduced the largest Iraqi salient, and recaptured several oil fields, inflicting severe losses on the enemy: 400 tanks and armored vehicles and 150 artillery pieces had been destroyed or captured; 8,000 Iraqis killed; 10,000 taken prisoner; and three divisions—two-thirds of the 4th Corps—wiped out. The Iranians had even treated themselves to capturing an intact battery of lethal SAM-6 surface-to-air missiles, which they would study to develop adapted countermeasures. Victory came at a price of 4,000 dead, largely from the ranks of the Pasdaran, and 12,000 wounded, but these losses were quickly made up for. The destruction of 200 tanks and as many armored personnel carriers was more bothersome, but these would partially be replaced by equipment captured from the enemy. Overall, this brilliant maneuver, the fruit of excellent combined arms coordination, was considered a textbook case, which would be taught in Iranian military academies and serve as a model for the rest of the war.

The euphoric Iranian generals organized flights over the battlefield to show the press the scale of the Iraqi army's defeat. General Shirazi enthusiastically proclaimed: "We are going to write our own military manuals from now on with absolutely new tactics, that Americans, British and French can study at their staff colleges."[6] Numerous regular army officers, conscious that this victory was theirs, held their heads up high again and took the liberty to make a few disagreeable comments about the Pasdaran. The latter realized they had been used as cannon fodder to allow for the success of their brothers in arms. They complained to their commander, Mohsen Rezaee, who notified Rafsanjani.

On April 9, 1982, the Iranian government announced the arrest of Sadeq Ghotbzadeh, Bani-Sadr's former minister of foreign affairs, accusing him of having plotted to assassinate the Ayatollah Khomeini with traitorous officers who had remained loyal to the old regime. Sadeq Ghotbzadeh had stepped down from his position and become a businessman long before Bani-Sadr's exile. He now vehemently denied the accusations and put himself in the hands of Ayatollah Khomeini, whom he had fervently supported. He had accompanied him in his French exile and faithfully served him from the first days of the Revolution, becoming the head of national radio and television. On express orders from Ali Khamenei and Akbar Hashemi Rafsanjani, he was sent to the notorious Evin Prison, where he was most likely tortured. A few days later, a filmed confession in which he admitted having wanted to overthrow the regime was broadcast on television. In his confession Ghotbzadeh denounced numerous officers, who were immediately arrested. The revolutionary courts intruded on the army units, instilling a climate of terror among army brass, who were far more afraid of the regime than their Iraqi enemies. The president of the republic and the speaker of Parliament saw this as an excellent opportunity to purge the regular army again, reminding its offi-cers where power truly rested. They knew that the Revolutionary Guards were now a military and political force with which to be reckoned. The situation naturally poisoned the already difficult relations between the regular army and the Pasdaran and put a temporary halt to operations on the front. Military high command used the opportunity to redeploy four divisions to Susangerd and Ahwaz in preparation for a future offensive.

On April 18, a day of celebration of the armed forces, the Ayatollah Khomeini made an appeasing speech and called for reconciliation be-tween the regular army and the Revolutionary Guards, recalling that all military personnel, no matter their affiliation, must be guided by the same desire to protect the nation and the Islamic Revolution. He did not, how-ever, pardon Sadeq Ghotbzadeh, who was now held incommunicado, or the seventy officers accused of participating in the plot. They were all dis-creetly executed the following summer. What could not be denied was that the regular army officers had gotten the message and would no longer dare to defy the regime or the Pasdaran. But many of them would also no longer be willing to risk their lives for the glory of the regime. Officers from the ranks of the Pasdaran would take advantage of this situation to impose themselves and monopolize the principal positions of power, durably transforming the makeup of the Iranian armed forces.

[Chapter 13]

New Mediation

In late April 1982 the Organization of Islamic Cooperation (OIC) attempted to mediate between Iran and Iraq under the leadership of the Tunisian Habib Chatty. His plan could be summarized in four points: 1) Iraqi withdrawal from the territory occupied since September 1980; 2) the establishment of a buffer force provided by OIC member states; 3) the creation of an international committee to arbitrate the Shatt al-Arab conflict; 4) the setting up of a commission to evaluate the damages suffered by Iran. To lend the OIC's proposal more weight, the Gulf Cooperation Council stated it was prepared to open a compensation fund for Iran. Seeking to break its isolation, Tehran responded favorably to these overtures. General Nejad publicly announced a message from the Iranian authorities stating that their army was defensive by nature and was therefore designed neither to continue the war nor invade its neighbors once its territory had been liberated. Nonetheless, the Ayatollah Khomeini remained inflexible regarding three demands: 1) Saddam Hussein had to go, 2) Iraq had to recognize its responsibility for the outbreak of hostilities, 3) Iraq had to repatriate the Shiites expelled in spring 1980. Naturally, the Iraqi dictator rejected these conditions across the board.

To make matters more complicated, the Algerian government quietly torpedoed the OIC's peace plan, priding itself that it could convince the Iranians to accept a ceasefire. Irritated by the Algerian authorities' arrogance, Saddam Hussein accused them of systematically favoring the Iranian side. He decided to teach them a lesson. On May 3, 1982, he ordered the commercial Gulfstream carrying Algerian foreign minister Mohammed Seddik Ben Yahia shot down. Ben Yahia was traveling to Tehran with several of his collaborators to convince the Iranian authorities to accept Algerian mediation and coordinate a mutual position for the upcoming OPEC meeting. Baghdad had easy access to the details of this regularly scheduled flight. As the Algerian Gulfstream approached the border between Turkey, Iran, and Iraq, it was brought down without warning by a long-range missile fired by a marauding Iraqi MiG-25.[1] There were no survivors. The Algerians unleashed their fury at both belligerents, without knowing exactly who to blame for the treacherous attack, since both the Iraqis and the Iranians accused each other of shooting down the plane.[2] Yet the message to the Algerian authorities was received loud and clear; from this point on, they no longer interfered in the conflict.

The International Community at a Loss

The United Nations (UN) had also failed to convince the belligerents to put an end to hostilities. A mere five days after the war's outbreak, the UN Security Council had unanimously adopted Resolution 479 asking both parties to abstain from resorting to force and calling on the international community to do everything in its power to avoid the conflict's expansion. For once Washington and Moscow had put aside their rivalry and immediately endorsed the resolution without endless quibbling, a clear sign of their concern regarding the situation. Since then UN Secretary General Kurt Waldheim had made every effort to convince Baghdad and Tehran to put down their weapons. On several occasions Saddam Hussein had said he was ready to agree to a "peace of braves" with the Iranian government if it recognized the borders set by international treaties. In other words, the Iraqi president was ready to put an end to the war if the Iranians gave up their claim to the Shatt al-Arab. Ali Khamenei and Akbar Hashemi Rafsanjani met each proposal with the scathing response that "the one who wants peace must first bring his troops back behind his borders." Disappointed by this dead-end dialogue, Olof Palme, the UN's special representative in the Middle East, shifted his focus to negotiations for prisoner exchanges, working closely with the International Committee of the Red Crescent (ICRC).

In the meantime the nonaligned countries, led by India and Cuba, shuttled between Tehran and Baghdad to try and find their own negotiated end to the conflict. They were no more successful than the UN, the OIC, or the Arab League. As the leader of the nonaligned, Indian prime minister Indira Gandhi condemned the use of violence and refused to take sides with either of the belligerents. She nonetheless reinforced India's economic ties with Iran, taking advantage of Tehran's isolation to impose trade conditions highly favorable to New Delhi. In exchange for oil purchased at a bargain price, India provided Iran with textiles and common consumer goods to supplement those delivered by Turkey. Yet the Indian authorities initially refused to ship Tehran any weapons. Beginning in 1985 Indian prime minister Rajiv Gandhi, who was far less scrupulous than his mother, gave in to Iranian commercial pressure and agreed to send Tehran "defensive" military equipment (primarily light boats and Soviet-designed torpedoes manufactured under license in India and used to arm Pasdaran gun boats).

Guarded Indifference in the Rest of the World

Pakistani president Zia-ul-Haq also unsuccessfully attempted to mediate between Baghdad and Tehran on several occasions. Despite his stated neutrality, he took advantage of geographic proximity and Iran's isolation to increase his volume of commercial exchanges with Iran tenfold over a few years, expanding Pakistan's revenue from forty million dollars in 1980 to 400 million in 1985. However, he refused to deliver Tehran weapons in order to preserve both his status as an arbitrator of the Islamic cause and his lucrative relationship with Saudi Arabia, which was hostile to Iran. This did not stop numerous Pakistani traffickers from clandestinely providing the ayatollahs with light weapons and spare parts for Chinese weapons, once the latter began reaching the front in vast quantities. For its part, the Pakistani army discreetly trained the Iranian pilots responsible for putting in service the F-6 and F-7 fighters delivered by China, which were identical to those used by the Pakistani air force.

The rest of Asia took a more guarded approach to the conflict. Japan did not dare endanger its extraordinary industrial boom by making any statement liable to upset the Middle Eastern nations that provided it with oil. The other Southeast Asian "dragons" (South Korea, Taiwan, and Singapore) also declared their neutrality, but discreetly supplied weapons and spare parts to the Iranians, who paid top dollar and in cash. In Africa and Latin America, only Brazil and South Africa got involved with the belligerents, securing outlets for their rapidly developing arms industries despite their façades of neutrality.

In the Gulf the belligerents' inflexibility revived the Gulf Cooperation Council's (GCC) security agenda. An internal security treaty was made by five of the six council members, authorizing their security forces to intervene on each other's territory to combat any destabilization effort operated from abroad. This agreement was coupled with bilateral defense treaties linking Saudi Arabia with the GCC's other members, which allowed Riyadh to increase its military cooperation with its neighbors. In 1983 a series of bombings on Kuwaiti and Saudi territories convinced the GCC leaders to establish the foundations of a common military force. This unit, named "Peninsula Shield," would comprise battalions provided by five of the six GCC member states, Kuwait having refused to participate. This symbolic military force, headed by a Saudi, was deployed in Hafar Al-Batin, Saudi Arabia, near the Iraqi and Kuwaiti borders. Tentative exercises were first carried out there in October 1983, revealing the mediocre abilities of a unit that would never see combat, including during the Second Gulf War of 1990–1991 (the unit did interfere to put down the Shiite rebellion in Bahrain in spring 2011).

Only Kuwait refused to be part of the force, continuing to reject the presence of foreign troops on its soil. Despite this strained situation, the Saudi generals were able to convince their other partners that it would be beneficial to develop an integrated air defense system using American technical support. Washington could thus coordinate the defense of the Persian Gulf's south shore and keep a closer watch on both belligerents' air activity.

Washington Initiates Rapprochement with Baghdad

In the late spring of 1982 U.S. secretary of state George Schultz implemented a new regional policy aimed to improve U.S. credibility in the Middle East. He hoped to distance himself from his predecessor, Alexander Haig, who had often been accused of ignoring the Arabs. Schultz's two priorities were to accelerate a settlement of the Palestinian problem—even if it meant putting pressure on Israel—and to support Iraq, in order to reduce the threat Iran posed to the Gulf monarchies. George Schultz had no compunction about making a potential alliance with Saddam Hussein to better contain Iran, for the Iraqis were now in a bad position. According to Pentagon analysts, the Iraqi army might not hold out much longer against Iranian troops' repeated attacks. Iraq's collapse would play into the Iranians' hands, naturally, but also into the Soviets', if they took the opportunity to launch a military intervention. Iranian—potentially even Soviet—military divisions would then be in a position to quickly and unexpectedly attack neighboring oil monarchies. There was no guarantee that the American Rapid Deployment Force on standby to be sent to the Gulf was enough to dissuade them, particularly if the Kuwaitis and Saudis continued to resist the presence of American troops on their soil. For all of the above reasons, the Iraqi shield had to be kept in place and Washington had to help, albeit discreetly, to avoid casting doubt on its stated neutrality. The American administration's position was neatly summed up by Brent Scowcroft, one of the Republican Party's most influential advisors: "[the] tilt toward Baghdad during the Iran-Iraq conflict [was] not out of preference for one of two reprehensible regimes, but because we wanted neither to win the war and were worried that Iraq would prove to be the weaker."[3]

Since the previous year several events had contributed to alleviating Washington's reservations about Baghdad. For one, the destruction of the Osirak nuclear power plant had implicitly put an end to Iraq's clandestine program to acquire nuclear military capability, which meant the Iraqi regime was no longer a vital threat to Israel. Next, the clergy's rise to power in Tehran had buried any hope of a rapprochement between Iran and the United States. Finally, King Hussein of Jordan and Egyptian president Hosni Mubarak's repeated entreaties had convinced Ronald Reagan that it was necessary for him to support Iraq.

The American president authorized the CIA to secretly provide military equipment to Iraq, on condition that it was not American-made.[4] Large quantities of Soviet-made weapons and ammunition were purchased on the gray market and delivered to Iraq. To convince the Iraqis that his proposal was in earnest, Ronald Reagan sent CIA veteran Tom Twetten to Iraq to give the authorities satellite photos of the front. A few weeks later Reagan persuaded Congress to remove Iraq from the list of states supporting terrorism. This decision made it possible to reestablish bilateral commercial ties, bank loans, and American investments in Iraq. It also paved the way for a potential resumption of diplomatic relations.

In fact, Washington had not waited until the spring of 1982 to initiate a rapprochement with Baghdad. On April 12, 1981, Morris Draper, a high-ranking diplomat, had traveled to the Iraqi capital to establish informal first contacts. Though he was received coolly, and his visit had not led to anything concrete, communication had been reestablished. The visit had also not gone unnoticed by Iranian intelligence services. As if by coincidence, the Iranian navy boarded and searched the *Western Sea,* an American oceanographic vessel suspected of being a spy boat, when it briefly strayed into Iranian territorial waters a few days later. With the hostage crisis fresh in everyone's mind, the incident led to a spike in tension. Washington demanded the immediate release of the nineteen crew members. After holding the Americans in its jails for a few days, Tehran freed them with a reminder to the U.S. government that it had committed to remain neutral toward both belligerents. The message was intended to be crystal clear: if the United States got too close to Iraq, it would have to bear the consequences.

The United States was not alone in revising its attitude toward the belligerents. In Moscow, the Kremlin faced a difficult dilemma: on the one hand, its members were inclined to maintain Saddam Hussein's regime under embargo to attempt to accelerate the end of hostilities; on the other, they could not allow Iraq to collapse. An Iraqi routing would be too detrimental to Soviet credibility in the region. Now the Soviets' advisors in Baghdad were sending back alarming reports emphasizing the Iraqi army's inability to contend with the Iranian combatants' persistence. Moreover, the Soviet leaders no longer had any illusions about the theocratic nature of the Iranian regime, which was daily proving more aggressive toward the USSR and openly arming the mujahidin in Afghanistan. It was clear to everyone in Moscow that the inspiring idea of opening up to Iran had had its day and that it was time to move on. Yet, the Politburo's elders were paralyzed by the approaching power shift at the Kremlin. Mikhail Suslov, the Party's ideologue, had died a few months earlier and, Leonid Brezhnev was at death's door. No one dared to make a decision that could be held against him when the time came to appoint the Party's new secretary general. Reacting to this immobilism, Marshall Ustinov, still the Iraqi regime's most faithful advocate, managed to convince his peers to accept that heavy weapons be urgently delivered to Baghdad. He reminded them that Iraq had proposed ceasefires on numerous occasions, all of which were rejected by the Iranian mullahs. Faced with Tehran's rigidity, Moscow was bound to honor its defense agreement with Baghdad. After all, he argued, Saddam had shown his good will toward the Kremlin by releasing 280 Communist officials from Iraqi prisons the previous month. Never mind that these Communist activists were sent directly to the front to fight the Iranian invader. . . . The Iraqi army soon started receiving T-72 and BMP-1 tanks, AT-4 Spigot antitank missiles, SAM-6 and SAM-9 surface-to-air missiles, thirty MiG-21s, and four Osa II missile boats to replace those sunk at the beginning of the war. But the Iraqis would still have to wait a while for the latest generation in weaponry.

Iranian Kurdistan

In early April 1982 Abdul Rahman Ghassemlou, the leader of the Iranian Kurds, launched an attempt to recapture the cities lost the previous fall. He succeeded in assembling 30,000 peshmergas, backed by the tanks and artillery pieces seized the previous year. Thanks to Baghdad's generosity, his combatants now had a significant number of machine guns, antitank rocket launchers, and recoilless guns.[5] Supported by part of the population, he took hold of the cities of Sanandaj, Saqqez, Bukan, and Mahabad, all of which were thus changing hands for the third time in less than a year. However, his troops made no headway outside Piranshahr, which was staunchly held by a regular army brigade. Further south, the PDKI leader did not even attempt to seize the Marivan garrison, which was unassailable since it had been reinforced during the winter. On the heels of this success, Ghassemlou contacted Bani-Sadr to offer him to return to Iran to establish a parallel government advocating the ouster of Imam Khomeini from the mountains of Kurdistan. The former president cautiously declined the offer, preferring to remain in his Parisian exile, an ideal setting to write his memoirs. Bani-Sadr knew that if he made the mistake of getting involved in openly contesting the mullahs' regime, he would lose the Supreme Leader's goodwill once and for all and would immediately become a target for killers dispatched by the SAVAMA, the ayatollahs' political police. The Ayatollah Khomeini had publicly denounced Bani-Sadr, but had thus far continued to extend his protection to him, for he had genuine affection for his former fellow-in-exile.

The Iranian authorities quickly launched a counteroffensive. General Shirazi headed the operation, which mobilized 80,000 men supported by 300 tanks, 150 artillery pieces, and fifty helicopters. In two months the Iranians regained control of the four cities they had lost and pushed the peshmergas back to their mountains, knowing that they would be out of commission for the summer because they would need to be at home to participate in their community's rural work. The peshmergas still found safe haven at home in the mountains, for the Iranians did not have enough troops to flush them out. However, Iranian soldiers fiercely clamped down on those who had supported the insurgents. General Shirazi earned both the nickname "man of iron" and the regime's gratitude by personally taking part in these operations.

[Chapter 14]

The Iranians Recapture Their Territory

On April 30, 1982, the Iranians launched the Beit ul-Muqaddas ("Holy City") offensive to recapture Khorramshahr and drive the Iraqis out of Khuzestan once and for all. General Nejad and General Shirazi mobilized every man available for this operation: twelve divisions positioned from Musiyan to Abadan, more than half of which were controlled by the Pasdaran, as well as eleven independent brigades.[1] They did not hesitate to call up battalions deployed on the Soviet, Afghan, and Pakistani borders, requisitioning every one of the air force's Boeings to transport them to the front lines. Overall, they had 200,000 men, 1,000 tanks, 600 cannons, and close to 100 helicopters.[2] Their weak point was their lack of air strike capacity. The air force was facing major logistical problems. Its munitions and spare parts had disappeared into thin air, equipment deliveries currently did not suffice to replace them, and its engineers had been unable to crack the codes to allow them to identify and manage the stocks of spare parts scattered over its bases.

Additionally the regime was still wary of its pilots and only authorized the absolute minimum number of sorties, favoring interception and reconnaissance missions, the only types of missions that did not pose any threat, since the aircraft assigned to them did not carry bombs powerful enough to destroy government bunkers. The Iranian military high command was counting on its batteries of Hawk surface-to-air missiles, which had been brought closer to the front, to prevent the Iraqi air force from flying over the battlefield. Iranian fighter planes were asked not to venture over the front to avoid friendly fire—their artillerymen had been ordered to systematically engage with any jets flying over their zone. Facing them, the Iraqis only had five divisions (the 3rd, 5th, 6th, 9th, and 14th) and ten autonomous brigades comprising 65,000 men, 500 tanks, and as many artillery pieces. Half of their forces were deployed in the area of Khorramshahr, with the other half staggered between Amarah and Hamid. However, the general commanding the 3rd Corps could rely on significant air support.

The Liberation of Khorramshahr

Shortly before dawn a battalion of parachutists was dropped on the Karun's western bank, near Darkhovin, to establish a bridgehead. The Iranian sappers immediately got to work building pontoon bridges. With the first light of day, hordes of Revolutionary Guards rushed to the other side of the river, encouraged by deafening "Allahu Akbars" played at top volume over dozens of loudspeakers. Thinking they were under attack from several enemy divisions, the Iraqis responsible for holding the sector took to their heels. The Iranian 88th Armored Division crossed the Karun and expanded the bridgehead toward Hosseinieh, but was careful to avoid seizing the town to prevent the Iraqis from panicking. The Iranian tactic was to leave the Iraqis in the dark about where the major assault would take place so that they would not know where to gather their troops.

While the 84th Division launched a diversionary attack on Fakkeh in the north of Khuzestan, the 30th and 77th Divisions moved in the center, in the Susangerd sector, and pushed the Iraqi 9th Division back to Hoveyzeh. Near Ahwaz the 21st and 40th Divisions forced the Iraqi 5th and 6th Divisions back beyond Hamid. General al-Qadhi, the commander of the Iraqi 3rd Corps, hesitated about how to respond and where to focus his effort to contain the Iranians. A visit from General Shamshal, the chief of staff of the armed forces, provided him a chance to ask for advice. The general pusillanimously responded, "I don't know. You are the corps commander, you decide."[3] The 3rd Corps' commander finally opted for an elastic defense with what remained of his armored and mechanized troops. The Iranians took advantage of the Iraqis' procrastination to commit their 23rd Special Forces Brigade and their 25th and 58th Infantry Divisions, which had thus far been held back as reinforcements.

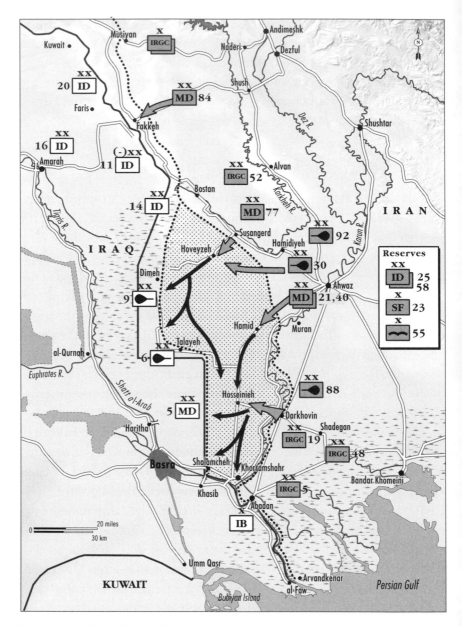

Iranian Holy City offensive (April 30–May 24, 1982)

During the night of May 7 to 8 the Iranians launched the second phase of their offensive. After a brutal artillery shelling, the Iranian divisions deployed between Susangerd and Muran overwhelmed the Iraqi 6th and 9th Armored Divisions and chased them to the border. The 9th Division disintegrated and—given its poor performance—was permanently removed from the Iraqi order of battle. Three days earlier Saddam had intervened to save its commander, General Tala al-Duri, a protégé whose loyalty and courage he valued, by appointing him to another command.[4] He replaced him at the last minute with General Kamal Latif, for whom he did not care, and who was held responsible for the defeat and executed. This anecdote is illustrative of the mind-set in Iraqi military high command at the time and explains certain generals' spinelessness.

A little further south, the 88th Armored Division raced toward the Iraqi border and seized control of Hosseinieh. Saddam Hussein had no choice but to have his troops retreat to Khorramshahr. The sector was defended by 35,000 men supported by one hundred tanks.

On May 12 the Iranians set up camp outside the city but held off on attacking to wait for the arrival of several Pasdaran divisions. Akbar Hashemi Rafsanjani had been perfectly clear: Khorramshahr had to be liberated by the Revolutionary Guards. They had been waiting for months for this well-deserved symbolic victory, which was to allow them to establish themselves as the driving element of the Iranian armed forces. The general staff took advantage of this respite to restock munitions, as well as drinking water, for the weather was becoming sweltering. It chartered buses to transport several thousands of young volunteers, who were sent straight to the front lines. Eventually the Iranians had assembled 80,000 men to attack the 35,000 Iraqis entrenched on the Persian Wall and inside Khorramshahr.

During the night of May 19 to 20 the Iranian artillery let loose, forcing the Iraqis to hole up in their positions. In the meantime the 55th Parachute Brigade, which had been carried by helicopter to the surroundings of Shalamcheh, took control of the town and destroyed the pontoon bridge over the Shatt al-Arab, isolating the Khorramshahr garrison. At dawn the Iranians assaulted the city. For forty-eight hours dozens of waves of fanatical Pasdaran crashed down on the Persian Wall. Mohsen Rezaee

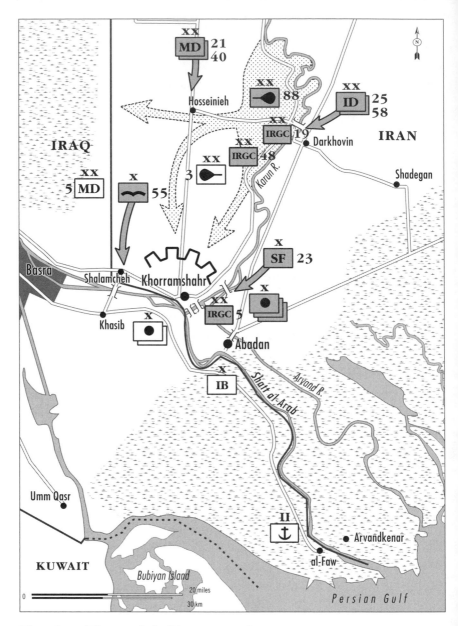

Liberation of Khorramshahr (May 8–24, 1982)

and Ali Shamkhani supervised operations. On the front lines they had read the troops a message from the Ayatollah Khomeini inciting the combatants to martyrdom. For this decisive battle they had called upon their best generals, who would fight like lions: Rahim Safavi, Hossein Kharrazi, and Mohammad Bagher Ghalibaf, all under twenty-five years old, but each in command of a division. Stunned by the fury, determination, and self-sacrifice of their assailants, the city's defenders felt like they had been transported back to the Dark Ages. On May 22 they began to flag. The exhausted men were nearly out of ammunition. The more enemy troops they killed, the more came at them.

The following night three Iranian divisions succeeded in breaching the Persian Wall, which had collapsed in several places under repeated artillery and tank fire. At dawn they spread out inside the city, while three other divisions encircled it, cutting off any potential retreat for the defenders. Iraqi pilots tried to break the Iranian troops' momentum by relentlessly strafing the columns of infantrymen. They failed to stop them, suffering heavy losses in the attempt (about thirty aircraft). On the ground the situation had turned into a rout. The panicked Iraqis abandoned their vehicles and tried to get to the Shatt al-Arab to cross on inflatable dinghies, makeshift rafts, or even by swimming. Barely 40 percent of them reached the opposite bank. The others were killed or captured. The few units that bravely tried to slow the Iranian advance were mercilessly wiped out. The galvanized Pasdaran were ready to make any sacrifice to give their leaders a victory. Nothing could stop them. By nightfall the Iranians had taken 12,000 prisoners. On May 24, 1982, the Iranian regime proclaimed the liberation of Khorramshahr, a city twice martyred. This saga would inspire the Iranian filmmaker Khosrow Sinai to make *Dar kouchehay-e eshq (In the Alleys of Love)*, an intimate, beautifully realized account of the battle that far surpasses the usual propaganda clichés. The loss of Khorramshahr was a terrible defeat for the Iraqis, who sustained 8,000 dead, 19,000 prisoners (including soldiers captured in other sectors), and more than 15,000 wounded, plus destroyed or seized equipment: 250 tanks, 300 other armored vehicles, and about 100 cannons. Though they had a victory to crow about, the Iranians also suffered heavy losses: between 12,000 and 15,000 dead, 25,000 wounded, and 400 tanks destroyed.

Strategic Withdrawal

The fall of Khorramshahr effectively ended the Iraqi president's crusade. Bitter but lucid, Saddam Hussein had to recognize his endeavor had failed. He now had to save face, find a way to put an end to the war, and sacrifice some scapegoats. He feared that the army and the party might hold him accountable for the disastrous toll: there were 30,000 dead, 35,000 prisoners, and twice as many wounded; half the ground forces committed to the invasion of Iran had been put out of commission; and the Iraqi army had lost 20 percent of its artillery, 40 percent of its aircraft, and 60 percent of its tank fleet. And all for naught, since the Iranian army had recaptured nine-tenths of the territory conquered. The Iranians had set up camp along the Shatt el-Arab and now threatened Basra. On May 28 they even launched two coordinated attacks on Qasr-e-Shirin and Sumer, hoping that the demoralized Iraqis would surrender the two towns without much resistance. The Iranian generals were mistaken. The Iraqi troops clung fiercely to their positions, knowing that the fall of these cities would open the path to Baghdad to their enemy.

Saddam Hussein took advantage of this timely success to regain control. He congratulated General Aziz, commander of the Qasr-e-Shirin and Sumer sectors, and cracked down on the officers he considered responsible for the Khorramshahr debacle to remind the others of their allegiance and duties. Upon his orders some twenty senior officers were relieved of their command. A military court immediately convened in Basra to try them. Ten were found guilty and executed, including generals al-Qadhi, Shitnah, and Latif, respectively the former commanders of the 3rd Army Corps and the 3rd and 9th Divisions. Several members of the military high command were dismissed or sidelined, notably General Shamshal, who was replaced as head of military high command (and of ground forces) by General Abdul Jawad Dhannoun, the former director of military intelligence. General al-Janabi was replaced as commander of the navy by his deputy General al-Kabi.

Meanwhile, the Iraqi president courted his minorities. He appointed a Kurd, Taha Maruf, vice-president of the Revolutionary Command Council. Though the position was purely honorary, the appointment reassured the Kurdish population. Several colonels of Kurdish or Shiite background were promoted to general. The regime also restored the Shiite mausoleums in Najaf and Karbala. Finally, Saddam started a national loan program to accelerate the completion of a number of large-scale construction projects, notably in the Kurdish provinces, and to create a compensation fund for war casualties, whose families were granted numerous social advantages. Saddam did not hesitate to have his smiling portrait printed on each national treasury bond to comfort the population and convince it to massively invest in this loan.

On June 6, 1982, the Israeli government, led by Menachem Begin, ordered the invasion of South Lebanon to chase down the Palestinian guerilla forces that had taken shelter there for over a decade. Begin's stated justification for the assault was the recent attack on his ambassador to London, which was attributed to the PLO, but actually executed by the notorious Abu Nidal, the Palestinian-born terrorist who always worked for the highest bidder. Saddam Hussein immediately latched on to this situation, which created a diversion at just the right time. Standing before a crowd of international journalists, he announced he was ready to put an end to hostilities with Iran and to bring his troops back to Iraq in order to send his army to fight the Israeli aggressor. Akbar Hashemi Rafsanjani, stunned by Saddam's naiveté, took him at his word and asked him by way of the media to let the Iranian army cross Iraq to Lebanon, hoping to drive the Iraqi dictator into a corner.

On June 10 Saddam Hussein unilaterally proclaimed a ceasefire and accepted the principal conditions decreed by Tehran: withdrawal from the conquered territories and payment of reparations via voluntary contributions made by the Arab states supporting Baghdad. He explicitly recognized the border delineation as defined by the Algiers Accord of 1975, took responsibility for starting the war—though he referred to an "imposed war"—and allowed that if Iranian troops were sent to Lebanon he would grant them right of passage. However, the Iraqi dictator categorically rejected two of the Iranians' demands: his stepping down and the repatriation of the 100,000 Shiites expelled to Iran before the beginning of hostilities. Saddam had taken a gamble on the Iranians proving rational and seizing the opportunity to put an end to the war now that their territory had been liberated and most of their demands met. If they were to decline, he counted on the active solidarity of his Arab allies, who should allow him to keep up a war of attrition, for he imagined that the Iranians could no longer launch large-scale operations against Iraq. Like the Iraqis, the Iranians were exhausted and had suffered major losses since the beginning of the war (50,000 dead and 5,000 prisoners). The most probable scenario, according to Saddam's chiefs of staff, was a return to the antebellum situation characterized by artillery duels and frequent border skirmishes.

One question remains unanswered to this day: did Saddam order the elimination of Shlomo Argov, the Israeli ambassador in London, to spark another war in the Middle East and give himself a handy reason to justify his ceasefire without losing face? It is a possibility, if one is to believe the persuasive hypotheses of Patrick Seale, an investigative journalist specializing in Middle Eastern affairs and the author of a remarkable biography of Abu Nidal, as well as those of historians Martin Van Creveld and Rob Johnson, who demonstrate that neither Syria, the PLO, Libya, nor Iran had anything to gain by triggering another war with Israel at that time, unlike the Iraqi president, who would be provided both with a convenient pretext to put an end to his war with Tehran and a means to punish Israel for the destruction of the Osirak nuclear power plant.[5] Yet nothing in the audiotapes seized in Baghdad in 2003 or in the transcripts of Saddam Hussein's interrogations has confirmed the theory.

In any case, the ceasefire proposal was staunchly supported by King Fahd of Saudi Arabia, who declared he was ready to pay fifty billion dollars cash to persuade the Iranian government to accept the Iraqi offer. This colossal sum was supposed to cover the damages Iran had suffered since the beginning of the war. Yet the Iranians proved to be fierce negotiators and demanded 150 billion dollars, probably in hopes of getting one hundred billion. Offended, the Saudi monarch withdrew his offer and more clearly aligned himself with Iraq. For the first time since the beginning of hostilities—and with Washington's blessing—he delivered directly to the Iraqi air force American-made precision-guided munitions to allow it to increase its bombing accuracy.

Despite Tehran's categorical refusal, Saddam Hussein ordered his troops to withdraw from the occupied territories in Iran and reposition themselves on the international border on June 20, 1982, thus taking the risk of opening the Iraqi plains and the road to Baghdad to the Iranians.

This strategic withdrawal was effective nine days later, putting an end to the war's second phase. The Iraqi president also convened the Ninth Ba'ath Congress, obtaining the party's full discharge for his management of the war at a time when criticisms were beginning to be heard. Nipping the rebellion in the bud, he eliminated several of his detractors as an example. Minister of Health Ibrahim Hussein, who had suggested that Saddam momentarily step down, was sent to the firing squad after a joke of a trial. Saddam Hussein took advantage of this new purge to impose a restrained party leadership and to restrict the Revolutionary Command Council to its first circle: Adnan Khairallah, his first cousin and minister of defense; Ali Hassan al-Majid, another cousin and the head of intelligence services; Barzan Ibrahim al-Tikriti, his half-brother and supervisor of the secret police; his son-in-law Hussein Kamel; Tariq Aziz, his minister of foreign affairs; Taha Yassin Ramadan, the commander of the Popular Army; Izzat Ibrahim al-Douri, deputy minister of defense; and Chief of Police Sabawi Ibrahim al-Tikriti. He told them that by returning to the positions held before September 22, 1980, he had stripped the Iranian regime of any moral justification for carrying on the war, thus putting the responsibility for its potential continuation on Tehran. If this were to happen, Tehran's expansionist ambitions would undoubtedly lead the major powers to stand up for Saddam. In this regard he proved clear-sighted. As a military attaché posted in Baghdad wrote at the time: "Psychologically, Iraq has already lost the war. The Khorramshahr defeat bodes poorly for Baghdad's capacity going forward to put a stop to the forced exporting of the Iranian Islamic Revolution."[6]

Rafsanjani and Khomeini Agree to Continue the War

The announcement of the ceasefire and the Iraqi withdrawal promptly led to a pivotal debate in Tehran. Should hostilities be continued and the war brought to the heart of Iraqi territory? Ayatollah Khomeini, faithful to his role as an arbiter, initially refused to pronounce himself, choosing instead to listen to both sides' arguments. Ayatollah Montazeri had the support of the majority of the clergy in stating that he was against continuing the war, arguing that after twenty months of deadly conflict, the population yearned for peace. Ali Khamenei was also against war. He had always prioritized the internal front and wanted to focus all his efforts on the struggle against the regime's opponents. The People's Mujahidin were still carrying out terrorist attacks in large cities, though their operational commander Moussa Khiabani had been killed a few weeks earlier. The Tudeh Communist Party militants, living semi-clandestinely, could still take up arms. In Kurdistan Province the peshmergas had been pushed back to the mountains, but not wiped out. The independence fighters in the provinces of Azerbaijan and Baluchistan had been put down, but it would only take a major setback elsewhere for the rebellion to rise again. More prosaically, Khamenei feared that a continued war against Baghdad could allow his rival Rafsanjani to gather laurels and increase his chances of imposing himself as the next Supreme Leader. Prime Minister Mousavi and Minister of Defense Salimi did not have a say in the matter. They were mere subordinates charged with implementing the mullahs' decisions. The army's leadership also had serious reservations, emphasizing the scale of the losses they had sustained. Devastated divisions had not been able to be reconstituted, despite the massive influx of new recruits.

Alone against everyone, Akbar Hashemi Rafsanjani insisted on continuing the war. As an astute psychologist and master manipulator, he put forward the decisive argument that the Ayatollah Khomeini hoped to hear: Saddam Hussein had to be punished and overthrown in order to give Iraqi Shiites a chance to seize power and turn Iraq into an Islamic Republic on the Iranian model. Every effort had to be made to humiliate the Iraqi dictator and precipitate the fall of the Ba'athist regime. The cost of reaching this strategic objective was a secondary matter. The speaker of Parliament cast doubt on Saddam's good faith and wagered that his army would not withdraw from all the territory conquered. Events proved Rafsanjani right, for the Iraqi troops kept control of a few ridges against the border, between Qasr-e-Shirin and Fakkeh, to protect access to Baghdad. The extension of combat therefore appeared legitimate to Rafsanjani, particularly since it would likely continue to stoke revolutionary fervor and unite the Iranian people around the mullahs while destroying the previous regime's social structure. Rafsanjani reminded the Supreme Leader that the Iranian army, which had repelled the best Iraqi troops, should not encounter major difficulties in bringing them to their knees.

By attacking immediately, the regime could turn the Iraqi withdrawal into a major Iranian victory.

With the help of the young head of propaganda, Mohammad Khatami, Akbar Hashemi Rafsanjani backed his analysis by flooding the Supreme Leader with statistics and reports showing that Iran had sufficient financial and demographic resources to deal the deathblow and bring down the Iraqi regime. In lobbying for the continuation of hostilities, the speaker of Parliament was actually maneuvering to reinforce the power he drew from his status as a war chief, which gave him authority and control over the entire state apparatus, as well as the country's economy. A prolonged war effort would allow him to increase his personal fortune; a victory over Iraq would allow him to impose himself as the country's uncontested leader after the Supreme Leader's death. On the other hand, the end of hostilities would probably lead him to lose his grip and would play into Ali Khamenei's hands. Once again, the core of Iranian politics was dominated by the relentless struggle for supreme power. Mohsen Rezaee and Ali Shamkhani, the heads of the Pasdaran, supported Rafsanjani, for they knew that continuing the war would bring them a degree of power to which they could not otherwise lay claim.

The Ayatollah Khomeini decided in Rafsanjani's favor and called on the other Iranian leaders to support his decision. General Shirazi announced his support for the speaker of Parliament. On June 22, 1982, he proclaimed: "The war will continue until Saddam is overthrown, so that we can go pray in Najaf, Karbala, and Jerusalem." Rafsanjani drove the point home by publicly stating that "the path to Jerusalem goes through Karbala and the elimination of the Iraqi Ba'athist regime."[7] To give the decision more weight, the Iranian government led the Iranian people to believe that the Iraqi army was still occupying a significant part of Iran, thereby justifying the war's continuation.

The Iranian military high command immediately started preparing a general offensive against Iraq. Its plan consisted of breaching the enemy layout at two distinct points, suffocating the Iraqi economy by isolating Basra and Kirkuk. The attacking units would then converge toward Baghdad, encouraging Shiite communities to rise up. If the Iraqi capital seemed inaccessible, they would return to Basra and install a revolutionary

Islamic government allied with Tehran, after having seized the oil fields near the Iranian border as war reparations. According to the Iranian strategists, this conjunction of events would lead to Saddam Hussein's downfall. To execute this plan, General Nejad and General Shirazi concentrated their best units in the zones selected to break through the enemy layout. In early July eight divisions (including two armored divisions) quietly gathered north of Basra; four others (including one armored division) deployed between Qasr-e-Shirin and Sumer to be in position to attack Khanaqin and Mandali. These twelve divisions, each of which consisted of 15,000 men, were supported by 800 tanks and 600 artillery pieces. The remaining six Iranian divisions were scattered along the front.

Facing them, the Iraqis also had eighteen divisions, backed by 1,000 tanks and 900 cannons, but the Iraqi divisions had little more than 8,000 men each. While the force ratio was in the Iranians' favor in terms of troop numbers, it was in the Iraqis' favor in terms of equipment, illustrating one of the war's major issues: the mullahs could only count on Iran's human potential, while Saddam banked on his tanks, cannons, helicopters, and planes to hold his positions.

On July 12, 1982, the UN Security Council unanimously adopted Resolution 514, calling on the two belligerents to put an immediate stop to hostilities. Concerned that the war was dragging on, the council's five permanent members had come to an agreement under the guidance of the Peruvian Javier Pérez de Cuéllar to issue a compromise statement that called for the "dispatch [of] a team of United Nations observers to verify, confirm and supervise the ceasefire and withdrawal . . . of forces to internationally recognized boundaries."[8] Saddam Hussein immediately accepted the terms of the resolution, while the Ayatollah Khomeini rejected it and called for the Iraqi people to rise up against him. In Iran television and radio pompously announced that a decisive battle was on the verge of being fought.

Figure 1: Upon his return from exile in February 1979, the Ayatollah Ruhollah Khomeini became the embodiment of Iranian resistance to foreign influence. His crusade against Saddam Hussein allowed him to consolidate the Islamic Revolution and bolster the power of the Iranian clergy. Credit: © Bettmann/Corbis

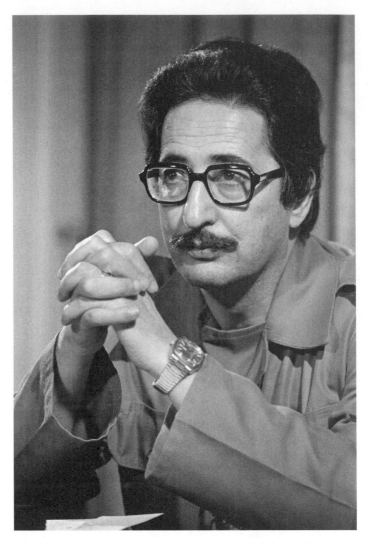

Figure 2: President Abol Hassan Bani-Sadr, who would be removed from office in June 1981, had to battle both the Iraqi invader and the Shiite clergy, which wanted to establish a theocracy in Iran. Credit: © Mahmoudreza Kalari/Sygma/Corbis

Figure 3: Through his duties as war chief, speaker of Parliament, and the regime's top money man, Akbar Hashemi Rafsanjani strove to reinforce his power and marginalize his rivals, particularly Ali Khamenei, while attempting to pull Iran out of its diplomatic isolation. Credit: © Mahmoudreza Kalari/Sygma/Corbis

Figure 4: Ali Khamenei (with turban and beard) inspects the front to show his rival Rafsanjani that he must reckon with him. This uncompromising cleric, elected president of the Republic in October 1981, sought to preserve the Islamic Republic against foreign influence. Credit: © Supreme Leader Ayatollah Ali Khamenei Office/ Handout/Corbis

Figure 5: Through his courage, charisma, and audacity, Mohsen Rezaee imposed himself as the "natural" commander of the Pasdaran, the famous Iranian Revolutionary Guards Corps, in the fall of 1981. He pursued a political career after the end of the Iran-Iraq War. Credit: Kaveh Kazemi/Hulton Archive/Getty Images

Figure 6: A merciless dictator and excellent tactician, Saddam Hussein ultimately proved to be a poor strategist. He considered himself the "Stalin of the Middle East." Each of his visits to the front was used for propaganda purposes. Credit: Keystone-France/Gamma-Keystone/Getty Images

Figure 7: Ali Hassan al-Majid, the head of the Iraqi secret service, was alone in daring to tell the truth to his first cousin Saddam Hussein—whom he closely resembled—each time that it proved necessary. He was given the macabre nickname of "Chemical Ali" after leading the repression of Iraq's Kurdish peshmergas in 1987–1988. Credit: Robert Nickelsberg/The LIFE Images Collection/Getty Images

Figure 8: General Adnan Khairallah was highly appreciated in the Iraqi military and was the country's minister of defense throughout the Iran-Iraq War. His first cousin Saddam Hussein thought of him as a brother and made him his closest advisor. He was killed in a suspicious helicopter accident in May 1989, probably at the instigation of Saddam's sons, who saw him as a rival. Credit: Thomas Hartwell/The LIFE Images Collection/Getty Images

Figure 9: An Iranian soldier watches the oil refineries of Abadan burn in September 1980, a few days after the outbreak of war with Iraq. The Iraqi offensive was aimed at the oil-rich Iranian province of Khuzestan. It would grind to a halt with the siege of Abadan in November 1980. Credit: © Henri Bureau/Sygma/Corbis

Figure 10: This photo, taken during the victorious Iranian counteroffensive of spring 1982, shows the infantry support role played by Iranian tanks (in this case, T-55s and T-62s delivered by Eastern Bloc countries). Instead of being at the tip of the assault, the tanks hold back, protected by an earthen rampart. Credit: AFP/Getty Images

Figure 11: Beginning in November 1982 the Iranian regime did not think twice about sacrificing tens of thousands of child soldiers in suicide offensives aimed at wearing down the Iraqi army, notably in the Battle of the Marshes, then later in the Battle of Basra. Credit: AP Photo/Ron Edmonds/© The Associated Press

Figure 12: Most of the Iranian offensives in Iraq, notably in the marshland zone, were repelled by the combined action of Iraqi air intervention, artillery, and tanks, as with Operation Kheibar in February 1984 (seen here). Iraqi leaders would not hesitate to make massive use of chemical weapons to push back Iranian assaults. Credit: © Jacques Pavlovsky/Sygma/Corbis

Figure 13: The mountainous Kurdish regions of Iran and Iraq were a full-fledged military front during the war between the two countries. Beginning in the spring of 1983 the Kurdish peshmergas in Masoud Barzani's KDP and Jalal Talabani's PUK would challenge the Iraqi army with the support of Iran. Credit: © Jacques Pavlovsky/Sygma/Corbis

Figure 14: In March 1986 Revolutionary Guards Corps combatants celebrate their victory after capturing the al-Faw peninsula. One year later the Battle of Basra would end in a bitter Iranian defeat. Credit: AP Photo/© The Associated Press

Figure 15: The "war of the tankers" became another symbol of the Iran-Iraq War, as seen here with the attack of the supertanker *Norman Atlantic* in December 1987. From March 1984 to July 1988 the belligerents attacked 430 commercial ships and sank seventy-two. Credit: AP Photo/© The Associated Press

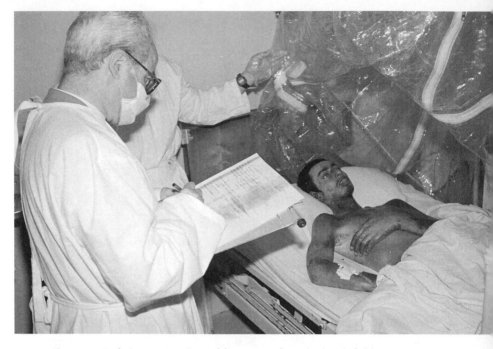

Figure 16: Early in 1988 Iranian soldiers gassed on the battlefield were sent to European hospitals to be treated and to prove to the international community that Iraq was heavily using chemical weapons. On March 16, 1988, the Iraqi army attacked the Kurdish town of Halabja with a massive chemical weapon strike to stop an Iranian offensive, indiscriminately killing civilians and soldiers. Credit: AP Photo/Greg English/© The Associated Press

Figure 17: Beginning in 1986 Iran mobilized women and trained them to use weapons and guard sensitive sites, replacing men sent to the front. The National Liberation Army's People's Mujahidin, who opposed the Iranian regime, followed suit, as seen in this photograph taken in a training camp in Iraq in the spring of 1988. Credit: © Jacques Pavlovsky/Sygma/Corbis

Figure 18: Iraqi prisoners of war prepare to return to Iraq in November 1988, three months after the August 20, 1988, ceasefire came into effect. Some of the 70,000 Iraqi prisoners of war and 45,000 Iranian prisoners of war would refuse to go home out of fear of reprisals. Credit: © Reuters/Corbis

[Chapter 15]

Blessed Ramadan Offensive

On July 13, 1982, in the middle of Ramadan, Tehran launched the "Blessed Ramadan" offensive, so named to stoke its combatants' fervor. This operation inaugurated the war's third phase. The offensive was initially directed at the Basra sector, held by the Iraqi 3rd Army Corps, which consisted of five divisions (the 3rd, 5th, 6th, 11th, and 15th). Shortly before midnight, the 30th and 88th Armored Divisions, backed by three mechanized divisions (the 21st, 40th, and 77th), rushed toward the Shatt al-Arab to cross the river over the Haritha Bridge about ten miles (about fifteen kilometers) north of Basra. The Iranian tanks advanced about ten miles (about fifteen kilometers) before being stopped at daybreak by violent counterattacks by Iraqi tanks. During the day a brutal tank battle unfolded under a scorching sun along the Shatt al-Arab's eastern bank. The Iraqi generals called in their air force, which mercilessly pounded the enemy columns. The Iranians were eventually pushed back to their initial positions. Though they had been severely thrashed, their armored and mechanized divisions were redeployed a little further north to participate in the offensive's second phase. During the night of July 16 to 17 they launched another attack, this time in the direction of al-Qurnah. This village, nestled at the confluence of the Tigris and the Euphrates, would provide an ideal bridgehead for the Iranians to cut off the only two roads between Basra and Baghdad, thus isolating the river city.

Iranian Troops Enter Iraq

The Iraqis yielded ground, attracting the enemy into a marshy area in which its vehicles would get bogged down. The Iranians fell into the trap, thinking that the area would be dry in the summer and would not hinder their advance. They were naturally unaware that two weeks earlier the

223

Iraqi command had decided to flood the marshes using irrigation channels from the Shatt al-Arab. The Iranian vanguard was immobilized and
caught in a net trap, attacked from three sides at once. Handicapped by
the darkness, Iranian tanks were forced to come in as close as possible to
support their infantrymen's advance, making themselves easy targets for
Iraqi tank crews and commandos. The Iraqis were armed with devastating
night-vision antitank missile launchers purchased from France at top
dollar. After thirty-six epic hours of battle, the Iranian divisions retreated
to their lines. Though shaken, the Iranian military high command moved
forward with its plan to allow the Pasdaran to take control of Basra.

Meanwhile, on July 17, which was the anniversary of the Ba'ath Party
coup in 1968, Saddam Hussein ordered his army to recapture Qasr-e-
Shirin. His troops ran against the defensive structures built by their own
engineering units the previous year and abandoned by Iraqi infantrymen
only three weeks earlier. They retreated after two failed assaults, having
suffered heavy losses. King Hussein came to the rescue and sent a contingent of Jordanian soldiers.

The Iranians launched another offensive in the Basra sector. This time,
they relied on their infantrymen to breach enemy lines and take control
of the bridges required to reach their objectives. Their soldiers were slowed
by minefields and water-filled trenches, torn apart by the artillery, and
finally repelled by tanks tactically entrenched behind the embankment
outside Basra. On July 23 the Iranians realized that they would not break
through in this sector and that they no longer had sufficient forces to
attack in the direction of Kirkuk. They decided to change strategies. Rather
than trying to reach the river, they settled for edging forward on a narrow
two-mile (three-kilometer) strip of land along the border, opposite Basra
and Haritha. As if to show the Ba'athist regime that the war was not over,
a car bomb exploded in Baghdad, killing twenty people. The attack was
claimed by the Iraqi Mujahidin movement, which was manipulated by the
Iranian secret service. Meanwhile, the Iraqis came to the conclusion that
they could contain the enemy by intelligently combining their forces.

On July 31 the Iranian command postponed its offensive long enough
to restock munitions and drinking water—its troops had consumed far
more water than projected over the previous two weeks. The generals also
needed to explain this stinging defeat to Akbar Hashemi Rafsanjani. The

failed offensive had cost them 12,000 dead and 300 tanks and gained them nothing, though the Iraqis had lost 150 tanks and 5,000 men (including 1,000 prisoners). The reasons for the rout were simple: the Iranians had severely underestimated the combativeness and motivation of the Iraqi soldiers—who were now fighting to protect their own territory—and the coordination between the regular army and the Pasdaran had been catastrophic. The military, struggling with low morale due to the bloody purge following the Ghotbzadeh case and the constant humiliation inflicted upon it by the Revolutionary Guards, had not shown much drive. General Nejad, who was furious to have been forced to lead an offensive he considered premature, even declared that he was prepared to resign if certain political leaders continued to interfere in the planning of operations. His criticism was clearly aimed at Rafsanjani. Nejad could allow himself this lèse-majesté, for he knew that he enjoyed the protection of the Ayatollah Khomeini and Ali Khamenei, both of whom were aware that the regime needed generals who combined his charisma and ability to plan complex operations. His position was reinforced by the blatantly obvious fact that the Revolutionary Guards lacked professionalism and training. Its human wave tactic had proven inadequate.

Akbar Hashemi Rafsanjani did not take long to react. Since he could neither dismiss General Nejad nor strip the regular army of the equipment required to reinforce the Revolutionary Guards, he provided the latter with the means to equip and train itself, without relying on the military's support. In mid-August he announced the creation of a Pasdaran ministry (the ministry was officially created by a vote in Parliament on November 7, 1982) and appointed his old friend Mohsen Rafighdoost at its head. Like Rafsanjani, Rafighdoost's background was among the traders of the bazaar. Secular, open, jovial, and friendly, he understood that anything could be bought so long as you were willing to spend enough money. His detractors protested that he was involved in trafficking, but could not deny his innate gift for negotiation. His many contacts—notably in the West—were supposed to ease his ability to negotiate the purchase of heavy equipment (tanks, cannons, missiles, river-crossing apparatus) to reinforce the Pasdaran units' weak arsenal. Rafsanjani chose Rafighdoost to take care of logistics and weapons supplies for the Revolutionary Guards, implicitly permitting him to get rich along the way. Mohsen

Rezaee and Ali Shamkhani, who were both living up to expectations, were confirmed as commander and deputy commander of the Pasdaran. They were assisted by Rahim Safavi and Mohammed Katibei, who had distinguished themselves during the recapture phase and were respectively charged with operations and intelligence. The Basij became a full-fledged component of the ministry, which was structured in ten regional commands and eight central management departments.[1]

Henceforth, the Pasdaran were given priority in the allocation of all captured and foreign-bought equipment. The speaker of Parliament had the parliamentary deputies adopt a series of measures offering a wide variety of advantages to young conscripts who chose to serve with the Pasdaran rather than the regular army: higher pay, longer leave, faster promotion, free access to university, and numerous public services. In the event of a Pasdaran recruit's death or infirmity, his family would be cared for by the Martyrs' Foundation. As a result, two out of three young men chose to serve with the Pasdaran, particularly since its training was said to be shorter and less difficult than the regular army's. The sons of prominent citizens, as well as those whose families enjoyed good connections in the clergy or the bazaar, generally chose this path, knowing that an assignment to the rear in the Pasdaran, in a general staff or a logistics unit, would be far more prestigious and less dangerous than an assignment to the front lines in a regular army division. After all, Iranian leaders were still using the human wave tactic to overwhelm the Iraqi army. Their limited financial resources prevented them from following Iraq in the frenetic race for armaments, and they were cynically aware that one hundred men would always come cheaper than a tank or an airplane.

Turning to military organization, Akbar Hashemi Rafsanjani created an ad hoc military high command responsible for supervising operations on the Iraqi front. It consisted of permanent representatives of the commanders of the ground forces, Pasdaran, navy, air force, and military police. This body's primary function was to bypass General Nejad, who was in the speaker of Parliament's crosshairs since he had acerbically criticized him. This new joint command supervised four regional commands, each of which was responsible for one sector of the front: Khuzestan, Fakkeh, Qasr-e-Shirin, and Kurdistan. These areas roughly lined up with the sectors held by the four Iraqi army corps on the other side of the border.

Rafsanjani also pushed to create a military branch of the Iranian Hezbollah ("the Party of God") called the "Quds Force." The Quds would be charged with special operations that could not be assigned to the Pasdaran. Its personnel was recruited from the Revolutionary Guards. Some were sent to Lebanon to blend into the Shiite community and supervise the implementation of the Lebanese Hezbollah, which was charged with fighting the Israeli military presence in Lebanon and protecting the local Shiite population, as well as carrying out special operations for Iran.

Oil Blockade

On August 12, 1982, Saddam Hussein retaliated for the Iranian offensive on his territory by establishing a maritime exclusion zone in the northern part of the Gulf. This maritime zone, which extended about fifty nautical miles around Kharg Island and included the Bushehr naval base, turned into a genuine war zone closed to maritime traffic. The Iraqi president had three objectives in mind. By attacking oil tankers, he intended to put pressure on Iran and force Tehran to accept a ceasefire. He also wanted to intimidate the shipping companies that delivered refined gasoline to Iran and exported its crude petroleum. This strategy produced the desired effect: the British insurance company Lloyd's, which insured most of global maritime traffic, tripled its risk premium for ships operating in Baghdad's maritime exclusion zone. Lastly, Saddam planned to force the Iranian leaders into error, hoping they would block maritime traffic on the Strait of Hormuz, which would cause the major powers to take action against Tehran. The Iranian government did not fall into the trap. It announced that it would not block the Strait of Hormuz. However, it decreed its own maritime interdiction zone, extending out approximately sixty nautical miles along its entire coastline. Any vessel that entered this zone without prior permission from the Iranian authorities would inevitably be attacked. This led maritime traffic to shift south, to a channel about twenty nautical miles wide and running along the Iraqi maritime exclusion zone. After a relatively calm year with attacks on only six commercial ships, the Persian Gulf was once again a high-risk area for maritime traffic.

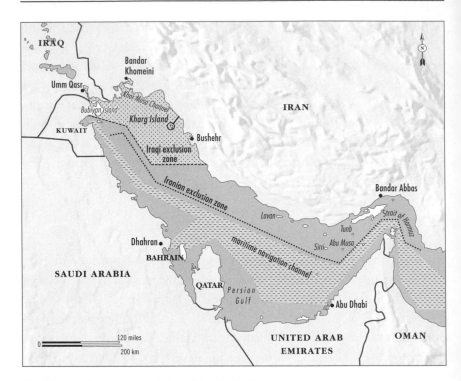

Maritime exclusion zones decreed by the belligerents

Beginning August 15 Baghdad committed its air force. MiG-23s and Su-22s based in Basra and Nasiriyah attacked tankers coming in or out of the Khor Musa channel leading to Bandar Khomeini. They sank a Greek cargo ship and a South Korean freighter in rapid succession. They were supported by the navy's Super Frelon helicopters, each of which was armed with two Exocet antiship missiles, which had been devastatingly effective in the Falklands War a few months earlier. The Super Frelons took off at dawn from Umm Qasr under the protection of fighter planes and traveled at very low altitude to a zone seventy-five miles (120 kilometers) from their base, near the mouth of the Khor Musa channel. Here, they tried to detect targets with their on-board radar. If they found one, they immediately fired their missiles and turned back to base, minimizing the chances of interception by enemy fighters. On September 4 they turned the Turkish freighter *Mar Transporter* into a floating wreck after an Exocet exploded in its engine room, setting off an inferno on board. The ship was towed to the nearest harbor and sent to the scrapyard without any further ado. A few weeks later the Super Frelons repeated their exploit at the expense of the Indian cargo ship *Archana* and the Greek oil tanker *Scapmount*. Yet the Iraqi strike capacity was limited by their lack of maritime patrol planes, the Super Frelons' narrow operating range, and, most dramatically, the lack of training of the MiG and Sukhoi pilots, who had not been taught to attack naval targets. Nonetheless, they were able to hit eight tankers by the end of 1982; two were severely damaged, while the other six were more lightly affected. The Iraqi authorities claimed a far more impressive rate of success in order to dissuade crews, ship owners, and insurers from sailing their ships to Iranian oil terminals.

The Iraqi navy contributed to the oil blockade in a more restricted fashion, limiting itself to nocturnal operations to avoid the Iranian air force. General al-Kabi, the navy's new commander, proved more enterprising and imaginative than his predecessor. He did not shy away from organizing harassing raids close to Iranian shores. On September 3 two Osa II missile boats came upon a convoy of twenty-five tankers escorted by two Iranian frigates. They succeeded in sinking one of the tankers and safely returning to their base in Umm Qasr. During the night of September 10 to 11 two Osa II boats conspicuously deployed near the Iranian port of Bushehr, hoping to attract some of the warships based there into the open sea. The trap worked. Two PF-103 corvettes rushed out of the naval base to intercept the Iraqi gunboats. They were immediately detected in the night-vision binoculars used by the crew of one of several Super Frelons that had discreetly arrived on site a few minutes earlier. This helicopter had positioned itself in ambush, hovering at water level ten nautical miles from Bushehr. It lifted a little and fired its two Exocet missiles. One missile hit one of the corvettes and sank it, killing the twenty crew members. The other corvette immediately returned to harbor. To shield themselves from the Iraqi navy's aggressive tactics, the Iranians deployed several missile boats on site and reinforced the escorts for merchant ships sailing to Kharg and Bandar Khomeini. Twelve days later a marauding Super Frelon managed to engage with the last operational PF-103 corvette and severely damage it. The Exocet that hit the PF-103 did not explode and the crew was able to wash up on shore.

The Iraqi navy had another trick up its sleeve: two batteries of CSSC-2 Silkworm surface-to-sea missiles able to strike naval targets within a range of fifty miles (eighty kilometers) from the coast that had been delivered by China early that year. The two batteries were positioned at the tip of the al-Faw peninsula to cover the area surrounding the Khor Musa channel. In the last months of 1982 at least eight of these missiles were fired, but did not hit their targets. Iraqi technicians would later modify their guidance system with the assistance of Soviet engineers to make them more accurate.

While harassing maritime traffic Baghdad also carried out multiple raids against Iranian oil installations. From August 15 to October 14, 1982, the Iraqi air force bombed the vast Kharg terminal seven times. At night Osa gunboats and Super Frelons fired their Styx and Exocet missiles at the giant oil tanks scattered across the island. The Iraqi regime even launched a salvo of three Scud-B missiles at the oil terminal. While damage was significant, the Shah's foresight prevented Iran's export capacity from being significantly affected. The Shah had demanded that the terminal be able to export six million barrels per day, or twice its oil production capacity at the time, in the expectation that it would double in the years to come. This high export capacity minimized the impact of Iraqi strikes and shortened loading time. Nonetheless, the Iranians dispatched several batteries of Hawk and anti-air defense missiles to the island. The fifteen Tomcats still operational were put in permanent rotation to provide operational watch over the oil terminal. One of these alert patrols repelled an Iraqi raid and shot down two MiG-23s and one Su-22 over the Gulf. Surface-to-air defense destroyed several Styx missiles before they hit their targets.

Since Kharg had become one of the most difficult targets to hit, the Iraqi air force and navy turned to the Nowruz, Bahregansar, Ardeshir, and Soroush oil platforms located in the northernmost part of the Gulf. The damage inflicted on these offshore facilities led to significant oil leaks, which soon turned into a major oil spill: 15,000 tons of crude oil poured into the Gulf every day while the Iranians tried for several weeks to seal off their installations. The bordering countries, concerned that their precious desalinization plants might become polluted, hired the famous Red Adair to attempt to contain the oil spill, but he failed.[2] The crude petroleum eventually dissolved in the sea, limiting the environmental impact on the Gulf coastline. After the offshore oil platforms, the MiG and Sukhoi pilots targeted the Bandar Khomeini refinery on a near-daily basis. Unable to put an end to these raids, Iran closed the refinery and halted construction on a new petrochemical complex financed by Japan. Its artillery retaliated by shelling the Basra refinery, forcing the Iraqis to close it.

Meanwhile, the Iranian air force continued its sporadic attacks on Iraq, targeting airfields, oil facilities, and power plants. Yet most of their raids were repelled by the increasingly effective Iraqi anti-air defense before they could reach their targets. Iranian pilots tried to get around the problem by flying at high altitude, but their bombings proved inaccurate. They also came up against Iraqi air-superiority fighters, which were eagerly awaiting them and shot down several Phantoms and Tigers. Yet the Iranians did not allow themselves to be bested and soon took their revenge. On September 16 an Iranian Tomcat brought down an Iraqi MiG-25 over the Gulf, using its formidable long-range Phoenix missile in this first instance of an F-14 pilot being credited with such an exploit. The first engagement between these two exceptional interceptors on February 15, 1982, had ended in a draw, with each aircraft damaging its opponent, but failing to down it. The Tomcat pilots improved their score by shooting down two other MiG-25s on December 1 and 4, 1982.

Contrary to Saddam Hussein's expectations, the Iraqi oil blockade only had a marginal effect on Iran; indeed, only 2 percent of the tankers serving Iranian terminals were affected. Nonetheless, Tehran took conservative measures to protect Kharg and limit the Iraqi blockade's impact as much as possible. Since the Bandar Khomeini terminal was too vulnerable, most oil traffic was brought back to Kharg, which became the terminus for supertanker convoys headed to Iran. A naval infantry brigade was deployed on the island to repel any attempt at an enemy landing. Some thirty barges and old cargo ships equipped with reflectors for amplifying radar signals were anchored close to the oil terminal, across from Iraq. These rusty vessels would serve as decoys to attract Iraqi navy and air force missiles. Concurrently, the capacity of the Lavan terminal, which was located out of the Iraqi air force's range on a small island 250 miles (400 kilometers) southeast of Kharg, was increased tenfold, to 250,000 barrels per day. As a result, only eight merchant ships travelling to Iran were hit in 1983. Iraqi Osa II gunboats ambushed a few tankers emptying Bandar Khomeini's last tanks. However, Iranian missile boats sank two other Osa II boats on April 12 and May 2.

Saddam Hussein tried to negotiate to open bases in Somalia, North Yemen, and Djibouti in order to attack maritime traffic to Iran from the rear. Saddam wanted to base the four frigates and six missile corvettes he had purchased from Italy on these bases and block maritime traffic to Iran by operating his navy from the Indian Ocean. Yet the Iraqi president came up against the hostility of Western nations, which pressured all three countries to turn down his request. While the Americans and Europeans wanted to help Baghdad counter Iranian radical Islamism, they had no intention of promoting the expansion of Ba'athist ideology.

Autumn Offensives

On October 1, 1982, the Iranian high command launched the Muslim Ibn Aqil offensive (named after a cousin of Imam Hussein who played an important part in the history of the Shiites) along a twenty-five-mile (forty-kilometer) front between Qasr-e-Shirin and Sumer, exactly where the second major attack had been planned to happen during the "Blessed Ramadan" offensive. The objective was simple: to simultaneously breach enemy lines in Khanaqin and Mandali in order to advance toward Baquba and threaten Baghdad. The Iranian generals committed two divisions (the 21st Mechanized and 81st Armored), their parachute brigade (the 55th), and six Pasdaran brigades. In total, they had 60,000 men, 300 tanks, and as many cannons. Their air force was largely grounded and would be of no use to them there. Facing them, the Iraqis had four divisions (the 7th and 8th Infantry, 12th and 17th Armored), supported by the 2nd Corps' artillery, for a total of 36,000 men, 400 tanks, and as many artillery pieces. They could count on air force and attack helicopter support. The Iranian military high command had no illusions about its capacity to reach Baghdad, but it hoped to gain ground and force the enemy to redeploy its troops around its capital, which would make it easier to break through elsewhere.

At dawn Iranian combatants overran Iraqi defenses along the hills lining the border between the two countries. They advanced about six

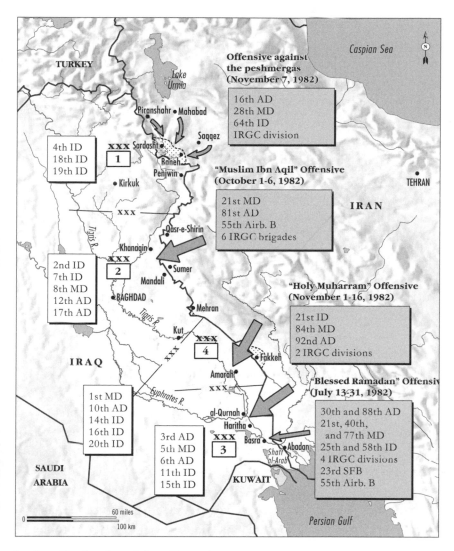

Iranian offensives from July to November 1982

miles (about ten kilometers) over the course of the day, but were violently counterattacked in the afternoon by armored formations of tanks and dismounted infantrymen. Lacking support from their own tanks, which had stayed back, the Iranian infantrymen were unable to withstand the enemy attack. Over two years of warfare, they had exhausted their stock of TOW missiles and could now only rely on Soviet-made antitank weapons, which were far less effective. They retreated under cover of night and regrouped. They assaulted again the next day, but were equally un-successful. For the first time in the war, the Iraqis used incapacitating CS gas to repel the Iranian human waves. The Iraqis were not yet using chem-ical weapons, but regular munitions normally used to suppress demon-strations. The Iraqi regime could easily make rapid deliveries of CS gas to the front, for it had stocked large quantities of it in Baghdad, barely sixty miles (less than one hundred kilometers) away.

Realizing that Baghdad would be directly threatened if his soldiers were to yield ground, Saddam Hussein traveled to the front to harangue his troops and exhort them to hold firm, no matter the cost. He massively committed his air force, which harassed enemy lines, suffering a few losses along the way (four MiGs, two Sukhois, and two Gazelles). The few Ira-nian Cobra helicopters that ventured over the front did not have the means to reverse the trend. Akbar Hashemi Rafsanjani, who understood this battle's crucial importance, also traveled close to the front to galvanize the Pasdaran. Having argued for hostilities to continue, he had to claim an operational success, even if it were only symbolic. He went against the military high command's advice and gave the order to commit all avail-able reserves to a final series of attacks to make the enemy yield.

Meanwhile, the UN Security Council adopted a new resolution (522) proposing that impartial observers be sent to oversee a ceasefire, which was now no more than idle fancy. As it had three months earlier, the Iraqi regime immediately accepted the resolution, but the Iranian delegation flatly rejected it. Since the resolution was based on Chapter 6 of the UN Charter, rather than Chapter 7—which would have allowed the recourse to force—the rejection had no effect beyond exacerbating the international community's disapproval. Locked in Cold War logic, the Security Coun-cil's permanent members had refused any resolution that could allow for the possible use of force to end the conflict.

During the night of October 5 to 6 30,000 Iranians launched another assault on Mandali. The impact was brutal, but the attackers were no more successful in seizing the town than they had been in the previous days. Combat continued throughout the day, the heat still considerable, as a deluge of artillery shells and incapacitating gas came down over the Iranians. Iraqi Gazelles and Mi-24s let loose, mercilessly strafing waves of gradually weakening infantrymen. In the late afternoon the Iranian command accepted that it would not be able to break through and put an end to the slaughter by ordering a tactical withdrawal to the ridges dominating Mandali to the east. To avoid getting trapped in the town, the Iraqis withdrew to the hills overlooking Mandali to the west. The narrow Mandali valley became a kind of no-man's-land, which the two belligerents would fight over for the rest of the war.

Though the Iranian combatants had succeeded in capturing a narrow strip of land 1.8 miles (three kilometers) long, their failure was obvious. They had been unable to seize either Khanaqin or Mandali, failed to break through the Iraqi layout, and suffered heavy losses: 6,000 dead and more than 15,000 wounded (versus 2,000 dead and some fifty destroyed tanks on the Iraqi side). More than a third of the forces committed were out of commission. This profoundly disappointing outcome promptly led to a command crisis between Rafsanjani and his generals. On the heels of General Nejad's criticisms two months earlier, the speaker of Parliament now had to face attacks from the military high command, who reproached him for having interfered in the conduct of operations. The Ayatollah Khomeini and Ali Khamenei, both delighted to remind Rafsanjani that he could not take every liberty, stepped in to defend the military. Even Mohsen Rezaee seemed to have misgivings, emphasizing the heavy losses among his Pasdaran. Rafsanjani realized he had to be less headstrong. He declared that, going forward, it would be wise to adopt an attrition strategy based on high-impact operations designed to weaken the enemy. He called an end to the massive attack tactic until the Pasdaran units were provided more appropriate and effective equipment.

In the wings of these discussions the speaker of Parliament convinced the Ayatollah Khomeini to order the resumption of the nuclear program. He sensed that the conquest of Iraq could prove far longer and more delicate than what he had imagined. If the war were to drag on, it would be good for Iran to have a nuclear power plant that could provide it with cheap electricity, but also fissionable material for the construction of one or several nuclear bombs. Rafsanjani was convinced that Iran needed to become a nuclear power, for reasons of prestige, energy independence, and dissuasion of aggressors of any stripe. The Shah had known as much. An assault like the Iraqis' could never be allowed to happen again. With the atomic bomb, Tehran could easily force Baghdad to put an end to the war.

These arguments were convincing, particularly since Rafsanjani swamped the Supreme Leader with statistics showing him that at the current price of oil, Iran would have the means to finance the program. Better yet, new uranium deposits had been found in Iran, providing it with relative self-sufficiency in terms of supply.

Ali Khamenei may have had some doubts regarding the theological compatibility with Islamic precepts of these weapons of mass destruction, but he fully understood how he could benefit from them if he were to replace the Supreme Leader. On October 19, 1982, Akbar Hashemi Rafsanjani revived the Iranian nuclear program with the Ayatollah Khomeini's blessing.[3] Teams of researchers and engineers were reconstituted and allocated vast resources. Construction on the Bushehr power station resumed. The Iranian regime's primary challenge was to find partners ready to support the rebuilding. None of the large nations that specialized in civil nuclear engineering wanted to help Tehran advance in this direction, including the Soviet Union, which no longer made any bones about its hostility toward the Iranian mullahs. France, which was at loggerheads with Iran over the Eurodif dispute, naturally refused to resume work on the factory. Germany was also contacted. While it refused to openly collaborate, it did not oppose having several of its engineers travel to Iran to provide it with their technical expertise.[4] After all, Iran remained Germany's primary commercial partner in the Middle East. Despite this discreet assistance, construction work on the Bushehr power station advanced slowly due to a lack of means and experienced scientists. Rafsanjani did not fool himself: Iranian nuclear capacity was still far off. This was another reason not to waste any time.

For his part, Saddam Hussein was determined to punish the Iranian regime for obstinately continuing the war. Since his army was not in a state to launch a large-scale counteroffensive, he ordered that the bombing of Iranian cities be intensified. On October 27 a salvo of three Scud-B missiles hit the city of Dezful. This was the Iraqi regime's first use of this ballistic missile, which is normally intended for deep retaliatory strikes. The message was clear: Iraq was ready to follow Iran in its escalation to total war.

Meanwhile, Tehran launched a new offensive called Holy Muharram, in reference to the month of Shiite mourning for the death of Imam

Muharram. This new offensive's objective was to repel the Iraqis in the direction of Amarah, on the central front, and to take control of the oil fields along the border. Applying new instructions, the Iranian generals no longer tried to overwhelm the enemy with human waves, using instead an infiltration tactic that was supposed to allow them to fragment the enemy layout.

On November 1, 1982, a Pasdaran division reinforced by several battalions of infantrymen snuck through enemy lines. The Iranian combatants overran some fifteen Iraqi strongholds. The next day they attacked enemy bunkers from the rear, while their tanks and artillery targeted the same strongholds. Their situation proving untenable, the Iraqis abandoned their positions to reestablish themselves on the other side of the border. The Iranians pushed their advantage and seized the ridges overlooking the Iraqi plain. Control of the road between Musiyan and Dehloran was now returned to the Iranians, but they still stopped short of Fakkeh, which the Iraqis maintained under artillery fire. If the Iranians made the mistake of taking Fakkeh, they would be ruthlessly crushed under a deluge of fire.

On November 6 Iranian units assaulted again, penetrating Iraq and taking a dozen border crossings. They continued by seizing the Abu Shirib and Bayat oil facilities, which produced a little over 30,000 barrels per day. The 1st and 10th Iraqi divisions counterattacked to recapture these installations, but failed, losing seventy tanks and some forty self-propelled guns in the attempt. When it began to rain, making the roads difficult to negotiate, the Iranian offensive came to an end. Yet its outcome was better than those of previous operations. Though the Iranians had lost 4,000 men, they had killed 3,000 Iraqis and taken 3,500 prisoner. They had pushed the Iraqis back to the other side of the border and even allowed themselves the luxury of establishing themselves in enemy territory. Rafsanjani could hold his head high again, particularly since the situation in Kurdistan had improved.

In mid-September the Iranian authorities had launched a new offensive in Kurdistan province to regain control of the border road between Saqqez and Piranshahr, in the heart of the PDKI's sanctuary. This road, which wound through the Gharbi Mountains, was the backbone of the peshmergas' logistics system, like the Ho Chi Minh trail had been for the

Vietcong. The peshmergas used this road for most of their weapon and equipment deliveries, traveling via the passes leading from the Iraqi border to the cities of Sardasht and Baneh. General Shirazi had mobilized 80,000 men divided in three regular divisions (the 16th Armored, 28th Mechanized, and 64th Infantry). Fierce fighting stretched on for several weeks, leaving 2,500 dead among the Pasdaran and twice that in the governmental forces. The Pasdaran and regular army soldiers occupied several sections of the strategic road but were unable to take control of Sardasht and Baneh. These two cities were still under the peshmergas' control when snow began to cover the area in late November, putting an end to the Iranian offensive.

Meanwhile, Abdul Rahman Ghassemlou had retreated to the Penjwin sector in Iraq. Saddam Hussein had granted an amnesty to Kurdish detainees and multiplied measures to benefit local populations in order to avoid facing a general insurrection in Kurdistan and making a delicate situation even more perilous.

The front stabilized during the winter of 1982–1983. Each belligerent improved its defensive positions to prevent the enemy from infiltrating its lines. On the Iraqi side, the engineering corps dug a network of trenches running along the front similar to those on the western front during the First World War. Blockhouses equipped with machine guns, mortars, and recoilless guns were built every 985 feet (300 meters) to provide infantrymen with invaluable support. Tank firing positions protected by earthen embankments were prepared at regular intervals along the front. Antitank ditches were dug in front of trenches protected by vast fields of mines and various traps. Electronic surveillance equipment, cameras, and thermal sensors were added to the overall system to detect any attempt at infiltration. Lateral tunnels were dug to facilitate bringing in reinforcements, supplies, and munitions, but also to allow infantrymen to get from one end of the layout to the other under cover. Logistic depots were built less than three miles (less than five kilometers) from the front lines so units could be more quickly resupplied. Further back, positions were created to assemble preset artillery and anti-aircraft defense to stop the enemy with a barrage of fire. New stretches of road were laid out and asphalted to connect the front lines to the main road along the Tigris.

The Iraqi sappers also took advantage of the winter lull to accelerate work on the defensive complex protecting the surroundings of Basra on the Shatt al-Arab's eastern bank. The twenty-mile (thirty-kilometer) canal dug as part of the defenses was now filled with water and connected to both the Shatt al-Arab and Fish Lake. Meanwhile, military high command accelerated the training of recruits and the creation of new units to make up for casualties and reinforce the front: four infantry divisions (the 21st, 22nd, 23rd, and 24th), a commando brigade (the 65th), and two Republican Guards brigades (one motorized infantry brigade and an armored brigade equipped with T-72 tanks). To resist growing pressure on the al-Faw peninsula, a 5th Army Corps was created under the command of General al-Jeboury to hold Basra's southern sector. The Iraqis placed operational responsibility in the hands of their army corps commanders rather than their division commanders.

On the Iranian side, defensive construction was less impressive and was limited to trenches scattered with bunkers used to shelter tanks and artillery. The Iranian generals could not see why they would waste their energy on building defensive works when they were on the offensive, set on advancing deeper into enemy territory. Their engineering corps built new command posts extremely close to the front and practiced crossing the Tigris and the Shatt al-Arab. To increase its offensive capacities, the Iranian command created two new shock troop divisions and turned the 23rd Commando Brigade into a special forces division under the administrative supervision of the Pasdaran.

Moscow and Beijing Hone Their Strategies

During the winter of 1982–1983 the Soviet Union radically changed its stance on the conflict. This reversal was brought about by several events. The first was the appointment of a new team at the head of the Kremlin. On November 10, 1982, Leonid Brezhnev died after a long illness and was replaced by Yuri Andropov. This former chairman of the KGB, also sick, was faced with escalating tension over the Euromissile crisis. He therefore decided to refocus Soviet policies on an orthodox line that favored unconditional support to allies of the Soviet Union, including Iraq. Once again, the Great Powers' positions were being dictated by Cold War agendas. This change of course was displayed in the appointment of a new Soviet ambassador to Baghdad, Viktor Minine, a strong supporter of Iraqi ideas. But the most significant factor pushing the Kremlin to tighten its bonds with Baghdad was Tehran's growing hostility toward Moscow. The theocratic Iranian regime had launched a ruthless witchhunt for the Tudeh Party's Communist activists. The party was banned in January 1983, and its members considered outlaws. In early February forty-five members of the Tudeh were accused of spying for the Soviet Union and arrested, convicted, and executed. Soon after the Iranians expelled Leonid Shebarshin, the KGB station chief in Tehran, and seventeen of his agents working at the embassy under diplomatic cover. How had it come to this?

A few months earlier, in June 1982, Vladimir Kuzichkin, a KGB agent in Baghdad, had decided to escape the Communist regime via Turkey, using a fake passport provided by the British secret service. Once in the hands of MI-6, the defector provided British authorities with the identities of the Soviet agents and their principal informers in Iran. The British passed this precious information on to the CIA, which decided to send it to the Iranians to deal the Soviet presence in Iran a severe blow.[5] The American authorities had still not given up hope of eventually rekindling diplomatic ties with Tehran; when the day came, this kind of small gesture might make a difference. The Iranian regime immediately expelled the Soviet spies and increased its support to Afghan freedom fighters, but held off from severing diplomatic ties with Moscow. Nonetheless relations between Tehran and Moscow were now at their lowest point since the fall of the Shah. Naturally this deterioration did not go unnoticed by American, Chinese, and Iraqi leaders, all of whom had their own reasons to be delighted.

Drawing the logical conclusions from these developments, the Kremlin cut off military assistance to Tehran. Weapon and ammunition shipments from Bulgaria were stopped, and those from Syria significantly slowed. Meanwhile, the Soviet leaders opened the floodgates of military assistance to Baghdad. The Iraqi army received 140 MiG-23 and Su-22 fighter bombers, about fifty Mi-17 and Mi-24 helicopters, several hundred T-72 tanks and BMP-1 armored vehicles, and about one hundred 2S1 and 2S3 self-propelled guns, as well as ten Il-76 transport planes, which carried some of this equipment to Iraq along with large quantities of spare parts and munitions. The Soviets were particularly generous in providing assistance because it provided significant revenue and was intended to convince the Iraqis that Soviet weapons were easily on a par with those made in the West.[6] From a political point of view, the Kremlin still put on a façade of neutrality, stating that, "the war between Iran and Iraq is absurd. It is irrational to want to prolong it."[7] Yet it defended Iraqi positions from the wings, quarantining the Iranian government. It was convinced that sooner or later the Iranian authorities would understand that it was in their interest to reestablish proper relations with the Soviet Union. When that time came, it would be up to them to come and plead for Soviet assistance. In the meantime, Moscow was determined not to do the Iranians any favors.

The break between Moscow and Tehran also forced the Chinese government to reconsider its position. In a mirror effect, Beijing now actively courted Tehran. Once again the Chinese stance consisted of going against Soviet interests by adopting the opposite position to the Kremlin's, while trying to conquer new markets. The deeply isolated Iranian regime proved receptive to Beijing's advances. The Iranians agreed to pay top dollar for Chinese-manufactured products (commercial exchanges would quintuple over the next three years), but especially for weapons and ammunition. To keep up appearances the Chinese authorities called on North Korea to serve as an intermediary between Beijing and Tehran. Most of the weapons delivered to Iran were officially supplied by North Korea, but were actually manufactured in China. In Pyongyang Kim Il Sung had no compunction about assisting Deng Xiaoping, given that China remained his primary protector and that his regime had already been delivering weapons to Iran for two years. Beginning in the first months of 1981 a large North Korean delegation had traveled to Tehran to offer to sell the Iranian regime arms and ammunition. The deal had been smoothly handled, and the Iranian military had received T-69 tanks, Type 59 cannons, rocket launchers, mortars, SAM-7 surface-to-air missiles, and even light motorboats that would allow the Pasdaran to form the beginnings of a naval force. China concurrently delivered Iran large quantities of spare parts, as well as twenty F-6 fighters (copies of the MiG-19) to be used for pilot training. In exchange, Iran paid cash and let Chinese experts inspect

Soviet-made modern weapons captured from Iraqi troops to allow China to copy their technology.[8]

Yet China continued to honor its contract with Iraq while supplying Iran. In the spring of 1983 it delivered to the Iraqi air force some thirty F-7 fighters (copies of the MiG-21), which would allow it to make up for the losses it had suffered. This "balanced" approach permitted the Chinese leaders to preserve their apparent neutrality while nurturing their relationships with both belligerents. China and North Korea were insidiously aware that it was in their interest for the conflict to last as long as possible, since its prolongation put both the United States and the Soviet Union in a delicate position while allowing their own countries to generate substantial revenue. From then on Beijing and Pyongyang would constantly supply both camps, carefully balancing their deliveries to maintain the status quo.

Chapter 16

Bloody Dawns

In January 1983 the Iranian government published a detailed map of the front in the press, showing seven pockets of Iranian territory that it asserted were controlled by the Iraqi army. It intimated that it might agree to undertake talks if Baghdad agreed to evacuate and recognize Iranian sovereignty over these few thousand square miles. Several of these pockets were part of Iraqi territory but had been claimed by Tehran since the beginning of the twentieth century. On January 27 Saddam Hussein rejected the proposal, but stated he was ready to go to Tehran to personally discuss the terms of a ceasefire with the Ayatollah Khomeini. His offer was hotly debated in Tehran. The Supreme Leader was tempted to accept, but Rafsanjani—now supported by Khamenei, who had come around to his position—insisted on rejecting it, judging that it would be humiliating to compromise with the Iraqi dictator, who deserved instead to be punished. The speaker of Parliament convinced his peers to launch a new offensive called Prelude, which was to deal a decisive blow to their enemy's morale and offer the Iranian regime a symbolic success a few days before the Islamic Revolution's fourth anniversary. On January 31 the Iranian government released a communiqué rejecting the Iraqi proposal. To make things perfectly clear, Ali Khamenei emphatically added that "the withdrawal of Iraqi troops is no longer the main condition for the end of hostilities. The issue now is to punish the Iraqi leaders."[1] Military high command was ordered to rapidly prepare an offensive to capture Fakkeh, then continue in the direction of Amarah to cut off the main road connecting Baghdad to Basra. Never mind that weather conditions were unsuitable, the point was to go on the offensive and pressure Saddam.

War of Attrition

Under the torrential downpour that fell during the night of February 6 to 7, 1983, two Pasdaran divisions attacked the Iraqi front lines on either side of Fakkeh to lure the Iraqis into believing they were launching a pincer attack on Amarah, a feint designed to make the Iraqis move their troops back to the rear. This would provide more favorable conditions for the principal attack on Fakkeh. Yet General Fakhri, who was responsible for the sector as commander of the 4th Corps, did not fall into the trap. He pushed back the Iranian assaults, relying on a solid defensive layout and motivated soldiers. The network of trenches built since the autumn proved effective. The masses of Iranian infantrymen, slowed by barbed wire and the barrage of fire, got bogged down in the mud, which treacherously concealed the mines and booby traps that decimated the first assault waves. The Iranians, soaking wet and shivering, and surprised by the level of resistance, called an end to the diversionary attack.

At dawn they launched the principal offensive on Fakkeh. Over three days 30,000 infantrymen tried to capture the town. They succeeded in penetrating the ruins of the small town at every attempt, but were caught in the fire from artillery and tanks entrenched in the neighboring hills. They were flattened under a deluge of shells. Unable to hold the position, the Iranians were forced to withdraw after sustaining heavy losses. Next they tried to attack the Iraqi trenches and put their cannons and tanks out of commission. The outcome was even worse: the Iranians were torn apart by the hail of bullets relentlessly sweeping the mounds of earth protecting Iraqi lines. At dusk on February 9 the Iranians decided to play their last card and committed the 92nd Armored Division, which they had previously kept back as a reserve. The Iranian command hoped that the tanks would be less vulnerable by night and more easily breach enemy lines. Two tank brigades assaulted the hill on top of which the Iraqi trenches had been dug, losing a few dozen vehicles in the attempt. The Iranian tanks overran the Iraqi trenches in a narrow sector roughly half a mile (barely a kilometer) wide, then pressed into enemy territory at daybreak. The steel behemoths advanced slowly, both to avoid getting bogged down and to save fuel now that they were cut off from their supply source. Lacking specific orders, the tank crews settled for crushing nests of resistance.

General Fakhri reacted immediately by committing his own armored reserve of four battalions of T-72 tanks, which proved far superior to the Iranian Chieftains and T-59s. He also called in support from artillery and helicopters, which flew over the battlefield, hunting down enemy tanks. The Iraqi tanks maneuvered to make a net trap around the Iranian vanguard and attack it from several sides at once. Meanwhile, several infantry brigades closed the breaches in the Iraqi trenches. The isolated Iranian tank crews defended themselves with a strength born of despair and retreated to their lines to avoid being wiped out. On February 11 Operation Prelude was adjourned. The Iranians had suffered a severe defeat, losing more than one hundred tanks and suffering 5,000 dead and 12,000 wounded (while the Iraqis lost 2,000 men and sixty tanks). Worse, the offensive, which was designed to sap the enemy's morale, had had the opposite effect: the unexpected victory had galvanized the Iraqi soldiers. The Ba'athist regime proudly displayed 1,000 Iranian prisoners and the wrecks of more than thirty tanks captured from the enemy in the streets of Baghdad.

Based on this defeat, Iranian command turned to an attrition strategy based on infantry and artillery. Tanks were stashed in the rear and would no longer be used other than to support the advance of infantrymen. Large-scale mechanized offensives had come to an end. Occasional attacks continued to be referred to as "offensives" for propaganda reasons and were numbered to maintain the illusion of permanent battle. The authorities hoped this would keep up their troops' fighting spirit. In a grandiloquent speech Rafsanjani proclaimed: "The war will continue no matter what happens!"[2] For the time being Iranian divisions burrowed along the front, generally half a mile (a kilometer) from the Iraqi trenches, just outside of enemy machine-gun range. For many months combat would follow a similar pattern to First World War combat, alternating artillery duels, shock attacks, and long periods of waiting. The Iranians used this period to test new harassment tactics. They sent their Pasdaran to assault enemy lines riding low-cylinder off-road motorcycles bought in Japan. During the approach stage each motorcycle driver zigzagged up to about 330 feet (100 meters) from the Iraqi trenches, kicking up a dust cloud to mask his advance. He then came to an abrupt stop so that the combatant riding with him could fire his RPG-7 rocket at an enemy stronghold. The crews that survived the retaliatory fire raced back to their lines.

Beginning in February 1983 the Iraqi president called on the international community to pressure the Iranian government to accept an end to hostilities. The UN, the OIC, and the Non-Aligned Movement once again came up against Tehran's inflexibility. The ICRC publicly denounced violations of international humanitarian law—the famous Geneva and Hague Conventions—and both sides' poor treatment of prisoners of war.

To show his unflagging support for his "great friend Saddam," King Hussein of Jordan undertook a tour of the front with the Iraqi president, inspecting the Jordanian contingent deployed there. He had his picture taken firing a cannon at Iranian positions. The photo was sent to all the capitals of the Middle East to incite Arab leaders to more actively commit to helping Iraq—at the very same time that the Ayatollah Khomeini solemnly asked the Gulf States to stop supporting Baghdad. For his part, General Adnan Khairallah ordered the construction of barrack buildings, mosques, and rec rooms equipped with televisions and VCRs to improve the comfort of the 400,000 Iraqi soldiers mobilized in the trenches or nearby. Mail service was improved. A rotation system was implemented so that each unit could train for six weeks in the rear, hold its positions for four months on the front, then enjoy two or three weeks of leave. With this system, Iraqi soldiers knew they had one in three chances of avoiding enemy offensives.

Dawn 1

The first major Iranian offensive of the spring of 1983 took place on April 10, when Iran launched Operation Al-Fajr 1 (literally, "Dawn 1") in the Fakkeh sector. Its objective was to regain control of this strategic crossroads. The Iranians went all out, committing three infantry divisions to the battle, which would last one week. Thanks to their artillery's constant hammering of Iraqi trenches, they captured several hills overlooking Fakkeh. Their infantrymen regained control of the town, eliminating snipers as they went. The operation was a success for the Iranian command. The generals proudly showed the media the 390 Iraqi prisoners captured, but carefully avoided mentioning the 6,000 fatalities sustained. In

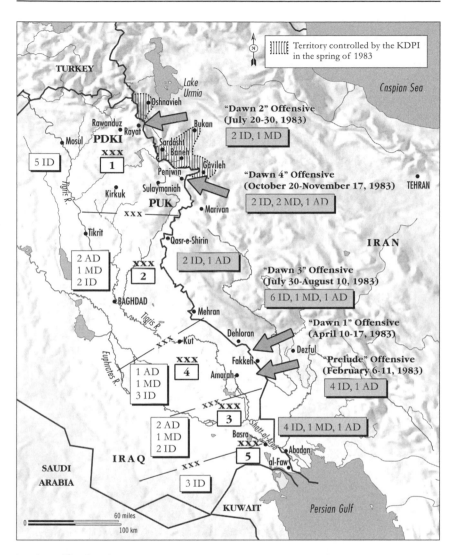

Iranian offensives in 1983

the Iraqi camp General Fakhri had chosen to yield a little ground to limit his losses. He reestablished his lines three miles (five kilometers) further, knowing that he still had Fakkeh in his cannons' sights, which allowed him to harass the logistics convoys following the border road. Baghdad retaliated by firing salvos of Frog and Scud missiles at the cities of Dezful, Andimeshk, and Shush, killing several hundred people. Following this display of strength, Tariq Aziz made an offer to Iran to negotiate an agreement under the authority of the United Nations on May 25, 1983. The proposal was to agree to stop bombing civilian populations. He was turned down flat. On June 7 Saddam Hussein suggested another one-month truce to mark the beginning of Ramadan. His offer was not made in hopes that Tehran would accept, but to show the Arab allies who financed him that he respected Islam's precepts, notably the Islamic calendar's holy month. To no one's surprise, the Iranian mullahs disdainfully rejected his offer, trumpeting their desire to soon pray in the "liberated" mosques of Najaf and Karbala.

Return to Kurdistan

To try and break the stalemate, the Iranians refocused all their efforts on Iraqi Kurdistan, hoping to arouse a general rebellion against the Ba'athist regime. But before they could penetrate the area, they had to regain control of their own Kurdish province by overrunning the peshmergas entrenched in the triangle between Sardasht, Baneh, and Bukan. In early spring General Shirazi mounted an offensive designed to deal a fatal blow to the Kurdish separatist movement. He mobilized 120,000 men supported by 400 tanks and 300 cannons. Overwhelmed by the governmental forces' firepower, the 20,000 peshmergas mobilized by Abdul Rahman Ghassemlou were forced to abandon the villages and valleys to once again seek shelter in the mountains. Over the next few weeks the Revolutionary Guards brutally cracked down in the area, claiming 5,000 lives. Yet they were not spared either. The twenty-eight-year-old General Mohammad Boroujerdi was killed by an antipersonnel mine during a search and sweep operation near Mahabad. He had participated in all the major Pasdaran offensives of the previous eighteen months and had distinguished himself by fiercely fighting the Kurdish rebels and covering up atrocities committed by some of his subordinates. By the end of June General Shirazi had reached his goal. He had taken control of nearly all of Iranian Kurdistan and put down the uprising of the peshmergas, who would henceforth only be able to carry out sporadic harassment raids. Shirazi could now enter Iraqi Kurdistan.

For its part, the PDKI only controlled the city of Baneh and the small town of Oshnavieh and Gavileh. Kurdish troops were now divided between several isolated pockets of resistance. Abdul Rahman Ghassemlou had sought shelter in Iraq and was moving between Halabja, Penjwin, and Gavileh. The overly self-confident Ghassemlou had made the mistake of combining two basically incompatible operational modes: static defense to protect his bases and mobile guerilla warfare to harass the enemy. Neither had truly paid off. Many of his former allies contested his leadership, and several of his lieutenants were assassinated in murky circumstances. He himself barely escaped an attack. The PDKI, isolated and pushed back against the Iraqi border, was now fighting for its survival.

The Iranian regime fully intended to exploit its advantage. On July 2, 1983, it launched the Dawn 2 offensive in the direction of the Rawanduz Valley in the north of Iraqi Kurdistan. While a Revolutionary Guards division seized Oshnavieh, where several groups of peshmergas had taken shelter, the 28th Mechanized Division left Piranshahr, supported by a Pasdaran division, and advanced in the direction of the pass forming the border with Iraq. The Iranian infantrymen were joined by 800 Kurdish combatants under the orders of the Barzani brothers. The objective was simple: to take control of the village of Haj Omran, located on the other side of the border, and home to one of the PDKI's operational headquarters. By eliminating this PDKI stronghold, Tehran hoped to allow the Barzani brothers' KDP, which it actively supported, to bolster its influence and convince the region's population to set off a general insurrection against the Iraqi regime. The Iranian strategy had basically remained unchanged for two decades, drawing on the same methods to apply pressure on Baghdad. If everything went as planned, the Iranians would continue to Rawanduz, thus threatening the oil area of Mosul.

On July 22 Iranian troops crossed the Piranshahr pass and overran the infantry brigade guarding it. They penetrated nearly ten miles (fifteen kilometers) into Iraqi territory, seizing Omran, Rayat, and Mount Kerman, which dominated the valley and provided an ideal lookout point from which to direct artillery fire. The PDKI's peshmergas fought desperately, but could not contain the assault. Several peshmerga leaders were able to escape, but the majority of the peshmergas were killed or captured and their families deported to prison camps in the south of Iran. The Barzani brothers' partisans participated in the violence, stoking the hatred between Kurdish clans. The Iraqi general staff had been immediately notified and deployed reinforcements to the area. Several commando battalions were airlifted to Rayat by helicopter to stop the Iranian breach while the 23rd and 24th Infantry Divisions made their way by road. On July 24 Saddam Hussein and Adnan Khairallah traveled to the front to personally assess the severity of the situation. The minister of defense took things in hand and directed operations. He launched a forceful counterattack with massive air force support. The Mi-24s recently delivered by the Soviet Union worked wonders as they hunted down infantrymen scattered on the surrounding mountains' arid slopes. One Mi-24 was shot down by a marauding Iranian fighter plane. A handful of Cobra helicopters also intervened to try to slow the Iraqi counterattack. One Cobra pulled off an unusual feat by using its on-board gun to shoot down a MiG-21 slowly flying over the battlefield at low altitude.

After three days of bitter combat that left several thousand dead, Adnan Khairallah stabilized the front and regained control of Rayat and Mount Kerman. He immediately ordered the construction of defenses and trenches identical to those protecting the rest of the front. The Iranians retained control of Omran and ten other villages. They entrusted their administration to the Shiites of the Supreme Council of the Islamic Revolution in Iraq (exiled former members of the Dawa Party), who would also persecute the local population and further stir up ethnic and sectarian resentment.

Despite this failure, the Iranians were determined to keep up the pace and take advantage of summer to continue to harass the Iraqi regime and provoke its downfall. On July 30, 1983, they launched the Dawn 3 offensive, now attacking in the center, on a wide front stretching about sixty miles (one hundred kilometers) from Mehran to Dehloran. The objective was to secure the border road connecting the two towns by seizing the Iraqi trenches dominating it. Once this initial objective was attained, the Iranian troops would attempt to breach the enemy layout in the direction of the Tigris and cut off the Baghdad-Basra road running along the river less than twenty miles (thirty kilometers) from the border. For this offensive Tehran mobilized 60,000 men assigned to five divisions (the

7th, 25th, and 58th Infantry, 30th Armored, and 40th Mechanized) and several independent brigades. Facing them, the Iraqis also had five divisions (the 1st Mechanized, 10th Armored, 2nd, 14th, and 20th Infantry). The Iraqis detected the Iranian preparations and took the initiative of operations. Attacking preemptively, two of their tank columns tore enemy infantry formations to pieces. Yet the tanks soon had to withdraw under a heavy barrage of fire. Now it was the Iranians' turn to launch an assault. For three days, with the support of T-59 and T-62 tanks, their infantry battalions succeeded each other in rushing the Iraqi front lines under a scorching sun and rolling artillery fire.

Every night Iranian commandos infiltrated Iraqi lines and took control of Iraqi outposts. Chinook helicopters flew by night with all their lights off to drop paratroopers behind the trenches so they could attack from the rear. On August 2 Iraqi infantrymen yielded ground and abandoned their trenches over a stretch of fifteen miles (about twenty-five kilometers) south of Mehran to reestablish their positions three miles (five kilometers) away, inside Iraqi territory. General Sultan Ahmad, commander of the 4th Corps, counterattacked with his remaining tanks. He struggled to contain the Iranian push, but succeeded, thanks to massive air force intervention and the arrival of the 12th Armored Division, deployed from the neighboring 2nd Corps.

The Iranians realized that they would not be able to breach Iraqi lines or reach the Tigris. Instead they chose to improve their positions around Mehran. On August 6 they assaulted the three hills overlooking this border city left in ruins by three years of war. Four days later they had taken control but had sustained heavy losses. On August 10 the Dawn 3 offensive ended with a mixed outcome. The Iranian army had succeeded in driving the Iraqis out of the heights overlooking the Mehran-Dehloran road, recapturing a narrow strip of land and pushing the Iraqis back a few miles (few kilometers). It had killed 6,000 Iraqis and captured 600, while destroying some sixty tanks and seizing 13,000 light weapons on the battlefield. On the other hand, the Iranians are believed to have sustained 7,000 dead and 15,000 wounded. At this rate, the hypothetical conquest of Baghdad would come at an exorbitant price that some Iranian leaders were no longer convinced they were willing to pay. Yet these limited gains lifted Iranian troop morale, which had been sapped by previous setbacks.

The Iraqis took revenge by firing more salvos of Scud missiles at Iranian cities. The Iranians retaliated by shelling Basra with their long-range artillery. Since the Iraqi Shiites had not risen up against Saddam's regime, Tehran no longer had any compunction about shelling them, though the Ayatollah Khomeini had previously resisted the idea. The United Nations Security Council promptly adopted a new resolution (540) demanding an immediate end to military operations and bombings directed at civilian populations. Once again Baghdad accepted the resolution and Tehran rejected it.

In early fall the center of gravity of operations shifted back to Iranian Kurdistan, where the Iranians launched the Dawn 4 offensive in the Marivan sector. The objective now was to seize the Penjwin Valley in which Abdul Rahman Ghassemlou had taken refuge. This valley was also used as the supply route for weapons and ammunition to the PDKI's last bastions. The Iranians hoped that by taking control of the valley they would cut off the peshmergas' supply chain and put an end to the Kurdish insurgency. During the night of October 19 to 20, 1983 several Pasdaran battalions attacked the Rashah Pass from the rear, coming through the mountains and overwhelming the soldiers guarding it. At dawn they were joined by the vanguards of the 29th and 64th Infantry Divisions, which had left Marivan in the night and were backed by a tank brigade and two mechanized divisions (the 21st and 28th). Their progress was slow, for the narrow road was soon congested by a huge column of vehicles. The divisions advanced at the pace of the infantrymen climbing the peaks overlooking the valley. They seized fifteen villages as they went.

At nightfall on October 22 the Iranian vanguard reached the outskirts of Penjwin and was met with the dogged resistance of the Iraqi 4th Infantry Division, which had been forewarned and had had time to take the necessary steps to reinforce its defensive perimeter. Iraqi military high command had expected an offensive in this sector. General Ma'ahir Abdul Rashid, commander of the 1st Corps, had preemptively gathered the 18th and 19th Infantry Divisions, artillery pieces, and several armored and mechanized brigades around Sulaymaniah. This substantial force allowed him to immediately counterattack. Fighting at the head of his troops, he led a mobile battle, pinning the enemy in place and outflanking it. By pushing the Iranians back to the Rashah Pass, he earned the nickname of the "Iraqi Rommel." MiGs and Sukhois called in for reinforcement slalomed between the mountains and relentlessly fired at the columns of Iranian vehicles, leaving a considerable number of burned-out shells in their path. Meanwhile, a Pasdaran division encircled the village of Gavileh, which was being used as a refuge by one of the last groups of PDKI peshmergas. The Revolutionary Guards assaulted the village by night and massacred the garrison that had been resisting government authorities for over two years. A handful of combatants managed to escape and weave their way along perilous mountain paths to take shelter in Iraq.

On November 6, 1983, the Iranians launched another attack on Iraqi lines. They committed two new Pasdaran divisions. Taking advantage of the bad weather that grounded the Iraqi air force, they took control of Penjwin and the mountainous salient sticking into Iranian territory between Marivan and Baneh. They then continued in the direction of Sulaymaniah. General al-Rashid, who was from the same tribe as Saddam Hussein and Adnan Khairallah, made a direct call to them and was granted the immediate dispatch of two Republican Guard shock battalions. Helicopters dropped these troops in front of the Iranian vanguard with a stock of chemical weapons. The Iraqis were not yet using neurotoxic agents, but regular mortar shells spreading mustard gas identical to that used during the First World War. Nonetheless, the gas took the Pasdaran by surprise, sending them pouring back in disarray and leaving about a hundred dead on the field. The Iraqi troops carefully chased them back, allowing them to entrench themselves in Penjwin. This was the first Iraqi use of chemical weapons since the beginning of hostilities. By authorizing their use Saddam Hussein was serving notice to the Iranian regime that Iraqi Kurdistan was a line; crossing that line would lead to an escalation in the conflict. Baghdad could not allow the region's precious oil resources to be threatened, particularly now that these were Iraq's principal source of revenue. The Iraqi government could not tolerate the kind of general insurrection the Iranians were trying to incite by gaining a foothold in the north of the country. Jalal Talabani, the head of the PUK, took the opportunity to up the ante and negotiate with Baghdad for a new agreement more favorable to the Kurds than the previous one. But he was shrewd enough not to push too hard and ensured Saddam Hussein that the PUK was neutral.

In mid-November the first snowfalls put an end to Dawn 4, which had also had mixed results. The Iranians had certainly succeeded in seizing a strategic pass and gaining about 180 square miles (a few hundred square kilometers), but at a heavy price. Five thousand of their soldiers were dead, 15,000 wounded. In the opposite camp, the Iraqis had "only" lost 2,800 men, sixty tanks, and twenty artillery pieces. They took advantage of the coming of winter to reinforce their defenses and turn Sulaymaniah and Halabja into strongholds. The 1st Army Corps now had five infantry divisions, with the 7th Division replacing the 4th, which had been decimated in battle. It could rely on the support of 1,000 PDKI peshmergas who served as auxiliaries while waiting to be able to return to Iran.

While the Iranians had improved their positions, they had not succeeded in seriously weakening their adversary. Insufficient logistics, lack of fire support (notably aerial fire support), and a dearth of sophisticated weapons (particularly missiles) had considerably reduced their offensives' effectiveness. Dissension and rivalries between the regular army and the Pasdaran had undermined their operations' coordination. The Iranian command had proved unable to conduct more than one major offensive at a time, giving the Iraqi army time to gather its strength. It had failed to create the conditions for a strategic surprise that would have allowed it to breach the front and outflank its enemy.

[Chapter 17]

Saddam's Ace in the Hole

The Iranians were completely in the dark about what would remain one of the Iraqi regime's best-kept secrets throughout the war: Baghdad was able to decode Iranian messages and thus anticipate most enemy offensives. Thanks to its decoding services, the Iraqi army was often optimally positioned to contain the Iranian steamroller. The Iraqis did not systematically know the details of the Iranians' plans—though this may have happened on a few occasions—but they did know the general direction of Iranian operations and where their principal units were deployed. In other words, they could see their opponent's cards. They could not neutralize its best cards, but they could prepare to block their effects. As would later be recognized by Major General al-Tarfa, a former head of Iraqi military intelligence services who spent the war examining Iranian military dispositions: "We were equal to the entire Iraqi Army and the Republican Guard because of the work we did gathering signal intelligence. . . . [We] were in a boxing match where the Iranians were blindfolded and our forces were not. We created the advantage with respect to the Iranians."[1]

The Iraqi army's intelligence services, and notably its technical branch, were the linchpin of this achievement. Yet this specialized branch had not distinguished itself during the first months of the war. At that time Iraqi experts could only fall back on Crypto-54 machines acquired a few years earlier from the Swiss Crypto corporation. The Crypto-54s provided only heavily fragmented decryption of Iranian messages intercepted by their "big ears." These "ears" were put in service with the assistance of some of the Soviet military advisors whom the Kremlin had kept in Iraq after the outbreak of hostilities, despite the Soviets' desire to punish Saddam. Naturally it was also convenient for the Soviet strategists to refine their own knowledge of the Iranian armed forces by helping Iraq.

The Iraqi Equivalent of Enigma

In the fall of 1981 a stroke of luck allowed the Iraqis to make a giant leap forward. An Iranian officer assigned to the 64th Infantry Division Staff deserted, taking along a war treasure that allowed him to negotiate his escape to Baghdad. His bargaining tool was a Crypto-52 enciphering machine manufactured by the above-mentioned Swiss corporation and used by the Iranian military high command to communicate with its troops. For more than two years the Iraqis would use the Crypto-52 to decrypt a significant volume of enemy messages. For Saddam Hussein it was an asset as valuable as the Enigma machine had been to Winston Churchill during the Second World War.

Interception work was further eased by the fact that the Iranians lacked discipline in their encryption and rarely changed their codes. Yet the Iraqi system had one major flaw: since the Pasdaran refused to use the telephone or the military high command's sophisticated methods of communication, their messages could neither be intercepted nor decrypted. Obsessed with secrecy, the Revolutionary Guards exclusively relied on dependable messengers to transmit their orders—which were always handwritten. The Iraqis could find out what the regular army was planning, but it was impossible for them to know the Pasdaran's plans. This was not a major problem as long as Iranian offensives involved the regular army, but once the Pasdaran started launching their own offensives without the army's support, the Iraqis were deaf and blind again and lost their ability to anticipate the enemy's moves.

In 1983 the Iranians acquired new Crypto T-450 machines, which gradually replaced their outdated Crypto-52s. The T-450s were entirely electronic modern encoders. The Iraqis promptly reacted by purchasing powerful Japanese-made computers to help them decrypt the messages exchanged by the Crypto T-450s. More than 1,500 Iraqi technicians were hastily sent to Japan to learn to use the computers. The Iraqis called on the KGB's best specialists to break the T-450's code. In return, Baghdad gave the USSR a near-intact Phantom, which had landed on its belly in Iraq after being lightly damaged by anti-aircraft defense.[2] Soviet engineers took it apart to unlock the secrets of its electronics and weapons system.

The Iranians modified their T-450 machines on several occasions. Each time, the Iraqis only took a few weeks to adapt and break the new enemy codes, using Soviet and Yugoslav specialists recruited at top dollar. This operation for the interception and decryption of Iranian communications, known as Project 858, would employ 2,500 analysts, linguists, and technicians until the end of the war. The only factor restricting the use of this mass of data was the limited number of linguists and analysts who mastered Farsi. At the beginning of hostilities only three men in the entire Iraqi army were able to read Farsi well enough to exploit the results of their spying; all three were assigned to the "Iran" office of military intelligence, which had merely six staff members. In 1983 the office was turned into a section consisting of more than thirty officers who had taken an accelerated training course in Farsi. These officers were buried under mountains of documents, which they could often only glance at in order to keep up with all the surveillance reports they received. They worked eighteen hours a day, seven days a week, to track down vital information that could have a crucial impact on the course of the war. Despite that, many messages remained unexploited for lack of time and sufficient personnel.

Three years later this "Iran" section had been replaced by a directorate employing eighty people and supervising several hundred linguists. Its head, General Wafiq al-Samarra'i, would play a key role in the Iraqi war effort. Like his men, he was not recognized or rewarded during the war in order to avoid divulging the existence of this operation, which was known only to a closed circle of insiders. All data were centralized by General al-Samarra'i, who then personally relayed them to the chief of staff of the armed forces and Saddam Hussein. Subordinate chiefs of staff and generals were voluntarily not in the loop. With an undeniable touch of humor, the Iraqi president named the operation "Muhammad." Just as the Prophet received the divine word, the Iraqi president could read into the Iranians' plans by decrypting their communications. He could impress his own generals by showing that he could read the enemy's thoughts and anticipate its reactions despite his lack of military background. By doing so he kept his subordinates fearful of him, reinforcing his grip on the army. Officers were afraid that if Saddam was gifted with extraordinary intuition that allowed him to foil the enemy's plans, he could probably also read people's minds and identify the dissemblers and traitors in his own camp. After the dictator's fall in 2003 many Iraqi officers questioned by the Americans stated that they were convinced that Saddam had extrasensory powers that allowed him to read his generals' minds like an open book.[3]

Accelerated Training

While trying to impress his generals, Saddam began to develop a real interest in military affairs. He was convinced he needed a better understanding to master the war's parameters, which would in turn allow him to assess the suitability of the plans he was proposed. He asked his cousin and minister of defense Adnan Khairallah to help him rapidly grasp the foundations of military thinking. Each day Khairallah shared some of his knowledge with him. The Iraqi president asked everyone he spoke to for a wealth of details about the organization and conduct of operations, never hesitating to bore them with basic questions that allowed him to learn "on the job." As can be heard in the audiotapes seized in Baghdad in 2003, the question "why?" became a leitmotif in his discussions with the chiefs of staff. Over the months Saddam learned and began to have a deeper comprehension of military affairs, feeling no compunction about correcting his generals and modifying their plans to stamp them with his seal. Though he was never able to establish himself as a strategist, he sometimes proved a decent tactician.

During this period Saddam Hussein became aware of the need to rely on a corps of professional officers who mastered the conduct of operations. He promoted talented young officers and appointed senior officers who had proven their worth in the war to leadership positions, including some who were not members of the Ba'ath Party.[4] He designated several generals who enjoyed significant prestige within the military institution to key positions: after fighting well in Kurdistan, Maher Abd al-Rashid was made commander of the 3rd Army Corps responsible for the crucial Basra sector; Khaled Daoud Nader became head of the engineering corps and took charge of reinforcing Iraqi defenses; and Aladdin Makki Khamas was assigned to supervise troop training and develop a new combat doctrine for the army. Hussein appointed first-class generals such as Sultan Hashim, Ayad Fayid al-Rawi, Ayad Khalil Zaki, and Salem Ali to the command of armored and mechanized divisions. Nonetheless, he also kept some generals who had proven mediocre, but were slavishly devoted to him. The most representative figure of this group is undoubtedly Tala al-Duri, who was one of the worst generals in the entire army—and certainly one of the most bloodthirsty and incompetent—but remained one of Saddam's faithful companions.

The dictator's indulgence also extended to his family. His eldest son Uday wanted to go to the air force academy to become a fighter pilot. Though Uday was a notorious psychopath physically unfit for service, his father intervened to allow him to enroll in the training course to become an attack helicopter pilot in the Republican Guard. Piloting Mi-24s like his many race cars, Uday Hussein terrified his colleagues, many of whom refused to fly with him. The chief of the air force had to personally step in to convince him to give up his vocation. As a consolation prize—and so he could later boast he had had military experience—Uday Hussein was made a "part-time" gunner on a helicopter and participated in a few low-risk missions at the end of the war, firing at a few fleeing Pasdaran columns.

Human Intelligence

The Iraqi army's intelligence service had more than its electronic surveillance system to gather information about its adversary. It also used a growing number of Iranian refugees and deserters. The brutal repression of Iranian Kurds and "Arabs" in Khuzestan drove some to seek shelter in Iraq. These men had seen a lot and could speak Farsi. They were able to translate the Iranian press and the Friday sermon. These open sources provided valuable information; Iranian newspapers were full of battle accounts tailored to maintain patriotic fervor. One of the military intelligence service's major coups was to recruit a senior Iranian air force officer vacationing in Turkey. The information he divulged permitted Iraqis to more effectively counter enemy air-superiority fighters.[5] The Iraqis have kept his identity secret to protect his family from reprisals.

General al-Samarra'i's men could also depend on the 400 commandos assigned to Unit 888, which was responsible for reconnaissance missions behind enemy lines.[6] These elite soldiers, who trained to hide in the most unlikely spots for several days to observe enemy movements, also carried out sabotage missions, most often against oil installations. Their operations contributed to disrupting the Iranian logistics chain and reducing the production of oil fields far removed from the front. To improve their knowledge of the Iranian military dispositions, Iraqi analysts also used photographs taken by their MiG-25Rs, which flew over the front at very high altitude, and satellite images parsimoniously handed over by the Kremlin. Beginning in the summer of 1986, they even received photos transmitted by the French commercial satellite *Spot,* apparently through an agreement made with the French DGSE (Direction générale de la sécurité extérieure; General Directorate for External Security), which allowed them to update their geological survey maps.[7]

The Iranians also had certain means of keeping tabs on the Iraqis, notably through an electronic interception system that the CIA and the Defense Intelligence Agency had set up for the Shah to spy on Iraq. This system relied on two ground stations located in Kurdistan and the Zagros Mountains, where they could receive military frequencies from over the Iraqi border, and three C-130 planes modified to intercept electromagnetic signals. These three Hercules planes used powerful oblique cameras to monitor Iraqi territory while remaining in Iranian air space.[8] However, most of the technicians employed in running the two ground stations and the three aircraft emigrated or were imprisoned after the Revolution. When hostilities broke out the Iranian regime freed some technicians and trained a few others, but it was not enough; Iran's monitoring apparatus was stuck in neutral throughout the war. The Iranians also failed to break the Iraqi army's codes. They sent their Phantoms on dangerous reconnaissance missions over enemy territory to attempt to gather more data. At least six planes were lost during these missions.

Unlike the Iraqis, the Iranians infiltrated few commandos behind enemy lines, both because of the density of the Iraqi defense network and because their operational model was not designed for this kind of procedure. Iranian intelligence services did have abundant sources among opponents to the regime in Baghdad (notably Kurds and Shiites) and deserters, as well as the many prisoners of war they ruthlessly intimidated and tortured to extract critical information. Prisoners who collaborated were given the possibility of marrying an Iranian woman. Those who wanted could even join the Badr Unit composed of Iraqi defectors, which was committed to the front lines for certain major Iranian offensives. Few survived.

Bargaining Chip

In January 1984 the Iraqi army was fully on the defensive, firmly entrenched along a 745-mile (1,200-kilometer) front. It only maintained control of a dozen square miles (a few dozen square kilometers) of Iranian territory, primarily around Qasr-e-Shirin. The Iranians, on the other hand, controlled several bridgeheads in Iraqi Kurdistan, but also in the sectors of Mehran and Fakkeh. Iranian strategists now tried to determine where they could attack to bring Saddam Hussein's regime to its knees. They had four options. The first was to mount a major offensive in Iraqi Kurdistan in order to seize its oil fields, cut off the Kirkuk-Dortyol pipeline, and dry up Iraq's revenue. This option presented two major difficulties. The first was that the Iranian army did not have the means to breach this mountainous region, which was easily defendable, and the second was that any threat to the Iraqi-Turkish pipeline would be interpreted as a casus belli by Ankara, which desperately needed the royalties from the pipeline to revive its economy. Iran depended on Turkey economically and could not take the risk of alienating it.

The second possibility would be to strike the Iraqi regime at its core, by attacking in the direction of Baghdad. Such an offensive, which would necessarily be mechanized, could only be considered with significant air support, a large number of tanks and self-propelled guns, and a wide variety of missiles, all of which the Iranian armed forces now lacked. Without these resources, any ill-conceived operation could turn into a disaster. Tehran had to shelve this plan for the time being. The third option would be to capture Basra. But seizing the city, which the Iraqis had turned into a fortress, currently seemed out of reach. The Iranian army could only consider taking Basra by crossing the Shatt al-Arab to attack the city from the rear, but it did not yet have the engineering resources to move enough troops over the river.

One solution remained: to make a sufficiently valuable territorial gain to justify continuing the war and to force Iraq to negotiate. What could be better than rich oil fields? Yet they needed to be accessible. Those in Kurdistan were not, and neither were those southwest of Basra, near the Kuwaiti border. However, the oil fields scattered in the marshlands north of Basra were ideal targets. In late January the Iranian military high command decided to capture them. To reach its goal, it mobilized two-thirds of its armed forces, or 400,000 men allocated to fifteen divisions, and conceived a complex plan intended to keep the enemy in the dark regarding the offensive's final objective.

On February 12, 1984, Iran launched Operation Tahrir al-Quds ("Liberate Jerusalem") in Iraqi Kurdistan, in the sector of Nosud, to deceive the Iraqi generals and lead them to send reinforcements to the north. In the heart of a snowstorm a division of Pasdaran specially trained for mountain combat crossed the Nosud Pass, overran Iraqi defense forces with little experience in winter conditions, and established a new bridgehead in Iraqi territory. Reinforced by a cohort of peshmergas following the Barzani brothers, the division advanced about nine miles (fifteen kilometers) toward Halabja and the Darbandikhan dam, which powered the Baghdad area. It was quickly stopped by a forceful Iraqi counterattack, which prevented it from capturing its two objectives. Nonetheless, the Iranians now controlled the three principal passes that allowed them to penetrate Iraqi Kurdistan. They also strengthened their hold on their own Kurdish province, in which Abdul Rahman Ghassemlou's PDKI was limited to harassing operations. The Iraqis reacted cautiously, informing their decisions with the interception of enemy communications, and opted not to send any additional reinforcements. They were convinced that they would face a major offensive somewhere else.

In mid-February Iranian command launched two other diversionary attacks, this time in the front's central sector. On February 16 three infantry divisions participated in the Dawn 5 offensive in the direction of the city of Kut. The Iraqis were well protected in their trenches and repelled successive assault waves over the course of five days. On the 21st two Iranian mechanized divisions mobilized for Dawn 6 tried to capture the town of Ali al-Gharbi on the Tigris, fifteen miles (twenty-five kilometers) from the border. The Iraqis were ready for them. Once again the Iranian infantrymen ground to a halt in front of their trenches. Bursts of machine-gun fire and precise mortar and tank bombardment stopped them dead. Losses in the Iranian camp were as heavy as they were futile, for the Iraqi military high command obstinately refused to dispatch any reinforcement from other sectors. Tehran had no idea that its trap had failed.

On February 22, 1984, the Iranian military high command launched Operation Kheibar, named after the Arabian fortress captured by the Prophet Muhammad one year before his triumphant entry into Mecca. Kheibar was the main offensive aimed at seizing control of the oil fields of the Majnoon Islands, but also at cutting off the Baghdad-Basra road between Amarah and al-Qurnah. The operation was to take place through the Hoveyzeh marshes extending from the border to the Tigris. The area was occupied by impoverished marshland Arabs, lakeside tribes of fishermen forgotten by the regime. These primarily Shiite locals were threatened with extinction by the oil industry, which lobbied for the draining of the marshes. For the time being this sanitization work had been limited to a narrow strip of a few miles (a few kilometers) to allow tanks to circulate along the Tigris's eastern bank. The Iraqi military had flooded the rest of the marshes to stop potential Iranian breaches between Haritha and Amarah and now only kept minimal defenses in this sector said to be impassable. The Iranian strategists thus chose to attack this very area, hoping to exploit one of the few weak points in the Iraqi layout. Their choice seemed particularly judicious in that this zone bordered the areas where both the 3rd and 4th Army Corps were deployed; the Iranians hoped the corps commanders would waste precious time by passing off responsibility for operations to each other. Given the stakes at play, the Iranians had mobilized six infantry divisions and kept three in reserve.

Operation Kheibar was personally headed by General Ali Jalali, the second-in-command of Iranian ground forces. The Ayatollah Khomeini had blessed him, and Rafsanjani had encouraged him, making clear that he could not afford to fail. To carry out his mission, General Jalali divided his forces in three groups of two divisions, each of which was charged with capturing an intermediate objective. The first two would infiltrate Iraq to the north and south of the marshes to allow the third to more easily seize the oil installations located in the center. Though they had decrypted the Iranians' messages, the Iraqis remained in the dark about their actual objective and tactics: four-fifths of the forces committed were Pasdaran and did not use any of the general staff's usual means of communication.

The Iranians Seize the Majnoon Islands

The Iranians attacked in the night of February 22 to 23, 1984, taking advantage of a heavy fog that masked their advance and a driving rain that kept most of the Iraqis inside their bunkers. Using a host of aluminum boats, each carrying one hundred combatants, the "north" maneuver group's two divisions crossed the border west of Hoveyzeh and took control of the lakeside villages of Beida, al-Sabkha, and al-Ajrada, which the Iraqis had left unprotected. They continued their advance, guided by locals and following narrow dykes interconnecting the fishing hamlets. Thirty-six hours later the two divisions' vanguard reached the edge of the marshes, two miles (a few kilometers) east of the Tigris, between al-Qurnah and al-Azair. The Pasdaran immediately established a bridgehead on this sandy area covering two square miles (a few square kilometers), then sent reconnaissance patrols toward the river to stop traffic on the Baghdad-Basra road. However, they lacked any significant support. Their heavy weaponry was limited to the machine guns and mortars they had carried on their backs or aboard the boats. Their RPG-7s could only slow down any potential tank counterattacks, not stop them.

The two "south" maneuver groups' infantry divisions infiltrated Iraq through the marshes and headed for the Shatt al-Arab under the cover of a thick fog. They soon came against the defense lines built by the Iraqi engineering corps to protect the triangular area between the international border, Fish Lake, and the Majnoon Islands, guarded by two infantry divisions solidly entrenched behind antitank ditches and embankments equipped with state-of-the-art detection equipment. Over several days the Iraqi infantrymen in this sector pushed back successive human wave assaults. Yet the Pasdaran eventually made a two-mile-wide (three-kilometer-wide) breach in the Iraqi layout south of the Majnoon Islands and reached the freshwater river connecting the islands to the Tigris.

Meanwhile, the "central" maneuver group's two divisions passed over the marshy border, crossed the lake aboard a flotilla of small boats, and captured the Majnoon Islands without firing a shot. These two sandy islands held the main installations for the oil field a Brazilian company had exploited for the past several years. Each island covered about ten square miles (a few square kilometers) and was spotted with derricks. The islands

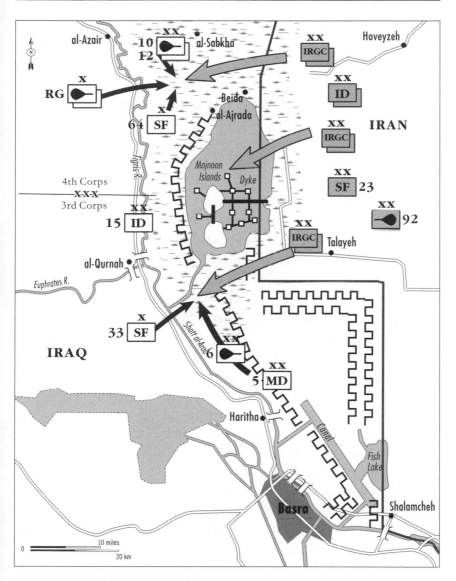

The first battle of the marshes (February 22–March 12, 1984)

were surrounded by numerous dykes and small artificial islands used as bases for oil drilling. These facilities were only guarded by a nominal garrison since their production had been stopped after the destruction of the Mina al-Bakr and Khor al-Amaya offshore platforms, which were linked to their oil deposits. The Pasdaran solidly entrenched themselves, also taking over the labyrinth of dykes connecting the two islands to the neighboring islets and readying themselves to repel an Iraqi counterattack.

After a moment of panic and a few hours of hesitation, the Iraqi generals reacted by ordering all available reinforcements sent to the marshes. In Basra General Fawzi Hamid al-Ali, the 3rd Corps' chief of staff, sent a reconnaissance force consisting of a brigade of T-62 tanks escorted by two mechanized battalions to the area to assess the scale of the Iranian breach and attempt to contain it. His counterpart with the 4th Corps followed suit, deploying one of his armored brigades to secure the road from Amarah to al-Qurnah. In the late afternoon these units engaged in combat with the Iranian vanguard. A fierce battle developed around the Iranian bridgehead. The Iraqi T-62s stampeded in every direction, crushing the Pasdaran entrenched in their individual holes dug in the sand. Dismounted infantrymen chased the survivors, forcing them back toward the marshes. About thirty tanks followed them in, but quickly got bogged down among the bulrushes, making easy targets for the Iranian reinforcements, which were arriving in continuous waves. The Iraqi crews were ordered to sabotage the tanks and join their comrades who had taken position on the edge of the marshes. The next day they were joined by a commando brigade; the day after that, by the vanguards of the 10th and 12th Armored Divisions, which had been sent in as reinforcements.

Further south the Iraqi 5th Mechanized Division's BMP-1s and the 6th Armored Division's T-62s had launched a forceful counterattack supported by the artillery and a constant stream of Mi-24s and Gazelles flying over the battlefield, mercilessly strafing the columns of Pasdaran. Helicopters airlifted a commando brigade nearby to reinforce the 5th and 6th Divisions. Only the battalions of infantrymen entrenched on the Majnoon Islands escaped the Iraqis' battering. They took advantage of the opportunity to reinforce their positions and start building bunkers with material brought in by barges and helicopters. To facilitate bringing in reinforcements, the Iranian sappers built a floating pontoon extending about six miles (about ten kilometers) between the Majnoon Islands and Iranian territory. This floating pontoon became a target for the Iraqi artillery. Each section destroyed would systematically be replaced, allowing for supplies for the two infantry divisions entrenched on the islands to continue flowing in.

On February 29, 1984, the Iranian military high command committed all its reserves to the battle in an attempt to hold the positions captured. The last three infantry divisions mobilized for Operation Kheibar (including the 23rd Special Forces Division), supported by the 92nd Armored Division's tanks, arrived to provide reinforcements on the marshy front extending over a width of about thirty miles (fifty kilometers). Taken by surprise, the Iraqis lost some ground before coming to grips with the situation. General Adnan Khairallah inspected the front and made three major decisions. He ordered that the Republican Guard be sent to the front to galvanize the troops shaken by the Iranians' resolve, that chemical weapons be used to repel the enemy, and that the high-tension line following the Tigris be run into the marshes to electrocute Iranian combatants fighting their way through the mire in waist-deep water. Beginning in the late afternoon of that day PC-7 Turbo Trainer planes that had recently been delivered by Switzerland began flying over the battlefield at low altitude. They looked like regular private planes, but they sprayed Tabun nerve gas over Iranian positions.[9] The Iraqi artillery also bombarded the marshes with chemical weapons derived from the notorious mustard gas used during the First World War. Concurrently the Iraqis released 200,000-volt electrical discharges into the marsh near the Iranian bridgehead. The combined effect of these attacks sowed panic in the Iranian ranks. Over a few hours thousands of Pasdaran were electrocuted or suffocated and drowned in the marshes. Iraqi tanks pushed back all those who tried to escape the area. One of the victims was General Mohammad Ebrahim Hemmat, who had distinguished himself as a Hezbollah fighter in Lebanon. Two days later, once they believed that the chemical weapons had dissipated, the Iraqis counterattacked in the direction of the border, wearing standard hygiene masks over their mouths. They eliminated the last pockets of resistance, making their way through the thousands of bodies that had floated back to the surface.

Further south General Ma'ahir Abdul Rashid also had the situation well under control. His 5th and 6th Divisions repelled the Pasdaran who had breached his layout. Al-Rashid also used chemical weapons. Though a headwind diminished the chemicals' effect, the Iranian infantrymen did not yet have appropriate protective equipment and ran as soon as they saw the gas clouds. Many of them were shot down by Iranian security units assigned to block their retreat. Others tried to escape through the marshes and met the same fate as their coreligionists.

In ten days the Iraqis methodically recaptured most of the territory initially lost, supported by an artillery barrage of phosphorus shells that horrifically burned the enemy. Only the Majnoon Islands remained in Iranian hands, for their troops were deeply entrenched there. Every night Chinook helicopters ferried Pasdaran reinforcements to the islands and evacuated the day's wounded. The Iraqis had neither the boats nor the amphibious means to recapture the islands. They attempted a helicopter assault, which turned into a disaster when eight of the Mi-8s committed to the operation were brought down by the Iranian anti-aircraft defense positioned on barges deployed around the islands.

For the moment the Iraqi generals had no choice but to prolong their defensive line on the edge of the marshes along the river's bank. Defending the two islands became a national cause for the Iranian regime, which sent its best battalions of infantrymen, its last portable SAM-7 missiles, light artillery, and, most importantly, the few gas masks and chemical protection suits it had available. President of the Republic Ali Khamenei traveled to the lake's Iranian shore to encourage the combatants charged with defending the fifty oil wells that the Pasdaran had seized.

On March 12, 1984, the Iraqi military high command, having realized it would not be able to expel the Iranians from the Majnoon Islands, proclaimed the end of the "first battle of the marshes." Overall the outcome was in its favor: more than 20,000 Iranians had probably been killed, gassed, or electrocuted, close to 30,000 had been wounded, and close to 1,000 captured. For their part the Iraqis had sustained only 3,000 fatalities and 9,000 wounded (as well as sixty tanks destroyed). However, they had just lost a sixth of their oil reserves. Fortunately the increase in the Kirkuk-Dortyol pipeline's capacity and the rapid progression of construction on the pipeline section connecting the oil fields in southern Iraq to the Saudi petroline thoroughly made up for this loss and allowed Baghdad to increase its oil exports by 20 percent (to 850,000 barrels per day, versus Iran's 1,900,000 barrels per day).

In Tehran the regular army's supporters criticized the use of human waves, which they considered foolish and uselessly dangerous. They put forward that it would be suicidal to attempt new offensives so long as Iran had not found a way to secure the sophisticated antitank and anti-air missiles it cruelly lacked. For their part the Pasdaran reproached the regular army for refusing to let them have its tanks and artillery. They also criticized Iranian pilots, who had not covered their retreat. Attempting to quell the controversy, Rafsanjani praised the Pasdaran's sacrifice and empathically declared: "Control of the Majnoon Island oil fields guarantees us more than sufficient oil reserves to make up for the war damages inflicted by the enemy."[10] Yet he insisted on continuing with the offensives, for he was convinced that the Iraqi regime was on the verge of toppling and would not withstand another staggering blow. For once the Supreme Defense Council did not back him. It ratified the end of major offensives and a return to trench warfare by a four-fifths majority. All large-scale operations planned for spring and summer were cancelled.

Meanwhile, Saddam Hussein refused to mount any offensive that could make Iraq look like anything other than the victim of Iranian fundamentalism. For the next year the front remained relatively calm, disrupted only by the occasional artillery duel, skirmishes between reconnaissance patrols (principally in Iraqi Kurdistan), and a single sizable operation (Dawn 7, from October 18 to 22, 1984) involving two divisions of the Iranian regular army in the Mehran sector. Once again the Iraqis decoded the Iranians' messages and easily repelled their assault.

Both sides took advantage of this lull to reinforce their orders of battle. The Iraqis established two new army corps: the 6th (General Fakhri), whose mission was to defend the Majnoon Islands sector, and the 7th (General Shawket), charged with replacing the 5th Corps (General al-Jeboury) that was now deployed to the Rawanduz Valley in the north of Iraqi Kurdistan to defend the al-Faw peninsula.[11] Military high command decreed the formation of fifteen new infantry divisions (the 25th to the 39th), which were optimized for defense and could only rely on limited artillery support (mortars and recoilless guns). The high command also created two naval infantry brigades (the 440th and 441st) responsible for defending the port of al-Faw and the Umm Qasr naval base, as well as a sixth commando brigade (the 66th). It assembled all the Republican Guard units in a single armored division named Hammurabi, in honor of the great Babylonian king. This elite division, whose command was entrusted to General Hussein Rashid, was allocated the most recent T-72 tanks and the GCT-AUF1 155 mm self-propelled howitzers just delivered by France. It had tremendous striking force. In total, Iraq had a little over 600,000 men on the front, distributed among thirty-eight divisions (six armored, three mechanized, and twenty-nine infantry).

The Iranians created six new Pasdaran divisions, including the 14th Mechanized Division, which was equipped with T-59 tanks delivered by North Korea, and two elite units assigned to the Revolutionary Guards: the "Master of Martyrs" 10th Assault Infantry Brigade and the "Ramadan" 20th Armored Brigade, equipped with T-69 tanks delivered by China. They turned the 55th Parachute Brigade into a full-fledged division and their 11th and 22nd Artillery brigades into divisions allocated most of the American-made self-propelled howitzers. The Pasdaran now made up 55 percent of Iranian ground forces, which totaled 750,000 troops distributed over thirty-one divisions (five armored, six mechanized, eighteen infantry, and two artillery). However, each Iranian infantry division had twice the number of infantrymen as an Iraqi division, giving Tehran greater striking force.

General Shirazi and General Jalali reorganized the Iranian layout. The infantry divisions were placed as a shield along the front, while the mechanized divisions were positioned as reserves, at the ready to rush to the site of an offensive. The artillery was staggered six miles (ten kilometers) behind the trenches in order to create a wall of fire in front of the infantrymen. Armored units were deployed behind the lines, twenty miles (thirty kilometers) from the front, ready to counterattack. Additional resources were allocated to the Majnoon Islands, where a second dyke was dug to connect the two islands to Iranian territory. A new regional command was instituted to manage the sector. Meanwhile, Iranian leaders turned their attention to Lebanon, which since the summer of 1982 had become a battle zone between the Islamic Republic and all those in the West who supported Iraq and wanted to precipitate the fall of the mullahs' regime. A flashback is required to understand this parallel front.

[Chapter 18]

The Lebanese Hostage Crisis

Six weeks after the Israeli invasion of Lebanon, just as Washington was showing signs of a rapprochement with Baghdad, David Dodge, president of the American University in Beirut, was kidnapped in the Lebanese capital on July 19, 1982. This would be the first in a long series of kidnappings intended to influence Western foreign policy in the Middle East.[1] Dodge's abductors demanded that the United States pressure Jerusalem to withdraw the Israeli army from Beirut. Washington refused to be blackmailed. On August 25, 1982, a multinational security force led by an American contingent landed in the Lebanese capital. Its mission was to stabilize the situation and allow Yasser Arafat's PLO to evacuate. At this point David Dodge was handed over to the Hezbollah, who took him to Iran. The American hostage was held in the notorious Evin Prison in the outskirts of Tehran for several months. David Dodge was a crucial bargaining chip for the Iranian regime, for a few weeks earlier Lebanese Christian Phalangists had kidnapped four Iranians in Beirut, including Ahmad Motevaselian, the head of the Revolutionary Guards in the Baalbek sector.

David Dodge was released in Damascus nearly one year to the day after his capture (July 21, 1983). According to the British journalist Con Coughlin, this unexpected release was due to Hafez al-Assad. The Syrian president allegedly interceded with the Iranian government to obtain Dodge's release in order to show Washington his good intentions.[2] The Americans were convinced that the Syrian authorities were being duplicitous regarding this kidnapping and had allegedly threatened Damascus with military retaliation if the hostage was not returned quickly and in good health. This respite proved short-lived. On August 29, 1983, the American contingent deployed in Beirut was struck by an initial wave of terrorist attacks. As with the attacks that would follow, responsibility for these bombings was claimed by the Islamic Jihad, a faction of the

Hezbollah Shiite militia under Iran's control. With the military front between Iran and Iraq apparently frozen, the mullahs had decided to open a new front in Lebanon through which they could indirectly weaken their Iraqi adversary.

France in Iran's Crosshairs

The French military presence in Lebanon within the multinational security force quickly became a new bone of contention pitting Paris against Tehran and Damascus. The Iranians and Syrians were hostile to the presence of French soldiers in what they considered their backyard, particularly since France had opposed Iran on several thorny issues and openly supported Iraq. On January 4, 1983, Tariq Aziz flew to Paris to negotiate a new payment schedule for the Iraqi debt, which now reached five billion dollars. Despite Iraq's financial difficulties, the Iraqi vice prime minister stated that he was ready to purchase twenty French Super Etendards equipped with the famous Exocet missile, a formidable tandem that had displayed its devastating effects in the Falkland Islands a few months earlier. The Dassault Corporation immediately stepped up. Its Super Etendard production line had been halted, but it offered to sell the Iraqis a new lot of twenty-four Mirage F-1s (EQ5 version) that were modified to allow each vessel to carry one Exocet missile. Dassault estimated it would take two years to carry out the modifications required. The deal was closed, but did not resolve the Iraqi military high command's pressing need to find an alternative solution while awaiting the arrival of the new Mirages, scheduled for early 1985. Dassault once again provided a solution by discreetly pressuring the French government to take a few Exocet-equipped Super Frelon helicopters from the French navy and "rent" the Iraqi air force a few Super Etendards in service with French naval aviation.

This proposal promptly set off an uproar in the navy, which was echoed by government figures who thought France was getting too involved with Iraq and would eventually pay the consequences. On May 26, 1983, François Mitterand decided in favor of delivering six Super Frelons to Baghdad and offering the Iraqis a two-year "rental" of five Super Etendards.[3] Five

Super Etendards were immediately taken from French units and reallocated to the Dassault Corporation. Six Iraqi pilots and thirty Iraqi mechanics arrived on the Landivisiau base to acquaint themselves with their future planes. Their presence did not go unnoticed; the press openly wondered what they were doing on French naval aviation's primary base.

During the summer Washington quietly pressured Paris not to deliver the Super Etendards, but its efforts were unsuccessful. Tehran also sent the French government a signal to let it know that the delivery of the Super Etendards to Baghdad would throw off the delicate military balance and would be interpreted as a casus belli. Several Iranian mullahs threatened France with terrorist attacks. In late August an Air France Boeing was hijacked to Tehran Airport. The situation was peacefully resolved after a week of negotiations. On September 21 the Pine Residence, which served as the French embassy in Beirut, was bombed, and five people were killed. Were the hijacking and bombing Tehran's final warnings? The next day six Super Etendards escorted by two Crusaders destroyed a Syrian artillery battery in the Chouf Mountains (Operation Sandre).

On October 7, 1983, the French government launched Operation Sucre. In the late morning five French fighter pilots carrying false passports and officially employed by the Dassault Corporation took off from Landivisiau aboard the Super Etendards rented to Iraq, headed for the Atlantic. Once in the air they changed direction and stopped in Cazaux, then in Solenzara, Corsica, where they arrived at nightfall. At dawn they headed for the Eastern Mediterranean. They landed on the aircraft carrier *Clemenceau*, which was cruising south of Cyprus as part of the Olifant Operation dedicated to watching the Lebanese coast. The aircraft carrier's deck was deserted, all personnel having been assigned to stay below deck. After refueling the planes took off in the direction of Iskenderun, Turkey, following a flight plan filed by a Dassault Corporation Falcon 50, which preceded them by a few minutes. They approached the Turkish coast at nightfall, flying at very low altitude to escape Syrian radar coverage. They flew along the Turkish-Syrian border, then entered Iraqi air space to finally land at Qayyarah Airfield West in northern Iraq.[4]

The next morning the Iraqi press was full of laudatory headlines vaunting the arrival of the Super Etendards, stating they would undoubtedly have devastating effects on Iranian oil traffic. Tehran openly threatened Paris. The French authorities, who had wanted to remain as discreet as possible regarding this affair, were furious. The French pilots immediately returned to France aboard the Dassault Corporation's Falcon 50. A Dassault technical crew stayed on site until the Iraqi crews trained at Landivisiau arrived. According to certain sources, the Iraqi authorities allegedly later convinced a French Super Etendard pilot to return to Iraq to help them and to fire AS-37 Armat antiradar missiles at Iranian targets. This pilot is said to have promptly left the French army and become a prosperous arms dealer.[5]

On October 23, 1983, two weeks after the Super Etendards arrived in Iraq, a booby-trapped truck crashed into the Drakkar building, which served as a residence for part of the French military contingent deployed in Beirut. Rescue teams removed the bodies of fifty-eight French parachutists from the building's ruins. Another suicide truck simultaneously destroyed the headquarters of the Marines deployed in the Lebanese capital, killing 242 Americans. The attackers had assaulted the two principal symbols of the Western military presence in Lebanon, both of which belonged to countries that supported Iraq. The bombings were attributed to the Islamic Jihad movement and the Hezbollah Shiite militia, which the CIA and DGSE knew to be under Tehran's orders. Both intelligence services had no doubt that Iran was behind the attacks. At the end of a whistle-stop visit to the Lebanese capital François Mitterrand made a conciliatory statement: "We are not Iran's enemies. France has not taken sides; it so happens that it has a friendship [with Iraq] and that it does not want to have enemies."[6] French minister of defense Charles Hernu was more vindictive, stating that the attack would not go unpunished. A few days later a French military jeep packed with 1,100 pounds (500 kilograms) of explosives was discovered parked outside the surrounding wall of the Iranian embassy in Beirut. It was successfully defused. This intimidation operation, approved by François Mitterrand, failed due to a lack of professionalism on the part of the specialist responsible for setting the explosives. In the heat of the moment he had simply forgotten to check that he had set the timer.[7] Nonetheless, the Iranians got the message. On November 9 Rafsanjani made a violent speech against the "little French Satan."

Raid on Baalbek

In Paris Charles Hernu and the military convinced François Mitterrand to retaliate, overruling Minister of Foreign Affairs Claude Cheysson, who wanted to be more prudent in handling the Lebanese militias. For several days the military high command had been preparing Operation Brochet, which was designed to strike one or several Hezbollah targets. The French high command initially considered targeting the Hotel Palmyra, where the militia's main leaders resided, but backed away from the likelihood of collateral damage and opted instead for the Sheikh Abdallah barracks near Baalbek, which served as a Hezbollah training camp. After several days of hemming and hawing over a potential joint American-French retaliation, the French decided to act alone.

In the late afternoon of November 17, 1983, eight naval aviation Super Etendards, led by Lieutenant Commander Hubert Rossignol, were catapulted from the deck of the aircraft carrier *Clemenceau,* which was cruising close to the Lebanese coast. They were closely escorted by two French Crusader fighters and, at a greater distance, two American F-14 Tomcats from the carrier USS *Eisenhower,* which was also cruising nearby. An EA-6B Prowler electronic warfare plane from the American naval group surreptitiously supported them by scrambling Syrian and Lebanese detection systems. The French pilots crossed over the Lebanese coast north of Beirut at very low altitude, leaving their escort fighters over international waters, ready to respond to any situation. Flying nap-of-the-earth, they crossed over the winding valleys of the Lebanon Mountains to burst into view over Baalbek. The Sheikh Abdallah barracks were soon in their sights, but instead of taking the barracks by surprise, as they expected, the French pilots found themselves in a trap. Anti-aircraft defense fire and anti-air missiles came at them from every direction. The pilots dropped their bombs on empty barracks and proceeded with a series of evasive maneuvers to avoid enemy fire.

Miraculously, all eight Super Etendards landed on the *Clemenceau's* deck undamaged that night. The French media picked up on the operation and criticized it as an embarrassing failure, embittering Admiral Bernard Klotz, who had commanded Operation Olifant from the aircraft carrier. Several months later he would learn through a Lebanese general and a leader of the Amal Shiite militia (Hussein Yatim) that a close collaborator of Claude Cheysson and very senior official at the French Ministry of Foreign Affairs had allegedly warned his Syrian contacts of an imminent French raid on Baalbek.[8] Having been alerted, the Shiite militia was able to evacuate the Sheikh Abdallah barracks and set up anti-aircraft defense around the target. This telephone conversation was allegedly intercepted by Lebanese and American wiretapping agencies.[9] It remains to be determined whether this now-retired senior official acted on his own behest or on orders from the minister, who was publicly known to be close to Lebanese and Syrian circles. There is currently no material proof to answer this question. The fact remains that this diplomat was never visibly sanctioned following the raid and was even appointed ambassador to Spain with the support of Claude Cheysson.[10] However, his progression in the order of the Legion of Honor has been permanently barred through Admiral Klotz's personal request to the grand chancellor of the Legion of Honor.[11]

American Retaliation

The United States also lost no time in responding to the October 23 bombing. On December 4, 1983, twenty Corsair and Intruder fighters based on the aircraft carriers *John Kennedy* and *Independence* bombed several Syrian surface-to-air missile batteries, as well as Hezbollah positions around Beirut. Though the raids were devastating, two American planes were brought down. Lieutenant Bob Goodman, one of the American navigators who ejected, was captured by Shiite militiamen. He was immediately transferred to Damascus, where Hafez al-Assad would release him a few weeks later to the Reverend Jesse Jackson, President Ronald Reagan's Democratic challenger, in the presence of the foreign press. Humiliated, Reagan publicly stated that he would mercilessly retaliate against any further Syrian or Iranian provocation.

The Iranians' response was not long in coming. On December 12, 1983, a terrorist bombing severely damaged the American embassy in Kuwait. Five other Western targets in the Kuwaiti capital were hit the same day, including the French embassy. A Kuwaiti Shiite organization supported by Iran claimed all six attacks. Convinced that he had to display the most unrelenting resolve, President Reagan ordered reprisals. On December 14, 1983, the American fleet opened fire on Hezbollah and Islamic Jihad positions along the Lebanese coast. The battleship *New Jersey*, a Second World War veteran, heavily bombarded Shiite militia bunkers and garrisons for several hours. The damages were considerable. Meanwhile, the American administration put in place Operation Staunch, which was intended to dissuade its allies from supplying Iran with weapons and ammunition by threatening the recalcitrant with economic and financial consequences.

On February 8 and 26, 1984, the battleship *New Jersey*'s guns fired again, crushing Hezbollah positions scattered through the Bekaa Valley with their shells. However, this proved to be a last stand. Conscious that he had nothing to gain from a constant cycle of retaliation with Iran and Syria, President Reagan had just ordered the American contingent's withdrawal from Beirut, in concert with the French authorities, who had taken stock of the Iranian regime's ability to do harm and also decided to pull out. Attacks on the French contingent of the multinational security force had multiplied since the raid on Baalbek. On December 21, 1983, the Islamic Jihad had given France ten days to leave Lebanon. Two days later Paris retaliated by expelling six Iranian diplomats suspected of preparing a series of terrorist attacks in France. During the night of December 31, 1983, while the French celebrated the new year and Charles Hernu was attending to the morale of French troops in Lebanon, two bombs exploded at the Saint-Charles train station in Marseille and in a high-speed train, killing five people. Three days later the driver of the French Consul in Beirut was assassinated. With 1984 having begun under such poor auspices, François Mitterrand was relieved to follow in his American counterpart's footsteps and order the withdrawal of the French contingent in Beirut. In Tehran the mullahs came to the conclusion that pressuring the West was an effective tactic. Yet they were aware that they had to be more careful with the Soviets, for the situation in Moscow had changed.

Yuri Andropov had died, and Konstantin Chernenko had replaced him in the Kremlin. The party ideologue's coming to power had not led to a new position on the Iran-Iraq War. Andrei Gromyko, who remained minister of foreign affairs, leaned heavily on Syria to convince

Hafez al-Assad to reopen the Kirkuk-Baniyas pipeline to allow Saddam Hussein to gather more revenue (and pay off his accumulated debts to the Soviet Union). The Syrian president stubbornly refused to make the slightest gesture that could be interpreted as a sign of weakness toward his great Iraqi rival. Judging that the timing was right, Tariq Aziz traveled to Moscow and told the Soviet minister of foreign affairs that Saddam Hussein intended to restore diplomatic relations with the United States. He offered his counterpart the following deal: Iraq would give up on the rapprochement with Washington if Moscow agreed to officially support Baghdad and forgive part of the Iraqi debt. Andrei Gromyko obligingly assured Aziz that arms shipments would continue and guaranteed a two-billion-dollar loan to finance the completion of major infrastructure work. However, he reminded Aziz that the Communist Bloc needed cash and would not be able to extend loans to Iraq ad infinitum. Most importantly, he explained that the Kremlin would not officially support Baghdad, for it intended to leave the door open to negotiations with Tehran.

The message was clear: Moscow would keep two irons in the fire in order to preserve its influence in the region. Back in Baghdad Tariq Aziz reported his discussions with Gromyko to Saddam Hussein. Irritated, the Iraqi president impulsively decided to play the American card and agreed to officially restore ties with Washington. A few months earlier the White House had taken the first step by having Ronald Reagan endorse National Security Decision Directive 114 (November 26, 1984), ordering the planning of measures to defend American interests in the Gulf and to prevent the military collapse of Iraq by any legal means, including restoring diplomatic relations between Washington and Baghdad if necessary.[12]

Tehran Punishes Washington

The Iranian mullahs were utterly determined to punish the Americans for their recent bombing of the Lebanese Hezbollah, but also for their sudden about-face in favor of the Iraqi regime. On March 16, 1984, William Buckley, the CIA station chief in Beirut, was spectacularly kidnapped by the Islamic Jihad. He was quickly transferred to Tehran, where he was interrogated and tortured. After months of silence, the Islamic Jihad revealed he had been "executed." According to accounts by other Western hostages held in Iranian jails, William Buckley is believed to have died of a heart attack brought on by an excessively forceful interrogation in June 1985.[13] His kidnapping convinced the American government that it had to play the Iraqi card to the hilt to more effectively fight the Iranian regime, which now represented absolute evil in the eyes of the neoconservatives that gravitated around the White House. Ronald Reagan charged his trusted friend Donald Rumsfeld with traveling to Baghdad to meet with Saddam Hussein, sound out his intentions, and offer to resume diplomatic relations between the two countries.

Donald Rumsfeld was a veteran of international politics who had served as Gerald Ford's secretary of defense and since moved into the private sector. He did not arrive in Baghdad empty-handed. The White House's envoy came with the promise of delivering up to two billion dollars in American government bank guarantees. Washington did not plan to deliver American weapons to the Iraqi regime, but it was ready to finance its war. The meeting was cordial, and the handshake between the two men was widely broadcast by the media. They agreed on principle to resume diplomatic relations between the two countries (both embassies would reopen on November 26, 1984). Yet, in substance, neither man had any illusions about the other's reasons for accepting this rapprochement. Saddam Hussein was as suspicious of the Americans as ever, but he needed their support to maintain pressure on the Gulf leaders and show the Soviets that he was not putting all his eggs in one basket. For his part, Donald Rumsfeld did not trust Hussein in the slightest, but knew that he was still the best barrier against the Iranians, as well as a firm adversary of the Syrian regime. The Iraqi dictator had welcomed him by giving him a videocassette of Syrian female soldiers tearing the heads of snakes off with their teeth. The subliminal message was clear: the Syrians, allies of the Iranians, were barbarians, and the United States was right to support Iraq. Donald Rumsfeld and Saddam Hussein would meet several times, sealing the agreement between their two countries.

The American government gave all its diplomatic support to Iraq. Most importantly, it provided invaluable help in terms of intelligence, supplying the Iraqis with satellite images taken by its reconnaissance satellites and data intercepted by its Airborne Warning and Control System (AWACS) and electronic surveillance planes patrolling over the Gulf. In Washington more than sixty Defense Intelligence Agency officers worked every day to provide Iraq with information, reconstructing battle orders and evaluating the Iranian units' offensive potential, while cataloging their electronic signature and radio frequencies.[14] Numerous CIA officers traveled to Baghdad to try to establish an information exchange with the Iraqi Mukhabarat, but their efforts were largely fruitless, for the Iraqi secret services refused to provide them with any data that could later be used against them. As Charles Cogan, former chief of the CIA Directorate of Operations' Near East-South Asia division, would later recognize: "This cooperation was never frank nor particularly good, but it continued until the end of the war because Iran had to be contained and the Gulf monarchies protected."[15]

In terms of material assistance, President Reagan signed two new directives authorizing the transfer of fragmentation bombs to the Iraqis. However, the American administration wanted to keep a low profile regarding the delivery of weapons to a country supported by the Soviet Union in order to avoid arousing concern in Congress. It therefore refused to sell Iraq tanks, artillery pieces, or fighter planes. The administration did authorize the sale of six Lockheed L-100s, the civil version of the famous C-130 military transport plane, which would allow the Iraqi air force to increase its tactical transport capacity and reinforce its logistics chain. The Iraqis took the opportunity to open commercial negotiations with the American Hughes Company to have it ship them eighty-six civil helicopters, which could easily be modified into attack helicopters. Iraq later sent their pilots to train in the United States on Jordanian passports.

Meanwhile, Iranians leaders could not directly attack American ships in the Persian Gulf for fear of military retaliation, so they turned once again to the Lebanese front to pressure Washington. In the span of a few weeks four American citizens were kidnapped in Beirut: Frank Regier, a professor at the American University; Peter Kilburn, a university employee; Jeremy Levin, a CNN correspondent; and Benjamin Weir, a Presbyterian minister. The Iranian government announced it had nothing to do with the kidnappings, but was in a position to help with the hostages' release. In other words, the American hostages' release needed to be negotiated via Tehran. Rafsanjani's conditions were that the United States pressure the Lebanese Phalangists to release the four Iranian prisoners they held; convince the Kuwaitis to pardon the Shiite activists sentenced for the terrorist attacks of December 1983; put an end to its rapprochement with Iraq; and return all the Shah's assets in the United States to Iran. The American administration flatly refused the Iranian regime's terms and stated that it was ready to mount a military intervention to avoid having an Iranian victory lead to the establishment of a Shiite government in Baghdad.

On September 24, 1984, the American embassy in Beirut was hit by a car bomb that killed twenty-four people and wounded several dozen, including the ambassador. The United States now considered itself at war with Iran. President Reagan authorized the CIA to act covertly to do harm to the Iranian regime and ordered the U.S. Navy to strengthen its layout near the Strait of Hormuz. In early January Father Lawrence Jenco, head of Catholic Relief Services, was kidnapped in Beirut. On March 8, 1985, a truck bomb killed more than eighty people in the Lebanese capital. The target was not a Western one for a change, but the building thought to contain Sheikh Mohammad Fadlallah, spiritual leader of Hezbollah and presumed culprit of several anti-American attacks. Many, including Robert Fisk, saw the hand of the CIA in this attack.[16] The Iranian mullahs were the first to suspect the CIA. Their response came quickly. On March 16 the American journalist Terry Anderson, correspondent for the Associated Press, was kidnapped. Three months later David Jacobsen and Thomas Sutherland, two local American notables, were also kidnapped. Twenty other Westerners would join them in Hezbollah's cells. Tehran now had a comfortable reserve of hostages with which to negotiate with Washington, Paris, London, and Berlin from a position of strength. Its demands remained unchanged. Negotiations were rendered more difficult by the fact that each country adopted a radically different strategy. Some, like Germany, would pay. Others, like the United Kingdom, would systematically refuse to give in to blackmail, no matter the consequences for their hostages. Three British citizens (Alec Collet, John Douglas, and Philip Padfield) were executed by their captors.

France Changes Course

In the spring of 1984 France became increasingly aware that Iraq was a troublesome ally, particularly since the Iraqi regime no longer seemed able to honor its debts and was beginning to face accusations from the international community of using chemical weapons. First Secretary of the Socialist Party Lionel Jospin came down in favor of restoring balance to France's policies toward the belligerents. For the first time the Elysée refused to receive Tariq Aziz during one of his many visits to Paris. The pace of arms shipments to Iraq slowed down. Signed contracts were honored, and weapon companies continued to deliver munitions and spare parts, but no further major deals were made.

François Mitterrand contacted the Syrian authorities to assure them that Paris wanted to put an end to the confrontational nature of its relationship with Damascus and Tehran. The message was passed on to the Iranian government. On July 31, 1984, an Air France Airbus was occupied by the Pasdaran during a stopover in Tehran. The Pasdaran took sixty hostages and threatened to execute them if Paris did not release Anis Naccache and his accomplices, all of whom were imprisoned in France. A crisis cell was immediately activated in Paris. Laurent Fabius, the new prime minister, charged his minister of foreign affairs Roland Dumas with leading negotiations with Tehran. Dumas promptly made contact with the Iranian Ministry of Foreign Affairs to begin discussions. He discovered that the hostage taking was only a pretext to initiate the first serious negotiations between the two capitals, with a view to eventual normalization. Ali Akbar Velayati put all the outstanding issues on the table, listing Iran's grievances toward France for Dumas: the dispute over the Eurodif loan, the offering of political asylum to Bani-Sadr and Massoud Rajavi, arms sales to Iraq, and the imprisonment of Anis Naccache.[17]

In early August the Airbus hostages were released. Dialogue between Paris and Tehran seemed reestablished. This unexpected crisis illustrated the struggle raging in Tehran between proponents of normalization with the West and radicals who rejected any opening to a foreign nation. For the former the attacks on France were merely a way to force Paris to negotiate, while the latter saw them as punishment of the "little Satan."

The Iranian authorities went so far as to declare they were prepared to buy large quantities of French weapons if France was willing to deliver them. Late in the year Engineer General René-Pierre Audran bypassed the president and prime minister and sent his deputy on an exploratory mission to Tehran, where he dangled the possibility of weapons contracts to his Iranian hosts. Audran, who had supervised arms sales to Iraq for several years at the General Delegation for Armament, probably felt too involved in Iraqi affairs to risk personally traveling to the Iranian capital. Once informed of his initiative, the French authorities immediately put a stop to it, telling Tehran they did not intend to ship Iran weapons until relations had been normalized. On January 25, 1985, René-Pierre Audran was assassinated in front of his home in La-Celle-Saint-Cloud by the Action Directe terrorist group. The French special services had no doubt that the attack had been planned in Tehran by the Revolutionary Guards, who were furious at losing potential weapon deliveries and wanted to punish the man they perceived as the symbol of French military assistance to Iraq.[18] Action Directe was probably commissioned by the Islamic Jihad (whose ties to Iran were patent), but allegedly only acted as a "service provider," following a well-established practice of "reciprocal favors" between extreme left European terrorist movements and the Middle Eastern terrorist group.[19] While definitive proof of this hypothesis is lacking, there is every indication that it remains the most likely.

Meanwhile, Roland Dumas had replaced Claude Cheysson as French minister of Foreign Affairs and taken over the Iranian question. François Mitterrand had charged him with settling the Eurodif dispute and smoothing out relations with Tehran. Mitterrand wanted France to communicate with both belligerents. For the first time the French government resisted the press campaign fomented by the military-industrial lobby to stigmatize France's change of policy and its allegedly dangerous decision to attempt a rapprochement with Tehran. The Elysée and the Ministry of Foreign Affairs stayed on course and slowed weapon deliveries to Iraq. But they did nothing tangible to repair their relationship with Tehran. Roland Dumas repeatedly contacted various Iranian officials, but they complained that the Eurodif situation had not moved forward.

On March 22, 1985, the Islamic Jihad kidnapped three French diplomats in Beirut: Vice-Consul Marcel Fontaine; Marcel Carton, head of protocol for the French embassy; and his daughter Dominique Pérez, a secretary with the French cultural services. The French chargé d'affaires in Tehran was immediately received by Rafsanjani, who told him that "the Iranian government has nothing to do with this hostage-taking, but it understands, knows, and can have influence on the kidnappers."[20] To prove that he was serious, Rafsanjani told him that Dominique Pérez, the only woman kidnapped, would be released. His statement was confirmed one week later. The message was utterly clear: hostages were released at Tehran's behest. A few days later the Iranian navy reminded France that it remained vulnerable in the Gulf by boarding and searching the container ship *Ville de Bordeaux* as it crossed the Strait of Hormuz. Paris immediately responded by ordering one of its dispatch boats deployed in the Indian Ocean to accompany French commercial ships sailing in Gulf waters (known as the Fil d'Ariane Mission).

On May 22, 1985, two months to the day after the first hostage takings, Jean-Paul Kauffmann, a journalist with *L'Evènemenent du Jeudi,* and Michel Seurat, a Centre National de la recherche scientifique (CNRS) researcher, were kidnapped in Beirut. Deeply shocked, the government entrusted Jean-Louis Bianco, secretary general of the Elysée; Hubert Védrine, diplomatic advisor to the president; and Jean-Claude Cousseran, a secret service insider, with resolving the hostage crisis. The three men unsuccessfully explored the Syrian option, while Roland Dumas continued direct negotiation of the Eurodif case with Tehran. Meanwhile, the secret services, who were convinced that Hezbollah was responsible for the kidnapping of French citizens, established the links between the Lebanese Shiite militia and the Islamic Republic. Yet the DGSE was abruptly cut out of the loop after the sinking of the Greenpeace flagship *Rainbow Warrior* by French intelligence was revealed in July.

From that point on Paris multiplied the number of intermediaries, ranging from Razah Raad, a French-Lebanese doctor with highly ambiguous connections, to Eric Rouleau, a former journalist and expert on the Middle East who had recently been appointed French ambassador to Tunisia with François Mitterrand's help. Their presence only served to make the hostages' release more complicated. Paris even sent a parliamentary mission to Tehran to try and identify new interlocutors—a surprising blunder, given that the French diplomats posted in Tehran constantly emphasized the obvious connection between the hostage takings and the Eurodif dispute and repeated that Akbar Hashemi Rafsanjani, Ali Akbar Velayati, and Mohsen Rafighdoost were the three most credible authorities with whom to negotiate.[21] Meanwhile, Tehran reiterated its demands: the settlement of the Eurodif dispute, the expulsion of Bani-Sadr and Massoud Rajavi, the curtailing of weapon deliveries to Baghdad, and the release of Anis Naccache. The Iranian government also repeated its offer to buy weapons from France. On December 7, 1985, a double bombing at the Galeries Lafayette and Printemps department stores in Paris lightly wounded forty-one people, as if to remind the French government that it urgently needed to speed up negotiations.

Paris Negotiates with Tehran

The next month, Paris offered Tehran the following terms for the release of the hostages and the normalization of bilateral relations: the French would initiate procedures to settle the Eurodif dispute and reimburse the first installment of the loan; Anis Naccache would receive a presidential pardon; and Iranian refugees in France would be prevented from participating in political activism. The Iranians told the French chargé d'affaires in Tehran that the offer was inadequate.

On February 3, 4, and 5, 1986, three bombings rocked the French capital (the Galerie du Claridge, the Gibert bookshop, and the Forum des Halles), causing thirty-five casualties but no fatalities. The explosive charges did not appear to have been designed to kill. These attacks were claimed by the Comité de solidarité avec les prisonniers politiques arabes et du Moyen-Orient (CSPPA; Committee of Solidarity with Arab and Middle East Political Prisoners), a previously unknown movement that also demanded the release of Anis Naccache and his men. The French authorities, which were hampered by rivalries between the DST (Direction de la surveillance du territoire; Directorate of Territorial Intelligence), the RG (Direction centrale des renseignements généraux; General Intelligence Directorate), and the DGSE, were unsure whether to blame the Iranians, the Syrians (because of French activism in Lebanon), or the Libyans (France and Libya were at war in Chad at the time). Pressure on the government was exacerbated by imminent French legislative elections to be held the following month.

To make matters more complicated, several mediators appointed by the RPR (Rassemblement pour la République; Rally for the Republic), then the principal opposition party, had rushed to Lebanon and Iran a few weeks earlier to negotiate the release of the hostages without consulting the French authorities. According to Roland Dumas, an envoy sent by Jacques Chirac allegedly outbid the socialist government's offer and asked the Iranians to delay the negotiations until the results of the legislative elections were announced.[22] Eric Rouleau, the French president's special envoy in Tehran, sent François Mitterrand an unequivocal diplomatic telegram stating that "the opposition has maintained regular relations with the Iranian government for three months . . . promising it a far more advantageous settlement than the one devised by the current government. The opposition is said to have warned the Iranians against any agreement that would favor the current majority in the eyes of the French public on the eve of the elections."[23] Jacques Chirac would later admit on a Europe 1 radio broadcast (January 6, 1987) that he had tried to make his humble contribution to resolving the situation before he was part of the government. Rafsanjani would drive the point home in a statement to the newspaper *Jeune Afrique* (July 19, 1987): "I confirm that the French right-wing did indeed send an important person to Tehran to negotiate with us before the French elections in March 1986."

This cacophony hardly facilitated the hostages' release. The Iranian government naturally took advantage of the poisonous atmosphere to drive up the bidding. With only a few days to go before the French legislative election of March 1986, an Antenne 2 television crew consisting of the journalists Philippe Rochot, Georges Hansen, Aurel Cornéa, and Jean-Louis Normandin was kidnapped in the heart of Beirut. Two other French nationals (Marcel Coudari and Camille Sontag) soon joined them in Hezbollah's cells. During the same period the Islamic Jihad announced the execution of Michel Seurat, who had been kidnapped the previous year in the Lebanese capital. It would later appear that the Shiite terrorist movement had sought to disguise that this frail and sick French researcher had probably been unable to withstand his detention conditions and had died of natural causes. His body was found only in 2005, during excavation work in Beirut's southern suburbs. In any case, nine French hostages were being held in Lebanon during this period. Their names were repeated daily on Antenne 2's 8:00 p.m. news to mobilize public opinion regarding their plight.

This series of kidnappings was accompanied by two more terrorist attacks in France. On March 17, 1986, the day after the legislative vote won by Jacques Chirac, a bomb exploded in the Paris-Lyon high-speed train, wounding nine people. Three days later the Point Show on the Champs-Élysées was targeted, leaving two dead and twenty-nine wounded. The new government had been warned: if it wanted the kidnappings and bombings to end, it had to negotiate. This may explain why the authorities chose not to arrest Imad Mughniyeh, a Hezbollah operational leader implicated in several attacks on French interests in Lebanon, whose presence in the greater Paris area had been revealed to the DGSE by Lebanese intelligence services.[24]

The message seemed to have gotten through to Jacques Chirac, who assigned a small team headed by Maurice Ulrich, his chief of cabinet, to negotiate directly with Tehran. The prime minister also brought in his friend Houphouët-Boigny, the president of Ivory Coast, who maintained excellent relations with the Shiite community in Abidjan, which was in turn on very good terms with Tehran. Chirac showed the Iranians his good intentions by agreeing to expel Massoud Rajavi, but specified that Bani-Sadr would continue to enjoy France's protection. Relations between the two countries began to thaw. On May 22 Jacques Chirac officially welcomed his Iranian counterpart Mir-Hossein Mousavi to Paris. Negotiations continued uninterrupted. France declared that it was ready to reimburse a first installment of the Eurodif loan; to discuss the reimbursement terms for the rest of the loan; to do its best to release Anis Naccache and his commando; to stop making weapon deals with Iraq; and to balance its relationships with the two belligerents.

On June 20, 1986, Philippe Rochot and Georges Hansen were released in Beirut. Negotiations continued into the summer, but were complicated by the presence of additional interlocutors on the French side, including Jean-Charles Marchiani, a close adviser to Minister of the Interior Charles Pasqua; Philippe Rondot, a former DGSE agent reassigned to the DST; and Alexandre de Marenches, the former head of the French secret services. Once again, coordination was not a strong suit among the French, giving the Iranians the impression that the people they were negotiating with were all pursuing different agendas. Matignon, the Ministry of Foreign Affairs, and the Ministry of the Interior did not seem to have the same priorities and did not agree on how much to trust the Iranians—and therefore on the ways and means to reach a successful outcome. Friction between Paris and Tehran rose again. The two parties had trouble agreeing on the exact amount of the Eurodif debt.[25]

Once again, the Iranian government claimed its right to access the enriched uranium, pointing to its shares in the Eurodif consortium. Worse, François Mitterrand refused to grant Anis Naccache a presidential pardon, calling into question the agreement negotiated two months earlier. The president of the republic's refusal was a way of taking revenge on the prime minister for the delaying maneuvers that had prevented an agreement between France and Iran before the legislative elections. The French hostages were now paying the price of having a cohabitation government. By early September the negotiations had reached a dead end. For the first time, several French oil tankers (the *Chaumont*, *D'Artagnan*, and *Brissac*) were attacked by Pasdaran gunboats in the Gulf, as if the Iranians wanted to remind the French authorities of their existence.

On September 8, 1986, a bomb exploded in the post office at Paris's city hall, killing one person and wounding twenty-one. The target was ripely symbolic, given that Jacques Chirac was concurrently prime minister and mayor of the capital. It would have been hard to ignore that the attack was a clear signal, particularly since it was claimed by the CSPPA, which continued to demand the release of Anis Naccache. Four days later a bomb at the Quatre-Temps department store at La Défense wounded fifty-four people. Two days after that an explosion at the Pub Renault on the Champs-Elysées killed two people. The next day a bomb exploded in the heart of Paris police headquarters, killing one person and wounding fifty-six. Finally, a terrorist attack devastated the Rue de Rennes on September 17. First aid workers reported seven dead and fifty-five wounded. Total casualties from this series of attacks, all claimed by the CSPPA, were thirteen fatalities and 300 wounded, many of whom were maimed. The next day Colonel Christian Gouttière, the defense attaché in Lebanon, was assassinated in Beirut.

The French authorities wrestled with the meaning of this series of attacks. Was it designed to pressure them into being more flexible in negotiations? Or was it due to a radical faction that wanted to torpedo the discussions and weaken the position of those in Tehran in favor of dialogue with the West? Regardless of the answer, Ali Akbar Velayati contacted Minister of Foreign Affairs Jean-Bernard Raimond on September 22 to offer to meet him and continue with negotiations. Talks accelerated. On October 27 the two parties agreed on the amount of the Eurodif debt, and Jacques Chirac committed to do everything he could to have Anis Naccache released. However, the French prime minister refused to accept the Iranians' request to receive enriched uranium. Jean-Claude Trichet, who was then the cabinet chief for the minister of finances and would later head the European Central Bank, traveled to Tehran to finalize the reimbursement terms for the first installment of the Eurodif loan.

On November 11, 1986, two French hostages (Marcel Coudari and Camille Sontag) were released in Lebanon. Six days later Georges Besse, CEO of Renault, was assassinated in front of his home. The attack was claimed by Action Directe. According to certain journalists and parts of the French secret services, the attack was commissioned by Iran in retaliation for its being denied access to the enriched uranium it considered its due.[26] Georges Besse had been the linchpin of the Eurodif project and had negotiated the terms of Iran's participation in the consortium. Since the advent of the Islamic Republic, he had been openly hostile to the resumption of nuclear cooperation with Iran. According to those who support this theory, Action Directe agreed to take responsibility for the attack in exchange for logistic support from terrorist movements operating for Tehran. If the Iranian government *was* behind the assassination, it was blowing hot and cold again. Nonetheless, on November 22, 1986, Paris paid Tehran a first installment of 330 million dollars toward to the Eurodif debt.[27] The next month an Iranian delegation was received in France. The journalist Aurel Cornéa was concurrently released in Beirut. There were now four French hostages in Lebanon, along with thirty other Western hostages whom Tehran used as bargaining chips when the profit motive alone was not sufficient to convince foreign representatives to help it reinforce its military potential.

Chapter 19

Money Has No Smell

Iran and Iraq took advantage of the lull on the front beginning in the spring of 1984 to restock munitions and acquire new weapons, as well as spare parts and motors. The latter market quickly became highly lucrative, as harsh weather conditions and the nature of the terrain led to countless breakdowns. The price of oil was still high enough to give both the Iranians and the Iraqis some room to maneuver, though their financial reserves were running out, forcing them to make drastic choices.

Iraq did not have much difficulty getting supplies, given that some thirty countries were willing to directly sell it the military equipment it required. These states were comfortable openly selling weapons to Iraq because it had been presented as the victim of the Republic of Iran's warmongering fanaticism since the summer of 1982. Three of these nations—the USSR, France, and China—met 85 percent of Iraq's needs. Initially, the Iraqi regime was primarily concerned with making its suppliers compete with each other to offer better prices. Once its resources began to diminish, its priority was to retain their trust. Tariq Aziz multiplied diplomatic tours to convince his creditors to stagger the Iraqi debt. He did not always succeed; some states, such as Spain and Portugal, quickly turned to Iran when Iraq was no longer able to promptly honor its debts. Fortunately, Baghdad could count on the GCC countries' financial support. This allowed the Ba'athist regime to avoid buying weapons from parallel-market arms traffickers.

Iran, on the other hand, was in a far more delicate position. Though the country was not subject to a formal UN embargo, it was under embargo from the United States, which threatened any nation that shipped war equipment to Tehran with economic retaliation. Only those who really had something to gain and knew they had nothing to fear or expect from Washington openly braved the American prohibition. These countries could be counted on one hand: Syria, Libya, China, and North Korea. Yet these four countries only met a third of Iran's military needs. Tehran was forced to be creative to find the other two-thirds. Alternating seduction, payoffs, and veiled threats, Iranian leaders managed to convince twenty-five other nations to provide them with military equipment or, failing that, to turn a blind eye to the activities of some of their corporations.[1] In many cases they had to purchase supplies on the parallel market at significantly higher prices. This put them in business with more or less reliable traffickers, as well as a few high-flying crooks who brazenly cheated them. One such individual was Benham Nodjoumi, who managed to sell the Iranians thirty-four crates of scrap iron by making them believe they contained TOW antitank missiles. Nodjoumi, who lived in London, chose to surrender to British authorities and serve a long prison sentence rather than face the Iranian assassins sent on his trail.

The Iranian government was most in need of ammunition and spare parts, but also light weapons to arm its masses of newly recruited infantrymen. The Iranians applied the same method to get their supplies, no matter who they were dealing with. The Supreme Defense Council convened in Tehran every week to examine the bids received. The Pasdaran were overrepresented because they knew that most of the equipment would wind up in their hands. Decisions were taken by consensus. When the council agreed to a bid, the Iranian bureau closest to the bidder was ordered to initiate negotiations with the dealer or his middleman. Tehran was apprised of the progress of discussions and arbitrated disagreements. Business in Europe was subcontracted through Tehran's backrooms in London and Frankfurt, with the knowledge that the British and German authorities would be indulgent toward Iran for the sake of their own commercial interests.

In this shadow market, London became the hub of arms sales to Iran. Tehran had decided to use London as a base for an important branch of the National Iranian Oil Corporation, which served as a screen to pay for its European purchases. The Iranian regime also operated through two shell corporations, both of which were well established in London: JSC International, registered in the Caribbean; and Metro International, 51 percent of whose capital was held by Iran, with the other 49 percent belonging to a group of Arab and Pakistani financiers. The system was operated by three individuals: Aziz Nezafatkhah, who was close to the Ayatollah Khomeini, served as the commercial attaché to the Iranian embassy in Great Britain, and was known as "Mister 10%"; Sadegh Tabatabai, who was the Supreme Leader's son-in-law and Ahmad Khomeini's close friend, and shuttled between London and Tehran; and Houshang Lavi, an Iranian businessman with far-reaching connections in the city.[2] In the United States the Iranians relied on Balanian Hashemi, an extremely rich businessman who had fled Iran after the fall of the Shah and was now trying to redeem himself by serving as the new regime's intermediary.

On the arms market, the Iranian regime stopped at nothing to corrupt those who could bring them interesting deals. It could rely on the cupidity of numerous intermediaries ready to ignore their own governments' prohibitions. Two individuals played a key role in supplying Iran while explicitly violating their countries' policies: the Saudi businessman Adnan Khashoggi and the American Frank Cradock. Another American citizen who hit the headlines for his audacity in similar dealings was Mark Broman, director of the American embassy in Paris's Office for Military Cooperation. Broman offered to sell the Iranians thirty Phantom fighters in service with the Egyptian air force, despite the fact that Egypt had taken sides with Iraq. His plan was to convince the Egyptians to purchase an equivalent number of F-16s by offering to buy back their Phantoms. These would then be fictively sold to Paraguay, where the corrupt American diplomat had numerous friends ready to bend any rules for a juicy commission. The deal was exposed and foiled. Its instigator was arrested and given a heavy sentence by an American court.

Business Is Business

Things were much simpler when Tehran dealt with the representatives of states reputed for being neutral and politically respectable. In Europe, Austria, Sweden, and Switzerland proved to be valuable partners who had the good taste not to be fussy so long as the petrodollars flowed into their coffers. Austria sold Iran 140 GHN-45 howitzers along with significant stocks of ammunition. Switzerland delivered fifteen PC-6 Turbo Porter utility aircraft, forty-seven PC-7 Turbo Trainer training aircraft, cryptology equipment, as well as large quantities of ammunition and electronic components for radars. Though it had passed legislation prohibiting the export of arms to nations at war, Sweden provided Iran a turnkey munitions factory, 300 portable RBS-70 surface-to-air missiles, and forty light motorboats, which were allocated to the Pasdaran's naval forces. This wave of orders was manna from heaven for the Karlskoga military-industrial complex, but also the Bofors Corporation, which indiscriminately sold colossal amounts of ammunition for its famous anti-air gun to both belligerents.

These illegal arms sales spurred a long legal investigation that led to the 1987 indictment of two Swedish CEOs, Mats Lundberg and Karl-Erik Schmitz, for serving as key middlemen on the European parallel market. Over the course of the investigation, Swedish customs uncovered the existence of a European cartel shamelessly supplying the mullahs' regime. This cartel provided more than 30,000 tons of gunpowder and explosives to Tehran, allowing Iran to manufacture mountains of ammunition in its Swedish-supplied factory. It had branches in the United Kingdom, France, Germany, Belgium, the Netherlands, Italy, Greece, Spain, Portugal, Austria, Switzerland, Finland, and even Norway.[3] A variety of European ports served as hubs for sending out the explosives: Zeebrugge in Belgium, Setubal in Portugal, Santander in Spain, Genoa and Talamone in Italy, and Piraeus in Greece. The cartel's representatives used several shipping companies and chartered two airlines: Scanco, which was headed by Karl-Erik Schmitz, and Santa Lucia Airways, which was registered in the Caribbean. Greece proved to be one of the main channels for moving shipments to Iran. A massive explosion that destroyed a factory in the suburbs of Athens in May 1987 was probably no accident: the factory produced munitions for Iran. Many suspected that the Iraqi special services were involved in the explosion. The Greek legal system quickly closed the case.

In order to surreptitiously sell such large quantities of explosives to Iran, the cartel needed to show the existence of a legal buyer who agreed not to cede them to a third party. The cartel drew up an end-user certificate, which enables one to obtain an export license. The Yugoslavs took care of this end of the deal, taking a 3 percent commission on each contract.[4] Concurrently, the Yugoslav government coolly shipped Iraq one training frigate, three minesweepers, one hundred D-30 guns, 300 mortars, tens of thousands of light weapons, and millions of shells, for a total value of over one billion dollars. The Yugoslav authorities had the best of both worlds.

Even Belgium let itself be tempted when Iran offered to pay generously for fifty old F-104 Starfighter interceptors the Belgian Air Force was trying to offload. Though Socialist parliamentarians intervened to prevent the sale at the last moment, the government merely held on to the planes' frames and sold the Iranians their jet engines. The engines were fitted to Iranian Phantoms (the F-4 and F-104 had the same engine). Though the Iranians failed to get the Belgian F-104s, they did get twelve Phantoms (F-4Ds) from South Korea and twelve F-5 Tigers from the Ethiopian government, which was ready to do anything to reap a few million dollars.

Iranian buyers ranged wide to procure weapons, covering Europe, the Middle East, and Asia, but also Africa and South America. South Africa and Brazil also became favored Iranian business partners. South Africa sold Tehran some thirty ultramodern 155 mm howitzers (G5) with the required stock of ammunition. Brazil provided close to 500 Cascavel and Urutu armored vehicles, as well as large quantities of shells.

In all, some forty nations contributed to the Iraqi and Iranian war efforts. At some point or other, half of them provided material support both to Iraq and Iran—including the five permanent members of the United Nations Security Council. In Europe, only Ireland can boast of having kept its hands clean. Every other state was implicated to various degrees in selling military equipment to one or often both of the belligerents. It took public disclosure of political-financial scandals to force certain countries, including France, to put their affairs in order.

The Luchaire Scandal

On February 28, 1986, shortly before the landmark legislative election that ushered in the Fifth Republic's first cohabitation government, the regional daily *La Presse de la Manche* revealed that the Luchaire Corporation had been smuggling munitions to Iran for several years. Three cargo ships loaded with munitions had just left the port of Cherbourg for Bandar Abbas in Iran. A few months earlier *Le Canard enchaîné* had nearly brought the case to light, but Roland Dumas, the satirical newsweekly's former lawyer, had convinced its editor Claude Angeli to forbear from doing so by telling him that revealing the scandal would complicate the release of the French hostages kidnapped in Lebanon.[5]

Yet as early as spring 1984, Admiral Pierre Lacoste, director of the DGSE, and General Armand Wautrin, head of Military Security (DPSD; Direction de la Protection de la Sécurité et de la Défense) had notified Minister of Defense Charles Hernu's cabinet of Luchaire's activities.[6] Luchaire was chaired by Daniel Dewavrin, the son of Colonel Passy, who had founded Free France's special services during the Second World War. Dewavrin thought his father's reputation would protect him from any legal procedure, particularly since there was no formal embargo prohibiting the sale of military equipment to Iran. Jean-François Dubos, a close advisor to the minister of defense and a member of his inner cabinet, had refused to request an investigation on several occasions, despite repeated warnings from the two senior officers. His attitude seemed especially surprising given that a few years earlier he had published a book condemning France's policy on arms sales.[7] On May 21, 1984, Admiral Lacoste had informed François Mitterrand of the scale of the traffic, which involved several hundreds of thousands of artillery shells. The president of the republic had dodged the issue by suggesting that the director of secret services speak directly to Charles Hernu. Hernu had been highly evasive and used the change of course decreed by the president to justify his cabinet's indulgence regarding this affair. Charles Hernu was soon forced to step down because of the *Rainbow Warrior* scandal, and the government decided to continue turning a blind eye to the Luchaire Corporation's activities.

On March 16, 1986, three days before the legislative election agitating the French political class, Paul Quilès, Charles Hernu's successor as minister of defense, pressed charges against the Luchaire Corporation for violating legislation on arms dealing, thus hoping to attenuate the case's negative impact on the electoral results. His efforts were insufficient; the Socialists lost the elections. The right returned to power, and André Giraud, the new minister of defense, ordered an immediate halt to all munitions deliveries to Iran. He asked Jean-François Barba, the comptroller general of the armies, to rapidly conduct a detailed investigation to get to the bottom of the Luchaire case. Barba had carte blanche to audit the accounts, be shown all relevant documents, and question everyone involved. He submitted his findings to the minister two months later. His conclusions were devastating for Charles Hernu, Jean-François Dubos, and Luchaire's CEO Daniel Dewavrin. It appeared that Luchaire had shipped Iran close to 500,000 155 mm and 203 mm shells by using fraudulent certificates stating Peru, Brazil, Thailand, Greece, or Yugoslavia as destinations. It also appeared that Charles Hernu had covered for the trafficking, of which he had been kept informed by Jean-François Dubos, one of his closest advisors. Other advisors had looked the other way.[8]

Several senior officials in the Ministry of Defense had lent Daniel Dewavrin's export requests additional credibility by helping him present them to the Commission interministérielle pour l'étude des exportations de matériel de guerre (CIEEMG; Interministerial Commission for Scrutiny of War Material Exports). More than one hundred million francs were allegedly paid to various middlemen in what arms companies modestly describe as "exterior commercial expenses." Finally, Jean-François Barba claimed that three million francs were allegedly paid to two key members of Hernu's circle, André Falcoz and François Diaz, both of whom were very close to the Socialists.[9] Nonetheless, Comptroller General Barba concluded that no money was directly paid to the party. Yet in a footnote to the report, Admiral Pierre Lacoste stated that he knew that a 3 percent commission on some of the contracts the Luchaire Corporation signed with Iran was supposed to be paid to the Socialist Party.[10] General Armand Wautrin also declared that he was certain that the arms trafficking had funded the Socialist Party, though he would later retract his statement, without providing a convincing reason for doing so.

Embarrassed, the government decided to keep quiet about the situation, until the newsweekly *L'Express* published the Barba Report in its January 16, 1987, edition to attract the law's attention to the case. The following October 17 examining magistrate Michel Legrand asked the Ministry of Defense to send him the report. In December 1987 he indicted Daniel Dewavrin and Jean-François Dubos for corruption, use of forged documents, and infringement of legislation on arms trading. Charles Hernu was not investigated, it having quickly become apparent that he had not personally stood to gain financially. Nonetheless, the case illustrated his ambiguous relationship with the arms industry. The investigation began in January 1988 and lasted seventeen months, during which Judge Legrand failed both to lift the classified status of certain key documents and to prove that the Socialist Party had received kickbacks. He soon realized that, given the numerous dysfunctions uncovered, he could not sentence Daniel Dewavrin and Jean-François Dubos without seriously damaging the Ministry of Defense's credibility.[11] On June 16, 1989, with the Socialists back in the government, the judge had no choice but to dismiss the case.

Why did the government treat the Luchaire case with such extreme caution? Perhaps because the company's suspected kickbacks were enjoyed by other political parties. Perhaps because it had to proceed cautiously with Iran, which was widely known to hold the key to the release of the French hostages kidnapped in Beirut. Perhaps, finally, because the French governments that succeeded one another from 1984 to 1989 knew that other French companies were implicated in smuggling military equipment to Iran. From 1983 to 1985, for instance, the Société nationale des poudres et explosifs (SNPE; National Company for Gunpowder and Explosives), whose primary shareholder was the state, had delivered 250 tons of gunpowder to Iran so it could manufacture its own ammunition. The SNPE allegedly delivered far more than that via the European gunpowder and explosives cartel, of which Guy Chevallier, a senior executive at the company, was the secretary general.[12] In 1987 the SNPE's general manager, Guy-Jean Bernardy, was dismissed by the minister of defense for having continued to sell gunpowder to Iran after the government had ordered him to stop all cooperation with the Islamic Republic.

Other companies shamelessly continued to play the Iranian card despite governmental warnings. The Manhurin Corporation delivered large quantities of small-caliber ammunition to Tehran; it allegedly even planned to build an ammunition factory in Iran. Matra sold Iran radar, as well as 2,000 braking systems for airborne bombs. Despite the fact that it was heavily involved in arms sales to Iraq, Thomson-CSF delivered 200 thermal night-vision cameras to equip Iranian air force planes. Even the DGSE allegedly shipped Iran Milan antitank missiles via its networks in the Afghan resistance to facilitate the release of the French hostages in Lebanon.[13] Finally, SNIAS (Aérospatiale) is said to have been on the verge of selling ATR-42 transport planes to the Iranian army, which would have used them for tactical transport. It allegedly pulled out at the last moment, after having received a governmental injunction to cease all contact with Iran around the time the Luchaire affair was coming to light. Perhaps Luchaire was actually the tree hiding the forest?

Chemical Weapons under Scrutiny

The profit motive also encouraged certain firms to help Iraq acquire large quantities of chemical weapons. Since the beginning of the war with Iran, the Iraqi regime had initiated a program for "special weapons," to be used exclusively in defending Iraqi territory in extreme emergencies. This discreet name served as a screen for chemical weapons, the use of which was prohibited by the Geneva Protocol of 1925.[14] Horrified by the gases' effects during the First World War, the international community had agreed to ban their use on the battlefield. Since then, only Italy had used them during the colonization of Ethiopia; the deterrence theory had otherwise been effective. Even at the height of the Second World War, all the belligerents resisted being dragged into the downward spiral and held back from using their stocks of chemical weapons.

The Iraqi chemical weapon program accelerated in the summer of 1982, when Iranian troops entered Iraq. At that point, the Soviet Union shipped Baghdad stocks of a vesicant, which was merely an improved version of the notorious First World War mustard gas.[15] Spain sold the Iraqi regime containers adapted for spreading chemical products, and Egypt sold it large quantities of empty shells. These were filled with gas in a plant in Samarra, south of Baghdad, and another in Akashat, near Rutba, on the Jordanian border. According to the accounts of former Iraqi generals, German, Belgian, Danish, Dutch, and even Lebanese companies provided chemical substances indispensable to the realization of this clandestine program, notably for the development of neurotoxic agents. These were particularly lethal because they were hard to detect and difficult to protect against.

By the fall of 1983 the Iraqi army had large stocks of blister gas and an initial batch of neurotoxic agents. A military command memorandum approved by the Iraqi president authorized recourse to chemical weapons and set forth the conditions for their use. A "life-size" experiment was even ordered to test the effectiveness of tabun on an Iraqi battalion, which was sacrificed for this trial run.[16] The minister of defense concurrently launched a program to acquire chemical protection equipment and ordered the addition of a chapter on maneuvering in contaminated areas to the force commitment doctrine. The first use of chemical weapons against Iranians came soon after.

Since Iran was unable to impose itself on the battlefield, its government tried to isolate the Iraqi regime by stigmatizing its blatant violation of the Geneva Protocol of 1925. No other nation had used poison gas in a major conflict since the First World War. Trying to justify itself, Baghdad fired back by accusing Tehran of outrageously violating international rules for the protection of prisoners of war. The ICRC ruled in Iraq's favor and decried the torture and intimidation visited upon Iraqi soldiers rotting in Iranian prison camps at the foot of the Caspian Mountains.

Iran persisted and referred the case to the United Nations Security Council, asking it to take sanctions against Iraq for using prohibited weapons that had killed more than 1,000 of its soldiers. To support its request, Tehran sent several dozen mustard gas and tabun victims to European hospitals. The doctors were categorical in their findings: the Iranians had been exposed to chemical weapons. A UN-mandated delegation of experts immediately traveled to the Iran-Iraq front, visited field hospitals, and confirmed that Baghdad was using poison gas. The Iraqi authorities feebly denied the charges, then adopted a prudent silence in the face of mounting evidence. General Khairallah, the minister of defense, eventually implicitly admitted to the facts, specifying that Iraq reserved the right to use any type of weapon to defend its territory. To try to appease the criticism streaming at Baghdad, he stated that these "special weapons" were only intended to be used on the battlefield and would not target civilian populations. He closely supervised their use to avoid any slip-ups. Only the commanders of the air force and Republican Guard were authorized to use them, in case of absolute necessity, after having consulted the military high command and receiving Saddam's personal agreement.[17] Nonetheless, Iraq's reputation was badly damaged by media coverage of chemical weapon use, and its credit on the international scene was diminished.

On March 30, 1984, the American and Soviet governments blocked a Security Council resolution denouncing Iraq for using poison gas on Iranian troops. Washington wanted to prove its conciliatory attitude toward the Iraqi regime as it prepared to resume diplomatic relations. Moscow wanted to avoid creating a precedent at a time when the Soviet army was accused of discreetly using chemical weapons on the Afghan front. Nonetheless, the White House was disturbed by pressure from a growing number of American congressmen who were shocked by Iraq's attitude and receptive to pro-Israeli lobbyists' requests that the government put an end to its rapprochement with Saddam. The controversy escalated when it was revealed that American companies had provided Baghdad with components used to manufacture chemical weapons.[18] The American administration responded by denouncing the use of chemical weapons and declaring a blanket embargo on the sale of the substances in question to both belligerents, calling on the international community to follow its example.[19] At the time, several Western companies, principally in Germany (notably Karl Kolb Gmbh), were supplying three Iraqi plants assembling chemical weapons under the guise of a pesticide manufacturing program.[20] Six months later the German government gave in to pressure from Washington and committed to reinforcing its export inspections, while recognizing that it could not legally prevent two German companies from trading with Iraq. To soothe its conscience, Germany sold Iran protective equipment against chemical weapons. Having lost its business relationships with several Western firms, the Iraqi government turned to East Germany, which agreed to cooperate, as attested to by two memos dated September 27, 1985, and March 10, 1986.[21]

For its part, Iran did not want to use chemical weapons. The mullahs were against using this kind of weapon on principle. It went against the Koran's precepts and was thus not included in the Revolutionary Guards' operational doctrine, which prioritized the use of infantry and did not make any provision for maneuvering mechanized troops in contaminated areas. In any case, Tehran had only an extremely limited stock of chemical munitions acquired under the Shah and did not intend to use them, to avoid increasing its isolation on the international scene and giving the Iraqis a legitimate excuse to unleash their own chemical weapons. Nonetheless, Akbar Hashemi Rafsanjani authorized the construction of a chemical plant in Bushehr to produce small quantities of blister gas as a precautionary measure. He also allotted funds to the purchase of protection equipment against the effects of chemical weapons, buying supplies from German, British, and Dutch companies. Early in 1985 most of the Iranian units deployed on the front line were equipped with gas masks, waterproof capes, decontamination kits, and atropine syringes. Photos of Iranian soldiers dug into their trenches with gas masks on their faces would be seen around the world, recalling images of the First World War.

[Chapter 20]

Total War

Since neither camp seemed able to take the advantage from a military standpoint, the Iraqi regime decided to play a new card to break the stalemate and convince the mullahs to put an end to the war. By bombing the Iranian population, it hoped to demoralize and force the Iranian people to pressure their government into accepting negotiations with Baghdad. The Iraqi regime had few scruples about targeting the civilian population since the explosion of a truck bomb in Baghdad on November 27, 1983, had killed about a hundred people. The Iraqis had blamed the attack on the Iranian special services and sworn to get revenge. Yet the Iraqi leaders' decision to bomb civilians repeated a mistake made by the Germans, Americans, and British during the Second World War. The bombing campaigns bonded the Iranian population to its leaders and boosted its determination to fight its demonized enemy to the bitter end. It also offered the Iranian armed forces precious respite, since Iraqi resources allocated to bombing civilians were not devoted to attacking military targets.

On February 1, 1984, the Iraqi government publicly announced its intention to bomb eleven Iranian cities located near the front, giving their inhabitants a few days' notice to evacuate. Tehran responded by threatening to shell the Iraqi cities within its artillery range. This was hardly enough to impress Saddam. On February 12 he launched the "war of the cities" by ordering a salvo of Scud missiles to be fired at Dezful. This initial operation left forty dead and close to 200 wounded.

The War of the Cities

The Iranians retaliated by bombing Basra, al-Faw, al-Qurnah, Mandali, and Khanaqin. The Iraqi government struck back with salvos of missiles fired at Abadan, Ahwaz, Susangerd, Andimeshk, Ilam, and Kermanshah.

The Iraqis could not use their artillery because most Iranian cities were outside cannon range and those that were too close to the front had been evacuated of their inhabitants. Instead, the regime decided to commit its air force. Tehran, Shiraz, and Esfahan were spared because they were out of range of Iraqi fighter planes and missiles. Iran did not have any ballistic missiles at its disposal and could only rely on its artillery and a few dozen Phantoms to strike back at Iraqi cities. Their pilots flew into enemy territory at very low altitude. They were careful to avoid the Baghdad sector, where their adversary had concentrated formidable surface-to-air defenses.

In late February Saddam Hussein proposed a truce, which Tehran rejected. Disappointed, he decided to make a symbolic strike against the Iranian capital, but also against Qom and Esfahan. Only his Tupolev bombers had the necessary range to reach these targets. Since the Tu-16s were considered too vulnerable for this mission, the Tu-22 Blinders were assigned. The air force high command remembered these bombers' mediocre performance at the beginning of the war and was not keen to risk sending them so far from their base. Yet it did as it was told. In early March several pairs of Tu-22s carried out nocturnal raids against the three Iranian cities. Tomcat patrols on twenty-four-hour air warning brought down three of the Tu-22s with Phoenix missiles. With his pilots left with only four operational Tu-22s, the air force chief of staff was compelled to scrap the attacks. The Iraqi president now had to find a way to end a bombing campaign that was turning to his disadvantage.

To break the deadlock, Saddam Hussein convened a high command meeting of his principal advisors and generals to find an alternative strategy. It quickly took shape. After having unsuccessfully targeted his adversary's military potential, followed by its industrial base and population, the dictator decided to attack its economy. His strategy was simple. It consisted in attacking oil tankers arriving to fill their tanks in Iran, at the risk of angering the Saudis and Kuwaitis, who feared this would give Iran a pretext to attack tankers coming to resupply in their ports. The Iraqi dictator knew that this campaign would be crossing a line and that he was radically shifting into a total war logic that could expose his own oil industry to Iranian retaliation. Yet he was convinced that he could force Iran to give up by drastically reducing its oil revenue. Tehran needed oil money to finance its war. Saddam also hoped that attacks on oil traffic would create a diversion, inciting the Iranians to stop bombing cities and focus on this new threat.

Lack of resources had previously limited the scale of Iraqi attacks on oil traffic. Iraq's Super Frelons did not have the range to strike beyond Kharg Island, and its Tupolev bombers had neither the missiles nor the bombing systems to allow for accurate attacks on naval targets. Yet over the previous few weeks Iraq had acquired an ideal combination of weapons to easily strike maritime traffic: France had rented it five Super Etendard fighter-bombers, which could fire the 200 AM-39 Exocet antiship missiles Iraq had bought at top dollar from Aérospatiale. At the time, the Super Etendard was one of the few combat aircraft able to fly right above sea level to fire an Exocet missile from a distance of twenty miles (thirty kilometers), giving it near-total protection from enemy fighters and anti-aircraft defense. These five aircraft had been assigned to the 81st Squadron based in Nasiriyah and were operational beginning on February 27, 1984. Their incorporation to the Iraqi fleet allowed the Iraqis to extend their striking range by 200 miles (300 kilometers) south of Kharg Island. Once the Super Etendards were delivered, the Super Frelon helicopters no longer fired Exocet missiles and were redeployed to lay Italian-made acoustic mines, principally around Kharg Island and in the Khor Musa channel.

Raid on Bushehr

Aware of the advantage its new striking force had given it, the Iraqi regime planned a raid that it had been eager to carry out for eighteen months: an attack on the Bushehr nuclear power plant. Satellite images provided by Washington showed that construction on the plant was advancing slowly but surely. The site was protected by a battery of Hawk missiles and a daunting concentration of anti-aircraft defenses. A classic air raid would have minimal chances of succeeding, and Scud missiles were not accurate enough to reach this kind of target. Only Super Etendards could hit Bushehr, thanks to their invaluable Exocet missiles, which could be fired from a safe distance. At nightfall on March 24, 1984, four Super Etendards took off in the direction of Bushehr. Their missiles had been set to lock on a static target the size of the structures sheltering the two future nuclear reactors. They flew over the Persian Gulf, skirted Kharg Island, and headed straight for the power plant. When they arrived twenty miles (thirty kilometers) from their objective, they set their radars to acquire the target, then fired a burst of missiles. They returned to base without any idea whether the raid had been successful.

Its outcome would only be revealed a few days later, through reconnaissance photos sent by American intelligence agencies. The news was disappointing—only secondary structures had been damaged. Yet the psychological toll on Iranian leaders was entirely real and led them to realize they would have to double their efforts to protect this crucial plant. The IAEA promptly turned its attention to the issue, suspecting Iran of wanting to build an atomic bomb, in violation of the Treaty on the Non-Proliferation of Nuclear Weapons (NPT), of which Tehran was a signatory. Once alerted, the media also jumped on the issue and accused the mullahs of trying to acquire a nuclear bomb. Due to the Bushehr power plant's strategic importance, the Iraqi air force attacked it six more times (twice in 1985, once in 1986, twice in 1987, and once in 1988). The most successful strike came in November 1986, when two Mirage F-1s severely damaged the protective dome of one of the plant's reactors with AS-30L missiles. The combined effect of these raids would result in more than four billion dollars' worth of damages and lead to a temporary halt in construction work.

The Tanker War

On March 27, 1984, a pair of Super Etendards took off on their first mission to find and strike oil tankers. The first direct hit was a mistake, striking the *Filikon L,* a Greek tanker carrying oil loaded in Kuwait. The ship had been sailing on the edge of the maritime exclusion zone. At the time Iraqi pilots did not have equipment to definitively identify their targets. Their radar screens only showed a dot of light, the shape of which varied according to the size of the ship targeted. Since Iraq did not have any maritime patrol aircraft to guide the way, Super Etendard pilots flew blind, merely following orders to engage with any ship traveling through the maritime exclusion zone. The second direct hit was a success, though it did not involve an oil tanker, but the South Korean cargo ship *Heyang*

Ilho, which was sunk while carrying supplies to an Iranian oil platform. Missions followed one another in rapid succession. On April 18 a Super Etendard hit the Panamanian tanker *Robert Star.* On April 25 the Saudi supertanker *Safina al-Arab* was set ablaze by the explosion of an Exocet after taking on a full load of Iranian crude at the Kharg terminal. Though the Saudis lambasted the Iranians, they had continued to do business with them. The Liberian tanker *Sea Eagle* was severely damaged on April 27, followed by another Saudi tanker, the *Al-Ahood,* on May 7. On May 13 the Iranian oil tanker *Tabriz* was hit.

Four other oil tankers were damaged by Exocet fire over the rest of the month of May. The mission profile was always identical. Nearly every day one or two Super Etendards took off from Nasiriyah shortly before dawn, searching for tankers that had arrived to load oil at the Kharg terminal during the night. They flew over the Gulf at moderate altitude escorted by a pair of Mirage F-1s and reached their sweep mission area within half an hour. Once there, they searched for a target on their radar. If they found one, they fired their single Exocet, praying for a direct hit. Yet they often returned to base unsuccessful, having failed to detect any tankers. To strike even further afield, the Iraqis also modified several Su-22 fighters to operate as refueling aircraft. The Su-22s doubled the striking range of the Super Etendards, all of which were equipped with in-flight refueling probes.

Early in May Tehran retaliated by attacking several Saudi and Kuwaiti tankers north of Bahrain—notably the 300,000-ton supertanker *Yanbu' Pride.* At the time, the Phantoms committed to these reprisal raids were only equipped with rockets and 20 mm shells, causing far lighter damages than those inflicted by the Iraqis. The Iranian pilots' operational methods were radically different from their adversaries'. They began by having an Orion maritime patrol aircraft fly over the zone. If it identified a target matching the desired criteria, a pair of Phantoms took off from the Bushehr or Bandar Abbas bases and headed straight for the target at low altitude. Once the two fighters had flown over the ship and verified its identity, they did two or three runs, firing their rockets and emptying their guns' magazines. At this stage of the conflict, the objective was not to sink ships, but to deliver a message to the Gulf monarchies: withdraw all support to Iraq, or the attacks will escalate. On May 16, 1984, Akbar

Hashemi Rafsanjani was more explicit in a statement to the international press: "We will not tolerate having difficulty exporting our oil from Kharg Island while other countries continue to easily export their oil. . . . The Persian Gulf will be accessible to all or to none."

The Fahd Line

Saudi Arabia reacted immediately. With the help of the United States, it implemented a no-fly zone extending far beyond its territorial waters. This area was demarcated by a "Fahd Line" along the naval exclusion zone established by Iran. This virtual line protected both Saudi oil installations— including those offshore—and the navigation channel connecting them to the Strait of Hormuz. A message was verbally conveyed to the Iranian regime, informing its leaders that it would be ill advised for them to cross this line. To reinforce King Fahd's staunch position, the United States announced with great fanfare that it was sending an air and sea group centered around the aircraft carrier *Midway* to the Gulf of Oman. The Iranian government decided to test the Saudis' resolve before the *Midway* arrived.

On June 5, 1984, a reconnaissance Orion crossed the Fahd Line and spotted two Saudi supertankers that had just left the Dhahran oil terminal in Saudi Arabia. Two Iranian Phantoms soon followed from their base in Bushehr, headed for the supertankers with the manifest intention of attacking them. They were immediately identified by AWACS, which promptly sent two Saudi F-15s in their direction. The F-15s quickly detected them. After having received confirmation of the order to engage, the two air-superiority fighters fired two Sparrow missiles at the Iranian planes. One of the Phantoms was obliterated, while the other was severely damaged and had to break combat to struggle back to base.[1] The furious Iranians decided to up the ante. Half an hour later six Phantoms took off from the Bushehr base, headed for the Saudi coast. Surveillance AWACS instantly detected them and conspicuously directed a formation of four Saudi F-15s and two F-5 Tigers to dissuade them from crossing the Fahd Line. The Iranians responded by committing six more Phantoms and six Tomcats, which were countered by an additional eight F-15s and eight Tigers from the Dhahran base. Within a single hour, forty Iranian and

Saudi fighters were aggressively maneuvering near the Fahd Line, aiming to intimidate, without actually firing. The Iranian fighters eventually ran short of fuel and were forced to turn back. King Fahd was exultant. The message had been received loud and clear. The Iranians took revenge five days later by attacking a Kuwaiti supertanker off the coast of the United Arab Emirates, out of the Saudi air-superiority fighters' range.

Despite the White House's security guarantees, the oil monarchies still refused to allow American troops on their soil. This irked the Pentagon, which thought that it would be easier to protect Saudi Arabia and Kuwait by having forces already on site. But Washington knew there was no use in antagonizing the Gulf leaders. The American administration's credibility was far from solid in the region. The United States needed to carefully play to the local monarchs' sensitivities to improve its image. To defuse the situation, Ronald Reagan told King Fahd that American armed forces would not directly intervene on Saudi soil unless specifically requested to do so by the kingdom. To ensure its ally's security, the American government signed a major arms deal with Saudi Arabia, providing for the delivery of M-1 tanks, Black Hawk helicopters, a new group of F-15 fighter jets, and 400 Stinger man-portable surface-to-air missiles.

The Air Force on the Front Line

Meanwhile, a new general had been appointed to head the Iraqi air force. Hamid Shaban was far better known for his talents as a strategist and a manager than as a pilot. Unlike his predecessor, he was not an apparatchik. He was convinced that the air force would play a decisive role in exhausting Iran. As a firm believer in air power, he developed a coherent strategy for using the air force and restructured it to orient Iraqi air missions toward fire support and deep strikes. He required qualified pilots to improve their skills at air-to-surface fire. An imaginative leader, Shaban lobbied for a certain number of outlandish projects that were met with much sarcasm. His principal asset was an ability to surround himself with competent, responsible people. He dismissed several of his subordinates and replaced them with individuals who had proven their worth.

He reoriented the air force's acquisition policy to prioritize the purchase of attack planes (MiG-23BNs, Su-22Ms, Su-25s, and Mirage F-1EQ5s).

He ordered the modification of previously delivered Mirage F-1s, which were strictly specialized in air-superiority missions, into deep-strike aircraft. He had heard about the merits of the Mirage F-1—which remained stable at very low altitude and was an excellent firing platform—from his own son, an accomplished Mirage pilot. General Shaban asked his mechanics to work with French technicians to modify the sixty Mirages in service so they could fire the most up-to-date air-to-surface munitions. Though he did not realize it, Shaban persuaded the French air force to follow his example and outfit itself with Mirage F-1 CTs optimized for attacking ground targets (which would be stunningly effective in the Chadian theater of operations).[2] Shaban also insisted that the new Mirage F-1s ordered from France be fitted with more reliable electronics, higher-capacity fuel tanks, and the most recent Exocet missiles. These initiatives encouraged Iraqi pilots to be more aggressive in facing off against their opponents, which were showing some muscle again after a long period of forced lethargy.

The Iranian air force had also acquired a more dynamic commander in Colonel Houshang Seddigh. His predecessor, Colonel Mojunpur, had paid the price for his excessive caution, but especially for the string of defections of dozens of pilots who had sought shelter in Turkey, Bahrain, Oman, and even Iraq. This new commander-in-chief had close ties to the clergy and enjoyed the regime's confidence. He convinced the Iranian authorities to allow his pilots to return to a regular training schedule. New recruits were initially trained in East Germany and Pakistan, then perfected their flying skills on twenty F-6 fighters delivered by China. These were copies of Soviet MiG-19s, which allowed young pilots to get accustomed to using combat planes on aircraft that were too obsolete to be committed to operations. Colonel Seddigh also succeeded in lifting the operational restrictions that had handicapped his fighter squadrons' effectiveness. Soon after his appointment, his pilots were reasserting their might, bringing down four Su-22s, two MiG-23s, two Mirage F-1s, and one MiG-25 over the front. The Iraqis modestly avenged themselves by attracting several enemy fighters into an ambush and shooting down one Phantom and one Tomcat. A precious Phoenix missile taken from the wreckage of the Tomcat was sent to Moscow to be studied by Soviet engineers.[3]

But Colonel Seddigh mostly reaped the benefits of a lucky combination of circumstances. His engineers had managed to crack the codes of the computerized system for managing the air force's spare parts, which had been locked by the Americans when they were expulsed from Iran. Thanks to this system, they were able to access an invaluable stockpile of hundreds of thousands of spare parts, which would allow them to keep half the fleet of Tomcats, Phantoms, and Tigers, which had survived four years of war, in the air for another two years. Meanwhile, Iranian "buyers" had obtained significant quantities of spare parts and munitions on the parallel market. Thanks to these combined factors, the Iranian air force had 140 operational fighters by the spring of 1984 (thirty Tomcats, sixty Phantoms, and fifty Tigers), nearly doubling what its fleet had been a year earlier.

With the outbreak of the oil tanker war, attacks on cities became less intense. The UN succeeded in imposing a moratorium on bombing civilian populations, which became effective on June 12, 1984. Beginning on June 24 Iraqi air raids resumed, now aimed at the Kharg terminal, through which 90 percent of Iranian crude oil exports passed. These attacks escalated over the summer. Iranian fighters shot down a Super Etendard on July 27, 1984.[4] The Iranians retaliated for the raids by multiplying attacks on oil tankers coming to load oil in Kuwait, Qatar, and the United Arab Emirates. Their Phantoms were now equipped with Maverick guided missiles, which caused far more extensive damage.

Mines in the Red Sea

During this period about ten commercial ships were damaged in the Red Sea by mines discreetly laid by "civilian" Libyan vessels. This was the fruit of Colonel Gaddafi's bid to contribute to the Iranian war effort by disrupting maritime traffic to the Yanbu oil terminal on Saudi Arabia's west coast.[5] The unruly Libyan dictator was trying to economically weaken the Egyptian government, with which he had a stormy relationship. The first drifting mines in the Red Sea led to an abrupt drop in maritime traffic along the Suez Canal, which Egypt relied on for a significant amount of its operating budget. To reassure President Mubarak, Washington held the massive Operation Bright Star military exercises in Egypt, near the

Libyan border, as a means of dissuading Colonel Gaddafi from continuing his attempts to destabilize the country. At Cairo and Riyadh's request, France sent four minesweepers to the Red Sea (Operations Grondin and Muge). For two months these ships would secure the approach to the Yanbu terminal and neutralize drifting mines.

Attacks on oil traffic in the Gulf continued through the fall. By late 1984 the Iraqi air force had hit forty-five commercial vessels, half of which were oil tankers; fourteen of these ships were sunk or sent to the scrapyard after having been irreparably damaged. Iraqi pilots fired eighty-five Exocets over the course of the year (versus forty-two in 1983), several of which hit the same target. According to Iraqi evaluations, two-thirds of the Exocets fired allegedly struck their targets, but 10 percent of them did not explode. The crude oil carried in the tankers' holds considerably attenuated the effect of the explosive charge, which was insufficient to ensure the destruction of heavy-tonnage ships.

Meanwhile, the Iranian air force sank only one ship and did more or less significant damage to thirteen others. Yet in the long run the effect of these attacks was limited, given that Iraq and Iran were both able to export nearly their total OPEC quotas in 1984 (1.2 and 2.3 million barrels per day, respectively). Baghdad was able to increase its oil exports by 18 percent during 1983; Tehran's exports dropped by 10 percent. The Iranian government's profit margin was halved because the Iranians had to substantially reduce the price of a barrel of crude oil to remain competitive in the face of rising insurance premiums for shipping companies sending their tankers to Kharg. To compensate for these drawbacks and limit risks taken by foreign ships, the Iranian authorities set up an oil tanker shuttle between Kharg and Lavan and the Strait of Hormuz.

Maintaining Troop Morale

Civilian and troop morale had been shaken by the bombing of cities, widespread destruction and shortages, constantly escalating casualties, but also the lack of a potential end in sight. Each belligerent used a different strategy to turn the situation around.[6] In Iraq the regime tried to reassure the people by reinforcing the cult of personality surrounding Saddam Hussein. Giant frescoes depicting the Iraqi dictator in glorious episodes of ancient history drawn from Babylon, the Caliphate, or the Crusades appeared on the walls of major cities. Saddam was represented as Nebuchadnezzar, Hammurabi, or Saladin, with a triumphant look and predatory smile, repelling the Persian lion on a chariot drawn by gleaming white stallions. Posters showing the dictator with farmers, workers, soldiers, but also foreign heads of state, were pasted all over the country. Eventually Iraqis joked that Iraq had 26 million inhabitants: 13 million citizens and 13 million portraits of Saddam.

The media deluged the population with comforting images of a hyperactive president, at ease in any setting, whether in the trenches with his generals or at the office with his ministers. Yet the media did not shy away from reporting the difficulties encountered on the front—though in minimized versions—to hammer home a simple message to the people: Iraq was fighting for survival, and everything possible had to be done to repel the invader. Government ministers and senior officials were encouraged to wear the same kind of fatigues as the military to show that the entire nation was mobilized. With the exception of soldiers, men were urged to regularly give blood and donate a day of their monthly wages to the state to subsidize the war effort. Women were invited to donate some of their jewelry. In a single year the state collected four tons of gold, which yielded 500 million dollars.

The population was called to volunteer to help drain the marshes to facilitate the building of defenses along the front. Children's books extolling the courage, heroism, and self-sacrifice of Iraqi soldiers were distributed in schools. Clips of Iranian soldiers killed on the front played over and over on national television. To compensate for the high number of fatalities, the regime promoted a policy aimed at increasing the birth rate by inciting each family to have at least five children. It encouraged young people between fifteen and seventeen years of age to follow a basic military training course, then to enroll before they were drafted. Deserving citizens were rewarded with a card that made them "Friends of Saddam." This valuable document paved the way to numerous material privileges: free health care, automatic access to higher education for members' children, and bank loans at preferential rates. The ultimate reward was that the "Friends of Saddam" were annually invited to meet the president and given a new suit for the occasion.

To confirm his legitimacy, Saddam Hussein organized general elections on October 20, 1984. Naturally, they were won by the Ba'ath Party. Conscious that he had to avoid falling into the sectarian trap that Tehran was laying for him, the Iraqi president reserved 40 percent of the seats in Parliament for Shiite deputies, reiterating in passing that the heart of Shiism was not in Iran, but in Iraq. This provocation angered Tehran, which made numerous sensational statements calling for the war to continue until Najaf and Karbala were liberated. The mullahs' extremism ultimately proved to be a tremendous asset for the Iraqi regime, which presented itself as the war's victim, despite the fact that Iraq had instigated it.

In adversity, the Iraqi people united behind their president. Their support was more readily achieved thanks to Saddam's unstinting efforts to promote a semblance of normality in Iraqis' everyday lives. Since the Iranian air force no longer seemed capable of bombing Baghdad, the capital's curfew was lifted. A significant part of the state's budget was devoted to buying manufactured products and common consumer goods. Stores were decently stocked, despite the fact that the volume of imports had dropped by half from 1982 to 1984. Agriculture was privatized to improve food supplies. Corporate and oil industry production was revived by the presence of one million Asian, Palestinian, and Egyptian technicians, as well as women, who replaced workers mobilized on the front. New developments were built in the suburbs of Baghdad to house the flood of refugees from combat zones. Major infrastructure projects continued, though they were considerably slowed by a lack of funds, forcing the government to devalue its currency and reduce civil servants' salaries. Iraq was now living on credit, thanks to the support of the oil monarchies, the United States, and all the countries that agreed to carry over its debt.

Saddam Hussein also took good care of his military. The standard of living of soldiers was improved by numerous perks. Following the Soviet model, medals were generously awarded. The most deserving officers were given one or several cars, sometimes even an apartment or a villa. Colonels and generals got Mercedes. Many years later some would brag with quavering voices that Saddam had given them one, two, maybe even three Mercedes as a reward for their amazing exploits.[7] The families of dead or disabled soldiers had the right to a pension, a plot of land, and an interest-free loan to build a house. However, the president was utterly merciless when it came to deserters and plotters, whose families were subjected to severe sanctions. In one instance, he ordered the execution of some fifty officers accused of having wanted to assassinate him at a reception at the officers' club in Baghdad on July 7, 1984.

Meanwhile, the Iranian regime relied on the cult of the martyr. A "fountain of blood" was erected on Tehran's central square to remind everyone of the sacrifice of the combatants fallen on the front. Streets, squares, and schools were renamed for the martyrs who died heroes' deaths and whose photos decorated walls. Newspapers overflowed with tales of their sacrifices. The general tone was aimed at making people feel guilty in order to incite as many combatants as possible to emulate the fallen. Iranian television constantly broadcast news pieces showing valiant Iranian fighters posing before the bodies of Iraqi soldiers. Processions of bearded Pasdaran stamped on huge American and Israeli flags draped over the capital's main avenues. Illustrated booklets narrating the exploits of martyrs fallen at the front were given away in schools and public buildings. The universities were closed and the students enrolled in the armed forces.

Everything was done to encourage austerity. Dress codes made black, the sign of mourning, the universal color for the whole population. Leaders promised their fellow citizens blood and tears, reminding them that this was a war that had been imposed upon them and that must be continued until victory. To motivate the troops, they evoked an imminent final offensive that would allow Iran to liberate its territory and the holy sites of Shiism. Beginning in 1985 Tehran would present each new year as the "decisive year" in which the war would come to an end. During Friday prayer the mullahs recalled the sacrifice of the Shiite saints and vaunted the martyrs' virtues. They guaranteed that those who died on the front would have immediate access to paradise, where they would be met with eternal glory and a cohort of houris, each more beautiful than the last.

For chaste, often unsophisticated, young soldiers who knew little other than the Koran's truth, this promise did not lack for appeal. Unlike Saddam, the Ayatollah Khomeini used religious sectarianism, presenting the continuing hostilities against Iraq as a legitimate crusade of Shiism versus Sunnism. He also did not hesitate to play to Iranians' nationalism, which proved a powerful factor in national unity. Reversion pensions were increased. Those disabled on the front were given priority to receive public employment. To encourage vocations, the Supreme Leader decreed a fatwa that authorized minors to enroll in the Basij without their parents' authorization, emphasizing that fighting for Islam was a moral obligation greater than work or education. The Martyrs' Foundation extended its services to young Basijis. Underprivileged families knew that if one or several of their children were killed in combat, their material situation would improve significantly. For large families without real prospects, this was a potent argument. Many young people would sacrifice themselves not for the glory of the regime but to offer their family a better future.

The regime also imposed strict observance of the precepts of Islam, giving the religious police full latitude to punish violators. Women's rights were further reduced, despite the fact that they were encouraged to replace men in factories, shops, public administrations, and private companies, always veiled in black. As in Iraq, they were invited to get rid of their jewelry to support the war effort. Their names were then published in the press to stimulate public generosity. Workers were urged to work without pay several days a month. Civil servants of age to be mobilized were incited to go to the front or pay a fraction of their salary to the state. Farmers were asked to make in-kind donations, however modest. Bartering was encouraged to avoid relying on the money machine. Electricity was cut several hours a day, and public administration budgets were drastically scaled back. Rationing became more severe, though those in power turned a blind eye to the expansion of the black market. The mullahs—and Rafsanjani in particular—knew that they had to go easy on the bazaar, which financed and supported them. To avoid a popular insurrection, the government subsidized staple products. All these efforts allowed the regime to observe strict budgetary orthodoxy so that it could devote one-third of GDP to the war effort. Knowing that it could not rely on any other outside aid, the government kept a currency reserve of approximately seven billion dollars to meet unexpected expenses. To show the people that it cared about them, the government ordered the construction of vast underground shelters intended to protect them from the devastating effects of Iraqi raids.

Yet the Islamic Republican Party experienced significant setbacks in the legislative elections held on April 15 and May 17, 1984—against expectations and despite the fact that it was supported by the Ayatollah Khomeini. This was a clear sign of the Iranians' weariness with the war and its deprivations. Though the IRP won the vote, the independent candidates' group, which gathered deputies from other parties, obtained an absolute majority of seats and demanded to debate the continuation of the war. Akbar Hashemi Rafsanjani was reelected speaker of the Majlis, but now had to negotiate with the other political groups, who opposed maintaining Mohammad Salimi as minister of defense. This was the parliamentarians' way of expressing a despondency that also appeared to be spreading to the military, based on the growing number of desertions. On August 29, 1984, two Iranian pilots defected with their Phantom fighter and sought shelter in Iraq. The Iraqis gave the plane to the Soviets to thank them for their valuable military aid.

Faced with discontent, the speaker of Parliament was forced to appoint a new minister of defense (Hussein Jalali) and tell the deputies his reasons for pursuing the war. He won their support following a stormy session, thanks to the decisive backing of the Ayatollah Khomeini and Hassan Rouhani, the chairman of the Majlis's Commission on Defense. By supporting Jalali's appointment, the ambitious thirty-six-year-old cleric Rouhani staked his political future on Rafsanjani, who would indeed fast-track his career. After the war Rouhani became vice-president of Parliament and secretary general of the Supreme National Security Council before joining the Assembly of Experts, then being appointed head negotiator on nuclear technology in Iran. Rouhani was elected president of the Islamic Republic on June 14, 2013, succeeding Mahmoud Ahmadinejad. In exchange for granting him his support, the Supreme Leader forced Rafsanjani to accept General Nejad as his personal representative to the Supreme Defense Council, knowing full well that the two men hated each other. This appointment was aimed to make Rafsanjani understand that he could no longer do whatever he liked and that he would not be able to win the war without the regular army's support. To make the message even clearer, the Ayatollah Khomeini had himself photographed embracing General Nejad. General Ismael Sohrabi was appointed chief of staff of the armed forces.

Meanwhile, Ali Khamenei took advantage of the situation to try to impose a new prime minister. But he had failed to take into account Rafsanjani's pugnacity. The speaker of Parliament convinced the Supreme Leader to keep Mir-Hossein Mousavi in position to thwart his great rival's influence. Offended that he had been disowned by the Supreme Leader, Ali Khamenei developed ever more radical rhetoric, rejecting on principle any sign of Iran's opening up to the outside world. This episode only served to exacerbate Ali Khamenei's resentment toward Mir-Hossein Mousavi, which culminated after the outcome of the 2009 presidential elections with his ordering the arrest of Mousavi, the reformist opposition candidate.

The Kurdish Independence Movement Forces Turkey into a Rapprochement with Iraq

For Ankara, the equation had radically changed since Iran had succeeded in shifting combat to the north of Iraq, near the Turkish border. The Turkish government was forced to prioritize security over its commercial interests, which led it to form closer ties with Baghdad and to distance itself from Tehran. In Turkey, Kurdish activists took advantage of this situation to establish rear bases in Iraqi territory. Since 1978 Turkey had had to contend with the activism of the Kurdistan Workers' Party (PKK), a Marxist organization founded by Abdullah Öcalan. After the 1980 coup d'état in Turkey, the PKK was banned and relentlessly suppressed by the generals. On August 15, 1984, Abdullah Öcalan turned to guerilla warfare, encouraged by Kurdish successes in Iraq and Iran. After harassing several Turkish garrisons, his peshmergas took refuge in the north of Iraq.

Since the Iraqi regime was bogged down in the war with Iran and unable to react, the Turkish army took things in hand. It launched several incursions onto Iraqi territory to attempt to wipe out the PKK's bases, but without much success. The Iraqi authorities had been notified, but could only admit their inability to locate and destroy the PKK's hideouts. Aware that he was unable to drive out the rebels, Saddam Hussein agreed to negotiate a mutual cooperation agreement with Ankara aimed at fighting the PKK. According to the terms of this agreement, signed on October 15,

1984, each of the two parties was authorized to enter and take military action on the other party's soil within a three-mile- (five-kilometer-) wide strip without prior notification. For the sake of maintaining a balance, Ankara attempted to negotiate a similar agreement with Iran. This proposal was met with the polite but firm refusal of President Ali Khamenei, who did not want to surrender an iota of his sovereignty to a lay regime allied with the Americans.

Chapter 21

The Year of the Pilot

On January 27, 1985, after more than two years of maintaining a defensive position on the ground, Iraq went on the offensive and attempted to recapture the Majnoon Islands and their precious oil fields. The operation was headed by General al-Rashid and General Fakhri, respectively the commanders of the 3rd and 6th Army Corps. They committed four of their best divisions and two commando brigades. While the divisions launched a large-scale clean-up operation to the north and south of the Majnoon Islands to flush out the Iranian combatants constantly infiltrating Iraqi lines, the special forces attacked the two islands after intense artillery preparation. Curled up in their boats, the commandos slalomed through the marshes and dashed for their target, dodging bursts of fire from anti-aircraft guns mounted on floating barges. They were counterattacked by the Pasdaran as soon as they landed. The fighting was extraordinarily fierce and ended in hand-to-hand combat, with the two sides rivals in tenacity. The Iranians sent in reinforcements along their dykes, overwhelming the attacking troops. At the end of the day the commandos had to abandon the northern island, but kept a bridgehead on the southern island, which was closer to their lines. They had regained control of about ten oil wells and immediately began building their own dyke so they could also bring in significant reinforcements.

On January 31 Iraqi command launched another attack. This assault was in the sector of Qasr-e-Shirin and was aimed at recapturing the line of peaks dominating Sumer. The Iraqis seized the area, but were driven out the next day by a violent counterattack, which cost the Iranians several battalions. On February 12 the Iraqis mounted a second attack, now in the direction of Mehran. Though they failed to capture the devastated city, they advanced four miles (seven kilometers) and entered Iran. Each of these attempts indicated that rearmament and the professionalization of the Iraqi officer corps were finally bearing fruit. Though the Iranians still had more men on the front, the Iraqis now had far superior firepower and mobility. They also had one tank for every one hundred soldiers, while the Iranian tank-to-soldier ratio was 1 to 500.

The Second Battle of the Marshes

The powers that be in Tehran were determined to take back the initiative. They agreed to a major offensive named Badr, in reference to the famous victory by the Prophet that had opened the road to Mecca. The operation was intended to rattle the Iraqi regime. Akbar Hashemi Rafsanjani convinced his peers to strike in the same place as the previous year—the heart of the Hoveyzeh marshes—to cut off the road to Baghdad and isolate Basra. According to him, the Iraqis would be taken by surprise. The speaker of Parliament also put forth another argument: in the marshes, the enemy's firepower would be considerably reduced, and its tanks would be useless; this would give Iranian infantrymen a better chance of gaining the upper hand. The Ayatollah Khomeini agreed, on condition that the operations be conducted both by the regular army and the Pasdaran.

The military high command fine-tuned its plans, having learned from its previous failures. Infantrymen, including those with the Pasdaran, were now equipped with gas masks, capes, and atropine syringes to protect themselves from the effects of chemical weapons. Their weaponry was better adapted. Each man now had a helmet, an assault rifle, and more grenades and antitank rockets. They were also better trained. The regime had consented to specific measures to improve cooperation between the regular army and the Pasdaran. Most of their gap-crossing equipment had been gathered near the attack sector. To deceive their adversary, the Iranian command ordered a series of exercises to be carried out across from the 3rd and 4th Corps, while the offensive was to take place in the marshy area held by the 6th Corps. Here, the Iranians had assembled eleven divisions that were to launch successive waves of assault on the enemy lines held by three infantry divisions.[1]

At nightfall on March 11, 1985, two Pasdaran divisions and three mechanized divisions quietly infiltrated the marshes and headed for the Tigris. At dawn they overran the Iraqi 35th Infantry Division. Overwhelmed by the Iranians' numbers and lacking artillery support, the defenders retreated to the river. Many were taken prisoner. The next day the Pasdaran reached the Tigris and began building three pontoon bridges a dozen miles (about twenty kilometers) south of al-Azair. In mid-afternoon a mechanized battalion crossed the river, reached the Baghdad-Basra road, and pressed south toward al-Qurnah. It established itself at the entrance of the village and took control of the bridge over the Euphrates, blocking potential reinforcements arriving from Basra. Further south two Pasdaran divisions left the Majnoon Islands and crossed the lake on landing craft to attack the Iraqi 4th Infantry Division with the support of their floating artillery. The Iraqi infantrymen resisted a few hours, but were finally overcome. Some held on to their positions and were surrounded, while others retreated toward the Tigris and waited for reinforcements.

The counterattack was coordinated by General Dhannoun, the Iraqi chief of staff. The 5th Mechanized Division left Basra along the Shatt al-Arab's west bank and recaptured al-Qurnah, while the 6th Armored Division traveled up the river's other bank to reinforce the 4th Infantry Division. Further north the 10th and 12th Armored Divisions overran the Iranian units that had crossed the Tigris. Even the Republican Guard Division left Baghdad and rushed to the combat zone. Meanwhile, army aviation's helicopters flew over the marshes, destroying landing craft carrying Iranian reinforcements, and high-altitude Tupolev bombers pounded the Pasdaran units' boarding sites on the Hoveyzeh marshes' eastern bank.

On March 13 an Iraqi commando brigade tasked with cutting off the Pasdaran's retreat was airlifted to the heart of the marshes by helicopter. It was joined by two other special forces brigades dropped off nearby by trucks. The next day the Iraqi counteroffensive progressed on every axis, supported by its artillery, which unleashed large quantities of chemical weapons. Though their effect was less devastating than the previous time, they contributed to disorganizing the Iranian combatants, who were not used to fighting with the limited mobility and vision imposed by their waterproof capes and the steamy gas masks over their faces. The Iraqi troops, which were better trained to maneuver in contaminated environments, pushed them back toward the marshes. However, the Iraqi 37th Tank Brigade fell into a fatal ambush. Iranian combatants came out of hiding at the last moment and fired their RPG-7 rockets at extremely close range, mercilessly picking off the Iraqi tanks one by one. These Iranian infantrymen fearlessly confronted Iraqi machine-gun and cannon fire to assault the T-62s.

On March 16 the Republican Guard arrived and joined the battle. Their T-72s charged at the Pasdaran, rolling over numerous infantrymen desperately trying to stop their advance. The Iraqi commandos who had infiltrated the marshes harassed the Iranians and cut off all escape routes; 2,000 Iranians were taken prisoner in less than forty-eight hours. Under pressure from Rafsanjani, the Iranian command committed its reserves, hoping to reverse the battle's outcome. But it was too late. The Iraqi divisions were advancing everywhere, liberating al-Ajrada, al-Sabkha, and Beida. They violently cracked down on the villagers, accusing them of collaborating with the enemy.

On March 18 Hosni Mubarak traveled to Baghdad to show his support for the Iraqi cause and encourage the Gulf monarchies to increase their financial participation in the war effort. This was the first trip to Iraq by an Egyptian president since Saddam Hussein had come to power. Saddam appreciated the gesture and ensured the Rais he would support his bid to have the Arab League's seat quickly moved back to Cairo.

By March 22 the Iraqis had recaptured all the territory lost at the beginning of the offensive and had inflicted heavy losses on their opponent: 10,000 dead, twice as many wounded, 2,000 prisoners, about a hundred armored vehicles destroyed, and a dozen transport helicopters brought down. Three Iranian divisions had been wiped out entirely, and four others severely trounced. In the Iraqi camp, 2,000 soldiers had been killed, 3,000 captured, and 6,000 wounded. Material losses were limited to one hundred tanks, eleven helicopters, and four PC-7 light aircraft (used to spread chemical weapons) shot down by anti-aircraft defense. Saddam Hussein boasted of his success in the media and lavished Mercedes on his generals. The Iraqi army's morale was at a high.

In Tehran the mood was morose. Criticism aimed at the speaker of Parliament streamed in from every direction, with many holding him responsible for the failure of an offensive that had weakened both the regular army and the Pasdaran. Ali Khamenei was unsparing with his rival, arguing that it would be best to end hostilities in order to definitively put down the regime's opponents, who continued to organize ter-

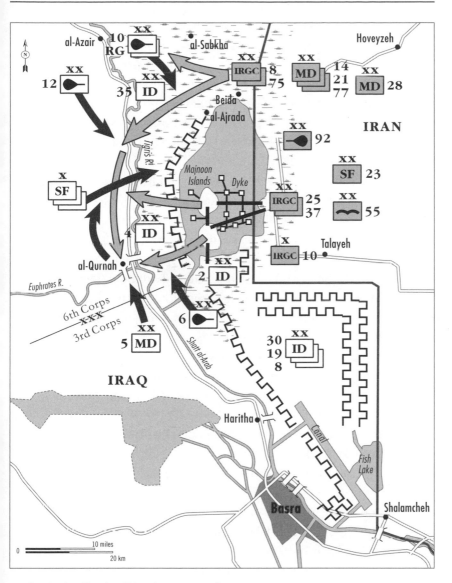

Iranian Badr offensive (March 11–22, 1985)

rorist attacks in major cities and harass security forces in those provinces seeking independence. The People's Mujahidin were particularly active again and carried out several spectacular attacks in the Iranian capital. Rafsanjani reacted by decreeing a temporary halt to major offensives and a return to the attrition strategy. He also made concessions to the regular army, which had been asking for months to put an end to the human wave tactic and return to classic mechanized combat.

Nonetheless, Rafsanjani continued to employ the rhetoric of the "final offensive" that would bring the Iraqi regime to its knees. Since the army was dragging its feet, he now relied on the Pasdaran. He summoned their minister Mohsen Rafighdoost and their commander Mohsen Rezaee to ask them to secretly prepare a large-scale offensive that would be exclusively conducted by the Pasdaran and the Basijis. To compensate for the regular army's absence, Rafsanjani committed to provide them with all the necessary means of support they had previously lacked. He obtained the Supreme Leader's permission to create an artillery command within the Revolutionary Guards, as well as a naval component. He gave orders to establish an engineering division charged with providing the means to quickly cross the Shatt al-Arab. He called for two regular army artillery brigades to be turned into full-fledged divisions, then transferred to the Pasdaran. He also authorized the creation of two new infantry divisions specialized in amphibious assault.

Finally, he entrusted the Pasdaran's naval branch to Colonel Ali Araki Hamadani and allocated him three commando brigades taken from naval infantry battalions. These were provided with one hundred patrol boats and high-speed motor boats bought from China, North Korea, and Sweden. These small boats were equipped with a cannon, a machine gun, and a rocket-launcher and were intended to harass maritime traffic around the Strait of Hormuz and support the Pasdaran's next offensive at the mouth of the Shatt al-Arab. The regular army generals were furious about these measures, but could not contest them: they had been approved by the Ayatollah Khomeini, who remained their most valuable supporter. Their room to maneuver was even more restricted by the fact that they had been pleading for modern equipment for months, notably for invaluable TOW antitank missiles, which could allow them to beat back Iraqi tanks.

Another War of the Cities

As soon as Operation Badr started, the Iraqi air force reacted to the Iranian offensive by launching a new bombing campaign aimed at the

Iranian industrial infrastructure. Having learned from experience, Saddam Hussein preferred to target the country's economic potential rather than its civilian population. But the Iranian government did not play by the same rules. It fiercely counterattacked, striking Baghdad with Scud-B missiles on March 14, 1985. This was the first time Iran used Scuds, which it had just received from Libya.[2] The spectacular initial attack caused extensive damage to downtown Baghdad. It was a major slap in the face to Saddam Hussein, who had always told his compatriots that the Iraqi capital was safe from an enemy strike. The dictator was all the more furious given that his own Scud missiles did not have the range to reach Tehran. Nonetheless, he ordered Frog and Scud missiles to be fired at several Iranian cities and asked Commander Shaban, the head of the air force, to find a way to regularly bomb Tehran. The Tupolev bombers did not seem like the solution, since they had been thrashed during the first phase of the war of the cities. A single option began to take shape: using MiG-25 interceptors, provided they were modified for bombing missions. The MiG-25 was the only other combat aircraft in service in the air force with sufficient operating range to carry out the mission without in-flight refueling. Theoretically, its cruising altitude and high speed kept it out of Iranian air-superiority fighters' reach.

The plan seemed feasible because the Soviets had designed an automated firing system to allow their MiG-25s to fire a tactical nuclear bomb weighing several dozen kilotons. Soviet engineers had later perfected the process to fire traditional 1,100-pound (500-kilogram) bombs. The Iraqi authorities promptly made contact with the Kremlin to negotiate the urgent delivery of several of these sophisticated release systems, as well as a stock of suitable bombs. Within a few days, the Iraqi air force had four modified MiG-25s at its disposal. They were deployed to the Kirkuk base, which was the closest to the Iranian capital. The missions began soon after. Every night, a MiG-25 carrying four bombs and two external fuel tanks took off from Kirkuk headed east. Flying over the mountains, it crossed the Iranian border after five minutes. It then jettisoned its external fuel tanks, climbed to an altitude of 60,000 feet (18,000 meters), and accelerated to more than twice the speed of sound.

At this velocity and altitude, it took no more than twenty minutes to reach the drop point located twenty-five miles (forty kilometers) from

Tehran. The fire-control computer and inertial navigation system automatically triggered the dropping of the bombs, leaving the pilot free to navigate the plane. The projectiles covered the last twenty-five miles (forty kilometers) along a ballistic trajectory while the pilot tipped his aircraft and returned to base. The entire mission lasted less than an hour. While this standoff fire was not accurate (the bombs often fell one to two miles [two to three kilometers] from the target), it considerably limited the risk of interception. Lack of accuracy was not a problem in that only the civilian population was targeted. Concurrently, Saddam Hussein decreed a no-fly zone over all of Iranian territory, leading to the interruption of most commercial flights to Tehran.

For four weeks the Iraqi MiG-25s dropped their bombs on Tehran every day. The cities of Tabriz, Shiraz, Esfahan, and even Qom were also hit. The Ayatollah Khomeini, who had been visiting the holy city, was hurried back to his bunker in the Tehran suburbs. None of the MiG-25s committed to this mission were shot down. Meanwhile, MiG-23s, Su-22s, and Mirage F-1s struck residential neighborhoods in cities near the front. During these missions Iranian fighters shot down two MiG-23s. To motivate his pilots, the Iraqi president emphatically decreed that 1985 would be "the year of the pilot."

The Iranian generals desperately requested Hawk surface-to-air missiles to try to repel the MiG-25 raids. Most city dwellers spent the night in underground shelters, while the more audacious climbed to the roofs of their buildings to watch the anti-aircraft defense's tracers draw lines across the sky. The Iranian air force retaliated by bombing Baghdad, Amarah, Kut, Nasiriyah, Mosul, Baquba, and even Tikrit, Saddam's native city. It lost two Phantoms over the Iraqi capital. The Iranians did not venture over Basra, for the city remained within range of their artillery and was defended by an exceedingly high concentration of surface-to-air missiles. For the time being, they spared the holy cities of Najaf and Karbala, as well as the Kurdish cities, in order to remain in their potential allies' good graces.

On April 21, 1985, Saddam Hussein once again called on the Iranians to put an end to the conflict. To reach a ceasefire, he proposed an end to the bombing of civilian populations, the withdrawal of both armies to the borders, the exchange of all war prisoners, and direct negotiations between the two countries to set the amount of reparations. The question of the Shatt al-Arab was no longer raised. The Iraqi dictator, who was in a rush to end a war that had lasted for far too long, was implicitly surrendering his claim on the river. But this was not enough to satisfy the Iranian leaders, who stubbornly reiterated their principal two conditions: the departure of Saddam Hussein and the repatriation of Iraqi Shiite refugees in Iran, whom they hoped would weaken the Ba'athist regime once back in Iraq. To drive the point home, another salvo of Iranian Scud missiles was fired at Baghdad. The Iraqi president replied by ordering a massive strike on Tehran, which left seventy-eight dead and 325 wounded in a single night. Exceptionally, this terror strike was carried out by four Tu-16 bombers, the only bombers capable of delivering a large number of bombs. The Tu-16s, which were equipped with jammer pods for this mission, flew by night and all safely returned to their base in Tammuz.

In May missile stocks ran low. In early June the strikes became rarer. Each side knew it would be unable to make the other yield and that it needed to hold on to a few Scuds as a safety. A new truce in the war of the cities was confirmed on June 15, 1985, under the aegis of the UN Secretary General, putting an end to the bombings that had killed 2,000 in Iran and 600 in Iraq. Yet this truce did not bring an end to hostilities. Following the government's instructions, the Iranian military high command planned a series of ground operations intended to keep up the pressure on Baghdad. Their goal was simple: to ruin the Iraqi regime by forcing it to maintain its overmanned army on the front.

From June 14 to 28, 1985, the Iranian generals mounted Operation Al-Quds 1 ("Jerusalem 1") to the north of the Majnoon Islands. This was not a proper offensive, but a succession of raids aimed at encroaching on enemy positions. One of these raids, conducted by a commando brigade, even succeeded in reaching the banks of the Tigris. Yet each raid was eventually pushed back by Iraqi firepower. For several months clashes in this sector were reminiscent of the ambushes associated with paddy field combat in the Indochina and Vietnam wars. Each night small groups of Iraqi soldiers would track down Iranian combatants trying to infiltrate Iraqi lines through the marshes, slaloming through the bulrushes on their small boats.

Applying their favorite tactic of striking in different places to surprise the enemy, the Iranians attacked the Qasr-e-Shirin sector on June 19. Operation Jerusalem 2, carried out by two infantry brigades, led to the destruction of a few bunkers and the capture of fifty Iraqi soldiers. The next day the Iranians launched Operation Fath ("Victory") in the Basra sector to test the strength of the local Iraqi layout. They quickly understood that it remained solid and that a frontal assault in this sector would be costly.

These harassment operations lasted through the summer. From July 26 to August 7 the Iranian generals conducted Operation Jerusalem 4 in the Mandali sector. During the last two weeks of September they launched Operation Jerusalem 6 between Mehran and Sumer. In October they multiplied skirmishes in the Qasr-e-Shirin sector, then once again shifted battle to the Hoveyzeh marshes. The coming of the rainy season put an end to their attempts, at least until the end of the year.

Guerilla Warfare in Iraqi Kurdistan

In 1985 Iraqi Kurdistan saw a resurgence of activity. In late January Jalal Talabani, the head of the PUK, denounced the neutrality agreement made with the Iraqi regime. He criticized Baghdad for its deal with Ankara, which allowed Turkey to hunt down PKK troops in Iraq. Aside from his commitment to the defense of the Kurdish cause, Talabani needed PKK leader Abdullah Öcalan's support to counter the influence of Talabani's principal rivals, the Barzani brothers and their KDP. The PUK's leader could no longer remain neutral once Abdullah Öcalan was attacked by Baghdad. Jalal Talabani also had a pragmatic understanding that he had to get along with the Iranians now established in Iraqi Kurdistan. The Iranians might well take over the entire region and become the only ones who could influence the Barzani clan.

Fearing a popular insurrection in the Kurdish provinces, Saddam Hussein proposed a general amnesty for the PUK's peshmergas on condition that they lay down their weapons. Jalal Talabani rejected the offer and went underground. He ordered his troops to attack symbols of power in the cities of Kirkuk, Erbil, and Sulaymaniah. In early March his 10,000 peshmergas were simultaneously fighting the Iraqi Popular Army, the

Barzani brothers' guerrilla fighters, and the PDKI survivors who had allied themselves with Baghdad. The situation rapidly descended into chaos, with each faction battling the others while fighting the Ba'athist regime. The Iraqi government gradually abandoned Abdul Rahman Ghassemlou's PDKI, which seemed increasingly marginalized.

In March, seeing that things were slipping out of his control, Ghassemlou broke with Baghdad and initiated a prudent rapprochement with Tehran. Through these alliances, the Iranian government hoped to neutralize the PDKI and put a definitive end to the Kurdish rebellion. Negotiations were conducted abroad and dragged on without leading to a formal agreement. They would nonetheless allow the Iranian government to reduce its military presence in the area, letting it commit additional divisions to Iraqi Kurdistan. In July 1988 Abdul Rahman Ghassemlou was assassinated by the Iranian special service, in the wings of yet another negotiation session. Tehran would subsequently sign a definitive agreement with his successor.

The Iraqi regime was now fighting against every one of the Kurdish factions. Fortunately for Baghdad, the factions remained divided and did not truly follow Tehran's instructions. Throughout the spring combat was limited to guerilla operations for the control of passes, plunging valleys, and isolated villages—the peshmergas did not yet have the means to face the Iraqi army in the open countryside and big cities. These battles, often fought in the mist at high altitudes, were captured in the poignant documentary *Living in the Clouds,* directed by the Iranian director Azizolah Hamidnejad.

In early July 1985 the Iranians launched Operation Jerusalem 3 in the direction of Sulaymaniah. Jalal Talabani's peshmergas created a diversion by seizing the old Hassan Beg fortress north of Kirkuk. They were chased out a few days later by Iraqi paratroopers. On July 14 the Iranian 30th Infantry Division left Penjwin, overran the Iraqi forces deployed outside it, and advanced about twenty miles (about thirty kilometers) along a narrow valley before being stopped by heavy barrage fire and air force intervention. A little further south the Iranian 35th Infantry Division unsuccessfully attempted to take control of Halabja. The town, which controlled access to the Darbandikhan dam, was locked down by several brigades of infantrymen. They did not yield an inch. For two weeks the

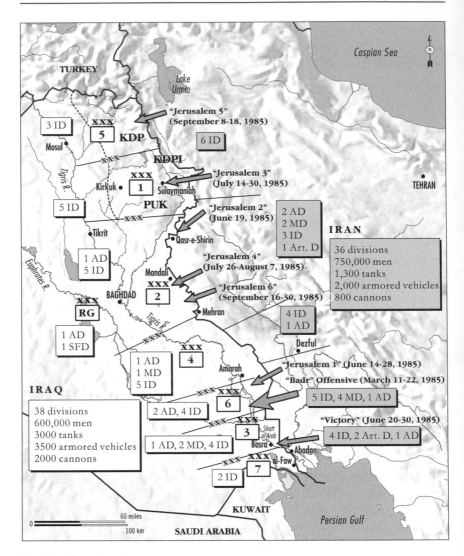

Iran-Iraq front in 1985

Iraqi army counterattacked, pushing the Iranians back about six miles (about ten kilometers).

Both sides used the month of August to reorganize their layouts. On September 8 the Iranians took back the initiative and launched Operation Jerusalem 5 in the north of Kurdistan. Supported by an armored brigade, artillery, and a few armed helicopters, an Iranian infantry division seized Rayat and continued advancing toward Rawanduz. It was stopped by the 23rd Infantry Division, which was guarding this small mountain city. In mid-September the Iraqi army launched a counteroffensive in this sector, using reinforcements from the 24th and 33rd divisions, backed by two tank brigades and one commando brigade. Faced with the Iraqis' manpower, the Iranians were forced to yield ground. On September 18 the front stabilized some twenty miles (some thirty kilometers) east of Rawanduz at the foot of a mountain range peaking at 11,800 feet (3,600 meters). Realizing that they lacked adequate forces, the Iranians did not mount any operations in Iraqi Kurdistan in the fall. However, they actively worked to bring the KDP and PUK together. But they were primarily concerned with internal policy questions.

The Presidential Election in Iran

During the summer Akbar Hashemi Rafsanjani had suggested postponing the presidential election planned for mid-August, arguing that the military operations underway would hamper the proceedings. The Ayatollah Khomeini opposed his suggestion and insisted that the election take place on the projected date. Khomeini believed nothing should hinder the democratic process; the Islamic Republic needed to be perceived as a model of democracy, both inside and outside the country. This was important not only for its image, but to preserve its popular legitimacy and its soldiers' support. The Iranian authorities brought ballot boxes to the front and organized rotations allowing each combatant to accomplish his civic duty. The electoral commission traveled to field hospitals to ensure that wounded and maimed soldiers could vote. On August 16, 1985, Ali Khamenei was reelected president of the republic with 88 percent of the vote, despite a headline-grabbing family scandal: a few weeks before the election, Khamenei's sister had fled to Iraq with her children and husband, Ayatollah Ali Tehrani, denouncing the "dictatorial" regime in Tehran. Bolstered by his reelection, Ali Khamenei put on his combat uniform and military cap and went on an inspection tour of the front, talking to numerous unit commanders. Rafsanjani realized that he would have to tread carefully with his rival, whose popularity was constantly growing in a country devastated by five years of warfare.

Chapter 22

Oil and the War Machine

The Gulf sovereigns were alarmed by the war's increasingly all-encompassing nature. They understood that Iraq probably wouldn't win, that Iran probably wouldn't lose, and that the only way to put an end to hostilities was by negotiating with Tehran. The war was starting to cost everyone too much. The heads of the GCC called on the two belligerents to be more flexible and openly received Iranian envoys in their palaces, infuriating Saddam Hussein, who accused them of sacrificing the Arab cause to their commercial interests. He was not entirely wrong—Sheikh Zayed, the president of the UAE, would have liked to increase trade with Iran.

Seeking to fortify his international stature, King Fahd of Saudi Arabia decided to intervene and impose himself as a mediator acceptable to both parties. He already had Saddam Hussein's trust, but he had to win the mullahs'. On May 18, 1985, having already quietly hosted Iranian Minister of Energy Hassan Ghafouri-Fard in Riyadh, Fahd sent his minister of foreign affairs, Prince Faisal, to Tehran to discuss a potential rapprochement between the two countries. There was no shortage of issues to discuss, including the Iran-Iraq War, guarantees of regional security, and OPEC. The Saudi envoy told his Iranian hosts that King Fahd would stop all aid to Iraq if Iran accepted a ceasefire. He also sounded them out about the price of peace. How much money did the Iranians expect to put an end to hostilities? The Saudis were prepared to bid very high to buy a return to calm in the region, particularly since they could rely on the solidarity fund the GCC had started for this purpose. In the meantime, as a gesture of goodwill, the Saudis gave the Iranians refined oil, which they had sorely lacked since the Iraqi air force had destroyed several of their refineries. Tehran appreciated the gesture and expressed its gratitude for the Saudi king's generosity.

As if by chance, Hezbollah picked this moment to release Hussein Farrash, the Saudi consul it had kidnapped in Beirut a few months earlier. Discussions could now proceed under better auspices. In an effort to be accommodating, Akbar Hashemi Rafsanjani proposed a plan by which the Gulf monarchies would stop all aid to Iraq and agree to contribute to Saddam Hussein's downfall, in exchange for which Iran would commit to holding off from promoting the radical Islamic fringe's rise to power in Iraq and to making peace with the new government, no matter its composition or persuasion. However, Iran would not compromise on one point: the ousting of Saddam Hussein. This was precisely the problem: the Gulf sovereigns all feared the Iraqi dictator and knew how brutal he was; none wanted to take a chance on committing to the risky and highly unpredictable process of his planned elimination. Nonetheless, King Fahd passed the proposal along to Washington. The Americans responded unambiguously: the administration had no credible plan to replace Saddam and refused to sacrifice him and scuttle its efforts at making a rapprochement with Iraq. Convinced that his alliance with Washington was vitally important, the Saudi monarch could not ignore the American diktat. He now had to tell the Iranian authorities that his initiative had fallen through.

Washington and Riyadh Agree on a New Oil Policy

Since King Fahd could not come to an agreement with Tehran, and it was increasingly urgent to put an end to this war, which was daily becoming more costly and detrimental to the Gulf's security, he changed strategies and accepted a proposal CIA director William Casey had made to him two years earlier. The plan was to economically suffocate not only Iran, but also the Soviet Union—the two countries the Saudi monarch most feared. How? Simply by opening the floodgates of Saudi oil wells to decrease the price of oil. The argument was irrefutable; Iran drew four-fifths of its revenue from oil sales. If its oil sales collapsed, Tehran would no longer be able to finance its war effort, given that the Islamic Republic had chosen to marginalize itself from the international banking system and could not count on any state for financial support. Nobody provided Iran with arms free of charge, not even Libya and Syria. Repercussions of the price drop on Iraq would probably be manageable, since Baghdad was waging its war on credit, relying on loans from the oil monarchies and major banks supported by American guarantees. The idea that Iraq would be more dependent on its financial backers was far from disagreeable to the Custodian of the Two Holy Mosques. Riyadh could make up for the drop in oil prices by increasing its production. With one of the largest oil reserves in the region, Saudi Arabia had an extraction potential of more than ten million barrels per day, which it was currently only exploiting at one-fifth of its capacity.

The royal family was strongly divided over the American proposal, with several princes fearing that by playing God, Riyadh could trigger a downward spiral that would durably weaken the kingdom. But King Fahd swayed the members of the Family Council by explaining that this strategy would allow them to sanction OPEC members—particularly Iran—that did not respect approved prices and offered unauthorized discounts to attract new clients, but also to wear out European oil producers who sold North Sea petroleum at prices far lower than those set by OPEC. He ultimately won the family over thanks to the decisive support of Prince Turki al-Faisal, head of Saudi intelligence services and a close friend of the director of the CIA. This was excellent news for William Casey and Ronald Reagan, who interpreted it as the successful realization of their plan to suffocate both Iran and the USSR. To reassure King Fahd, the highest American authorities reiterated their commitment to defend the Saudi monarchy under any circumstances, repeating the pledge President Roosevelt had made to King Ibn Saud aboard the U.S. cruiser *Quincy* forty years earlier.

Since 1982 various reports had pointed out the exhaustion of the Soviet economy, which was handicapped by its bureaucratic system, the increase in the price of raw materials, the dramatic surge in its military budget due to the exorbitant cost of its intervention in Afghanistan, and especially the arms race the Kremlin had shrewdly been lured into by the White House (the famous "Star Wars" program). These reports showed that Moscow was financing its tottering empire through massive oil exports. The Soviet Union primarily functioned as a closed circuit and did not have any significant sources of revenue aside from its gold sales, which served as a reliable indicator of its economic problems. From 1980 to 1984 the Kremlin had quadrupled its gold sales, a clear sign of the catastrophic state of its finances.

The American administration was convinced that the best way to bring the Soviet system to its knees was to cause a collapse in oil prices. Several of its analysts had shown that the USSR would lose one billion dollars for every dollar decrease in the price per barrel of oil. American strategists crunched the numbers and concluded that they had to convince Saudi leaders to follow them in this endeavor, which also served Saudi interests, since King Fahd considered the Soviets "the true infidels."[1] This strategy would also allow them to dry up Soviet investments in natural gas, which appeared to be oil's principal competition. The timing seemed particularly good, given that the United States had reduced its energy dependency on the Gulf and that Washington needed to boost American industry by promoting consumer spending through affordable oil. To accentuate the strategy's effects, the American government allowed its currency to drop, further diminishing oil revenue, which was negotiated in dollars, and facilitating its own exports (the dollar would lose 37 percent of its value over eighteen months). The Iranian argument was only the tip of the iceberg, but it was the one that convinced the Saudis.

As agreed, King Fahd ordered the floodgates opened as of July 1985. Oil poured forth, reaching six million barrels per day by the end of the summer, nine million by the end of the fall, and ten million in January 1986. After having peaked at thirty-five dollars in late 1982, then stabilized around twenty-nine dollars for nearly three years, the price per barrel began plummeting, eventually dropping below the symbolic ten-dollar bar. In the spring of 1986 Vice President George Bush, looking out for American oil companies, agreed with King Fahd to moderately increase the price per barrel and stabilize it around fifteen dollars.

These developments were met with utter dismay in Iran, Iraq, and the Soviet Union. Rafsanjani, who held the purse strings in Tehran, quickly realized the scale of the disaster. State revenue dropped by two-thirds over a few months, just as the government was preparing to launch another series of offensives on the Iraqi front. These operations could now only rely on the Pasdaran's courage and self-sacrifice—air and mechanized support was expensive. Prime Minister Mousavi found ingenious means of contending with growing shortages of everyday consumer goods. In Baghdad, Saddam Hussein let the American and Saudi ambassadors know that he was furious. Yet he had a pragmatic understanding that this drain in oil revenue was far more damaging to his adversary than it was to him. He was also aware that the oil pipeline section connecting Basra to the freshly inaugurated Saudi petroline would allow him to significantly increase his oil export volume. Most importantly, he was promised new loans and bank guarantees, which allowed him to continue his war against the Ayatollah Khomeini on credit. He also convinced the Americans to provide the Iraqis with more intelligence support. In Moscow, the Soviets squandered their gold reserves to compensate for the loss of oil revenue. This episode undoubtedly contributed to persuading them to change their policies.

The Soviets Change Tactics Again

Mikhail Gorbachev's coming to power following Konstantin Chernenko's death in March 1985 signaled another turning point in the USSR's stance toward the belligerents. The Kremlin's new master quickly dismissed the old guard's leaders and put in place a younger directorate that would gradually apply a policy of glasnost (transparency) and perestroika (restructuring). In the early summer of 1985 Andrei Gromyko stepped down and was replaced by Eduard Shevardnadze, the former secretary general of the Georgian Communist Party and another devotee of reformist doctrines. Keenly aware that the Soviet economy was on the verge of collapse, Gorbachev and Shevardnadze focused on reorienting Soviet policy based on three priorities: withdrawing the Soviet army from Afghanistan; de-escalating tension with the West; and redefining cordial relations with the Third World.

The nexus of these objectives led them to reassess their relations with the Middle Eastern states. Moscow no longer wanted to put ideological confrontation first, but rather to favor long-term interests by banking on fruitful economic partnerships with Middle Eastern nations. The USSR was on the verge of bankruptcy: it had to open up to new markets, including those outside the traditional arms sector, in order to bring in desperately needed currency. This new policy required the USSR to reestablish good relations with Egypt. It also implied a move toward the cash-rich Gulf monarchies. Most importantly, it demanded that the Soviets restore cordial relations with Iran, which was perceived as a far more captive market than Iraq. It was also the USSR's direct neighbor, which facilitated economic exchanges and the delivery of Iranian fuel to isolated Soviet regions in Central Asia. Perhaps most importantly, Iran could influence the Afghan guerilla movement as Moscow tried to disengage from Afghanistan.[2] The rapprochement between Moscow and Tehran seemed especially pertinent given that Akbar Hashemi Rafsanjani was trying to build economic partnerships to break Iran's isolation. As part of this initiative, Iranian technocrats had traveled to Moscow the previous year to ensure the Kremlin that Iran wanted to rekindle commercial ties between the two countries despite the ideological differences opposing the two capitals.

Nonetheless, there was a gulf between theory and practice, and relations between Moscow, Baghdad, and Tehran continued to bear the weight of habit and reciprocal mistrust. Both the Iraqi and Iranian regimes went about testing the new Soviet direction, each in its own manner. As soon as Gorbachev was elected, Tariq Aziz took his pilgrim's staff and flew to Moscow. He told Soviet authorities that Saddam wanted to meet the Kremlin's new strong man to make a fresh start on consolidating bilateral relations and obtain more arms. Iraqi generals were eager for the latest jewels of Soviet industry: MiG-29 and Su-27 fighters, T-80 tanks, BMP-2 infantry fighting vehicles, SS-23 ballistic missiles, and the latest generation of anti-aircraft systems (SA-11/12/13/14). On December 16, 1985, Saddam Hussein arrived in Moscow on an official visit, which he hoped would be decisive. He had not set foot in the Soviet capital since 1978, when he was still only the regime's number two.

Despite the pomp and red carpet, the reception was ice cold. Not a single official photo was taken to commemorate this encounter, which was qualified as "frank and friendly" by the local press. In less diplomatic terms, this bears witness to a stormy meeting during which both heads of state dug in their heels. Annoyed with Saddam's presumptuousness, Mikhail Gorbachev reproached his Iraqi counterpart for not taking Soviet interests into account. He told him that the USSR needed cash assets and could no longer afford to extend him credit. He also reminded him that Baghdad could not hope to enjoy Moscow's unconditional support after restoring cordial relations with Washington. Overall, the Soviet leader let Saddam know that Iraq was no longer one of his priorities. Having fallen out, the two men would never meet again. The only two points on which they agreed remained the pressing need for a ceasefire and the continuation of Soviet military assistance to Iraq. On this last score, Saddam did not go home empty-handed. He was promised that he would be shipped fifty-four Su-25 assault aircraft, the notorious "tank killer," known for its exploits on the Afghan front, and 300 old-generation Scud-B ballistic missiles. Since their range was too short to reach Tehran, these missiles, renamed "Al-Hussein," were later modified to strike the Iranian capital by Iraqi engineers assisted by Soviet technicians. For the rest, the Iraqis would have to wait.

The Iranians adopted a strategy of indirect approach. As soon as Gorbachev came to power, Rafsanjani gave a conciliatory speech aimed at the USSR, stating that, "We are inclined to have good relations with the Soviet Union."[3] Following the Soviets' lack of response, Iranian leaders decided to strike a different note. On September 30, 1985, four Soviet diplomats (Arkady Katkov, Oleg Spirin, Valery Mirikov, and Nikolai Svirsky) were kidnapped in Beirut. As with the American, French, and British hostages, the operation was claimed by the Islamic Jihad, a faction of Hezbollah controlled by Tehran. The next week Arkady Katkov's mutilated body was found near the Soviet embassy. The message could not have been clearer: Iran wanted to enter into negotiations with the Soviet Union, but was not afraid of the Soviets. Moscow was not about to let itself be intimidated. In a few hours several mechanized divisions were deployed along the Iranian border, while the Soviet air force multiplied intimidation missions along the border, violating Iranian air space several times. Two Soviet MiG-27s were shot down by Iranian interceptors.

Though it was committed in Afghanistan, the Soviet army remained capable of threatening Iran along its northern border, which had been left underprotected to focus on the Iraqi front. Both sides ultimately exercised restraint to avoid escalating the conflict. In Lebanon the KGB and GRU simultaneously went to work to locate the Soviet diplomats' captors. Once they had succeeded, a team of Spetsnaz soldiers—elite commandos known for their ferocity—arrived in the capital to conduct a reprisal operation.[4]

Several Hezbollah officials were mysteriously assassinated over the next few days. One of the victims' heads was allegedly delivered to the Iranian embassy. The strong-arm method seemed to bear fruit: the Iranian authorities requested to negotiate with the Kremlin. Prime Minister Mousavi traveled to Moscow in late November to try to put an end to the crisis. Common ground was quickly reached, and the three surviving diplomats were released.

Two months later Georgy Korniyenko, a deputy foreign minister and member of the Soviet Communist Party's Central Committee, came to Tehran to meet Akbar Hashemi Rafsanjani and Ali Khamenei, Iran's two most influential leaders aside from the Ayatollah Khomeini. This was the first time that such a high-ranking Soviet official traveled to Iran since the advent of the Islamic Republic. The Iranians were perfectly aware of this and treated their guest with every consideration. He informed them that Mikhail Gorbachev and Eduard Shevardnadze wished to restore cordial bilateral relations. As a sign of good will, Tehran called off the trials of members of the Tudeh Party. Now that each party had had a chance to assess the other's determination, discussions moved forward on sturdy foundations and concentrated on economic questions. The two governments also agreed to build a new railway connecting their countries and to reestablish air traffic between the two capitals. On a diplomatic level, Moscow proposed to discreetly become Tehran's advocate on the United Nations Security Council. The Soviet authorities were prepared to act as mediators to facilitate the conclusion of a ceasefire between the belligerents.

Their analysis remained unchanged: the war's continuation was counterproductive for the Soviet Union. This was the logic behind the Soviets' refusal to deliver weapons to Tehran as long as the conflict dragged on. However, the Kremlin lured the Iranian government with an offer to provide the Iranians sophisticated weapons and cooperate with them in the nuclear sector as soon as hostilities ended. The proposal was appealing, but the Ayatollah Khomeini refused to accept it: he could not conceive of conceding the status quo to Saddam Hussein. The Iraqi dictator had to be humiliated and punished, no matter the cost. Though the Rafsanjani-led proponents of openness tried to tell the Supreme Leader that this was a unique opportunity to reinforce the Islamic Republic in the long term, he refused to be swayed. He even took the liberty of sending a thank-you note to Mikhail Gorbachev suggesting that he convert to Islam.

Objective Kharg

Raids on oil traffic continued uninterrupted over the course of 1985. They escalated, beginning in February when the Iraqi air force put the first Mirage F-1EQ5s equipped with Exocet missiles in service alongside its three operational Super Etendards (a fourth was grounded following damage from an air-to-air missile blast). The Mirages were tremendously effective in the hands of Saddam's pilots, who were now trained well enough to fire their missiles in optimal conditions. They were assigned to the 81st Squadron, which was redeployed to the al-Wahda advanced base near Basra. On February 14, 1985, a Mirage F-1EQ5 sank the Liberian tanker *Neptunia* off the coast of Bushehr. This initial success was the first of many. Thanks to a pair of large external fuel tanks, the Mirage F-1EQ5s had a superior range to the Super Etendards, which allowed them to reach targets 400 miles (600 kilometers) from their base. They could attack ships cruising north of Qatar. In theory, their in-flight refueling probes could allow them to go much further, but the limited number of Mirage F-1EQ5s in service dissuaded General Shaban to equip them with the buddy-buddy in-flight refueling systems Mirages require to carry a nacelle to refuel another aircraft in flight.

The Iranians reacted by putting an ever-increasing number of decoys around Kharg Island, ranging from rusty old cargo ships waiting to be scrapped to barges equipped with radar amplifiers that decoyed the Iraqi Exocets' homing heads. Most significantly, they created an alternative oil terminal 400 miles (600 kilometers) southeast of Kharg, near Sirri Island, not far from the Strait of Hormuz—and theoretically out of the Iraqi air force's range. This floating terminal consisted of three 400,000-ton supertankers secured to each other and used to store crude oil. Foreign tankers could load this oil into their tanks without venturing deep into Gulf waters, thereby avoiding the war zone and the extra premium imposed by insurance companies. The Iranians implemented a tanker shuttle between Kharg and Sirri to supply the floating terminal. The eight tankers

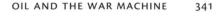

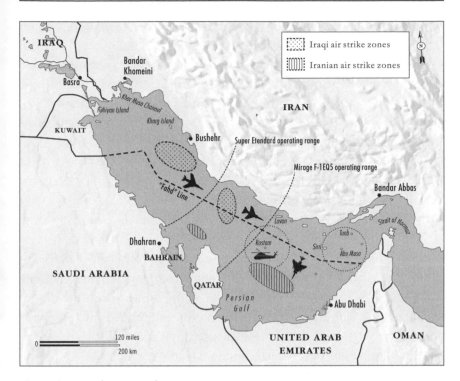

The tanker war (1984–1985)

assigned to this thankless, dangerous task sailed under the Iranian flag, maintaining radio silence.

They transferred the oil brought to Kharg terminal by pipeline to the supertankers anchored off Sirri. This stratagem allowed Iran to avoid offering a discount on the price of crude oil loaded in Sirri. The Islamic Republic did need to acquire old oil tankers to replace those that might be sunk, for the shuttle system required a just-in-time strategy between the two terminals. The Iranians secured their biggest tankers to old cargo ships, using the latter as shields against missile blasts rather than sending them to the scrapyard. It was of little importance whether these ships burned or sank, so long as the tanker they were protecting was saved. Over the course of five months, the Iraqis fired sixty-two Exocets, but hit only eighteen tankers. Most of the other missiles hit decoys or old decommissioned ships.

The Iranians retaliated for these attacks with occasional raids on oil traffic. They only targeted ships sailing east of Qatar, out of range of Saudi interceptors, and were careful to avoid any attacks on commercial vessels belonging to members of the United Nations Security Council. These attacks were rare due to the Iranian air force's priority on bombing Iraqi cities and industrial infrastructure. Its stock of ammunition was also running low. Having practically run out of Maverick missiles, Phantom pilots resumed rocket attacks and did not hesitate to fire their Sidewinder infrared-homing air-to-air missiles. These small missiles, attracted to the heat of the combustion gas from the tankers' boilers, exploded at the level of their exhaust stacks, damaging the bridge and sometimes starting a fire.

The Phantoms were backed by navy helicopters, which had been redeployed to Abu Musa Island and Iranian oil platforms off the coast of the United Arab Emirates. These thirteen helicopters harassed tankers passing nearby (three SH-3 Sea Kings armed with Maverick missiles of the same type as those fired by the Phantoms and ten AB-212s equipped with AS-12 wire-guided missiles delivered by France at the end of the Shah's reign). Their operational mode was simple: when the Abu Musa Island or Rostam oil platform surveillance radar detected a potential target, a helicopter scrambled to identify it. If the Iranian authorities decided to strike, another helicopter armed with missiles or rockets took off and headed to attack the target. However, these attacks were limited by the surveillance radars' range (about sixty miles [about one hundred kilometers]).

The rest of the Iranian navy focused its activities on keeping the Strait of Hormuz under surveillance and escorting the few tankers that continued to load oil at the Kharg terminal.[5] These ships were particularly vulnerable because the Iraqis were decoding Iranian navy messages and knew where to strike to have optimal chances of making a direct hit. Aside from these escort missions, Iranian warships rarely strayed from the coast. After the arrest and execution of Captain Bahram Afzali, who had been accused of collusion with the Tudeh Party, the navy had been denigrated and subjected to a purge, which did not inspire its leaders to take the initiative. The appointment of Captain Mohammed Hussein Malekzadegan to the head of the admiralty in the summer of 1985 reinvigorated the institution, which was aware that it was in competition with the Pasdaran's recently created naval branch. Though he was close to the clergy, the new admiral was first and foremost an experienced and audacious sailor respected by his peers. He was ready to take risks to impose himself and prove the navy's value to the country's political authorities.

Meanwhile, the Iraqi strategy evolved. In June 1985 the remaining Super Etendards were discreetly brought back to France, having been replaced by Mirage F-1EQ5s. The shuttle system between Kharg and Sirri and the growing number of floating decoys had made it more unpredictable to attack oil tankers. With the agreement of the military high command, General Shaban decided to mount a direct assault on the Kharg terminal. He now had more modern attack aircraft fitted with countermeasures intended to more effectively block the surface-to-air missiles deployed on the island. He also knew that the Iranians were nearly out of Hawk missiles, which they only rarely fired now. To apply his strategy, General Shaban built a replica of the Kharg terminal far from prying eyes, on an island in the middle of a lake in northwest Iraq. Here, his pilots practiced attacking the target from every angle and in every configuration. On August 14, 1985, he launched his offensive on Kharg Island. He had decided to attack at 3 p.m., knowing that, in this sweltering stretch of the summer, most of the anti-aircraft battery and missile operators would be napping. The heat at this time of day would also keep the early warning fighter patrol on the ground. At 2:30 p.m. six Su-22Ms took off from Basra, followed by two Mirage F-1s. After skirting Kharg Island to the south, the eight fighter-bombers burst into view over their objective at low altitude. They accelerated to maximum speed, released decoy flares, and separated into three groups, each of which targeted a different jetty. They dropped their 550-pound (250-kilo) parachute bombs and immediately turned back to their base, while Iranian guards shaken out of their lethargy randomly fired a few SAM-7s.

A few minutes later a reconnaissance MiG-25 flew over the island at high altitude to evaluate the damage. The toll was disappointing. Though several oil tanks were on fire and a jetty had been damaged, oil-loading operations did not seem to have been affected. Once again the Shah's foresight had paid off and the Kharg terminal's superfluous installations had proven their weight in gold. General Shaban stubbornly continued the raids on Kharg Island, intent on damaging as many oil installations as possible and reducing Iran's export capacity. He was particularly determined given that Saddam Hussein, who was stoically watching oil prices gradually drop, had ordered him to escalate the bombing campaign in order to to dry up the Iranian economy.

On September 20, 1985, Ali Khamenei responded from Tehran by threatening to block the Strait of Hormuz. However, his warning did not have any material effect, for the Iranians lacked the means to durably prevent navigation through the strait. Naturally, they could disrupt maritime traffic by laying drifting mines or launching harassment raids, but they knew that these actions would inevitably lead Western powers to intervene. Thus they moderated their attacks on oil traffic. In 1985 Iran attacked only twelve oil tankers and sank a single one.

Over the last four months of 1985 the Iraqi air force conducted about sixty raids on Kharg Island, averaging one nearly every two days. To attempt to take their enemy by surprise, the pilots emerged over their targets at different times of day and from various directions. The Iranians fired Hawk missiles increasingly rarely and desperately tried to acquire more on the parallel market. However, their Tomcats were very much in evidence and shot down three Mirage F-1s and one Su-22. Though these raids allowed the Iraqis to reduce the Kharg terminal's operating capacity by 40 percent, the remaining 60 percent was enough to handle the exporting of most of Iran's oil production. Attacks on oil tankers were also not critical. In 1985 the Iraqi air force hit only thirty tankers (excluding numerous decoys), or barely 3 percent of those that had come to load oil in Iran; only eleven of those hit were sunk—or scrapped, for many shipping companies sent only their oldest ships to the Gulf and their low value did not justify expensive repairs. Through these two operations, the Iraqis succeeded in reducing the amount of oil exported by Iran by 12 percent in one year. This was not enough to ruin the Iranian economy. However, the combined collapse of the price of a barrel of oil and of the dollar had diminished Tehran's revenue by a third in a few months, having a far greater effect on the Iranian war effort than Iraqi attacks on oil traffic. Economic warfare proved effective. It would be decisive in the year to come.

Chapter 23

The Slaughter of the Child Soldiers

The photos have been seen around the world: fired-up young Iranian teens preparing to storm Iraqi lines wearing uniforms several sizes too big and red headbands with white letters spelling out "Allah is the greatest." They have come to represent the horror and perversity of the Iran-Iraq War, underscoring the tragic use of child soldiers in contemporary wars. While the Iraqi regime also enrolled sixteen- and seventeen-year-old teenagers to compensate for losses in the Popular Army, particularly at the end of the war, it did not do so systematically. Iran's use of child soldiers is particularly shocking due to its massive scale and the fact that for several years children as young as twelve were used as mere cannon fodder, sent on what often amounted to suicide missions to open the way for the rest of the army. Beginning in the spring of 1982 the Pasdaran drew from the Basij's reserves to make up for their losses and increase the size of their battalions. At the time, the Basij militia consisted of 150,000 individuals, a third of whom were adults of draft age. The remaining two-thirds were teenagers eager to serve their country. The adults were charged with guarding sensitive areas or were incorporated in the Pasdaran divisions' instruction and supply units. The young Basijis were directed to combat units.

The Sacrifice of the Basijis

Beginning in primary school, "educators" recruited by the regime taught children the virtues of sacrifice. Defending the nation was presented as a holy cause. These propaganda campaigns intensified in middle school. At the age of twelve, young boys were invited to join the Basij. Volunteers were given basic military training for two weeks, then sent to the front for one or two months—generally long enough to participate in an offensive.

Beginning in 1985, the initial training period was extended to three weeks in order to increase recruits' chances of survival. Once on the front, they were supervised by an imam and received further training. Most were merely equipped with a few grenades; only the oldest and most skillful were given a rifle or machine gun. On the eve of the attack the boys' hands were tattooed with henna to symbolize their union with God in view of their probable martyrdom. To bolster their courage, their commander gave them each a golden plastic key said to open the door to paradise. The regime had rushed to order more than one million keys from toy manufacturers. Since their time on the front was so brief, the young Basijis were not even given ID tags to identify their bodies if they were killed.

The Basijis' drive was supposed to serve as an example to the soldiers. After this initial period on the front, they returned to middle school to take regular classes until the next major offensive or the following vacation, during which they would be sent back to the front for a few weeks. The pattern would repeat until the boys were killed or became old enough to be assigned to a Pasdaran division. Those who wanted to leave could do so, but the social pressure was so intense that few followed this route. Some even developed a taste for combat. The Ministry of Education's primary goal was no longer teaching, but mobilizing children for the war effort. Everything was focused on this; teachers who opposed the policy were sanctioned.

Basij mobilization intensified with the major offensives of 1984–1985. The Basijis came to make up 20 percent of the troops committed—with the proportion sometimes much higher. For instance, the Pasdaran minister recognized that 57 percent of fighters involved in the conquest of the Majnoon Islands were children.[1] Ten thousand were allegedly killed or wounded during the battle. Their exploits were broadcast on television. Akbar Hashemi Rafsanjani solemnly invited all boys ages twelve and up to participate in the holy war. The Ayatollah Khomeini regularly met with their representatives, never denying the risks entailed, but charming them by vaunting their courage and reminding them that martyrdom would guarantee them a prominent place in paradise. He enjoyed being photographed with them, conversing with them, and listening to their remarks. The Iranian director Morteza Avini's documentary *Enamoured of Love,* which describes the complex relationship between the Basijis and the Supreme Leader, adroitly shows that what took place was not fanaticizing in the strict sense of the term, but a paternalistic, mystical relationship.

By the beginning of 1986, 300,000 Basijis had experienced battle. Another million had undergone military training. This rotation of fresh troops provided the Iranian military high command with 150,000 combatants to add to the 500,000 Pasdaran and soldiers on the front. For certain offensives, military command could even mobilize up to 200,000 Basijis, or 30 percent of the armed forces' total strength. In the Basra sector, Pasdaran and regular army soldiers never attacked Iraqi positions until they had been preceded by a minimum of three waves of young volunteers.

Contrary to common belief, these young Basijis were not all sons of illiterate peasants. The findings of Iranian and British sociologists who interviewed young Basijis in Iraqi prison camps or in Iran after the war reveal diverse social backgrounds and motivations.[2] The Basij also included many boys from the working and middle classes. Most of them had gone to school. One in three boys in middle school joined the Basij, most often at fourteen. Enrollment was facilitated by the fact that parental authorization was not required.

Boys ignored the dangers and enrolled for four principal reasons. The first was mysticism and religious devotion, which made martyrdom seem like a natural choice, colored by heroism and romanticism. Teenagers were not totally aware of the danger and imagined they could escape death. And should they fail to do so, death was idealized, as described by Ali, a child soldier interviewed by Ian Brown: "If we weren't here [in the Iraqi prison camp], we would be martyrs and that would be the best thing for us, but we didn't get the chance to be martyrs so we'll stay here. . . . It's better for me to be in Iraq because I'm closer to the Saints." Another former boy soldier expanded on the same idea: "We are Shiite Muslims, not Sunni. Only a small proportion of Muslims are Shiite, but ours is the true faith. Since the beginning of Islam, we have been fighting and dying for our rights. Imam Ali became the leader of the Muslims, but was martyred while reading the Qur'an. We are not afraid to be martyred for Islam . . . , like Imam Hussein."[3] Religious devotion combined with a powerful devotion to the family: many Basijis knew that the state would take care of their parents and siblings if they were to perish. They were prepared to sacrifice themselves to offer their family a better future.

Another reason for enrolling was patriotism. Steeped in stories vaunting the grandeur of eternal Persia from an early age, many children dreamed of being among the country's liberators. This was young Ahmed's case: "I'm not very religious so I don't know much about the subject [of martyrdom]. It's true that martyrdom is important to Shiites—we all learn about the Imams and how they died—but I didn't go to war to die for Islam. I went to defend Iran and I think most of my friends went for the same reason. . . . No one influenced my decision. At fourteen I could decide things for myself and I wanted to go to war, so I went."[4]

Social pressure was a potent third factor. In a conservative patriarchal society based on the virtue of age and the preeminence of elders, many teenagers sought to impress their parents, classmates, teachers, or even their fiancées. They saw war as an adventure, nearly a game, which would allow them to achieve glory. Young Samir's account is enlightening: "[The] boys who attacked the Iraqis were a very important weapon for the army, because they had no fear. We captured many positions from the Iraqis because they became afraid when they saw young boys running towards them shouting and screaming. Imagine how you would feel. Lots of boys were killed, but by that stage you were running and couldn't stop, so you just carried on until you were shot yourself or reached the lines." Another boy was lucid in his assessment of the situation: "I was too young to fight. I was a little boy who wanted to play with guns. When they gave me a real one I'd never been happier. But when I went to fight and shoot people, I was petrified."[5]

Finally, some boys joined the militia out of opportunism, to obtain social status and a few privileges, gain easier access to higher education, then find a job in the administration, while earning significant wages along the way. A married sixteen-year-old Basiji (the legal age of marriage was fifteen) received a monthly salary of 7,000 toman, the equivalent of an average civil servant's wages. The director Mehran Tamadon perfectly captures these diverse motivations in his film *Bassidji* (2009), which tells the epic story of these boys during the war and explores their persistent influence on Iranian society.

The regime shrewdly used these various motives to steer young Basijis toward specific types of missions. Mystics and religious fanatics were generally chosen for suicide missions, notably those requiring the boys to walk by night, unarmed, carrying only their keys to paradise and a Koran as they crossed Iraqi minefields to set off the mines and open the way for the Pasdaran. Patriots were used for more complex infiltration missions. The others were all used as light infantry to surprise and harass the enemy. Iraqi soldiers were stunned by the sight of children rushing toward their lines on bicycles, half-hidden by the dust kicked up by their bikes, then throwing a volley of grenades in their direction. An Iraqi officer described these traumatic episodes: "They chant 'Allahu Akbar' and they keep coming, and we keep shooting, sweeping our 50 mm [*sic*] machine guns around like sickles. My men are eighteen, nineteen, just a few years older than these kids. I've seen them crying, and at times the officers have had to kick them back to their guns. Once we had Iranian kids on bikes cycling towards us, and my men all started laughing, and then these kids started lobbing their hand grenades and we stopped laughing and started shooting."[6]

The adolescent death toll was extremely high. Due to the lack of reliable registers—because the child soldiers were only considered part-time auxiliaries—the exact number of fatalities remains unknown to this day. According to the most reliable estimates, at least 80,000 Iranian child soldiers were killed, and at least as many were maimed.

The Iranians Capture the Al-Faw Peninsula

At the beginning of 1986 Akbar Hashemi Rafsanjani was determined to strike a decisive blow to dismiss criticisms from all those in Tehran exasperated by the stalemate of a war now entering its sixth year. The situation was exacerbated when the Iraqis recaptured the entirety of the south isle of the Majnoon Islands in mid-January. Feeling pressure on every front, the speaker of the Majlis realistically assessed the circumstances. The Iranian navy and air force were on the defensive. Iraqi pilots could now strike more or less wherever they wanted. The West was proving increasingly nervous, threatening to intervene in the Gulf if the situation should deteriorate. The Iranian regime's only asset remained its plethora of ground forces, which still held a numerical advantage, despite a lack of tanks and reliable equipment. The army could still occasionally overwhelm the enemy. Yet it had to strike quickly, for financial reserves were running out. Intent on celebrating a victory on the Revolution's seventh anniversary, Rafsanjani put on his war-chief garb and summoned the generals to prepare the launch of a major offensive in February. The objective was simple: to cross the Shatt al-Arab and conquer the al-Faw peninsula, thereby cutting Iraq off from its supplies from the Gulf, preventing Baghdad from exporting oil to Kuwait and Saudi Arabia, and positioning Iranian troops to attack Basra from the rear. God permitting, the Iranians hoped to be able to take the city through a pincer movement. Even if they failed, they would at least pin the Iraqis in place, weakening them by causing maximum casualties and material losses.

The Iranian regime spared no expense to execute this ambitious plan, mobilizing every last man available. Thanks to the exceptional enlistment of 200,000 Basij boys, the Iranians had close to one million men on the front, two-thirds of whom were combatants. For this meticulously prepared offensive, one-fifth of the troops was sent to the front lines near al-Faw. Over the preceding months a large quantity of river-crossing equipment had discreetly been brought to the Shatt al-Arab's eastern bank. The most noticeable components, such as pontoon bridge parts and self-propelled ferries recently purchased in China, were stored in river cities such as Khorramshahr and Abadan. Further south hundreds of skiffs and boats with capacities of up to thirty combatants were camouflaged in the marshes. The newly created 41st Assault Pioneer Division relentlessly practiced river crossing on the Arvand, the arm of the Karun surrounding the Abadan Peninsula and running into the Gulf. The 33rd Artillery Division was deployed along the river to provide fire support at the principal crossing points. The 21st and 77th Mechanized Divisions, which had been turned into infantry divisions, performed numerous landing exercises on Caspian Sea beaches. Four other infantry divisions were moved closer to the front and stood ready to carry out diversionary attacks, then to reinforce the bridgehead. These eight divisions were put under the command of Mohsen Rezaee, the head of the Pasdaran, who had been entrusted with the weighty task of supervising the offensive's first phase. On the other side, the Iraqi 7th Corps only had 15,000 men distributed between the 15th and 26th Infantry, both second-rank divisions, and the 441st Naval Infantry Brigade, which was responsible for guarding the ruins of the port of al-Faw.

The Iranians' preparations did not go unnoticed by the Iraqis' "big ears" or their reconnaissance troops, who sent alarmed reports to military high command. Yet the chiefs of staff ignored the reports, assuming the Iranians were feinting and that their attack would come either in Basra or in the sector of the Majnoon Islands, to regain recently lost ground. General Mahmoudi Shahin, head of military intelligence, was utterly convinced of it: intercepted Iranian communications showed a significant increase in activity south of the Majnoon Islands; the Iranians had rounded up six of their strongest divisions in the area, including the 30th and 92nd Armored; they had started exercises and sent large stocks of munitions to the sector. Faced with this evidence, Chief of Staff of the Armed Forces General Dhannoun decided to put the 3rd and 6th Corps on high alert. Naturally, Dhannoun did not know that these carefully studied movements and the shrewdly maintained hubbub were designed to deceive him regarding the Iranians' actual intentions. General Shawket, the commander of the 7th Corps, had absolutely no idea what was about to hit him. He considered himself protected by the Shatt al-Arab, which was more than half a mile (close to one kilometer) wide in his sector. The seasonally inclement weather did not encourage him to increase the number of patrols along the riverbanks.

At nightfall on February 9, 1986, the Iranians launched the Dawn 8 offensive, which was named "Dawn" as a reminder of the previous Dawn offensives' successes. North of Basra the Iranian 12th Infantry Division went to work in the driving rain, creating a diversion by attacking the Iraqis' entrenched positions south of Fish Lake. Over several hours waves of fiery young Basijis stormed the enemy defenses, backed by the Iranian artillery's rolling fire. With the support of an engineering brigade, an infantry brigade from the 12th Division simultaneously launched a surprise attack and captured Umm al-Rassas Island, which splits the Shatt al-Arab at Khorramshahr. In a few hours the Iranian sappers built a pontoon bridge between the riverbank and this three-mile-long (several-kilometer-long) island. Reinforcements moved in over the bridge. At 10 p.m. the Iranians began crossing the river at two separate points: the first was close to Siba, 1.8 miles (three kilometers) southwest of Abadan, over a wide sandbank that eased operations; the second was further south, nine miles (fifteen kilometers) from al-Faw, on a relatively narrow bend in the river (1,300 feet [400 meters]). Frogmen had already swum across the Shatt al-Arab to secure the two bridgeheads, now reinforced by thousands of Pasdaran who had crossed the river aboard rubber dinghies delivered by India a few weeks earlier. Meanwhile, the 3rd Naval Infantry Brigade landed on the south of the peninsula on either side of al-Faw, supported by the continuous fire of a dozen Pasdaran gunboats spraying bullets at the few Iraqi strongholds guarding the sector.

The river-crossing operations at Siba were the most spectacular. By the end of the night a first pontoon bridge was in service, allowing the 21st and 77th Divisions' motorized units to cross the river and make speed to their objectives. Further south the Iranian sappers built an innovative bridge composed of large blocks of polystyrene supporting metal spans. The bridge proved solid enough to allow the Pasdaran's artillery division and logistics trucks to get across. During the day the pontoon bridge's sections were taken apart and hidden along the riverbanks to protect them from enemy artillery and air strikes. At dawn they were reassembled to allow river-crossing operations to resume. For weeks soaking wet, freezing cold Iranian sappers slaved away to tirelessly assemble and reassemble the bridge, which they succeeded in preserving from Iraqi attacks.

Unable to intercept Pasdaran communications, the military high command in Baghdad was taken by surprise. General Dhannoun was reassured by soothing reports from the 7th Corps commander and ordered the 15th Infantry Division to regain control of Umm al-Rassas Island with the support of a commando brigade. The Iraqis recaptured the island after thirty-six hours of fierce combat. Further north the Iraqi 11th Division firmly held its ground, repelling every assault by the Iranian 12th Division. Meanwhile, General Dhannoun had ordered the Republican Guard's armored division to leave Baghdad for Basra and push back the Iranians on the Shatt al-Arab's Iraqi bank. He also dispatched all available engineering support in the Basra sector to a point twelve miles (twenty kilometers) southeast of the city to erect a first line of defense guarded by the 5th Mechanized Division. The air force was grounded due to continuing poor weather conditions.

The Iranians took advantage of these two days to enlarge their bridgeheads. After seizing Siba, the 77th Division turned toward Basra. It soon came up against the Iraqi 5th and 15th Divisions' vanguard, while a mo-

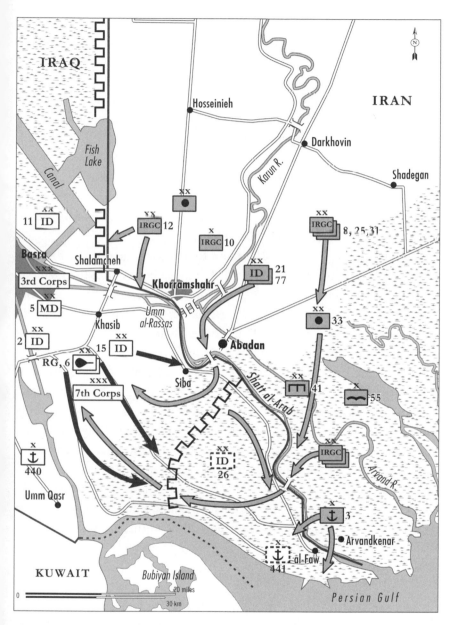

The Iranians capture al-Faw (February 9–March 11, 1986)

torized detachment sent in the direction of the Umm Qasr naval base was repelled by the 440th Naval Infantry Brigade. The 21st Division followed the road parallel to the Shatt al-Arab toward al-Faw, cleaning out Iraqi points of resistance in rapid succession. Despite the bad weather, paratroopers were airlifted across the peninsula by helicopter to encircle retreating Iraqi troops. Meanwhile, the 3rd Naval Infantry Brigade's commandos destroyed the radar at the peninsula's southern tip, partially blinding Iraqi missile boats and fighter planes. The Iranians deployed two Silkworm missile batteries that had been freshly delivered from China to the peninsula (two other batteries were installed near the Strait of Hormuz). These missiles would prevent any sortie by Iraqi ships and be a permanent threat to maritime traffic headed for neighboring Kuwait.

On February 12 General Dhannoun took advantage of a brief sunny spell to dispatch reconnaissance aircraft, which allowed him to grasp the breadth of the enemy breakthrough. He obtained Adnan Khairallah and Saddam Hussein's authorization to use chemical weapons. At the first lull in the weather two PC-7 Turbo Trainers agilely took off from Basra, flew over the al-Faw peninsula at low altitude, and sprayed clouds of mustard gas over enemy lines. Meanwhile, the commander of the 7th Corps was granted the urgent deployment of two reinforcement divisions (the 2nd Infantry and 6th Armored) to hold the line of defense he was building southeast of Basra. The 26th Division had collapsed, making reinforcements urgently necessary. Groups of crazed soldiers in tattered uniforms attempted to escape their pursuers through the salt marshes. Four days into the offensive, Dawn 8 was a success. The Iranians controlled the al-Faw peninsula. They had suffered 600 fatalities and 2,000 wounded, versus 5,000 dead or wounded among the Iraqis, and another 1,500 captured.

The Iraqis Counterattack

On February 14 the rain came to an end, making way for a few days of bright sunshine. The Iraqis took advantage of the good weather to massively commit their air force over the al-Faw peninsula. While Iraqi fighters strafed Iranian trenches, their assault aircraft struck the pontoon bridges across the Shatt al-Arab, damaging the bridge near Abadan. Iranian sappers had to be devilishly inventive and work themselves to the bone to put it back in service. Iraqi Tupolev bombers flattened Iranian infantry assembly areas with carpet bombing. Iranian interceptors responded by shooting down a Tu-22 bomber, a Super Frelon helicopter, and six fighters, including two Egyptian Mirage-Vs sent to reinforce the Iraqi front. Iranian anti-aircraft defense was equally successful, destroying a Tu-16 heavy bomber with Hawk missiles fired from Abadan.

On February 16 Iraqi intelligence services were still persuaded that the crossing of the Shatt al-Arab was only a diversionary attack.[7] Consequently, General Dhannoun refused to commit additional reinforcements south of Basra; General Shawket had to make do with the troops already on the field. His artillery relentlessly pounded the enemy's front lines, alternating chemical and traditional shells. On the other side, three Iranian divisions (the 8th, 25th, and 31st) relieved the thrashed Pasdaran.

On February 18 Iraqi military high command finally accepted that the principal Iranian offensive was the one they were facing on the al-Faw peninsula. Given the gravity of the situation, Saddam Hussein traveled to Basra with Adnan Khairallah to assign responsibilities. While the minister of defense coordinated operations, Deputy Chief of Staff General al-Jeboury took the head of the column charged with regaining control of the coastal road along the Gulf. General Shawket was given command of the column set to advance along the Shatt al-Arab. Saddam entrusted General Ma'ahir Abdul Rashid with the most delicate mission. He liked the general and trusted that his approach could turn the situation around. He offered him the command of the Republican Guard, which was assigned to follow the central road, a route that wound through salt marshes and palm groves to al-Faw. The faster the Guard advanced, the better it could support the other two columns. Aware of the mission's difficulty, Saddam authorized his protégé to use chemical weapons without conferring with him. He also promised him that he would allow his youngest son Qusay to marry his daughter if he returned victorious.[8] Motivated by the prospect of this family alliance and the wealth of privileges that would accompany it, Ma'ahir Abdul Rashid immediately traveled to the Republican Guard's assembly point, harangued his troops, and rushed toward the enemy like a Bedouin tribal chief lured by the plunder.

On February 21 the three Iraqi columns advanced in parallel along the three roads converging toward al-Faw. To the north, General Shawket reached Siba. The Iranians entrenched in the town resisted with all their might. They knew that surrendering this position meant losing the principal bridgehead connecting them to Abadan. General Shawket was equally aware of Siba's strategic importance. He laid siege and ordered his artillery to mercilessly shell the garrison. In the center, General Rashid progressed less quickly than he had hoped. It had started to rain again, turning the salt marshes into a vile quagmire. Tanks got bogged down and infantrymen sank into the mud up to their knees, their advance made even more difficult by the fact that wearing gas masks made them breathless, while the condensation on the masks practically blinded them. They frequently had to engage in hand-to-hand combat to destroy nests of resistance. In these conditions they only progressed two or three miles (four or five kilometers) a day. The Republican Guard soldiers had been trained for mechanized combat, not trench warfare. Nonetheless, General Rashid methodically edged forward. To the south, General al-Jeboury advanced along the coastal road more quickly. He easily overwhelmed the Iranian infantrymen, outflanking them and forcing them to retreat toward al-Faw. On February 23 his stampede was brought to an abrupt halt by salvos of TOW missiles. The Iraqi tank crews were particularly astonished, given that their leaders had ensured them that the Iranians no longer had any TOW missiles. Clearly they had managed to rebuild their stock.

In four days the Iraqis had succeeded in pushing the front line back a dozen miles (twenty kilometers) east. It now extended from Siba to the peninsula's southern coast, facing Bubiyan Island, which belonged to Kuwait. In Tehran Akbar Hashemi Rafsanjani lowered his ambitions, stating that Iran must keep hold of the al-Faw peninsula, but omitting any further mention of seizing Basra. However, he warned the Kuwaiti authorities to keep Bubiyan Island off limits to Iraq. Saddam's troops could easily have infiltrated this desert island only fourteen miles (a few kilometers) from the Umm Qasr base. Once on the island, the Iraqis could effortlessly reach the al-Faw peninsula less than three miles (five kilometers) away and attack Iranian positions from the rear.

Fully aware of the potential dangers he faced, the Kuwaiti monarch was confronted with his own contradictions. Having always objected to the presence of foreign troops on his soil, he had no one to rely on to protect it. He complied with Rafsanjani's demand and let Saddam Hussein know that Bubiyan Island was a line that could not be crossed. Should Saddam ignore the warning, Kuwait would immediately suspend all material and financial support to Baghdad. King Fahd of Saudi Arabia repeated this warning on his own behalf, making it that much more persuasive. The humiliated Iraqi president would not forget this incident four years later. Meanwhile, he gave strict orders that Bubiyan Island could not be used to mount offensive strikes, though he authorized his special forces to infiltrate it and discreetly observe Iranian activity around al-Faw. He also authorized his air force to continue flying over Bubiyan to avoid Iranian anti-aircraft defense. The Kuwaitis looked the other way.

On February 24, 1986, the United Nations Security Council adopted a resolution (582) calling for the immediate implementation of a ceasefire, followed by international mediation of all aspects of the conflict. With the exception of the Chinese, the council's permanent members were beginning to seriously worry about the turn of events. Both in Western chancelleries and the Kremlin, experts interpreted Iran's taking of al-Faw as a portent of an Iraqi defeat. This would have catastrophic consequences on the geopolitical balance in the Gulf region, forcing the major powers to directly intervene. As usual, Baghdad immediately accepted the terms of this umpteenth resolution, and Tehran rejected it.

Combat Shifts to Iraqi Kurdistan

On February 25, 1986, Iran launched offensive Dawn 9 in the Penjwin sector of Iraqi Kurdistan. The Iranian attack was intended to force Baghdad to send heavy reinforcements to this stretch of the front, which was weakly guarded by the Iraqi army, relieving Iraqi pressure in the al-Faw area. Once again the Iranian government relied on the Pasdaran to preserve the surprise effect. In the midst of a snowstorm, the 30th Infantry Division, backed by several groups of peshmergas, left its entrenchments and headed toward Sulaymaniah along a mountain road leading out of Penjwin. Its commander was counting on the fog and snow to mask the advance of his troops as long as possible and prevent enemy air intervention. A little further south, the 35th Infantry Division left the Nosud Pass at the same time and moved to attack Halabja.

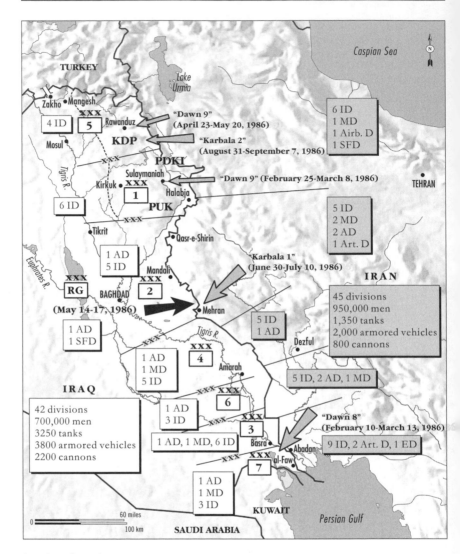

Iran-Iraq front in 1986

Over the first three days the Pasdaran from Penjwin drove back the freezing Iraqi soldiers that had been charged with guarding access to the steep valley leading to Sulaymaniah. They were able to seize the village of Chuarta, which controlled access to Sulaymaniah as well as to peaks from which they could guide their artillery fire. On February 28 they came up against Sulaymaniah's defenses. The city was well guarded by the Iraqi 27th Division. Meanwhile, the Pasdaran assigned to capture Halabja were stymied by mountain troops. The Iraqis counterattacked, backed by Kurdish fighters allied with the regime. Once again, chaos and rivalry reigned within the Kurdish resistance.

In early March the weather improved and the sun came out over the entire front. General Shaban, commander-in-chief of the Iraqi air force, took the opportunity to put one of his many ideas into practice: converting his Ilyushin 76 four-engine transport jets into bombers. Over several weeks these aircraft flew over the Kurdish front and the al-Faw peninsula at 20,000 feet (6,000 meters), out of range of light anti-aircraft defense and SAM-7s, bombing enemy lines with pallets consisting of several dozen fifty-gallon (200-liter) tanks of napalm connected to an altimeter detonator set to explode 330 feet (one hundred meters) above ground. Though primitive, this method caused heavy casualties among Iraqi combatants panicked by the deluge of fire.

By March 8 General al-Khazraji, head of the Iraqi 1st Corps, had recaptured some of the ground lost in the Sulaymaniah and Halabja sectors. He had lived up to his reputation as an excellent tactician and had not spared himself, his men, or his enemy. Exhausted and out of ammunition, the Iranians momentarily put a halt to their offensive in Iraqi Kurdistan.

Meanwhile, to the south of Basra, the Iraqi counteroffensive continued in the direction of al-Faw. The three mechanized columns plodded forward, preceded by the artillery's rolling fire. The Iraqis had gathered their most modern cannons and rocket launchers—purchased in Austria, South Africa, France, and Brazil—to pound the Iranian positions. Each artillery piece fired up to 600 shells a day, or one shot every two minutes, twenty-four hours a day. As soon as they gained a few miles (few kilometers), the Iraqis were counterattacked by human waves of fanaticized young Basijis who were trying to recapture the lost ground. Nonetheless, General Shawket's column seized Siba, then the neighboring bridgehead, destroying the floating bridge near Abadan. The head of the Iraqi 5th Mechanized Division, General Ali Jassem Hayani, was killed during the battle. His division was stopped three miles (five kilometers) further by bunkers located on the side of the road.

On March 13 the three worn-out columns linked up in the middle of the salt marshes. The dramatically divided terrain favored the Iranians in the defensive position. The front stabilized here. Engineering troops immediately began preparing a network of trenches and strongholds, building the new front line. Both sides claimed victory and took advantage of this respite to reconstitute their forces. The casualties had been terrible. The Iranian toll was 10,000 dead and 25,000 wounded, one-third of them gassed.[9] The Iraqis suffered 3,000 dead and 9,000 wounded, not to mention the 1,500 soldiers captured at the beginning of the offensive. They had also lost sixty tanks, fifty other armored vehicles, forty artillery pieces, and twenty aircraft.

The Iranians were still in control of a 150-square mile (400-square kilometer) bridgehead, which would allow them to wear down their adversary, despite the fact that they had to reorganize to direct their logistics to their only remaining floating bridge six miles (ten kilometers) north of al-Faw. Though the Iraqis regularly attacked the bridge, its polystyrene structure proved extremely hard to sink. Each section the Iraqi air force managed to destroy was soon replaced. The Pasdaran built two other lower-capacity floating bridges nearby, which served to deliver troops and ammunition to the front, as well as to evacuate the dead and wounded. Given this logistic chain's limited capacity, the Iranian command restricted its forces at the bridgehead to two infantry divisions, supported by an artillery division and an engineering division. Pasdaran forces rotated to keep up personnel levels year-round.

In the Iraqi camp military high command was satisfied to have contained the Iranian offensive and partially repelled it, thereby saving Basra, Umm Qasr, and the precious pipeline carrying Iraqi oil to Saudi Arabia. Saddam Hussein congratulated General Rashid and General al-Jeboury, but strongly admonished General Shawket, who had been taken by surprise by the Iranian attack. Shawket's drive during the counterattack saved his life. He was nonetheless replaced at the head of the 7th Corps by General al-Jeboury. The Iraqi president also punished General Shahin, head of military intelligence, by replacing him with General Sabar al-Duri, in whom he had utter confidence.

Combat on the al-Faw peninsula continued at a less sustained rate throughout the rest of the year, turning into trench warfare aimed at harassing the enemy. The Iraqis kept five divisions on site—including one armored division—to contain the 40,000 Iranians deployed in the sector.

In late April Iran took advantage of the thaw and more clement weather to launch the second phase of Operation Dawn 9 in Kurdistan and try once again to diminish Iraqi pressure on the southern front. On April 23 the 64th Infantry Division, the 23rd Special Forces Division, and the 55th Parachute Division overran the Iraqi battalions guarding the Rawanduz sector. The Iraqi troops' collapse was accelerated by a rear attack by hordes of peshmergas hurtling down the mountains. The Barzani brothers intended to use this attack to mark out their territory and impose themselves as the champions of the Kurdish cause at a time when Tehran was attempting to reconcile them with their great rival Jalal Talabani. For five days Iranian forces progressed toward Rawanduz despite the sporadic intervention of Mirage F-1s based in Mosul. On April 29 they were stopped three miles (a few kilometers) from the city by a powerful Iraqi counterattack. In early May the Iranians dispatched their 2nd Infantry Division, considered one of the best in the army, to the area. For once, they bet on quality rather than quantity, mobilizing their elite infantrymen for this offensive, which was designed to open the way to the Mosul oil fields. The Iraqis were forced to send two additional infantry divisions.

On May 15 1,000 peshmergas, backed by Iranian paratroopers who had infiltrated behind Iraqi lines, took hold of the town of Mangesh, north of Mosul and about twenty miles (about thirty kilometers) from the Turkish border. The Kirkuk-Dortyol pipeline, which ran nearby, was directly threatened. Baghdad reacted immediately by dispatching an armored brigade, a mountain brigade, and a special forces brigade supported by attack helicopters. These three brigades struggled, but eventually regained control of Mangesh with the help of Kurdish partisans faithful to the regime. Conscious of the need to increase protection of the crucial pipeline, the Iraqi authorities doubled the amount of Popular Army troops in the region and armed volunteer Arab farmers to patrol the sector. At the same time the Iranian air force launched a raid against the Zakho Bridge at the Iraqi-Turkish border, which was used by tanker trucks bringing Iraqi oil to Turkey. The warning was clear: Iran was no longer holding back from striking oil traffic between Iraq and Turkey. On May 20 the Iranians, still getting nowhere outside Rawanduz, ended the Dawn 9 offensive to focus on new operations.

Chapter 24

Deadlock

The taking of the al-Faw peninsula by the Iranians forced Syrian president Hafez al-Assad to come to a worrisome realization. He suddenly found himself concerned that his Iranian allies would win. An Iranian victory would probably lead to a radical Shiite regime in Baghdad, which was as unacceptable to the Syrian president as it was to his Arab neighbors. Assad sent Tehran a firm message, reminding the Iranian leaders that "the land of Iraq is Arab and we will not allow anyone to occupy it."[1] Misunderstandings between the two capitals had accumulated over the last few months, contributing to the peremptory nature of Assad's message. Tehran's repeated criticism of the Soviet Union put Damascus in a delicate position vis-à-vis Moscow. Even more troubling, the Iranians had challenged Syria's hegemonic ambitions in Lebanon since the Israeli withdrawal of 1985 by launching a clandestine campaign to increase their influence there. The time had come to tell the Iranian regime not to overstep certain limits. To make his message clear, Hafez al-Assad ordered the immediate suspension of all military equipment shipments to Tehran, making a cargo ship full of weapons and ammunition turn back. The Iranians felt compelled to react. They abruptly stopped delivering oil to Syria, forcing the Syrians to buy oil at full price on the spot market. And as if by coincidence, Hezbollah intensified its operations against pro-Syrian militias in Lebanon.

Hafez Al-Assad Ups the Ante

Frustrated by the Iranian attitude, President Assad openly displayed his exasperation and made repeated overtures to Amman and Riyadh. King Hussein of Jordan seized the opportunity and immediately tried to promote a rapprochement between Syria and Iraq, which would benefit all the Arab nations. Syria's rallying to the Arab cause would certainly not change the situation from a military perspective, but it would contribute to further isolating Iran on the international scene and allow Iraq to use the Kirkuk-Baniyas pipeline again, significantly increasing its oil revenue. On April 12, 1986, the Jordanian monarch undertook a mediation trip during which he met the Syrian and Iraqi presidents. His good offices were supported by King Fahd, who offered Syria an annual delivery of 2.5 million tons of oil free of charge, twice what Iran had been giving it, in exchange for joining the Arab consensus. It was an attractive offer, but Hafez al-Assad wanted to up the ante. He discreetly resumed contact with Tehran and suggested that they send an envoy to Damascus to find some common ground At the same time he suggested a possible reconciliation with Saddam Hussein, though he still had fundamental divergences with his Arab rival.

In late April Iran's Deputy Minister of Foreign Affairs Ali Mohammad Besharati traveled to the Syrian capital and negotiated the terms of a new understanding with Vice President Abdul Halim Khaddam. Discussions were complicated by the intervention of the Kremlin, which wanted to keep Syria away from Iran. After several stormy sessions, the Syrian and Iranian delegations finally arrived at the terms of a new agreement. In exchange for Syria maintaining its alliance with Tehran, Iran committed to outbidding the Saudis and putting a halt to all hostile actions against Syrian interests in Lebanon. Tehran offered to ship Syria a bonus first installment of 2.5 million tons of oil by late summer, then resume regular deliveries under more advantageous conditions for Damascus.[2] Akbar Hashemi Rafsanjani also guaranteed the Syrian president in writing that if Saddam Hussein were to be eliminated, Iran would do nothing to install an Islamic regime in Baghdad and would let the Iraqi people decide on its future alone.

Now that he had been reassured, President Assad confirmed his alliance with the Islamic Republic and resumed his weapon shipments to Tehran. Nonetheless, in an attempt to preserve his relations with Saudi Arabia, he hosted an Iraqi delegation that had come to negotiate the Kirkuk-Baniyas pipeline's potential reopening, leading King Hussein and King Fahd to believe Assad would be prepared to reconcile with Saddam Hussein if Saddam were to make the first move. But the Iraqi dictator did not fool himself regarding Hafez al-Assad's good intentions. He was not about to humiliate himself before his rival. He told the Jordanian and Saudi monarchs that it was premature to consider a reconciliation between Iraq and Syria.

On June 13, 1986, all pretenses were dropped: President Assad announced that "Iran and Syria had just decided to preserve their shared strategic interests," adding that the Syrian-Iraqi pipeline would not be reopened. The meeting between Saddam Hussein and Hafez al-Assad was postponed. A brief meeting was eventually held at the Iraqi-Syrian border on April 26, 1987, but did not yield the slightest tangible outcome.

Meanwhile, events had moved quickly. In April 1986 Saddam Hussein asked his chiefs of staff to plan an operation that would ensure Iraq captured Iranian territory, which it could then exchange for the al-Faw peninsula. The Iraqi generals immediately set to work. Since Iranian forces were concentrated on the north and south of the front, the Iraqis decided to strike in the center. Making meticulous use of the information provided by their surveillance services, they identified a weak point in the Iranian layout located at the Mehran salient. A single 84th Mechanized Division brigade and one 25th Infantry Division battalion—a little less than 5,000 men—guarded this devastated city and its surroundings. To engage with them, the Iraqis deployed two divisions (the 17th Armored and 37th Infantry), reinforced by a commando brigade and a Republican Guard T-72 tank brigade. The Iraqis had 25,000 men, 250 tanks, and about 100 cannons, or 5 to 1 superiority—enough to win.

On May 14, 1986, General Ibrahim (2nd Corps) launched his troops against Mehran. The dismounted infantry progressed methodically, supported by artillery and tanks. The Iranians retreated toward the nearby Zagros Mountains. By May 17 General Ibrahim controlled the area. Following Saddam's instructions, he expanded his bridgehead by a dozen miles (about twenty kilometers) around Mehran in order to capture enough ground to exchange for the al-Faw pocket. Ibrahim then ordered his troops to firmly entrench themselves and sent the Republican Guard armored brigade back to Baghdad, replacing it with two infantry brigades that had arrived as reinforcements.

On the Road to Karbala

Against all expectations, an Iranian counteroffensive was slow to materialize. In Tehran leaders clashed over the appropriate response to Saddam's offer of a territorial exchange. But the primary cause for the revival of factional antagonism was the Supreme Leader's flagging health. Now eighty-six, the Ayatollah Khomeini was severely ill. His doctors suggested a risky surgical intervention, which they considered the only chance to save his life. While his entourage was in favor of surgery, Ali Khamenei, Akbar Hashemi Rafsanjani, and Ali Montazeri were against it, underlining that the Supreme Leader's untimely death would galvanize the Iraqis. His demise could also incite the majority of Iranians exhausted by the war to accept a compromise with Saddam Hussein. More than anything else, the three men needed the Supreme Leader to arbitrate their disagreements and appoint his successor. The trio therefore agreed to put off the surgery.

With the question of surgery settled, they turned to Saddam's proposal. Ayatollah Montazeri wanted to avoid unnecessary casualties and was thus more or less in favor. His two rivals formed an alliance to stand in his path and declared that they wanted to continue the war until the Iraqi dictator was ousted. Having convinced the Ayatollah Khomeini to support them, they got their way. Yet Rafsanjani and Khamenei continued to disagree on a major issue: the former was convinced that Iran needed to open up to the outside world to come out of isolation and win the war, while the latter was persuaded that the Iranian people would only be victorious by relying on their faith in God and the principles of the Islamic Revolution, which imposed the rejection of compromise with foreign powers. Twenty-five years later, this politico-theological debate remains unsettled, leading to repeated crises between Tehran and the international community.

The speaker of Parliament and the president of the republic finally rejected Saddam's offer and ordered their generals to prepare a series of "decisive" offensives to crush the Iraqi army once and for all. These were named "Karbala" because they were designed to lead to the liberation of the Shiite holy city, followed by the fall of the Ba'athist regime.

On June 30, 1986, Tehran launched the Karbala 1 offensive in the Mehran sector to recapture the territory recently seized by the Iraqis. Chief of Staff of the Armed Forces General Sohrabi had mobilized 100,000 men divided across eight divisions. For forty-eight hours, the "Imam Ali," "Karbala," and "Rasulullah" divisions followed waves of young Basijis in mercilessly battering the Iraqi layout. Once it was sufficiently weakened, they were joined by the 40th and 84th Mechanized Divisions, supported by the 11th Artillery Division and the 81st and 88th Armored Divisions' tanks. These combined forces overran the defenders, who scattered back to the Iraqi border. On July 3 Rafsanjani traveled to the front to rouse the troops and proclaim the liberation of Mehran. Iraqi military command immediately mounted a powerful counterattack, which was stopped by the dogged intervention of thirty Cobras. The Iranians had been unable to gather so many attack helicopters for a single battle in three years—one would have thought a bounty of spare parts and missiles had miraculously landed on their doorstep (see Chapter 25).

Several dozen T-62 and T-72 tanks were quickly immobilized or destroyed. Pushing his advantage, General Sohrabi committed his strategic reserve of two elite Pasdaran brigades: the "Master of Martyrs" 10th Infantry and the "Ramadan" 20th Armored. Their perfectly timed intervention forced General Ibrahim to sound the retreat, a decision which led him to be called back to Baghdad to be stripped of his command and summarily executed for cowardice in the face of the enemy. Saddam Hussein liked to occasionally make an example to maintain a climate of terror within the army. After all, this was the man who told his generals, "When soldiers no longer fight for the love of their leader, then they must fight by fear."[3] General Aladdin Makki would later bear witness to the fact that Iraqi officers were far more afraid of Saddam than of the enemy.[4]

By July 10 the Iranians had recaptured all of the territory lost seven weeks earlier and had even improved their positions. The cost was admittedly high (3,000 dead and 9,000 wounded), but their losses were much lower than those sustained in previous offensives. The Iraqis reported 1,000 dead, 1,200 prisoners, 3,000 wounded, eighty tanks destroyed, and six helicopters downed. Combined with the casualties from the Dawn 8 and 9 offensives, more than 30,000 Iraqi soldiers had been lost since the beginning of the year. At this rate Baghdad would not be able to maintain its defensive layout along the front much longer. Saddam Hussein had learned his lesson: he would no longer venture onto Iranian soil until he thought he was capable of dealing the deathblow. On July 16 he had himself reelected secretary general of the Ba'ath Party and president of the Revolutionary Command Council. The objective was to display the Iraqi population's support for its "dear President" in order to persuade Tehran that the Iraqis were determined to resist the Persian invader to the end. A week later the Iraqi president sent an open letter to Iran's leaders offering them an honorable peace. Once again, their response was scathing. At the same moment —and for the first time—Washington explicitly condemned Iraq's use of chemical weapons.

Sensing that the tide was turning, Akbar Hashemi Rafsanjani responded in contradictory ways, stating on the one hand that "a new Iraqi regime might not have to pay for the war damages inflicted on Iran" and on the other that "650,000 Iranians are assembled at the front with their finger on the trigger, ready for the final assault."[5] He had actually decided to shift the operational center of gravity to Iraqi Kurdistan to support the Kurdish rebellion, but especially to counter Turkey in this strategic region.

Escalating Tension between Tehran and Ankara

Beginning in late spring the PKK took advantage of the weakening of the Iraqi army to launch a new harassment campaign on Turkish positions from northern Iraq. On August 13, 1986, Abdullah Öcalan's peshmergas destroyed a military post in southeast Anatolia and killed twelve Turkish soldiers. Two days later Ankara retaliated with a massive reprisal raid over the border, killing 165 PKK fighters. On August 23 1,000 Turkish soldiers entered Iraqi territory on a manhunt that uncovered some forty Kurdish combatants, some of whom were supported by Tehran. That was all it took to spark a crisis between Iran and Turkey. The Iranian authorities considered that the Turkish government had crossed a line by carrying out a military intervention in Iraq. But the Kurdish question was not the sole reason for Iran's frustration with Turkey. Also bothering the Iranians were Turkey's flagrant advantage in their commercial exchanges and the mediocre quality of Turkish consumer goods sold for top dollar in Iran. The Iranians, whose revolution had partially been inspired by a desire to escape the influence of foreign powers, were frustrated at having made themselves economically dependent on Turkey. Nonetheless, the Ayatollah Khomeini openly criticized the Turkish regime and, in an act of supreme sacrilege, declared Ataturk to be an iniquitous tyrant. The Turkish government responded by increasing its material support to Iraq, but did not ship Baghdad weapons. It gathered 30,000 men at the Iraqi border and 20,000 at the Iranian border.

Ali Khamenei also lashed out at his Turkish counterpart, warning him against any territorial ambition and accusing him of disrespecting Islamic values. Turkish president Kenan Evren immediately responded with a speech declaring that Islamic fundamentalism was as significant a threat as communism. Yet he knew that he had to restrain himself, for his government was daily growing more concerned about the impact that a potential crisis might have on the country's stability, given that 1.5 million Iranian refugees were living in Turkey. The security authorities, who feared a resurgence of Muslim fundamentalism, estimated that the Iranian secret service had infiltrated 10,000 agent provocateurs in Turkey, all allegedly only waiting for orders to mount a major destabilization operation.

Manouchehr Mottaki, Iran's ambassador to Ankara, took a menacing tone and stated that the Kirkuk-Dortyol pipeline would become a legitimate Iranian military target if Turkey continued its military operations in Iraq. To lend his statement weight, Iranian military high command launched the Karbala 2 offensive in the direction of Rawanduz on August 31, 1986. A breakthrough in Rawanduz would open the road to Erbil, then to Mosul and its precious pipeline. Three regular army divisions (the 28th Mechanized, 55th Parachute, and 64th Infantry), supported by several Pasdaran divisions, advanced along the mountainous road leading to Rawanduz. They seized several important bridges, but were stopped short by the city's defenses. The Iraqi 23rd and 33rd divisions, supported by the 5th Corps' artillery, repelled the Pasdaran's repeated assaults. Air intervention and several reinforcement battalions brought by helicopter beat the Iranians back about six miles (ten kilometers).

Meanwhile, at the other end of the front, the Iranians launched a commando operation named Karbala 3. At nightfall on September 1 several Pasdaran companies left al-Faw aboard helicopters and hydroplanes to assault the Khor al-Amaya offshore platform. This former oil terminal had been out of service since the beginning of the war but served as a base to a small garrison responsible for maintaining the early warning radar that kept maritime and aerial traffic at the mouth of the Shatt al-Arab under surveillance. The Pasdaran took control in a few hours. They destroyed the radar, permanently blinding the Iraqi navy, which could no longer follow the movement of Iranian ships responsible for supplying the al-Faw bridgehead. A few days later 200 Iraqi paratroopers were dropped from helicopters onto the Khor al-Amaya platform and recaptured it following a bloody battle.

On September 7 the Iranian military high command called a halt to its Karbala 2 offensive, assuming that Ankara had understood its resolve, but continued to actively support Kurdish guerilla warfare. A Pasdaran company attacked a water reprocessing plant and a classification yard near Kirkuk in tandem with peshmergas led by Jalal Talabani, who had now allied himself with Tehran. A parachute company assaulted the Dukan Dam, leaving Kirkuk without power for several days. Finally, a group of commandos guided by the Barzani brothers' peshmergas infiltrated Iraq and reached the Zakho Bridge on the border with Turkey. They used mortars to destroy two tanker trucks, closing the strategic road for forty-eight hours. These operations forced Baghdad to deploy Republican Guard units to Kurdistan, though they would have been far more useful on the front.

On September 22, 1986, the Iranian regime held an impressive military parade in Tehran to commemorate the sixth anniversary of the war's outbreak, creating an occasion to display its strength and resolution to journalists invited to cover the event from all over the world. The generals had assembled several hundred tanks and self-propelled howitzers, their few remaining Scud missiles, and brand-new chemical decontamination vehicles delivered by Germany. A dozen Tomcats, twenty Tigers, and thirty Phantoms flew over the thousands of soldiers who had been brought to parade through the capital. This display of power surprised military experts, who had underestimated the Iranian armed forces' remaining material potential. In the fall Iran mounted a few limited attacks around Qasr-e-Shirin and the Hoveyzeh marshes to assess the enemy's defenses and to exploit potential local weaknesses. All these attempts were easily beat back by Iraqi troops, but they pressured Baghdad, keeping the regime guessing about the location of Iran's next major operation. Meanwhile, the war had reached a stalemate, both on the ground and in the air.

Hunting Season Begins

During the first months of 1986 the Iraqi air force, busy defending the al-Faw peninsula and the mountains of Kurdistan, slowed the rate of its attacks in the Gulf. Once the Kharg oil terminal's anti-aircraft defense began firing Hawk missiles again, the air force ended its bombing campaign against the island. Only the squadron equipped with Mirage F-1EQ5s tirelessly pursued its mission, tracking oil tankers shuttling between the Kharg and Sirri terminals. These pilots left blindly, on an open air-superiority mission toward the zones through which enemy oil tankers were supposed to pass. They carried a significantly improved version of the Exocet, which increased their attacks' effectiveness. In 1986 they hit twenty-seven oil tankers and sank eight. After the battle of al-Faw ended, they were joined by Su-22s and MiG-23s and bombed about twenty more tankers. With time, the Iraqi pilots became increasingly predictable. Their sweep mission area covered an oval sector extending between Bushehr and the Fahd Line. They generally appeared there at dawn or twilight, nearly always following the same course. This routine made them easier to intercept. In just a few weeks, Iranian Tomcats significantly improved their score, downing one Mirage F-1EQ5, three Su-22s, and four MiG-23s in this area. Several pilots achieved more than five victories, which qualified them as "aces," notably the record holders Fazlollah Javidnia, Jalil Zandi, and Fereidoun Ali-Mazandarani.[6] Contrary to tradition, these pilots were not given any particular publicity or authorized to paint symbols of their victories on their aircraft, for official propaganda wanted to minimize the regular army's exploits to emphasize those of the Pasdaran.

Propaganda was particularly quiet about the air force because the regime remained suspicious of its pilots. In the popular imagination, the war had to be won by the Guardians of the Revolution, not former henchmen of the Shah. Many Iraqi aircraft shot down by Iranian air-superiority fighters were credited to Pasdaran alleged to have brought them down with portable SAM-7s, heavy machine guns, or even Kalashnikovs. The fighter pilots were politely requested not to take offense and to keep their exploits to themselves, unless invited to do otherwise by the regime, which happened exceedingly rarely, since Iranian propaganda preferred to honor the dead than the living. Those who defied these rules were grounded and sometimes even imprisoned for a few weeks. The first documented exploits by Iranian pilots were only disclosed under President Khatami, twelve years later, in a manner carefully supervised by the regime. Several Iranian historians ran afoul of the authorities by relating these accomplishments, but also for reestablishing the air force and regular army's roles in battles supposedly only fought by the Pasdaran. To this day there is no official record of the victories achieved by Iranian air-superiority fighters. Several "aces" have been "erased" from the collective memory for daring to displease the authorities. In fall 2012 the broadcast of a documentary series devoted to Tomcat pilots' exploits was interrupted due to pressure from the Revolutionary Guards—despite the fact that it was produced by Iranian television.

On the other hand, Iraqi pilots could exaggerate their feats for propaganda purposes without incurring their superiors' wrath. Captain Moukhalad Abdul Karim proudly painted fourteen Iranian insignia on the side of his plane, claiming many fictional exploits, while official authorities would later only credit him with two confirmed victories. His bragging cost him the command of a base and promotion to general. Nonetheless, photographs of his Mirage F-1 were seen all over the world and contributed to the aircraft and its missiles' stellar image—much to the delight of the Dassault and Matra companies. The Iraqi air force also stood to gain from Karim's claims, for they enhanced a reputation otherwise undermined by persistently poor statistics. Iranian air-superiority fighters had brought down a little more than 150 Iraqi aircraft since the beginning of the war, while Iraqi fighters had only destroyed fifty Iranian aircraft. In fact, many Iraqi generals would later bear witness that no Iraqi pilot officially achieved the five victories required to claim the title of "flying ace." However, three pilots each obtained four officially recognized victories: Samir Abdul Razak (flying a MiG-21); Ali Sabah (Mirage F-1); and Mohommed Rayyan (MiG-23).

Despite their losses, the Iraqi pilots pushed on with their attacks on oil traffic, forcing Tehran to increase the Lavan terminal's capacity and to add two new storage supertankers to the Sirri floating terminal. Iran installed a pumping station in Genaveh, along its coast, which was connected to the Kharg terminal by a flexible pipeline that carried the refined fuel that the Islamic Republic imported onto the continent for its domestic needs. The Iranians regularly announced their intention to open two new oil terminals: the first near the Bandar Abbas naval base, the second in the port of Jask on the Gulf of Oman. These two plants were intended to prevent tankers from having to enter the Persian Gulf, but required a new pipeline to be built through the southern part of Iran to transport oil extracted in Khuzestan. This expensive construction project was only completed after the war.

In early May General Shaban, who had 340 combat aircraft at his disposal,[7] launched another wave of attacks on the Iranian oil infrastructure, setting refineries as his priority target. He succeeded in setting fire to the Tehran refinery, which had become the largest in the country after the Abadan refinery was destroyed early in the war. He damaged the Genaveh pumping station and destroyed part of the oil stored in the Ahwaz oil depots. He also bombed the Esfahan steelworks, several electric and thermal power plants, and the Parchin munitions plant southeast of Tehran. The Iranian government responded by firing four Scud missiles at Baghdad and nineteen Oghab missiles at Amarah and Basra. The Oghabs were the first surface-to-surface missiles locally assembled by Iranian industry, with the assistance of North Korean engineers. Since the beginning of the year North Korea had helped Iran assemble 300 Oghab missiles (these North Korean copies of Soviet Frog-7s were said to have a range of fifty miles [seventy kilometers]). Following General Shaban and Adnan Khairallah's advice, Saddam Hussein did not let himself be lured into another war of the cities. Instead, he continued attacks aimed at damaging the Iranian economy. Nonetheless, his air force occasionally bombed Iranian airports, destroying one Boeing 737 and two Boeing 747 refueling planes at Shiraz Airport.

The Mirages Strike in the Gulf

For several weeks General Shaban had carefully planned several daring raids far away from the Gulf. To deceive the enemy, he ordered several strikes against the Kharg terminal early in the summer. On August 12, 1986, he stepped up activities and launched a spectacular raid on the Sirri floating terminal. Six Mirage F-1EQ5s took off at dawn from their base in al-Wahda, headed southeast toward the northern tip of Qatar. The first two planes, each armed with two 900-pound (400-kilo) bombs, were tasked with striking the target, while the other four would refuel them in flight. Saudi air control, which was probably informed of the operation, discreetly turned a blind eye. After being refueled off the coast of Kuwait, then of Bahrain, the two pilots responsible for the attack descended right above sea level and accelerated to maximum speed. They set their course directly on their target, which was located 500 miles (800 kilometers) from their starting point. They burst into view above Sirri, sank the tanker *Azarpod,* and damaged two other supertankers. They returned to their base without encountering any Iranian air-superiority fighters and refueled in-flight again off the coast of Qatar. On August 29 Iraqi pilots repeated their exploit, this time by attacking the Lavan oil terminal. For this operation, twelve Mirages took off from al-Wahda: two were filled with electronic warfare equipment to scramble Iranian radars, four were armed with bombs, and six were loaded with fuel for in-flight refueling. The formation followed the same flight path as the previous time, merely turning off a little earlier. The attackers easily dodged the Iranian antiaircraft defense's inaccurate fire, bombed the terminal, and sank the tanker *Mokran.*

The expansion of Iraqi strikes convinced Tehran to extend its shuttle system to Larak, a small island off of Bandar Abbas at the mouth of the Strait of Hormuz. Here, the Iranians had anchored several supertankers side by side—including the *Seawise Giant,* then the largest ship in the world at a length of 1,500 feet (460 meters) and a weight of 700,000 tons—to store the oil transported from Kharg Island. This new floating terminal, which was supposed to be out of Iraqi air-superiority fighters' range, was intended to allow for an increase in oil traffic and reassure

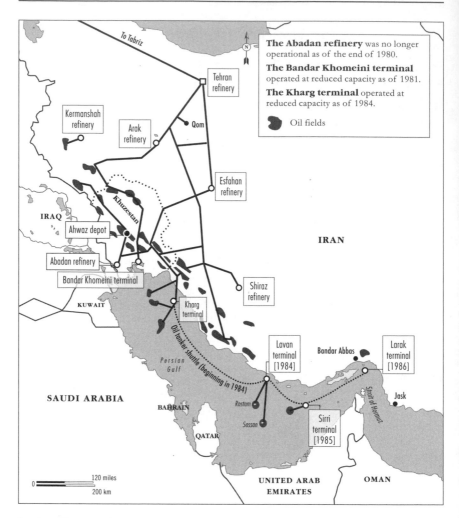

The Abadan refinery was no longer operational as of the end of 1980.

The Bandar Khomeini terminal operated at reduced capacity as of 1981.

The Kharg terminal operated at reduced capacity as of 1984.

Oil fields

Iranian oil network

shipping companies, which were concerned about the escalation of violence in Gulf waters.

From October to November General Shaban resumed bombing Kharg while planning new raids. On October 6 and 7 two Tomcat patrols intercepted assailants near Kharg terminal and shot down three Mirage F-1s, while a fourth was destroyed by a Hawk missile. Not to be outdone, the Phantom pilots tore one MiG-23 and two Su-22s out of the sky. Iraqi raids continued for several weeks, alternating MiGs, Sukhois, and Mirages.

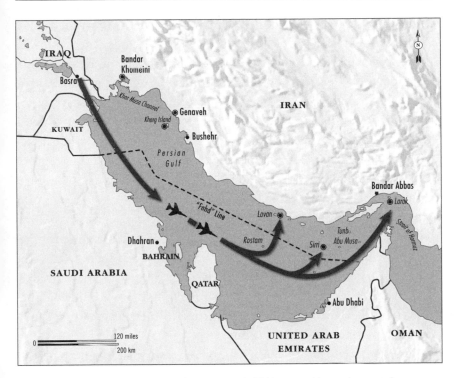

Mirage F-1 long-range strikes in the Persian Gulf (August–November 1986)

Iraq's relentlessness paid off, severely damaging a pier and several loading docks, which were out of service for several months. In November General Shaban mounted a series of raids against the Sassan, Rostam, and Rakhsh Iranian oil platforms off the shores of the United Arab Emirates. Once again, the Mirage F-1EQ5s were put to work, refueling in flight on the way there and back. Iran retaliated by sending its Phantoms to bomb the Emirati Abu al-Bukhoosh oil field and accused Abu Dhabi of having allowed Iranian fighters in its airspace. The Iranian government would later apologize for this "mistake" and would compensate the UAE, as well as the families of those killed during the attack, who included two French nationals working for Total.

On November 25, 1986, General Shaban took the Iranians by surprise again by striking the brand-new Larak floating terminal. This was the most distant raid ever conducted by the Iraqi air force: three Mirage F-1EQ5s, each carrying four bombs, took off from al-Wahda before daybreak, preceded by nine other Mirage F-1s fitted with in-flight refueling pods and two Mirage F-1s fitted with jammer pods. These fourteen Mirages were armed with Magic II air-to-air missiles to defend themselves. On the whole, they followed the same path as the previous raid on the Sirri terminal, with the exception that they passed far south of the terminal. The three Mirages responsible for the strike then followed a semi-circular path that led them to follow the Emirati coast and emerge over their target 775 miles (1,250 kilometers) from their base. They immediately separated, targeting the supertankers that served as floating terminals and the tankers being loaded. Total panic broke out aboard the ships. Technicians immediately interrupted refueling operations to limit the risk of fire. The supertanker *Antarctica* was wrecked, and four other tankers were severely damaged. After having dropped their bombs, the three Iraqi pilots even allowed themselves the luxury of two additional weapon deliveries, during which they strafed the ships with their 30 mm guns. They then turned back and returned to their base without incident, having spent four hours in flight.[8]

Furious at having let themselves be taken by surprise, the Iranians dispatched significant anti-aircraft defenses to protect the Larak terminal and ordered the Phantoms based in Bandar Abbas to permanently be on patrol in this sector. They responded to the Iraqi strikes by firing their four last Scuds at Baghdad and intensifying their attacks on maritime traffic in the eastern part of the Gulf. Given their low number of operational fighter planes (one hundred at most),[9] the thirteen Phantoms available for strikes in the Gulf (seven in Bushehr; six in Bandar Abbas) had to carry out early warning patrols and could no longer truly disrupt maritime traffic. Over the course of a year they attacked only ten oil tankers, sinking two. The Sea King and AB-212 helicopters based in Abu Musa and on the Rostam and Sassan oil platforms picked up the slack; twenty tankers were damaged and three others scrapped following their attacks.

Even the navy made a few nocturnal sorties to harass tankers. In October and November two Vosper-class frigates left their base in Bandar Abbas at nightfall and discreetly joined the dense traffic in the Strait of Hormuz to fire their Sea Killer missiles at four supertankers coming from Kuwait and the UAE. By daybreak the frigates were back at harbor. During the day, other navy ships carried out multiple inspection missions on boats transiting through the Strait to try to intercept weapon shipments to Iraq. When their searches were successful, they appropriated the freight. For instance, they seized a shipment of T-69 tanks and artillery pieces from a Chinese cargo ship.

The Pasdaran did not lag behind; they soon launched their first maritime raids. On September 16 several fast patrol boats based in the Tunb Islands and Abu Musa sprayed the Kuwaiti tanker *Al Funtas* with bullets, firing several salvos of rockets. The damaged ship had to sail to the closest port to be repaired.

Both countries' oil infrastructures suffered badly over the course of 1986. Most refineries and pumping stations were bombed; ninety-six commercial ships were attacked, three-quarters of which were tankers; sixteen were sunk or had to be scrapped. According to Lloyd's, ninety-three other ships were immobilized in the Gulf because their owners did not want to risk an overly dangerous crossing. This was a shortfall for both belligerents. The Iranian government recorded a 5 percent drop in its oil production and an 8 percent drop in its crude exports, despite the fact that it rationalized its industry and multiplied the shuttles between its loading terminals. Yet the real death knell for the Iranian economy was the collapse of the price of oil combined with the drop of the dollar and the discounts offered its clients. In less than a year, Tehran lost more than half its oil revenue. For its part, the Iraqi government compensated for the loss of revenue through the financial assistance of the Gulf nations, a 15 percent increase in production, and a 30 percent rise in exports.

For the first time since 1981, Iranian gross domestic product was barely superior to Iraqi GDP, though its population was three times greater. Rationing had to be intensified. The armed forces found it increasingly difficult to attract new recruits and reconstitute decimated divisions. For the first time, women—often war widows—were trained to use weapons so they could replace militiamen previously assigned to protect sensitive facilities in urban areas. Photos of these women, wearing black abayas and face veils as they fired pistols or Kalashnikovs, were published around the world. The regime had to use coercive measures to force new recruits to enlist. Civil servants and university professors were given basic military training in a few weeks so they could take administrative and logistic positions at the front. The length of military service was extended from twenty-four to thirty months. Desertions rapidly increased—including from Akbar Hashemi Rafsanjani's immediate entourage. On August 12, 1986, the pilot and copilot of a military utility Falcon-50 assigned to the speaker of Parliament's personal use fled the regime and landed in Baghdad. The regime's top money man's concerns were exacerbated by the fact that there was no hope of financial assistance from abroad and that he had just lost a precious channel for war supplies.

Chapter 25

The Iran-Contra Affair

On November 3, 1986, the Lebanese magazine *Ash-Shiraa* revealed that the American government was clandestinely shipping weapons to Iran to facilitate the liberation of American hostages in Lebanon. The news set off an uproar in the United States, whose government prided itself on never negotiating with hostage takers. Congress immediately demanded that the White House explain itself, underlining the embargo forbidding all sales of military equipment to Iran. Faced with pressure from a wide variety of sources, Ronald Reagan was forced to justify his actions in a televised address: "My purpose was . . . to send a signal that the United States was prepared to replace the animosity between [the US and Iran] with a new relationship. . . . The most significant step which Iran could take, we indicated, would be to use its influence in Lebanon to secure the release of all hostages held there."[1] His explanation did not suffice to quell the furor in Congress, which called for the creation of an investigatory commission chaired by Senator John Tower. The commission explored the dark corners of power for three months, interviewing hundreds of individuals. Its 500-page report lifted part of the veil on the affair that rocked Reagan's authority.

The matter had begun in 1984, a few weeks after Reagan's triumphant reelection. In Germany, former CIA officer Theodore Shackley was approached by Manucher Ghorbanifar, an Iranian known to Western intelligence services for his years of involvement in arms trafficking to Tehran. Ghorbanifar claimed to be close to the Iranian prime minister and told Shackley that the "moderate" factions wanted to resume dialogue with the United States to rescue Iran from its diplomatic isolation. In fact, he was not speaking exclusively for the moderates, but for everyone in Tehran who agreed with Rafsanjani and Mir-Hossein Mousavi's conviction that the Islamic Republic had nothing to gain from maintaining its isolation. On the contrary, these individuals believed Iran needed to rekindle its ties with the West, yet without making the slightest ideological concession. To lure Shackley, Manucher Ghorbanifar suggested that Iran would be willing to trade Soviet-made equipment—notably the notorious T-72 tank worrying Western military commands at the time—for the precious antitank and anti-air missiles Iranian troops desperately needed. As a bonus, the mullahs could intervene with Hezbollah to facilitate the liberation of the American hostages. The idea gained traction in Langley, to the point that in the spring of 1985, the CIA wrote the White House a memorandum recommending a change of policy on Iran. Anticipating the Ayatollah Khomeini's death, the American intelligence agency suggested resuming more constructive relations between Washington and Tehran to prepare for the future.

The Israeli Connection

Meanwhile, Michael Leeden, the assistant to Ronald Reagan's national security advisor, Robert McFarlane, told his boss about a proposal he allegedly received from the Israeli prime minister during a trip to Jerusalem on May 5, 1985.[2] Shimon Peres purportedly informed Leeden of an Iranian offer to purchase large quantities of TOW antitank and Hawk anti-air missiles. Israel proposed to serve as an intermediary by using its arms traffic network to Iran, but wanted the green light from the highest American authorities. If they agreed, the Israeli government said it was prepared to transfer the United States the money Iran paid to purchase the weapons. In exchange, the United States would have to commit to shipping the Israeli army an equivalent number of latest-generation missiles at no cost. The Israelis saw this operation as a way to modernize Tzahal's inventory without spending a shekel and to reactivate the Iranian network put on standby by Menachem Begin and Ariel Sharon after Hezbollah's first spectacular terrorist attacks against Israeli occupation troops in Lebanon. Since then, Tzahal had withdrawn from most of Lebanese territory and the Israeli government was seeking to resume dialogue with Tehran to negotiate the repatriation of more Iranian Jews to Israel. With a little luck, Israel could even take advantage of the opportunity to increase its own weapons shipments to Iran and reap additional revenue. Jerusalem had everything to gain from convincing Washington to agree to this arrangement.

The convergence of these various elements persuaded Robert McFarlane to open negotiations with the Iranians, with the aim of exchanging weapons for hostages. A similar arrangement had led to the resolution of the first hostage crisis in fall 1980. Robert McFarlane undoubtedly thought that Ronald Reagan and CIA director William Casey would accept the idea of such an exchange since they had already endorsed a similar scheme five years earlier. In June Robert McFarlane smoothly convinced William Casey to back his plan. In mid-July he visited Bethesda Hospital, where Ronald Reagan had just been operated on for colon cancer. The recovering president gave his agreement, convinced that he was working to protect his unjustly kidnapped compatriots. Secretary of State George Schultz and Secretary of Defense Caspar Weinberger were fiercely opposed to the clandestine operation, which they considered detrimental to the United States' interests, but they had no choice but to follow the president's decision.

Feeling confident, the national security advisor informed the Israeli government that the highest American authorities had agreed to the shipping of military equipment to Iran. As agreed, Israel would take the arms directly from its own inventory and deliver them to Tehran by airplane and ship. These shipments would supplement those Israel carried out on its own behalf. The United States would replenish Israeli stockpiles once it had received the money from the transaction. The whole operation had to remain secret. In Israel, David Kimche, director general of the Ministry of Defense; Amiram Nir, a special advisor to the prime minister; and the ubiquitous Jacob Nimrodi, the former defense attaché to Tehran under the Shah, served as intermediaries between the American government and the Iranian authorities, working through the arms dealer Manucher Ghorbanifar, the same man who had directly approached the Americans a few months earlier and had solid connections both in Iran and Israel. The Saudi arms dealer Adnan Khashoggi was also in the loop.

Arms for Hostages

On August 20, 1985, the first delivery of one hundred TOW missiles arrived in Iran. It was followed three weeks later by an additional 400 missiles. On September 15 the Islamic Jihad freed Pastor Benjamin Weir in Beirut. In mid-November Israel shipped Iran eighteen Hawk missiles with the White House's blessing. But the missiles were not the version requested by the Iranian regime, which refused to free any hostages if the missiles delivered did not meet their requirements. To make matters more complicated, Manucher Ghorbanifar imposed a 40 percent increase on the price of the equipment delivered. Furious, the Iranians threatened to put a stop to the operation. Robert McFarlane, discouraged and increasingly contested in circles of power, stepped down on December 5, officially citing family reasons. He was replaced by Admiral John Poindexter, who discovered the situation upon taking office. He decided to continue his predecessor's operation, but suggested doing so without Ghorbanifar's services, dealing directly with the Iranians. At this stage one of the affair's key figures was brought in: Lieutenant Colonel Oliver North, a marine responsible for antisubversion efforts with the National Security Council. North proposed to use the money paid by the Iranians to finance the Contras, the anti-Communist guerillas fighting the Sandinista regime in Nicaragua. Admiral Poindexter and William Casey were won over by the idea, which allowed them to bypass Congress and undermine a Marxist dictatorship threatening their backyard without costing the American taxpayer a cent.

Over the few weeks that the new team settled in, negotiations between Washington, Jerusalem, and Tehran collapsed. On January 12, 1986, for the first time since the beginning of the Iran-Iraq War, the Pasdaran boarded and searched a ship flying the American flag, the *President Taylor*, in the Strait of Hormuz. After a full search, the ship was allowed to continue on its way, but the American authorities had been warned: Tehran would not hesitate to attack American interests in the Gulf if the weapon deliveries were suspended. Washington understood the message and resumed shipments, now working without intermediaries. In February 1,000 TOW missiles and large quantities of spare parts for Hawk missiles arrived in Iran on flights directly chartered by the CIA. Annoyed by the

Americans' delays, the Iranians upped the ante by refusing to free more hostages. They demanded more missiles, as well as the release of Shiite prisoners in Kuwait and fifty Hezbollah combatants held by the Israelis in South Lebanon. The Israeli authorities were delighted at this opportunity to get back into the negotiations and re-impose themselves as middlemen for weapon shipments. The Iranians also asked the Americans to provide them with information about the Iraqi layout.

Discussions were complicated by the American raid on Iran's ally, Libya. On April 15, 1986, fifty U.S. air force and U.S. navy aircraft bombed several symbolic targets of the Libyan regime (Operation El Dorado Canyon) after Libya had ordered the deadly bombing of a Berlin nightclub in which several American servicemen had been killed. Two days later the American hostage Peter Kilburn and the British hostages John Douglas and Philip Padfield were executed in Lebanon. To ease tensions, Vice President George Bush traveled to Kuwait to pressure local authorities to release some of the Shiite prisoners sentenced to death following the December 1983 terrorist attacks. He persuaded the Emir of Kuwait to agree not to execute them. Yet this was not enough to convince the Iranians to return to the negotiating table. Going for broke, Admiral Poindexter authorized a delivery of 500 TOW missiles to Tehran—this time through the Israeli network. He also created a small team of American experts, which he sent to the Iranian capital to directly negotiate the freeing of the hostages outside of Manucher Ghorbanifar's stranglehold on the situation. He gave his predecessor Robert McFarlane a chance to come back into the game by appointing him head of the delegation.

These were the first American government representatives to travel to Iran since the severing of diplomatic relations between the two countries. On May 25, 1986, the small group of experts met with representatives of the Iranian government in Tehran. The Iranians were surprised, for they had not expected to see an American delegation turn up in their country. Negotiations stagnated while the stunned Iranians referred every American proposal to their superiors. Growing irritated with the waste of time, the former national security advisor finally backed the Iranians into a corner: either they immediately freed a hostage as a show of goodwill or the American party would walk away. The Iranian government proved unable to secure a hostage release in a few hours and the American delegation returned to Washington empty-handed.[3]

Yet dialogue was not broken and negotiations continued at a faster pace. On July 26 Father Jenco was released in Beirut. A week later the American government sent Iran another batch of spare parts, which allowed the Iranian army to put close to one hundred Hawk missiles back in service. In mid-September an Iranian delegation discreetly traveled to Washington to further discussions, which then continued in Germany in October. On October 28 another batch of 500 TOW missiles was delivered to Iran. On November 2 David Jacobsen was released in Beirut after spending more than a year and a half in captivity. He would be the last American hostage freed during the war; the next day the Iran-Contra scandal became worldwide news, putting the American administration in an extremely delicate position. In fifteen months the United States had only obtained the release of three hostages (out of five), in exchange for delivering Iran 2,500 TOW missiles and the equivalent of 300 Hawk missiles.

Conflicts of Interest in Tehran

Why did this affair hit the headlines at the very moment when negotiations seemed to be coming to a favorable resolution and the Iranian army was finally getting the missiles it had desperately been trying to acquire for years? Simply because certain individuals in Tehran had organized leaks to scuttle the negotiations. The rapprochement between Iran and the United States worried members of the Iranian faction that advocated self-sufficiency. They were concerned to see the Islamic Republic draw closer to the former tutelary power. This faction, headed by Ali Khamenei, Ayatollah Montazeri, and a few others, also noticed that this rapprochement reinforced Rafsanjani's stature and put him at an advantage in the race to succeed the Supreme Leader. From their perspective, it was crucial to torpedo this opening to the United States. Was it pure happenstance that Mehdi Hashemi, Ayatollah Montazeri's son-in-law, was later identified as the source of the leaks that allowed *Ash-Shiraa* to publish its scoop? Hashemi was arrested on superficial charges, then discreetly tried, sentenced, and executed for high treason, which further marginalized Ali Montazeri and left him no chance of succeeding the Ayatollah Khomeini. The Ayatollah was naturally perfectly aware of the "arms for hostages" exchange and extended his moral authority over it.

In the eye of a scandal, the White House had no choice but to put an end to the attempted rapprochement with Iran and order Israel to follow suit. The Israeli government's role as an intermediary had also come to light, complicating the geopolitical situation for Washington. The Israelis had just sold the Iranians 1,000 TOW missiles on their own behalf and were upset to lose the prospect of selling them Gabriel antiship missiles and one hundred old Skyhawk fighter-bombers the Israeli air force wanted to offload. Yet once the Americans put on the pressure, the Israelis had no choice but to obey, particularly since they were trying to move on from the Pollard affair, which had poisoned their relationship with the United States. A few months earlier, Jonathan Pollard, a Jewish analyst working for the U.S. navy's intelligence services, had been caught red-handed divulging highly classified information to Israeli intelligence services.[4] Heartsick, recently elected Prime Minister Yitzhak Shamir declared: "the war between Iraq and Iran is nothing less than folly. . . . Iraq and Iran, both of them, are extreme enemies of our country. We strongly support American action to prevent this ugly war from spilling over."[5] In Washington responsibility for the hostage negotiations was taken away from the National Security Council and the White House and put back in the hands of the secretary of state. George Schultz finally had his revenge, though he would not succeed in obtaining the hostages' release.

For their part the Iranians were furious. Over a few weeks six more Americans were kidnapped in Beirut, raising the total number of American hostages to eight. The American government was left with the bitter feeling of having been duped. It was back to square one. The president and his advisors came to the conclusion that from here on out they would need to be as firm as possible with Iran and no longer shrink from confrontation—including military confrontation, if necessary.

A Disastrous Outcome for Washington

In Baghdad Saddam Hussein fulminated against the Americans, accusing them of double-dealing. He called Ronald Reagan and Donald Rumsfeld every name under the sun, as can be heard on the audiotapes that systematically recorded all his conversations. In late 1985 he grew even more furious when he learned that Washington had given Tehran satellite images showing detailed Iraqi military deployment along the front, which had helped Iran capture the al-Faw peninsula. Yet the Iraqi president remained pragmatic. He knew that for the time being he had to tread softly with the White House, since the Kremlin appeared to be moving away from him and the Europeans were objecting to selling him arms, using his country's insolvency as a pretext. Ever the shrewd politician, he decided to make his American interlocutors feel guilty by asking them to increase their financial assistance and technical cooperation. The Americans sheepishly gave the Iraqis more and more intelligence data, allowing them to refine their perception of the Iranian layout. They also turned a blind eye to Iraq's massive use of chemical weapons. Walter Lang, a former officer with the U.S. Defense Intelligence Agency, later recognized that at the DIA, "the use [of chemical weapons] against military objectives was seen as inevitable in the Iraqi struggle for survival."[6]

In Washington the Iran-Contra scandal took its course. Ronald Reagan managed to save himself and avoid impeachment proceedings. Nonetheless, the Tower Commission severely criticized him for not having exercised enough control over his national security advisor's activities. Admiral John Poindexter and Secretary of Defense Caspar Weinberger did not fare as well: they were forced to resign. Robert McFarlane, the brains behind the scheme, attempted suicide and was later sentenced to two years' probation for abuse of authority. Once elected president, George Bush Sr., the vice president during Iran-Contra, rehabilitated all three men and even hired John Poindexter to work for him. William Casey escaped public disgrace by dying of cancer on May 6, 1987, only a few days before his scheduled appearance before Congress. He was replaced at the head of the CIA by William Webster. Lieutenant Colonel Oliver North was found guilty of three felonies for lying to Congress and obstructing justice. He was sentenced to a three-year suspended prison term. Two years later the charges against him were vacated, freeing him to try his luck as a neoconservative politician and then to become a bestselling author.

On the fringes of this affair, the American justice system brought to light several lucrative Tehran-bound trafficking networks, one of which was based on the aircraft carrier *Kitty Hawk*, then stationed in the Gulf. One of the pursers had organized a network by which the ship's Tomcats' spare parts and electronic components were misappropriated and delivered to Iran via a New York import-export company and a shell company in London.[7] This equipment, valued at seven million dollars, had been removed from the *Kitty Hawk* during a stopover in New York, then fictitiously sold to the import-export company, which had shipped it to London, then to Tehran using false export documents. The members of the network pled guilty and were sentenced to long prison terms.

As for the American hostages still held captive in Lebanon,[8] they would wait to be freed until 1991, once all the Shiite detainees implicated in the terrorist attacks in Kuwait and Europe and against the Israeli army in South Lebanon were released, the Lebanese civil war was over, the Shah's assets had been returned, and the Iranian president Rafsanjani had publicly encouraged the reinvestment of Western capital in his country.

[Chapter 26]

All-Out Offensives

In the late fall of 1986 the Iranians prepared another offensive intended to bring Saddam Hussein to his knees. Since Baghdad remained out of range, the Iranian army targeted Basra. Its leaders were convinced that the Ba'athist regime could not survive losing Iraq's second biggest city. They hoped that the fall of Basra would set off a Shiite insurrection in southern Iraq. They had massed 360,000 soldiers nearby, which were divided into thirteen divisions (ten infantry, one commando, one armored, and one artillery), in addition to the 40,000 troops deployed in the al-Faw pocket. The offensive was postponed several times while the regular army and the Pasdaran argued over the method of operations. General Shirazi had proposed a large-scale envelopment maneuver, which he deemed safer and less costly, though it would undoubtedly take longer. Mohsen Rezaee, acting as the spokesman for the Pasdaran, argued for a frontal assault on Basra, which would be more expensive but faster.

The time factor was particularly crucial because the Ayatollah Khomeini had recently decreed a fatwa asking the armed forces to defeat Iraq before March 21, 1987, the next Nowruz, or Persian New Year. This unusual step on the Supreme Leader's part was obviously aimed at motivating the troops, but also at increasing pressure on Rafsanjani to win or negotiate. The war had lasted too long. Extending it was becoming counterproductive. The mullahs' power was now firmly established over a fragmented society that no longer had the means to contest the clergy's stranglehold on public affairs. The opposition parties had been wiped out or muzzled and the Kurdish, Azeri, and Baloch separatist movements put down. Now the authorities needed money to satisfy the people and guarantee social peace. The continuing hostilities were impoverishing Iran. It was urgent to oust Saddam.

The Assault on Basra

Following a heated meeting of the Supreme Defense Council, Rafsanjani imposed the idea of a frontal attack on Basra. The attack would be in two phases: troops would cross the Shatt al-Arab at Khorramshahr to attack the city from the rear, coming from the south, while the main assault would come from Shalamcheh and Hosseinieh, along the river's eastern bank. During the night of December 24 to 25, 1986, Rafsanjani set off Operation Karbala 4. The 21st Infantry Division, which had been renamed "Prophet Muhammad," crossed the Shatt al-Arab and landed on Umm al-Rassas Island and the three islets of Bouarim, Tawila, and Fayaz. The division commander, General Ahmad Kossari, was supported by the 41st Engineering Division. His infantrymen immediately ran up against Iraqi troops and were mowed down by their machine guns and mortars. By dawn the Iranians had barely advanced. General Kossari, conscious of his mission's importance, ordered additional reinforcements deployed. Over thirty-six hours more than 30,000 Pasdaran disembarked on the bridgehead. The Iraqi military high command lost no time in responding, ordering its air force to bomb the floating bridges installed across the Shatt al-Arab. It entrusted the counterattack to the 7th Corps, which was currently assigned to defending the al-Faw peninsula. General Ma'ahir Abdul Rashid, now an ally of Saddam's family, was in the heart of the action. Heading the 6th Armored Division, he launched a vast outflanking maneuver that wiped out the Iranian soldiers scattered along the river, while some of the 7th Corps' divisions left their trenches twelve miles (twenty kilometers) away to storm the Iranian bridgehead.

Fierce combat raged for forty-eight hours. Knowing that Basra's fate was in their hands, the Iraqis seemed unstoppable. On December 27 General Rashid still had full control of the area. His combatants wiped out the remaining pockets of resistance after regaining control of Umm al-Rassas Island and the three neighboring islets. In seventy-two hours they had slaughtered more than 8,000 Iranian fighters, taking only 200 prisoners. The rest had scrambled back across the river. By comparison, the Iraqis' losses were minor: 800 dead and 2,000 wounded. Glowingly proud of this stunning victory, General Rashid swaggered before his rivals, who often criticized him for bypassing high command and directly obtaining support from Saddam. The dictator was in no position to complain: Ma'ahir Abdul Rashid had just handed him a memorable victory, which he promptly began referring to as the "Battle of the Great Day."

In Tehran, on the other hand, criticism of Rafsanjani streamed forth from all quarters, including from Ali Khamenei, Ayatollah Montazeri, and General Nejad, the former chief of staff of the armed forces. The Ayatollah Khomeini even considered removing Rafsanjani as commander in chief of the armed forces, then thought better of it. In ill health, Khomeini needed to rely on the man whom he saw as the only mullah able to stay the course through thick and thin—at least so long as the war lasted. He also knew that the Pasdaran would not understand if he sidelined Rafsanjani—and the Pasdaran were now the country's most powerful force. The speaker of Parliament was therefore able to pursue his initial plan to attack Basra. Alone against the rest of the regime, he staked his all on committing every available combatant to the battle. He knew his political future depended on it. The fight would be all-out and merciless. A single catchphrase prevailed: defeat the enemy at any cost. While the Battle of Khorramshahr in 1982 has often been compared to the Battle of Stalingrad, the Battle of Basra in early 1987 can easily be likened to Verdun: for several months, the belligerents would wear each other down through a hellish confrontation in which they drove their countries' best and brightest into muddy trenches.

The "Mother of All Battles"

On January 8, 1987, Akbar Hashemi Rafsanjani launched the Karbala 5 offensive in the sector east of Basra, across from Fish Lake and the artificial channel. Beginning in 1984 the Iraqis had significantly expanded the military layout there. Aside from a succession of minefields, antitank ditches, barbed wire, ramparts, bunkers, and trenches, the sappers had erected a curving embankment around the bridges connecting Basra to the Shatt al-Arab's eastern bank from the town of Tanuma. The system was supplemented by an electronic early warning system able to detect approaching assailants. General Tala al-Duri, commander of the Iraqi 3rd Corps, had three divisions in the sector: the 8th Infantry to the north of Fish Lake; the

11th Infantry between the lake's southern tip and the Shatt al-Arab; and the 5th Mechanized, further back near Tanuma. His four other infantry divisions and 3rd Armored Division were deployed a little further north, on the other side of the artificial channel. The city of Basra and the western bank of the Basra-Umm Qasr channel were guarded by several Republican Guard special forces divisions and Popular Army brigades.

At dusk the Iranian 92nd Armored Division engaged with the 8th Iraqi Division, aiming to pin it in place along the border. As soon as night fell the 58th and 77th Pasdaran divisions crossed Fish Lake aboard flat-bottomed boats and disembarked on the other bank, in the middle of the marshes, in order to attack the 8th Division from the rear. They then continued to the artificial channel. Once this maneuver was accomplished, a Pasdaran brigade crossed the canal aboard rubber dinghies and established a half-mile-wide (one-kilometer-wide) bridgehead on the opposite bank, north of Tamura. Concurrently, the 23rd Special Forces Division crossed Fish Lake to establish a second bridgehead facing Tanuma. It was counterattacked by the 5th Mechanized Division.

Meanwhile, further south, three Pasdaran divisions rushed to attack a small quadrangle covering about five square miles (twelve square kilometers) wedged between the Shatt al-Arab, the area south of Fish Lake, and the Jassem Canal, twelve miles (twenty kilometers) east of Basra. Though the Iraqis had expected and prepared for the offensive, they were surprised by the mass of enemy troops: 40,000 combatants, a majority of whom were teenagers, crushed their defenses. At dawn the 11th Division's infantrymen retreated to a second line of defense erected 1.8 miles (three kilometers) back, near the village of Du'aiji. General Abd al-Wahed Shannan, the division commander, had rallied his troops there and deployed his last brigade.

For forty-eight hours the Iraqis counterattacked with the limited means at their disposal. Cloudy skies forced their air force to fly at low altitude, making it more vulnerable to Iranian anti-aircraft defense: five of its fighters were shot down, while a Tu-16 was destroyed over Shalamcheh by a Hawk missile. The Pasdaran advanced on every front. In the north the 8th Division was surrounded and collapsed. Its general, Abrahim Ismael, was taken prisoner. In the south the Iranians overran the Iraqi second line of defense and seized the village of Du'aiji.

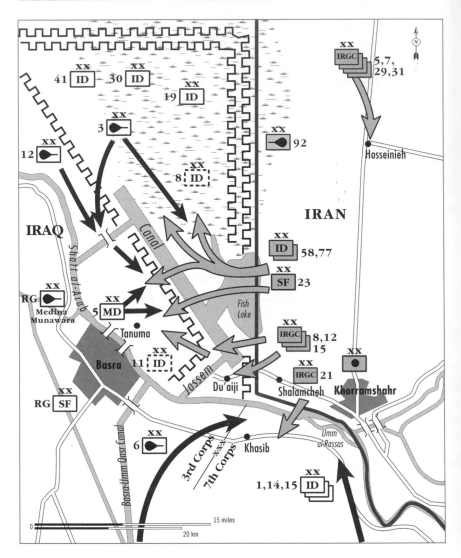

Battle of Basra (December 25, 1986–April 11, 1987)

On January 11 General al-Duri authorized the 11th Division to withdraw behind the Jassem Canal, which connected the artificial channel to the Shatt al-Arab. The waterway formed a natural line of defense, which brought the Basijis to a stop. The Iranian vanguard was now only ten miles (sixteen kilometers) from Basra, within cannon range. Furious that General al-Duri had ordered a withdrawal without his authorization, Saddam

Hussein stripped him of his command. Though the dictator had always forgiven al-Duri's past mistakes, he now needed a genuinely competent individual to supervise the defense of Basra. He appointed Diah ul-Din Jamal as his replacement, a Shiite general who had won his confidence by swearing that he would sooner die than let his native city fall into Iranian hands. Without conferring with General Dhannoun, Saddam Hussein gave General Jamal his operational orders. Dhannoun was offended. The situation grew tense, and Saddam dismissed his chief of staff of the armed forces, asking his entourage who could replace him. Given the circumstances, no one was eager for the job. None of the generals in the high command volunteered. Saddam eventually chose by default, appointing Saladin Aziz, a retired general whose name had been given to him by his advisors. Aziz was an intellectual trained by the British. He had proven himself against the Kurds in the early 1970s and left active duty a few months before the outbreak of war with Iran. Having been summoned out of retirement, he was immediately received by the president, who promoted him to his new appointment. The next day Saddam Hussein, Adnan Khairallah, and General Aziz traveled to Basra to personally assess the situation. The Iraqi dictator authorized the use of chemical weapons and decided to commit the Republican Guard's "Medina Munawara" armored division to the battle. Realizing that Basra could fall, he ordered its inhabitants to evacuate and asked his generals to prepare a second line of defense along the Euphrates to prevent the Iranians from advancing to Baghdad.

In addition, on January 12 the Iraqi president reignited the "War of the Cities" in a knee-jerk effort to punish the Iranian government and discourage it from continuing its offensive on Basra. The Iraqi air force was directed to abandon its fire support missions on the battlefield and its attacks on oil traffic in the Gulf to bomb thirty Iranian cities, including Tehran, Qom, and Esfahan. Though located far from the front, these three cities were raided over several weeks by the ten MiG-25s modified for this type of mission. One MiG-25 was shot down near Esfahan on February 15, 1987. The Iraqis also fired several salvos of Scud missiles at Dezful, Ahwaz, and Kermanshah. The Iranians promptly retaliated by firing Oghab missiles at the Iraqi cities near the front and Scud missiles at Baghdad.[1] North Korea had recently delivered twenty Scuds to Iran and was preparing to ship eighty by the fall. The Iranians retaliated with their artillery, their long-range cannons pounding Basra, Mandali, Khanaqin, and Sulaymaniah. As with previous episodes in the War of the Cities, the latest urban bombing campaign did nothing to shake the belligerents' resolve.

During the night of January 13 to 14, 1987, the Iranians launched the Karbala 6 offensive in the sector of Sumer. Their goal was to seize the strategic barrier of Mandali, which controlled the road to Baghdad, but especially to force the Iraqis to deploy their reinforcements in this direction, making Basra more vulnerable. General Shirazi personally headed the operation, committing 100,000 men and 600 tanks divided over seven divisions (the 11th Artillery, 25th and 35th Infantry, 40th and 84th Mechanized, and 81st and 88th Armored) to this diversionary battle. For the first time, his general staff also used small drones to fly over the enemy layout, which allowed the Iranians to preserve their precious reconnaissance planes.[2]

The Iraqis had only three infantry divisions facing their opponent. The general in charge of the sector also had three more divisions staggered along the border, but these could not move from their positions without leaving a wide opening in the Iraqi layout. His only operational reserves were the 10th Tank Division and the Republican Guard's "Hammurabi" Armored Division. In five days the Iranians overran the Iraqi defenses and captured several hills overlooking the abandoned town of Mandali, but failed to break through. The Iraqis counterattacked with their two armored divisions. For the first time in four years the belligerents engaged in a real tank battle. The Iraqis got the upper hand over their adversaries; the Iranian T-59s and T-69s were no match for the Iraqi T-72s, particularly since the former's tank crews painfully lacked training and motivation. Some had never even fired a shell before, due to Iranian rationing of what had become rare commodities. Yet the Iraqi tank crews were unable to follow through on their success and were beaten back by salvos of TOW antitank missiles. In the final tally each side lost 200 tanks.

On January 17 Saddam Hussein convened his main generals in Baghdad to organize the counteroffensive, which began the next day in the region of Basra. The 3rd Armored Division headed for the marshlands to regain control of the eastern bank of the artificial channel and isolate the Iranian infantrymen entrenched on the other bank, across from Basra. Meanwhile, the 5th Mechanized Division, the 12th Armored Division, and the "Medina Munawara" tank division reduced the two enemy bridgeheads established on each side of Tanuma and pushed the Iranian combatants back into the water. Many did not know how to swim and drowned.

On January 21, with the front appearing to have stabilized, the Iraqi president addressed the Iranian people in a solemn radio broadcast in which he renounced his territorial claims and proposed a comprehensive peace plan for Iran and Iraq. The plan was based on four principles: the total and reciprocal withdrawal of armed forces to the internationally recognized borders, the exchange of all prisoners of war, the rapid signing of a nonaggression treaty, and noninterference in each country's interior affairs. Tariq Aziz traveled to Moscow, while Taha Yassin Ramadan traveled to Beijing to ask the Soviet and Chinese authorities, respectively, to pressure Tehran to accept the peace plan. At this stage only the Soviet Union and China seemed able to influence the Iranian regime. Yet, once again, the Iranians proved inflexible. Parallel negotiations conducted by the Organization of Islamic Cooperation and the nonaligned countries were equally fruitless.

On January 23 Ali Khamenei declared that Iran would refuse to negotiate as long as Saddam Hussein remained in power. Rafsanjani went one step further and stated he was prepared to purchase weapons from the United States, hoping to drive a wedge into the complex relations between Baghdad and Washington. While he was at it, he visited the southern front to inspect his troops and galvanize them for the resumption of combat, asking them for a final push. In a burst of lyricism, he qualified the offensive as "the mother of all battles."[3] He called in four additional Pasdaran divisions. The Iranians now had 150,000 combatants standing by to cross the Jassem Canal and the artificial channel and press on to Basra. General Jamal had only 40,000 men to fend them off, but they were supported by 600 tanks and 400 cannons.

On January 29, 1987, the frenzied Iranians crossed the Jassem Canal and rushed the enemy positions. Their commander, Mohsen Rezaee, ran from one end of his layout to the other to encourage his troops. For seventy-two hours the human waves succeeded each other without interruption to submerge the enemy defenses. The losses were tremendous, but the Iranians did not seem to be deterred. Iraqi soldiers watched the bodies pile up in front of their machine guns. Iranian combatants could even weave their way to the foot of the Iraqi trenches by taking cover behind walls of mangled bodies, then throw their grenades. Next the Iranians made their way over these macabre obstacles and emptied their magazines at their adversaries, gradually pushing them back.

On February 1 the Pasdaran broke through the Jassem Canal, forcing the Iraqis to withdraw to their next-to-last line of defense. The Iranians were now only seven miles (twelve kilometers) from Basra and could see its outlying areas and some of its buildings. In Tehran, Rafsanjani reveled in his success and pressed his generals to commit all their reserves to the battle. Yet now that the troops were not as tightly locked in battle, combat ground to a halt because the Iraqi artillery could carry out devastating barrage fire without worrying about striking its own soldiers. Iraqi firepower was so intense that the shell-battered landscape was lastingly altered. Twenty-five years later, aerial views of the sector still revealed an area riddled with craters. To further disrupt the Iranian attack, the Iraqis massively resorted to battle gas and called in their heavy Ilyushin 76 four-engine jets, which flew high above the battlefield and dropped pallets of napalm canisters, horribly burning Iranian soldiers. On the Iranian side, with logistics flagging and a limited stockpile of shells, the Pasdaran could only count on their numbers to bear them to victory.

At the Gates of Basra

On February 11, 1987, on the occasion of the eighth anniversary of the Islamic Revolution, the Ayatollah Khomeini broke his silence and made a public speech in which he compared the war to "a holy crusade that must continue until the final victory and the departure of the tyrant of Baghdad." He invited young Iranians to join the army and go to the front without delay, for the Iraqis were repelling one assault after another. Mohsen Rezaee was granted additional reinforcements to make up for losses. On the other side, General Jamal was given two new infantry divisions from the 6th and 7th Corps to relieve his exhausted infantrymen.

On February 19 the Pasdaran's commander, eager to take action, committed all his forces to another assault. Once again, the clash was infernal. Iraqi firepower initially succeeded in holding back the enemy, but the Pasdaran and Basijis were so driven that they managed to breach the Iraqi layout at several points. To avoid being surrounded, Iraqi troops were forced to withdraw to the last line of defense protecting Basra, five miles (eight kilometers) from the city. In Baghdad, General Aziz hesitated regarding the approach to follow. Overwhelmed by how events were developing, he proved incapable of adapting to the new realities of the war he was discovering. On the field General Jamal traveled to the front lines, adjusting his layout with the assistance of Adnan Khairallah. He lifted the soldiers' spirits and accelerated the evacuation of civilians.[4] Jamal's ammunition depots were well stocked and he considered his defensive layout flawless.

On February 23 Mohsen Rezaee launched his troops at the last Iraqi line of defense. The frenetic Iraqis beat back the human waves one after another. Their tanks were all put to work tearing apart the infantrymen assaulting their positions in tight ranks. On February 26 the Iranians, exhausted and running out of ammunition, decreed the end of Karbala 5. Tehran let its troops catch their breath for a few weeks, long enough to reorganize and reinforce. This operational break led to the end of urban bombings, which had killed 3,000 in Iran and 1,000 in Iraq over the course of six weeks. Saddam Hussein took advantage of the lull to replace General Aziz with General Nizar al-Khazraji, who had previously been the commander of the 1st Corps. This brilliant, charismatic, humble, and highly professional officer could also be utterly ruthless when required. Adnan Khairallah, who had pushed for his appointment, appreciated his uprightness and talent. Khairallah was convinced that al-Khazraji's presence at the head of the armed forces would allow Iraq to reverse the trend and regain the initiative.

On March 3 Iran mounted the Karbala 7 offensive in Iraqi Kurdistan to maintain pressure on Iraq. Concurrently, the Turkish army launched a large-scale operation against the PKK on Turkish territory. The Turkish government immediately notified the Iranian regime that it would not allow it to seize Kirkuk or Mosul. Rafsanjani played for time, fully aware that the force ratio was unfavorable to him both on the military and the economic planes. He knew that Turkey was turning a blind eye to the weapon shipments Libya and Syria were still sending to Iran via its territory. Determined to ease tensions, he traveled to Ankara and invited President Evren to visit Tehran as soon as possible. Meanwhile, the Iranian 28th and 46th divisions had advanced about ten miles (fifteen kilometers) across a snowy landscape in the direction of Rawanduz with the support of KDP peshmergas. On March 9 with the city within their sight, they were ordered to stop their advance. The Iranian regime did not want to vainly provoke the Turkish government. The two nations had taken great care to avoid clashing since the late seventeenth century, including during the two world wars. It would have been foolish to challenge this policy in pursuit of highly debatable advantages.

During the month of March Iranian troops maintained the siege of Basra and prepared a last-ditch offensive. Their inadequate logistics chain was struggling to keep combatants supplied with food, drinking water, and ammunition. For their part, the Iraqis pounded enemy lines with their artillery and reinforced their own defenses. Saddam Hussein lucidly imagined the worst and reassured his generals: "As the supreme leader of the Iraqi state, I can tell you very clearly that even if Basra were to fall it would not be the end of the world. . . . We would continue to fight, and even if they reached the doors of the Palace of the Republic in Baghdad, we would still fight them until we pushed them back across the border. They are exhausted. We are strong. We will win."[5]

During the night of April 6 to 7 Iranian command finally attacked (Operation Karbala 8): 40,000 Pasdaran attempted to breach the last line of defense protecting access to Basra. Despite their courage and determination, they failed. The Iraqis had mastered defensive combat and had terrifying firepower at their disposal. Their Katyusha rocket launchers and ultramodern cannons relentlessly hammered the assailants. Each time their infantrymen had to give a little ground, their tank crews counterattacked and regained the territory lost. This bloodbath lasted four days. On April 9 and 12 the Iranian regime went against its principles and tried to win the battle by using chemical weapons for the first time. At nightfall Iranian artillery poured phosgene gas in the Iraqi 3rd Army Corps' sector. These bombings caused only minimal Iraqi losses (twenty dead and 200 wounded) and did not suffice to break the defensive layout around Basra. They did, however, alert the Iraqi intelligence services, who informed Saddam Hussein that Iran was developing a tabun production

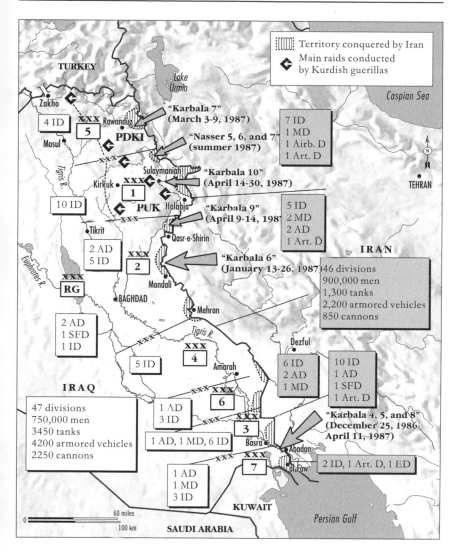

Iran-Iraq front in 1987

plant in Marvdasht, near Shiraz, with the help of North Korean techni-cians.[6] Iraq retaliated by spraying the assailants with mustard gas.

Meanwhile, Tehran had launched another diversionary attack (Karbala 9) in the sector of Qasr-e-Shirin. For four days the Iranian 25th and 84th Divisions battled the Iraqi 21st Division and took control of four strategic hills dominating the road to Baghdad. Yet the Iraqis did not fall into the trap and merely reorganized their defenses with what was on hand, without deploying additional reinforcements.

In mid-April the worn-out and demoralized Iranians ended the assault and put a stop to the Battle of Basra, which had lasted a little over three months and cost them terrible losses: at least 40,000 fatalities and twice as many wounded.[7] The Pasdaran had been hit particularly hard. A quarter of their most hardened officers were killed in the battle, including General Hossein Kharrazi, cut down by the explosion of an Iraqi shell. Rattled, they retreated to their positions and kept up the siege of Basra. The Iranian government tried to tone down this frightening toll by publicizing the 1,750 prisoners (including two generals and ten colonels) and twenty-seven square miles (seventy square kilometers) they had captured and by emphasizing the extent of Iraqi losses: 10,000 dead, not to mention the 150 tanks destroyed and the ten aircraft brought down by their anti-aircraft defense (principally attack helicopters). Despite the losses incurred, Saddam Hussein was delighted: Basra, which had been on the verge of falling, was saved. He congratulated his generals for this "superb victory" and named it "the Great Harvest" for the impressive number of Iranians killed.

Hungry for revenge, the Iranians launched the Karbala 10 offensive in Kurdistan on April 14. They wanted to show the Iraqis that their army could still shake them up. But their heart was no longer in it. For two weeks three of their divisions, supported by a few thousand PUK peshmergas, gained a few square miles (a few square kilometers) in the sectors of Sulaymaniah and Halabja, without succeeding in taking either of these cities. The facts were unavoidable: the exhausted Iranian army no longer had the necessary resources to maintain these costly all-out offensives. The Iraqi army was probably not ready to go back on the offensive, but it was strong enough to durably resist Iranian military pressure. The stalemate on the terrestrial front was total. This was a setback for Akbar Hashemi Rafsanjani, who had publicly committed to defeating Iraq by the end of March 1987. Bitter and frustrated, the Iranian speaker of Parliament was forced to come up with a new strategy.

[Chapter 27]

Iran Changes Strategy

In April 1987 the Supreme Defense Council convened in Tehran under Rafsanjani's chairmanship to define a new strategy. Its task was urgent; for the first time since the beginning of the war, Pasdaran were demonstrating in the capital's streets, demanding an end to hostilities. Iran's intelligence agencies even reported that in the quietest sectors of the front, fraternization had taken place across battle lines. The Pasdaran were supported by Ayatollah Montazeri, who readily appeared at their side. To ease tensions, the government promoted a dozen Pasdaran to general and announced increased pensions for the families of martyrs fallen on the battlefield. Following fraught debates, the government and the military agreed to return to a war of attrition and to escalate air and naval strikes against maritime traffic. Iranian strategists believed this would force the oil monarchies to reduce their financial support to Baghdad. They also hoped to push the great powers to pressure Saddam Hussein to suspend his attacks on oil traffic, which would allow Iran to bolster its economy and military. On the front, this new strategy entailed maintaining the siege of Basra and creating a Kurdish sanctuary to exhaust the Iraqi army and force it to divide its forces between opposite ends of the front line. Iran's leaders clearly perceived that the war would now play out in the long term and that its human and financial cost needed to be attenuated to make it more acceptable to the population.

In Baghdad, Saddam Hussein and his advisors had also drawn the necessary conclusions from the battle of Basra. The time had come for them to regain the upper hand and impose their pace on the Iranians. They agreed to increase their attacks on oil traffic in order to suffocate the Iranian economy, preventing Tehran from rebuilding its weapons and ammunition stocks. They also maintained hope of pushing the mullahs to make a mistake by inciting them to block the Strait of Hormuz, which would immediately lead the great powers to intervene. They agreed to establish a powerful and mobile battle corps able to spearhead a future counterattack aimed at recapturing lost territory (Iran controlled a dozen pockets of land along the border in Iraq, totaling a little over 775 square miles [over 2,000 square kilometers]).

Military, Diplomatic, and Commercial Maneuvers

In late April Iran conspicuously deployed two batteries of Silkworm anti-ship missiles on Qeshm Island in the Strait of Hormuz, near the Bandar Abbas naval base.[1] The Revolutionary Guards announced the creation of a "special" maritime intervention zone controlling the strait and under Pasdaran command. Meanwhile, the navy increased patrols to prevent any incursion into the maritime exclusion zone, which it was charged with enforcing. Every day a frigate deployed at the strait's entrance questioned commercial ships about their destination and cargo. Those that were suspicious were inspected or even fired at by a second frigate positioned in ambush. The Iranian authorities aimed to show the international community that it was in a position to block the Strait of Hormuz if necessary.

The Iraqi regime intensified its attacks on oil traffic. Iraqi Mirage F-1EQ5s had a field day, firing forty-two Exocets in two months, thirty of which made direct hits. No ships were sunk, but thirty were so seriously damaged that they had to be scrapped. Iranian oil exports dropped by 20 percent during this period, forcing Iran to acquire fifteen new oil tankers. The Mirages were backed by Su-22M fighters armed with new Kh-29 Kedge antiship missiles recently delivered by the Soviet Union. These planes used two specially converted transport Il-76s to refuel in flight. The Iraqis took advantage of their extended striking range to harass Iranian oil platforms off the coasts of Qatar and the United Arab Emirates.

For their part, the Iranians damaged twenty tankers. In most instances the tankers were attacked by gunboats following a proven procedure. The boats would appear from behind in the dark, dash along the ship's flanks at full speed, then machine-gun it for ten minutes and fire a few rockets right above the waterline. After having repositioned themselves to the back of the boat, they concentrated their fire on the engine room and the crew's quarters, hoping to set them ablaze. They disengaged once they ran out of ammunition. The Iranians now practically never used their air force to attack oil tankers. The priority for their few remaining operational Phantoms was air-superiority missions. Anyhow, Iran's stock of Maverick missiles had run out, and Iranian engineers had failed to turn their navy destroyers' standard surface-to-air missiles into antiship missiles. Missions against oil traffic were taken over by a few naval aviation helicopters armed with the last A-12 missiles, but these attacks were rare.

While the navy and Pasdaran kept up their harassment strategy in the Strait of Hormuz, Minister of Foreign Affairs Ali Akbar Velayati traveled to Moscow to reassure Eduard Shevardnadze of the Soviet Union's new importance in Tehran's eyes. While the encounter was cordial, it did not yield any concrete results. The Soviet minister of foreign affairs criticized his Iranian counterpart for increasing attacks on oil traffic in the Gulf, which could only favor the United States' influence in the region. He also condemned Iran's support of the Afghan mujahidin. Despite its statements of good intentions, the Islamic Republic rankled Moscow by continuing to back the Afghan guerilla fighters. Meanwhile, the Soviets made unabashed overtures to the Gulf monarchies. The Soviet vice-minister of foreign affairs made a tour of the region and denounced Iran's rigidity. In Kuwait, he offered to provide Emir Jaber with military equipment at a good price.[2] He also agreed to make three Soviet tankers available to transport part of the oil produced in Kuwait. The Kremlin was convinced that the mullahs would never dare to attack Soviet vessels because they feared economic and military reprisals.

Realizing that the Kremlin was not yet ready to ally itself with Iran, Akbar Hashemi Rafsanjani turned again to the United States, offering to resume diplomatic relations if the American administration agreed to modify its policy on Tehran. Yet Secretary of Defense Caspar Weinberger, who remained angry about the hostage crisis, dampened Rafsanjani's hopes, believing that it was illusory to attempt to establish a relationship with allegedly moderate factions in Iran. Weinberger announced the reinforcement of the American naval presence in the area and warned Iran's leaders that the United States would retaliate against any Iranian provocation. The British government declared that it was sending three additional warships to the Gulf to protect its commercial vessels. These three ships reinforced the Armilla flotilla, which had been patrolling the Gulf since the summer of 1982. With one missile destroyer, two frigates, one replenishment oiler, and one auxiliary ship in the area now, London hoped its deployment could simultaneously promote Britain's arms sales policy. The British gambit paid off: Saudi Arabia, which was unsure of Washington's reliability and did not want to put all its eggs in the American basket, ordered forty-eight Tornado fighter planes from the United Kingdom.

Meanwhile, Tariq Aziz made his own trip to the Kremlin to evaluate the extent of the rapprochement between Moscow and Tehran. He took advantage of the opportunity to ask his hosts to deliver the ultramodern equipment Iraqi generals were impatiently awaiting. The Soviet authorities were of two minds. On the one hand, they wanted to cut the war short and did not wish to send Tehran overly negative signals. On the other, they were in desperate need of cash and told themselves that giving the Iraqi army the means to improve its situation on the field would make the Iranian government realize that it was in its best interest to accept the ceasefire for which they had long been calling. Following intense negotiations, the Kremlin authorized the sale to Iraq of fifteen MiG-29 interceptors, thirty Su-25 assault aircraft, about forty Sam-13 surface-to-air systems, as well as several hundred Spigot antitank missiles. Moscow made the equally crucial decision to provide Baghdad with a continuous flow of ammunition and spare parts. Tariq Aziz and his Soviet counterparts also extended the friendship and cooperation treaty the two countries had signed in 1972.

For its part, China committed to delivering Iraq four H-6D long-range bombers, which were actually copies of the Tupolev-16 armed with C-601 antiship missiles, the airborne version of the notorious Silkworm missile. Thanks to these aircraft, the Iraqi air force would be able to strike close to the Strait of Hormuz while remaining at a safe distance. During the same period Beijing provided Iran with sixty F-7 fighters (the local copy of the MiG-21) and ten surface-to-air missile batteries derived from the Sam-2 and Sam-3, all of which were channeled through North Korea. The Chinese authorities were still putting business first, while ensuring the Iraqi and Iranian leaders of their best intentions. Determined to make strategic headway in the Gulf, the Chinese also made an agreement with King Fahd: in return for guaranteed access to Saudi oil, they committed to selling Riyadh CSS-2 Dongfeng-3 conventionally tipped ballistic missiles, which would allow the Saudi kingdom to increase its dissuasive power on Iran.[3] These missiles lacked accuracy, but they could reach Tehran with their 1,500-mile (2,500-kilometer) strike range, and their two-ton explosive charge was sufficient to cause considerable damage to urban targets. King Fahd was convinced that adding this type of missile to his arsenal would prevent the belligerents from firing their own missiles at Saudi territory.

On May 8, 1987, the freighter *Ivan Korotoyev* was attacked by Pasdaran gunboats shortly after it crossed the Strait of Hormuz, though it was clearly flying the Soviet flag. This deliberate attack annoyed the Kremlin, which upped the ante by announcing it would send a dozen warships to the Gulf.[4] The following week, the Soviet tanker *Marshall Chuikov,* one of the three the Kremlin had "rented" to Kuwait, was damaged by a drifting mine near the maritime exclusion zone decreed by Iran. In Moscow annoyance gave way to anger, and the Soviet authorities informed the Iranian regime that another attack against Soviet ships would be interpreted as an act of aggression and lead to severe retaliation against Iran. No further Soviet ships were attacked. However, the number of oil tankers targeted—particularly Kuwaiti vessels—increased. The Kuwaiti authorities had reasons for particular concern. Early in the year Iran had brazenly fired two Silkworm missiles at Kuwait from the al-Faw peninsula to demonstrate that it remained capable of striking it if necessary. Several terrorist attacks had echoed these threats and wreaked havoc in the emirate.

Worried by this turn of events, Emir Jaber asked the five permanent members of the United Nations Security Council to take over the Kuwaiti flotilla of oil tankers. France, the United Kingdom, and China refused, but the Soviet Union accepted. Caught off-guard, the United States reacted immediately. Robert Murphy, the assistant secretary of state for Near Eastern and South Asian affairs, committed to registering eleven of the twenty-two Kuwaiti oil tankers as American-flagged vessels, sparking a controversy in Congress, which was against the initiative. Though preliminary contacts had been made in the previous weeks, Washington had put off responding definitively because it believed U.S. legislation prevented its vessels from escorting foreign ships. Now the American administration reassured Emir Jaber, answering that the flag transfer would indeed take place, but would require a few weeks.

The Attack on the USS Stark

At nightfall on May 17, 1987, an American AWACS plane patrolling the Saudi coastline to prevent Iranian incursions detected an Iraqi jet plane approaching above Bubiyan Island. It immediately alerted American ships in the southern part of the Gulf to be on their guard. Since the beginning of the year, the Iraqi air force had already attacked twelve vessels sailing on the edge of the maritime exclusion zone decreed by Iran. Three days earlier a Mirage F-1 from the al-Wahda base had approached within firing range of the *Coontz* destroyer, probably mistaking it for an Iranian oil tanker. After having made its identity known, the American destroyer had shined its fire control radar on the F-1, and the plane had flown away. The next day another American destroyer, the *David Ray*, had been subjected to a false attack in the same zone, this time by an Iranian fighter plane.

At 8:50 p.m. the AWACS crew asked the Iraqi jet to identify itself and turn back, for it was headed straight for the Perry-class frigate USS *Stark* (4,200 tons), which was cruising northeast of Bahrain. Receiving no response, the American air traffic controller repeated his warning and directed a patrol of Saudi F-15s toward the Iraqi plane. The controller was surprised because Iraqi Mirage F-1s generally complied with AWACS orders. This approaching jet was flying more slowly and much higher than Mirages did. Yet the *Stark*'s commanding officer Captain Glenn Brindel was initially not concerned. Since his electronic early warning systems were not detecting any signal suggesting that his ship was being targeted by enemy fire control radar, he did not put his crew on alert or set off any specific countermeasures. At 9:09 p.m. the *Stark*'s radio operator sent the Iraqi jet a message informing it that it had just penetrated the protective bubble extending twenty nautical miles around the ship and asking it to identify itself, failing which the *Stark* would activate its interception systems. At the same moment the Iraqi pilot fired his two Exocet missiles at the target he had just locked on, then turned back to base. The American vessel's shipboard system detected the missiles' acquisition radar one minute later. The ship's chief petty officer immediately called for action stations and set off countermeasures, but it was too late. At 9:12 p.m. the frigate *Stark* was directly hit on its port side by two Exocet missiles in rapid succession. Both missiles tore through the ship's hull just above the waterline. One of the two detonated, devastating the middecks, while the other started a fire, which the crew would take more than twenty-four hours to contain. To save his vessel from sinking, Captain Brindel had no choice but to flood part of the starboard holds to make the ship list and prevent it from taking on too much water. Fortunately, the *Stark*'s motors were still functional, and the ship was able to struggle back to Middle East Task Force headquarters at the Bahrain naval base. The attack killed thirty-seven crew members and seriously injured twenty-one.

This was the first time during the Iran-Iraq War that an American warship was hit by antiship missiles. Washington immediately demanded that Baghdad explain itself. Furious, Congress blamed the White House and set up an investigatory commission. Some congressmen opposed to the policy of rapprochement with Iraq even insinuated that the attack may have been Saddam Hussein's response to the Iran-Contra scandal, pointing to similarities with the USS *Liberty* incident twenty years earlier.[5] The *Stark*'s captain was court-martialed, found guilty of severe negligence, and relieved of his command.

The Iraqi regime promptly claimed the attack had been an error and humbly apologized. Saddam Hussein personally wrote to Ronald Reagan to ensure him that the incident was a tragic mistake and that the Iraqi pilot genuinely thought he was firing at an enemy ship crossing the war zone at its own risk. Baghdad committed to generously compensating the victims. The White House accepted the apology and decided to move on. Nonetheless, it set out to understand what had truly happened. It sent a team of inspectors to Baghdad to untangle the events. The Iraqis proved extremely cooperative, with two exceptions. They refused to show the American investigators the plane involved in the attack and did not allow them to interrogate the pilot who flew the mission. The American experts were convinced the plane was a Mirage F-1EQ5 (they were unaware that this type of Mirage cannot carry two Exocets) and that its pilot had been punished and put out of sight or possibly eliminated.

The Iraqis did not provide any information that might contradict these conclusions. They reached an agreement with the American military authorities to implement a stringent identification procedure to avoid any further mistakes of this kind.[6] The U.S. navy hardened its rules of engagement, now authorizing fire at any presumed hostile aircraft entering the security zone. Some American sailors verged on paranoia, fearing a Pasdaran suicide attack, particularly in the Strait of Hormuz. As a precautionary measure, the Iraqis momentarily suspended their raids in the Gulf.

For the next twenty years the official story told by journalists and historians was that the frigate *Stark* was attacked by a Mirage F-1. The truth did not come out until after the fall of Saddam Hussein, thanks to interviews with several exiled Iraqi generals and the discovery of audiotapes of meetings attended by the Iraqi dictator. Once again, the tapes bear witness to the Iraqi air force commander's wild imagination. In the summer of 1986 General Shaban received an unhoped-for gift: a Falcon 50 brought by the Iranian deserters who had piloted Rafsanjani on his official trips. Shaban suggested turning this three-engine corporate jet into a deep-strike aircraft. His technical services made contact with the Dassault Company, which produced the Falcon 50 and was more than ready to help Iraq, its top foreign client. Iraq asked the French airplane manufacturer to equip the Falcon 50 with the attack radar used for the Mirage F-1EQ5, external fuel tanks, electronic countermeasures, and—most importantly—two hardpoints beneath the wings allowing it to carry and fire two Exocet missiles.

These modifications were to be carried out in Iraq, as quickly as possible, by a team of French technicians. The aircraft was ready by the early spring of 1987. Its original livery was preserved to trick Iranian pilots who might otherwise intercept it. Two highly experienced transport pilots had been trained on its weapons system and immediately began flying attack missions against the Larak terminal. The Falcon 50's range allowed it to fly directly to its target without refueling in-flight. It used the airway normally reserved for commercial flights to operate more discreetly. Once close to its target, it descended to a low altitude and fired its two missiles at stand-off range, thereby escaping Iranian air-superiority fighters.[7] When they were not attacking the Larak terminal, the Falcon's two crews flew harassment missions against maritime traffic in the Mirage F-1's sweep mission area. The USS *Stark* incident took place during one of these missions.

These are the known facts: on May 17, 1987, the Falcon 50 took off at 8 p.m. from its base in Kut—not from al-Wahda, the base where the Mirage F-1EQ5s were stationed. Its pilot, headed for the Falcon's usual sweep mission area off the coast of Bahrain, ignored the AWACS messages. At 9 p.m. he saw an echo on his radar. He fired his first missile at twenty nautical miles from his target and the second when he was only fifteen nautical miles away. He immediately turned back and returned to his base without waiting to see the results of his strike.[8] His superiors did not punish him, for they knew that the procedure for this type of mission entailed the possibility of error. According to General al-Abousi, this highly experienced transport pilot carried out many other missions aboard the Falcon 50. This pilot, with close ties to the former regime, has kept his identity secret out of fear of reprisals from the Shiite administration currently in power in Baghdad.

While all the evidence now indicates that the attack on the frigate *Stark* was a mistake, it remains unclear whether the incident was voluntary or accidental. While Saddam Hussein certainly had several reasons to be angry at the America administration, none of the recorded conversations he had with his generals give any indication of a plot.[9] On the contrary, Iraq's leaders were surprised to learn of the attack on the American frigate. Some panicked, fearing military retaliation from the United States. Tariq Aziz insisted that Saddam Hussein immediately contact President Reagan to apologize and dispel any doubt regarding this regrettable "accident" (the word he used). Every Iraqi general questioned since the dictator's fall has confirmed that the attack was an accident, though it would have cost nothing to accuse Saddam Hussein after his death. If Saddam did order a deliberate attack on an American ship, he proved a first-rate actor and never told his generals, though he was having long conversations with them about various details of military operations at the time.

According to General Sadik and General al-Abousi, the Falcon 50's pilot was convinced he was dealing with an oil tanker headed to Iran to stock up. He may have rushed to fire his missiles to avoid returning to base empty-handed and to prove his valor to the Mirage F-1 pilots, who formed a privileged caste within the air force. He did not have an IFF (Identification Friend or Foe) system to determine whether his target was friend or foe. While the ship targeted was actually on the outside edge of the Iranian war zone, the Falcon's flight instruments were not working properly that day and showed it inside the zone, making it a legitimate target. According to these two generals, the Iraqi leadership hid the pilot's identity from the commission to avoid revealing the Falcon 50's existence, which the regime considered a secret asset. Ultimately, everything points to the theory that the frigate *Stark*'s crew had the misfortune of being in the wrong place at the wrong time under the command of a reckless captain.[10]

Mines in the Gulf

In late May 1987 four oil tankers sailing in the narrow channel leading to the Kuwaiti al-Ahmadi terminal, most of them Kuwaiti, were damaged by mines in rapid succession. Laden with oil, the ships were forced to follow the channel to avoid running into the shallows. A team of American divers was called in as reinforcements. Their exploration of the area yielded a veritable minefield. These were not mere drifting mines, but moored mines immersed at the right depth to be detonated exclusively by fully loaded tankers. They had been laid a few days earlier by Iranian Sea Stallion helicopters operating from the al-Faw peninsula, 50 miles (80 kilometers) away. The operation had probably not lasted more than two hours. Its objective was simply to maintain pressure on Kuwait, which was considered the weak link in the GCC, in order to convince Emir Jaber to take a tougher stance toward the Iraqi regime. The Iranians, who had a stock of several thousand mines (including 600 Italian depth mines detonated by electromagnetic influence), intended to show the GCC oil monarchies that they would not hesitate to pollute the entire Gulf if the GCC continued to support Baghdad.

Calling the West for help again, Emir Jaber asked Washington to accelerate the registration of his oil tankers as American-flagged vessels. Paris and London reacted at once and promised to send several minesweepers to the Gulf. The request annoyed the American admirals, who considered mine warfare a subordinate task, which they had passed on to their NATO allies since the end of the Vietnam War. While they agreed to send their six remaining minesweepers to the Gulf, their transfer to the area would take several weeks. In the meantime, they dispatched Galaxy military cargo planes to carry eight Sea Stallion helicopters equipped with ultrasensitive sonar equipment to their Diego Garcia base. The helicopters were then loaded onto the amphibious assault ship *Raleigh,* which was docking at the base and was scheduled to depart soon for the Gulf.

Beginning June 20 Iraq resumed air attacks on oil traffic in the Gulf for two weeks. Yet early in July Baghdad declared a unilateral moratorium on attacks in the Gulf to encourage Iran to accept the peace plan proposed by the Security Council's five permanent members on June 23. The plan basically followed the terms put forward by Saddam Hussein five months earlier (immediate end to hostilities, withdrawal of armed forces to internationally recognized borders, exchange of all prisoners of war), but called for mediation by the United Nations Secretary General and added two new clauses favorable to Iran: the creation of an impartial organization charged with investigating the circumstances surrounding the outbreak of hostilities and the recognition of Iran's right to receive reparations for damage inflicted. This time, the Soviet Union and China unreservedly supported the agreement and attempted to convince Tehran to accept it.

On July 20, 1987, the Security Council unanimously adopted Resolution 598, which included the new peace plan's proposals in full and ordered a complete team of impartial observers to be sent to the region to supervise the ceasefire as soon as the resolution was accepted by both belligerents. Breaking with its response to previous peace proposals, the Iranian regime did not formally reject the plan, understanding that it had to keep a door open for an honorable exit if its new strategy did not deliver the expected effects. Foreign naval presence in the Gulf was constantly being reinforced, limiting the Iranian navy's room to maneuver. Rafsanjani realized that his hardline policies were now threatening to lead to a Western military intervention against Iran.

Aware of the escalating tension, the Soviet Union sent its UN ambassador Yuli Vorontsov to both belligerents to convince them to accept the ceasefire and prevent an onslaught of Western ships in the Gulf. Though they were sincere reformists, Mikhail Gorbachev and Eduard Shevardnadze remained prisoners of Cold War logic, which continued to dictate the great powers' actions in the Middle East. The Iraqis were not receptive to the Soviet initiative, for they were convinced that the Soviets were merely waiting for the right time to carry out a change of alliance that seemed more perceptible by the day. Refused an audience with Saddam Hussein, Yuli Vorontsov had to make do with an informal meeting with Tariq Aziz. Vexed, the diplomat went on to Tehran where, contrary to his expectations, he received a warm welcome. News traveled fast—the Iranians had understood that the relationship between Moscow and Baghdad was on the rocks and fully intended to take advantage of that. They informed Vorontsov of their extreme reservations regarding the Security Council's resolution—they did not want to appear to be surrendering to joint pressure from Western and Arab chancelleries—but they assured him that the Iranian authorities wanted to develop closer ties with the Kremlin.

The Al-Anfal Campaign

While tension escalated in the Gulf, terrestrial operations continued in Iraqi Kurdistan. The situation had taken a new turn since the spring, after the Iranian government had succeeded in brokering an agreement between Jalal Talabani (PUK) and Masoud Barzani, now the sole leader of the KDP following his brother Idris's death of a heart attack in January 1987. For the first time since the beginning of the war, the Kurdish opposition to the Ba'athist regime was united under Iranian leadership. It consisted of 30,000 peshmergas with some fifty tanks, one hundred light artillery pieces, and 1,000 machine guns. The PUK carried out several raids on the cities of Erbil, Sulaymaniah, Kirkuk, and Mosul (Operations Fath 4, 5, 6, and 7), while the KDP participated in the Iranian Karbala 7 offensive, then harassed the Iraqi garrisons on Kurdistan's northern border near Rawanduz, Haj Omran, and Zakho. The PUK and KDP also made an agreement with Mahmoud Othman's Kurdistan Democratic Socialist Party (KDSP), which was supported by Damascus and whose insurgents were very active on the Turkish-Syrian border. Yet these alliances remained fragile.

For the first time since the beginning of hostilities, the Iraqi government was faced with a united front, which prevented it from using its usual tactic of pitting one faction against another. More worrisome was the fact that the Iraqi Kurds had negotiated an alliance with the Shiite Dawa Party, which remained highly active throughout the rest of the country. Its members became the eyes and ears of the Iraqi opposition and organized bloody attacks on the regime. On April 9 a commando succeeded in attacking the presidential convoy near Mosul, in the heart of the Kurdish region. Saddam Hussein escaped the attack, but his chauffeur and ten of his guards were killed. This was the straw that broke the camel's back. To this point, the Iraqi dictator had believed it was possible to win over the Kurdish population by playing to Iraqi nationalism. He now abandoned this approach and adopted a vicious repression and scorched earth policy. He named it Anfal (literally "the spoils") in reference to the eighth Sura of the Koran, which authorizes fighters for God to dispossess the adversaries of their land.

Hoping this approach would allow him to permanently eradicate the Kurdish problem, Hussein appointed the chief of the intelligence service, his cousin Ali Hassan al-Majid, proconsul of the provinces of Iraqi Kurdistan, with full powers to punish the population and crush the rebellion. To assist al-Majid in his task, Saddam gave him full authority over the 1st and 5th Army Corps deployed in the area. The Iraqi divisions immediately established a cordon sanitaire extending between Halabja, Sulaymaniah, Kirkuk, Erbil, Mosul, and Rawanduz, which served as a buffer zone to contain peshmerga and Pasdaran offensives. Kurds were no longer permitted to live beyond the cordon sanitaire, next to the border.

In directive SF/4800, dated June 20, 1987, Ali Hassan al-Majid went even further, ordering that, "Every male aged 15 to 70 will be executed after having been interrogated by the security services to try to learn useful information." To apply this terror strategy, the military high command mobilized vast reinforcements taken from other areas of the front; fourteen infantry divisions were charged with patrolling the region and tracking down the pershmergas. They were backed by two Republican

Guard divisions and several commando brigades. A third of the Iraqi army (250,000 men) was now concentrated in Kurdistan.

In the course of a few weeks the Iraqi government destroyed hundreds of villages, deporting their inhabitants to squalid swampland in the south of the country, between the Tigris and Euphrates. Every Kurd not affiliated with the Iraqis and found in possession of weapons was considered a rebel and executed. Before being evacuated, some villages were bombed by artillery or air. Roundups and punitive expeditions were carried out in the region's large cities. A forced Arabization policy forbade the teaching of Kurdish in schools and heavily sanctioned any citizen caught speaking the language. For each Iraqi soldier shot or killed in a terrorist attack, several dozen hostages were executed. Jalal Talabani's partisans were specifically targeted and decimated by the repression, which left several thousands dead by the spring of 1987. While this scorched earth policy undeniably increased the governmental forces' room to maneuver in Kurdistan, it reinforced the Kurdish people's yearning for independence and its determination to take arms and fight the Ba'athist regime, as powerfully depicted in Fariborz Kamkari's superb film *The Flowers of Kirkuk* (2010).

Meanwhile, the Turkish army continued intervening in the north of Iraq to hunt down the PKK. In early June Turkish president Kenan Evren traveled to Tehran to meet with Iranian leaders and attempt to appease the tensions that had been undermining bilateral relations between the two countries for close to two years. They agreed to a five-point agreement stipulating that the two parties would: 1) not interfere in their respective internal affairs, 2) refuse to take any official position potentially detrimental to the other party, 3) commit to not broadcast radio or television programs hostile to the other party, 4) reinforce cross-border cooperation in the field of security, and 5) commit to actively fight Kurdish groups operating on the other party's territory.

The Iranians took advantage of the Iraqi army's commitment to Operation Anfal to improve its positions on the northern front. During the summer it seized Mawat and launched several Operation Nasser raids in the direction of the Dukan Dam. After the summer the terrestrial front remained calm for the rest of 1987, with the exception of the occasional artillery duel and a few coups de main to keep the enemy on its guard.

The Gordji Affair Forces France to
Intervene in the Gulf

On January 13, 1987, French journalist Roger Auque was kidnapped in the capital of Lebanon. This kidnapping led to a decisive reorientation of French policy on Iran. Both Jacques Chirac's government and French public opinion could no longer rationalize holding talks with hostage takers. The idea took root that this situation would have no end, for each step toward normalization was followed by another terrorist attack or hostage taking. Frustration was at a peak. Here too, opinions varied between those who criticized the Iranian authorities' cynicism and those who saw it as proof of a fierce struggle between the regime's different factions. Nonetheless, Charles Pasqua was able to impose a hardline policy on Iran. To guard himself against any further terrorist campaigns, the minister of the interior implemented exceptional measures to protect the French. Management of the Iranian situation was shifted from the diplomatic corps to the police.

On February 17, 1987, a repented Tunisian Islamic fundamentalist contacted the DST and stated he was ready to turn in the terrorist network responsible for the terror attacks on the French capital in 1986. The informer had originally been recruited by Iranians while studying at Qom University. He claimed to be disappointed by the Ayatollah Khomeini's blindness and to want to put an end to the attacks vainly bloodying France. He identified the entire terrorist network headed by Fuad Ali Saleh, a Tunisian whom he had met in Qom. Saleh claimed to be close to Ayatollah Montazeri. He had been recruited by Islamic fundamentalist networks controlled by Tehran. In return for this precious information, the informer was given French nationality and a new life in North America.[11] The informer's revelations brought to light the central role played by the Iranian embassy in organizing these attacks. They identified a certain Wahid Gordji, officially an interpreter with the embassy, as the likely coordinator of the terrorist attacks carried out in 1986. According to the informer, Gordji had actually been the Iranian secret service's agent in Paris since the early eighties.[12]

One can legitimately wonder what really pushed this Tunisian Islamic fundamentalist close to Iranian power to reveal his former comrades' identities to the French authorities. Isn't it conceivable that this was a case of provocation or score settling between Iranian factions? Every hypothesis remains feasible. The case was referred to antiterrorism magistrate Gilles Boulouque. For three months the DST investigated and closed in on the suspects. On June 3, 1987, the police arrested fifty-seven individuals, half of whom were expelled under emergency procedures. At the last minute Wahid Gordji took refuge in the embassy and escaped the roundup. He was allegedly warned that the arrests were imminent by a French diplomat then responsible for the Iranian dossier at the Quai d'Orsay.[13] The Ministry of Foreign Affairs and the Ministry of the Interior were on the worst of terms, in complete disagreement about how to manage the Iranian situation. Given this deleterious context and the animosity between Jean-Bernard Raimond and Charles Pasqua, it is not unlikely that leaks were planned to avoid humiliating the Iranian representation in France and further damaging bilateral relations. The French judicial authorities did not share this point of view, however, and decided to place the Iranian embassy under conspicuous surveillance to prevent the escape of Wahid Gordji. Charles Pasqua was triumphant.

In late June Jacques Chirac sent Tehran an ultimatum stipulating that if Wahid Gordji had not presented himself before examining magistrate Gilles Boulouque by July 16, all the Iranian diplomats in France would be expelled. Chirac had radically moved on from the conciliatory statements he was making a few months earlier. However, the prime minister added that he was ready to exchange Wahid Gordji for all the French hostages held in Lebanon. In early July Iran responded by threatening to kidnap the twelve French diplomats still in Tehran. The French police immediately retaliated by besieging the Iranian embassy. On July 13 Pasdaran gunboats in the Gulf fired their cannons and rockets at the French container ship *Ville d'Anvers*. The message was crystal clear: Tehran would not give an inch and was ready to attack French interests. The next day, while the Bastille Day garden party was in full swing outside the Elysée, the Pasdaran surrounded the French embassy in Tehran. The memory of the American embassy hostage crisis was suddenly on every French mind. A four-month "war of the embassies" was to follow. French public opinion became heated and strongly critical of the mullahs' regime. Former president Valéry Giscard d'Estaing even came out of his usual reserve to state that "France must not normalize its relations with Iran, which is in the grip of religious passion and fanaticism."[14]

Operation Prométhée

On July 17, 1987, France officially broke off diplomatic relations with Iran. The president of the republic launched Operation Prométhée by deploying a French naval task force to cruise off the Iranian coast. The group had a dual mission: on the one hand, to put pressure on Iran to force it to free the French diplomats and end the war of the embassies; on the other, to protect French merchant traffic in the Gulf. On July 30 the aircraft carrier *Clémenceau*, armed with its forty aircraft, the frigates *Suffren* and *Duquesne*, and the tanker *Meuse*, set sail from Toulon for the Indian Ocean. They followed in the wake of the frigate *Georges Leygues*, which had urgently cast off a week earlier, and were themselves followed by the minesweepers *Garigliano*, *Cantho*, and *Vinh-Long* and the support ship *Garonne* a few days later. The ships all reached the area during the first two weeks of August, joining the tanker *Marne* and the corvettes *Protet*, *Bory*, *Doudart de Lagree*, and *Schoelcher*. These fourteen ships now formed Task Force 623, commanded from the *Marne* by Admiral Jacques Lanxade, who was seconded by Admiral Hervé Le Pichon aboard the *Clémenceau*. Task Force 623 was divided into three Task Groups: TG 623–1 comprised the frigate *Georges Leygues* and the four corvettes, and patrolled the Gulf to escort French-flagged commercial ships; TG 623–2 comprised the aircraft carrier *Clémenceau*, the frigates *Suffren* and *Duquesne*, and the tankers *Meuse* and *Marne*, and was deployed in the Gulf of Oman to maintain a deterrent presence against Iran; and TG 623–3 comprised the three minesweepers and the support ship *Garonne*, whose mission was to neutralize the mines Iran laid near the Strait of Hormuz. The task force was supported by an Atlantic maritime patrol plane based in Djibouti. The crews had flexible rules of engagement, which authorized them to open fire at the mere suspicion of hostile intent, though they had first to positively identify their potential target. Meanwhile, Operation Prométhée's command planned an air campaign targeting Iranian bases and oil installations, notably Kharg terminal. French Naval Aviation pilots stood ready to attack. The Iranians were made aware of the fact.

The French military presence apparently proved dissuasive enough to prevent any further terrorist incidents in France and any attacks on French ships traveling in the Gulf.[15] The only serious incidents consisted of French Crusaders intercepting Iranian maritime patrol planes that came too close to the naval task force. The Iranian P-3 Orions always retreated soon enough for the French aircraft not to have resorted to using their weapons.

In the meantime, the French government tried to negotiate with Iranian emissaries to find an honorable end to the crisis. Charles Pasqua brought up the French hostages held in Lebanon and once again offered to use Wahid Gordji as a bargaining chip. The Iranians were in favor of the idea, but requested a second installment of the Eurodif debt. They also demanded the release of Anis Naccache and his henchmen. Jacques Chirac agreed to the prisoner exchange and, in principle, to another financial transaction. He further committed to granting a presidential pardon to Anis Naccache if he were elected president of the republic the following spring. According to the journalists Pierre Favier and Michel Martin-Roland, Jean-Charles Marchiani, the prime minister's *missus dominicus* to the Iranian authorities, allegedly confirmed that Anis Naccache's release was verbally agreed to between Tehran and Jacques Chirac's government.[16]

On November 27, 1987, the journalists Roger Auque and Jean-Louis Normandin were freed in Beirut. The next day the French police broke its siege of the Iranian embassy in Paris. Wahid Gordji immediately surrendered to the French authorities. He was interrogated for a few hours by Magistrate Boulouque, who did not press any charges. He was then put on a plane and expelled to Iran. While these events occurred the Pasdaran ended their siege of the French embassy in Tehran. The war of the embassies was over. A few days later Paris paid Tehran 330 million dollars as a second installment in the Eurodif dispute.[17] Negotiations continued. It appears that Jacques Chirac, then running for president, promised Iran that he would reestablish it as a shareholder in Eurodif, giving it access to enriched uranium through the Tricastin plant, if all the French hostages still held in Lebanon were released by the second round of the French presidential election.[18] This was a highly alluring offer to the Iranian government, which had relaunched its nuclear program and was desperately trying to acquire enriched uranium.

While the last three French hostages (Marcel Fontaine, Marcel Carton, and Jean-Paul Kauffmann) were released on May 4, 1988, between the two rounds of the presidential election pitting Jacques Chirac against François Mitterrand, this was not enough to secure Chirac's victory. His defeat by the incumbent put an end to the first cohabitation between the Socialists and the RPR. The Gordji affair had surfaced again during the televised debate between the prime minister and the president following the first round of the election. After Jacques Chirac stated that Wahid Gordji's release had been the magistrate's decision alone, François Mitterrand contested this version, claiming that Magistrate Boulouque had received instructions from the government. When his prime minister asked him, "Can you really look me in the eye and contest my version of the facts?" François Mitterrand responded, "Looking you in the eye, I contest it." Two years later Magistrate Boulouque committed suicide, humiliated by this affair and disgusted by its political exploitation.

[Chapter 28]

The Gulf Set Ablaze

At the height of the war of the embassies between Paris and Tehran, Washington mounted Operation Earnest Will to escort American-flagged ships crossing the Gulf. Launched on July 21, 1987, Earnest Will was the largest naval escort operation since the end of the Second World War. The eleven Kuwaiti ships affected by this measure (eight oil tankers and three liquefied natural gas [LNG] tankers), now renamed and flying the stars and stripes, were each put under the supervision of an American commander supported by a few U.S. navy reservists. From a political perspective, the idea was to show the oil monarchies that they could count on the United States to ensure their security. In contrast to its actions in Lebanon three years earlier, the White House would not back down and would remain in the region no matter what happened. The U.S. navy had chosen to rely on the well-tried method of convoys. A cruiser, a destroyer, and two frigates would escort convoys of oil tankers and LNG tankers from Kuwait to the mouth of the Strait of Hormuz in the Gulf of Oman. The first convoy left the Kuwaiti al-Ahmadi terminal on the evening of July 21. The 800-mile (1,300-kilometer) route ran the length of the maritime exclusion line decreed by Iran and passed near small islands and oil platforms turned into fortresses by the Pasdaran.

Admiral Harold Bernsen, the commander of the Middle East Task Force, believed that American warships' dissuasive presence would suffice to avoid a confrontation with Iran. Aware that they could not attack these convoys head-on, the Iranians fell back on a strategy of indirect action. On July 24 the supertanker *Al-Rekkah,* which had just been renamed the *Bridgetown,* hit a mine, which caused serious damage and forced the ship to turn back. The rest of the convoy continued on its way, with lookouts carefully observing the surface of the water to spot other mines. The incident took place off the coast of Saudi Arabia, eighteen miles (thirty kilometers) from Farsi Island, which was controlled by Iran. In fact, the convoy had entered a real minefield, which had not existed a few days earlier. Though the Iranians fiercely denied any involvement in the incident, no one was fooled. This was a direct affront to the United States, which was being tested by Tehran from its very first convoy.

The United States Takes Direct Action

Convinced that Iran would need to be taught a lesson sooner or later, the Pentagon accelerated the shipping of antimine equipment to the Gulf and deployed important naval reinforcements to the region. It dispatched one of its amphibious groups, headed by the helicopter carrier *Guadalcanal*, to the area off the shores of the United Arab Emirates. The aircraft carrier *Constellation*, which was scheduled to return to the United States, was ordered to remain in the Gulf of Oman with the aircraft carrier *Ranger*. The aerial task force aboard these two sea giants totaled 170 aircraft, more than Iran was able to launch from all its bases combined. The battleship *Missouri* stood ready to cross the Strait of Hormuz to bring its devastating firepower to the Gulf. With thirty-two Tomahawk cruise missiles and nine 406 mm cannons with a range of over eighteen miles (thirty kilometers), this modernized battleship (aboard which Japan's official surrender had been signed in September 1945) could pulverize any coastal installation. Lastly, Admiral Bernsen was granted the deployment of five missile-carrying hydrofoils, which he considered ideally suited to countering the Iranian Combattante II-class fast attack craft.

The U.S. navy now had fifty warships in the region, with an additional twenty-three French and British ships present. Iran had only four frigates, one corvette, a few support ships, and ten missile boats to oppose them. Its three venerable destroyers no longer had any military value; their weapons systems were out of commission. Iran's other warships had been sunk or damaged during the hostilities. Rear Admiral Malekzadegan, commander of the Iranian Navy, did have five amphibious assault ships to supply garrisons scattered around the Gulf, but also to discreetly lay mines. The only air support he could rely on was limited to a dozen Phantom fighters, six Tomcat interceptors, and three Orion maritime patrol aircraft. Hassan Ali, the commander of the Pasdaran's naval branch, had sixty armed motor boats, which were like gnats in the face of the Western warships. He also commanded a handful of helicopters and twenty Pilatus PC-7 training aircraft delivered by Switzerland, which he threatened to turn into suicide planes crammed with explosives. The specter of kamikazes abruptly reappeared in the minds of the American admirals, who loosened their ships' rules of engagement, authorizing them to fire at any presumed hostile aircraft that entered their security perimeter of twenty nautical miles. As a precautionary measure, Admiral Dennis Brooks, who was supervising the entire operation from the cruiser *Long Beach* in the Sea of Oman, planned a campaign of air strikes aimed at destroying Iran's air and navy bases, as well as its batteries of Silkworm missiles.

Yet before reaching such extremes, the United States was determined to react by beating Iran at its own game. In late July, with the agreement of the CIA and the White House, the Pentagon launched Operation Prime Chance. Since Kuwait and Saudi Arabia still refused to have American bases on their soil, the United States secretly set up two mobile floating bases in the Gulf, from which its special forces could monitor Pasdaran naval activity and respond to their attacks on maritime traffic. Two large "civil" barges were placed in the Gulf's international waters. Both were legally chartered by Kuwait and officially intended for oil platform maintenance. The first, named *Hercules,* was deployed in the northern part of the Gulf, between Farsi Island, which belonged to Iran, and the Saudi coast. The second, which was registered under the name *Wimbrown 7,* was anchored much farther south, close to the Emirati coast, about eighteen miles (thirty kilometers) from the Sirri and Abu Musa islands.

While they looked perfectly harmless from the outside, these two barges were actually veritable floating fortresses worthy of a James Bond movie. Each barge had a camouflaged hangar containing one Black Hawk transport helicopter and two AH-6 Cayuse attack helicopters. On deck, the barges kept two stocked patrol boats, which could carry two navy SEAL strike forces.[1] Each barge also had radar and a highly sophisticated electronic warfare system. They were defended by Stinger portable surface-to-air missiles and radar-guided Phalanx cannons with a very high rate of fire, which could destroy aircraft, gunboats, and sea skimmers. In a worst-case scenario, the barges had enough ballast and armor to resist bomb and missile impacts. They were accompanied by a tug that put up a smokescreen by constantly moving them. During the day, they attended to maintenance work, keeping up a harmless appearance. But they came to life at nightfall. Navy SEALs boarded the patrol boats and were lowered into the water, while two Cayuse helicopters took off on surveillance missions. Their deployment aboard the barges was worthy of a spy film.

Donald Isbell, one of the Cayuses' pilots, recalled:

We were with the US Army's 160th Special Operations Aviation Regiment. We were all qualified commandos known as the Night Stalkers. We were the first army pilots to be permanently equipped with night-vision goggles, since we only flew at night. We left our base at Fort Campbell, Kentucky, on a huge C-5 Galaxy plane that was also transporting our helicopters and supplies. Before we left, I had to take a sleeping pill dosed for the duration of the flight. I fell asleep shortly after takeoff and woke up fifteen hours later, shortly before we landed by night at Thumrait Air Base in the Sultanate of Oman. I wasn't exactly as fresh as a daisy, but I was in good enough shape to help the mechanics take our helicopters off the plane and quickly get them ready to fly. Two hours after landing, we took off in our helicopters to land on a frigate about to cross the Strait of Hormuz. In the days leading up to our transfer, we had refined our flight plans. Two days later, we took off at night to land on our barge and begin our mission. We only brought out the helicopters and took off—always at night—when we were certain there were no Soviet satellites overhead. We were guided by the air traffic control team aboard the barge. Our helicopter had been modified so it could move as quietly as possible, skimming the sea. We could hover barely 500 meters (1,600 feet) from an Iranian oil platform with all our lights off and go undetected. We had an observation mast above the rotor, which allowed us to examine our target with enlarged infrared images. Sometimes we received orders to attack and sink an Iranian gunboat that had just attacked one of our oil tankers. That was easy to do because we had a powerful 30 mm gun and two rocket pods. We were practically invincible. The principal two risks were accidents, which were always a possibility due to the extreme flight conditions, and the Pasdaran's Stinger missiles.[2]

Most of the time, the armed helicopters did not intervene directly, but handed the mission over to the navy SEAL teams, who operated equally stealthily.[3] The operation's primary goal was not to neutralize the Pasdaran, but to monitor their activities to anticipate their coups de main and catch them red-handed while laying mines. In pursuit of these objectives, the helicopters based on the *Hercules* and *Wimbrown 7* barges occasionally deployed aboard a frigate to remain unpredictable and extend their operating range.

On August 4 Tehran pointedly launched air and sea maneuvers in the Strait of Hormuz to hamper the convoys and taunt their escorts. The Iranians used these maneuvers to unveil a midget submarine recently delivered by North Korea, as well as radio-controlled motorboats full of explosives, which could potentially be propelled at Western warships at top speed. Admiral Brooks responded by sending several of his destroyers to patrol the area of the strait on the edge of the Iranian exclusion zone. Undeterred, the Iranian government dispatched a Phantom toward the aircraft carrier *Constellation*. The Phantom was immediately intercepted by a Tomcat patrol, which fired two missiles in its direction, forcing it to flee. On August 10 a supertanker owned by Texaco was damaged by a mine in the Sea of Oman, outside the Gulf. The same day several dozen drifting mines were spotted in the Strait of Hormuz, slowing maritime traffic.

Tensions with Tehran escalated a notch, exacerbated by an incident one week earlier, when some Shiite worshippers—probably controlled by the Iranian secret service—had provoked bloody riots during the pilgrimage to Mecca, leaving more than 400 dead and 700 wounded. The Saudi king reacted immediately. He demanded the United States provide him with more assistance so he could better control the Fahd Line, whose defensive umbrella he extended to the neighboring monarchies. Under pressure, the Pentagon broadly increased the number of satellite reconnaissance missions to keep the Iranian layout under close surveillance and attempt to detect new minefields. Its famous U-2 and SR-71 spy planes left from Incirlik in Turkey and Kadena in Japan to fly over the Gulf night

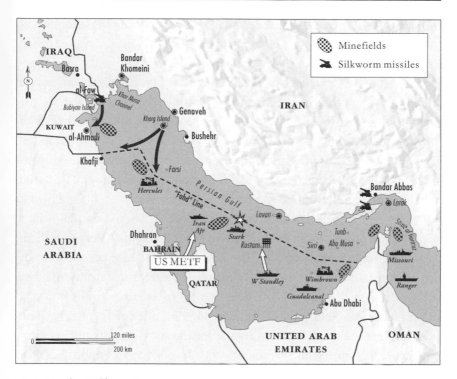

Unrest in the Gulf in 1987

and day, remaining at high altitude and out of range of Iranian anti-air defense. Meanwhile, the U.S. navy minesweepers, now ready to start their mission, began mine disposal operations in the Strait of Hormuz with the help of French and British vessels—and five dolphins trained to detect underwater mines and brought from the United States at great cost.

Iran Defies the U.S. Navy

On August 30, 1987, the Iraqi air force resumed its attacks in the Gulf after a seven-week interruption. Soviet mediation had failed, and the Iraqi regime had come to the conclusion that it needed to hit the Iranian economy harder to force Tehran to fold. Its Mirage F-1s and Su-22s went back to striking oil tankers coming to stock up in Iran. Over the course of a few days they damaged ten ships and the Kharg, Lavan, Sirri, and Larak installations. Tomcats guarding the oil terminals brought down one Mirage and one Su-22. The tanker war reached a peak in September, with forty-one Iraqi and seventeen Iranian attacks. Lloyds was forced to raise the insurance premiums for ships crossing the Gulf by 50 percent.

Iran retaliated by increasing the frequency of its attacks to one or two a day and firing another salvo of Silkworm missiles from the al-Faw peninsula onto Kuwaiti territory. One of the missiles landed in the bay of Kuwait City, a stone's throw from the city, within view of its astounded inhabitants. The Iranians also laid more mines in the Gulf. Two ships struck drifting mines near Farsi Island. One of these, which was registered in Panama, sank like a stone. On September 7 the Belgian and Dutch governments announced that they were sending a binational flotilla of four minesweepers to the Strait of Hormuz and that the British had given them a guarantee of logistical support. The next day Italy announced that it was also sending a naval force to the Gulf (three frigates, three minesweepers, and one replenishment oiler) in reaction to a Pasdaran gunboat attack on an Italian container ship five days earlier. Despite the fact that several of its tankers had been attacked by the Pasdaran, Germany put the protection of its commercial agreements with Iran first and announced that it was limited by constitutional provisions preventing it from carrying out external military operations. Its only concession was to reinforce its naval presence in the Mediterranean as part of a NATO mission to replace the American 6th Fleet vessels now redeployed in the Gulf.

In the meantime, UN Secretary General Javier Pérez de Cuéllar undertook a mediation trip to Tehran and Baghdad. Feeling that the tide was turning, Ali Khamenei and Akbar Hashemi Rafsanjani stated they would be ready to accept Resolution 598 once an international commission had officially established Iraq's responsibility for starting the war. Paris and Washington opposed their proposal. Both governments wanted to punish Iran, albeit for different reasons. To justify its decision, the White House soon released details of an encounter between the U.S. navy and the Iranian amphibious assault ship *Iran Ajr* to prove Iran's duplicity.

On September 21, 1987, the *Iran Ajr* discreetly left its base in Bandar Abbas, weaving between the Iranian coast and Qeshm Island in the direction of the Sirri terminal. It was immediately detected by the U.S. navy, most likely thanks to a nuclear attack submarine on an observation mission close to the Iranian base. It was then followed by satellite. Once night fell the *Iran Ajr* shifted course toward international waters. The *Wimbrown 7* barge's Cayuse helicopters and patrol boats picked up the chase. In the middle of the night, after having refueled on board the frigate *Jarrett*, the American pilots caught the *Iran Ajr* laying mines in the heart of the international navigation channel, fifty miles (eighty kilometers) northeast of Bahrain. With their motors running at slow speed, they used their infrared cameras to film the *Iran Ajr* for several minutes. Once their superiors considered the evidence sufficiently damning, they ordered the helicopters to attack. The two Cayuses immediately fired salvos of rockets at the engine room to prevent the ship from moving, then sprayed its deck with bullets to keep the crew from coming out. Two navy SEAL teams transported by helicopter from the *Guadalcanal* assaulted the ship and took control of it in less than half an hour. Five Iranian sailors were killed during the attack. The remaining twenty-six were taken prisoner. The American frogmen searched the ship, discovered another dozen mines ready to be laid, and seized valuable documents regarding the Iranian navy. The prisoners and the dead were transferred to the Middle East Task Force's headquarters in Bahrain, while the ship was scuttled in open water. Images of the sheepish Iranian crew and the *Iran Ajr* laying its mines were seen all over the world, exposing Tehran's responsibility for the mines in the Gulf. This was a blow to the mullahs. Even China was forced to denounce Iran's attitude in order to guarantee its oil supply from Saudi Arabia. To make matters worse, the Pasdaran had attacked a British oil tanker, the *Gentle Breeze*, the same day. Prime Minister Margaret Thatcher immediately closed the Iranians' London "office," which had been responsible for discreetly negotiating the purchase of weapons and ammunition in Europe.

Meanwhile, the Iraqi air force escalated its attacks on Iranian oil terminals. During a raid against Larak at the mouth of the Gulf, it damaged the *Seawise Giant*, the biggest supertanker in the world, which Iran used as a floating reservoir. On September 29 a Mirage F-1EQ5 was shot down over Lavan by one of the American-made Stinger missiles the Iranians had received from the Afghan mujahidin. The pilot ejected and was rescued thirty-six hours later by an American helicopter, which brought him to the *Guadalcanal*. He was sent back to Iraq, where he immediately returned to combat at the helm of one of the new Mirage F-1EQ6s recently delivered by France. The F-1EQ6 was another improved version of the Mirage, with higher-performance electronics and a greater operating range, which allowed it to better engage with Iranian Phantoms and Tomcats patrolling over the Gulf.

In late September Moscow took another decisive step in its rapprochement with Tehran. During the opening session of the General Assembly of the United Nations in New York, Eduard Shevardnadze advocated appeasement and criticized Washington and Paris's hawkish policies. The Iranian leaders breathed a sigh of relief; Saddam Hussein was enraged. The indefatigable Tariq Aziz returned to Moscow, both to attempt to get his Soviet counterpart to yield and to tell him the Iraqi president's position. He was met with a wall of coldness. The Kremlin had not forgotten the way Saddam Hussein had treated Yuli Vorontsov two months earlier. Saddam's right-hand man even tried to use his Christianity to soften Shevardnadze, reminding him of the Kremlin's historical role as a protector of Christians in the East. His efforts were in vain. In the meantime, the Soviet diplomats failed to convince the Iranian regime to be more flexible, despite threatening to decree an embargo. The Iranians were not easily fooled. They knew perfectly well that the war allowed numerous respectable companies to make significant profits by trading with them. They sensed that economic sanctions were still relatively far off, which left them some room to make headway in the Gulf.

On October 2, 1987, French warships discovered another minefield off the coast of the small emirate of Fujairah, laid by dhows, traditional boats used for trafficking between Iranian and Emirati shores. The next day Iran gathered fifty Pasdaran gunboats near Kharg Island, at the other end of the Gulf, and sent them toward the small Saudi port of Khafji, which is located close to the Kuwaiti border. The objective was not to invade Saudi Arabia, but to test King Fahd's resolve by carrying out a raid on his coastlines. The flotilla was immediately detected by the AWACS on duty, which simultaneously alerted Saudi military high command and American Middle East Task Force headquarters in Bahrain. Admiral Bernsen instantly rerouted one of his ships to intercept the flotilla, while the Saudi admiralty dispatched one frigate and four missile boats to the area. Since the ships would potentially arrive too late, Minister of Defense Prince Sultan ordered twenty F-15 fighters and the first Tornados delivered by the United Kingdom to fly over the Iranian gunboats. For his part, the king immediately contacted Tehran and warned the Iranians that his planes and ships would fire without warning on any motorboat that crossed the Fahd Line. The speed of the Saudi response and the scope of forces engaged convinced the Iranian authorities to cancel the operation and call back their naval forces.

Seeing that they could not directly attack Saudi territory, the Iranians changed their plans. On the night of October 8 they sent three gunboats, escorted by their last PF-103 class corvette, to attack the American barge *Hercules*. The moment the barge's crew detected the attacking flotilla, its commander ordered action stations. The barge's three helicopters took off and the two patrol boats were launched. The American pilots sped toward the assailants to attempt to intimidate them. One of the Pasdaran boats opened fire on one of the helicopters, prompting an immediate counterattack from the other two aircraft. The boat was sunk and the other two were severely damaged. The Iranian corvette, which had stayed back, was spared. The Iranians disengaged and returned to Farsi Island.

On October 13 the Iranian frigate *Alborz* taunted the U.S. navy again, firing its cannon at the Liberian oil tanker *Atlantic Peace,* which was cruising barely one nautical mile from the destroyer *Kidd.* Because American ships were only mandated to protect American-flagged merchant ships, the *Kidd* was not authorized to retaliate. Two days later a Silkworm missile fired from al-Faw hit the Liberian supertanker *Sangari* while it was loading at the al-Ahmadi terminal. The next day the Iranians attacked again and fired another Silkworm at the same terminal. This time the missile directly hit the supertanker *Sea Isle City,* which had recently been reregistered under the American flag. Its commander and several officers, all of whom were American, were severely injured. Once informed, President Ronald Reagan ordered reprisals.

The American Navy Retaliates

On October 19, 1987, the U.S. navy launched Operation Nimble Archer. In the early afternoon it sent a radio ultimatum to the Pasdaran entrenched on two oil platforms in the heart of the Rostam oil field, forty-three miles (seventy kilometers) south of the Lavan terminal (to which the platforms were connected by an underwater pipeline), giving them twenty minutes to evacuate. General Colin Powell, who was then the U.S. deputy national security advisor, later stated that the navy did not directly strike the battery of Silkworm missiles at the tip of the al-Faw peninsula in order to avoid creating the impression that the U.S. was directly allying itself with Iraq. No longer in service since they had been heavily damaged by the Iraqi air force, the two oil platforms were now exclusively used as landmarks for Iranian gunboats and helicopters harassing maritime traffic. At exactly 2 p.m. with the ultimatum having gone unheeded, the destroyers *Kidd, Hoel, Leftwich,* and *John Young,* which were cruising a few nautical miles away, opened fire on the two targets. The destroyers were protected by the cruiser *William Standley* and a pair of Tomcats responsible for repelling any air incursion. For an hour and a half the American destroyers fired a little more than 1,000 large-caliber shells, ravaging the two installations. An Iranian Phantom sent to the rescue turned back as soon as its pilot realized the scope of the American layout. Following the shelling a navy SEAL team landed on one of the oil platforms and destroyed it with explosives. The operation ended in mid-afternoon so that it could make the headlines in Washington the next morning. The Iranian government later instituted proceedings with the International Court of Justice (ICJ) in the Hague, requesting that it sanction the American navy's destruction of the Rostam oil platform and the amphibious boat *Iran Ajr,* which it qualified as acts of piracy.[4]

On October 22 the Iranians, furious following their humiliation, fired a last Silkworm missile at the Kuwaiti al-Ahmadi oil terminal. The explosion caused significant damage along the main pier. The Iranian artillery simultaneously shelled the Kuwaiti island of Bubiyan, while the Pasdaran made repeated incursions onto the island. Emir Jaber realized he had to put his foot down to dissuade Iran from pursuing its strategy of intimidation. He accepted the assistance of the United States, which transported several of its battalions to Bubiyan Island to prevent the Iranians from capturing it. Emir Jaber also authorized the American navy to redeploy its floating naval base *Wimbrown 7* in Kuwait's territorial waters, since its position in the southern part of the Gulf had been rendered unnecessary by the destruction of the Rostam platform. Lastly, he accepted that "civilian" advisors install a battery of Hawk missiles on his soil and that two more barges manned by American crews be deployed along his shoreline to protect the al-Ahmadi terminal. These barges were equipped with radar amplifiers and could decoy any further Silkworm missiles fired at oil complexes. The innovative tactic the Iranians had devised to protect the Kharg terminal was now turned against them.

Meanwhile, Iraq was pulling no punches in its attacks on Iran. In late October its planes hit the oil refineries in Tehran, Tabriz, and Bandar Khomeini particularly hard. Though Iranian air-superiority fighters were able to bring down four of the MiG-23s and two of the Su-22s assigned to the strikes, the blow to the Iranian economy was severe, depriving it of the capacity necessary to refine the fuel required by its armed forces. Prime Minister Mousavi found himself forced to import more gas, further reducing Iran's financial reserves. The Iranian government took revenge by firing five Scuds at Baghdad. The Iraqi regime did not fall into the trap and continued its attack on Iranian economic potential undeterred.

From October 28 to November 1 Yuli Vorontsov made a final mediation trip to try and move the situation forward. This time Saddam Hussein did receive him, airing his grievances with the masters of the Kremlin and vehemently rejecting any fallacious interpretation of Resolution 598. To make the pill less bitter, the Soviet diplomat assured him that the Soviets would continue providing military assistance to the Iraqi army. In Tehran, Vorontsov was cordially received by the Iranian authorities, who expressed that they were ready to discuss the methods of applying the resolution, but did not give an inch on the crux of the matter. In their eyes, Saddam had to pay the price for his aggression and be designated as the aggressor bearing sole responsibility for the horrible war that had devastated the Persian Gulf for more than seven years. The weary Soviet ambassador recognized his mediation's failure, though his efforts did allow the USSR to impose itself as an interlocutor acceptable to both parties. This was a success for Mikhail Gorbachev and Eduard Shevardnadze in and of itself, for it benefitted their respective statuses and confirmed their idea that they would do well to pursue their policy of opening up the USSR to the Middle East and the Third World. Yet ten days later the Iranian government chose to show that it remained in control of its territory by brazenly shooting down a Soviet MiG-25 on a reconnaissance mission over Iran.

Over the last two months of 1987 the belligerents continued their attacks in the Gulf, playing hide-and-seek with the thirty Western and Soviet warships sailing between al-Ahmadi and the Strait of Hormuz, though the pace of Iranian attacks fell off. The Americans' firm stance seemed to have paid off. Pasdaran gunboats, which were now responsible for most of the attacks, were careful only to assault unescorted ships. On December 7 Tehran fired a ninth and last Silkworm at al-Ahmadi; the missile was decoyed by one of the barges positioned in front of the oil terminal. The minesweepers deployed in the Gulf continued their mine-clearing mission, counteracting more than eighty mines. With a touch of fatalism, those involved began to ask themselves how much longer this absurd war would last.

[Chapter 29]

The Halabja Massacre

Early in 1988, with the war entering its eighth year, lack of material and financial means pushed the Iranians to forgo their usual winter offensive. State coffers were now nearly empty, and with legislative elections coming up, Akbar Hashemi Rafsanjani did not want to provoke another bloodbath potentially damaging to his image in Parliament. The front remained relatively calm, with the exception of a few harassment operations by the Pasdaran, principally in Iraqi Kurdistan.[1] Nonetheless, the government was forced to extend the duration of military service to counter the drop in troops due to the previous year's colossal losses, the growing number of desertions, and the toll of real and imagined diseases in the trenches. Always ready to make waves, Ayatollah Montazeri proposed merging the regular army with the Revolutionary Guards, incurring both armies' wrath. Each organization was attached to its distinctiveness and privileges, a fact the government used to its advantage by putting them in competition, thus ensuring that neither would attempt a coup. The Supreme Defense Council headed by Hassan Rouhani opposed Montazeri's proposal and continued to prepare the next large-scale operation, which was to take place in Iraqi Kurdistan as soon as the snow melted.

The Iraqi Army Ups the Ante

The Iraqi army took advantage of this respite to reinforce itself and refine its training through the efforts of General Aladdin Hussein Makki Khamas, who introduced a new combined arms combat doctrine. Two new Republican Guard divisions ("Nebuchadnezzar" and "al-Faw") were added to the order of battle to provide a greater reserve of shock troops. Throughout the winter Iraqi troops tirelessly carried out exercises in an

433

area of marshland between the Tigris and Euphrates where their sappers had created terrain similar to that on the al-Faw peninsula. Iraqi units succeeded each other in the marshes to develop the best tactics to isolate, then breach, the enemy layout. Iraq's weaponry was modern, abundant, and well suited to mechanized combat. In the best units aging equipment was replaced with new tanks, armored vehicles, and cannons. The Republican Guard now became a full-fledged battle corps, consisting of six elite divisions able to rapidly maneuver and deliver a devastating shock effect on any sector of the front.[2] It had the best equipment, a large number of trucks, and its own fire support (artillery and helicopter). It could rely on flawless logistics. This qualitative leap also affected the command structure, where the professionalization of the officer corps had borne fruit.

Naturally, the military high command still included some apparatchiks and old fossils, but overall the colonels and generals in command were competent and eager. General al-Khazraji, the chief of staff of the armed forces, headed a far more effective force than his predecessor had. The 1988 Iraqi army had little in common with the 1980 army. For the first time since the beginning of the war, Iraq had nearly as many troops on the front as Iran, with a little more than 800,000 men. They were divided in eight army corps comprising fifty divisions (seven armored, three mechanized, and forty infantry). Iraq was also completing construction work on new roads, which improved troop supplies, and, most importantly, on a six-lane highway between Baghdad and Basra, which zigzagged along the Euphrates and would allow Iraqi forces to shift from the northern to the southern front in less than forty-eight hours by using an armada of 3,000 tank transporter trailers. Saddam Hussein and his generals were convinced that the time had come to go back on the offensive and liberate the territory conquered by Iran. To do so, they would need to be able to rapidly concentrate their forces without leaving their enemy time to regain its footing. Meanwhile, Iraq continued its strikes on Iran's oil infrastructure and the supertankers that came to load at the Lavan, Sirri, and Larak terminals.

Tehran Starts the War of the Capitals

During the first two months of the year the Iraqi air force attacked twenty ships and bombed Kharg Island, which still served as a hub for the "shuttle" of oil tankers supplying the Larak floating terminal. Iraqi aircraft occasionally fell into ambushes laid by Iranian air-superiority fighters. On February 9 Iranian Captain Hossein Khalili shot down three Mirage F-1s with his Tomcat; four others would fall to his comrades' fire over the next two weeks, while the Iranian air force did not record any losses. On February 15 Captain Ismaeli pulled off an impressive feat near the Strait of Hormuz by using one of the last operational Phoenix missiles to destroy one of the four Tu-16 heavy bombers delivered to Iraq by the Chinese. When they were far from their base Iraqi pilots could only try to escape by flying low to the sea, relying exclusively on their countermeasures.

On February 27, 1988, the Iraqi air force devastated Tehran's oil refinery. The Iranian authorities retaliated by bombing Baghdad, both to show the Iraqi government that they could strike at its heart and in hopes of luring it into another war of the cities, which would relieve pressure on the oil industry. They also wanted to let the Iraqis know that they had a new stock of missiles, courtesy of North Korea. On February 28 three Scud-Bs struck the Iraqi capital, with a fourth hitting Tikrit, Saddam Hussein's native city, in an open act of provocation. The Iraqi dictator took up the challenge and ordered a new type of missile to be fired at Tehran the following day. With this intimidatory salvo of five missiles Hussein showed the Iranians and the rest of the world that he had acquired missiles able to strike directly at Tehran—or Israel and other countries in the region, if that should prove necessary. For two and a half years the Iraqi engineers of Program 144 had worked with Soviet scientists to modify the Scud-Bs delivered by Moscow from 1985 to 1988, doubling their range (400 miles/650 kilometers) by halving the weight of their warheads (1,100 pounds/500 kilos).[3]

The missiles were named Al Hussein in honor of the Shiite imam. They allowed Saddam Hussein to concentrate his air force on attacking the Iranian oil infrastructure, further increasing pressure on his adversary. Saddam found the timing particularly appropriate given that the Iranians were preparing to elect a new Parliament; he hoped this new terror campaign would bolster the parties in favor of ending hostilities. Saddam decided to commit his last Tupolev 22s and the few MiG-25s modified for high-altitude bombing missions to what would be the final episode of the war of the cities. These aircraft carried out about forty night raids on Tehran, Qom, Shiraz, and Esfahan; two Tu-22s and three MiG-25s were shot down by Iranian air-superiority fighters. The Iranians mobilized a handful of Phantoms, whose crews braved the Iraqi capital's anti-aircraft defense to bomb Baghdad and its suburbs.

For fifty-two days running Iraq fired three or four Al Hussein missiles a day at Tehran, striking both by day and by night. Tehran's inhabitants were shocked by the brutality and regularity of the Iraqi strikes, as shown in Marjane Satrapi's remarkable animated film *Persepolis* (2007). Fearing chemical attacks, countless city dwellers sought shelter in the country, further disrupting the country's economic activity and public services. In a few weeks a third of Tehran's population fled the city. As a precautionary measure, the Ayatollah Khomeini was evacuated to a medical clinic in the provinces.

The Iranians retaliated by firing one or two Scuds a day at Baghdad. The bombings finally came to an end when munitions ran short. On April 20, 1988, the belligerents called off the strikes following an agreement brokered by the UN secretary general; Iran had only five Scuds left and Iraq ten Al Husseins. In all, the Iraqis are believed to have fired 193 missiles (189 Al Husseins and four Scud-Bs) at the principal Iranian cities, three-quarters of them at Tehran. The Iranians are said to have launched seventy-seven Scud-Bs at Iraqi cities and an additional hundred or so Oghab rockets at villages near the border;[4] 1,500 Iranian civilians were killed, versus 300 Iraqis.

In New York, the Security Council's permanent members exerted themselves to convince the belligerents to accept Resolution 598. On March 5 the United States, France, and the United Kingdom proposed a total embargo on arms sales to Iran and Iraq. The Soviet Union and China vetoed the proposal. Four days later the Soviet authorities came before the Security Council to submit a resolution calling for an immediate end to combat. This proposal, which emphasized Baghdad's responsibility for the war's outbreak, did not meet with the approval of the Council's other members. Washington, Paris, and Beijing did not want to ostracize the Iraqi regime.

The Gassing of the Kurds

On March 13, 1988, Iranian Generals Sohrabi and Shirazi launched a wide-scale offensive in Iraqi Kurdistan. The offensive's two sections were called "Victory 7" and "Holy City 3." The former aimed to seize the Dukan Dam, about twenty miles (thirty kilometers) north of Sulaymaniah. The latter targeted the town of Halabja, which prevented access to the Darbandikhan Dam a little to its south. The Iranians hoped to increase pressure on the Ba'athist regime by taking control of the country's two largest hydroelectric dams and depriving Iraq of a significant portion of its electricity. Once again, the Iranian regime was using an asymmetric strategy. Since Tehran could not significantly reduce Iraq's oil exports, it attacked its electric resources, which its oil industry required to function at full capacity. To achieve their objectives, the Iranian generals mobilized nineteen divisions (fourteen infantry, two mechanized, and three artillery) on the northern front—half of their armed forces. They gathered their best shock troops, notably the 23rd Commando Division and the 55th Parachute Division, in the north and left the rest of the front to be held by a thin array of infantrymen supported by five armored divisions and their remaining 1,200 tanks. Opposing them, the Iraqis had the 1st and 5th Corps' fifteen infantry divisions, respectively commanded by General Kamel Sajid and General Tala al-Duri.

On March 14 the 55th Parachute and 84th Mechanized divisions overcame formidable barrage fire to wipe out the Iraqi 43rd Division, breach the front line, and capture Halabja. Iranian troops pushed on toward the Darbandikhan Dam, but were stopped by massive intervention of Iraqi aircraft and reserve troops. Meanwhile, a little further north, two Pasdaran divisions deployed near Mawat overpowered Iraqi defenses and seized the Dukan Dam. The 66th Commando Brigade, which was assigned to defend the dam, retreated before the Iranian steamroller without having received permission. Its commander, Colonel Jafar Sadeq, was immediately called to Baghdad for debriefing. Though he knew Sadeq and appreciated his courage, Saddam Hussein proved intractable and had him executed. Other officers involved in the battle of Halabja followed Sadeq into the grave. Now that it was preparing to mount another offensive in the al-Faw sector, the Iraqi regime was intent on motivating its troops, including through fear.

Saddam Hussein decided to make a show of punishing those he considered responsible for their setback in Kurdistan, beginning with Halabja's Kurdish population, whom he accused of having colluded with the enemy to facilitate its capture of this small high plateau city located barely ten miles (a few kilometers) from the border. Saddam ordered his cousin Ali Hassan al-Majid, the proconsul of the Kurdish provinces, to intensify the Anfal Campaign and raze Halabja with chemical weapons and artillery shelling. Saddam hoped to kill two birds with one stone by eliminating as many of the Kurdish rebels and Iranian soldiers entrenched in Halabja as possible. As for the rest of population, too bad. The audiotapes prove Saddam Hussein's responsibility for the massacre without a doubt.[5] In the middle of a meeting, Saddam is heard losing his temper and repeating, "Kill them all!" The Halabja massacre would provide the grounds for his death sentence. Saddam did not deny giving this order during his 2004 trial. Instead, he explained that it was a "defensive measure against Iranian aggression." As for Hassan al-Majid, he earned the macabre nickname "Chemical Ali" for his role in the massacre.[6]

In the early morning of March 16, 1988, ten MiG-23s flew over Habjala at low altitude and dropped containers of napalm, which set fire to part of the city and surrounded it with huge walls of fire. Several Pilatuses soon appeared overhead, spreading a lethal cocktail of chemical agents containing mustard gas, phosgene, and tabun and sarin nerve gases. The artillery then finished off the carnage by battering the city for several hours. In the late afternoon Iranian journalists who were nearby to cover the taking of Halabja entered the city and discovered an open-air charnel house. Their photos of the painfully contorted bodies of women and children were quickly seen around the world, contributing to the isolation of the Iraqi regime. These images also convinced the international community that it was urgent to put an end to hostilities. Iranian emergency services counted more than 3,000 dead, but it was impossible to calculate the exact proportion of civilians. Many others would die subsequently. The massacre's toll remains debated to this day, but is estimated to be between 3,000 and 5,000 dead and close to 10,000 wounded. The Iraqis tried to exonerate themselves by claiming that the Iranians had also fired chemical shells at Halabja in their attempt to seize the city. These allegations, repeated by the Anglo-Saxon press at the time and confirmed by Iraqi generals years later, have contributed to the persistent controversy surrounding the attribution of blame for this tragic massacre.[7] What cannot be denied is that the gassing of Halabja brought the Iranian offensive to a sudden halt, the large number of military casualties having convinced Tehran of the potentially devastating effect of further chemical attacks. The regular army and the Pasdaran, who had captured 230 square miles (600 square kilometers) in three days and reinforced their grasp on Sulaymaniah, now dug in to their new positions and awaited the Iraqi counteroffensive.

Defying all expectations, the Turks were the next to react. Ankara spoke up and threatened to close its border with Iran if Tehran continued its offensive in Iraqi Kurdistan. Closing the border would have deprived the Iranian regime of one of its principal lifelines and accelerated its economic ruin. Yet the Iranian government did not let itself be intimidated by this threat or the fact that it was in a pre-election period and took a hardline position with its neighbor. On March 27 the Iranian air force bombed the Habur border post, which served as the primary border crossing between Turkey and Iran, in the first direct Iranian attack on Turkish soil since the beginning of the war. Ankara immediately dispatched several divisions to the area and multiplied the number of air patrols, threatening military intervention. Its warning was heeded. The commercial traffic vital to Iran was not interrupted and the Turkish government faced no further provocation.

The Iraqi Army Recaptures the Al-Faw Peninsula

The Iranian offensive's relative success left the Iraqi government facing a dilemma regarding the best possible use for the mechanized battle corps it had patiently rebuilt over the last eighteen months. Should it immediately counterattack in Iraqi Kurdistan to reduce the Iranian hold there and recapture the Dukan Dam, as the Iranians expected? Or would it be better to strike elsewhere, where their adversary was not necessarily well prepared for the impact of a major offensive? Following a long meeting, Saddam Hussein, his son-in-law Hussein Kamel, Adnan Khairallah, and General al-Khazraji chose the latter option. The terrain in Kurdistan was not well suited to armored maneuvers, and the 3,860 square miles (10,000 square kilometers) of mountains and high plateaus controlled by the Kurdish rebels made it difficult to coordinate a wide-scale offensive. The Iraqi government decided to hold up on the northern front and focus all its efforts on the southern front to recapture the al-Faw peninsula, which was the Iranian layout's weak point. By regaining control of the peninsula, Iraq could increase its oil exports using the new oil pipeline section connecting Basra to the Umm Qasr naval base, which could now accommodate the loading of medium-tonnage tankers.

The Iraqi government conceived an elaborate deception plan to maximize its chances of taking the Iranians by surprise. It conspicuously moved several divisions from the central front and sent them in the direction of Kirkuk and Sulaymaniah. It increased the number of exercises and amount of radio activity in that sector. The minister of defense traveled to the area to inspect the troops and did not contradict the war correspondents accompanying him when they speculated that an offensive in Kurdistan was imminent. He ordered his commandos to intensify reconnaissance missions in the sector. Meanwhile, Adnan Khairallah discreetly deployed five Republican Guard divisions south of Basra. These were joined by three divisions from the 3rd and 4th Army Corps. All troop movements took place at night, under radio silence. In two weeks the military high command managed to gather 100,000 men on the edge of the al-Faw peninsula, as well as 2,500 armored vehicles (including 1,200 tanks), 1,400 cannons, and one hundred attack helicopters. These forces were divided in twelve divisions (three armored, two mechanized, six infantry, and one special forces), all heavily armed and well trained.

The Iranians only had two diminished infantry divisions to face them, supported by an artillery division and a few sapper battalions. Their total strength in the area barely reached 20,000 men, one hundred tanks, and 150 cannons. The balance of power was massively in the Iraqis' favor. To stack the odds further in their favor, the Iraqis decided to attack on the first day of Ramadan and take advantage of the fatigue of Iranian combatants absorbed by fasting and prayer. They knew that the Iranian command traditionally organized a major troop rotation to allow soldiers on the front to visit their families at the beginning of the holy month. By striking during the rotation, they hoped to catch the Iranians at their lowest force level, before replacement troops had arrived. Naturally, they named the offensive Ramadan al-Mubarak ("blessed Ramadan"). The Iranians did not suspect a thing. They remained convinced that the Iraqi counteroffensive would take place in Kurdistan. Not anticipating any threat on the southern front, they gave the soldiers stationed there a special day of rest to properly celebrate the beginning of the month of fasting.

At 4:30 a.m. on April 17, 1988, shortly after the call to prayer signaling the beginning of Ramadan, the Iraqi armada started toward the Iranian lines. Their plan was simple: a classic pincer movement aimed to break through the enemy layout at both ends in order for troops to converge toward its center of gravity (al-Faw) and encircle the trapped units. General Ayad Fayid al-Rawi, the head of the Republican Guard, commanded both the Iraqis' right wing and the overall operation. The five Republican Guard divisions charged with taking control of the coastal road running along the al-Faw peninsula's southern coast were under General al-Rawi's orders. Further north, General Ma'ahir Abdul Rashid commanded the left wing, comprising four divisions of the 7th Corps charged with advancing along the Shatt al-Arab in the direction of al-Faw.[8] General Rashid had been assigned the most delicate mission, for the Iranians were firmly entrenched along the river. Once again, Ma'ahir Abdul Rashid paid the price for his arrogance and outsize ambition. Many of his peers would not have minded seeing him in a difficult spot.

In a few hours the lead units broke through the array of Iranian troops, which was overwhelmed by formidable barrage fire. To further disorganize the enemy, General al-Rawi ordered a massive chemical strike against its outposts. Yet the wind unexpectedly picked up and suddenly changed directions, pushing the poison clouds toward Iraqi lines. This unexpected turn of events killed nearly 200 soldiers and severely injured several hundred more.[9] In the meantime, the Iraqi air force destroyed the three pontoon bridges over the Shatt al-Arab, isolating the Iranian troops on the peninsula. Its pilots had perfected a new bombing tactic, which proved to be highly effective. Su-22Ms at stand-off range fired Kedge missiles guided by a laser beam emitted by Mirage F-1s equipped with ATLIS targeting pods. The results were spectacular; the components of the pontoon bridges sank in rapid succession. In addition, Iraqi pilots destroyed two of the principal bridges over the Karun River at Khorramshahr, preventing the Iranians from sending reinforcements to al-Faw.

The navy also participated in the recapture of the peninsula: 200 frogmen swam across the Shatt al-Arab to carry out diversionary attacks, while several navy infantry battalions landed along the coastal road to support the Republican Guard's advance. They were backed by saturation fire from two Polnocny-class amphibious assault ships converted into rocket-launcher ships. The Iranian conscripts yielded ground at every point and retreated toward al-Faw. Attack helicopters flew over the columns of fleeing troops, mercilessly machine-gunning them, turning their retreat into a rout. Saddam Hussein's eldest son Uday played at making war by emptying his guns from aboard one of the helicopters.

By the evening of April 17 the Iraqis had advanced about twenty miles (about thirty kilometers), surpassing all their objectives for the day. The following day, they captured al-Faw. Victory was total. The Iraqi military high command was even surprised by the extent of its success: in thirty-six hours, its elite troops had recaptured the bridgehead that had resisted them for over two years. They had killed close to 5,000 Iranians and taken a little more than 10,000 prisoners, seizing all the Iranian tanks and cannons abandoned on the battlefield. Iraqi troops had also gotten hold of the precious Silkworm missile battery that had harassed the Kuwaiti al-Ahmadi terminal for over a year. Despite this impressive outcome, the Iraqis had only lost 800 combatants and twenty armored vehicles. Saddam Hussein euphorically distributed Mercedes to his officers. He even made a surprise visit to Mecca the following day, undertaking a conspicuous pilgrimage to publicly thank God for granting him such a great victory. The trip served as a pretext for Saddam to thank King Fahd for his unfailing financial support, while showing he was a "good Muslim" and silencing all those who criticized him for his notorious lack of piety.

The Iraqi success had an immediate impact on Iran, which could no longer fire Silkworm missiles at Kuwaiti territory. On April 20 the mullahs ordered a Scud missile to be fired at the al-Ahmadi terminal, showing Emir Jaber they could still reach it if necessary, even if it meant adding oil to the fire.[10] For in the meantime, the Persian Gulf was ablaze again.

[Chapter 30]

The Destruction of Iran Air Flight 655

On April 14, 1988, the missile frigate USS *Samuel Roberts* struck a mine on the edge of the maritime navigation channel while escorting a convoy of oil tankers off of Bahrain. The explosion blew a twenty-six-foot (eight-meter) hole close to the ship's stern, causing major damage and igniting a fire that took several hours to control. Fortunately, no one was killed or severely injured. The *Samuel Roberts*'s commander reacted perfectly, stopping the motors and stabilizing the ship to isolate the breach. Soon a team of mine-clearance divers sent to the area detected other mines around the damaged frigate. The *Samuel Roberts* had sailed into a trap laid about twenty-five miles (about forty kilometers) from Farsi Island, which was still occupied by a Pasdaran garrison. While neutralizing the remaining mines, the divers noticed they had the same serial number as those seized on the *Iran Ajr*. The frigate *Samuel Roberts* was towed to Bahrain, then sent back to the United States aboard a heavy-lift ship.

The White House promptly decided to respond to the provocation. On April 16 recently appointed National Security Advisor General Colin Powell proposed to attack the two Iranian oil platforms serving as Pasdaran bases, a plan which had been vetted by the Pentagon. Once again, General Powell chose not to strike Iranian territory in order to avoid a military escalation that he would not be able to fully control.[1] He was particularly cautious, given his awareness that as the first black general to reach his level of responsibility, he would not be allowed to make any mistakes. The next day his plan was approved by President Reagan, who immediately informed members of Congress.

Air and Sea Battle in the Gulf

On April 18, 1988, U.S. Admiral Anthony Less launched Operation Praying Mantis from his new headquarters aboard the *Coronado* off Abu Dhabi. Like the voracious insect, the U.S. navy would carefully choose its prey. For the prior few weeks Admiral Less had simultaneously headed the naval forces present in the Gulf and the Middle East Task Force (METF) based in Bahrain. He commanded fifteen warships divided into four task forces. The first, led by the aircraft carrier *Enterprise,* was cruising in the Sea of Oman near the Strait of Hormuz. Its mission was to provide the operation's air cover. The second, led by amphibious assault ship *Trenton,* was to attack one of the two Iranian oil platforms, while the third, led by the cruiser *Wainwright,* struck the other platform. The last, comprising two destroyers and one frigate, would repel any Iranian naval sortie from the Bandar Abbas naval base. Each of the task forces supported the others and stood ready to respond to any hostile action. To face them, Rear Admiral Malekzadegan could only rely on four missile frigates, one Combattante II-class fast attack craft, a handful of gunboats, and three Orion maritime patrol aircraft. All his other vessels were either out of service or out of range.

At 9 a.m. the *Trenton* arrived before the Sassan platform, fifty miles (eighty kilometers) south of the Lavan terminal, escorted by the destroyers *Merrill* and *McCormick.* The crew radioed the platform to give its entrenched Pasdaran twenty minutes to evacuate. Remembering the destruction of the Rostam platform seven months earlier, the Pasdaran complied and escaped aboard a tug they had used as a tender. At 9:20 a.m. the American ships opened fire with their cannons. An hour later marines were carried by helicopter from the *Trenton* and dropped on the scorched platform to search for documents left behind by the Pasdaran. They then blew up the installation's remains.

At 9:30 a.m. the cruiser *Wainwright,* accompanied by the frigates *Bagley* and *Simpson,* initiated the same procedure to attack the Nasser platform, which was forty nautical miles away, near the floating terminal at Sirri. Yet events unfolded slightly differently. Having been alerted, the Pasdaran were not taken by surprise and had had time to prepare. While part of the garrison evacuated the platform during the grace period, a group of fighters who had chosen to sacrifice themselves remained on site, hoping to inflict the maximum amount of damage on the Americans. For over an hour the platform was subjected to heavy bombing, which ravaged its superstructures and killed some of the combatants who had stayed behind. When the American flotilla approached to land navy SEALs, the survivors rushed to their remaining batteries of 23 mm guns and fired at the helicopters and ships within range. The American vessels immediately moved back, then opened fire again with their shipboard artillery. The *Trenton*'s Sea Cobra battle helicopters were called in to strike the Iranian batteries with rockets and Vulcan cannons. Their attack's impressive results put a quick end to any resistance, but not before one of the Sea Cobras was shot down. This would be the only American loss of the day. The American flotilla cautiously retreated, leaving the Nasser platform in flames, but making no attempt to take control of it.

Determined to get revenge, Iranian Rear Admiral Malekzadegan ordered his naval units in the sector to attack the nearest American ships, whether military or civilian. After receiving the green light from Tehran, he ordered the frigates *Sahand* and *Sabalan* to leave Bandar Abbas to engage combat with the enemy fleet. Given their awareness of the disproportion of the forces in the field, the Iranian sailors did not lack for courage or panache. They were ready to meet their fate, hoping to find the chink in the U.S. navy's armor that would allow them to inflict substantial damage. Malekzadegan also requested air force support and put the Silkworm missile batteries on alert.

Around noon three gunboats that had departed from Abu Musa sped toward the cruiser *Wainwright*'s task force. The Pasdaran fired a Stinger missile as the frigate *Simpson*'s helicopter flew overhead. The pilot released his decoy flares, avoided the missile, and alerted the aircraft carrier *Enterprise,* which immediately launched a squadron of fighter-bombers to deal with the threat. Meanwhile, three Pasdaran gunboats attacked the British supertanker *York Marine,* having found no other potential target, then headed for the Mubarak oil field off Abu Dhabi to attack the Scan Bay oil platform, which belonged to an American oil company. The Pasdaran's watchword was "an eye for an eye, a tooth for a tooth."

Around 1 p.m. Operation Praying Mantis took a different turn. The Iranian missile boat *Joshan,* which had been cruising near the Lavan oil

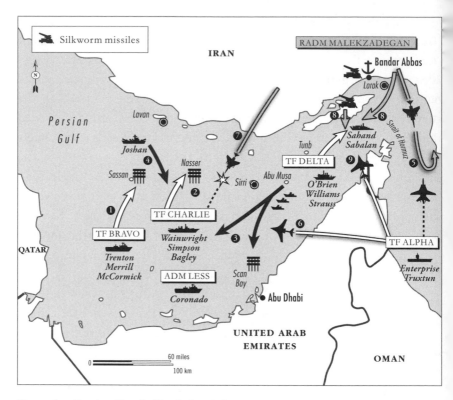

Operation Praying Mantis (April 18, 1988)

terminal, arrived within sight of the Nasser platform. It detected the *Wainwright* on its radar, ignored its injunctions, and fired a Harpoon missile at it, narrowly missing. The American cruiser and its two escort frigates immediately retaliated by firing a broadside of four Harpoon missiles, three of which made direct hits. This was the first U.S. navy engagement involving antiship missiles. The *Joshan* was destroyed, but its wreck remained afloat. The frigates *Bagley* and *Simpson* approached to collect the few survivors and sink the *Joshan* with their cannons. In the meantime, five Phantoms took off from Bandar Abbas and sped toward the *Enterprise* and its escort, which were cruising in the Sea of Oman. The planes were immediately detected by a Hawkeye surveillance plane, which directed an eager Tomcat patrol toward them. The Iranian pilots were not kamikazes at heart and chose to beat a cautious retreat, knowing they would never get close enough to the aircraft carrier to fire their missiles.

In the early afternoon the attack squadron from the *Enterprise* spotted the Pasdaran gunboats near the Scan Bay platform. The squadron commander, Lieutenant Commander James Engler, immediately requested authorization to open fire. Thanks to the American armed forces' real time communications network, the request was transferred to the general commanding Centcom in Tampa, Florida, then to the secretary of defense and the chairman of the Joint Chiefs of Staff at the Pentagon, and finally to the national security advisor and the president. Three minutes after having called in, Lieutenant Commander Engler received direct confirmation of the order of commitment from President Reagan, who was following the operations live from the White House crisis room. The eight Intruders and Corsair IIs immediately went on the attack, spending the next twenty minutes hunting down the Iranian gunboats, whose small size and maneuverability made them elusive targets. The American pilots eventually succeeded in sinking three gunboats, while the others returned to their base in Abu Musa without further ado.

Meanwhile, further west, the cruiser *Wainwright* had detected two rapidly approaching Iranian Phantoms. It locked its fire control radar on them and ordered them to turn back. Receiving no response from the Phantoms, it fired two Standard missiles at them in rapid succession. One of the fighters immediately withdrew and managed to escape the missile fired at it. The other fighter maneuvered, but was severely damaged by the explosion of the second missile. Its pilot struggled back to Bandar Abbas and landed on one engine, his plane's airfoils and empennage in shreds.

Yet the battle was not over. At 4 p.m. the missile frigate *Sahand* entered the Strait of Hormuz and headed straight for the destroyer *Joseph Strauss* and the frigate *Jack Williams*, ignoring their orders to withdraw. Four Intruders dispatched from the *Enterprise* soon flew over the *Sahand* and tried to intimidate it into turning back. The frigate responded by firing three surface-to-air missiles at the assault aircraft, then two Sea Killer missiles aimed at the American ships. The U.S. navy ships and aircraft released their decoy flares, dodged the missiles, and immediately retaliated. The destroyer *Joseph Strauss* fired a Harpoon missile and made a direct hit, while the Intruders dropped four laser-guided Skipper bombs. The bombs tore the Iranian frigate apart, reducing it to a floating wreck. It was destroyed half an hour later when it was hit with two more Harpoon missiles and two electro-optic guided Walleye bombs fired by two other sections of Intruders and Corsair IIs called in as reinforcements. The pulverized frigate *Sahand* sank in a few minutes.

The Iranians had not said their last word. They retaliated by firing Silkworms from Qeshm Island. The frigate *Jack Williams* and the destroyer *Joseph Strauss* were forced to activate their Phalanx Close-In Weapons System to avoid a salvo of five Silkworm missiles. The frigate *Gary,* which was positioned as a radar guard on the other side of the Strait of Hormuz, dodged two other Silkworms. At twilight the Iranian frigate *Sabalan* burst into view in front of the American destroyers, ready to engage combat. It immediately fired a Sea Killer missile at the frigate *Jack Williams*—which it had just acquired on its radar—and a Sea Cat missile at a formation of Intruders headed to intercept it. The same causes producing the same effects, the *Sabalan* was soon struck by two laser-guided Skipper bombs. One detonated in the engine room, starting a terrible fire, while the other shattered its stern. Now immobilized, the *Sabalan* seemed on the verge of sinking. The American naval aviation pilots requested Washington's authorization to finish it off. Clearance was denied by Secretary of Defense Frank Carlucci, who had consulted with President Reagan and General Powell and decided to show clemency to avoid provoking an uncontrollable escalation of violence. In any case, the operation's outcome was undeniable. In a single day, the U.S. navy had destroyed two platforms used as Pasdaran bases, sunk a frigate, a missile boat, and three motor boats, and severely damaged another frigate and a Phantom interceptor. Fifty-seven Iranian sailors and twenty Pasdaran had been killed. The engagement remains the U.S. navy's most significant naval battle since the end of the Second World War. At 8:30 p.m. Admiral Less informed the Iranians that they had his authorization to tow the frigate *Sabalan* to its base in Bandar Abbas. It would stay there for repairs for three years and return to service in 1991.

The next day Akbar Hashemi Rafsanjani told the Iranian media that "time [was] now against Iran."[2] Should his words be interpreted as an announcement of the imminent end of hostilities? Probably, given the political context in Tehran at the time. Ten days earlier the first round of legislative elections had left the chairman of Parliament's faction trailing in the upcoming runoff against Mehdi Karroubi, the secretary general of the Association of Combatant Clerics (a leftist populist religious party) and the beneficiary of significant popularity as the head of the Martyrs' Foundation. Karroubi advocated a rapid end to the war and the export of the Islamic Revolution to the rest of the community of believers, following the ideological line of marginalized Ayatollah Montazeri.

Sick and increasingly weak, the Ayatollah Khomeini had been unable to intervene in the electoral battle. Mohammad Khatami, who still held Iran's propaganda portfolio, had felt the tide turning and joined the Association of Combatant Clerics, distancing himself from the Combatant Clergy Association to which Rafsanjani and Khamenei belonged. Isolated, Rafsanjani and Khamenei decided to form an alliance to face the rising young guard. They knew that they now had to find a way to put an end to the war that had allowed them to take power but had lasted too long. The loss of the al-Faw peninsula had also been a severe blow to Iranian morale. Though there is no hard evidence to support this theory, it is conceivable that Rafsanjani deliberately sacrificed part of the Iranian navy to demonstrate the disproportion of the forces in the field and justify the upcoming acceptance of a ceasefire. According to his new rhetoric, Iran could continue the war against Iraq indefinitely, but could not fight the United States at the same time.

On April 19 the American government announced that it was extending its protection to all maritime traffic in the Gulf. In case of absolute necessity, American warships were authorized to use force to protect ships of all nationalities if they were under attack by Iranian forces. Tehran immediately put an end to its harassment of maritime traffic to avoid repeating the slap in the face of Operation Praying Mantis. In early May the Iranian navy's command deployed its three venerable destroyers, *Babr*, *Palang*, and *Damavand*, in the Strait of Hormuz. The three ships' weapons systems were no longer operational. The maneuver fooled no one: the emperor had no clothes and everyone knew it, both in Tehran and Baghdad.

The Iraqis Recapture Their Other Lost Territories

In the second round of Iranian legislative elections held on May 13, 1988, Mehdi Karroubi's Association of Combatant Clerics won 60 percent of the seats in Parliament. This was a severe setback for Akbar Hashemi Rafsanjani, who had to bargain both with the Association of Combatant Clerics and independent parliamentarians hostile to continuing the war in order to retain the chairmanship of Parliament and reappoint his government. Mehdi Bazargan, a member of the opposition and one of Bani-Sadr's former prime ministers, published an open letter to the Ayatollah Khomeini criticizing Rafsanjani for having failed to negotiate at the right time and accusing him of being solely responsible for the continuation of a war Bazargan saw as contrary to the principles of Islam. While forty of his supporters were immediately arrested, Bazargan himself remained untouchable thanks to the protection of Ayatollah Montazeri.

Having been hit hard, the flagging Supreme Leader leaned once again on Rafsanjani, publicly reaffirming his trust in him and renewing his appointment as commander-in-chief of the Iranian military. Since a scapegoat was needed to explain the two humiliating defeats the Iranian army had just experienced on land and at sea, Rafsanjani dismissed General Sohrabi from his position as chief of staff of the Iranian armed forces and replaced him with General Ali Shahbazi. While the general was not a genius, he was close to the Pasdaran and had spent the last two years in the Supreme Leader's cabinet, advising the Ayatollah Khomeini and his son Ahmad on military matters. To the mullahs, he had the advantage of being an ideologically safe bet. To Rafsanjani, he was an unassuming general who would not balk at taking responsibility for defeat when the time came for the Iranians to resolve themselves to accepting a ceasefire.

A few days later the Soviet army began withdrawing from Afghanistan, which accelerated the rapprochement between Tehran and Moscow. The Iranian regime, which was reassured to see Soviet troops leaving a neighboring Muslim country, no longer opposed an "official" normalization of relations with the USSR. The Kremlin tried to persuade Iran's leaders that it was urgent to declare a ceasefire to stabilize the region and avoid another confrontation between American and Iranian forces, which would only reinforce the U.S. grip on the Gulf. Rafsanjani, Khamenei, Karroubi, Rezaee, and Mousavi were convinced the Kremlin was right, but the Ayatollah, whose lucidity was diminishing by the day, continued to oppose the ceasefire.

While combat proceeded on the ground front, and tension remained dangerously high in the Gulf, Mikhail Gorbachev welcomed Ronald Reagan to Moscow on May 29, 1988, for a four-day summit during which the two heads of state were to discuss numerous issues, including those related to establishing reciprocal confidence measures between the two superpowers. The Soviet leader allegedly offered to pressure Iran to end the Iran-Iraq War if Washington pressured Pakistan and Saudi Arabia to facilitate the Soviet withdrawal from Afghanistan. The two men are said to have agreed to Gorbachev's proposal with a handshake. For once, the "win win" approach seemed to prevail, heralding the end of the Cold War.

Meanwhile, Saddam Hussein had decided to strike while the iron was hot and launch his victorious troops against the Iranians in the sector of Fish Lake, east of Basra. The operation had a dual objective: to eliminate any threat to the river city and to force the Iranians to accept the cease-fire agreement by dealing another decisive blow to their morale.

On May 25, 1988, Iraqi military high command launched Operation Tawakalna ala Allah ("Trust in God"), which comprised 150,000 men and fourteen divisions, supported by 3,000 armored vehicles and 1,500 cannons.[3] Since traveling to Mecca, Saddam Hussein had decided to give his offensives a religious connotation to increase popular fervor and convince the oil monarchies to continue supporting him. The Iranians had five infantry divisions totaling 50,000 men, ninety tanks, and 150 cannons in the area. Beginning at dawn, the Iraqi steamroller advanced toward the Iranian lines with air support. Taken by surprise, the Pasdaran doggedly resisted and called their interceptors to the rescue. Yet the Iranian planes retreated as soon as the new Iraqi MiG-29s delivered by Moscow appeared. A MiG-29 accidentally destroyed by Iraqi surface-to-air defense during this operation would be the only MiG-29 lost during the war. Later in the day Iraqi General Jamal (3rd Corps) obtained permission to launch a chemical attack on enemy positions. He exclusively used neurotoxic agents, which had the advantage of being only mildly persistent and therefore barely slowed the advance of his own troops, who were equipped with chemical protection suits. The Pasdaran had only gas masks, which were useless against the poisonous drops of VX and tabun scattered by Iraqi artillery. Many died clutching their cannons and machine guns.

By the end of the day the Iraqis had crushed the Iranian trenches and forced their enemy back six miles (ten kilometers). The next day they routed the Iranians and pushed them all the way to the border. Republican Guard tanks charged panicked Pasdaran, who fled in disorder after abandoning their equipment. Meanwhile, Iraqi troops flushed the Pasdaran out of the marshlands thirty miles (fifty kilometers) further north. The Iraqis' success was total. In barely sixty hours they had recaptured a crucial pocket of land, killed more than 6,000 Iranians, and seized incredible amounts of weapons and ammunition.

On May 27, 1988, the Iraqi flag was raised over the Iranian town of Shalamcheh, located barely six miles (ten kilometers) west of Khorramshahr, for the first time in six years. Iraqi soldiers had stopped pushing forward while awaiting orders. The previous evening Saddam Hussein had held a crucial meeting with his most valuable generals to decide on the rest of the operation. Despite the stunning victories in al-Faw and Shalamcheh, the Iraqi president anticipated a long war, which could drag on until the Ayatollah Khomeini's death. He gave himself eighteen months to drive the Iranians out of Iraqi territory. His analysis was rational and based on tangible factors. He had learned a great deal in eight years and now mastered many variables. His generals were very cautious, wanting to avoid underestimating the enemy's counterattack capacity. Nizar al-Khazraji, who had long commanded the northern front before becoming chief of staff of the armed forces, argued for an offensive in Iraqi Kurdistan to eradicate any threat to the oil zones of Kirkuk and Mosul. Adnan Khairallah thought it more urgent to attack in the center to secure the access to the Iraqi capital. Saddam Hussein was inclined to start by recapturing the Majnoon Islands to recover their oil fields and increase Iraqi revenue. After extensively debating each option's pros and cons, the three men agreed to focus the principal effort on the center and southern fronts, while reorganizing their forces on the northern front to launch the occasional attack in the sector. They ordered the construction of new roads to bypass Kurdish militia bastions and ease armored units' movements toward the mountainous area. Their key principal was flexibility. Each corps was placed on alert and ordered to prepare to rapidly go on the offensive if necessary.

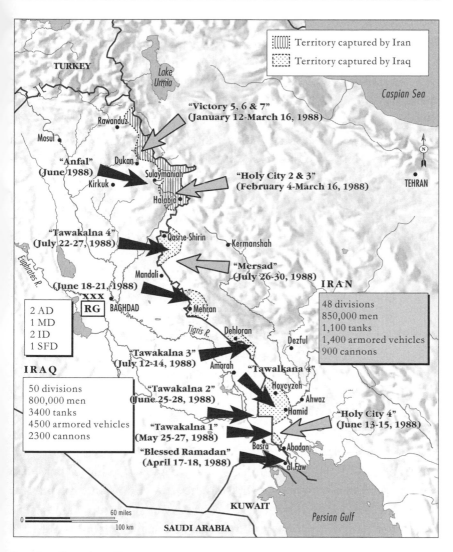

Iran-Iraq front in 1988

On the other side, the Iranians' hearts were no longer in it. The troops were heavily demoralized. Nonetheless, General Shahbazi and General Shirazi had managed to mount a sizeable attack to recapture Shalamcheh on June 13. For two days three Pasdaran brigades, backed by one hundred tanks, made multiple frontal assaults and broke through the Iraqi layout.

They were immediately counterattacked by the Republican Guard, which recaptured the border town. The same day the Iraqi military high command launched several raids in Kurdistan to regain control of various objectives, including several passes. Having little regard for General Sajid, the commander of the 1st Corps, General al-Khazraji personally headed operations. The Iraqis seized the Dukan Dam, but Halabja continued to hold out. A division of Pasdaran had entrenched themselves in its burned ruins among the dead bodies. According to General al-Hamdani, the Iraqi regime now came to a simultaneous truce with Jalal Talabani and Masoud Barzani.[4] By this agreement, Baghdad committed to exclusively targeting Iranian troops deployed in Iraqi Kurdistan in return for the Kurdish militia's agreement to cease expanding its presence. Once again, Saddam Hussein was willing to be pragmatic to reach his main objective: driving the Iranians out of Iraq.

On June 18 the Iraqi army launched an offensive against the Mehran salient on the central front, working in close coordination with Massoud Rajavi's People's Mujahidin. Since being forced to leave France, the charismatic leader of the armed opposition to the mullahs' regime had taken shelter in Iraq and founded the National Liberation Army of Iran (NLAI), which was equipped by Baghdad. This troop of highly motivated auxiliaries comprised 20,000 men provided with armored vehicles and light artillery. The Iraqi government, which frowned upon the NLAI's presence on its soil, seized this opportunity to send it to fight in Iran. With the support of an Iraqi armored division, the People's Mujahidin took four days to wipe out a Pasdaran division, seize Mehran, and establish a bridgehead reaching twelve miles (twenty kilometers) into Iranian territory. For Baghdad this was primarily a diversionary maneuver to attract as many Iranians as possible to the sector and thin their defenses on the rest of the front. The trap worked, convincing General Shirazi to send several divisions toward Mehran. Saddam took the opportunity to play another card.

At dawn on June 25 the Iraqi president launched Operation Tawakalna ala Allah 2 in the direction of the Majnoon Islands and the Hoveyzeh marshes, which were defended by 40,000 men and four infantry divisions. Saddam committed 160,000 men divided in fourteen divisions and backed by more than 1,000 cannons.[5] Four armored divisions were at the ready to rush into the breaches opened by the infantry to the north and south of the Majnoon Islands and encircle Iranians entrenched in the marshes. Once again, the Iraqi offensive began with massive artillery shelling, followed by a chemical attack and air strikes by "tank killer" Su-25s. Already demoralized by their previous setbacks, Iranian troops yielded before the heavy firepower. In eight hours Iraqi special forces aboard amphibious armored combat vehicles took control of the southern Majnoon Islands, which had resisted them for over three years. Iranian soldiers fled toward the border in disorder.

The Iraqi generals were surprised by their own success. To fully encircle the Iranians, they had helicopters transport the 42nd Parachute Brigade to the rear of enemy lines. By June 28 they had seized the entire zone and were in control of a bridgehead in Iranian territory; 3,000 Pasdaran had been killed, 8,000 wounded, 4,000 captured, and all the others had vanished into thin air, searching for their units or a way to get back home. This additional defeat precipitated a collapse of morale in the Iranian camp. While Tehran could still claim a few pockets in Iraqi territory, primarily in Kurdistan, its armed forces had lost their fighting spirit. Even the Pasdaran asked the government to put an end to hostilities. Desertions reached a record high. Ali Khamenei ordered all combatants to do their duty and immediately report to the front. Without naming them, Rafsanjani criticized all those who had contributed to isolating Iran by opposing the policy of openness that he had advocated for years. The atmosphere in the halls of power became poisonous, with each player trying to exonerate himself of responsibility for the accumulation of defeats. In Baghdad, however, optimism was the order of the day. A jovial Saddam Hussein declared: "Today's battle was the last of a long series of very difficult confrontations. The final victory is now very close, God willing."[6] An unexpected tragedy at the other end of the Gulf would contribute to proving him right.

The Destruction of an Iran Air Airbus

At sunrise on July 3, 1988, the USS *Vincennes* was cruising near Abu Musa Island toward the Strait of Hormuz, escorted by the frigates *Sides* and *Montgomery*, on the way to accompany another convoy of oil tankers headed for Kuwait. The *Vincennes* was a state-of-the-art Ticonderoga-class guided-missile cruiser (567 feet/173 meters long and 10,000 tons), which had just arrived in the Gulf equipped with the brand-new Aegis combat system. The core of this entirely automated system was a highly powerful three-dimensional electronically scanned array radar, which could simultaneously track several dozen targets thanks to its pair of radar-guided 127 mm turrets and two artillery batteries able to rapidly fire off the sixty Standard surface-to-air missiles in the ship's hull. This jewel of technology, known to its crew as the "Robocruiser," was initially conceived to intercept waves of Soviet bombers attempting to saturate U.S. navy defenses. Captain William Rogers, the vessel's commander, was proud to be at the helm of the most modern ship cruising in the sector. Granted, his crew lacked training, and most of his officers had only recently graduated from the Naval Academy, but all had received top grades and showed a lot of drive. Every one of them was itching for an opportunity to prove himself.

Sailing beside the *Vincennes,* the USS *Montgomery,* a frigate fifteen years its senior, paled in comparison. Yet it was the *Montgomery* that detected a gathering of thirteen Pasdaran gunboats at 6:30 a.m. and determined they were maneuvering to attack a group of tankers fifty nautical miles away from the American ships' position. The *Vincennes*'s captain ordered action stations, sped up his ship, and took the initiative to engage with the Iranian boats, if only to break the monotony of these escort missions that did not suit his aggressive temperament. Rogers dreamed of doing battle and earning the same decorations as his peers who had served in Operation Praying Mantis two months earlier. For two hours the cruiser traveled northeast as fast as its turbines could carry it, trying to intercept the Iranian boats, which had not yet detected it or its escort of two frigates. However, its course brought it dangerously close to the naval exclusion zone decreed by Iran. By 8:40 a.m. the *Vincennes* was forty nautical miles north of its assigned position.

The METF officer on watch in Bahrain called it to order and asked it to resume its regular course. Playing for time, William Rogers answered that he had sent the ship's helicopter on a reconnaissance flight and could not turn back without it. A few minutes later the helicopter was hit by bursts of automatic weapon fire as it flew over the Iranian boats. The *Vincennes*'s captain immediately claimed the right of self-defense and requested authorization to pursue the gunboats, which were moving north in the direction of Iranian territorial waters. Having difficulty assessing the situation in the field, the METF officer gave him leave to do as he thought fit. In fifty minutes the *Vincennes* came within range of the gunboats, which were attempting a disorderly escape. At 9:39 a.m. it opened fire on them with its cannons. Two minutes later the *Vincennes* entered Iranian territorial waters, but its crew was so absorbed by the chase that it did not notice. The *Vincennes* also ignored its escorts' warnings. Though they were concerned that Rogers was overstepping orders, the frigates' lower-ranking commanders felt they lacked the stature to chastise the officer they saw as an arrogant cowboy who listened to no one.[7]

For the next half an hour the captain and his officers were gathered in the cruiser's operations room, fully engrossed by their battle with the gunboats. The tension was palpable. For the moment, no direct hit had been made—the rapid, easily maneuverable gunboats were slaloming to avoid the shells landing all around them. The Iranians had received orders to retreat and did not counterattack. On board the *Vincennes* the excitement of combat was suddenly replaced by anxiety. The captain realized that by entering enemy territorial waters, he had exposed the ship to potentially legitimate attack. The intelligence officer on board reminded him that naval intelligence had circulated a memo a few days earlier warning that the Iranians would probably attempt a high-profile action on the Fourth of July to seek revenge for their humiliation two months earlier.

The officers began to wonder if the *Vincennes* might be headed into a trap. Feeling uncertain, the captain ordered his crew to ceasefire so his helicopter could land and the ship could turn back toward international waters. At this point the cruiser was sixty nautical miles from its regular route, near Qeshm Island, which was home to a battery of Silkworm missiles. The battery did not engage combat, following strict orders from Tehran to avoid vainly provoking the U.S. navy. Despite their saber rattling, the mullahs were perfectly aware of the highly uneven balance of power. Rafsanjani knew very well that he had nothing to gain by sparking a major confrontation with the United States.

Fifty miles (eighty kilometers) away, the Iran Air Airbus A-300, providing a daily connection to Dubai, took off from Bandar Abbas at 10:17 a.m., carrying 290 people (274 passengers and sixteen crew). It was immediately detected by the *Vincennes*'s radar, whose transponder initially classed it as a "civilian contact." Two minutes later, several of the *Vincennes*'s operators misinterpreted radar signals—probably due to their lack of training and the stress on board—and determined that the plane was descending while gaining speed, the standard profile for an air attack against a ship. The Airbus, which was carefully following the airway for commercial aviation, was actually still ascending to reach its cruising altitude of 14,750 feet (4,500 meters), for the flight across the Strait of Hormuz that took only half an hour.

While maneuvering to engage the Pasdaran gunboats, the *Vincennes* had positioned itself on the flight path of Iran Air Flight 655, which it would not normally have encountered. The young officer responsible for the interception system interrogated the transponder again, which now classed the contact as "civilian or military," adding to the general confusion.[8] Worried voices burst out in the operations room, which had been left in darkness to facilitate the operators' work. Several suggested the aircraft might be an Iranian Phantom or Tomcat posing as a commercial flight, since the Bandar Abbas airport also served as a military air force base with about ten of these fighters. The specter of the attack on the USS *Stark* loomed large on everyone's mind. At 10:20 a.m. the *Vincennes*'s radio operator sent a warning to the approaching aircraft over two international emergency frequencies, the military (243.0) and civilian frequencies (121.5). He received no answer. Given their short flight time, Iran Air 655's crew had probably remained on Bandar Abbas and Dubai's frequencies, without engaging the emergency frequencies.

Meanwhile, confusion reigned in the *Vincennes*'s operations room. Several experienced radar operators reexamined the radar data and concluded that the worrisome contact was indeed gaining altitude, not losing it. A naval officer then consulted the schedule of commercial flights and did not find a flight at that time; Flight IR655 was on the schedule, but thirty minutes later. No one on board stopped to think of the thirty-minute time difference between Bahrain (which served as a reference for the U.S. navy's ships) and Iran (from which the Airbus had taken off).[9] At 10:22 a.m. the *Vincennes* sent another message over both emergency frequencies, asking the approaching aircraft to identify itself, warning it that it would be shot down if it entered a safety zone of twenty nautical miles from the cruiser, which was still sailing in Iranian waters. Tension aboard the ship reached a new peak. The Americans steeled themselves to be hit by one or several missiles. In the operations room, documents flew in every direction and the crew frantically busied itself without taking the time to reflect. Captain Rogers did not even consider checking his escort vessels' radar data. How could the commander of the most modern ship in the fleet stoop to ask their help?

At 10:23 a.m. the cruiser sent a final radio warning. Having received no response one minute later, the captain of the *Vincennes* ordered his men to open fire. The young fire controlman was under so much pressure that he frenetically pushed the wrong button several times until his more experienced noncommissioned officer showed him the right one; two SM-2 Standard missiles immediately hurtled out of the ship and sped toward the Iranian Airbus at three and a half times the speed of sound. The plane was smashed to tiny pieces and disappeared from radar screens at 10:25 a.m., only eight minutes after its takeoff from Bandar Abbas, while it was a mere eight nautical miles from the *Vincennes*. At that distance, a Phantom would have already fired its missiles. The *Sides* and *Montgomery*'s crews were bewildered. Their captains, who had clearly identified the radar echo as that of a commercial flight, were stunned to witness this unexpected missile launch—during the seven minutes the engagement had lasted, Captain Williams had neither consulted nor warned them. This tragic mistake was the result of an accumulation of human errors combined with a deficient man-machine interface.[10] It was certainly not the intentional attack or American provocation that the Iranian authorities continue to claim it was.

Revenge, Iranian Style

Tehran reacted immediately by accusing Washington of having committed a war crime. A few days later the Iranian minister of foreign affairs filed a complaint before the International Court of Justice in the Hague, requesting it to sanction what he deemed "a barbaric act having cost the life of 300 innocents." Ronald Reagan expressed his sincere regrets for this terrible human tragedy, but refused to apologize, stating that the *Vincennes*'s captain had taken the "appropriate defensive measures."

He emphasized that the tragedy would never have taken place if Iran had agreed to apply UN Security Council Resolution 598. This statement, which was loudly decried by the mullahs, would give rise to a conspiracy theory according to which the United States intentionally shot down the Iran Air Airbus to accelerate the end of the Iran-Iraq War. Supporters of the theory point to the fact that Captain Rogers was never sanctioned; instead, he was awarded the Legion of Merit following his command period. This is seen as an indication that he was following orders.[11]

The theory does not hold up to common sense, let alone a meticulous examination of the facts. Every account collected after the events underlines Rogers's pathological behavior, the crew's lack of training, the ambient stress, the confusion in the operations room, and the unfortunate sequence of human errors that led to the order to fire. William Rogers was ostracized by his peers and sidelined as soon as his command ended. Many navy personnel have recognized that he was only decorated to prevent the United States from losing face. An investigative commission headed by the retired Rear Admiral William Fogarty was charged with examining the incident's circumstances and concluded that it was a mistake due to what the military call "the fog of war," noting that the captain had acted to defend his ship.[12] Many aspects of the report are highly critical of William Rogers and emphasize the long series of errors that led to his deadly decision to open fire. A final point speaks against the premeditation theory: the downing of Iran Air's Airbus could have easily provoked another escalation between Tehran and Washington.

While the Iranian government did not openly retaliate for the destruction of the Airbus, it did not hesitate to warn the American authorities that it would not tolerate further incidents of this type and reminded them of the right of self-defense recognized by the United Nations charter. Five months later, on December 21, 1988, a Boeing 747 operated by the American airline Pan Am (Flight 103) exploded over Lockerbie, Scotland, killing 270 people. After three years of investigation, the FBI concluded that Flight 103 had been the target of a terrorist attack ordered by Colonel Gaddafi's Libyan regime and that Gaddafi was probably seeking revenge for the 1986 American raid on Tripoli. In 2003 the Libyan dictator recognized that his regime's intelligence services were responsible for the attack and paid compensation to the victims' families in return for the lifting of international sanctions on Libya and its reinstatement to the United Nations.[13]

Yet, following the fall of Colonel Gaddafi in 2011, another hypothesis was finally made public. A high-ranking officer of the Libyan secret service who had joined the opposition declared that while Gaddafi had indeed ordered an American commercial airliner to be sabotaged, the bombing's real instigator had been the Iranian regime, which was seeking revenge for the destruction of the Iran Air Airbus. According to his theory, Iran was aware that it could manipulate Gaddafi and exert various types of pressure on him. Naturally, in order to protect this source's life, his identity has been kept secret by the new Libyan regime and all those who have had access to his account. Since then, a secret U.S. Defense Intelligence Agency report has been declassified under the Freedom of Information Act. The February 1991 report was assembled while the FBI investigation was ongoing and has been heavily redacted to preserve the sources' anonymity. It states that the Iranian regime ordered the Lockerbie bombing. Pages 49 and 50 identify Ali Akbar Mohtashamipur, an Iranian secret service official close to Rafsanjani, as the individual who paid the Libyan authorities ten million U.S. dollars to carry out the attack.[14]

If the report is accurate (which cannot be stated with absolute certainty), why didn't Washington use it to officially reveal Tehran's responsibility for the bombing? There appear to be several answers. First, it seems that the American administration did not have enough proof at the time to solidly support such an accusation. Mention of the Iranian hypothesis could have weakened the Libyan lead, allowing both those who ordered the bombing and those who carried it out to avoid legal responsibility, and damaging the victims' case. Rivalries between American agencies unquestionably did not benefit the investigation. While the White House certainly wanted to facilitate the settlement of the Lockerbie case before the International Court of Justice, it may also have tried to avoid stigmatizing the Iranian regime at a time when it seemed to be opening up a little following the Ayatollah Khomeini's death. And it undoubtedly sought to protect several well-placed sources. At the end of the day, the American administration probably took a realistic and pragmatic approach, keeping this case as a wild card, which may have helped it to negotiate with Tehran for the release of American hostages in Lebanon.

Yet the Iranian vendetta did not stop there. On March 10, 1989, William Rogers's wife miraculously survived a car bomb near the U.S. naval base in San Diego while her husband was still at the helm of the *Vincennes*. This was the first attack of this type on American soil, long before all those that would receive major news coverage. Following this incident, the American administration entered into protracted negotiations with the Iranian regime to reach a settlement of the *Vincennes* episode. In 1996 the United States paid 131.8 million dollars to the Iranian government (including 61.8 million dollars to compensate the victims' families) in exchange for Iran dropping its claim before the International Court of Justice.[15] Looking back, one thing seems certain: the accidental destruction of the Iran Air Airbus convinced the Iranian regime that it could not afford to fight both Iraq and the United States. It also convinced Saddam Hussein that the time had come to deal the decisive blow that would make Tehran fold.

Chapter 31

Endgame

On July 12, 1988, after a week of intense preparation, Saddam Hussein launched Operation Tawakalna ala Allah 3 in the direction of Dehloran, on the central front. With a total of 140,000 men supported by 1,000 tanks and 1,000 cannons, the 4th Corps and Republican Guard reinforcements attacked Iranian positions in a sector approximately sixty miles (one hundred kilometers) wide.[1] In a single day the Iraqis recaptured their frontier oil fields, which the Iranians had occupied for more than five years. The next day they broke through the enemy layout at several points and penetrated deep into Iranian territory without encountering significant resistance. At nightfall they seized Dehloran, which gave them control of a bridgehead larger than the whole of all the Iranian pockets of resistance in Iraqi Kurdistan. On July 14, as Iraqi troops chased routed Iranian units and expanded their hold on enemy territory, Saddam Hussein threatened Tehran that he would attack in the south in the direction of Ahwaz and take control of Iran's oil wells if the Iranian army did not immediately withdraw from Iraqi Kurdistan. Facing total disaster in their ranks, the Iranians had to take the ultimatum seriously. In three days three of their infantry divisions had been wiped out and their infantrymen had abandoned 570 armored vehicles and 320 cannons; 10,000 soldiers were killed or wounded and 5,000 captured. The others had vanished into thin air. In Khuzestan, the Iranian generals were left with a mere 200 tanks to face the 1,000 tanks that the Iraqi army could now throw into battle at every offensive.

Ayatollah Khomeini Approves the End of Hostilities

During the night of July 14 to 15 Iran's leaders gathered for an emergency meeting in Tehran to evaluate the situation. It was now clear that Iran would be headed for disaster if it obsessively pursued a war that had turned to its disadvantage. The ailing Ayatollah Khomeini did not attend the meeting, but let its forty participants know that he wanted them to speak their minds with an exclusive focus on the interests of the Islamic Republic. Once again he reminded them that religious principles sometimes needed to be suspended to protect the regime. By doing so, he gave the mullahs and generals free rein to objectively assess a situation that was getting worse by the day. The government had pushed too far, and the people were no longer behind it. The losses had been too great. Iran's money had run out. Recent setbacks had demonstrated the armed forces' inadequacy. The navy and air force were no longer capable of facing a Western air and sea intervention. The specter of a resumption of the war of the capitals tempered even the most bellicose spirits. But most importantly, Iran needed to come out of isolation to revive its economy and begin rearming, a process that would take several years. Over the course of an eight-hour meeting, the Iranian leaders made two major decisions: they accepted Saddam Hussein's proposal and agreed to put an end to the war, knowing that they would have to convince the Supreme Leader to take responsibility for this decision.

On July 15 Akbar Hashemi Rafsanjani publicly announced the withdrawal of Iranian troops from Iraqi Kurdistan. The very next day, Iranian divisions deployed in the region began a hurried withdrawal, starting in Halabja, then Penjwin, Haj Omran, and Rayat. On July 17, which was the twentieth anniversary of the Ba'ath Party's rise to power, Saddam Hussein listed the five conditions required for a comprehensive, just peace: 1) direct negotiations between the two parties; 2) an immediate start to United Nations cleanup of the Shatt al-Arab; 3) a guarantee of free navigation in the Gulf for Iraq; 4) the end of Iranian attacks on maritime traffic; and 5) prisoner exchange. To show his good faith and allow the Iranian government to save face, the Iraqi president ordered his troops to retreat to the international border and to abandon recently conquered territory in Iran.

For his part, Rafsanjani visited the Ayatollah Khomeini to explain the situation and ask him to accept the ceasefire. Rafsanjani knew that he was playing all or nothing with his political future. He apologized to the Supreme Leader for not having defeated the Great Satan (Saddam Hussein and the United States), acted contrite, and put his fate in Khomeini's hands, declaring he was ready to step down from all his positions if demanded. Though weak, the Ayatollah Khomeini was lucid. He thanked Rafsanjani for his frankness and reassured him that the Islamic Republic still needed him—his energy, vision, and connections—to set the country back on an even keel and preserve the regime. Knowing that his days were numbered, the Supreme Leader told Rafsanjani he would take sole responsibility for the war's failure in order to protect him and his other protégé, Ali Khamenei.

The same day the Soviet ambassador to the United Nations began a final mediation tour in the Middle East. A day later, while Yuli Vorontsov was still in Baghdad, Ali Khamenei sent a letter to the UN secretary general to inform him that Iran had decided to unconditionally accept the terms of Resolution 598, which the Security Council had adopted a year earlier. The letter stipulated that the ceasefire would be effective one month later. The Iranian government intended to minimize the role of Soviet diplomacy by accepting the ceasefire before the Kremlin's representative arrived in Tehran. With the war coming to an end, the Iranians knew they would now be able to do business with Moscow. Major arms and nuclear energy deals were already on the horizon. It was therefore essential for the Iranians not to appear to be indebted to the Soviets. They had been defeated on the battlefield, but they remained excellent negotiators.

On July 19 Tariq Aziz welcomed the Iranians' announcement on behalf of the Iraqi regime, but declared that military operations would continue until the Iranians' intentions were confirmed. A few hours later a dozen MiG-29s and Mirage F-1s ambushed Iranian air-superiority fighters over the Kharg terminal. The Iranians lost one Phantom and two Tomcats, one of which was shot down by a Mirage piloted by Captain Ali Sabah, scoring his fourth officially recognized victory. This engagement convinced Colonel Mansour Sattari, commander-in-chief of the Iranian air force, to put an end to air operations and save what was left of his fleet. His aircraft in flying condition had been reduced to a handful of Tomcats, some twenty Phantoms, and as many Tiger IIs. The next day the Ayatollah Khomeini addressed one of his last major speeches to the international press and accepted the ceasefire: "Taking this decision was more painful and deadly to me than drinking a cup of poison. I trusted in God and

drank the cup of poison to satisfy His decision to stop this bloodbath . . .
I had sworn to fight until my last breath. . . . It would have been more
bearable to me to accept death and martyrdom, but I had to accept the
enlightened opinion of all the military experts."[2]

Final Clashes

UN Secretary General Javier Pérez de Cuéllar immediately invited the
Iraqi and Iranian ministers of foreign affairs to meet in New York to begin
negotiating the terms of the ceasefire. The Iranian delegation notified him
that it would refuse any direct negotiation with Iraqi representatives, for
Tehran considered Saddam Hussein's regime illegitimate.

Since the mullahs were shilly-shallying, Saddam went back on the offensive. On July 22 he launched Operation Tawakalna ala Allah 4 in the
sectors of Qasr-e-Shirin on the central front and Hoveyzeh on the southern
front. This high-impact operation aimed to put pressure on Tehran by
capturing new territory. Saddam committed all his armored and mechanized divisions and the entire Republican Guard. The Iranians did not
have much to pit against these twelve Iraqi divisions comprising more
than 2,000 tanks and 3,000 other armored vehicles. Once again, they were
routed. In four days the Iraqis advanced about thirty miles (about fifty
kilometers) and took more than 8,000 prisoners. In the center, they
captured Qasr-e-Shirin and advanced to Sar-e-Pol-e-Zahab and Geilan
Zarb, opening the road to Kermanshah. In Khuzestan, they took control
of Hoveyzeh and drove through to Hamid, reaching the banks of the
Karun River, some twenty-five miles (forty kilometers) from Ahwaz.

This was the context for Tariq Aziz and Ali Akbar Velayati's first individual meetings with Javier Pérez de Cuéllar in New York on July 26.
Discussions quickly came up against three stumbling blocks: acceptance
of direct negotiations; recognition of the validity of the 1975 Algiers Accord; and prisoner exchanges, for prisoners on both sides refused to return to their native country, either for ideological reasons or out of fear
of retaliation. To increase the pressure on Tehran, Saddam played his final
card: Operation Eternal Light. On July 26 he launched Massoud Rajavi's
People's Mujahidin along the recently reopened road to Kermanshah. In
doing so, he hoped to kill two birds with one stone: to reignite revolt in

Iran and get rid of the troublesome NLAI. Saddam may even have been deliberately trying to wipe out the NLAI to remove a potential subject of tension with Tehran and smooth the path to future normalization.

For the first twenty-four hours the People's Mujahidin advanced about sixty miles (about one hundred kilometers) without encountering any sig nificant resistance. Concerned that the insurrection was coming back to life, the furious Iranian government launched a merciless counterattack, Operation Mersad ("Ambush"), whose sole credo was to take no prisoners. Over three days General Shahbazi and General Shirazi committed their last armored and mechanized forces against the column of mujahidin. The NLAI tried in vain to call the Iraqi air force to the rescue. The Iranians killed several thousand mujahidin and pushed the survivors back to Iraqi lines. This episode led to an unexpected political development in Tehran. Having come to know many of these mujahidin in prison a decade earlier, Ayatollah Montazeri openly protested the massacre and strongly criticized the Ayatollah Khomeini for having failed to oppose their elim- ination. Montazeri only succeeded in drawing the Supreme Leader's ire and the mullahs' sarcasm. He was definitively sidelined. Ali Khamenei and Akbar Hashemi Rafsanjani were exultant. Though they had lost the war, they had permanently removed their rival in the struggle to succeed the Supreme Leader.

In the final days of July Baghdad launched a last series of raids against Iranian oil installations and the Bushehr nuclear power station, which was still under construction. On August 6 the Iranians yielded to military and diplomatic pressure and accepted direct negotiations. That day Saddam Hussein addressed an interminable speech "to the Iraqi people, the Arab nation, and the world," in which he rejoiced in his "very great victory" and gave his agreement for the ceasefire to come into effect, so long as Tehran expressly recognized all the terms and Baghdad recovered the navigation rights it enjoyed on the Shatt al-Arab prior to the outbreak of hostilities. By doing so, he implicitly recognized the validity of the Al- giers Accord, thereby putting an end to the absurd and atrociously bloody war he could have avoided.

The next day the Iranian government confirmed the terms of the cease- fire, accepted direct negotiations, and recognized the right of free passage on the Shatt al-Arab. Combat stopped soon after the announcement, and the Iraqis gradually withdrew from the territories they had recently occupied. At dawn on August 20, 1988, the ceasefire officially became effective along the front, which basically followed the international border. After seven years and eleven months, the war was over. A United Nations-mandated peacekeeping force of 350 observers immediately positioned itself along the ceasefire line to monitor the peace and report the many incidents that would take place over the following months. This Military Observer Group established by Security Council Resolution 619 (August 9, 1988) was headed by the Swede Jan Eliasson, who was the UN secretary general's representative, and the Yugoslav Major-General Slavko Jovic. The group was composed of military observers from twenty-six countries and was not open to those from Arab nations or permanent members of the Security Council. It was dismantled in February 1991 at the beginning of the Gulf War.

The end of hostilities did not spell the end of problems for a number of countries heavily involved in the conflict, including those that remained in a painful diplomatic standoff with the Iranian regime, which still held many Western hostages. This was obviously the case both for the United States, which had just displayed its military might in the Gulf, and for France.

Paris and Tehran Settle Their Accounts

In the summer of 1988 François Mitterrand came to the conclusion that he needed to settle the Iranian question. He charged Roland Dumas, who had returned to head the Ministry of Foreign Affairs, with settling the Eurodif dispute once and for all, no matter the cost. Following Dumas's advice, the government reestablished diplomatic relations with Tehran and made a heavily publicized announcement that it was repatriating the air and sea group (now headed by Admiral Guy Labouérie), which had now spent more than a year in the north of the Indian Ocean. Had its dissuasive presence been sufficient to convince the Iranian government to be more measured in its dealings with France? Or did it only have a marginal effect, leaving most of the work to be accomplished through negotiations? The answer probably lies somewhere between the two.

The French authorities were relieved to see the Iran-Iraq War come to an end. Though Iraq's debt to France had risen to over four billion dollars, Baghdad remained an acceptable commercial partner. Nonetheless, the government refused to agree to the new arms deals eagerly requested by Saddam Hussein. French arms industrialists ultimately had to make do with the seventeen billion dollars they had accumulated over the course of hostilities, not to mention the five billion dollars they had collected during the 1970s and the colossal profits French oil, construction, and nuclear energy companies had reaped in Iraq. This economic boon should not overshadow the cost of France's relationship with the two belligerents: thirteen French nationals were taken hostage, about one hundred were murdered (including the diplomats and military personnel killed in Lebanon), and close to 500 were wounded or maimed in terrorist attacks. In retrospect, this ambiguous position was emblematic of certain unscrupulous industrialists' fraudulent practices, of governmental intrusion in the justice system, and the abstruse manner in which political parties were financed at the time.

In September 1989, a few months after Roland Dumas traveled to Tehran to participate in the commemoration of the tenth anniversary of the Islamic Revolution, France and Iran agreed on the terms of a final settlement of the Eurodif dispute. In July 1990 François Mitterrand granted Anis Naccache and his henchmen the presidential pardon that he had previously opposed. On December 29, 1991, the two countries signed a definitive agreement. France paid Iran a last installment of several hundred million dollars in full settlement of the Eurodif debt.[3] Iran was formally reestablished as a shareholder in the company after having compensated Paris for canceling the Framatome nuclear power plant commission. According to this agreement, Iran would not have the right to enriched uranium produced by the Eurodif factory, but would receive its share of the revenue generated through its participation in the international consortium.[4] On December 23, 2006, Iran's profits were placed in escrow after the UN Security Council passed Resolution 1737, which froze the assets of the Atomic Energy Organization of Iran as part of the international campaign to prevent Iran from clandestinely acquiring the atomic bomb. The dispute is now null and void, as Eurodif was dissolved in 2012 after the permanent closing of the George-Besse factory in Tricastin.

French-Iranian relations took a turn for the worse on August 7, 1991, when an Iranian commando assassinated Shapour Bakhtiar, the former Iranian prime minister who had sought refuge in France. One of the commandos, Ali Vakili Rad, was arrested, tried, sentenced, and imprisoned by the French. His two accomplices managed to escape to Iran. This case would poison French-Iranian relations until May 18, 2010, when Ali Vakili Rad was pardoned and expelled to Iran, two days after the Iranian government freed Clotilde Reiss, a young French academic who had been arbitrarily arrested in Tehran during the demonstrations against the contested reelection of Mahmoud Ahmadinejad in June 2009. Eight days before Clotilde Reiss's release, the French authorities had quietly freed Majid Kakavand, an Iranian engineer arrested in France in 2009. Suspected of being involved in the Iranian nuclear program and facing an extradition request from the United States, Kakavand was allowed to return to Tehran.

A Terribly Deadly War

Human and material losses on both sides of the Iran-Iraq War were horrific. However, they were overestimated, for it was in both sides' interest to exaggerate the number of victims—albeit for different reasons. For Baghdad, it was a matter of proving to the Gulf monarchies that Iraq had valiantly played its role as a shield against Shiite revolutionary expansionism in order to convince them to give up their financial claims on Iraq in return for the blood spilled. The Iraqis also needed to prey on the conscience of the West and the Soviets to encourage them to deliver the regime more arms under favorable payment terms. For Tehran, the point was to reinforce the general focus on Iran's suffering to justify the end of hostilities, increase the sense that Shiites were victimized by Sunnis, and demonize Iraq by blaming it for the extremely brutal internal repression that Iran had carried out throughout the war.

As soon as hostilities came to an end both sides released unverifiable statistics in a morbid attempt to outdo each other. Iraq claimed the loss of more than 350,000 men, while Iran mourned at least 600,000. Analysts and journalists hurriedly repeated these figures, rounding them up to one million dead. *One million,* a nice round figure! Years later, thorough research based on a comparison of the losses from each battle with field studies and generals' accounts reduced this figure by one-third. In an interview with the daily *Al Hayat* (December 1, 2002), General al-Khazraji, who was chief of staff of the armed forces in 1987–1988 and took refuge in Lebanon after breaking with Saddam Hussein, confirmed that the Iraqi army had "only" lost 125,000 men during the war, rather than the 325,000 claimed by the regime.

The war's total human toll stands at 680,000 dead and missing (180,000 Iraqis and 500,000 Iranians) and more than 1.5 million wounded and maimed. The Iran-Iraq War remains by far the most deadly war in the history of the Middle East. Yet the commonly held idea that the proportion of civilian victims was inordinately high (fueled by images of devastated cities) is also false: 85 percent of the dead were soldiers (3.5 times more Iranians than Iraqis). The number of civilians killed by bombings only accounts for 3 percent of the overall death toll. The remaining 12 percent of civilian losses were Kurds killed by both the Iraqis and the Iranians. About 115,000 soldiers are said to have been taken prisoner (70,000 Iraqis and 45,000 Iranians). Their exact number remains impossible to establish, for several thousand prisoners died in captivity, while others were exchanged during the hostilities, changed sides, or refused to go home.[5]

Another reason for the revised, lower toll of deaths and casualties during the war is that while the offensives were extremely deadly, there were more lulls in combat than actual fighting. Over nearly eight years of war soldiers only physically clashed a quarter of the time, with the other three quarters devoted to waiting and preparing for the next offensives. The conflict was thus proportionally less deadly than the First World War, to which it has often been compared. The principal belligerents in the First World War lost an average of 4 percent of their population in four years, while Iran and Iraq lost 1.3 percent of their populations over eight years.

Material losses were also extensive, roughly equivalent to what the Arab and Israeli armies lost during the Six-Day War and the Yom Kippur War combined. Yet these losses were spread over close to eight years, rather than a single month, creating the impression of an endless war of attrition. In total, 9,000 armored vehicles, including 4,600 tanks (2,500 belonging to Iraq, 2,100 to Iran) were destroyed, as well as 1,650 artillery pieces, 950 aircraft (including 485 combat planes: 305 belonging to Iraq, 180 to Iran), and thirty warships, not to mention seventy-two commercial ships crossing the Gulf.

A meticulous analysis of the intensity of human and material losses reveals that the pace of military operations more or less followed the price of oil (intense when it was high; mild when it was low). This conclusion provides after-the-fact confirmation of the cardinal importance of the economic war and any strategy that prioritized targeting oil, which was both belligerents' near-exclusive source of revenue.

This assessment would not be complete without including the war's financial cost, which is estimated at approximately 1,100 billion dollars (1988 dollars, twice its current value), 40 percent of which were spent by Baghdad and 60 percent by Tehran. Due to Iran's isolation and lack of outside financial assistance, Rafsanjani focused on economizing and waged the war like "a good family man"—at least on a financial level. Ultimately, the Iranian regime suffered far more from the combined effect of the collapse of oil prices and the drop of the dollar than from the attacks on its oil tankers and terminals. However, Rafsanjani was far more liberal with the only cheap resource he had in abundance: his soldiers' lives. Unlike Rafsanjani, Saddam Hussein waged war on credit, drawing on loans from the oil monarchies, bank guarantees from the United States, and payment deferments allowed by the Soviets and the West. He proved more sparing with his soldiers' lives, knowing that they remained the best shield to preserve his power. Yet this colossal expense slowed the economic and social development of both countries, which were left considerably weakened by the terrible war that Saddam Hussein continued to affirm was wholly justified under FBI interrogation. He stated:

> What do you do when your neighbor torments your cows, damages your farm, and disrupts your irrigation system? Iran had violated the Algiers Accords and seriously interfered in Iraqi politics.... Khomeini was a religious fanatic persuaded that every leader was like the Shah of Iran—easy to overthrow. Kho-

meini thought he could do the same thing in Iraq. . . . Iraq had no choice but to start the war, in order to put an end to Iran's interference. I must insist on this point, because it is essential. . . . All this was done for the good of the people and humanity. The people love men for their actions. It also loves symbols, and I am a symbol given that my portrait can be found in the homes of Iraqis all over the country. . . . What is important is not what people say or think of me today, but what they will think in 500 or 1,000 years.[6]

Epilogue

The moment the ceasefire came into effect, Saddam Hussein cried victory. He announced the construction of an imposing triumphal arch in Baghdad representing two steel fists holding a pair of crossed swords. This monument, named the Swords of Qadisiyyah, came to represent his defeat of the eternal enemy. The Iraqi dictator did not hesitate to proclaim that he was "certain that in 1,000 years, our people will remember this historic victory over our adversary."[1] Yet beyond the bravado, Saddam was perfectly conscious of having won a Pyrrhic victory. He knew that Iraq's finances were in a catastrophic state. In fact, he was faced with a no-win situation: he could demobilize the army and reintegrate a large number of former soldiers into civilian life, many of whom were affected by the war and destined to join the ranks of the unemployed, or keep the army as it was, with the knowledge that doing so would require him to find a way to keep the military occupied while finding new revenue to finance its upkeep. The size of the armed forces had quadrupled over the last eight years, but oil revenue had diminished by 50 percent.

On August 24, 1988, Tariq Aziz and Ali Akbar Velayati began direct peace negotiations in Geneva. Meanwhile, the Iraqi army took advantage of the end of hostilities with Iran to turn against the Kurdish militia and mercilessly hunt down PUK, KDP, and KDSP peshmergas, sparking outrage around the world. On September 3 "Chemical Ali" proudly announced the end of Operation Anfal and the total liberation of Iraqi territory, proclaiming the eradication of the Kurdish rebellion. The combat in late August, during which 400 Iraqi soldiers had been killed, had provoked a massive exodus of peshmergas and their families (more than 100,000 people) to Turkey, Syria, and Iran.

On September 22 Iran withdrew the Pasdaran from the Farsi, Abu Musa, and Greater Tunb islands and participated in demining operations in the Strait of Hormuz. On September 25 the United States ended the Earnest Will naval convoy operation and announced that it was reducing its naval presence in the Gulf.[2] On October 1 Iran reestablished diplomatic relations with Saudi Arabia, Kuwait, and Bahrain, as well as most European nations, including the United Kingdom, which immediately withdrew the Armilla Patrol from the region. Three weeks later Tehran ended its tanker shuttles and announced that the Kharg terminal was reopening to maritime traffic. Baghdad increased the port of Umm Qasr's export capacity while waiting for the Mina al-Bakr and Khor al-Amaya terminals to be rebuilt. Lloyd's followed by reducing its insurance rates for ships crossing the Persian Gulf to prewar levels. The Iranians and Iraqis began rebuilding the Abadan and Basra refineries. By the end of the year Iran and Iraq's oil production would grow to more than two million barrels per day, which financed the reconstruction of their destroyed infrastructures.

In a speech before the Iranian Parliament on November 19 Akbar Hashemi Rafsanjani excluded the possibility of renewed hostilities. Five days later Tehran and Baghdad exchanged their wounded prisoners, opening the way to a full prisoner exchange, a process that would take twenty-one months. On December 29 the two governments agreed to create a joint military commission to consolidate the implementation of the ceasefire and avoid incidents that could reignite the conflict. Both sides' armed forces returned to their prewar positions.

On February 14, 1989, the Ayatollah Khomeini issued a fatwa (religious decree) sentencing the British writer Salman Rushdie to death for blasphemy after the publication of his famous *Satanic Verses*. The Supreme Leader was undoubtedly trying to create a diversion from Iran's defeat by Iraq, as well as detract attention from Iranian internal problems and affirm the strength of Shia Islam so as to present himself as the champion of the Muslim world. By doing so, he forced the entire Iranian political class to radicalize itself again, putting a sudden halt to the overtures made to the West. To the bitter end, the old lion would prove uncompromising with all those he accused of playing into the hands of the United States and authoritarian secular Islamic regimes.

On May 5, 1989, Adnan Khairallah, Iraq's charismatic minister of defense, was killed in the explosion of his helicopter during an inspection tour in Kurdistan. His death immediately gave rise to an abundance of rumors. One theory blamed Saddam Hussein, positing that Saddam wanted to get rid of his first cousin because his growing popularity was overshadowing his own. Today most accounts, including those of former generals, blame Saddam's sons and one of his sons-in-law.[3] Uday, Qusay, and Hussein Kamel allegedly agreed to eliminate the man they saw as their main rival to succeed the dictator. In the event of Saddam's death, the three men planned to create a younger executive committee to replace their father and father-in-law. By losing Adnan Khairallah, Iraq lost one of its best generals and one of the very few people able to reason with Saddam Hussein. His death was accompanied by the sidelining of General Ma'ahir Abdul Rashid, who was suspected of harboring excessive ambitions.

On June 3, 1989, the Ayatollah Khomeini died of internal bleeding at the age of eighty-six. Saddam Hussein exulted in the news, hoping that Khomeini's death would accelerate Iran's normalization process and allow him to move forward with other projects. Legend has it that the Supreme Leader called Akbar Hashemi Rafsanjani and Ali Khamenei to his deathbed so he could take advantage of his last moments of lucidity to appoint them to their future roles. The truth appears more prosaic. When the two men entered the Ayatollah Khomeini's bedroom, he was no longer able to speak. This gave them a few minutes to divide power between themselves. At that moment Rafsanjani made the only mistake of his long political career. He allowed Ali Khamenei to succeed Khomeini as Supreme Leader, despite the fact that he had excellent arguments to claim the position for himself: he was older (fifty-four, while Khamenei was forty-nine), more qualified and charismatic, and had far better connections than his rival. Yet these were precisely the assets that persuaded him that he would enjoy more power as president. He was certain that he would gain the upper hand by using his network, his fortune, and the institutions, and that Ali Khamenei lacked the charisma to match the Ayatollah Khomeini's influence. The rest is history. Both men were made ayatollahs. After waiting for so long, they had finally reached the top rung of Iranian power. They would share it for many years. The Assembly of Experts appointed Ali Khamenei as the new Supreme Leader, while Akbar Hashemi Rafsanjani was elected, then reelected, president of the Republic, before being appointed to head the Expediency Discernment Council, then the Assembly of Experts.

Now that they no longer needed Mir-Hossein Mousavi, the two men modified the Constitution to do away with the position of prime minister. Mousavi slipped into obscurity for twenty years, then returned to politics at the head of the opposition in the 2009 presidential election. While Akbar Hashemi Rafsanjani apparently remained the regime's most influential figure, Ali Khamenei always had the last word on the most crucial issues. The rivalry has shifted into hatred and remains relevant twenty-six years later, though Rafsanjani has been marginalized by the Supreme Leader and lost some of his luster—which has not prevented him from continuing to pull a few strings. The duel will only come to an end with the death of its protagonists. In the meantime, younger leaders will have replaced them.

As soon as he was elected president Akbar Hashemi Rafsanjani focused on Iran's economic recovery by giving its citizens a single watchword: "Get rich!"[4] For his part, Saddam Hussein struggled with his Arab neighbors to raise the price of oil and increase his OPEC production quotas so he could finance a military apparatus that was becoming more expensive by the day. He openly threatened Emir Jaber of Kuwait, who insisted on maintaining very low oil prices and refused to forgive the financial debt Iraq had accumulated during the war, while King Fahd had been wise enough to forgive the debt across the board. On August 20, 1990, Iraq withdrew from its last occupied territories in Iran, putting a definitive end to the war between the two countries. Eighteen days earlier Saddam Hussein had invaded Kuwait, setting off "the mother of all battles." But that's another story.

A New Geopolitical Situation

Let's return to the Iran-Iraq War. In the late summer of 1988 Ba'athist Iraq emerged as the primary military power in the Gulf. Baghdad had four times as many tanks, armored vehicles, and cannons and six times as many combat aircraft as Tehran. After the slaughter of the summer offensives the Iraqi army, which now comprised fifty divisions, even surpassed the Iranian army in terms of troop numbers. Iran's generals announced that it would take them ten years to regain strategic parity with Iraq, which they estimated would require the acquisition of 2,500 tanks, 2,000 artillery pieces, and several hundred combat aircraft.[5] The Iraqi army was also three times stronger than all the Gulf Cooperation Council's armies put together. Feeling invulnerable, Saddam Hussein was confident that he had achieved regional leadership. The oil monarchies drew the conclusion that they needed to buy more weapons and accept Western military forces on their soil to protect themselves from Iran's desire for revenge and Iraq's voracity.

In psychological terms, the war acted as a catalyst on Saddam Hussein. The dictator discovered his interest for military matters, learning as he went, which would later lead him to bypass his chiefs of staff. Believing that he was competent enough to do without his generals' advice, Saddam would make the disastrous decision to invade Kuwait. He was convinced that his fierce determination had led to his victory over Iran and that he had been right not to yield. He considered that the United States had been inconstant, showing its weak character and fickleness. He further believed that the Gulf monarchies would never dare to contest his leadership.

In Tehran, the ceasefire had left a bitter taste of defeat. The mullahs felt humiliated that they had been forced to concede the status quo and that an eight-year war had yielded only their failure to defeat a state three times smaller than their own. Nonetheless, the regime had succeeded in reaching one of its primary goals: it had durably established itself in Iran.

Paradoxically, Turkey emerged as the war's primary beneficiary. The conflict allowed it to redress its economy (it had earned twelve billion dollars by selling the belligerents consumer goods, plus the commission on weapons transiting through its territory), stockpile cheap oil, establish its regional stature, and bolster its relationship with the United States. Its construction companies were contracted for numerous reconstruction projects, both in Iraq and Iran. The only cloud on the horizon was that the war had reinforced Kurdish nationalism and driven the PKK to launch a relentless guerilla war, which would claim 35,000 lives over nearly thirty years.

The conflict's other beneficiary was undoubtedly King Fahd of Saudi Arabia, who had allowed his kingdom to emerge as the Gulf's third major power after Iraq and Iran. Before the war, Saudi Arabia had merely been seen as a gigantic reserve of oil and dollars. It was now recognized as a regional power and an essential player. The Custodian of the Two Holy Mosques had shrewdly maneuvered to contain Iran without directly confronting it, get in Iraq's good graces while making Baghdad dependent on him, reinforce his strategic alliance with the United States, and open up to China and the Soviet Union.

As for the United States, France, and Great Britain, they had realized they needed to establish—or in the case of Britain, reestablish—a military presence in the Gulf to secure their energy sources. By agreeing with Saudi Arabia to radically reduce oil prices, the United States had precipitated the Soviet Union's economic collapse and lastingly weakened Iran.[6] The Americans, French, and British did not come gladly to the Gulf, but they soon reaped the benefits of their presence by making large-scale energy and weapons deals. The network of alliances forged at this time remains relevant in dealing with the current Iranian and Iraqi crises.

The war had mixed effects on the Soviet Union. Weapons sales to the belligerents had allowed the USSR to collect some forty billion dollars, which had helped it meet immediate economic needs, but the irreparable damage to the relationship between Moscow and Baghdad meant the Kremlin had lost a major ally in the region. Despite the efforts of Yevgeny Primakov, indefatigable advocate of Russian-Arab relations, to put the pieces back together, Saddam Hussein had understood that he could no longer truly count on the Kremlin, though it would continue to honor existing contracts. Saddam paid a heavy price for this deteriorated relationship when Moscow dropped him altogether during the Kuwait crisis. On the other hand, the Russians had managed to become closer with Iran. As a testament to this spectacular thawing of relations between Moscow and Tehran, a large Iranian delegation accepted the Kremlin's invitation to visit the Soviet Union from June 20 to 23, 1989. The trip included the first face-to-face encounter between Rafsanjani and Mikhail Gorbachev. The two leaders immediately connected. After discussing the reinforcement of commercial and energy relations between their two countries,[7] they agreed to sign a huge arms contract by which the USSR committed to delivering Iran large quantities of state-of-the-art equipment.[8] In the early 1990s Gorbachev and Rafsanjani would also agree to have the Soviet Union take over construction of the Bushehr nuclear power plant.

While they had gained a major commercial partner, the Russians had not found an ally to replace Iraq. The Iranians continued to be suspicious of the Soviets. They had not forgotten that part of their country had remained under Russian, then Soviet, influence for close to a century. The mullahs were determined not to fall back under the Kremlin's control and regularly warned their Russian interlocutors not to meddle in Iranian affairs. On a regional level, Moscow could pride itself on having extended its influence by opening a dialogue with the Arab monarchies, though these exchanges remained discreet. Nonetheless, Kuwait, Saudi Arabia, Qatar, and the United Arab Emirates had reached a better understanding of the Soviet Union. They realized that the USSR was not necessarily aiming to destabilize the region and that it might in fact be in the Soviets' best interest to stabilize it. Indeed, Moscow was concerned by the resurgence of agitation in Muslim republics and sought to avoid Islamic protest spreading there. This change of attitude led Kuwait, the United Arab Emirates, and Oman to establish diplomatic relations with Moscow.

Like the USSR, China and North Korea had taken advantage of the war to do good business with Iran and Iraq (twelve billion dollars' worth of weapons and ammunition delivered to both belligerents) and reinforced their commercial presence in the Gulf. By buying large amounts of Iranian oil, Beijing had gradually imposed itself as one of the rare capitals that could put pressure on Tehran.

The lifting of the Iraqi threat for a few years had allowed Israel to chase the PLO out of Lebanon, but at what cost? In the Arab nations, Iran's defeat bolstered the modernist camp against the Islamic fundamentalists, putting the brakes on the political Islam disseminated by Tehran. Political Islam would only return to the forefront in a more nationalist iteration, with the rise to power of the Justice and Development Party (AKP) in Turkey, followed by the spread of Arab revolts in 2011.

What Military Lessons Can Be Retained?

The Iran-Iraq War was the twentieth century's last total war, by which we mean a war in which two nations fight each other without restrictions and commit all their human, material, economic, and political potential. This hellish confrontation mobilized up to two million soldiers, 10,000 armored vehicles (half of which were tanks), 4,000 artillery pieces, and 1,000 aircraft at one time. It can be seen as a distillation of twentieth-century warfare, with aspects reminiscent both of the First World War (trench warfare, human waves, gas attacks) and the Second World War (use of armored vehicles, bombing of cities, economic warfare), as well as of the Israeli-Arab conflict (jet plane battles over the desert, extensive use of missiles) and wars of insurrection such as those in Algeria and Vietnam (ambushes in rocky hillsides, infiltration through marshland). The most prosaic combat techniques were used side by side with the most sophisticated.

This war demonstrated that quality did not always make up for quantity, and vice versa. It showed once again that it is impossible to win without a clear sense of the objectives sought and a coherent strategy based on an appropriate forces employment doctrine. It served as a reminder of the importance of military intelligence, troop training and motivation, flexibility of the chain of command, and awareness of the environment, both in terms of weather and terrain. The Iranians and Iraqis did not fight the same way in summer and in winter, in the city and in the mountains, in desert areas and in marshlands. The war also underlined the crucial role played by the engineering corps (defensive construction, crossing the Hoveyzeh marshes and Shatt al-Arab) and logistics. Without a reactive and well-developed supply chain and colossal stockpiles of ammunition, the Iraqi army would probably not have held the front throughout the war. Iranian offensives failed because the Pasdaran ran out of ammunition at the decisive moment, just as their adversary was weakening.

The Iran-Iraq War was also characterized by the normalization of chemical weapons and ballistic missiles (more than 480 Scuds were fired by both belligerents), which had a significant psychological impact despite the fact that they were relatively inaccurate and ten times less deadly than regular artillery. Nonetheless, the risk of chemical weapon proliferation convinced the United Nations to adopt an international convention banning their use, manufacture, and storage. This convention, adopted on January 13, 1993, led to the destruction of stocks and the implementation of highly intrusive verification measures, which now apply to practically every nation, including the five permanent members of the Security Council. Ultimately, neither the Iranians nor the Iraqis derived a decisive advantage from their massive violations of the law of war and international human rights law.

On land, the Iranians proved more imaginative than the Iraqis in developing innovative tactics, particularly in the realm of light infantry. This did not prevent them from losing the war. Rivalries and lack of coordination between the regular army and the Pasdaran were responsible for many of their failures, proving that command unity remains one of the fundamental principles of warfare.

In the air, the Iraqis showed an unbridled imagination, developing innovative tactics and readily converting their transport and reconnaissance planes to carry out combat missions. The Iranians attempted to use guided drones, but were not able to pursue this project due to lack of funds. Contrary to commonly held beliefs, aerial activity was sustained throughout the entire conflict, though Iranian pilots gradually reduced the pace of their sorties due to lack of munitions and spare parts.[9] Electronic warfare and in-flight refueling played a determining part. The intensity of air combat during the conflict is attested to by the roughly 900 aircraft destroyed more than a third of which were flown by air-superiority fighters). Iranian pilots dominated the skies, achieving a total of 244 victories versus seventy for the opposing camp. While close to three-quarters of the Iraqi aircraft destroyed were brought down by Iranian air-superiority fighters, 60 percent of Iranian aerial losses were due to Iraqi surface-to-air defense. Friendly fire proved inevitable, costing each side a dozen aircraft.

In the naval realm, combat confirmed the redoubtable effectiveness of Exocet and Harpoon-type missiles, which could race toward their targets along the water line. The Iraqis used these weapons immoderately, firing more than 500 Exocets during the conflict. On the other hand, Silkworm missiles proved too big, too slow, easy to decoy, and generally ill suited for air and sea combat. The clashes that took place in the Gulf in 1987 and 1988 demonstrated that it was impossible to durably ban navigation in the Strait of Hormuz, no matter the effort exerted by Iran. During this standoff Western sailors rediscovered mine warfare and convoy escorts, which they had not been exposed to since the end of the Second World War. These lessons remain profoundly relevant at a time when Iran is threatening once again to close this strategic strait in case of a military intervention on its soil.

Finally, the Iran-Iraq War served as a laboratory for weapon manu-
acturers to test their new technological finds. Strides in the fields of missiles and electronic warfare were the most significant advances of those
eight years. Their use in real conditions showed manufacturers that a
weapon system's sophistication also needed to translate to simplicity of
operation—a weapon that is overly fragile or too complicated to apply in
fail-safe mode is useless. In many cases, the combatants' best friend turned
out to be simplicity. The intensive use of Scud-type missiles convinced certain manufacturers to begin designing antimissile systems. In 1991
American troops in the Gulf were protected by the first Patriot missiles,
which were famously designed to strike Iraqi Scud, Al Hussein, and Al
Abbas missiles in flight.

Are the Political Lessons Applicable Today?

The consequences of the Iran-Iraq War remain perceptible to this day,
whether in the radicalization of the Iranian regime and the revival of its
nuclear program or the marginalization of Iraq.

In Iran, the war served as a framework and excuse for the brutal power
struggle that continues to rage a quarter of a century later. It allowed the
most radical members of the clergy to gradually eliminate the nonreli-
gious revolutionary fringe (Bazargan, Bani-Sadr), the idealist religious
movement (Montazeri), the radical opposition (Peykar, People's Mujahidin, Communist Party), and the insurrectionary movements demanding
independence for the Kurdish, Baloch, and Azeri provinces. The war allowed the clergy to take power in the summer of 1981 and maintain a
stranglehold on it to the present day. However, veterans—particularly Pasdaran veterans—have since formed an increasingly powerful pressure
group. They have sought to take political and economic power to at long
last claim their slice of the pie, criticizing the clergy and the powerbro-
kers of the Bazaar for dodging combat and getting rich off their backs
during the war. Mahmoud Ahmadinejad used this populist platform to
get elected president of the Republic in June 2005.

Faced with internal disorder, rampant pauperization due to economic sanctions, and the reformist opposition's failure to overcome its
byzantine quarrels and offer a credible and durable alternative, certain

charismatic Pasdaran figures who rose to prominence during the wa
might succumb to the temptation of Bonapartism, particularly in case o
the death of the current Supreme Leader, Ali Khamenei. This militaris
faction would naturally receive support from the Revolutionary Guards
which seems more than ever to be the true arbiter of Iranian politics. Mos
Iranians today appear to be awaiting a strong, pragmatic, and coheren
government that would protect the country from outside interference, senc
the clergy back to the mosques (so that they stop presiding over worldly
matters and the minutiae of daily life), and reopen Iran to the outside
world to allow for the economic development of a country that has been
living in near-autarky for more than thirty years.

The current regime probably allowed the election of a more outwardly
acceptable president of the Republic than Mahmoud Ahmadinejad to
avoid just such a power play and lay the groundwork for a more constructive dialogue with the West, which could eventually lead to a lifting of
economic sanctions and the normalization of diplomatic relations with
Washington. This seems to be the direction favored by President Barack
Obama and European leaders. Yet while Hassan Rouhani has long cam-
paigned for opening up Iran to the outside world, he remains a product
of the Iranian clerical system that shaped him and to which he belongs.
Like his mentor Rafsanjani, he will not hesitate to use doubletalk and
asymmetric methods if necessary. Once again, one must not confuse "reformist spirit" with "need for openness." However, Western normalization of relations with Iran would appease tensions in the Gulf and allow
energy strategy diversification, as well as the resolution of numerous
thorny issues, notably in Syria and Lebanon. There are three potential obstacles to normalization: first, the lashing out of Iranians in the case of
an unexpected upheaval (e.g., the death of the Supreme Leader, new protests, a Pasdaran power play, etc.); next, obstruction by the American Congress, which is caught in a systematic campaign to denigrate President
Obama's initiatives; finally, the openly stated opposition of Israel and
Saudi Arabia, which fear their regional positions could be weakened.

No matter who winds up on top in Iran, a careful study of the Iran-
Iraq War will provide the keys to deciphering the regime's current and
future behavior. First, despite its customary saber rattling, the Iranian
leadership is perfectly rational and pragmatic and thoroughly understands
the notions of ratio of power and deterrence. It systematically manipu-

lates external tensions to internal ends, rallying its troops and reinforcing one faction's influence over another's. The rivalry between Rafsanjani, Khamenei, and Montazeri has given way to political struggles between younger leaders (Khatami, Rouhani, Ali Larijani, Ghalibaf), but the logic of the conquest of power remains the same. Any military intervention against Iran would only reinforce the regime by uniting the population behind it, rather than weakening it. The Iranian government also remains careful with its money. It is aware that many states are prepared to buy its oil, or even sell it weapons, but none are ready to lend it money. In other words, economic war—now referred to as "economic sanctions"—works with Tehran. So long, of course, as the instigator has enough time for sanctions to take effect and is ready to truly dry up the Iranian economy, at the risk of making its population pay the price.

It is also important to remember that the Iranian government practices asymmetric warfare and does not hesitate to strike first to take its opponent by surprise. Iran has a real ability to do harm. During the war it readily used other states and militias to carry out kidnappings and terrorist attacks, attacked oil infrastructures, and laid mines and fired missiles in the Gulf. Iran could conceivably undertake similar actions now or in the future if it thought that it were in its interest or if it felt forced to do so. Finally—and this is probably the crucial point—the war showed that the Iranian government only yielded when it was convinced that its adversary was on the verge of doing it great harm, either militarily or economically. Experience shows that before engaging in a process of direct or indirect confrontation with the Iranian regime, whether in Syria, Lebanon, Iraq, Iran (with strikes against its nuclear program, for instance), or elsewhere, a state must carefully analyze the impact of its actions, notably their harmful consequences. This does not imply that it is wrong to act, merely that one must be conscious of all of an action's potential repercussions and be ready to respond to them with the suitable resources. A confrontation with Iranian power must by no means be taken lightly and entered upon impulsively or as a gamble. Such a decision should result from a thoroughly considered strategy aimed at achieving truly crucial objectives.

Let's turn to Iraq. The American withdrawal in 2011 exacerbated the power struggle that had been reinitiated by the dismantling of the Ba'ath Party in 2003. Shiites, Sunnis, and Kurds are battling for control of the country and its resources. After monopolizing power under Saddam, the Sunnis are now on the losing end, for Iraq's oil fields are located primarily in Shiite and Kurdish provinces. It is no surprise to see many Sunnis lose hope, become radical, and turn to terrorism, particularly since they are supported by Arab states worried about the potential appearance of a Shiite axis between the Mediterranean and Tehran. The Iraqi crisis could endure; every one of Iraq's neighbors has an objective interest in maintaining a weak Iraqi state while ensuring it a minimum of stability. A powerful Iraq is frightening, but to its neighbors the idea of a failed and dismantled Iraq is even more disturbing. In this poisonous context, Iraqi leadership in any form could be tempted to reestablish national unity based on the three sacred causes that Baghdad has always used to manipulate the Iraqi people: the "reconquest" of the Kurdish provinces, of Kuwait (still quietly claimed as Iraq's nineteenth province), and of the Shatt al-Arab, which certain Iraqis dream of recapturing in its entirety. The two first options now seem out of reach. Turkey guarantees the security of the Iraqi Kurds, with whom it has made commercial and energy agreements vital to its economy. Through a far-reaching accord signed with Abdullah Öcalan in March 2013, Turkey committed to protecting the Kurds in exchange for the PKK giving up arms. The United States guarantees Kuwait's security and would be ready to go back to war to protect this oil-rich, key bridgehead in the Gulf.

That leaves the question of the Shatt al-Arab, which is constantly put back on the table by the populist Iraqi press. Tehran's attempt to acquire the nuclear bomb or, at least, "nuclear capacity," may simply be an attempt to avoid history repeating itself. Despite its repeated denials, the Iranian government is convinced that it must do everything in its power to avoid another tragedy like the war with Iraq. This explains why development of the nuclear program is one of the rare consensual subjects in the otherwise heavily divided Iranian political class. If the atomic bomb had been invented after the First World War, it is more than likely that the most damaged European states would immediately have sought to acquire it.

APPENDIXES

NOTES

SOURCES

ACKNOWLEDGMENTS

INDEX

Chronology

636

The Arabs defeat the Persians at the Battle of al-Qadisiyyah near Najaf, in Iraq. The Arab caliphate now extends over the entire region.

680

The Shiite Imam Hussein is defeated at the Battle of Karbala, in Iraq. The Sunni Caliphate triumphs and controls Iraq until the Mongol invasions (thirteenth through fourteenth centuries).

1503

Shia Islam becomes Persia's official religion under Shah Ismail I. Ismail establishes the Shia holy cities of Qom and Mashhad to compete with those of Najaf and Karbala in Iraq. The wars between the Persian and Ottoman empires begin.

1555

The Treaty of Amasya is signed: Persia renounces any claim to Iraq and the Shatt al-Arab.

1639

The Treaty of Qasr-e-Shirin confirms the terms of the Treaty of Amasya. Persians and Ottomans clash over control of the province of Khuzestan-Arabistan.

1746

The Treaty of Constantinople confirms previous treaties: Iraq and the Shatt al-Arab belong to the Ottoman Empire. Arabistan becomes an Ottoman protectorate.

1837

Emir Haji Jabir Bin Mirdao founds the Emirate of Muhammara (Khorramshahr), which includes most of Arabistan.

1847

May 31: The Treaty of Erzerum provides the first precise delimitation of the border between the Ottoman and Persian empires. The Ottoman Empire retains control of Iraq and the Shatt al-Arab. The Persian Empire gains Khuzestan (Arabistan) and obtains the right of free navigation on the Shatt al-Arab. The Shah of Persia recognizes the Emirate of Muhammara's autonomous status.

1913

November 4: The Constantinople Protocol sets the border between the Ottoman and Persian empires. The only notable difference between the Constantinople Protocol and the previous treaties is that the islets on the Shatt al-Arab come under Persian control.

1920

December: After the fall of the Ottoman Empire, the League of Nations grants the United Kingdom a mandate over Iraq. The Qajar Dynasty's Persian Empire collapses. London suspends support to the Emirate of Muhammara. Russian troops occupy the north of Persia.

1924

Reza Khan Pahlavi seizes power and has himself crowned Shah of Iran. The following year, he reconquers the Emirate of Muhammara, which becomes part of the province of Khuzestan.

1930

June 30: Iraq gains its independence and becomes a Hashemite monarchy governed by King Faisal. Iraqi nationalism develops in the Iraqi army. Tensions increase between Iraq and Iran.

1937

July 18: The Treaty of Tehran confirms the 1913 Constantinople Protocol, but states that the river border between Iraq and Iran runs along the thalweg on a narrow stretch of the Shatt al-Arab between Khorramshahr (Muhammara) and Abadan.

1941

April–May: The British army suppresses a pro-German military coup d'état in Iraq.

September: The United Kingdom and the Soviet Union occupy Iran and overthrow the Shah. He is replaced by his son Mohammad Reza Pahlavi, who becomes the new Shah of Iran. Occupation troops leave Iran in 1946.

1958

July 14: General Abd al-Karim Qasim overthrows the Iraqi monarchy and establishes closer ties with the Soviets. He is overthrown by Abdel Salam Aref (in 1963), who is in turn assassinated and replaced by his brother Abdel Rahman (in 1966). There are violent clashes with Iraqi Kurds and there is a resurgence of tensions between Iraq and Iran.

1967

June: Baghdad breaks diplomatic relations with Washington at the end of the Six-Day War.

1968

July 17: The Ba'ath Party takes power in Iraq. General al-Bakr becomes president. He is assisted by Saddam Hussein, who is appointed second-in-command of the Revolutionary Command Council.

1969

April 19: The Shah reneges on the Treaty of Tehran (1937), claims shared sovereignty of the Shatt al-Arab, and actively supports Iraqi Kurd militias.

1970

March 11: The Iraqi government grants autonomy to the Kurds, who still enjoy the material support of the Shah of Iran. Saddam Hussein becomes vice president of the Republic. There is a final break between the Syrian and Iraqi branches of the Ba'ath Party after Hafez al-Assad takes power in Damascus.

1971

December: The United Kingdom completes its withdrawal from the Gulf. Oman, the United Arab Emirates, Qatar, and Bahrain declare independence. Iran seizes three small islands near the Strait of Hormuz claimed by the UAE (Abu Musa, Greater and Lesser Tunbs). The United States and the United Kingdom invest Iran as "policeman" of the Gulf. Massive American and British arms shipments to the Iranian army begin.

1972

April 9: Signing of the Friendship and Cooperation Treaty between Iraq and the USSR. Moscow delivers modern weapons to Baghdad. The Iraqi government begins a special partnership with France in order to diversify its supply sources.

June 1: The Iraqi oil industry becomes nationalized. The Ba'athist regime launches an ambitious program to reform and modernize Iraqi society.

June 18: Saddam Hussein travels to Paris to secure a French-Iraqi oil agreement.

1973

October 6–25: Iraq participates in the Israeli-Arab Yom Kippur War and develops closer ties with the Gulf monarchies.

1974

March: Mustafa Barzani's KDP (supported by Iran, the United States, and Israel) declares the independence of Iraqi Kurdistan. Heavy combat between the Iraqi army and Kurdish rebels ensues. Several thousand Iranian infantrymen fight beside the Kurdish peshmergas.

June 27: Iran and France sign a civil nuclear cooperation agreement.

December: France agrees to deliver sophisticated weapons to Iraq. It concurrently accepts a one-billion-dollar loan from the Shah of Iran to build the Eurodif nuclear enrichment plant.

1975

March 6: The Algiers Accord between the Shah and Saddam Hussein is signed. Iraq recognizes shared sovereignty of the Shatt al-Arab. The new river border between the two countries is the subject of a protocol appended to the Treaty of Neighborly Relation, which is signed in Baghdad on June 13. Now lacking any external support, the Kurdish rebellion collapses. Jalal Talabani takes the opportunity to found the PUK, the rival to Mustafa Barzani's KDP.

June 24: The Saïda Agreement is signed, by which the Lebanese Shiite community recognizes the authority of the Iranian clergy represented by the Ayatollah Khomeini, who has been in exile in Iraq since 1964.

November 18: Iraq and France sign a civil nuclear cooperation agreement.

1978

October 5: The Ayatollah Khomeini leaves Iraq to take asylum in France, at Neauphle-le-Château.

December: Protests against the Shah's regime peak in Iran.

1979

January 16: Mohammad Reza Pahlavi leaves Iran. Shapour Bakhtiar steps in as acting prime minister.

February 1: The Ayatollah Khomeini makes a triumphant return to Tehran. This is the beginning of the Islamic Revolution in Iran. There is an acceleration of the Iraqi nuclear program.

April 2: The Islamic Republic of Iran is proclaimed. Anti-Western purges become increasingly violent. Several Kurdish, Arab, Azeri, and Baloch regionalist factions become dissident movements.

April 9: Iran denounces the nuclear cooperation agreement with France and demands reimbursement of the loan granted by the Shah. This is the beginning of the Eurodif dispute, which will sour French-Iranian relations for a decade. France increases its military assistance to Iraq.

May 5: The Islamic Revolutionary Guards Corps (IRGC) is created.

July 16: Saddam Hussein takes power in Baghdad and launches major purges in the army and Ba'ath Party.

July 28: Saddam Hussein denounces a Syrian plot to overthrow him. The failure of the projected union between Iraq and Syria pushes Syria to ally itself with Iran.

August–September: There are informal attempts at a rapprochement between Washington and Tehran.

October 22: The United States grants the Shah asylum.

October 30: Saddam Hussein puts the question of the Shatt al-Arab's status back on the table.

November 4: The American Embassy in Tehran is attacked: about fifty Americans are held hostage for more than fourteen months.

November 7: The Basij Corps is created in Iran. Mohammad-Ali Rajai (who has close ties to the clergy) replaces Mehdi Bazargan (secular) at the head of the Iranian government.

November 20: There is a bloody hostage taking in Mecca. Major tensions grow between Sunni and Shiite communities.

December 3: The Iranian Constitution is adopted, establishing an Islamic Republic and providing for the balance of power between secular and religious institutions. Tension between Iraq and Iran revives.

December 26: The Soviet army invades Afghanistan.

1980

January 23: The "Carter Doctrine," aimed at securing the Middle East, is announced.

January 25: Bani-Sadr is elected president of the Republic in Iran. Internal struggles escalate between progressives and the Islamic Party for actual control of power.

April 1: There is a failed assassination attempt on Tariq Aziz in Baghdad, which is blamed on a Shiite Iraqi. Ayatollah al-Sadr, leader of the Iraqi Shiite community, is executed. Tension escalates between Iraq and Iran.

April 7: The United States breaks diplomatic relations with Iran.

April 24: Operation Eagle Claw to free the hostages in Iran is a fiasco.

July 9–10: A failed military plot in Iran leads to bloody purges in the army. The fight against Kurdish, Arab, Baloch, and Azeri rebels intensifies.

July 16: Saddam Hussein asks his chiefs of staff to prepare for war.

July 18: Anis Naccache, the head of an Iranian commando unit that attempted to assassinate Shapour Bakhtiar, and exiled in France, is arrested.

August 5–6: Saddam Hussein travels to Saudi Arabia to inform King Khalid that he has decided to wage a "military crusade" against Iran.

September 4: The Iranian artillery shells Iraqi border positions. This is the beginning of a war of attrition that will last until the outbreak of hostilities.

September 17: Saddam Hussein denounces the Algiers Accord of March 6, 1975.

September 22, 1980: Beginning of the Iran-Iraq War. The Iraqi army launches an air offensive and penetrates about twenty miles (about thirty kilometers) into Iranian territory. There are confused reactions on the international scene.

September 28: The UN Security Council adopts Resolution 479, calling for the belligerents to put an end to hostilities. Saddam Hussein states he is prepared to call off his offensive if Iran accepts comprehensive negotiation.

September 30: The United States announces it is dispatching one cruiser and four AWACS in the Gulf. The Iranian air force bombs the Iraqi Osirak nuclear reactor. Iraqi troops grind to a halt outside Khorramshahr, Ahwaz, and Dezful.

October 1: Saddam Hussein unilaterally decrees a one-week operational break. Iran decrees a maritime blockade of Iraq.

October 12: The Iranian government establishes the Supreme Defense Council to more closely supervise the army's activity and reinforce the IRGC's power.

October 14: Beginning of the Iraqi army's siege of Abadan.

October 24: The Iraqis take control of Khorramshahr.

November 18: A mediation mission is undertaken by Olof Palme, the United Nations special representative to the belligerents.

November 27–29: The Iranians reinforce their maritime blockade by winning an air and sea battle at the mouth of the Shatt al-Arab. The Iraqi navy is out of commission.

December 10: The Iraqis are now on the defensive. **End of the war's first phase.**

December 24: The Iraqis massively bomb the Kharg oil terminal and open a new front in Iranian Kurdistan.

1981

January 5–8: The first Iranian counteroffensive fails.

January 15: The Iraqi army penetrates Iranian Kurdistan.

January 19: In Algiers, Washington and Tehran agree to the terms of the release of the American hostages. They are freed the next day, while Ronald Reagan is being sworn in at the White House.

April 1: There is general insurrection in Iranian Kurdistan, supported by Baghdad.

April 4: A spectacular Iranian air raid on the Iraqi H-3 base succeeds.

April 12: In Baghdad, first discussions between Americans and Iraqis are held.

May 25: The Gulf Cooperation Council (GCC) is created.

June 7: The Israeli air force destroys the Iraqi Osirak nuclear reactor.

June 20: In Iran, President Bani-Sadr is removed from power. One month later, he escapes to France with Massoud Rajavi, head of the People's Mujahidin.

June 21: The Iranian minister of defense dies in a plane accident.

June 28: The leaders of the Iranian Islamic Party are killed in a terrorist attack attributed to the People's Mujahidin. The clergy reacts by taking power in Tehran.

July 3: Saddam Hussein proposes another truce.

July 28: Mohammad-Ali Rajai is elected president of the Republic of Iran. He and his prime minister are killed in a terrorist attack one month later.

September 4: French ambassador Louis Delamare is assassinated in Beirut. This is the beginning of a series of terrorist attacks against French interests in Lebanon.

September 26–30: The Iranian Eighth Imam offensive takes place in Khuzestan. The Iraqis raise the siege of Abadan and retreat to the west bank of the Karun.

October 2: Ali Khamenei is elected president of the Republic of Iran. Akbar Hashemi Rafsanjani elected speaker of Parliament. Mir-Hossein Mousavi is appointed prime minister, occupying the position throughout the war.

October–November: A large-scale Iranian offensive is conducted against the Kurdish peshmergas.

November 29–December 7: Iranian Jerusalem Way offensive takes place in the sector of Susangerd. The Iranians liberate Bostan and advance in the direction of Hamid.

December 15: Saddam Hussein proposes a "peace of braves."

December 16: A Shiite putsch in Bahrain fails.

December 12–24: The Iranian Break of Dawn offensive is conducted in the sector of Qasr-e-Shirin. The Iranians liberate Geilan Zarb and Sar-e-Pol-e-Zahab.

1982

March 21–30: The Iranians claim their first major victory over the Iraqis in the sector of Fakkeh (Operation Undeniable Victory).

April 8: Syria closes the Kirkuk-Baniyas pipeline and its border with Iraq. Baghdad and Ankara make an agreement to double the Kirkuk-Dortyol pipeline's capacity.

April 9: Sadeq Ghotbzadeh, Bani-Sadr's former minister of foreign affairs, is arrested in Iran. The regular army in Iran is brought to heel.

May 3: Iraq shoots down the plane transporting the Algerian minister of foreign affairs en route to Iran.

April 30–May 24: The Iranians recapture Khorramshahr during the Holy City offensive.

June 6: Israel invades South Lebanon (Operation Peace for Galilee).

June 10–20: Saddam Hussein unilaterally proclaims a ceasefire, calling on the Iranians to ally their forces with his own to fight Israel in Lebanon. The Iranians refuse. Nonetheless, Saddam Hussein orders the Iraqi army's withdrawal to the border. **End of the war's second phase.**

June 22: Iran announces that it will continue the war until the fall of the Iraqi regime.

June 25–27: The Iraqi president takes advantage of the 9th Ba'ath Congress to purge the party and reorganize army command.

July: The United States initiates a prudent rapprochement with Baghdad. It removes Iraq from the list of state sponsors of terrorism. Western hostages start being taken in Lebanon. The USSR resumes arms deliveries to Iraq.

July 12: The UN Security Council adopts Resolution 514, calling for the belligerents to respect the ceasefire: Baghdad accepts it; Tehran rejects it.

July 13–31: Iranian Blessed Ramadan offensive is launched in the sector of Basra.

August 12: Saddam Hussein announces an oil blockade on Iran and decrees a maritime exclusion zone around Kharg Island. Tehran responds by setting its own maritime exclusion zone in the Gulf.

August 18: The creation of the IRGC Ministry (effective November 7) is announced.

August 25: The multinational security force intervenes in Beirut.

September: Heavy combat ensues in Iranian Kurdistan between the Iranian army and the Iranian Kurdish peshmergas.

September 11: Naval engagement occurs outside the Bushehr navy base.

October 1–6: The Iranian Muslim Ibn Aqil offensive is launched in the sector of Mandali.

October 4: The UN Security Council adopts Resolution 522 (unsuccessfully).

October 19: The Iranian nuclear program resumes.

November 1–16: The Iranian Holy Muharram offensive is conducted in the sector of Amarah.

December: Yuri Andropov succeeds Leonid Brezhnev in the Kremlin. The USSR changes its stance, ostracizing Iran and firmly supporting Iraq. China now openly supports Iran.

1983

January 4: Tariq Aziz negotiates the purchase of new French weapons and agrees with Paris on a new payment schedule for the Iraqi debt.

February 6–11: Following the Iranian Prelude offensive in the sector of Fakkeh, Iran opts for an attrition strategy.

February 15: The KGB resident in Tehran is expelled from Iran. Relations between the USSR and Iran reach a new low. China and North Korea form closer ties with Iran.

April: Tehran launches a large-scale operation against the peshmergas in Iranian Kurdistan.

April 10–17: The Iranian Dawn 1 offensive is launched, also in the sector of Fakkeh.

April 12–15: Naval engagements occur between Iraqi and Iranian patrol boats.

May 25: Baghdad proposes to suspend the bombing of civilian populations.

June 7: Saddam Hussein proposes a one-month truce to coincide with Ramadan.

July 20–30: The Iranian Dawn 2 offensive is launched in the direction of Iraqi Kurdistan.

July 30–August 10: The Dawn 3 offensive is launched in the sector of Mehran.

August 29: The first terrorist attacks on the Western contingents deployed in Lebanon occur.

September 22: French naval aviation bombs Syrian positions in Lebanon (Operation Sandre) in retaliation for the bombing of the French diplomatic mission in Beirut.

October 9: The five Super Etendards rented by France arrive in Iraq, all equipped with Exocet missiles. Iran considers that France has crossed a line.

October 15: The first GCC military exercises are conducted.

October 20–November 19: Iran launches Dawn 4 offensive in the direction of Iraqi Kurdistan. Chemical weapons are first used by the Iraqi army.

October 23: Terrorist attacks are carried out on the French (Drakkar) and American contingents stationed in Beirut (300 dead).

October 31: The UN Security Council adopts Resolution 540 (unsuccessfully).

November 9: Rasfanjani delivers a violent indictment of France.

November 17: French naval aviation bombs a Hezbollah barracks in Baalbek, in Lebanon (Operation Brochet). A series of terrorist attacks in France ensues.

December 4: U.S. naval aviation destroys several Syrian surface-to-air missile batteries in Lebanon.

December 12: Attacks on the French and American embassies in Kuwait are carried out.

December 14: The U.S. navy begins bombings of Hezbollah positions in Lebanon (final bombings on February 26, 1984).

December 20: Donald Rumsfeld meets Saddam Hussein in Baghdad. They agree on the principle of reestablishing diplomatic relations between the United States and Iraq.

1984

February 1–2: Second meeting between Donald Rumsfeld and Saddam Hussein in Baghdad is conducted.

February 12–15: Iranian Liberate Jerusalem offensive is launched in Iraqi Kurdistan. Iraq retaliates by setting off the "war of the cities" (until June 12).

February 16–22: Dawn 5 and 6 offensives occur between Kut and Amarah.

February 22–March 12: Iranian Kheibar offensive is launched in the sector of the Majnoon Islands. Neurotoxic gases are first used by the Iraqis.

February 28: France decides to adjust its policy toward the belligerents, adopting a more balanced position, including reducing arms deliveries to Iraq.

March 16: The CIA bureau chief in Beirut is kidnapped.

March 24: Donald Rumsfeld pays a third visit to Baghdad. The Iraqi air force attacks the Iranian nuclear power plant being built in Bushehr for the first time.

March 27: The first attack by Iraqi Super Etendards on Iranian oil traffic occurs. The tanker war begins.

May 17: Rafsanjani wins the second round of the legislative elections in Iran.

June 1: The Security Council adopts Resolution 552 (unsuccessfully).

June 5: Saudi air-superiority fighters shoot down an Iranian Phantom. Saudi Arabia implements an air and sea exclusion zone (Fahd Line). The United States announces it is sending an air and sea group to the Gulf of Oman.

July 9–September 20: Libya lays drifting mines in the Red Sea.

July 31: An Air France Airbus is hijacked by Iranian IRGC soldiers. Direct negotiations between France and Iran begin, covering the Eurodif dispute, the expulsion of Massoud Rajavi, the liberation of Anis Naccache, the suspension of French weapons sales to Iraq, and potential arms deliveries to Iran.

August 15: PKK guerilla warfare in Turkey begins.

September 20: Bloody attack on the American embassy in Beirut is carried out.

October 15: Turkey and Iraq agree to allow the Turkish army to pursue the PKK in Iraq. Kurdish guerilla fighters rise against the Iraqi regime.

October 18–22: Iranian Dawn 7 offensive in the sector of Mehran is launched.

November 26: Diplomatic relations between Washington and Baghdad are reestablished.

1985

March 11–22: The Iranian Badr offensive in the sector of the Majnoon Islands ends in an Iraqi victory thanks to the intensive use of chemical weapons.

March 11–June 15: The second episode of the "war of the cities" takes place.

March 22: A series of kidnappings of French nationals begins in Lebanon as French-Iranian negotiations collapse.

April 21: Saddam Hussein proposes a roadmap for ending the war.

June: The United States and Saudi Arabia agree on a new oil strategy to stifle Iran and the Soviet Union. Riyadh heavily increases its oil output, leading to the collapse of the price of oil.

June 14–28: Iranian Operation Jerusalem 1 north of the Majnoon Islands is waged.

June 19: Iranian Operation Jerusalem 2 around Qasr-e-Shirin is waged.

June 20–30: Iranian Operation Victory is waged in the sector of Basra.

July 14–30: Operation Jerusalem 3 is waged in Iraqi Kurdistan.

July 26–August 7: Operation Jerusalem 4 is waged in the sector of Mandali.

August 14: The Iraqi air force begins a four-month bombing campaign against the Kharg oil terminal.

August 16: In Iran, Ali Khamenei is reelected president of the Republic.

August 20: The first American missiles are delivered to Iran as part of Iran-Contra.

September: There is an escalation of tension between Moscow and Tehran after the kidnapping of four Soviet diplomats in Beirut (September 30). Mikhail Gorbachev decides to cautiously form closer ties with Iran.

September 8–18: Iranian Operation Jerusalem 5 is waged in Iraqi Kurdistan.

September 16–30: Operation Jerusalem 6 is waged between Sumer and Mehran.

October 23–November 7: Iranian Operation Ashura is waged in the Hoveyzeh marshes.

October 24: The pipeline between Iraq and Saudi Arabia is opened.

December 16: Saddam Hussein meets Mikhail Gorbachev in Moscow.

1986

January 6–14: The Iraqis recapture part of the Majnoon Islands.

January 12: An American ship is intercepted for the first time by the Iranian navy in the Strait of Hormuz.

February 9–March 13: The Iranians take control of the al-Faw peninsula (Dawn 8).

February 24: The UN Security Council adopts Resolution 582 (unsuccessfully).

February 25–March 8: First phase of the Iranian Dawn 9 offensive is launched in Iraqi Kurdistan.

February 28: The Luchaire affair (sales of French munitions to Iran) is brought to light in France.

April 15: The Americans raid Libya.

April 23–May 20: Second phase of the Dawn 9 offensive is waged in Iraqi Kurdistan.

May: France declares it is prepared to pay Iran for the Eurodif debt. It expels Massoud Rajavi, who finds shelter in Iraq. Two French hostages are freed in Beirut. The degradation of the Ayatollah Khomeini's health provokes a political crisis in Tehran.

May 14–17: The Iraqis seize a pocket of Iranian territory around Mehran and propose to exchange it for the al-Faw peninsula.

May 25: An American delegation secretly travels to Tehran to accelerate "arms for hostages" negotiations as part of Iran-Contra.

June 30–July 10: The Iranians liberate the Mehran pocket after the Karbala 1 offensive.

August 12: The first Iraqi raid on the Sirri floating oil terminal is carried out.

August 23: The Turkish military makes incursions in Iraqi Kurdistan.

August 29: The first Iraqi raid on the Lavan oil terminal is carried out.

August 31–September 7: The Iranian Karbala 2 offensive is waged in Iraqi Kurdistan. Iran conducts raids on the Iraqi-Turkish border.

September 1–2: The Karbala 3 offensive is conducted against the Kohr al-Amaya terminal.

November 3: The Iran-Contra scandal is revealed.

November 22: France pays Iran a first installment of the Eurodif loan following a series of terrorist attacks in Paris. A French hostage is freed in Beirut.

November 25: Iraq conducts first raid on the Larak floating oil terminal.

December 24–27: The Karbala 4 offensive is launched in the sector of Basra.

1987

January 8–February 26: Karbala 5 offensive is waged on Basra. A command crisis occurs among the Iraqi chiefs of staff. A new episode of the "war of the cities" is launched.

January 13–26: Karbala 6 offensive is waged in the sector of Mandali.

January 21: A new peace plan is proposed by Saddam Hussein. Iran responds by firing two Silkworm missiles at Kuwait.

February 13: The Iranian minister of foreign affairs' visit to Moscow marks a further step toward the rapprochement between the USSR and Iran.

March 3–9: Karbala 7 offensive is waged in Iraqi Kurdistan. There is a second Turkish military incursion against the PKK in Iraq. Jalal Talabani (PUK), Massoud Barzani (KDP), and Mahmoud Othman (PSK) agree to unite the Kurdish resistance against the Iraqi regime. Saddam Hussein launches Operation Anfal against the Kurdish insurrection.

April 2: Washington commits to reregistering eleven Kuwaiti oil tankers to fly the American flag. London announces the reinforcement of the Armilla Patrol in the Gulf.

April 6–11: The Karbala 8 offensive, the final Iranian assault on Basra, is launched.

April 9–14: The Karbala 9 offensive is conducted in the sector of Qasr-e-Shirin. Iraq and the USSR renew their Friendship and Cooperation Treaty.

April 14–30: The Karbala 10 offensive is waged in Iraqi Kurdistan. Iran ends its all-out offensives and returns to the war of attrition. **End of the war's third phase.**

April 15: The USSR reregisters three Kuwaiti oil tankers to fly the Soviet flag.

May 8: The Kremlin announces that it is sending a war flotilla to the Gulf.

May 6–20: The first oil tankers are damaged by Iranian mines.

May 17: The frigate USS *Stark* is attacked by an Iraqi Falcon 50.

June–July: The Gordji affair breaks out in France. The "war of the embassies" between Paris and Tehran begins. France breaks diplomatic relations with Iran on July 17 and deploys its air and sea group in the Gulf (Operation Prométhée).

July 20: The UN Security Council's five permanent members agree on a comprehensive peace plan to put an end to the Iran-Iraq War (Resolution 598).

July 21: The United States announces it is sending major naval reinforcements to the Gulf and launches operations Earnest Will (escorts for American ships) and Prime Chance (surveillance of IRGC naval activity). Numerous incidents between the U.S. navy and Iranian air and sea forces take place.

August–September: Iranian launches attacks in Iraqi Kurdistan (Nasser 5, 6, and 7).

September 2–5: The UN Secretary General carries out a mediation mission in Iraq and Iran. Iran fires three Silkworm missiles at Kuwait.

September 7–8: The Netherlands, Belgium, and Italy announce that they are sending warships to the Gulf.

September 21: The U.S. navy captures the Iranian ship *Iran Ajr* while it is laying mines off of Bahrain.

October 3: The U.S. and Saudi navies repel an IRGC flotilla off of Khafji.

October 8: The U.S. navy sinks an IRGC gunboat and damages two others near the American floating base *Hercules*.

October 15–16: Iran fires two more Silkworm missiles at Kuwait. The American supertanker *Sea Isle City* is severely damaged.

October 19: The United States launches Operation Nimble Archer (destruction of the Iranian Rostam offshore oil platform).

October 22: Iran fires another Silkworm missile at Kuwait, which accepts the U.S. offer to provide military assistance.

October 28–November 1: Another Soviet attempt is made to mediate between Baghdad and Tehran.

November 27–28: The "war of the embassies" between Paris and Tehran ends. France allows Wahid Gordji to return to Iran. Iran lifts the siege on the French embassy in Tehran. Two French hostages are freed in Beirut. France pays Iran a second installment of the Eurodif loan.

December 27–28: Iran fires a Silkworm missile at Kuwait.

1988

January 12–February 26: Iranian Victory 5 and 6 and Holy City 2 operations are carried out in Iraqi Kurdistan. The Iraqis intensify Operation Anfal.

February 28: Iran fires a salvo of Scud missiles at Baghdad. Iraq retaliates by firing Al-Hussein missiles at Tehran. The "war of the capitals," which rages until April 20, begins.

March 13–16: In Iraqi Kurdistan, the Iranians seize Halabja and the Dukan Dam during the Victory 7 and Holy City 3 offensives.

March 16: Iraqi launches chemical attacks on the small town of Halabja.

April 14: The frigate USS *Samuel Roberts* is seriously damaged by a mine in the Gulf.

April 17–18: The Iraqis liberate the al-Faw peninsula (Operation Blessed Ramadan).

April 18: During an air and sea battle in the Gulf, the U.S. navy sinks several Iranian navy ships and destroys two offshore platforms used by the IRGC (Operation Praying Mantis).

April 20: Iran fires a Scud missile at Kuwait.

May 4: The last French hostages in Lebanon are released between the two rounds of the French presidential election. After being reelected, François Mitterrand decides to pardon Anis Naccache and settle the Eurodif dispute once and for all (France pays off the balance of the loan in a final installment on December 29, 1991).

May 13: The leftist conservative religious opposition wins the second round of the legislative elections in Iran, putting Rafsanjani in a difficult position.

May 15: The Soviet army begins withdrawing from Afghanistan.

May 25–27: The Iraqi Tawakalna 1 offensive is waged in the sector of Basra.

May 29–June 2: The American and Soviet presidents meet in Moscow to discuss the crisis in the Gulf.

June 13–15: The Iranian counteroffensive in the sector of Basra fails.

June 15–30: The Iraqi army regains ground in Iraqi Kurdistan.

June 18–21: The People's Mujahidin capture Mehran.

June 25–28: The Iraqis recapture the Majnoon Islands (Tawakalna 2).

July 3: The cruiser USS *Vincennes* shoots down an Iranian Air Airbus in the Gulf.

July 12–14: The Iraqi Tawakalna 3 offensive is waged in the sector of Dehloran.

July 15: The Iranian government decides to end the war.

July 17: Saddam Hussein lists his conditions for accepting the ceasefire.

July 18: Iran accepts the terms of UN Security Council Resolution 598.

July 20: The Ayatollah Khomeini publicly takes responsibility for the ceasefire, stating that making this decision was like "drinking a cup of poison."

July 22–27: The Iraqi army attacks on the central and southern fronts to increase pressure on Tehran (Tawakalna 4 offensive).

July 26–30: The Iranian army crushes a final offensive by the People's Mujahidin in the direction of Kermanshah (Operation Mersad).

August 6: Iran unconditionally accepts the ceasefire.

August 20: The ceasefire becomes effective, monitored by a UN force of observers. **End of the Iran-Iraq War.**

August 24: Direct negotiations between Iraq and Iran begin in Geneva.

September 3: The Iraqi army announces that it has reconquered all the Iraqi territory previously in the hands of the Kurdish insurrection.

September 25: The American Operation Earnest Will and the French Operation Prométhée in the Gulf end.

October 25: The Kharg terminal reopens. Maritime oil traffic in the Gulf is back to normal.

November 19: The Iranian authorities rule out the possibility of renewed hostilities.

November 24: Prisoner exchanges begin.

December 29: A mixed Iraqi-Iranian military committee is created to consolidate implementation of the ceasefire.

1989

February 14: The Ayatollah Khomeini decrees a fatwa for blasphemy against Salman Rushdie, creating a diversion from Iran's defeat.

May 5: Adnan Khairallah, the Iraqi minister of defense, dies, bolstering Saddam's sons' position within the family clan.

June 3: The Ayatollah Khomeini dies. Ali Khamenei becomes the new Supreme Leader (June 4), while Akbar Hashemi Rasfanjani is elected president (July 28). Negotiations to finalize a peace agreement are accelerated.

1990

August 20: Eighteen days after Iraq invades Kuwait, the Iraqi army withdraws from the last occupied Iranian territories, and both parties proceed to exchange the final prisoners of war.

1991

February: The UN ceasefire monitoring force leaves the Gulf.

[Appendix B]

Iraq and Iran in 1980

TABLE B.1

A COMPARISION OF IRAQ AND IRAN IN 1980

	IRAQ	IRAN
Size	438,000 km / 166,000 sq. miles	1,648,000 km / 636,300 sq. miles
Primary type of terrain	Plains and marshes	Mountains and high plateaus
Climate	Semi-desert	Arid
Population (1980)	13 million inhabitants	39 million inhabitants
Language	Arabic	Persian
Principal ethnic groups	Arab: 80%	Persian: 55% Azeri: 25%
	Kurd: 18%	Kurd: 10% Arab: 2%
	Turkmen: 2%	Baloch: 3%
Religions	Shia Muslim: 54%	Shia Muslim: 85%
	Sunni Muslim: 43%	Sunni Muslim: 13%
	Chaldean Christians: 3%	Other: 2%
Capital	Baghdad	Tehran
Institutional arrangements	Presidential Republic	Islamic Republic
Number of provinces	18	30
Currency	Iraqi dinar	Rial
GNP (1980)	$45 billion	$110 billion
Defense budget (1980)	$2.8 billion (6.5% of GNP)	$4.5 billion (4% of GNP)
Total military personnel (1980)	250,000 troops (1.9% of population)	290,000 troops (0.7% of population)
Military service	24 months	18 months
Average number of draft-age men	135,000 men/year	420,000 men/year

Note: Iraq and Iran have a 905-mile (1458-km) shared border.

[Appendix C]

Military High Command

Iraqi High Command

President and Commander-in-Chief of the Armed Forces: Saddam Hussein.

Minister of Defense: Adnan Khairallah.

Chief of Intelligence Services: Ali Hassan al-Majid (proconsul for Iraqi Kurdistan beginning in 1987).

Chief of Defense: Abdoul Jabar Khalil Shamshal (1980–1982), Mohammed Abdel Jawad Dhanoun (1982–1986), Saladin Aziz (January–February 1987), and Nizar al-Khazraji (1987–1988).

Head of Operations: Abdel Jabar Assadi (1980–1982), Abdel Jawad Dhanoun (1982–1986), Nizar Abdel Karim Khazraji (1986–1987), and Hussein Rachid Mohammed (1987–1988).

Head of Popular Army: Taha Yassin Ramadan.

Director of Army Intelligence: Abdul Jawad Dhanoun (1980–1982), Mahmoudi Shahin (1982–1986), and Sabar al-Duri (1986–1988).

Commander of the Air Force: Mohamed Jessam al-Jeboury (1980–1984) and Hamid Shaban (1984–1988).

Commander of the Navy: Aladdin Hammad al-Janabi (1980–1982) and Abid Mohammed al-Kabi (1982–1988).

Commander of the 1st Army Corps: Mohammed Fathi Amin (1980–1982), Maher Abd al-Rashid (1982–1984), Nizar al-Khazraji (1984–1986), and Kamel Sajid Aziz (1987–1988).

Commander of the 2nd Army Corps: Abdallah Abdel Latif (1980–1981), Mustafa Aziz (1981–1982), Mohammed Fathi Amin (1982–1983), Zia Tawfik Ibrahim (1983–1986), and Abdel Satar Mouaïni (1986–1988).

Commander of the 3rd Army Corps: Saadi Toumah Abouri (1980–1981), Salah al-Qadhi (1981–1982), Saadi al-Jaburi (1982–1984), Maher Abd al-Rashid (1984–1986), Tala al-Duri (1986), and Diah ul-Din Jamal (1987–1988).

Commander of the 4th Army Corps: Hisham Sabah al-Fakhri (1981–1983) and Tabet Sultan Ahmed (1983–1987).

Commander of the 5th Army Corps: Saadi al-Jaburi (1984–1985), Diah ul-Din Jamal (1985–1986), and Tala al-Duri (1986–1988).

Commander of the 6th Army Corps: Hisham Sabah al-Fakhri (1984–1986) and Sultan Hashem Ahmed (1986–1988).

Commander of the 7th Army Corps: Shawket (1985–1986), Saadi al-Jaburi (1986), and Maher Abd al-Rashid (1986–1988).

Commander of the Republican Guard: Hussein Rashid Mohammed (1985–1987) and Ayad Fayid al-Rawi (1987–1988).

Iranian High Command

Supreme Leader: The Ayatollah Khomeini.

President of the Republic and theoretical head of the armies: Abol Hassan Bani-Sadr (1980–1981), Mohammad-Ali Rajai (1981), and Ali Khamenei (1981–1988).

Speaker of Parliament and effective head of the armies: Akbar Hashemi Rafsanjani.

Minister of Defense: Mostafa Chamran (1980–1981), Mohammad Salimi (1981–1984), and Hussein Jalal (1984–1988).

Minister of Islamic Revolutionary Guards Corps: Mohsen Rafighdoost (as of 1982).

Chief of Staff of the Armed Forces: Hossein Chaker (1980), Valliolah Fallahi (1980–1981), Qasim Ali Zahir Nejad (1981–1984), Ismael Sohrabi (1984–1988), and Ali Shahbazi (1988).

Commander of Ground Forces: Valliolah Fallahi (1980), Gassim Ali Zahir Nedjad (1980–1981), and Ali Shirazi (1981–1988).

Commander of the Air Force: Javad Fakouri (1980–1981), Mohammad Hasan Mojunpur (1981–1983), Houshang Seddigh (1983–1986), and Mansour Sattari (1986–1988).

Commander of the Navy: Bahram Afzali (1980–1983), Esfandiyar Hosseini (1983–1985), and Mohammed Hussein Malekzadegan (1985–1988).

Commander of the Islamic Revolutionary Guards Corps (IRGC): Ali Khamenei (1980–1981) and Mohsen Rezaee (1981–1988).

Deputy Commander of the IRGC: Ali Shamkhani (1981–1988).

IRGC Head of Operations: Rahim Safavi (1981–1988).

Commander of the IRGC's Naval Branch: Ali Araki Hamadani (1985–1988).

Commander of the Basij: Hassan Rahmani.

Other notable officers who headed IRGC divisions: Hossein Kharrazi, Mohammad Bagher Ghalibaf, Ahmad Kazemi, Mohammad Boroujerdi, Mohammad Ibrahim Hemmat, and Ahmed Kossari.

Military Forces

TABLE D.1

FORCES AT THE OUTBREAK OF HOSTILITIES

RAQ	IRAN
250,000 troops	290,000 troops
Ground forces	
210,000 troops	215,000 troops
12 divisions	
6 independent brigades	7 divisions
7 independent brigades	
1,750 tanks	1,710 tanks (1,150)
2,350 other armored vehicles	1,900 other armored vehicles (1,300)
1,350 artillery pieces	1,100 artillery pieces
Aerial forces	
25,000 troops	50,000 troops
18 squadrons	23 squadrons
295 combat aircraft	421 combat aircraft (200)
300 helicopters	835 helicopters (240)
including 58 attack helicopters	including 200 attack helicopters (80)
Anti-aircraft defense	
10,000 troops	[part of ground forces]
9 brigades	16 battalions
260 SAM launchers	230 SAM launchers
2,000 anti-aircraft guns	600 anti-aircraft guns
Naval forces	
5,000 troops	25,000 troops
17 warships	25 warships
14 missile boats	3 destroyers, 4 frigates, 4 corvettes
3 amphibious assault ships	9 missile boats
	5 amphibious assault ships

Note: The figures in parentheses indicate the approximate number of Iranian armored vehicles or aircraft that were operational at the beginning of the war.

Iraq

ARMY

180,000 troops divided in 12 divisions, 41 combat brigades, and 14 artillery brigades (1 per division and 2 independent surface-to-air missile
brigades). The 12 divisions were divided into 5 armored divisions (3rd,
6th, 9th, 10th, and 12th), 2 mechanized divisions (1st and 5th), and 5
infantry divisions (2nd, 4th, 7th, 8th, and 11th). The combat brigades
were divided into:

— **15 infantryman brigades:** 2nd, 3rd, 4th, 5th, 18th, 22nd, 23rd, 28th, 29th,
36th, 39th, 40th, 111th, 112th, and 113th.
— **8 mechanized brigades:** 1st, 8th, 14th, 15th, 20th, 23rd, 24th, and 27th.
— **14 armored brigades:** 6th, 9th, 10th, 12th, 16th, 17th, 25th, 26th, 30th,
34th, 35th, 37th, 43rd, and 45th.
— **3 special forces brigades:** 31st, 32nd, and 33rd.
— **1 parachute brigade:** 42nd.

Each armored division (270 tanks) was supported by a surface-to-air
mobile defense brigade, by an artillery brigade (fielding about 40 self-
propelled guns and about 30 multiple rocket launchers), and a reconnaissance regiment.

Each mechanized division (180 tanks) was supported by an artillery brigade fielding about 60 artillery pieces.

Each infantry division was supported by an artillery brigade fielding
about 60 artillery pieces and by a battalion of about 30 T-54 tanks.

Each mechanized brigade fielded about 100 armored personnel carriers
and about 30 T-55 tanks.

Each armored brigade fielded about 100 tanks and about 40 armored
vehicles for infantry combat.

EQUIPMENT:

— **1,750 main battle tanks:** 100 T-72s, 800 T-62s, 400 T-55s, and 450 T-54s.
— **550 light armored reconnaissance vehicles:** 150 PT-76s, 200 EE-9 Cascavels, 110 Panhard M-3s, and 90 AML-90/60s.
— **1,800 armored personnel carriers:** 200 BMP-1s, 500 OT-64s, 450
OT-62s, 200 BTR-60s, and 450 BTR-152s.

— **1,350 artillery pieces:** 530 towed field guns (15 203 mm B-4s, 40 152 mm D-20s, 250 130 mm M-46s, 205 122 mm D-30s, and 20 105 mm M-101s), 160 self-propelled guns (120 Su-100s and 40 Su-152s), 60 BM-21 multiple rocket launchers, and 600 120 and 160 mm heavy mortars.

— **Antitank capacity:** AT-3 Sagger, SS-11, Milan, and Hot missiles.

— **Ballistic capacity:** 26 Frog-7 launchers and 18 Scud-B launchers (stock of 160 Frog-7 missiles and 120 Scud-B missiles).

DEPLOYMENT:

In the north, facing Iranian Kurdistan:

— 1st Army Corps (HQ in Kirkuk).

PENJWIN SECTOR:

— 7th infantry division: 28th, 39th, and 40th infantryman brigades.

KIRKUK SECTOR:

— 11th mountain infantry division: 111th, 112th, and 113th infantryman brigades.

IN THE CENTER, BETWEEN QASR-E-SHIRIN AND DEZFUL:

— 2nd Army Corps (HQ in Baghdad—ACP in Khanaqin).

FACING QASR-E-SHIRIN:

— 6th armored division: 16th, 25th, and 30th tank brigades (T-62).

— 8th infantry division: 3rd, 22nd, and 23rd infantryman brigades.

FACING SUMER:

— 4th infantry division: 5th, 18th, and 29th infantryman brigades.

— 12th armored division: 15th mechanized brigade and 9th tank brigade (T-55).

— 10th Republican Guard tank brigade (T-72).

FACING MEHRAN:

— 2nd infantry division: 2nd, 4th, and 36th infantryman brigades.

— 37th tank brigade (T-55) detached from the 12th armored division.

IN THE SOUTH, FACING KHUZESTAN:

—3rd Army Corps (HQ in Basra).

FACING DEZFUL:

— 10th armored division: 24th mechanized brigade, 17th and 45th tank brigades (T-62/T-55).

FACING SHUSH:

— 1st mechanized division: 1st and 27th mechanized brigades, 34th tank brigade (T-55).

FACING AHWAZ:

— 9th armored division: 14th mechanized brigade, 35th (T-62) and 43rd (T-55) tank brigades.

— 5th mechanized division: 20th and 23rd mechanized brigades.

FACING KHORRAMSHAHR:

— 3rd armored division: 8th mechanized brigade, 6th and 12th tank brigades (T-62).

— 26th tank brigade (T-55) detached from the 5th mechanized division.

GENERAL REINFORCEMENTS:

— 31st, 32nd, and 33rd special forces brigades, in Baghdad.

— 42nd parachute brigade, scattered between Baghdad and Kut.

— 147th artillery brigade equipped with Scud-B ballistic missiles.

— 148th artillery brigade equipped with Frog-7 ground-to-ground missiles.

POPULAR ARMY

60,000 troops (all members of the Ba'ath Party) divided in small units the size of a company or a battalion, exclusively equipped with light weapons, whose principal missions consisted of protecting the regime, guarding certain public buildings, maintaining a military presence throughout the territory, monitoring the regular army, and reinforcing it in case of war.

AIR FORCE

25,000 troops (including army aviation personnel detached to the air force) divided over 11 air bases: Baghdad international airport, Baghdad (al-Rasheed), Baghdad (al-Muthana), Basra (al-Wahda), Kirkuk (al-Hourrya), H-3 (al-Wallid), Kut (Abou Oubaïda), Mosul (Firnas), Nasiriyah (Ali Ibn Abou Talib), Tammuz, and Tikrit (home of the air force academy). A twelfth base (Saddam), located in the north of Iraq near Mosul, became operational in 1981 to land Mirage F-1s. A thirteenth base (al-Bakr), built north of Baghdad between Samarra and Balad, became operational in 1984.

EQUIPMENT:

— **295 combat aircraft:** 54 MiG-23s, 135 MiG-21s, 4 MiG-21Rs, 68 Su-20/22s, 16 Su 7s, 12 Tu-22s, and 6 Tu-16s. The fighters were equipped with AA-2 Atoll (all), AA-8 Aphid (MiG-23), and Matra R-550 Magic-1 (MiG-21MF) air-air missiles.

— **31 transport planes:** 1 Tu-124, 3 Falcon 20s, 10 An-12s, 9 An-24s, 2 An-26s, and 6 Il-76s (more than 10 An-2s stockpiled).

— **180 training aircraft:** 9 MiG-23Us, 24 MiG-21Us, 7 Su-7Us, 2 Tu-22Us, 8 Jet Provosts, 50 L-39 Albatros, 40 L-29 Delphins, and 40 Zlins (principally distributed between Tikrit and Baghdad).

— 60 combat aircraft warehoused: 20 Hunters, 27 MiG-21s, 5 MiG-17s, and 8 Il-28s.

ARMY AVIATION (DETACHED TO THE AIR FORCE)

ASSETS:

300 helicopters: 42 Alouette IIIs, 39 Gazelles, 10 Super Frelons, 3 Pumas, 18 Mi-24s, 144 Mi-8s (including about 30 detached to air bases for missions to recover bailed pilots), 12 Mi-6s, 32 Mi-4s. About 60 of these helicopters (Alouette III, Gazelle, and Mi-24) were equipped for anti-tank combat.

ANTI-AIRCRAFT DEFENSE

10,000 troops, operating 9 surface-to-air brigades and 26 Soviet-made surveillance radars, coordinated by a next-generation system by the French company Thomson/CSF.

TABLE D.2

DEPLOYMENT OF IRAQI AIR FORCE COMBAT UNITS

(18 SQUADRONS)

Squadron	Allowance	Mission	Location
1st	16 Su-20s	Attack	Kirkuk
5th	18 Su-22s	Attack	Mosul
7th	18 MiG-21F/Ps	Air superiority	Baghdad
8th	16 Su-7, 7 Su-7Us*	Attack	Kut
9th	18 MiG-21MFs	Air superiority	Mosul
10th	12 Tu-22s, 6 Tu-16s, 2 Tu-22Us	Bombing	Tammuz
11th	20 MiG-21MFs	Air superiority	Baghdad
14th	16 MiG-21bis*	Air superiority	Kut and Basra
17th	7 MiG-21Fs, 12 Mig-21Us	Advanced training	Tikrit
27th	12 MiG-21Ps + 12 MiG-21Us + 8 Mi-23Us	Advanced training	Baghdad
29th	18 MiG-23BNs	Attack	Kut
37th	16 MiG-21bis	Air superiority	Kirkuk
39th	18 MiG-23Es	Interception	Tammuz
44th	16 Su-22s	Attack	Kirkuk
47th	16 MiG-21bis	Air superiority	Kirkuk
49th	18 MiG-23BNs	Attack	Nasiriyah
70th	12 MiG-21MFs + 4 MiG-21Rs	Air superiority / Reconnaissance	Baghdad
109th	18 Su-22s	Attack	Basra

* The 8th and 14th squadrons were dissolved in 1984, and their aircraft, then obsolete, were scrapped.

TABLE D.3

DEPLOYMENT OF IRAQI AIR FORCE TRANSPORT UNITS

(3 SQUADRONS)

Squadron	Allowance	Location
3rd	1 Tu-124, 3 Falcon 20s	Baghdad
23rd	10 An-12s, 9 An-24s, 2 An-26s	Baghdad
33rd	6 Il-76s	Baghdad

TABLE D.4
DEPLOYMENT OF IRAQI ARMED HELICOPTERS (3 REGIMENTS)

Unit	Allowance	Location
1st regiment	Alouette III, Gazelle	Mosul & Kirkuk
2nd regiment	Alouette III, Gazelle	Basra & Rumaila
4th regiment	Mi-24	Baghdad

SURFACE-TO-AIR ASSETS:
— 5 **static brigades** covering the sectors of Baghdad (145th), Tammuz (146th), Basra (148th), Umm Qasr (149th), and Kirkuk (195th). These 5 brigades fielded 40 batteries of surface-to-air missiles, comprising 120 SAM-2 launchers and 80 SAM-3 launchers.
— 4 **mobile brigades** (155th, 162nd, 175th, and 185th) charged with protecting the armored divisions and certain sensitive sites, fielding 24 SAM-6 missile triple launchers, 36 SAM-9 missile launchers, and 40 ZSU-23x4 self-propelled weapon systems carrying a turret with radar-guided 23 mm quad guns.
— About 100 SAM-7 portable missile launchers and 2,000 anti-air guns for close defense of sensitive bases and targets, ranging in caliber from 23 to 100 mm (ZSU-23x2, ZSU-57x2, M53, Bofors-40, S-60, KS-18, and KS-19).

NAVY
5,000 troops (including naval infantry) divided over three naval bases: Basra, Umm Qasr, and al-Faw.

ASSETS (45 LIGHT SHIPS FIELDING 5,000 TONS AND 1,500 NAVY TROOPS):
— 14 **missile boats** (6 Osa Is—registered R-12 to R-17—and 8 Osa IIs—registered R-18 to R-25).
— 3 **Polnocny-class LSM amphibious assault ships** (*Atika, Ganda,* and *Nouh*), each able to carry eight light armored vehicles and 350 infantrymen.
— 10 P-6 torpedo boats.

— 13 light patrol boats (4 Kraljevikas, 3 SO-1s, 4 Zhuks, and 2 Poluchats).
— 5 minesweepers (2 T-43s and 3 Evguenias).
— 4 naval infantry battalions charged with protection of bases.
— 1 frogmen group.

DEPLOYMENT:

Basra: 6 torpedo boats, 3 light patrol boats, 3 minesweepers, and 1 naval infantry battalion.

Umm Qasr: 14 missile boats, 7 light patrol boats, 4 amphibious assault ships, 2 naval infantry battalions, 1 frogmen group, and all the Super Frelon helicopters armed with Exocet missiles.

al-Faw: 4 torpedo boats, 3 light patrol boats, 2 minesweepers, and 1 naval infantry battalion.

Iran

ISLAMIC REVOLUTIONARY GUARDS CORPS (IRGC)

30,000 troops divided in companies and battalions, exclusively equipped with light weapons, whose missions consisted of fighting against counterrevolutionary activity, maintaining a military presence throughout the territory, and monitoring the regular army and reinforcing it in case of attacks on Iranian territory. The Islamic Revolutionary Guards Corps, supported by a political bureau and an economic bureau, was divided into four separate branches:

— Central command (protection of Tehran).
— Provincial command.
— Border surveillance.
— Training.

ARMY

185,000 troops divided over 7 divisions, 29 combat brigades, 5 artillery brigades (11th, 22nd, 33rd, 44th, and 55th), and 3 reconnaissance regiments. The 7 divisions were divided into 3 armored divisions (16th, 81st, and 92nd), 3 mechanized divisions (21st, 28th, and 77th), and 1 motorized infantry division (64th). The combat brigades were divided into 13 armored brigades, 9 mechanized, 4 motorized infantry, 1 mountain infantry, 1 special forces, and 1 parachute.

Each armored division (360 tanks) was supported by an artillery brigade fielding about 100 self-propelled guns and a reconnaissance regiment equipped with Scorpion light tanks.

Each armored brigade fielded 120 tanks and about 40 armored personnel carriers.

Each mechanized brigade fielded close to 150 armored personnel carriers.

EQUIPMENT:

— **1,710 main battle tanks:** 850 Chieftains, 460 M-60A1s, 400 M-47/48 Pattons (+ 175 repair tanks).
— **250 Scorpion light armored reconnaissance vehicles**.
— **1,650 armored personnel carriers:** 650 M-113s, 600 BTR-60s, and 400 BTR-50s.
— **1,100 artillery pieces:** 545 towed field guns (25 203 mm M-115s, 150 155 mm M-114s, and 370 105 mm M-101s), 485 self-propelled guns (25 203 mm M-110s, 60 175 mm M-107s, and 400 155 mm M-109s), and 70 122 mm BM-21 multiple rocket launchers.

Antitank capacity: TOW and Dragon missiles.

DEPLOYMENT:

IN TEHRAN:

— 21st mechanized division: 1st, 2nd, 3rd, and 4th mechanized brigades (BTR-60).
— 15th mountain infantry brigade.
— 23rd special forces brigade.

IN QAZVIN:

— 16th armored division: 1st, 2nd, and 3rd tank brigades (M-60).

IN SHIRAZ:

— 37th tank brigade (M-48).
— 55th parachute brigade.

IN THE SECTOR OF KURDISTAN, FACING IRAQ AND TURKEY:

— 28th mechanized division: 1st tank brigade (M-48), 2nd, and 3rd mechanized brigades (M-113).
— 64th motorized infantry division: 1st, 2nd, and 3rd infantryman brigades.

IN THE SECTOR OF KERMANSHAH, FACING IRAQ:

— 81st armored division: 1st, 2nd, and 3rd tank brigades (Chieftain), in Kermanshah.
— 84th mechanized brigade (M-113), in Khorramabad.
— 1st army aviation brigade (Cobra), in Kermanshah.
— One mechanized battalion (detached from the 77th mechanized division), in Mehran.

IN THE PROVINCE OF KHUZESTAN:

— 92nd armored division: 1st, 2nd, and 3rd tank brigades (Chieftain).
— 138th and 141st mechanized infantry battalions, detached from the 21st mechanized division.
— 151st fortification battalion defending the city of Khorramshahr, reinforced by a naval infantry battalion.
— Two tank battalions detached from the 37th and 88th tank brigades.
— 22nd and 55th artillery brigades.
— A detachment of the 2nd army aviation brigade in Shiraz (Cobra).

IN THE NORTHEAST, FACING THE SOVIET UNION AND AFGHANISTAN:

— 77th mechanized division: 1st tank brigade (M-47), 2nd, and 3rd mechanized brigades (BTR-50).
— 30th motorized infantry brigade (BTR-60).

IN ZAHEDAN, FACING AFGHANISTAN AND PAKISTAN:

— 88th tank brigade (Chieftain).

ANTI-AIRCRAFT DEFENSE (DETACHED TO THE ARMY)

DETECTION ASSETS:

Network of American-made Westinghouse AN/TPS-43 and British-made Marconi S-330 and S-404 modern surveillance and acquisition radars, managed from an air operations center in Tehran.

SURFACE-TO-AIR ASSETS:

— 16 four-battery anti-aircraft defense battalions, fielding:
— 37 fixed batteries of Hawk missiles (long range), each comprising four triple launchers (twelve missiles per battery) [1,800 Hawks in total]
— 20 mobile batteries of Rapier missiles (short range), each comprising

three quadruple launchers (twelve missiles per battery) [800 Rapiers in total]
— 7 fixed batteries of Tigercat missiles (short range), each comprising three triple launchers (nine missiles per battery) [400 Tigercats in total]
— **600 fixed and mobile anti-air guns** (ZSU-23x2, ZSU-23x4, Oerlikon-35x2, Bofors-40, ZSU-57x2).

ARMY AVIATION (DETACHED TO THE ARMY)
ASSETS:
— **56 planes:** 40 Cessna 185 Skywagons, 10 Cessna O-2 Skymasters, and 6 Cessna 310s.
— **730 helicopters:** 200 antitank combat AH-1 Cobras, 142 AB-205s, 44 AB-206s, 260 Bell-214s, 84 CH-47 Chinooks. These helicopters were divided among two army aviation brigades (1st and 2nd) deployed in Kermanshah and Shiraz and several independent battalions positioned with the principal garrisons. Only a quarter of the CH-47 Chinooks and a third of the other helicopters were operational at the outbreak of hostilities (approx. 240 aircraft).

AIR FORCE
50,000 troops (versus 75,000 under the Shah) divided among 9 air bases: Tehran (Mehrabad), Tabriz, Hamadan (Nojeh), Dezful (Vahdati), Bushehr, Shiraz, Esfahan, Bandar Abbas, and Shah Bahar. A tenth base (Omidiyeh) located close to Bandar Khomeini, near the Iraqi border, became operational in 1981 to serve as a home for the 5th wing. Seven airports with landing strips of at least 9,800 feet (3,000 meters) could receive detachments: Abadan, Ahwaz, Jask, Kermanshah, Manzariyeh, Mashhad, and Zahedan.

EQUIPMENT:
— **421 combat aircraft:** 77 F-14A Tomcats, 178 F-4D/E Phantoms, 140 F-5th/F Tiger IIs, 20 RF-4Es, 6 P-3 Orions. Only half of these aircraft were operational at the outbreak of hostilities. The fighters were equipped with AIM-9E/J Sidewinder, AIM-7E Sparrow, and AIM-54 Phoenix air-air missiles, two-thirds of which were warehoused.
— **105 transport planes:** 56 C-130E/Hs (four in electronic warfare ver-

sions), 18 Fokker F-27s, 14 Boeing 707s (eight in KC-135 in-flight refueling versions and two in electronic warfare versions), 11 Boeing 747s (three in in-flight refueling versions), 3 Falcon 20s, 1 Falcon 50, and 2 Jet Stars.

— **70 helicopters:** 18 AB-205s, 10 AB-206s, 2 CH-47 Chinooks, and 40 Bell-214s assigned to air bases for pilot rescue missions.
— **48 training aircraft** (Beech Bonanza F-33).
— 24 combat aircraft warehoused (F-5A/B).

NAVY

25,000 troops (including naval infantry) divided over four naval bases: Bandar Abbas, Bushehr, Kharg, and Khorramshahr. A fifth base, located on the Caspian Sea (Rasht), served as a naval academy but did not have any warships. A sixth base (Bandar Chabahar) was being built on the Gulf of Oman, not far from the Pakistani border.

ASSETS (61 SHIPS TOTALING 55,000 TONS, 35 HELICOPTERS):
— **3 destroyers** (2 Allen Sumner and 1 Battle): *Babr, Palang,* and *Damavand.*
— **4 Vosper Mk-5 missile frigates:** *Alvand, Alborz, Sabalan,* and *Sahand.*
— **4 PF-103 corvettes:** *Bayandor, Naghdi, Milanian,* and *Kahnamvie.*
— **9 Combattante II missile boats:** *Kaman, Zoubin, Khadang, Paykan, Joshan, Falakhon, Shamshir, Gorz,* and *Gardouneh.*
— **5 amphibious assault ships (LST),** each able to carry ten armored vehicles and 180 infantrymen: *Iran Ajr, Hengham, Tomb, Larak,* and *Lavan.*
— 14 hydroplanes (8 SRN-6s and 6 BH-7s), each able to carry 60 infantrymen.
— 7 patrol boats (4 Capes and 3 PGM-71s).
— 5 minesweepers.
— 4 cargo ships.
— 3 replenishment oilers: *Bandar Abbas, Bushehr,* and *Kharg.*
— 3 logistics ships: *Delvar, Charak,* and *Chiroo.*
— **35 helicopters:** 7 RH-53 Sea Stallions, 14 AB-212s, and 14 antisubmarine SH-3 Sea Kings (principally based in Bandar Abbas).
— 3 naval infantry battalions (1,500 naval troops).

TABLE D.5

DEPLOYMENT OF IRANIAN AIR FORCE COMBAT AIRCRAFT
(23 WINGS)

Squadron	Allowance	Mission
1st wing (Tehran–Mehrabad)		
11th	8 RF-4Es, 14 RF-5As	Reconnaissance
12th	24 F-4Es	Air superiority / bombing
13rd	24 F-4Es	Air superiority / bombing
2nd wing (Tabriz)		
21st	20 F-5E/Fs	Tactical support
22nd	20 F-5E/Fs	Tactical support
23rd	20 F-5E/Fs	Tactical support
3rd wing (Hamadan–Nojeh)		
31st	16 F-4Es, 8 RF-4Es	Air superiority / reconnaissance
32nd	16 F-4Es	Air superiority / bombing
33rd	16 F-4Es	Air superiority / bombing
4th wing (Dezful–Vahdati)		
41st	20 F-5E/Fs	Tactical support
42nd	20 F-5E/Fs	Tactical support
43rd	24 F-5E/Fs	Support / training
6th wing (Bushehr)		
61st	20 F-4Es	Air superiority / bombing
62nd	20 F-4Es, 4 RF-4Es	Air superiority / bombing
7th wing (Shiraz)		
71st	16 F-4Ds	Attack in depth
72nd	19 F-14As	Interception
73rd	19 F-14As	Interception
8th wing (Esfahan)		
81st	20 F-14As	Interception
82nd	19 F-14As	Interception
9th wing (Bandar Abbas)		
91st	12 F-4Es	Air superiority / bombing
92nd	6 P-3F Orions	Anti-ship combat
10th wing (Shah Bahar–Kangan)		
101st	14 F-4Ds	Air superiority / training
102nd	16 F-5E/Fs	Tactical support

TABLE D.6
DEPLOYMENT OF IRANIAN AIR FORCE TRANSPORT PLANES
(7 SQUADRONS)

Squadron	Allowance	Location
11th	12 C-130s	Tehran
12th	16 C-130s	Tehran
13rd	6 Boeing 707s, 8 KC-135s, 11 Boeing 747s	Tehran
14th	1 Falcon 50s, 3 Falcon 20s, 2 Jet Stars (VIP)	Tehran
15th	18 Fokker F-27s	Tehran
71st	14 C-130s	Shiraz
72nd	14 C-130s	Shiraz

DEPLOYMENT:

Bandar Abbas: 3 destroyers (*Babr, Palang,* and *Damavand*), 4 missile frigates (*Alvand, Alborz, Sabalan,* and *Sahand*), 5 amphibious vessels (*Iran Ajr, Hengham, Tomb, Larak,* and *Lavan*), 5 minesweepers, 2 patrol boats, 4 cargo ships, 3 oil tankers, 2 logistics vessels, and 2 naval infantry battalions.

Bushehr: 4 corvettes (*Bayandor, Naghdi, Milanian,* and *Kahnamvie*), 6 missile boats (*Kaman, Khadang, Falakhon, Shamshir, Gorz,* and *Gardouneh*), 2 patrol boats, 8 hydroplanes, and 1 logistics vessel.

Kharg: 3 missile boats *(Zoubin, Paykan, Joshan),* 1 patrol boat, 3 hydroplanes, and 1 naval infantry detachment.

Khorramshahr: 2 patrol boats, 3 hydroplanes, and 1 naval infantry battalion.

Reinforcements in Both Camps (1981–1988)
Iraq
ARMY

STRENGTH:

Increase from 180,000 troops (1980) to 540,000 troops (1988) at a rate of 45,000 troops per year. These forces included a corps of foreign volunteers of approximately 25,000 troops (12,000 Egyptians, 8,000 Jordanians, and 5,000 citizens of other Arab states). The regular army was reinforced by the Popular Army, which grew from 60,000 troops (1980) to 650,000 troops (1988), an increase of 75,000 troops per year. One-third of the Popular Army was permanently assigned to the front, by rotation, primarily in the infantry divisions (of which it formed the basic structure), the border guard brigades, and the training brigades. Overall, the regular army and the Popular Army could array a maximum of 750,000 troops on the front in 1988.

UNITS:

5 army corps and 40 divisions—34 regular (33 infantry and 1 armored) and 6 Republican Guard (2 armored, 1 mechanized, and 3 motorized infantry).

1981: 4th Army Corps (HQ in Amarah).

> 14th, 15th, and 16th infantry divisions.
>
> 3 training brigades.
>
> 20 border guard brigades (numbered 101 to 120 and deployed facing Saudi Arabia, Kuwait, Syria, Turkey, and Iranian Kurdistan).

1982: 17th armored division equipped with Chieftain, Scorpion, and Patton tanks seized from the Iranian army.

> 18th, 19th, and 20th infantry divisions.
>
> 64th special forces brigade.
>
> Dissolution of the 9th armored division (following the battle of Khorramshahr).

1983: 5th Army Corps (HQ south of Basra).

> 21st, 22nd, 23rd, and 24th infantry divisions.
>
> 1st Republican Guard motorized infantry brigade.
>
> 2nd Republican Guard armored brigade.
>
> 65th special forces brigade.
>
> 3 additional training brigades.

1984: 6th Army Corps (HQ north of Basra).

> 7th Army Corps (HQ south of Basra).
>
> 25th, 26th, 27th, 28th, 29th, 30th, 31st, and 32nd infantry divisions.
>
> Creation of the Republican Guard's Hammurabi armored division, equipped with T-72 tanks and AUF-1 self-propelled howitzers, grouping the 1st motorized infantry brigade and the 2nd and 10th Republican Guard armored brigades.

Naval infantry battalions were grouped in two naval infantry brigades (440th and 441st).

66th special forces brigade.

1985: Gathering of three commando brigades in a Republican Guard special forces motorized division.

33rd, 34th, 35th, 36th, 37th, 38th, and 39th infantry divisions.

224th artillery brigade equipped with Scud-B ballistic missiles, then Al Hussein ballistic missiles (in 1988).

1986: Creation of a HQ for the Republican Guard Army Corps, based in Baghdad and controlling the Guard's divisions, as well as all the ground-to-ground missile brigades (147th, 148th, and 224th).

40th, 41st, 42nd, 43rd, and 44th infantry divisions.

1987: Medina Munawara armored division of the Republican Guard (T-72 tanks).

Baghdad infantry division of the Republican Guard (in the capital).

45th, 46th, and 50th infantry divisions.

1988: Nebuchadnezzar mechanized division of the Republican Guard.

EQUIPMENT:

— **3,250 main battle tanks:** 500 T-72s delivered by the USSR; 500 T-55s and 500 T-62s delivered by the USSR, Poland, and Romania; 1,000 T-59s (T-55) and 500 T-69s (T-62) delivered by China; 250 T-55s delivered by Egypt; and a few AMX-30s delivered by France.

— **500 light armored reconnaissance vehicles:** 150 OT-65s (BRDM-1) delivered by Hungary, 100 BRDM-2s delivered by the USSR, 100 Panhard UTM 800 "Hots" delivered by France, 100 SK-105 Kürassiers delivered by Austria, and 50 EE-3 Jararacas delivered by Brazil.

— **3,000 armored personnel carriers:** 1,600 EE-11 Urutus delivered by Brazil; 800 BMP-1s delivered by the USSR, Poland, and Romania; 400 OT-62s and OT-64s delivered by Poland and Czechoslovakia; 100 AMX-10Ps delivered by France; and 100 MOWAG Rolands delivered by Switzerland.

— **1,500 artillery pieces:** 900 towed field guns (300 122 mm D-30s delivered by the USSR, Poland, Romania, and Yugoslavia; 300 130 mm Type-59s—copy of the M-46—delivered by China; 100 155 mm G-5s delivered by South Africa; and 200 155 mm GHN-45s delivered by Canada and Austria), 180 self-propelled guns (80 155 mm GCT-AUF1s delivered by France, 70 122 mm 2S1s and 30 152 mm 2S3s delivered by the USSR), 120 multiple rocket launchers (60 127 mm ASTROS IIs, 30 180 mm ASTROS SS-40s, and 30 300 mm ASTROS SS-60s delivered by Brazil) and 300 120 and 160 mm heavy mortars delivered by Yugoslavia.

— **Antitank capacity:** Delivery of several thousand Sagger and Spigot missiles by the USSR. Delivery of several thousand Hot and Milan missiles by France.

— **Ballistic capacity:** Delivery of 18 Scud-B launchers and 400 missiles by the USSR beginning in 1985 (half of which the Iraqis would convert into Al Hussein missiles with longer range but lighter loads).

AIR FORCE

STRENGTH:

Increase from 25,000 troops (1980) to 40,000 troops (1988).

UNITS (15 NEW COMBAT SQUADRONS AND 3 NEW HELICOPTER WINGS):

1981: 79th fighter squadron equipped with Mirage F-1EQs.

87th air superiority squadron equipped with MiG-25Ps.

1982: 97th reconnaissance squadron equipped with MiG-25Rs.

3rd helicopter wing equipped with Pumas, "Hot" Gazelles, and BO-105s.

1983: 91st attack squadron equipped with Mirage F-1EQs.

59th attack squadron equipped with MiG-23BNs.

1984: 63rd fighter squadron equipped with MiG-23MLs.

69th attack squadron equipped with Su-22Ms.

81st attack squadron equipped with Super Etendards, then Mirage F-1EQ5s.

89th attack squadron equipped with Mirage F-1EQs.

107th squadron equipped with PC-7 Turbo Trainers armed for chemical warfare.

4th helicopter wing equipped with Mi-17s, Mi-24s, and BO-105s.

1985: 73rd fighter squadron equipped with MiG-23MLs.

1986: 96th air superiority squadron equipped with MiG-25Ps.

115th attack squadron equipped with Su-25s.

1987: 116th attack squadron equipped with Su-25s.

5th helicopter wing equipped with BO-105s and Hughes 300/500/530s.

1988: 114th attack squadron equipped with Su-25s.

6th fighter squadron equipped with MiG-29s.

EQUIPMENT:

— **440 combat aircraft:** 97 Mirage F-1EQs (15 B versions for training) and 24 Mirage F-1EQ5s (equipped for firing Exocet missiles) delivered by France; 5 Super Etendards rented from France from 1983 to 1985; 30 MiG-21bis, 86 MiG-23s (18 BN versions for ground attack and 68 MF/ML versions for interception), 40 MiG-25s (24 P versions for interception and 16 R versions for reconnaissance), 54 Su-22Ms, 54 Su-25s, and 15 MiG-29s delivered by the USSR; and 30 F-7s (MiG-21) and 4 H-6Ds (Chinese copy of the Tu-16 equipped to fire C-601 anti-ship missile) delivered by China (via Egypt). Most of these aircraft were armed with a new generation of air-air missiles: Matra Super 530 and R-550 Magic-1 (Mirage F-1), AA-6 Acrid (MiG-25), AA-7 Apex (MiG-23), and AA-11 Archer (MiG-29).

— **260 helicopters:** 40 "Hot" Gazelles, 10 Pumas, and 6 "Exocet" Super Frelons delivered by France, 18 Mi-17s and 40 Mi-24/25ss delivered by the USSR, 60 BO-105s delivered by Germany (via Spain), 30 Hughes-300s and 56 Hughes-500/530s delivered by the United States.

— **162 training aircraft:** 16 MBB-223 Flamingos delivered by Germany, 48 AS-202s delivered by Italy, 24 L-29s and L-39s delivered by Czechoslovakia, 50 PC-7 TurboTrainers delivered by Switzerland, 24 EMB-312 Tucanos delivered by Brazil.

— **19 transport planes:** 2 Tu-124s and 10 Il-76s delivered by the USSR, 6 Lockheed L-100s (civilian copy of the C-130) delivered by the United States, 1 Falcon-50 (ex-Iranian).

ANTI-AIRCRAFT DEFENSE

STRENGTH:

Increase from 10,000 troops (1980) to 15,000 troops (1988).

EQUIPMENT:

Delivery of 400 57 mm S-60 anti-aircraft guns by Hungary. Resupply of SAM-2/3/6/7/9 missiles by the USSR and the Eastern Bloc countries. Delivery of 60 "Roland" systems and 20 "Crotale" systems by France.

Delivery of SAM-13/14s by the Soviet Union beginning in 1988.

NAVY

STRENGTH:

Constant (5,000 troops).

VESSELS (11 LIGHT SHIPS):

1981: 3 Nestin minesweepers delivered by Yugoslavia.

1982: 1 training frigate *(Ibn Marjid)* delivered by Yugoslavia.

1982–1984: 4 OSA II missile boats, 2 P-6 torpedo boats, and 1 Polnocny-class LSM amphibious assault ship delivered by the USSR.

— 11 warships purchased by the Iraqi navy from Italy at the beginning of the war, but kept under embargo in Italian ports for the duration of the conflict:

— 4 Lupo missile frigates *(Hittin, Thi Qar, Al-Qadisiya,* and *Yarmouk).*

— 6 Assad missile corvettes *(Moussa Ben Nussaïr, Tariq Ibn Ziad, Abdulla Ben Abi Sarh, Khalid Ind Walid, Saad Inb Abi Wacade,* and *Saladin Al-Ayoori).*

— 1 replenishment oiler *(Agnadeen).*

COASTAL DEFENSE:

Delivery of CSSC-2 Silkworm antiship missile land batteries by China, as of 1982.

Iran

ARMY (INCLUDING ARMY AVIATION AND ANTI-AIRCRAFT DEFENSE)

STRENGTH:

Increase from 185,000 troops (1980) to 280,000 troops (1988), or a little more than 10,000 troops per year, and from 7 to 16 divisions.

UNITS:

1981: Transformation of the 88th armored brigade into the 88th armored division equipped with Chieftain, then T-55 and T-62 tanks (delivered by Libya).

Transformation of the 84th mechanized brigade into the 84th mechanized division equipped with Soviet-made equipment captured from the Iraqi army.

1982: Creation of 4 regional HQs responsible for Kurdistan, Khuzestan, and the sectors of Qasr-e-Shirin and Mehran.

Creation of 3 infantry divisions (30th, 40th, and 58th).

Transformation of the 30th motorized infantry brigade into the 30th armored division equipped with T-59 tanks delivered by North Korea (under the supervision of the IRGC).

1983: Transformation of the 23rd special forces brigade into the 23rd commando division.

1984: Transformation of the 11th artillery brigade into the 11th artillery division.

1985: Transformation of the 55th parachute brigade into the 55th parachute division.

Transformation of the 22nd artillery brigade into the 22nd artillery division.

1986: Transformation of the 33rd artillery brigade into the 33rd artillery division (under the supervision of the IRGC).

1987: Transformation of the 44th artillery brigade into the 44th artillery division (under the supervision of the IRGC).

1988: Transformation of the 55th artillery brigade into the 55th artillery division (under the supervision of the IRGC).

Given the inadequate number of tanks and armored vehicles, several mechanized divisions would be downgraded into regular infantry divisions.

EQUIPMENT:

See the section below regarding the IRGC, since most of the equipment delivered was taken by the IRGC.

ISLAMIC REVOLUTIONARY GUARDS CORPS (IRGC)

STRENGTH:

Increase from 30,000 troops in 1980 to 700,000 troops in 1986, followed by a slight drop to 600,000 troops in 1988, or a little more than 100,000 troops per year. Half of the Pasdaran served on the front (by rotation) in units detached from the IRGC. The IRGC was **reinforced, when necessary, by the Basij** (literally "mobilization") **militia**, which recruited youth between twelve and seventeen years old and adults without military obligations. This militia had 600,000 young fighters as of 1986, of which a maximum of one-third were present in the IRGC divisions, by short-term rotation (two or three months), to participate in large-scale offensives.

UNITS (32 DIVISIONS, INCLUDING THREE ARTILLERY):

1981: 4 infantry divisions (5th, 7th, 8th, and 9th).

1982: Creation of the Ministry of the IRGC.

9 infantry divisions (11th, 12th, 15th, 17th, 18th, 19th, 25th, 27th, and 29th). 30th armored division equipped with T-59 tanks (from the regular army).

1983: 4 infantry divisions (31st, 34th, 36th, and 37th).

1984: 4 infantry divisions (48th, 52nd, 57th, and 59th).

Master of Martyrs 10th assault infantry brigade.

1985: 14th mechanized division equipped with T-59 tanks.

2 infantry divisions (66th and 71st).

Ramadan 20th armored brigade equipped with T-69 tanks.

351st artillery brigade equipped with Scud-B ballistic missiles (delivered by Libya, then North Korea).

Creation of a naval command and artillery command within the IRGC.

1986: 2 infantry divisions (75th and 82nd).

41st assault pioneer division plus 2 armored brigades (38th and 72nd). 33rd artillery division (detached from the regular army).

3 naval infantry brigades (1st, 2nd, and 3rd) created from the transformation of the naval infantry battalions (detached from the navy).

26th Silkworm antiship missile brigade.

1987: 1 infantry division (91st).

44th artillery division (detached from the regular army).

1988: 55th artillery division (detached from the regular army).

The IRGC's 27 infantry divisions were identified by the following numbers and names: 5th Nasser, 7th Valiasr, 8th Najaf, 9th Badr, 11th Momenim, 12th Ghaem, 14th Hossein, 15th Hassan, 17th Abitaleb, 18th Ghadir, 19th Fajr, 25th Karbala, 27th Rasulullah, 29th Akram, 31st Ashura, 34th Sajjad, 36th Ansar, 37th Noor, 48th Fatah, 52nd al-Qods, 57th Abolfazi, 59th Agheel, 66th Vali-ye-Amr, 71st Ruhollah, 75th Zafar, 82nd Saheb al-Amr, and 91st Baghiatallah. As of 1984, these divisions were gradually gathered into 9 army corps named: "Badr," "Najaf," "Karbala," "Ramadan," "al-Qods," "Fatah," "Hamzeh," "Noor," and "Zafar."

EQUIPMENT:

— **850 main battle tanks:** 100 T-55s, 100 T-62s, and 100 T-72s delivered by Libya, 100 T-55s and T-62s delivered by Bulgaria, and 300 T-59s (T-55) and 150 T-69s (T-62) delivered by China and North Korea.

— 180 EE-9 Cascavel light armored reconnaissance vehicles delivered by Brazil.

— **630 armored personnel carriers:** 50 BTR-60s delivered by Bulgaria, 100 BTR-60s and 180 BMP-1s delivered by Libya, and 300 EE-11 Urutus delivered by Brazil.

— **470 artillery pieces:** 410 towed field guns (40 105 mm Oto Melaras—licensed by the Chinese NORENCO company—and 150 130 mm Type-59s—a Chinese copy of the M-46—delivered by North Korea, 50 155 mm Soltam M-71s delivered by Israel, 30 155 mm G-5s delivered by South Africa, and 140 155 mm GHN-45s delivered by Austria), and 60 multiple rocket launchers (20 107 mm Type-63s and 40 122 mm BM-11s) delivered by North Korea.

— **3,000 107 and 120 mm mortars** delivered by China and North Korea.

— **100 light patrol boats** built by Iran (30 MIG-G/S) or delivered by China (10 CAT-14s), North Korea (20 IPS-16/18s), and Sweden (40 Boghammas). All these patrol boats were armed with a cannon or machine gun, two torpedo tubes, and/or one rocket launcher.

— **Antitank capacity:** Delivery of RPG-7 and AT-3 Sagger missiles by Libya, Syria, and Bulgaria. Resupply of TOW missiles by Israel, South Korea, and the United States.

— **Anti-air capacity:** Resupply of Hawk missiles by Israel, South Korea, and the United States. Delivery of SAM-2/3s by China and portable SAM-7s by the USSR, Bulgaria, North Korea, Syria, and Libya. Delivery of 300 RBS-70 portable surface-to-air missiles by Sweden.

— **Ballistic capacity:** Delivery of 6 Scud-B ground-to-ground missile launchers by Libya, accompanied by a supply of 26 missiles (1985). Iran manufactured 300 Oghab (Frog-7) missiles with the assistance of North Korea (1986). Delivery of 100 Hwasong-5 (Scud-B) missiles by North Korea (1987).

— **Antiship capacity:** Delivery of CSSC-2 Silkworm antiship missile land batteries by China as of 1986.

AIR FORCE

STRENGTH:

Drop from 50,000 troops (1980) to 35,000 troops (1988).

UNIT:

5th wing comprising the 51st, 52nd, and 53rd squadrons based in Omidiyeh and equipped with warehoused F-5A/B (in 1981), then F-6 (as of 1983) and F-7 fighters (as of 1987), which were not engaged in combat.

EQUIPMENT:

— **104 combat aircraft:** 12 F-4Ds delivered by South Korea, 12 F-5A/Es delivered by Ethiopia, 20 F-6s (MiG-19) and 60 F-7s (MiG-21) delivered by China.

— 24 CH-47 Chinook helicopters delivered by Italy.

— 15 PC-6 Turbo Porter utility aircraft delivered by Switzerland.

— 45 PC-7 Turbo Trainer training aircraft delivered by Switzerland.

NAVY

STRENGTH:

Drop from 25,000 troops (1980) to 15,000 troops (1988).

UNITS:

As of 1986, transformation of the three naval infantry battalions into three naval infantry brigades, which were placed under the supervision of the IRGC.

VESSELS (8 LIGHT SHIPS AND 4 LOGISTICS VESSELS):

1981: 5 Combattante II missile boats awaiting delivery by France at the outbreak of the Islamic Revolution (*Khanjar, Neyzeh, Tabarzin, Derafsh,* and *Kalat*) and 2 logistics vessels delivered by Pakistan (*Souru* and *Silim*).

1982: 2 logistics vessels delivered by Pakistan (*Sirjan* and *Dayer*).

1988: 3 hydroplanes delivered by South Korea.

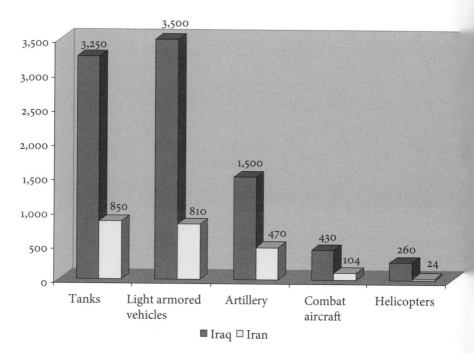

Graph D.1 War equipment deliveries in Iraq's favor

Regarding the artillery, it should be noted that Iran was delivered 3,000 mortars.

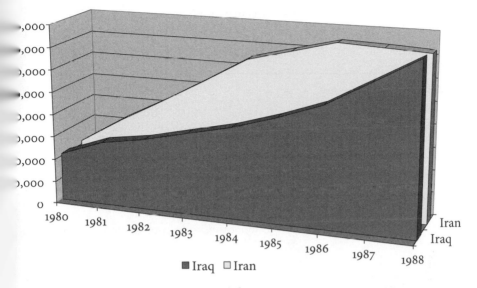

Graph D.2 Increase in manpower in Iran's favor

The Balance of Power in April 1988

Iraq

ARMY

— 7 armored divisions (3rd, 6th, 10th, 12th, 17th, Hammurabi, Medina Munawara).

— 3 mechanized divisions (1st, 5th, Nebuchadnezzar).

— 41 infantry divisions: three Republican Guard (al-Faw, Baghdad, and Tawakalna); 8 1st category (2nd, 4th, 7th, 8th, 11th, 14th, 15th, and 16th); 15 2nd category (18th, 19th, 20th, 21st, 22nd, 23rd, 24th, 25th, 26th, 27th, 28th, 29th, 30th, 31st, and 32nd); and 15 3rd category (33rd, 34th, 35th, 36th, 37th, 38th, 39th, 40th, 41st, 42nd, 43rd, 44th, 45th, 46th, and 50th).

DEPLOYMENT:

5th Corps (Rawanduz): 23rd, 33rd, 38th, and 45th infantry divisions.

1st Corps (Kirkuk): 4th, 7th, 24th, 27th, 34th, 36th, 39th, 43rd, 44th, 46th, and 50th infantry divisions.

TABLE D.7
THE BALANCE OF POWER IN APRIL 1988

IRAQ	IRAN
800,000 troops	850,000 troops
51 divisions	48 divisions
	(Army: 16—IRGC: 32)
3,400 tanks	1,100 tanks
4,500 other armored vehicles	1,400, other armored vehicles
2,300 artillery pieces	900 artillery pieces + 3,000 mortars
360 combat aircraft, divided in 30 squadrons	60 combat aircraft (+ 100 out of commission), divided in 18 squadrons
140 attack helicopters	40 attack helicopters (+ 50 out of commission)

2nd Corps (Baghdad): 16e, 21e, 22e and 28e infantry divisions.
4th Corps (Amarah): 2nd, 18th, 20th, 29th, and 32nd infantry divisions.
6th Corps (Majnoon): 25th, 31st, and 35th infantry divisions.
3rd Corps (Basra): 8th, 11th, 19th, 30th, 41st, and 42nd infantry divisions.
7th Corps (al-Faw): 14th, 15th, 26th, 37th, and 40th infantry divisions.
Mechanized field corps: 3rd, 6th, 10th, 12th, and 17th armored divisions— 1st and 5th mechanized divisions—Republican Guard.

AERIAL FORCES
— 4 Mirage F-1 squadrons (79th, 81st, 89th, and 91st).
— 7 MiG-21 squadrons (7th, 9th, 11th, 27th, 37th, 47th, and 70th).
— 6 MiG-23 squadrons (29th, 39th, 49th, 59th, 63rd, and 73rd).
— 3 MiG-25 squadrons (87th, 96th, and 97th).
— 1 MiG-29 squadron (6th).
— 1 Su-20 squadron (1st).
— 4 Su-22 squadrons (5th, 44th, 69th, and 109th).

— 3 Su-25 squadrons (114th, 115th, and 116th).

— 1 Tu-16 and Tu-22 squadron (10th).

Iran

ARMY

— 5 armored divisions (16th, 30th, 81st, 88th, and 92nd).

— 4 mechanized divisions (14th, 28th, 77th, and 84th).

— 32 infantry divisions (5th, 7th, 8th, 9th, 11th, 12th, 15th, 17th, 18th, 19th, 21st, 23rd, 25th, 27th, 29th, 30th, 31st, 34th, 36th, 37th, 40th, 48th, 52nd, 57th, 58th, 59th, 64th, 66th, 71st, 75th, 82nd, and 91st).

— 1 parachute division (55th).

— 1 pioneer assault division (41st).

— 5 artillery divisions (11th, 22nd, 33rd, 44th, and 55th).

TABLE D.8

USE OF BALLISTIC MISSILES

	Number of missiles fired by Iraq on Iranian targets	Number of missiles fired by Iran on Iraqi targets
1980	10 (all Frog-7s)	—
1981	54 (all Frog-7s)	—
1982	26 (23 Frog-7s, 3 Scud-Bs)	—
1983	37 (4 Frog-7s, 33 Scud-Bs)	—
1984	63 (38 Frog-7s, 25 Scud-Bs)	—
1985	113 (31 Frog-7s, 82 Scud-Bs)	18 (all Scud-Bs)
1986	—	27 (19 Oghabs, 8 Scud-Bs)
1987	27 (all Scud-Bs)	99 (81 Oghabs, 18 Scud-Bs)
1988	193 (4 Scud-Bs, 189 Al Husseins)	181 (104 Oghabs, 77 Scud-Bs)
Total	523 (160 Frog-7s, 174 Scud-Bs, 189 Al Husseins)	325 (204 Oghabs, 121 Scud-Bs)

Note: Some sources list a higher number of Scud missiles fired by Iraq, erroneously including Frog-7 missile fire in their statistics. These missiles were nearly exclusively aimed at cities, killing approximately 4,000 civilians (Iranian and Iraqi) and wounding 12,000. Only a few missiles were directed at military objectives (air bases, headquarters, oil terminals). During this period, Iran also fired 9 Silkworm missiles and 1 Scud missile at Kuwait.

AERIAL FORCES

— 3 F-14 Tomcat squadrons (72nd, 81st, and 82nd).

— 7 F-4 Phantom squadrons (11th, 12th, 31st, 61st, 71st, 91st, and 101st).

— 5 F-5 Tiger squadrons (21st, 22nd, 41st, 42nd, and 102nd).

— 1 F-6 squadron (51st).

— 2 F-7 squadrons (52nd and 53rd).

[Appendix E]

Armed Opposition

Opposition to the Iraqi Regime

KURDISTAN DEMOCRATIC PARTY (KDP)

Leader: Masoud Barzani (supported by Iran).

Maximum strength (from 1986 to 1988): 45,000 peshmergas (a third of whom were permanently mobilized) with a few tanks, light artillery pieces, recoilless guns, machine guns, antitank missiles, and SAM-7s.

Zone of activity: Northern part of Iraqi Kurdistan.

PATRIOTIC UNION OF KURDISTAN (PUK)

Leader: Jalal Talabani (supported by Iran and Syria).

Maximum strength (from 1986 to 1988): 12,000 peshmergas with a few tanks, light artillery pieces, recoilless guns, machine guns, antitank missiles, and SAM-7s.

Zone of activity: Southern part of Iraqi Kurdistan.

KURDISTAN DEMOCRATIC SOCIALIST PARTY (KDSP)

Leader: Mahmoud Othman (supported by Syria).

Maximum strength (from 1986 to 1988): 1,500 peshmergas equipped with light weapons.

Zones of activity: Mosul and the border area with Syria.

Opposition to the Iranian Regime

THE PEOPLE'S MUJAHIDIN OF IRAN (MUJAHIDIN E-KHALQ)

Leader: Massoud Rajavi (in exile in France from 1981 to 1986, then in Baghdad).

Maximum strength (from 1981–1983 to 1987–1988): 15,000 fighters, with a few tanks and several dozen light artillery pieces, recoilless guns, machine guns, antitank missiles, and SAM-7s.

Zones of activity: Tehran, Shiraz, Tabriz, and the provinces of Iranian Azerbaijan until 1983–1984, then in the Iraqi border zone as of 1987.

PEYKAR (DISSIDENT MARXIST WING OF MUJAHIDIN E-KHALQ)

Leader: Hossein Ruhani (arrested in 1982).

Maximum strength (from 1980 to 1982): 3,000 fighters equipped with light weapons.

Zones of activity: Tehran and the provinces of the Caspian Sea and Iranian Azerbaijan.

PEOPLE'S FEDAYEEN (FEDAYAN-E KHALQ)

No charismatic leader, heavily decentralized movement.

Maximum strength (from 1980 to 1983): 5,000 fighters equipped with light weapons.

Zones of activity: Iranian Kurdistan and Baluchistan.

DEMOCRATIC PARTY OF IRANIAN KURDISTAN (PDKI)

Leader: Abdul Rahman Ghassemlou (assassinated in July 1988).

Maximum strength (from 1980 to 1983): 30,000 peshmergas with a few captured tanks and light artillery pieces, recoilless guns and machine guns.

Zone of activity: Iranian Kurdistan.

ORGANIZATION OF REVOLUTIONARY TOILERS OF IRANIAN KURDISTAN, BETTER KNOWN AS KOMALA

Leaders: Saafar Chafyih and Nawshirwan Mustafa.

Maximum strength (from 1980 to 1983): 5,000 peshmergas equipped with light weapons.

Zone of activity: Iranian Kurdistan.

ARAB FRONT FOR THE LIBERATION OF AL-AHWAZ
(SUPPORTED BY IRAQ)

Strength in 1980: A few hundred militiamen rapidly suppressed in the weeks following the Iraqi invasion.

Zone of activity: Khuzestan.

[Appendix F]

Foreign Military Assistance

Iraq

Approximate value of all deliveries of war equipment to Iraq: 80 billion dollars (1988 dollars).

USSR (APPROXIMATE VALUE: 30–45 BILLION DOLLARS)

Training of Iraqi personnel in all fields. Presence of Soviet "military advisors" in Iraq. Agreement for reconditioning Soviet-made war equipment. Beginning in spring 1982, delivery of 280 combat aircraft (MiG-21, MiG-23, MiG-25, MiG-29, Su-22, and Su-25), 58 Mi-17 and Mi-24/25 helicopters, 12 Tu-124 and Il-76 transport planes (including one modified for aerial surveillance), 1,000 tanks (T-55, T-62, and T-72), 500 BMP-1 armored transport vehicles, 100 BRDM-2 armored reconnaissance vehicles, 150 D-30 towed field guns, 100 2S1 and 2S3 self-propelled guns, 18 Scud-B launchers and 300 ground-to-ground missiles, 4 OSA II missile boats, 2 P-6 torpedo boats, 1 Polnocny-class amphibious assault ship, several million various shells and munitions, several tens of thousands of light weapons, several thousands of trucks and light vehicles, several thousand AT-3/4 antitank missiles, SAM-2/3/6/7/9/13/14 surface-to-air missiles, and AA-2/6/7/8/11 air-air missiles.

FRANCE (APPROXIMATE VALUE: 17 BILLION DOLLARS)

Training of Iraqi pilots and technicians flying French aircraft. Presence of French technicians in Iraq. Rental of 5 Super Etendard planes equipped with Exocet missiles (from 1983 to 1985). Throughout the entire conflict, delivery of 121 Mirage F-1EQ combat aircraft (including 24 equipped for firing Exocet missiles), 56 helicopters (40 Gazelle "Hot," 10 Puma, and 6 Super Frelon "Exocet"), 10 AMX-30 tanks, 100 Panhard UTM-800 "Hot" light armored reconnaissance vehicles, 100 AMX-10P armored vehicles,

o GCT-AUF1 cannons, 60 Roland surface-to-air systems, several Cro-
ale surface-to-air missile batteries (via Saudi Arabia), electronic war
quipment, several million various shells and munitions, several thousand
Iot and Milan antitank missiles, several hundred Exocet ground-to-sea
missiles, Roland surface-to-air missiles, AS-30L air-to-ground missiles,
nd air-air missiles (Magic-1 and 2, Super 530).

CHINA (APPROXIMATE VALUE: 6 BILLION DOLLARS)
Delivery of 1,500 T-59/T-69 tanks and 300 Type-59 towed field guns (beginning in 1981), CSSC-2 Silkworm antiship missile batteries (in 1982),
50 F-7 fighters (from 1983 to 1985), 4 H-6 bombers (in 1988), as well as several tens of thousands of light weapons and several million various shells
and munitions.

ITALY (APPROXIMATE VALUE: 3.6 BILLION DOLLARS)
Basic training of a number of Iraqi pilots. Undelivered order of 11 war-
ships (4 frigates, 6 corvettes, and 1 replenishment oiler). Delivery of 48
AS-202 training aircraft (from 1981 to 1983), several million mines (via
Singapore), and large quantities of various shells and munitions.

EGYPT (APPROXIMATE VALUE: 3 BILLION DOLLARS)
Sent about 50 Egyptian pilots, several hundred technicians, and several
thousand "volunteers" to the Iraqi front. Sent the 71st fighter squadron
equipped with Mirage Vs to the Iraqi front (beginning in 1986). Supplied
large quantities of spare parts for Soviet-made equipment. Delivery of
250 T-55 tanks, a wide variety of munitions, and AA-2, AT-3, and SAM-7
missiles beginning in 1982. Delivery of 30 obsolete Su-7 fighters (used as
decoys on Iraqi airfields).

BRAZIL (APPROXIMATE VALUE: 1.7 BILLION DOLLARS)
Delivery of 24 of 50 Tucano training aircraft ordered (from 1986 to 1988),
50 EE-3 Jararaca light armored reconnaissance vehicles, and 1,600 EE-11
Urutu armored vehicles (beginning in 1981), several hundred E-25 and
E-50 trucks, 120 multiple rocket launchers (ASTROS II, ASTROS SS-40,
and SS-60, beginning in 1985), and spare parts for EE-9 Cascavel light armored vehicles.

YUGOSLAVIA (APPROXIMATE VALUE: 1.2 BILLION DOLLARS)

Training of a number of Iraqi sailors. Beginning in 1981, delivery of training frigate, 3 minesweepers, 100 D-30 towed field guns, 300 heav' mortars, several hundred thousand various shells and munitions, and sev' eral tens of thousands of light weapons.

ROMANIA (APPROXIMATE VALUE: 1 BILLION DOLLARS)

Beginning in 1981, delivery of 300 T-55 and T-62 tanks, 200 BMP-1 armored vehicles, 100 D-30 towed field guns, several tens of thousands o: light weapons, several hundred trucks and light vehicles, as well as large quantities of various shells and munitions and AA-2, AT-3, and SAM-7 missiles.

POLAND (APPROXIMATE VALUE: 900 MILLION DOLLARS)

Beginning in 1981, delivery of 200 T-55 and T-62 tanks, 100 BMP-1 armored vehicles, 200 OT-62 and OT-64 armored personnel carriers, 100 D-30 towed field guns, several tens of thousands of light weapons, several hundred trucks and light vehicles, as well as large quantities of various shells and munitions and AA-2, AT-3, and SAM-7 missiles.

CZECHOSLOVAKIA (APPROXIMATE VALUE: 800 MILLION DOLLARS)

Beginning in 1981, delivery of 24 L-29 and L-39 training aircraft, 200 OT-62 and OT-64 armored vehicles, light weapons, as well as large quantities of shells and AA-2, AT-3, and SAM-7 missiles.

AUSTRIA (APPROXIMATE VALUE: 350 MILLION DOLLARS)

Delivery of 100 SK-105 Kürassier armored reconnaissance vehicles (in 1981) and 200 GHN-45 towed field guns (beginning in 1984, via Gerald Bull's Canadian company).

HUNGARY (APPROXIMATE VALUE: 300 MILLION DOLLARS)

In 1981, delivery of 150 BRDM-1 light armored vehicles and 400 S-60 anti-air guns.

UNITED STATES (APPROXIMATE VALUE: 250 MILLION DOLLARS)

Cooperation in the field of military intelligence, notably in terms of space and radar imaging and ELINT-SIGINT data. Delivery of 6 L-100 transport planes (in 1985), 86 Hughes 300/500/530 helicopters (beginning in 1986), and large quantities of fragmentation bombs.

SOUTH AFRICA (APPROXIMATE VALUE: 200 MILLION DOLLARS)

Delivery of 100 G-5 towed field guns and related munitions (beginning in 1986).

GERMANY (APPROXIMATE VALUE: 150 MILLION DOLLARS)

Training of Iraqi military doctors. Delivery of several hundred tank transporters and Mercedes trucks. Beginning in 1982, delivery of 60 BO-105 helicopters equipped with Hot antitank missiles, via Spain.

SPAIN (APPROXIMATE VALUE: 150 MILLION DOLLARS)

Delivery of BO-105 helicopters on behalf of Germany, several thousand light weapons, several hundred 106 mm recoilless guns, several hundred Land Rover Santana jeeps, as well as large quantities of munitions.

SWITZERLAND (APPROXIMATE VALUE: 100 MILLION DOLLARS)

Delivery of 100 MOWAG Roland armored personnel carriers (in 1981), 50 Pilatus PC-7 Turbo Trainer training aircraft (from 1982 to 1985), small caliber munitions, and cryptography equipment.

UNITED KINGDOM (APPROXIMATE VALUE: 60 MILLION DOLLARS)

Enrollment of Iraqi cadets in British military academies. Basic training of a number of Iraqi pilots. Delivery of 300 Land Rovers, guided artillery radar systems, and spare parts for Chieftain and Scorpion tanks captured from the Iranian army.

SWEDEN (APPROXIMATE VALUE: 50 MILLION DOLLARS)

Delivery of large quantities of munitions for Bofors anti-air guns.

BELGIUM (APPROXIMATE VALUE: 40 MILLION DOLLARS)

Delivery of light weapons and small-caliber munitions.

SINGAPORE

Supply of Italian-designed naval mines.

CANADA

Hosting of Iraqi cadets. Cooperation in the field of artillery.

CHILE

Supply of fragmentation bombs.

JORDAN

Transit agreement for the delivery of weapons from other countries. Agreement for the temporary parking of Iraqi combat aircraft on Jordanian territory. Delivery of Magic and AIM-9 Sidewinder air-air missiles. Loan of about ten Mirage F-1 fighters. Deployment of several thousand Jordanian "volunteers" and a mechanized brigade on the Iraqi front. Detachment of about 15 Jordanian fighter pilots and about 50 technicians to the Iraqi air force.

GERMAN DEMOCRATIC REPUBLIC (GDR)

Training of pilots.

SAUDI ARABIA AND KUWAIT

Transit agreements for the delivery of weapons from other countries. Agreements for the temporary parking of Iraqi combat aircraft on Kuwaiti and Saudi territory. Delivery of American-made bombs and munitions. Significant financial assistance.

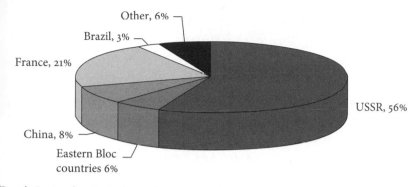

Graph F.1 Iraq's principal suppliers

MOROCCO AND NORTH YEMEN

Deployment of "volunteers" to the Iraqi front. Detachment of a few Moroccan Mirage F-1 pilots to the Iraqi army as instructors.

TURKEY

Transit agreement for the delivery of weapons from other countries. Military cooperation agreement to fight the Kurdish armed opposition. Enrollment of Iraqi cadets in Turkish military academies.

JAPAN

Cryptography and electronic interception equipment.

Iran

Approximate value of overall deliveries of war equipment to Iran: 24 billion dollars (1988 dollars).

CHINA (APPROXIMATE VALUE: 3 BILLION DOLLARS)

Delivery of 200 T-59/T-69 tanks and 80 F-6/F-7 fighters (beginning in 1983); CSSC-2 Silkworm antiship missile batteries (in 1986); SAM-2 and SAM-3 batteries (in 1987); 10 CAT-14 light patrol boats; 1,000 mortars; millions of various shells, mines, and munitions; as well as several tens of thousands of light weapons.

NORTH KOREA (APPROXIMATE VALUE: 3 BILLION DOLLARS)

Presence of North Korean "military advisors" in Iran. Assistance agree ment for the manufacturing of Frog-7 ground-to-ground missiles. Agree ment to recondition Soviet-made equipment captured from the Iraqi army Beginning in 1981, delivery of 250 T-59 tanks; 190 towed field guns (Type-59 and Oto Melara/Norenco); 60 multiple rocket launchers (Type-63 and BM-11); 2,000 mortars; 20 IPS-16/18 light patrol boats; a midget submarine several hundred SAM-7 surface-to-air missiles; recoilless guns; 100 Scud-B ground-to-ground missiles (beginning in 1987); millions of various shells, mines, and munitions; as well as large quantities of light weapons.

LIBYA (APPROXIMATE VALUE: 2.5 BILLION DOLLARS)

Supply of spare parts for Soviet-made equipment captured from the Iraqi army. From 1981 to 1984, delivery of 300 T-55, T-62, and T-72 tanks; 280 BTR-60 and BMP-1 armored vehicles; 6 Scud-B ground-to-ground missile launchers (in 1985, with 26 missiles); several thousand tank shells and RPG-7s; and several hundred AT-3 and SAM-7 missiles.

ISRAEL (APPROXIMATE VALUE: 2 BILLION DOLLARS)

From 1980 to 1986, supply of spare parts for various types of missiles, M-48 and M-60 tanks, for F-4 fighters, and AH-1 and Bell-212 helicopters. De- livery of jammer pods, telecommunication and jamming devices, 2,500 TOW antitank missiles, several hundred Sidewinder air-air missiles, 68 Hawk surface-to-air missiles, 50 Soltam M-71 guns, 150 M-40 antitank guns, several hundred jeeps, several thousand light weapons, and several hundred thousand shells (tanks and artillery).

USSR (APPROXIMATE VALUE: 1.5 BILLION DOLLARS)

Transit agreement for the delivery of arms coming from other countries, notably via the port of Bandar-e Anzali on the Caspian Sea. Presence of Soviet "military advisors" in Iran. Training of Iranian military personnel to use Soviet-made armored vehicles and artillery pieces. Agreement for the reconditioning of Soviet-made equipment captured from the Iraqi army. Delivery, beginning in 1981, of SAM-7 surface-to-air missiles, hundreds of trucks and light vehicles, several tens of thousands of light weapons, and large quantities of munitions for Soviet armored vehicles and artillery pieces captured from the Iraqi army.

SOUTH KOREA (APPROXIMATE VALUE: 1.2 BILLION DOLLARS)

Beginning in 1981, supply of large quantities of spare parts for M-48 and M-60 tanks, F-4 and F-5 fighters, and AH-1 helicopters. Delivery of 12 F-4D fighters in 1983, several thousand light weapons and several hundred TOW antitank missiles, Hawk surface-to-air missiles, and AIM-7E/F Sparrow and AIM-9J/L Sidewinder air-air missiles.

BULGARIA (APPROXIMATE VALUE: 840 MILLION DOLLARS)

Supply of spare parts for all Soviet-made equipment. In 1981, delivery of 100 T-55 and T-62 tanks, 50 BTR-60 armored vehicles, and large quantities of light weapons, shells, rockets, and all types of munitions, notably RPG-7s and AT-3 and SAM-7 missiles.

SYRIA (APPROXIMATE VALUE: 800 MILLION DOLLARS)

Agreement to allow approximately 2,000 Iranian fighters to join the ranks of Hezbollah in South Lebanon, facing Israel. Supply of spare parts for all Soviet-made equipment. As of 1981, delivery of large quantities of light weapons and all types of munitions, notably RPG-7s and AT-3 and SAM-7 missiles.

PORTUGAL (APPROXIMATE VALUE: 760 MILLION DOLLARS)

Delivery of large quantities of shells and all types of munitions.

SPAIN (APPROXIMATE VALUE: 730 MILLION DOLLARS)

Supply of spare parts for F-4 and F-5 fighters. Delivery of Land Rover light vehicles built under license in Spain and large quantities of munitions (notably for the air force).

UNITED STATES (APPROXIMATE VALUE:
650 MILLION DOLLARS)

As of 1981, delivery of spare parts for helicopters, F-4, F-5 and F-14 fighters, and AIM-54 Phoenix missiles. From 1984 to 1986, delivery (via Israel) of 2,500 TOW antitank missiles, 18 Hawk surface-to-air missiles, and spare parts used to modernize 300 Hawk missiles. Supply of satellite imagery.

UNITED KINGDOM (APPROXIMATE VALUE:
600 MILLION DOLLARS)

Agreement to modernize the air detection network. Supply of spare parts and motors for Chieftain and Scorpion tanks, electronic components for Rapier surface-to-air missiles and electronic countermeasure systems.

SWEDEN (APPROXIMATE VALUE:
600 MILLION DOLLARS)

Delivery of a turnkey munitions factory, 300 portable RBS-70 surface-to-air missiles (in 1986), 40 Boghamma high-speed patrol boats, large quantities of shells for Bofors anti-air guns, and 1,300 tons of gunpowder and explosives for the manufacturing of munitions and shells.

ITALY (APPROXIMATE VALUE: 500 MILLION DOLLARS)

Delivery of 24 CH-47 Chinook helicopters (beginning in 1981), spare parts for helicopters, 13 coastal radars, electronic warfare systems, and large quantities of gunpowder (at least 5,300 tons) for the manufacturing of munitions. Undelivered order of 7 patrol boats.

FRANCE (APPROXIMATE VALUE:
480 MILLION DOLLARS)

Delivery (from 1982 to 1986) of 500,000 155 and 203 mm artillery shells (Luchaire), 2,000 bomb-braking systems (Matra), 200 thermal imaging cameras for aircraft (Thomson-CSF), small-caliber munitions (Manhurin), and large quantities of gunpowder (SNPE) for the manufacturing of munitions.

AUSTRIA (APPROXIMATE VALUE: 480 MILLION DOLLARS)

Delivery of 140 GHN-45 (Noricum) towed field guns and related munitions, via Libya (beginning in 1987).

BRAZIL (APPROXIMATE VALUE: 450 MILLION DOLLARS)

From 1982 to 1986, delivery of 180 Cascavel armored cars, 300 EE-11 Urutu armored vehicles, and several tens of thousands of artillery shells.

SWITZERLAND (APPROXIMATE VALUE: 430 MILLION DOLLARS)

Delivery of 15 Pilatus PC-6 Turbo Porter utility aircraft (in 1983), 45 Pilatus PC-7 Turbo Trainer training aircraft (as of 1984), spare parts for radar equipment and anti-air guns, encrypting equipment, and large quantities of small-caliber munitions.

GREECE (APPROXIMATE VALUE: 350 MILLION DOLLARS)

As of 1981, supply of vast quantities of spare parts for F-4 and F-5 fighters and AB-205/206 helicopters. Delivery of munitions and gunpowder for manufacturing shells.

SOUTH AFRICA (APPROXIMATE VALUE: 100 MILLION DOLLARS)

Delivery of 30 G-5 towed field guns and related munitions (beginning in 1987).

ETHIOPIA (APPROXIMATE VALUE: 70 MILLION DOLLARS)

Delivery of 12 F-5A/E fighters in 1986.

BELGIUM (APPROXIMATE VALUE: 50 MILLION DOLLARS)

Delivery of gunpowder and explosives and fighter plane engines.

ARGENTINA

Delivery of several thousand light weapons.

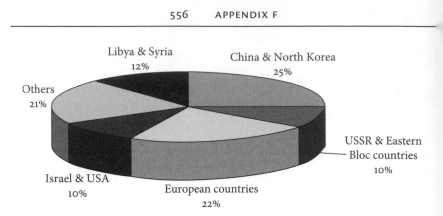

Graph F.2 Iran's principal suppliers

GERMANY

Delivery of several hundred Mercedes trucks (via Switzerland) and large quantities of small-caliber munitions (Werner). Negotiations for the potential delivery of Transall transport planes and 6 Type 209 submarines.

GERMAN DEMOCRATIC REPUBLIC (GDR)

Training of Iranian fighter pilots.

TAIWAN

Supply of spare parts for F-5 fighters and M-48 tanks beginning in 1981.

SINGAPORE

Supply of munitions and light weapons.

INDIA

Delivery of 2,000 inflatable boats for the Iranian engineering corps and of 200 torpedoes for IRGC gunboats.

PAKISTAN

Training of Iranian instructors on F-6 and F-7 fighters.

TURKEY

Transit agreement for the delivery of arms coming from other countries. Delivery of spare parts for F-4 and F-5 fighters.

[Appendix G]

Oil

Iraq

BEFORE THE OUTBREAK OF THE WAR

OPEC PRODUCTION QUOTA: 3.2 MILLION BARRELS PER DAY /
THEORETICAL PRODUCTION CAPACITY OF 4 MILLION BARRELS PER DAY.
— Oil fields around Basra: 60 percent of total production.
— Oil fields around Kirkuk-Mosul: 40 percent of total production.

REFINERY CAPACITY: 310,000 BARRELS PER DAY.
— Basra refinery: 140,000 barrels per day.
— Daurah (Baghdad) refinery: 80,000 barrels per day.
— Baiji refinery: 60,000 barrels per day.
— Kirkuk refinery: 30,000 barrels per day.

THEORETICAL EXPORT CAPACITY: 5.2 MILLION BARRELS PER DAY.
— Mina al-Bakr offshore terminal: 2.2 million barrels per day (destroyed in November 1980).
— Kohr al-Amaya offshore terminal: 1.8 million barrels per day (destroyed in November 1980).
— Kirkuk-Dortyol pipeline (via Turkey): 650,000 barrels per day.
— Kirkuk-Baniyas pipeline (via Syria): 550,000 barrels per day (closed after April 1982).

PUTTING INTO SERVICE OF NEW EXPORT CHANNELS DURING THE WAR

1982: Putting into service of a fleet of tanker trucks to Aqaba (in Jordan) and Dortyol (in Turkey): 50,000 barrels per day.
1984: New Kirkuk-Dortyol pipeline (in Turkey): 400,000 barrels per day (work began in 1982—capacity of 600,000 barrels per day in 1988).

1985: Pipeline section connecting the oil fields in southern Iraq to Yanbu (in Saudi Arabia) via the Saudi "Petroline": 500,000 barrels per day (work began in 1983—capacity of 1 million barrels per day in 1988).

1987: Beginning of construction on the Baiji-Basra pipeline (capacity of 500,000 barrels per day) connecting Iraq's northern and southern oil fields. This section of the pipeline was not put into service until after the war.

Iran

BEFORE THE OUTBREAK OF WAR

**OPEC PRODUCTION QUOTA: 4.4 MILLION BARRELS PER DAY /
THEORETICAL PRODUCTION CAPACITY OF 6 MILLION BARRELS PER DAY.**

— Oil fields in Khuzestan: 65 percent of total production.
— Oil fields throughout the rest of the country: 20 percent of total production.
— Offshore oil fields: 15 percent of total production.

REFINERY CAPACITY: 1.2 MILLION BARRELS PER DAY.

— Abadan refinery: 600,000 barrels per day (destroyed in November 1980).
— Tehran refinery: 200,000 barrels per day (heavily damaged in 1988).
— Bandar Khomeini refinery: 140,000 barrels per day.
— Esfahan refinery: 80,000 barrels per day.
— Tabriz refinery: 80,000 barrels per day.
— Shiraz refinery: 40,000 barrels per day.
— Arak refinery: 40,000 barrels per day.
— Kermanshah refinery: 20,000 barrels per day.

THEORETICAL EXPORT CAPACITY: 7.525 MILLION BARRELS PER DAY.

— Kharg terminal: 6 million barrels per day (reduced capacity after 1984).
— Bandar Khomeini terminal: 1.5 million barrels per day (capacity reduced by half after 1981—Out of commission after 1983).
— Lavan terminal: 25,000 barrels per day.

TABLE G.1
OIL REVENUE 1978–1988

	1978	1979	1980	1981	1982	1983	1984	1985	1986	1987	1988
Average price of barrel of oil	$15	$18	$36	$34	$35	$30	$29	$27	$14	$17	$18
IRAQ											
Average production (in millions of barrels per day)	2.6	3.5	2.6	0.9	1	1.1	1.2	1.3	1.5	2	2.4
Average quantity of oil exported (in millions of barrels per day)	2.4	3	2	0.7	0.8	0.7	0.85	1	1.3	1.5	2
Annual revenue from exported oil (in billions of dollars)	13	19.5	26	8.5	10	7	8.5	9.5	6.5	9	13
IRAN											
Average production (in millions of barrels per day)	5.2	3.2	1.5	1.3	2	2.3	2.2	2.1	2	2.2	2.3
Average quantity of oil exported (in millions of barrels per day)	4.6	2.7	0.8	0.9	1.6	2	1.8	1.6	1.5	1.35	1.6
Annual revenue from exported oil (in billions of dollars)	25	17.5	10.5	11.5	20	21.5	19	15.5	7.5	8	10

PUTTING INTO SERVICE OF NEW EXPORT CHANNELS
DURING THE WAR

1984: Implementation of an oil tanker shuttle to the Lavan terminal, whose export capacity is increased to 250,000, then 1 million barrels per day.

1985: Sirri floating terminal (1.5 million barrels per day) connected to Kharg by an oil tanker shuttle.

1986: Larak floating terminal (2 million barrels per day) connected to Kharg by an oil tanker shuttle.

1987: Beginning of construction on the Bandar Abbas and Jask terminals, which were not put in service until after the end of the war.

Data in Graphs G.1 and G.2 show the effectiveness of Iraqi attacks on Iranian oil tanker traffic from 1983 to 1987 (resulting in a 25 percent drop in Iranian exports over this period) and the close relationship between oil revenue and the intensity of military ground operations. Three phases can be clearly identified:

— The initial phase of the Iraqi offensive (1980–1981), characterized by a significant revenue differential to Iraq's benefit;

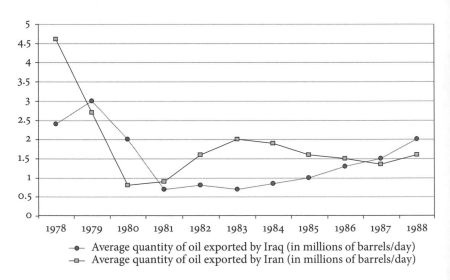

—•— Average quantity of oil exported by Iraq (in millions of barrels/day)
—□— Average quantity of oil exported by Iran (in millions of barrels/day)

Graph G.1 Iraqi and Iranian oil exports during the war

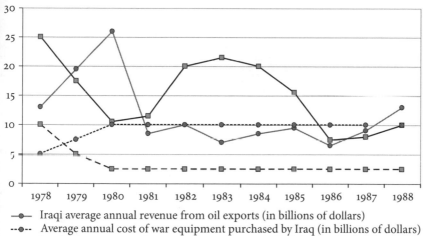

—●— Iraqi average annual revenue from oil exports (in billions of dollars)
--●-- Average annual cost of war equipment purchased by Iraq (in billions of dollars)
—■— Iranian average annual revenue from oil exports (in billions of dollars)
—■·— Average annual cost of war equipment purchased by Iran (in billions of dollars)

Graph G.2 Iraqi and Iranian oil revenue during the war

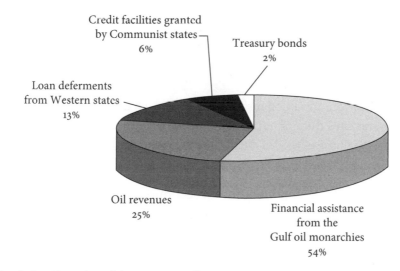

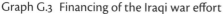

Graph G.3 Financing of the Iraqi war effort

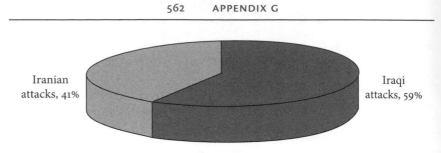

Graph G.4   Oil Tankers attacked in the Gulf

TABLE G.2

FINANCING OF THE IRAQI WAR EFFORT

Loans granted by Gulf oil monarchies*	80 billion dollars
Iraqi oil revenue**	38 billion dollars
Loan deferments granted by various Western states	20 billion dollars
Credit facilities granted by various communist states	9 billion dollars
Treasury bonds issued by the Iraqi central bank	3 billion dollars
Total	**150 billion dollars**

* Saudi Arabia: $60 billion; Kuwait: $15 billion; UAE and Qatar: $5 billion.
** From September 1980 to July 1982, 30 percent of Iraqi oil revenue was earmarked for the country's war effort. This proportion increased to 40 percent from August 1982 to February 1986, and to 50 percent from March 1986 until the end of the war.

— The phase of Iranian offensives (1982–1986), characterized by a significant revenue differential to Iran's benefit;
— The final phase of the Iraqi counteroffensive (1988), once again characterized by a clear revenue differential to Iraq's benefit.

The Iraqis fired more than 500 Exocet missiles during the war. Only two-thirds of the vessels attacked were oil tankers. More than half the attacks on maritime traffic took place in 1987 and 1988. These attacks killed 420 sailors and severely wounded 425 others. The six countries most affected by the attacks were Liberia (60), Iran (48), Panama (46), Cyprus (43), Greece (32), and Kuwait (16). The five permanent members of the United Nations Security Council were mostly spared: United Kingdom (6), France (5), United States (3), USSR (2), China (1). In tonnage, the belligerents neutralized the equivalent of a quarter the number of cargo ships sunk during the Battle of the Atlantic in the Second World War.

TABLE G.3
TOLL OF THE WAR OF THE TANKERS

	Number of ships attacked		Number of ships sunk or damaged beyond repair
	By Iraq	By Iran	
1981	5	0	1
1982	14	0	6
1983	8	0	5
1984	25	14	8 (1 by Iran)
1985	31	13	12 (1 by Iran)
1986	57	41	16 (5 by Iran)
1987	83	79	19 (9 by Iran)
1988	29	31	5 (2 by Iran)
Total	252	178	
Total	430*		72 (54 by Iraq and 18 by Iran)

*The British Lloyds Bank would later publish a slightly higher toll (543), for its total included commercial ships destroyed or immobilized in the Shatt al-Arab at the beginning of the war, as well as all the vessels subjected to hostile behavior on the part of the belligerents, including in those incidents that led to no damage. Naturally, Lloyds needed to justify a tenfold increase in its insurance premiums.

International Naval Presence in the Gulf

Fall 1987–Summer 1988

AMERICAN PRESENCE

Rear Admiral Dennis Brooks (replaced by Rear Admiral Anthony Less in February 1988) supervised the entire American air and sea layout from the missile cruiser *Long Beach,* which comprised up to **54 warships** (including 2 aircraft carriers, 1 helicopter carrier, 1 battleship, 5 cruisers, 6 destroyers, and 12 frigates), 160 combat aircraft, and 70 helicopters.

➤ **Middle East Task Force,** in the Gulf (HQ in Bahrain)—Rear Admiral Harold Bernsen: 1 command ship (*Lassalle*—replaced by the *Coronado* in 1988), 1 helicopter carrier (*Guadalcanal*—replaced by the *Okinawa* in 1988), 1 cruiser (*Standley*—replaced by the *Wainwright* in 1988), 1 destroyer (*Kidd*—replaced by the *O'Brien* and the *McCormick* in 1988), 6 frigates (*Flatley, Hawes, Jarret, Klakring, Rentz,* and *Stark*—replaced by the *Bagley, Halyburton, Jack Williams, Samuel Roberts, Simpson,* and *Stump* in 1988), 1 amphibious assault ship (LPD *Raleigh*—replaced by the LPD *Trenton* and LSD *Portland* in 1988), 4 replenishment oilers (*Acadia, Kilavea, Navasota,* and *St Louis*), 6 minesweepers (*Enhance, Esteem, Fearless, Illusive, Inflict,* and *Grapple*), and 5 missile-carrying hydrofoils (*Hercules, Taurus, Aquila, Aries,* and *Gemini*).

➤ **Carrier battle group** deployed in the Gulf of Oman: 1 aircraft carrier (*Ranger*—replaced by the *Enterprise* in 1988), 1 missile cruiser (*Gridley*—replaced by the *Truxtun* in February 1988, then the *Vincennes* in May 1988), 3 destroyers (*Leftwich, John Young,* and *Auchanan*—replaced by the *Chandler, Merrill,* and *Joseph Strauss* in 1988), 2 frigates (*Peary* and *Holt*—replaced by the *Gary* and *Sides* in 1988), 2 replenishment oilers (*Shasta* and *Roanoke*), and 1 auxiliary ship *(Camden).*

→ USS *Constellation* **carrier battle group** in the north of the Arabian Sea, then sent back to the United States in November 1987: 1 aircraft carrier *(Constellation)*, 1 cruiser *(Reeves)*, 1 destroyer *(Cochrane)*, 2 frigates *(Crommelin* and *Cook)*, 2 replenishment oilers, and 1 auxiliary ship.

→ **Battle group** deployed in the Gulf of Oman, then sent back to the United States in February 1988: 1 battleship *(Missouri*—replaced by the *Iowa* in December 1987), 2 missile cruisers *(Long Beach* and *Bunker Hill)*, 1 destroyer *(Hoel*—replaced by the *Montgomery* in December 1987), 2 frigates *(Schofield* and *Curts)*, 3 replenishment oilers *(Hassay-ampa, Kansas City,* and *Wichita)*, and 1 auxiliary ship *(Niagara Falls)*.

FRENCH PRESENCE

Admiral Jacques Lanxade commanded **Task Force 623** (Operation Prométhée) from the replenishment oiler *Marne*. TF-623 consisted of **14 warships** (including 1 aircraft carrier and 3 missile frigates), 38 combat aircraft, and 8 helicopters.

→ **Task Group 623–1** deployed in the Gulf: 1 missile frigate *(Georges Leygues)* and 4 avisos *(Protet, Bory, De Lagree,* and *Victor Schoelcher)*.

→ **Task Group 623–2** (carrier battle group) deployed in the Gulf of Oman: 1 aircraft carrier *(Clémenceau*—Admiral Le Pichon), 2 missile frigates *(Suffren* and *Duquesne)*, and 2 replenishment oilers *(Marne* and *Meuse)*.

→ **Task Group 623–3** deployed in the Strait of Hormuz: 3 minesweepers *(Garigliano, Cantho,* and *Vinh-Long)* and 1 auxiliary ship *(Garonne)*.

SOVIET PRESENCE

Indian Ocean squadron—**11 warships** deployed in the Gulf: 1 command ship *(Dauriya)*, 2 missile destroyers *(Boevoy* and *Stoyky)*, 1 frigate *(Grisha)*, 1 amphibious assault ship (LST *Tortsev)*, 3 minesweepers (Natya-class— nos. 737, 913, and 918), and 3 replenishment oilers.

BRITISH PRESENCE

Armilla patrol—**9 warships** deployed in the Gulf and the Strait of Hormuz: 1 missile destroyer *(Edinburgh)*, 2 frigates *(Andromeda* and *Brazen)*, 4 minesweepers *(Bicester, Brecon, Brocklesby,* and *Hurworth)*, 1 replenishment oiler *(Brambleleaf)*, and 1 auxiliary ship *(Abdiel)*.

ITALIAN PRESENCE

7 warships deployed in the Gulf and the Strait of Hormuz: 3 frigates (*Grecale, Perseo,* and *Scirocco*), 3 minesweepers (*Milazzo, Sapri,* and *Vieste*), and 1 replenishment oiler *(Vesuvio).*

BELGIAN AND DUTCH PRESENCE

5 warships deployed in the Strait of Hormuz: 4 minesweepers (*Breydel, Bovesse, Hellevoetsluis,* and *Maassluis*) and 1 auxiliary ship *(Zinnia).*

TOTAL

100 warships (including 3 aircraft carriers, 1 helicopter carrier, 1 battleship, 5 cruisers, 10 destroyers, 20 frigates, and 23 minesweepers), **200 combat aircraft,** and **about 100 ship-borne helicopters.**

Air and Sea Forces Present during Operation Praying Mantis (April 18, 1988)

AMERICAN

Commanded by Rear Admiral Anthony Less from the command ship *Coronado,* with **17 warships** (including 1 aircraft carrier, 2 cruisers, 5 destroyers, and 5 frigates), **86 combat aircraft,** and **31 helicopters.**

→ **Task Group Alpha** deployed in the Gulf of Oman: nuclear-powered aircraft carrier *Entreprise* (28 F-14s, 28 A-7s, 12 A-6s, 4 EA-6Bs, 10 S-3s, 4 E-2s, and 6 SH-3s), missile cruiser *Truxtun,* destroyer *Chandler* (2 SH-2s), frigates *Gary* and *Sides* (4 SH-60s), 2 replenishment oilers, and 1 auxiliary ship.

→ **Task Group Bravo** deployed in the Gulf, off the UAE: amphibious assault ship LPD *Trenton* (4 AH-1s, 2 UH-1s, and 4 CH-46s) and destroyers *Merrill* and *McCormick* (2 SH-60s).

→ **Task Group Charlie** deployed in the Gulf, close to the Sirri terminal: missile cruiser *Wainwright* and frigates *Bagley* and *Simpson* (1 SH-2, 2 SH-60s).

→ **Task Group Delta** deployed in the Gulf, close to the Strait of Hormuz: frigate *Jack Williams* (2 SH-60s) and destroyers *O'Brien* and *Joseph Strauss* (2 SH-60s).

TABLE H.1
LOSSES IN OPERATION PRAYING MANTIS

US Navy	Iranian Navy
1 Sea Cobra helicopter	2 oil platforms destroyed (Sassan and Nasser)
	1 missile boat sunk *(Joshan)*
2 dead (crew)	1 frigate sunk *(Sahand)*
	1 frigate severely damaged *(Sabalan)*
	3 Boghammar high speed patrol boats sunk
	(3 others damaged)
	1 Phantom fighter damaged
	57 dead, 110 wounded

IRANIAN

Commanded by Rear Admiral Mohammed Hussein Malekzadegan from his HQ in Bandar Abbas, with **11 warships** (3 destroyers, 4 frigates, and 4 patrol boats, including 1 missile boat), a few gunboats, and **20 combat aircraft.**

↣ **In open water on the Gulf, off the UEA:** missile boat *Joshan* (Combattante II) and 6 Boghammar high-speed patrol boats (IRGC).

↣ **At Bandar Abbas:** missile frigates *Alvand, Alborz, Sabalan,* and *Sahand;* destroyers *Babr, Palang,* and *Damavand* (lacking any genuine military value); patrol boats *Parvin, Bahram,* and *Nahid* (lacking any genuine military value); amphibious assault ships LST *Hengham, Tomb, Larak,* and *Lavan;* replenishment oilers *Bandar Abbas, Bushehr,* and *Kharg;* 91st squadron equipped with 8 F-4E Phantom fighter-bombers; and 92nd squadron equipped with 3 P-3F Orion maritime patrol aircraft.

↣ **At Shah Bahar:** 101st squadron equipped with 8 F-4D Phantom fighter-bombers.

↣ **On air patrol near Bandar Abbas:** 2 F-14A Tomcats detached from the 81st squadron.

War Losses

Aircraft Losses

IRAQ

305 combat aircraft destroyed (including 218 shot down by Iranian fighters and 4 by Iranian Cobra helicopters): 82 MiG-23s, 78 MiG-21s, 64 Su-20/22s, 46 Mirage F-1s, 9 MiG-25s, 9 Tu-22s, 5 Tu-16s, 4 Su-7s, 3 Su-25s, 3 Hunters, 1 Super Etendard, 1 MiG-29.

150 helicopters destroyed (including 24 shot down by Iranian fighters and 25 by Iranian Cobra helicopters): 40 Mi-8s, 32 Mi-24/25s, 30 Gazelles, 15 Mi-17s, 6 Alouette IIIs, 6 Mi-4s, 5 BO-105s, 5 MD-500s, 4 Mi-6s, 4 Bell 214s, 3 Super Frelons.

8 transport planes destroyed (including 2 shot down by Iranian fighters): 3 An-12s, 3 An-24s, 1 An-26s, 1 Il-76s.

IRAN

180 combat aircraft destroyed (including 55 shot down by Iraqi fighters): 90 F-5 Tiger IIs, 80 F-4 Phantoms, 9 F-14 Tomcats, 1 P-3 Orions.

250 helicopters destroyed (including 13 shot down by Iraqi fighters): 100 AH-1 Cobras, 85 AB-212/214s, 53 AB-205/206s, 12 CH-47 Chinooks.

15 transport planes destroyed (including 2 shot down by Iraqi fighters): 8 C-130 Hercules, 2 Fokker 27s, 2 Boeing 747s, 1 Boeing 737, 1 Boeing 707, 1 Airbus A-300 (shot down by the USS *Vincennes*).

Causes of Aircraft Losses

AIR WAR
IRAQ

Iraqi fighter pilots are thought to have shot down 73 aircraft, including 70 Iranian aircraft (55 combat aircraft, 13 helicopters, and 2 transport

TABLE I.1

WAR LOSSES

RAQ	IRAN
Casualties (Total: 680,000 dead and missing)	
Approximately 180,000 dead and missing	Approximately 500,000 dead and missing
125,000 military	380,000 military and IRGC
5000 civilians	80,000 Basijis
50,000 Iraqi Kurds	10,000 civilians
	30,000 Iranian Kurds
Approximately 520,000 wounded and maimed	Approximately 1,300,000 wounded and maimed
70,000 prisoners of war captured by the Iranian army	45,000 prisoners of war captured by the Iraqi army
Equipment losses	
2,500 tanks*	2,100 tanks**
2,100 other armored vehicles	2,300 other armored vehicles
650 heavy artillery pieces	1,000 heavy artillery pieces
305 combat aircraft	180 combat aircraft
(+ 100 others severely damaged)	(+ 120 others severely damaged)
150 helicopters	250 helicopters
(+ 50 others severely damaged)	(+ 150 others severely damaged)
8 transport planes	14 transport planes
15 warships:	15 warships:
2 Osa I missile boats	2 frigates (Sahand and Sabalan***)
5 Osa II missile boats	2 corvettes (Milanian and Kahnamvie)****
6 P-6 torpedo boats	2 Combattante II-class missile boats (Paykan and Joshan)
1 minesweeper	1 amphibious vessel (Iran Ajr)
1 Polnocny-class LSM amphibious assault ship	3 patrol boats
13 light patrol boats	3 minesweepers and 2 hydroplanes
	44 light patrol boats

  * Including 400 T-54, T-55 and T-62 tanks captured by the Iranian army.
  ** Including 600 Chieftain, Scorpion, T-55, T-59 and T-62 tanks captured by the Iraqi army.
  *** Though severely damaged, the frigate Sabalan was repaired after the war.
  **** Another corvette was severely damaged.

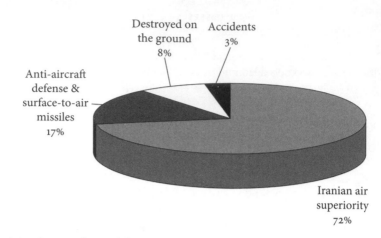

Graph I.1 Causes of aircraft losses, Iraq

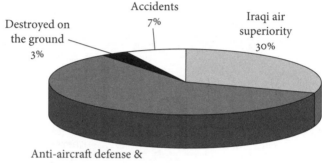

Graph I.2 Causes of aircraft losses, Iran

TABLE I.2

VICTORIES BY IRAQI PILOTS (2 OR MORE VICTORIES)

Pilot	Fighter types	Number of kills
Ali Sabah*	Mirage F-1	4
Samir Abdul Razak	MiG-21	4
Mohommed Rayyan	MiG-23	4
Moukhalad Abdul Karim**	Mirage F-1	2
Omar Goben	MiG-21	2
Ahmad Salem	Mirage F-1	2

  * Ali Sabah is credited with two unconfirmed additional victories, which would make him the only Iraqi flying ace of the conflict.
  ** Only two of the fourteen victories claimed by Moukhalad Abdul Karim have been confirmed by official authorities.

TABLE I.3

VICTORIES BY IRANIAN PILOTS (3 OR MORE VICTORIES)

Pilot	Fighter types	Number of kills
Fazlolah Javidniya*	F-14	12
Jalil Zandi**	F-14	11
Fereidoun Ali-Mazandarani	F-14	9
Abolfazel Mehreganfar	F-14	6
Hassan Harandi	F-14	6
Shahram Rostami	F-14	5
Hossein Khalili	F-14	5
Jamshid Afshar	F-14	5
Jalil Moslemi	F-14	5
K. Sedghi	F-14	5
Toufanian	F-14	5
Mohamed Masbough***	F-14	4
Yadolah Khalili	F-14	4
Abbas Afkhami	F-4	4
Aliasghar Jahanbakhsh	F-14	3
E.M. Peyrovan	F-14	3
Hashem All-e-Agha	F-14	3
Yadolah Javadpour	F-5	3
Yadolah Sharifi Raad	F-5	3
Siavash Bayani	F-4	3

* Fazlolah Javidniya has the world record for victories with Phoenix missiles.

** Jalil Zandi was killed in an automobile accident shortly after the end of the war.

*** Mohamed Masbough is the only pilot on record to have shot down three fighter planes with a single missile.

Note: Several Phantom pilots who could have claimed the title of flying ace allegedly had their victories erased by the regime. Others who still hold positions in the Iranian armed forces have not had their names released due to censorship. Accounts differ regarding another pilot (Aliyah Hoda), who is credited with six victories by certain sources, while others state he left active service after the outbreak of hostilities.

planes), 2 Syrian MiG-21Rs (reconnaissance), and 1 Algerian Gulf-stream (military utility).

➤ **MiG-21 pilots: 32 victories** (21 planes and 11 helicopters)

➤ **MiG-23 pilots: 21 victories** (19 planes and 2 helicopters)

➤ **Mirage F-1 pilots: 15 victories** (exclusively combat aircraft)

→ **MiG-25 pilots: 5 victories** (exclusively planes, including 1 Algerian Gulfstream)

Helicopter pilots are thought to have shot down 20 helicopters (10 AH-1 Cobras, 9 AB-214s, and 1 AB-205s).

IRAN

Iranian fighter pilots are thought to have shot down 250 aircraft, including 244 Iraqi aircraft (218 combat aircraft, 2 transport planes and 24 helicopters), 2 Soviet MiG-25s and 2 MiG-27s, as well as 2 Egyptian Mirage 5s.

→ **F-14 pilots: 144 victories** (47 MiG-23s, 32 Mirage F-1s, 24 MiG-21s, 20 Su-20/22s, 7 MiG-25s, 5 Tu-22s, 1 Tu-16, 1 Super Etendard, 1 Mi-24, 1 Super Frelon and 4 Soviet MiGs, and 1 Egyptian Mirage).

→ **F-4 pilots: 80 victories** (29 MiG-21s, 21 MiG-23s, 19 Su-20/22s, 2 Mirage F-1s, 2 An-24s, 2 Mi-24s, 1 Tu-22, 1 Hunter, 1 Bell-214, 1 Super Frelon, and 1 Egyptian Mirage).

→ **F-5 pilots: 26 victories** (12 Mi-24s, 6 Mi-8s, 5 MiG-21s, 2 Su-20s, and 1 MiG-25)

Cobra helicopter pilots are said to have shot down 4 combat aircraft (2 MiG-21s, 1 MiG-23, and 1 Su-22) and **25 helicopters** (10 Gazelles, 7 Mi-24/25s, 5 Mi-17s, and 3 Mi-8s).

Financial Cost

The conflict's total financial cost to Iran and Iraq was approximately 1,100 billion dollars.

TABLE J.1
FINANCIAL COST OF THE WAR TO IRAQ

Loss of oil revenue	160 billion dollars (35%)
Debt (financing of the war effort)	110 billion dollars (24%)
Damage to infrastructure	90 billion dollars (20%)
Purchase of war equipment	80 billion dollars (18%)
Compensation of casualties' families	9 billion dollars (2%)
Construction of new pipelines	3 billion dollars (~1%)
Total:	452 billion dollars (1988)

Sources: Paul Rivlin, "The Reconstruction of the Iraqi Economy and the Weight of History," *Orient* 3 (2004): 369–383; Kamran Mofid, *The Economic Consequences of the Gulf War* (London: Routledge, 1990); Anthony Cordesman, *The Lessons of Modern War: The Iran-Iraq War* (Boulder, CO: Westview Press), 3–4.

TABLE J.2
FINANCIAL COST OF THE WAR TO IRAN

Loss of oil revenue	350 billion dollars (54%)
Damage to infrastructure	180 billion dollars (28%)
Loss of industrial revenue	35 billion dollars (5%)
Compensation of casualties' families	25 billion dollars (4%)
Purchase of war equipment	20 billion dollars (3%)
Expenses related to war effort	20 billion dollars (3%)
Importing of refined petroleum products	12 billion dollars (~2%)
Increase in insurance premiums (oil trade)	3 billion dollars (~1%)
Total:	645 billion dollars (1988)

Sources: Paul Rivlin, "The Reconstruction of the Iraqi Economy and the Weight of History," *Orient* 3 (2004): 369–383; Kamran Mofid, *The Economic Consequences of the Gulf War* (London: Routledge, 1990); Anthony Cordesman, *The Lessons of Modern War: The Iran-Iraq War* (Boulder, CO: Westview Press), 3–4.

NOTES

CHAPTER 1: ESCALATION

1   *Jeune Afrique,* March 26, 1980.
2   As can be seen in a report by the Iraqi military attaché to Tehran dated April 19, 1979, seized by the American army in 2003, and now kept at the Institute for Defense Analysis in Washington under shelf number SH-GMID-D-000-845.
3   Quoted by Paul Balta, *Iran-Irak: Une guerre de 5000 ans* (Paris: Anthropos-Economica, 1988), 136.
4   The Algiers Accord had led to an Iran-Iraq Treaty on International Border and Good Neighborly Relations, signed in Baghdad on June 13, 1975.
5   Balta, *Iran-Irak,* 136.
6   Agence France-Press (hereafter AFP), April 6, 1980.
7   Mohammad al-Sadr was hanged on April 8, 1980. His son-in-law and second cousin Muqtada al-Sadr, nicknamed "Billy the Kid" by many Iraqis, would later take arms against the Americans and would become one of the leaders of the Shiite community after the fall of Saddam Hussein in 2003.
8   AFP, April 18, 1980.
9   The Iranian air force had lost a third of its personnel in eighteen months.
10 General Oveisi was assassinated in Paris by an Iranian commando on February 7, 1984. Shapour Bakhtiar was murdered by Iranian killers on August 6, 1991, after having been the target of an aborted assassination attempt on July 18, 1980.
11 As documented in a report analyzing the political, military, and economic situation in Iran and given to Saddam Hussein by his intelligence services on June 30, 1980, audio transcript SH-GMID-D-000-842, Conflict Records Research Center (CRRC), National Defense University (NDU), Washington, DC.
12 Quoted by Kevin Woods in his *Saddam's Generals—Perspectives of the Iran-Iraq War* (Alexandria, VA: Institute for Defense Analyses), 60–61.
13 *Le Monde,* July 18 and 19, 1980.
14 As heard on the audiotapes dated August 16, 1980, and seized in Baghdad.
15 During the six months that preceded the official outbreak of war, 524 border skirmishes were recorded.
16 The full transcript of this crucial meeting, which is particularly representative of Saddam Hussein's management style, can be found in the CRRC's oral archive collection under shelf number SH-SHTP-A-000-835.
17 AFP, September 17, 1980.

18   See Appendix D for a detailed list of the military forces on the field, both on the Iraqi and Iranian sides.

19   The equipment in question consisted of T-54, T-55, and T-62 tanks; BTR-152 and BTR-60 armored vehicles; D-30 and M-46 towed field guns; Su-100 and Su-152 self-propelled guns; AK-47 assault rifles; RPG-7 grenade launchers; MiG-21, Su-7, and Su-20 fighters; Mi-8 helicopters; SAM-2 and SAM-3 surface-to-air missiles; Osa I and Osa II missile boats; and P-6 torpedo boats. British equipment, which was largely obsolete, was limited to trucks, old towed field guns, and some twenty warehoused Hunter fighter jets.

20   From the moment he came to power, Saddam Hussein privileged the engineering corps, using it to implement his policy of major public works. Since this corps was not perceived as a potential threat (sappers do not have access to heavy weaponry), it largely escaped the purges that plagued the rest of the army. It thus became a refuge for the most brilliant officers who wanted to have a career without compromising themselves with the Ba'ath Party.

21   Before the Revolution, the Iranian military police and border guard force still consisted of a paramilitary force 75,000 strong, principally responsible for keeping the country under surveillance. It gradually disintegrated and was replaced by the Pasdaran.

22   In fact the Iraqi army came out on top only in terms of antitank combat, thanks to massive deliveries of French HOT and Milan missiles, then considered the best in the world.

23   Ahmad Madani, Taghi Riahi, and Mostafa Shamran, successively, held the defense portfolio, while generals Mohammed Vali Qarani, Nasser Farbood, and Hussein Shakari followed each other as army chief of staff.

CHAPTER 2: SADDAM'S QADISIYYAH

1   For a full account of aerial operations during the first phase of the war, see the remarkable volume by Tom Cooper and Farzad Bishop, *Iran-Iraq War in the Air* (Atglen, PA: Schiffer Publishing 2000), 72–110.

2   Under the Shah, many Iranian pilots had gone to Israel to refine their training.

3   This plan owed a great deal to Commander Abbas Doran, one of the most talented Phantom pilots, who proved to be one of the best tacticians in the Iranian air force. He would lead numerous attack and reconnaissance missions over Iraq before being shot down over Baghdad on July 21, 1982, during a raid targeting the convention center where the summit of nonaligned countries was to take place.

4   During the first four days of the war, the Iraqis lost twenty-five combat aircraft (eight MiG-21s, five MiG-23s, four Su-20s, three Su-22s, two Su-7s,

one Hunter, one Tu-16, and one Tu-22). The Iranians lost fifteen fighter planes (eight F-4 Phantoms and seven F-5 Tigers).

5   The inhabitants of Qasr-e-Shirin, like those of other border towns, had been evacuated two weeks earlier, with the first artillery clashes.

6   *Le Monde*, September 29, 1980.

CHAPTER 3: HOW DID IT COME TO THIS?

1   Iraq's image in the West had deteriorated following the case of the "Baghdad hangings," when the Ba'athist regime publicly hanged fifteen Iraqis accused of spying for Israel in January 1969.

2   The Shiite Al-Dawa Party (literally, "The Call") was created in the late 1960s by Ayatollah Mohammad al-Sadr to promote the establishment of an Islamic state in Iraq.

3   The 1977 assassination of Mostafa Khomeini, the ayatollah's eldest son, probably on SAVAK orders, only increased Khomeini's hatred for the Shah of Iran.

4   The Baloch people, concentrated near the Afghan and Pakistani borders, are a minority made up of farmers and mountain people who practice Sunni rites, like the Kurds, and unlike the rest of the Iranian population, which is primarily Shiite.

5   The People's Fedayeen demanded autonomy for the Iranian provinces and the establishment of a Marxist state. They were closely tied to the Palestinian revolutionary movements.

6   General Ahmed Hassan al-Bakr died on October 4, 1982, in his Baghdad villa. His death came at an opportune moment for Saddam Hussein, when the Iraqi army was being mangled by the Iranian army and the figure of General al-Bakr could have appeared as a providential recourse to many Iraqis.

7   According to statements made to the author by former Ba'athists, Saddam Hussein frequently told those in his entourage that "fear and violence are tools to be used wisely."

CHAPTER 4: DID THE UNITED STATES PUSH
SADDAM TO ATTACK?

1   Abol Hassan Bani-Sadr and Jean-Charles Deniau, *My Turn to Speak: Iran, the Revolution and Secret Deals with the US* (Washington, DC: Brassey's, 1991), 70ff.

2   Dilip Hiro, *The Longest War* (New York: Routledge, 1991), 71.

3   BBC Worldwide Monitoring Service, March 22, 2009.

4   Paul Balta, *Iran-Irak: Une guerre de 5000 ans* (Paris: Anthropos-Economica 1988), 196.

5   Several participants in these events have confirmed this theory to me Richard Murphy, former American ambassador to Saudi Arabia; Mark Hambley, the United States consul general in Riyadh at the time; and Judith Yaphé, the former head of the CIA analysis division's Iraq office.

6   Lawrence Potter and Gary Sick, *Iran, Iraq and the Legacies of War* (New York: Macmillan, 2004), 173. Former Ba'ath leaders confirmed this information in interviews with the author.

7   Quoted by Balta, *Iran-Irak*, 240.

8   As described by Charles Cogan, former CIA director of operations for the Middle East, in an interview with the author.

9   Bruce Laingen, quoted by Bill James in his remarkable volume *The Eagle and the Lion—The Tragedy of American-Iranian Relations* (New Haven, CT: Yale University Press, 1988), 276.

10 Ibid., 290–291. This information was confirmed by Charles Cogan, former CIA director of operations for the Middle East.

11 The Iranian authorities would later accuse these technicians of having sabotaged certain electronic components of Tomcat fighters and Phoenix air-to-air missiles on orders from the Pentagon, lest they fall into the wrong hands in working order.

12 Ayatollah Morteza Motahhari (fifty-nine years old) was shot on May 1, 1979, while Mohammad Mofatteh (fifty-one years old) was mowed down by his attackers on December 18, 1979. These two assassinations were conveniently attributed to a dissident faction of the People's Mujahidin.

13 After diplomatic relations were broken off, the Swiss embassy in Tehran represented American interests, while the Pakistani embassy in Washington represented Iranian interests in the United States.

14 For an exhaustive analysis of this mission, see the excellent narrative by Charles Cogan in his remarkable history *La République de Dieu* (Paris: Jacob-Duvernet, 2008), 88–98.

15 Warren Christopher, *Chances of a Lifetime* (New York: Scribner, 2001), 108–111.

16 Pierre Péan, *La Menace* (Paris: Fayard, 1987), 11–15.

17 Gary Sick, *All Fall Down: America's Tragic Encounter with Iran* (New York: Random House, 1985), 245–246.

18 This now declassified memorandum can be consulted at the American National Archives in the collection of CIA documents in the HNO 1999 series.

19 Jimmy Carter, "Situation in Iraq and Iran, Remarks Concerning the Conflict, September 24, 1980," *The American Presidency Project*, ed. Gerhard Peters and John T. Woolley, http://www.presidency.ucsb.edu/ws/?pid=45129.

20   As related by Iranian president Abol Hassan Bani-Sadr in his book *L'Espérance trahie* (Paris: Édition Papyrus, 1982).

21   Mark Bowden, *Guests of the Ayatollah* (New York: Atlantic Monthly Press, 2006), 563ff.

22   Anthony Cordesman, *The Iran-Iraq War and Western Security* (London: Jane's Publishing, Royal United Services Institute for Defense Studies, 1987), 115. F-14 parts were delivered to Iran via a front organization staffed by former U.S. Navy technicians and based outside of the United States.

23   Larry Everest, "Iran-Iraq: Helping Both Sides Lose the War," *Press for Conversion!* 51 (May 2003): 30–31. On Haig's actions, personal interview with Mark Hambley, London, LSE, September 24, 2010.

24   As recognized by Yevgeny Primakov, former Russian minister of foreign affairs, in *Russia and the Arabs: Behind the Scenes in the Middle East from the Cold War to the Present* (New York: Basic Books, 2009), 309. The USSR launched the *Cosmos* 1208 (August 28, 1980), 1209 (September 3), 1210 (September 19), 1211 (September 23), and 1212 (September 26) satellites. All these satellites were positioned at low orbit and only remained in space for two weeks.

25   Hélène Carrère d'Encausse confirmed this in an interview with the author: defending the Kurdish people was always a constant of Soviet policy.

26   *Pravda,* October 1, 1980.

27   Aryeh Yodfat, *The Soviet Union and Revolutionary Iran* (London: Croom Helm, 1984), 123.

28   In May 1981, Moscow and Tehran signed an agreement to give their military cooperation an official framework.

29   After the fall of the USSR, Russian test pilots admitted to having flown this F-14. Centre d'Exploitation du Renseignement Militaire (CERM).

30   Primakov, *Russia and the Arabs,* 312.

31   Iran had been one of the first states to recognize the People's Republic of China's membership in the UN. In Iran, China was perceived as a counterbalance to the USSR's influence. In China, Iran was seen as a barrier to the Soviet push toward the Gulf and the Indian Ocean.

32   *Beijing Information,* October 6, 1980.

CHAPTER 5: FRANCE SIDES WITH IRAQ

1   Agence France-Presse (AFP), September 24, 1980.

2   Iraq would soon become Dassault's best customer in the Middle East. Following this initial contract for the sale of forty Mirage F-1EQs, a second contract was signed in 1979 for the sale of twenty-nine additional aircraft (delivery beginning in 1983). A third contract for twenty-four Mirage F-1EQ5s

optimized for firing Exocet missiles was signed in 1983 (and delivered upon two years later). A final lot of twenty-eight Mirage F-1EQs was delivered in 1988 to partially make up for war losses. From 1981 to 1988, Dassault delivered a total of 121 Mirage F-1s (106 single-seaters and fifteen two-seaters) to Iraq, which proved to be its best export customer over this period. In total, the Mirage F-1s acquired in France and the Mirage F-1s "loaned" by Jordan equipped four Iraqi air force squadrons (the 79th, 81st, 89th, and 91st). Negotiations were also carried out for the delivery of Mirage 2000s and Alpha Jet training planes but dragged on—due to Iraq being over-indebted by the war effort—and were interrupted by the outbreak of the Second Gulf War in August 1990.

3   AFP, September 5, 1975.

4   Pierre Péan, *La Menace* (Paris: Fayard, 1987), 97.

5   As a volunteer in the army during the final months of the Second World War, Valéry Giscard d'Estaing had met the Shah of Iran when he had served as his chauffeur during a visit to the front. The future French president had been won over by his charisma.

6   Valéry Giscard d'Estaing, *Le Pouvoir et la vie,* vol. 1 (Paris: Compagnie 12, 1989), 112–113.

7   José Garçon, "La France et le conflit Iran-Irak," in *Politique étrangère* 2 (IFRI, 1987–1992), 359.

8   John Chipman, "Europe and the Iran-Iraq War," in *The Iran-Iraq War: Impact & Implications,* ed. Efraim Karsh (London: JCSS-MacMillan, 1989), 220.

9   Hans-Dietrich Genscher, "How Bonn got Iran off the Hook," *The Middle East Journal* (December 1988): 20–22.

10 CERM archives.

CHAPTER 6: THE ARABS DIVIDED

1   Ralph King, *Irak-Iran: La guerre paralysée* (Paris: Éditions Bosquet, 1987), 80.

CHAPTER 7: ISRAEL BANKS ON IRAN AND TURKEY BENEFITS FROM THE WAR

1   *Washington Post,* October 29, 1987.

2   Paul Balta, *Iran-Irak: Une guerre de 5000 ans* (Paris: Anthropos-Economica), 1988, 220.

3   Pierre Péan, *La Menace* (Paris: Fayard, 1987), 25.

4   *Washington Post,* November 6, 1987.

5   Tom Cooper, Ahmad Sadik, and Farzad Bishop, "La guerre Iran-Irak: les combats aériens—1re partie," *Avions*, special issue no. 22 (2007): 64–65.

6   Ronen Bergman, *The Secret War with Iran* (New York: Free Press, 2008), 40–48; Trita Parsi, *Treacherous Alliance: The Secret Dealings of Israel, Iran and the US* (New Haven, CT: Yale University Press, 2007), 104–108; Jane Hunter, "Israeli Arms Sales to Iran," *The Washington Report on Middle East Affairs* (November 1986).

7   The junta returned power to civilians in December 1983 and ended the state of siege in 1984, after having instituted a constitution tailor-made to preserve the army's central role.

CHAPTER 9: STALEMATE

1   *Le Monde,* October 22, 1980.

2   Agence France-Presse, November 9, 1980.

3   At the time, the U.S. Navy's Mideast force was deployed in the Gulf (two destroyers, two frigates, and one command ship), and its 7th Fleet was in the Indian Ocean (composed of the aircraft carriers *Midway* and *Eisenhower,* the helicopter carrier *New Orleans,* two attack submarines, three missile cruisers, two destroyers, four frigates, three landing crafts, and one fleet train). The Royal Navy had only the destroyer *Coventry* in the area, while the French navy could rely on the presence of the dispatch boats *Commandant Rivière, Victor Schoelcher,* and *Bouvet.* Together, the Saudi and Emirati navies had four corvettes and fifteen missile boats.

CHAPTER 10: THE INITIATIVE CHANGES SIDES

1   The Turkish authorities certainly detected the presence of the Iranian fighters in their air space, but given their very brief presence (about fifteen minutes), the Turks probably preferred to look the other way to avoid a diplomatic incident potentially disruptive to the two countries' commercial relations. According to a former Turkish diplomat's account, Ankara let Tehran know that the Turkish government would no longer tolerate the slightest violation of its air space.

2   This base would be retroceded to the Egyptians only a few months later as part of the Camp David Accords.

3   Several dozen technicians were killed in the attack, including one Frenchman, whose family was discreetly paid restitution by the Israeli government.

4   This can be heard in the audiotapes dated mid-June 1981 and seized in Baghdad in 2003.

CHAPTER 11: THE MULLAHS TAKE POWER

1   George Cave, the CIA bureau chief in Tehran at the time, confirmed Bani-Sadr's version in an interview with the author. He admitted that he had attempted to enroll Bani-Sadr, without suspecting he would be elected president of the Republic four months later.

2   Akbar Hashemi Rafsanjani's enemies pointed out that he had conveniently left the IRP's headquarters fifteen minutes before the explosion. Some did not hesitate to suggest that he was possibly responsible for the bombing that killed some of his most serious rivals. Others assumed that he was not to blame for the attack but had been told about it and decided to take advantage of it. A final group did not believe he was guilty and credited him with insolent good luck.

3   Maurice Vaïsse, *La Puissance ou l'influence? La France dans le monde depuis 1958* (Paris: Fayard, 2009), 389.

4   Notably Tom Cooper and Farzad Bishop in *Iran-Iraq War in the Air, 1980–1988* (Atglen, PA: Schiffer Publishing, 2000), 127–128.

CHAPTER 12: FIRST VICTORIES

1   *Kayhan*, September 27, 1981.

2   Edgar O'Ballance, *The Gulf War* (London: Brassey's, 1988), 69. This episode would lead to acute controversy between the two countries' authorities and the International Committee of the Red Crescent.

3   Quoted in ibid.

4   As has been confirmed to the author by several credible sources.

5   Kevin Woods, ed., *Saddam's Generals: Perspectives of the Iran-Iraq War* (Alexandria, VA: Institute for Defense Analyses and National Defense University of Washington, 2011), 124.

6   Quoted in O'Ballance, *The Gulf War*, 82.

CHAPTER 13: NEW MEDIATION

1   Tom Cooper and Farzad Bishop, *Iran-Iraq War in the Air 1980–1988* (Atglen, PA: Schiffer Publishing, 2000), 134.

2   The highly reliable Flight Safety Foundation's report does not leave much doubt that the Iraqis were responsible.

3   Brent Scowcroft and George Bush, *A World Transformed* (New York: Vintage, 1999), 305.

4   See the testimony of Howard Teicher, a staff member of the National Security Council, in *USA v. Carlos Cardoen* (1995), which can be consulted at the

National Security Archive, Washington, D.C., in the series "Iraq: Declassified Documents of US Support for Saddam Hussein."

5 The Iraqi regime would always carefully avoid delivering heavy weapons to the PDKI, ensuring they would not later be turned against its own troops.

CHAPTER 14: THE IRANIANS RECAPTURE THEIR TERRITORY

1 The nine divisions directly involved in the offensive were the 30th, 88th, and 92nd Armored Divisions; the 21st, 40th, 77th, and 84th Mechanized Divisions; and the 25th and 58th Infantry Divisions.

2 The 2nd Helicopter Brigade had twenty-six Cobras, thirty-four AB-212/214s, twenty-two AB-206s, and sixteen CH-47s.

3 General Makki, a direct witness to the scene, describes the incident in Kevin Woods, ed., *Saddam's Generals: Perspectives of the Iran-Iraq War* (Alexandria, VA: Institute for Defense Analyses and National Defense University of Washington, 2011), 114.

4 General al-Duri was hated by his peers, who deemed him incompetent, but would later be appointed to the command of the 3rd and 5th Army Corps. General al-Hamdani later accused him of being responsible for a third of the Iraqi army's losses during the war (Woods, *Saddam's Generals*, 16).

5 Patrick Seale, *Abu Nidal: A Gun for Hire* (New York: Random House, 1992), 224–227; Martin Van Creveld, *Tsahal—Histoire critique de la force de défense israélienne* (Monaco: Éditions du Rocher, 1998), 423; Rob Johnson, *The Iran-Iraq War* (London: Palgrave Macmillan, 2011), 67–68.

6 Interview with the author, anonymous source.

7 Quoted in Paul Balta, *Iran-Irak: Une guerre de 5000 ans* (Paris: Anthropos-Economica, 1988), 162.

8 UNSC Resolution 514 (1982).

CHAPTER 15: BLESSED RAMADAN OFFENSIVE

1 The ten regional commands were assigned to the cities of Tehran, Esfahan, Rasht, Mashhad, Tabriz, Bandar Abbas, Kermanshah, Shiraz, and the regions of Khuzestan and Kurdistan. The eight management departments were respectively responsible for personnel, planning, acquisition, operations, intelligence, the military justice system, security, and reconstruction.

2 Red Adair would become known to the general public a few years later by spectacularly putting out the Kuwaiti oil fires lit by the Iraqi army during the 1991 Gulf War.

3   Edgar O'Ballance, *The Gulf War* (London: Brassey's Defence Publisher 1988), 90.

4   *Jane's Defence Weekly,* June 24, 1984.

5   John Parker, *Persian Dreams: Moscow and Tehran since the Fall of the Sha* (Washington, DC: Potomac Books, 2009), 16–17.

6   In an article published on May 24, 2003, in the Soviet military journal *Kra: naia Zvezda,* General Mokrous estimated that weapons sales to Iraq the. made up 65 percent of revenue generated by Soviet arms exports.

7   *Pravda,* June 17, 1983.

8   As revealed by the *International Herald Tribune* on April 4, 1984.

CHAPTER 16: BLOODY DAWNS

1   Quoted by Paul Balta in *Le conflit Irak-Iran, 1979–1989,* notes et études doc- umentaires, no. 4889 (La Documentation française, 1989), 61.

2   *Kayhan,* February 14, 1983.

CHAPTER 17: SADDAM'S ACE IN THE HOLE

1   General Mizher Rashid al-Tarfa, quoted in Kevin Woods, *Saddam's Gen- erals: Perspectives of the Iran-Iraq War* (Alexandria, VA: Institute for De- fense Analyses and National Defense University of Washington, 2011), 102.

2   Ibid., 95.

3   Rashid al-Hamdani, quoted in Woods, *Saddam's Generals,* 60.

4   Notably Lieutenant Colonel Rashid al-Hamdani, one of the first officers to be assigned to the Republican Guard who was not a member of the Ba'ath Party. Al-Hamdani was made a general at the end of the war and would then command the Hammurabi Armored Division. He later became one of the few military advisors to whom Saddam Hussein was willing to listen.

5   Interview with General al-Tarfa in Woods, *Saddam's Generals,* 98.

6   The unit's name was changed to Unit 999 in the spring of 1986.

7   According to audio recording SH-GMID-D-000–076, dated June 17, 1986, Conflict Records Research Center (CRRC) Project (Washington, DC: Na- tional Defense University/Institute for National Strategic Studies).

8   As told to the author in Washington, DC, on October 27, 2011, by George Cave, CIA station chief in Tehran at the time of the Iranian Revolution.

9   These planes, grouped in the 107th Squadron, were fitted with external fuel tanks equipped with an aerial application system identical to those used in agriculture.

10   *Le Monde,* March 30, 1984.

11 The 1st Corps (General al-Khazraji), based in Kirkuk, remained responsible for Kurdistan. The 2nd Corps (General Ibrahim) remained responsible for the central sector. The 3rd Corps (General al-Rashid) remained responsible for the Basra sector, while the 4th Corps (General Ahmad) defended the portion of the front between Kut and Amarah.

CHAPTER 18: THE LEBANESE HOSTAGE CRISIS

1 From 1982 to 1989 ninety-six Western hostages were kidnapped in Lebanon, including twenty-five American nationals, sixteen French, twelve British, seven Swiss, and seven German; eight were murdered or died due to lack of medical care during their confinement. The remaining hostages were freed after being held for various lengths of time. Terry Anderson, the Associated Press's Middle East correspondent, was held the longest: six and a half years.

2 Con Coughlin, *Hostage: The Complete Story of the Lebanon Captives* (London: Little Brown, 1992), 36.

3 Claude Angeli and Stéphanie Mesnier, *Notre ami Saddam* (Paris: Olivier Orban, 1992), 122–139.

4 Based on the author's interviews with former French Super Etendard pilots who have chosen to remain anonymous. Interviews conducted in Paris, June 2007.

5 Jean Guisnel, *Armes de corruption massive—Secrets et combines des marchands de canon* (Paris: Éditions La Découverte, 2011), 155; Philippe Vasset, *Journal intime d'un marchand de canons* (Paris: Fayard, 2008), 29–34.

6 AFP, October 26, 1983.

7 This was confirmed to the author by Admiral Pierre Lacoste, who was then director of the DGSE.

8 Jean-Pierre Otelli, *Pilotes dans la tourmente—Raid sur Baalbek* (Levallois-Perret: Éditions Altipresse, 2005), 74. These statements have been confirmed to the author by several trustworthy sources.

9 As was confirmed to the author by a former head of Lebanese electronic surveillance services under condition of anonymity.

10 Otelli, *Pilotes*, 99.

11 This information was confirmed by Admiral Pierre Lacoste.

12 Joyce Battle, ed., *Shaking Hands with Saddam Hussein: The U.S. Tilts toward Iraq, 1980–1984*, National Security Archive Electronic Briefing Book No. 82 (Washington, DC: NSA, February 25, 2003), http://nsarchive.gwu.edu/NSAEBB/NSAEBB82/.

13 William Buckley's body was never returned by his captors. It was found by chance in 1991 during roadwork in the Shiite zone near the Beirut airport.

14   Larry Everest, "Iran-Iraq: Helping Both Sides Lose the War," *Press for Conversion* 51 (May 2003): 30.

15   Interview with the author in Rome on March 5, 2009.

16   Robert Fisk, *Pity the Nation: The Abduction of Lebanon* (New York: Atheneum, 1990), 581.

17   Roland Dumas, *Affaires étrangères (1981–1988)* (Paris: Fayard, 2007), 349–357.

18   Pierre Péan, *La Menace* (Paris: Fayard, 1987), 133; Péan's analysis has been confirmed by several trustworthy sources.

19   These agreements are convincingly documented in Patrick Seale's remarkable *Abu Nidal: A Gun for Hire* (New York: Random House, 1992).

20   Péan, *La Menace,* 135.

21   Dumas, *Affaires étrangères,* 349–357.

22   Ibid., 353.

23   Diplomatic telegram from Tehran no. 217, March 13, 1986, quoted in Péan, *La Menace,* 184–185.

24   This was confirmed to the author by a former head of Lebanese electronic surveillance services under condition of anonymity. Imad Mughniyeh would be assassinated by Mossad in Damascus on February 12, 2008.

25   At the time the French estimated the "net" debt at 750 million dollars (after deduction of part of what Tehran owed for the cancelled construction of the civil nuclear power station), while the Iranians demanded two billion dollars.

26   See Dominique Lorentz's book *Secret atomique, ou la véritable histoire des otages français au Liban* (Paris: Les Arènes, 2002), 32–33; Roger Faligot and Jean Guisnel's *Histoire secrète de la Vᵉ République* (Paris: La Découverte, 2006), 252; and David Carr-Brown's documentary film, *La République atomique,* broadcast on Arte on November 14, 2001.

27   *Le Matin,* November 24, 1986; Lorentz, *Secret atomique,* 141.

CHAPTER 19: MONEY HAS NO SMELL

1   See Appendix F for a detailed list of nations that armed Iran and/or Iraq.

2   All this information has been confirmed by the accounts of former Iranian diplomats and is taken from Walter de Bock and Jean-Charles Deniau's *Des armes pour l'Iran* (Paris: Gallimard, 1988).

3   de Bock and Deniau, *Des armes pour l'Iran,* 73ff.

4   Ibid., 113.

5   Ibid., 205.

6   This has been confirmed to the author by Admiral Pierre Lacoste.

7   Jean-François Dubos, *Vente d'armes: Une politique* (Paris: Gallimard, 1974).

8   For an overview of notable figures implicated in this case, some of whom would later hold important positions, see the Barba Report, which was published in its entirety by Walter de Bock and Jean-Charles Deniau in the appendix to *Des armes pour l'Iran.*

9   Jean Guisnel, *Charles Hernu ou la République au coeur* (Paris: Fayard, 1993), 493-496.

10 Barba Report, in de Bock and Deniau, *Des armes pour l'Iran,* 253. Information was confirmed to the author by Admiral Pierre Lacoste.

11 Gilles Gaetner, "L'affaire Luchaire," *L'Express,* March 30, 1995.

12 All the information in this paragraph is drawn from de Bock and Deniau, *Des armes pour l'Iran.*

13 Roger Faligot and Jean Guisnel, *Histoire secrète de la Ve République* (Paris: La Découverte, 2006), 254; see also Jean-Christophe Notin's *La Guerre de l'ombre des Français en Afghanistan: 1979-2011* (Paris: Fayard, 2011).

14 The Geneva Protocol of June 17, 1925, which was not adopted by Iran and Iraq, did not, however, prohibit the production, acquisition, and storage of chemical weapons. In 1993 it was replaced by an international convention forbidding both the possession and use of chemical weapons.

15 Derek Wood, "Gulf Chemicals Could Be Soviet," *Jane's Defence Weekly,* March 31, 1984.

16 As attested to by an audiotape played by Williamson Murray on the occasion of the London School of Economics seminar in London, September 23-24, 2010.

17 Interview with General al-Khazraji, *Al-Hayat,* Beirut, December 28, 2002.

18 Seymour Hersh, "US Aides Say Iraqis Made Use of a Nerve Gas," *New York Times,* March 30, 1984.

19 "Chemical Weapons and the Iran-Iraq War," *Department of State Bulletin* no. 2085, Washington, April 1984, 65-66.

20 *Newsweek,* August 27, 1984.

21 The memos are held in the Stasi archive at the Woodrow Wilson Center in Washington under references BsTu-ZA-HA-I-13558.

CHAPTER 20: TOTAL WAR

1   This successful interception owed a great deal to Captain Bill Tippin, a U.S. Air Force exchange officer, who was flying in the rear position of one of the Saudi F-15s that day and was the de facto head of the operation.

2   Interview with former French Air Force general Yvon Goutx, Paris, September 10, 2012.

3 Tom Cooper and Farzad Bishop, *Iran-Iraq War in the Air 1980–1988* (Atglen, PA: Schiffer Publishing, 2000), 156.

4 A Tomcat and a Phantom pilot each claimed the destruction of this Super Etendard, numbered "67" in French Naval Aeronautic nomenclature, though it remains impossible to determine which of the two actually brought it down.

5 Paul Balta, *Iran-Irak: Une guerre de 5000 ans* (Paris: Anthropos-Economica, 1988), 170.

6 For an exhaustive sociological analysis, see chapters 5 and 6 of Shahram Chubin and Charles Tripp's excellent *Iran and Iraq at War* (London: I.B. Tauris, 1988).

7 The author witnessed this when interviewing several of these officers. The most cynical among them pointed out that these cars, which were almost certainly fitted with microphones to record their conversations, were actually more of a curse than a blessing.

CHAPTER 21: THE YEAR OF THE PILOT

1 This 200,000-man force was divided between four regular army infantry divisions (the 21st, 28th, 55th, and 77th) and six Pasdaran divisions (the 8th, 14th, 17th, 23rd, 30th, and 31st). The 92nd Armored Division provided in-depth defense of Iranian lines.

2 The six launcher vehicles and twenty-six Scud-B missiles delivered by Libya were gathered in the 351st Artillery Brigade, which was placed under Pasdaran control.

CHAPTER 22: OIL AND THE WAR MACHINE

1 See the illuminating account in Eric Laurent's *La Face cachée du pétrole* (Paris: Plon, 2006), 183–195. This analysis has been confirmed to the author by reliable American, Emirian, Iraqi, and Saudi sources.

2 The principle of Soviet withdrawal from Afghanistan was made official by the Politburo on October 1985 (and implemented on May 15, 1988).

3 Quoted in John Parker, *Persian Dreams: Moscow and Tehran since the Fall of the Shah* (Washington, DC: Potomac Books, 2009), 20.

4 This information, which is referred to by William Burgess in his *Inside Spetsnaz—Soviet Special Operations: A Critical Analysis* (Novato, CA: Presidio Press, 1989), was confirmed to the author by former French and American secret service agents posted in Beirut.

5 In 1985 the Iranian navy inspected more than 300 ships suspected of delivering arms to Iraq.

CHAPTER 23: THE SLAUGHTER OF THE CHILD SOLDIERS

1   Sepehr Zabih, *The Iranian Military in Revolution and War* (New York: Routledge, 1988), 220.

2   Farhad Khosrokhavar, *L'islamisme et la mort: Le martyr révolutionnaire en Iran* (Paris: L'Harmattan, 1995); Ian Brown, *Khomeini's Forgotten Sons: The Story of Iran's Boy Soldiers* (London: Grey Seal Books), 1990.

3   Brown, *Khomeini's Forgotten Sons*, 46 and 86.

4   Quoted by Efraim Karsh in *The Iran-Iraq War* (Oxford: Osprey, 2002), 64.

5   Brown, *Khomeini's Forgotten Sons*, 90–91.

6   Karsh, *The Iran-Iraq War*, 62. The guns were not 50 mm, but 12.7 mm.

7   See General al-Hamdani's account in Kevin Woods, ed., *Saddam's Generals: Perspectives of the Iran-Iraq War* (Alexandria, VA: Institute for Defense Analyses and National Defense University of Washington, 2011), 70.

8   Qusay Hussein would indeed marry General Rashid's daughter a few months later.

9   Though the number of gassed soldiers was high, the number of deaths directly linked to chemical weapons (700) remained proportionally low, bearing witness to the many constraints of their implementation, notably those related to weather conditions.

CHAPTER 24: DEADLOCK

1   Quoted in Charles Caret, "L'alliance contre nature de la Syrie baassiste et de la République islamique d'Iran," *Politique étrangère* 2 (summer 1987): 385.

2   Under the terms of this new agreement, 30 percent of the oil Iran delivered to Syria would be free of charge and 70 percent would be supplied at a highly preferential rate (versus 20 percent and 80 percent previously).

3   Quoted by General al-Hamdani in Kevin Woods, ed., *Saddam's Generals: Perspectives of the Iran-Iraq War* (Alexandria, VA: Institute for Defense Analyses and National Defense University of Washington, 2011), 51.

4   Alladin Makki, quoted in Woods, *Saddam's Generals*, 115.

5   Quoted in the *Washington Post*, August 27, 1986; *Keyhan*, August 30, 1986.

6   At the end of the war these three pilots were respectively credited with twelve, eleven, and nine victories.

7   About one hundred MiG-21s, eighty MiG-23s, sixty Mirage F-1s, sixty Su-20/22s, thirty MiG 25s, and six Tupolev bombers.

8   See the detailed account by General Alwan al-Abousi in Woods, *Saddam's Generals*, 201–202.

9   Forty Phantoms, forty-five Tigers, and fifteen Tomcats.

CHAPTER 25: THE IRAN-CONTRA AFFAIR

1   Speech delivered to American media representatives, November 13, 1986, *NBC News,* November 24, 1986.

2   Three years earlier Michael Leeden had founded the Washington-based Jewish Institute for National Security Affairs, a lobby group intended to protect Israeli interests in Congress.

3   In his remarkable article, "Why Secret US-Iran Arms for Hostages Negotiations Failed," *Washington Report on Middle East Affairs* (Sept.–Oct. 1994), George Cave, one of the delegation's members, provides a detailed account of the discussions that took place in Tehran from May 25 to 28, 1986.

4   Sentenced to life imprisonment for high treason, Jonathan Pollard is still serving his time. His case remains a source of friction between Washington and Jerusalem.

5   Quoted in Joseph Alpher, "Israel and the Iran-Iraq War," in Efraim Karsh, ed., *The Iran-Iraq War,* 161.

6   Patrick Tyler, "Officers Say US Aided Iraq in War Despite Use of Gas," *New York Times,* August 18, 2002.

7   Tom Cooper and Farzad Bishop, *Iran-Iraq War in the Air, 1980–1988* (Atglen, PA: Schiffer Publishing, 2000), 225.

8   The remaining hostages were Edward Tracy, Frank Reed, Jesse Turner, Joseph Cicippio, Thomas Sutherland, Alan Steen, Robert Polhill, and Terry Anderson. The eighth American hostage, William Higgins, a lieutenant colonel of the Marine Corps serving as enior Military Observer with the United Nations Truce Supervision Organization (UNTSO) in South Lebanon at the time of his capture, was executed by his abductors during his captivity.

CHAPTER 26: ALL-OUT OFFENSIVES

1   During this latest episode of the War of the Cities, the Iraqis fired twenty-seven Scud-Bs, while the Iranians fired thirteen Scuds and eighty-one Oghabs (Frog-7s).

2   These Mohajer drones, modeled after the Israeli Scout drones successfully used by the Israelis during the 1982–1985 Lebanese War, looked like big remote-controlled toys equipped with powerful cameras. Several were destroyed by Iraqi anti-aircraft defense.

3   Saddam Hussein would use this same expression four years later to refer to the battle between his army and the international coalition formed to liberate Kuwait.

4   In two months Basra's population dropped from 1 million to 150,000. Refugees were directed to Baghdad and northern Iraq via the Euphrates road, while military reinforcement reached Basra via the Tigris road.

5   From audio recording SH-SHTP-A-000–634, dated March 28, 1987, Conflict Records Research Center (CRRC) Project (Washington, DC: National Defense University/Institute for National Strategic Studies).

6   As can be heard on audio recording SH-GMID-D-001–125, dated April 14, 1987, CRRC Project.

7   American sources, based on the study of satellite images of the battlefield, would later estimate there were 50,000 dead, which is probably slightly high, given the analysts' inability to distinguish the dead from the wounded. The low ratio of wounded to dead is due to the inadequate medical chain, which was unable to evacuate many of the wounded because of the way the troops were interlocked and the particular configuration of the battlefield.

CHAPTER 27: IRAN CHANGES STRATEGY

1   At the time Iran had one Silkworm launcher and a stock of twenty-eight missiles.

2   Kuwait soon purchased 150 T-84 tanks and 120 BMP-2/3 armored vehicles from the USSR.

3   Saudi Arabia received nine launchers and thirty missiles in January 1988.

4   The fleet included one command ship, one Krivak-class missile frigate, two Sovremeny-class destroyers, one amphibious assault ship, three minesweepers, and three oil tanker tenders.

5   On June 8, 1967, during the Six-Day War, the Israeli air force and navy intentionally attacked the spy ship the USS *Liberty* off al-Arish. For a full account of the incident, see my book, *Tsahal: nouvelle histoire de l'armée israélienne* (Paris: Tempus Perrin, 2008), 240–242.

6   Despite this procedure, two similar incidents were narrowly avoided on January 28 and February 13, 1988. The attacks avoided were on the assault ship *Portland* and the destroyer *Chandler*, stationed off of Bahrain and Qatar, respectively.

7   See the detailed account by Ahmad Sadik and Tom Cooper, "Un Falcon 50 lance-missiles," *Le Fana de l'aviation* 470 (Jan. 2009): 41–45.

8   See General Alwan al-Abousi's account in Kevin Woods, ed., *Saddam's Generals: Perspectives of the Iran-Iraq War* (Alexandria, VA: Institute for Defense Analyses and National Defense University of Washington, 2011), 205–206.

9   As heard on the audiotapes, notably the tape recorded May 27, 1987 (SHSHTP-A-000–958), Conflict Records Research Center (CRRC) Project (Washington, DC: National Defense University/Institute for National Strategic Studies).

10 Alwan al-Aboussi, quoted in Woods, *Saddam's Generals*, 204–206.

11 Pierre Péan, *La Menace* (Paris: Fayard, 1987), 237–244.

12 In 1985 the police prefecture had requested the expulsion of Wahid Gordji and about ten other Iranian nationals without requesting the authorization of the government, which was careful to tread softly with Tehran at that time. Péan, *La Menace*, 237–244.

13 "France: les démons de l'islamisme," *Aujourd'hui le Maroc*, Jan. 25, 2005; see also http://fr.wikipedia.org/wiki/Wahid_Gordji.

14 Antenne 2, 8 p.m. *Nightly News*, July 24, 1987, INA Vidéo.

15 For a detailed account of the French navy's activities in the Gulf, see Dominique Guillemin, "L'action de la Marine nationale pendant la guerre Iran-Irak," in *Le Pétrole et la Guerre* (Brussels: Peter Lang, 2012), 335–362.

16 Pierre Favier and Michel Martin-Roland, *La Décennie Mitterrand*, vol. 3 of *Les Défis* (Paris: Le Seuil, 1996), 432–433.

17 Dominique Lorentz, *Secret atomique, ou la véritable histoire des otages français au Liban*. (Les Arènes, 2002); see also http://fr.wikipedia.org/wiki/Eurodif; http://www.iran-resist.org/article167.

18 Ibid.

CHAPTER 28: THE GULF SET ABLAZE

1 The name navy SEAL refers both to an acronym for the U.S. navy frogmen's "Sea, Air, and Land" operational methods and the nickname "seal."

2 Interview with the author in Rome on May 13, 2008. The AH-6 Cayuses were replaced by OH-58 Kiowa helicopters beginning in January 1988.

3 See Commander Gary Stubblefield's enlightening account in *Inside the US Navy SEALs* (Osceola, WI: MBI Publishing, 1995), 154–170.

4 Following interminable proceedings, the ICJ decreed on November 6, 2003, that it could not settle the dispute and held each country equally responsible.

CHAPTER 29: THE HALABJA MASSACRE

1 These were Operations Victory 5 and 6, then Holy City 2, which took place between January 12 and February 26, 1988.

2 The divisions in question were the "Hammurabi" and "Medina Munawara" armored divisions, the "Nebuchadnezzar" mechanized division, the "Tawakalna" special forces division, and the "Baghdad" and "al-Faw" motorized infantry divisions.

3 Moscow delivered 300 Scuds to Baghdad from 1985 to 1987, then another 118 in 1988. Two Scuds were required to make one Al Hussein.

4 One hundred forty-one missiles struck Tehran, twenty-three fell on Qom, twenty-two on Esfahan, four on Tabriz, and three on Shiraz; sixty-two missiles struck Baghdad, nine fell on Mosul, five on Kirkuk, and one on Tikrit.

5   See in particular the audiotapes recorded on March 15, 1988, and catalogued as SH-GMID-D-000–468.

6   The Iraqi authorities in 2007 sentenced Ali Hassan al-Majid to death for his involvement in the massacre, as well as for his central role in the Anfal Campaign.

7   See the *Washington Post,* March 24, 1988, and the *Economist,* April 2, 1988. The most exhaustive, impartial investigation remains Joost Hilterman's *A Poisonous Affair: America, Iraq and the Gassing of Halabja* (New York: Cambridge University Press, 2007).

8   The 1st Mechanized, 6th Armored, and 2nd and 7th Infantry were under General Rashid's orders to carry out this maneuver. Three other infantry divisions (14th, 15th, and 26th) were kept at the center of the order of battle to pin the Iranian divisions in place and facilitate their encirclement.

9   This was confirmed to the author in an interview conducted in Washington, DC on October 27, 2011 with Ali Alameri, an Iraqi surgeon who was then doing his military service in a field hospital near Basra and treated numerous severely gassed Iraqi soldiers.

10 Unlike the Silkworm, the Scud missile's range allowed it to reach the Kuwaiti al-Ahmadi terminal from Iranian soil.

CHAPTER 30: THE DESTRUCTION OF IRAN AIR FLIGHT 655

1   Colin Powell would enter the history books three years later as chairman of the Joint Chiefs of Staff during the 1991 Gulf War, and would later be appointed secretary of state by George W. Bush, who would manipulate him to launch Bush's personal crusade against Saddam Hussein in 2003.

2   *Keyhan,* April 19, 1988.

3   These forces were divided into four armored divisions (the 3rd, 6th, "Hammurabi," and "Medina Munawara"); two mechanized (the 5th and "Nebuchadnezzar"); seven infantry (the "al-Faw," 8th, 11th, 19th, 30th, 41st, and 42nd), and the "Tawakalna" Special Forces Division.

4   Ra'ad Majid Rashid al-Hamdani in Woods, *Saddam's Generals,* 84.

5   These forces were divided into four armored divisions (the 3rd and 12th, "Hammurabi," and "Medina Munawara"); six infantry (the 25th, 31st, 35th, 41st, 42nd, and "al-Faw"); three mechanized (the 1st, 5th, and "Nebuchadnezzar"); and the "Tawakalna" Special Forces Division.

6   AFP, June 27, 1988.

7   During Operation Praying Mantis the U.S. navy had gone to great lengths to avoid entering Iranian territorial waters.

8   In the tense atmosphere on board, the officer had shifted his transponder into "military" mode, forgetting that most commercial flights and military

aircraft were equipped with a dual transponder allowing them to answer both civilian and military air traffic controllers. An experienced air traffic controller would not have made this mistake.

9   Bahrain Standard Time is Coordinated Universal Time (UTC) plus three hours, while Iran Standard Time is UTC plus 3.5 hours.

10   As was confirmed to the author in an interview conducted in Rome on February 15, 2012, with Sandy Guptill, a retired Marine Corps colonel and former air traffic controller charged with synthesizing the lessons drawn from the *Vincennes* incident. See also John Barry and Roger Charles, "Sea of Lies," *Newsweek,* July 13, 1992; Richard Saltus, "A Tragic Error Led to New Insights on Behavior Crisis," *Boston Globe,* February 28, 1994; "The Other Lockerbie," *BBC News,* April 17, 2000; "Air Emergency: Mistaken Identity," *National Geographic Channel,* season 3, episode 3, July 28, 2006.

11   Ibid.

12   William Fogarty, "Formal Investigation into the Circumstances Surrounding the Downing of Iran Air Flight 655 on 3 July 1988" (Washington, DC: U.S. Dept. of Defense, July 28, 1988).

13   Benjamin Barthe, "Le Libyen Al-Megrahi disparaît avec ses secrets," *Le Monde,* May 21, 2012.

14   Pan Am Flight 103 Investigation–DOI 910200.

15   International Court of Justice ruling of February 9, 1996.

CHAPTER 31: ENDGAME

1   The Iraqi order of battle consisted of two armored divisions ("Hammurabi" and "Medina Munawara"); three mechanized divisions (the 1st, 5th, and "Nebuchadnezzar"); six infantry divisions (the 2nd, 18th, 20th, 29th, 32nd, and "al-Faw"); and the "Tawakalna" Special Forces Division. Iranian forces present totaled 40,000 men in four divisions (two mechanized and two infantry).

2   Reuters, July 20, 1988.

3   France is said to have paid more than one billion dollars to settle the Eurodif debt (see Dominique Lorentz, *Secret atomique* [Paris: Les Arènes, 2002], 141; and Jean-Xavier Péri, "L'Iran détient 10% du Tricastin: le contentieux Eurodif," *Le Dauphiné libéré,* March 5, 2008).

4   See the data regarding the Eurodif affair collected on www.iranwatch.org, which is maintained by the Iranian opposition.

5   1989 ICRC reports; see also *Los Angeles Times,* December 26, 1989.

6   *La Chute: Interrogatoires de Saddam Hussein par le FBI,* preface and commentary by Pierre-Jean Luizard (Paris: Éditions Inculte/Actes Sud, Temps réel collection, 2010), 27–36.

EPILOGUE

1   See the transcript of audiotape SH-SHTP-A-001–631 (late 1988), Conflict Records Research Center (CRRC) Project (Washington, DC: National Defense University/Institute for National Strategic Studies).

2   By January 1989 the U.S. navy had only fourteen warships in the region, including one cruiser and six destroyers and frigates, but no aircraft carriers.

3   See General al-Hamdani's enlightening account in Kevin Woods, ed., *Saddam's Generals: Perspectives of the Iran-Iraq War* (Alexandria, VA: Institute for Defense Analyses and National Defense University of Washington, 2011), 42. Several journalists specializing in the murky depths of Iraqi politics had come to the same conclusion: see Sandra Mackey, *Iraq and the Legacy of Saddam Hussein* (New York: W. W. Norton, 2002), 322; and Andrew and Patrick Cockburn, *Out of the Ashes: The Resurrection of Saddam Hussein* (New York: Harper, 1999), 155–156.

4   As Bernard Hourcade points out in his remarkable volume *Géopolitique de l'Iran* (Paris: Armand Colin, 2010), 139.

5   *Jane's Defence Weekly,* February 4, 1989.

6   Other nations were also affected, such as Algeria, where bankruptcy led to civil war.

7   From 1989 to 1990 the volume of commercial exchanges between Iran and the USSR would triple, growing from 500 million to 1.5 billion dollars.

8   According to the terms of the contract signed on June 20, 1989, the USSR shipped Iran fifty-four MiG-29 interceptors, twenty-four Su-24 fighter-bombers, 480 T-72 tanks, 400 BMP-2 infantry fighting vehicles, 210 2S1 self-propelled howitzers, 200 S-200 anti-aircraft systems, 700 SA-15 surface-to-air missiles, and several thousand RPG-29 and AT-4 Spigot antitank missiles.

9   Though there are no available statistics, experts estimate that the Iraqi air force carried out at least 500,000 combat sorties during the conflict, versus 100,000 for the Iranians.

SOURCES

Archives

SERVICE HISTORIQUE DE LA DÉFENSE
(Château de Vincennes, France)
[Historical Department of the Ministry of Defense]:
Files 1997 Z 331/2 and 1997 Z 720/9 (consulted by special authorization of the director of Memory, Heritage and Archives at the Ministry of Defense), containing the situation reports, intelligence memoranda, orders of battle, and summary reports prepared by the *Centre d'exploitation du renseignement militaire* (CERM) [Military Intelligence Exploitation Center] on the Iran-Iraq War from 1980 to 1988.

WOODROW WILSON INTERNATIONAL CENTER FOR SCHOLARS (WASHINGTON, DC):
Oral archive kept by the Woodrow Wilson Center in Washington as part of the Cold War International History Project, which deals with the Iran-Iraq conflict (1980–1988) and provides firsthand perspectives on the nature of the American government's involvement in the war. These archives were publicly presented during an international conference held on July 19, 2004, at the Woodrow Wilson Center's headquarters.
Archives of the STASI (secret service of the former German Democratic Republic) relating to the Iran-Iraq War, obtained in Berlin thanks to the research of Bernd Schaefer, senior scholar at the Woodrow Wilson Center. These archives contain highly interesting details regarding the cooperation between former Eastern Bloc countries and Iraq and Iran. They can be consulted at the Woodrow Wilson Center, after filing a request via the Web site: www.cwihp.org.

NATIONAL DEFENSE UNIVERSITY /
INSTITUTE FOR NATIONAL STRATEGIC STUDIES
(WASHINGTON, DC):

Oral archives held by the National Defense University in Washington (NDU) as part of the Conflict Records Research Center (CRRC) project, which include all the magnetic audiotapes and documents captured by the U.S. army upon the taking of Baghdad in 2003. These tapes have recordings of conversations (in Arab and in English) between Saddam Hussein and the individuals he met with from 1979 to 2002. As soon as he came to power, the Iraqi Rais ordered that all his conversations, including those with his generals, be systematically recorded "for posterity." This essential documentary archive, which is currently being translated into English, can be consulted on site under certain conditions by contacting the CRRC at CRRC@ndu.edu. A selection of these audiotapes was compiled in *The Saddam Tapes,* published by Cambridge University Press in 2011.

List of the Most Interesting Audio Transcripts

REFERENCE—DATE—SUBJECT:

SH-GMID-D-000–842—June 30, 1980—Report analyzing the political, military, and economic situation in Iran.

SH-SHTP-A-000–835—September 16, 1980—Meeting between Saddam, the Ba'ath National Command, and the Revolutionary Command Council regarding the start of the war.

SH-SHTP-D-000–847—September 23, 1980—Meeting between Saddam and his generals to discuss the war.

SH-PDWN-D-001–021—October 6, 1980—Meeting between Saddam and Iraqi officials to discuss the war.

SH-MISC-D-000–695—October 12, 1980—Meeting between Saddam and his generals regarding Iraqi positions at the beginning of the war.

SH-SHTP-D-000–623—October 17, 1980—Meeting between Saddam and his generals.

SH-SHTP-D-000–826—October 31, 1980—Meeting between Saddam and his generals.

SH-MISC-D-000–827—October 1980—Meeting of the Iraqi generals to discuss the progress of the war.

SH-SHTP-D-000–856—November 1, 1980—Meeting between Saddam and his generals to prepare the army for the new offensive.

SH-PDWN-D-000–566—November 1980—Meeting between Saddam and the chiefs of staff to discuss the progress of the war.

SH-IISX-D-000–841—January 1, 1981—Report on the evaluation of the Iranian military threat.

SH-IZAR-D-000–278—February 28, 1981—Report by the chiefs of staff on the battle of al-Khafajiyah and discussion of the potential use of chemical weapons.

SH-SHTP-A-000–571 and SH-SHTP-A-000–910—Mid-June 1981—Meeting between Saddam and his closest advisors on the attack of Osirak by the Israeli air force and the decision to rebuild the nuclear reactor.

SH-IZAR-D-001–086—September 26, 1981—Report on military operations in the 10th Division's sector.

SH-SHTP-A-000–561—Late 1981—Meeting between Saddam and his generals to discuss the progress of the war.

SH-SHTP-A-000–628—February 1982—Meeting between Saddam and his advisors on the state of relations between Iraq and Syria.

SH-GMID-D-000–531—April 1982—Report by Iraqi intelligence on Iranian movements.

SH-SHTP-A-000–710—July 21, 1982—Meeting between Saddam and his ministers to discuss Iranian advances in Iraqi territory.

SH-SHTP-D-000–864—September 1982—Meeting between Saddam and his generals concerning the progress of recent battles.

SH-PDWN-D-001–029—May 11, 1983—Meeting between Saddam and the commander of the Iraqi army on the progress of the war.

SH-AFGC-D-000–094—November 1, 1983—Memorandum between the General Command of Iraqi Armed Forces and the Directorate of Military Intelligence on the use of chemical weapons.

SH-SHTP-A-000–627—Fall 1983—Meeting between Saddam and his generals to discuss the progress of the war.

SH-SHTP-A-001–035—July 7, 1984—Meeting between Saddam and the heads of the air force to assess aerial forces' performance.

SH-SHTP-A-000–735—October 18, 1984—Meeting between Saddam and Iraqi officials to discuss the progress of operations.

SH-AADF-D-000–747—December 1984—Report on Iraq and Iran's military activity during the war.

SH-RPGD-D-000–706—January 1985—Report on Iranian military activity.

SH-IZAR-D-000–781—January 1985—Report on military activity in the 4th Corps' sector.

SH-GMID-D-000–649—February 1985—Report on the overall situation on the front.

SH-GMID-D-000–663—February 1985—Meeting between military intelligence and the Directorate of Operations on Iranian military activity.

SH-GMID-D-000–744—June 1985—Report on the positions of Iranian troops.

SH-SPPC-D-000–540—February 1986—Meeting between Saddam and his generals concerning plans for the war's progress.

SH-GMID-D-000–076—June 17, 1986—Report by military intelligence on the potential use of the French civil observation satellite *Spot* for military purposes.

SH-GMID-D-000–746—August 1986—Report on Iranian military activity.

SH-SHTP-D-000–411—September 12, 1986—Meeting between Saddam and the regime's political and military executives to determine the position to adopt following Iranian missile attacks on Iraqi cities.

SH-MISC-D-000–449—October 29, 1986—Meeting of the chiefs of staff to discuss the deployment of Iranian forces along the Iraqi border.

SH-SHTP-D-000–608—November 1986—Meeting between Saddam and his generals regarding delivery of weapons to Iran by Israel and the United States.

SH-SHTP-A-000–555—November 15, 1986—Meeting between Saddam and the Revolutionary Command Council regarding President Reagan's speech on American arms sales to Iran.

SH-SHTP-A-000–556—Late November 1986—Meeting between Saddam and his ministers on the implications of American arms sales to Iran.

SH-MISC-D-000–264—December 27, 1986—Report on Iraqi and Iranian losses during the "Battle of the Great Day."

SH-SHTP-A-000–733—1987—Meeting between Saddam and his advisors regarding the establishment of a potential ceasefire.

SH-SHTP-A-000–896—March 6, 1987—Meeting between Saddam and the members of the Revolutionary Command Council on the state of Iraq and the use of chemical weapons.

SH-SHTP-A-001–023—Meeting between Saddam and members of the Ba'ath Party regarding the progress of the war and the need to target Iranian cities.

SH-GMID-D-000–133—March 1987—Saddam's decision to use chemical weapons against the Iranians and Kurdish rebels in the region of Kurdistan.

SH-SHTP-A-000–634—March 28, 1987—Meeting between Saddam and the corps commanders to discuss the "Battle of the Great Day."

SH-GMID-D-001–125—April 14, 1987—Report on Iran's use of chemical weapons against Iraqi troops.

SH-SHTP-A-000–958—May 27, 1987—Meeting between Saddam and officials of the regime concerning the attack on the American frigate USS *Stark*.

SH-IAZR-D-001–087—June 4, 1987—Report on the battle of Mandali.

SH-GMID-D-000–087—July 6, 1987—Military intelligence report on the Lebanese al-Kataibi factory manufacturing chemical weapons for Iraq.

SH-GMID-D-000–898—October 1987—Report on Iran's chemical capacity and the alleged use of these weapons against Iraqi troops.

SH-SHTP-V-000–612—1988—Meeting between Saddam and his generals regarding the role of the Republican Guard and efforts to reconquer the Majnoon Islands.

SH-GMID-D-000–708—January 1, 1988—Report analyzing the overall situation in the Gulf.

SH-GMID-D-000–468—March 15, 1988—Plans to counter Iranian and Kurdish attacks in the sector of Halabja and losses inflicted by chemical attacks.

SH-IZAR-D-000–655—March 20, 1988—Orders launching the second Operation Anfal against Iraqi Kurds.

SH-SHTP-A-000–568—April 1988—Meeting between Saddam and his closest advisors to determine where the general counteroffensive will be launched.

SH-GMID-D-000–902—May 1, 1988—Meeting between Saddam and the chiefs of staff relating to plans for deception, chemical attacks, and Operation Anfal.

SH-PDWN-D-000–730—May 26, 1988—Meeting of the chiefs of staff relating to the general situation, notably in al-Faw, and the war's military and diplomatic aspects.

SH-SHTP-D-000–538—June 27, 1988—Meeting between Saddam and his generals to discuss the progress of the war.

SH-SHTP-A-000–568—July 1988—Meeting between Saddam and his generals to discuss the liberation of al-Faw.

SH-SHTP-A-000–816—August 9, 1988—Meeting between Saddam and members of the Ba'ath Party discussing the Iraqi victory.

Interviews

Abdulla, Abdulkhaleq, director of the Al Khaleej Research Center, specialist on the Gulf Cooperation Council (Dubai: May 28, 2009; Rome: December 2, 2009; Manama: December 13, 2009; Cambridge: July 8, 2010).

Abu-Jaber Kamel, former minister of foreign affairs for Jordan (regular contact since 2007).

Alameri, Ali, Iraqi surgeon (Washington: October 27, 2011).

Alani, Ali, Iraqi colonel (Rome: March 26, 2009).

Alani, Mustafa, director of National Security and Terrorism Studies Department at the Gulf Research Center and specialist on the Iran-Iraq War (regular contact since 2009).

Al-Assad, Wael, director of Disarmament and Multilateral Relations at the League of Arab States (Amman: June 24, 2009; Rome: October 29, 2009; Wilton Park: December 1, 2010 and May 22, 2012).

Al-Faisali, Shehab, Iraqi commodore (Rome: November 26, 2007).

Al-Hameedawi, Akram, Iraqi colonel (Rome: November 27, 2007).

Al-Jabouri, Najim, Iraqi general, former officer of the anti-air defense forces (Washington: October 26, 2011).

Al-Jeboury, Mohamed, Iraqi colonel (Rome: October 9, 2009).

Al-Marashi, Ibrahim, sociologist specialized on the Iran-Iraq war's impact on Iraqi society (London: September 24, 2010).

Al-Sabah, Thamer (Sheikh), chairman of Kuwait's National Security Apparatus (Rome: March 31, 2010).

Al-Samawi, Abdul, Iraqi general (Rome: October 9, 2009).

Al-Shamlan, Asaad, director of the Riyadh Institute for Diplomatic Studies, specialist in the Gulf's geopolitics (Rome: December 3, 2009; Manama: December 12, 2009).

Al-Sultan, Khudhair, Iraqi colonel (Rome: April 1, 2008).

Al-Suwaidi, Jamal, director general of the Emirates Center for Strategic Studies and Research (Abu Dhabi: May 26, 2009).

Al-Windawi, Mouayad, Iraqi academic specialized in the Iran-Iraq War, close to generals who fought Iran (Wilton Park: December 2, 2010).

Al-Zayani, Abdullatif, Bahraini general (Rome: November 2, 2009).

Ashton, Nigel, British specialist on Jordan and its role in the Iran-Iraq War (regular contact since 2010).

Babood, Abdullah, specialist on the Gulf Cooperation Council (regular contact since 2009).

Barzegar, Kayhan, Iranian academic, director of the Institute for Middle East Strategic Studies in Tehran (Rome: December 2, 2009).

Basbous, Antoine, director of the Observatory of Arab Nations (regular contact since 2006).

Bishop, Farzad, specialist in aerial operations during the Iran-Iraq War (regular contact since 2010).

Brom, Shlomo, retired Israeli general responsible for military matters at the Institute for National Security Studies in Tel-Aviv, heavily involved in the Iraqi and Iranian dossiers (regular contact since 2007).

Byrne, Malcolm, responsible for the development of the oral archives relating to the Iran-Iraq War (London: September 24, 2010; Washington: October 26, 2011).

Cave, George, CIA bureau chief in Iran during the Islamic Revolution (Washington: October 27, 2011).

Carrère d'Encausse, Hélène (Paris: March 23, 2011).

Chubin, Shahram, Iranian academic specializing in the Iran-Iraq War (Wilton Park: December 1–2, 2010; Washington: October 26, 2011).

Cogan, Charles, CIA director of operations for the Middle East from 1978 to 1984 (regular contact since 2000).

Cooper, Tom, specialist on aerial operations during the Iran-Iraq War (regular contact since 2010).

Cordesman, Anthony, expert in military affairs and former advisor to the American administration on Gulf-related matters (Washington: October 25, 1998; Rome: March 4, 2009).

Enghusen, Mareike, historian specialized in the role of child soldiers during the Iran-Iraq War (London: September 23, 2010).

Farhang, Mansour, Iranian ambassador to the United Nations from 1979 to 1980 (Washington: October 26, 2011).

Guptill, Sandy, retired Marine Corps colonel, former air traffic controller in the Gulf (Rome: February 15, 2012).

Hambley, Mark, former American diplomat stationed in the Gulf during the Iran-Iraq War (London: September 24, 2010).

Hassan-Yari, Houchang, Iranian historian specialized in contemporary conflicts, professor at the Royal Military College of Canada (regular contact since 2008).

Heisbourg, François, former diplomatic advisor to Charles Hernu (regular contact since 2012).

Hourcade, Bernard, research director at the CNRS, stationed in Tehran during the Iran-Iraq War (regular contact since 2006).

Irdaisat, Mahmoud, Jordanian general, director of the Jordanian Center for Strategic Studies (regular contact since 2007).

Isbell, Donald, retired U.S. army colonel who led many special missions in the Gulf in 1987–1988 (regular contact from 2007 to 2009).

Javedanfar, Meir, Israeli specialist on relations between Israel and Iran (London: September 23, 2010).

Kadry Saïd, Mohamed, retired Egyptian general responsible for military matters at the Al-Ahram Center for Political and Strategic Studies in Cairo (regular contact since 2007).

Kalinovsky, Artemy, specialist in relations between the Soviet Union, Iraq, and Iran (London: September 24, 2010).

Kamrava, Mehran, director of the Center for International and Regional Studies at Georgetown University in Doha (Istanbul: June 5–6, 2008).

Khalil, Ayman, director of the Arab Institute for Security Studies in Amman (regular contact since 2008).

och, Christian, research director at the Gulf Research Center (regular contact since 2008).

.acoste, Picrre, former head of France's General Directorate for External Security [1982–1985] (regular contact since 1999).

Mack, David, director of the "Middle East" office at the State Department in Washington at the beginning of the war (Washington: October 27, 2011).

Malovany, Pesach, retired colonel, responsible for monitoring the Iraqi army for Israeli military intelligence during the Iran-Iraq War (Washington: October 28, 2011; Tel-Aviv: July 5, 2012).

Moadab, Shahidi, former ambassador and researcher in international relations at University of Paris IV-Sorbonne (Paris: January 20 and March 24, 2011).

Monem, Saïd, Abdel, political specialist with expertise in inter-Arab relations, former director of the Al-Ahram Center (Cairo: February 6, 2008).

Murphy, Richard, U.S. ambassador to Saudi Arabia from 1981 to 1983, then assistant secretary of state for Near Eastern and South Asian Affairs from 1983 to 1989 (London: September 24, 2010; Washington: October 26, 2011).

Nadimi, Farzin, Iranian academic specialized in energy matters during the Iran-Iraq War (London: September 24, 2010; Washington: October 27, 2011).

Najem, Hani, Iraqi general (Rome: September 22, 2008).

Natali, Denise, specialist on the Kurdish question (Washington: October 26, 2011).

Newton, David, ambassador who reopened the American embassy in Baghdad during the Iran-Iraq War (Washington: October 27, 2011).

Noori, Salah, Iraqi general (Rome: March 27, 2009).

Radchenko, Sergey, specialist in relations between the Soviet Union, Iraq, and Iran (Washington: October 27, 2011).

Rangwala, Glen, researcher at Cambridge University, specialized in the financing of the Iraqi war effort during the Iran-Iraq War (London: September 24, 2010).

Sariolghalam, Mahmood, Iranian professor specialized in the Iran-Iraq War (Cambridge: July 9, 2010).

Savranskaya, Svetlana, specialist in relations between the Soviet Unior Iraq, and Iran (Washington: October 27, 2011).

Seale, Patrick, specialist on Syria (regular contact from 2003 until hi death in 2014).

Seif, Armin, specialist in relations between Iraq and Iran at Cambridg University (London: September 23, 2010).

Shaker, Mohamed, former Egyptian diplomat, former director of the Egyptian Council for Foreign Affairs (regular contact from 2008 tc 2012).

Talmage, Caitlin, specialist on the Iran-Iraq War at the Massachusetts Institute of Technology (London: September 23, 2010).

Tomay, Hani, Iraqi colonel, young special forces officer during the Iran-Iraq War (Rome: February 28, 2011).

Tripp, Charles, professor at the London School of Oriental & African Studies, specialist on Iraq and the Iran-Iraq conflict (regular contact since 2009).

Veliotes, Nicholas, American ambassador in Jordan and in Egypt during the Iran-Iraq War (Washington: October 26, 2011).

Woods, Kevin, responsible for the conservation of the Saddam Hussein oral archives at the National Defense University, responsible for numerous interviews with Iraqi generals (London: September 24, 2010; Washington: October 27, 2011).

Yaphe, Judith, former CIA agent charged with monitoring the Iran-Iraq War (regular contact since 2010).

Yasseen, Fareed, Iraqi ambassador to France (Paris: January 28, 2010; Wilton Park: December 1, 2010).

Reports and Studies

Atlas of Iran-Iraq War. 2nd ed. Tehran: IRGC Ministry, 2010.

Balta, Paul. *Le conflit Irak-Iran: 1979–1989.* Notes et études documentaires no. 4889. Paris: La Documentation française, 1989.

Barba, Jean-François. *Rapport du Contrôle général des Armées sur l'affaire Luchaire.* In *Des armes pour l'Iran,* edited by Walter De Bock and Jean-Charles Deniau. Paris: Gallimard, 1988.

Battle, Joyce, ed. *Shaking Hands with Saddam Hussein: The US Tilts toward Iraq 1980–1984.* National Security Archive Electronic Briefing

Book No. 82. Washington, DC: National Security Archive. Document declassified under the Freedom of Information Act, February 25, 2003, http://nsarchive.gwu.edu/NSAEBB/NSAEBB82/.

Bergquist, Ronald. *The Role of Airpower in the Iran-Iraq War*. Maxwell Air Force Base, Montgomery, AL: Airpower Research Institute, Air University Press, 1988.

Cordesman, Anthony. *The Iran-Iraq War and Western Security*. London: Jane's Publishing, Royal United Services Institute for Defence Studies, 1987.

Gamlen, Elizabeth. *US Military Intervention in the Iran-Iraq War*. Peace Research Report no. 21. University of Bradford, 1989.

Islamic Republic of Iran. *The Imposed War: Defence versus Aggression*. 5 vols. War Information HQ and Supreme Council, 1982–1987.

The Iran-Iraq War: A Reference Aid. Report No. DDB-2600–5954–88. (Report intended for Congress, declassified under the Freedom of Information Act). Simi Valley, CA: Ronald Reagan Library, Defense Research Reference Series, 1988.

Karsh, Efraim. *The Iran-Iraq War: A Military Analysis*. Adelphi Papers no. 220. London: International Institute for Strategic Studies, 1987.

King, Ralph. *The Iran-Iraq War: The Political Implications*. Adelphi Papers no. 219. London: International Institute for Strategic Studies, 1987.

Pelletiere, Stephen, and Douglas Johnson. *Lessons Learned: The Iran-Iraq War*. Carlisle, PA: Strategic Studies Institute, U.S. Army War College, 1991.

Rajee, Farhang. *Iranian Perspectives on the Iran-Iraq War*. Gainesville: University Press of Florida, 1997.

Royal United Services Institute for Defence Studies. *The War in the Gulf*. Whitehall Paper. London: Royal United Services Institute for Defence Studies, 1988.

Sabin, Philip, ed. *Operation Morvarid*. London: Dept. of War Studies, King's College, 2006.

Tower, John. *The Tower Commission Report*. (Official report of the Tower Commission on the Iran-Contra scandal). New York: Times Books, 1987. Extensive excerpts can be found online at http://www.presidency.ucsb.edu/PS157/assignment%20files%20public/TOWER%20EXCERPTS.htm.

Woods, Kevin, ed. *Saddam's Generals: Perspectives of the Iran-Iraq War.* Alexandria, VA: Institute for Defense Analyses and National Defense University of Washington, 2011.

Books

Aeschimann, Eric, and Christophe Boltanski. *Chirac d'Arabie: Les mirages d'une politique française.* Paris: Grasset, 2006.

Angeli, Claude, and Stéphanie Mesnier. *Notre ami Saddam.* Paris: Olivier Orban, 1992.

Ashton, Nigel, and Bryan Gibson, eds. *The Iran-Iraq War: New International Perspectives.* London: Routledge, 2013.

Balta, Paul. *Iran-Irak: Une guerre de 5000 ans.* Paris: Anthropos-Economica, 1988.

Barzin, Nader. *L'Iran nucléaire.* Paris: L'Harmattan, 2005.

Basbous, Antoine, and Annie Laurent. *Guerre secrète au Liban.* Paris: Gallimard, 1987.

Benraad, Myriam. *L'Irak.* Idées reçues. Paris: Le Cavalier Bleu, 2010.

Bergman, Ronen. *The Secret War with Iran.* New York: Free Press, 2008.

Bill, James. *The Eagle and the Lion: The Tragedy of American-Iranian Relations.* New Haven, CT: Yale University Press, 1988.

Bonnet, Yves. *Vevak au service des ayatollahs: Histoire des services secrets iraniens.* Boulogne-Billancourt: Timée-éditions, 2009.

Bowden, Mark. *Guests of the Ayatollah.* New York: Atlantic Monthly Press, 2006.

Brown, Ian. *Khomeini's Forgotten Sons: The Story of Iran's Boy Soldiers.* London: Grey Seal Books, 1990.

Bulloch, John, and Harvey Morris. *The Gulf War: Its Origins, History and Consequences.* Methuen London Ltd, 1989.

Burgess, William. *Inside Spetsnaz—Soviet Special Operations: A Critical Analysis.* Novato, CA: Presidio Press, 1989.

Cadiot, Jean-Michel. *Quand l'Irak entra en guerre.* Paris: L'Harmattan, 1989.

Chubin, Shahram, and Charles Tripp. *Iran and Iraq at War.* London: I. B. Tauris, 1988.

Cogan, Charles. *La République de Dieu: Regards d'un Américain sur les Etats-Unis et l'islam.* Paris: Jacob-Duvernet, 2008.

Cockburn, Andrew, and Patrick Cockburn. *Out of the Ashes: The Resurrection of Saddam Hussein.* New York: Harper, 1999.

Cooper, Tom, and Farzad Bishop. *Iran Iraq War in the Air, 1980–1988.* Atglen, PA: Schiffer Publishing, 2000.

———. *Iranian F-4 Phantom II Units in Combat.* Combat Aircraft no. 37. Oxford: Osprey Publishing, 2003.

———. *Iranian F-14 Tomcat Units in Combat.* Combat Aircraft no. 49. Oxford: Osprey Publishing, 2004.

Cooper, Tom, and Farzad Bishop, with Ahmad Sadik. *Iraqi Fighters.* Houston, TX: Harpia Publishing, 2008.

Cooper, Tom, and Farzad Bishop, with Babak Taghvaee and Liam Devlin. *The Modern Iranian Air Force.* Houston, TX: Harpia Publishing, 2010.

Cordesman, Anthony, and Abraham Wagner. *The Iran-Iraq War: The Lessons of Modern War.* Vol. 2. Boulder, CO: Westview Press, 1990.

Coughlin, Con. *Hostage: The Complete Story of the Lebanon Captives.* London: Little, Brown, 1992.

Coville, Thierry. *Iran: la révolution invisible.* Paris: Éditions La Découverte, 2007.

Creighton, John. *Oil on Troubled Waters: Gulf Wars 1980–1991.* London: Echoes, 1992.

Dawisha, Adeed. *Iraq: A Political History from Independence to Occupation.* Princeton, NJ: Princeton University Press, 2009.

De Bock, Walter, and Jean-Charles Deniau. *Des armes pour l'Iran.* Paris: Gallimard, 1988.

De Guttry, Andrea, and Natalino Ronzitti. *The Iran-Iraq War and the Law of Naval Warfare.* Cambridge: Grotius Publications, 1993.

Dekker, Ige, and Harry Post. *The Gulf War of 1980–1988.* Dordrecht (Netherlands): Martinus Nijhoff Publishers, 1992.

Djalili, Mohammad-Reza. *Iran: L'illusion réformiste.* Paris: Presses de Sciences Po, 2001.

Dubos, Jean-François. *Vente d'armes: Une politique.* Paris: Gallimard, 1974.

Dumas, Roland. *Affaires étrangères (1981–1988).* Paris: Fayard, 2007.

El Azhary, M.S., ed. *The Iran-Iraq War.* New York: St. Martin's Press, 1984.

Faligot, Roger, and Jean Guisnel. *Histoire secrète de la Ve République.* Paris: Éditions La Découverte, 2006.

Farrokh, Kaveh. *Iran at War.* Oxford: Osprey Pub, 2011.

Favier, Pierre, and Michel Martin-Roland, *La Décennie Mitterrand.* Vol 3 of *Les Défis.* Paris: Le Seuil, 1996.

Fisk, Robert. *Pity the Nation: The Abduction of Lebanon.* New York: Atheneum, 1990.

Gibson, Bryan. *Covert Relationship: American Foreign Policy, Intelligence and the Iran-Iraq War 1980–1988.* Santa Barbara, CA: PSI Reports, Praeger, 2010.

Giscard d'Estaing, Valéry. *Le Pouvoir et la vie.* Vol. 1. Paris: Compagnie 12, 1989.

Guisnel, Jean. *Armes de corruption massive: Secrets et combines des marchands de canon.* Paris: Éditions La Découverte, 2011.

———. *Charles Hernu ou la République au cœur.* Paris: Fayard, 1993.

Hilterman, Joost. *A Poisonous Affair: America, Iraq and the Gassing of Halabja.* New York: Cambridge University Press, 2007.

Hiro, Dilip. *The Longest War: The Iran-Iraq Military Conflict.* New York: Routledge, 1991.

Hourcade, Bernard. *Géopolitique de l'Iran.* Paris : Armand Colin, 2010.

Hourcade, Bernard, with Jean-Pierre Digard and Yann Richard. *L'Iran au XXᵉ siècle.* 2nd ed. Paris: Fayard, 2007.

Hubac, Olivier. *Irak: Une guerre mondiale de 1980 à nos jours.* Paris: La Martinière, 2006.

Johnson, Rob. *The Iran-Iraq War.* London: Palgrave Macmillan, 2011.

Karsh, Efraim. *The Iran-Iraq War 1980–1988.* Oxford: Osprey Publishing, 2002.

Katzman, Kenneth. *The Warriors of Islam: Iran's Revolutionary Guards.* Oxford: Westview Press, 1993.

Kaul, Kapil. *Tanker War: Aspect of Iraq-Iran War 1980–88.* Leicester: Stosius/Advent Books, 1989.

Khadduri, Majid. *The Gulf War: Origins and Implications of the Iraq-Iran Conflict.* Oxford: Oxford University Press, 1988.

Khosrokhavar, Farhad. *L'islamisme et la mort: Le martyr révolutionnaire en Iran.* Paris: L'Harmattan, 1995.

King, Ralph. *Irak-Iran: la guerre paralysée.* Paris: Éditions Bosquet, 1987.

King, Ralph, and Efraim Karsh, eds. *The Iran-Iraq War and the First Gulf War.* London: Routledge, 2006.

aurens, Henry. *L'Orient arabe à l'heure américaine*. Paris: Hachette Littératures, 2008.

——. *Paix et guerre au Moyen-Orient*. 2nd ed. Paris: Armand Colin, 2005.

aurent, Eric. *La face cachée du pétrole*. Paris: Plon, 2006.

evinson, Jeffrey, and Randy Edwards. *Missile Inbound: The Attack on the USS Stark in the Persian Gulf*. Annapolis, MD: U.S. Naval Institute Press, 1997.

orentz, Dominique. *Secret atomique, ou la véritable histoire des otages français au Liban*. Paris: Les Arènes, 2002.

Luizard, Pierre-Jean. *Comment est né l'Irak moderne*. Paris: CNRS Editions, 2009.

——. *La question irakienne*. Paris: Fayard, 2002.

Mackey, Sandra. *Iraq and the Legacy of Saddam Hussein*. New York: W. W. Norton, 2002.

Marshall, Jonathan, Peter Dale Scott, and Jane Hunter. *The Iran Contra Connection*. New York: South End Press, 1987.

Maull, Hanns, and Otto Pick, eds. *The Gulf War: Regional and International Dimensions*. London: Printer Publishers, 1989.

Mofid, Kamran. *The Economic Consequences of the Gulf War*. New York: Routledge, 1990.

Nonneman, Gerd. *Iraq, the Gulf States and the War*. London: Ithaca Press, 1986.

Makinsky, Michel, ed. "L'Iran ou la révolution permanente." *Les Cahiers de l'Orient* 99 (summer 2010).

Malovany, Pesach. *Milhamot Bavel HaHadasha* (The wars of modern Babylon). Tel-Aviv: Maarachot, IDF publications, Stematzky, 2010.

McDowall, David. *A Modern History of the Kurds*. London: I. B. Tauris, 2007.

Navias, Martin, and E. Hooton. *Tanker Wars: The Assault on Merchant Shipping during the Iran-Iraq Conflict*. London: I. B. Tauris, 1996.

O'Ballance, Edgar. *The Gulf War*. London: Brassey's Defence Publishers, 1988.

Otelli, Jean-Pierre. *Pilotes dans la tourmente: Raid sur Baalbek*. Levallois-Perret: Editions Altipresse, 2005.

Parham, Ramin, and Michel Taubmann, *Histoire secrète de la révolutio* *iranienne*. Paris: Denoël, 2009.

Parker, John. *Persian Dreams: Moscow and Tehran since the Fall of th* *Shah*. Washington, DC: Potomac Books, 2009.

Parsi, Trita. *Treacherous Alliance: The Secret Dealings of Israel, Iran an* *the US*. New Haven, CT: Yale University Press, 2007.

Péan, Pierre. *La Menace*. Paris: Fayard, 1987.

Pelletiere, Stephen. *The Iran-Iraq War: Chaos in a Vacuum*. New York Praeger, 1992.

Perlmutter, Amos, Michael Handel, and Uri Bar-Joseph. *Two Minutes ove* *Baghdad*. 2nd ed. London: Frank Cass, 2003.

Potter, Lawrence, and Gary Sick. *Iran, Iraq and the Legacies of War*. New York: Palgrave Macmillan, 2004.

Primakov, Yevgeny. *Au cœur du pouvoir: Mémoires politiques*. Paris: édition des Syrtes, 2002.

———. *Russia and the Arabs: Behind the Scenes in the Middle East from the Cold War to the Present*. New York: Basic Books, 2009.

Rajaee, Farhang, ed. *Iranian Perspectives on the Iran-Iraq War*. Miami: University Press of Florida, 1997.

Razoux, Pierre. *Tsahal: nouvelle histoire de l'armée israélienne*. Paris: Tempus Perrin, 2008.

Rondot, Philippe. *L'Irak*. Collection "Que sais-je ?" Paris: PUF, 1995.

Roux, Jean-Paul. *Histoire de l'Iran des origines à nos jours*. Paris: Fayard, 2006.

Ryan, Paul. *The Iranian Rescue Mission: Why It Failed*. Annapolis, MD: Naval Institute Press, 1985.

Saint-Prot, Charles. *Histoire de l'Irak*. Paris: Ellipses, 1999.

Sassoon, Joseph. *Saddam Hussein's Bath Party: Inside an Authoritarian Regime*. Cambridge: Cambridge University Press, 2011.

Scowcroft, Brent, and George Bush. *A World Transformed*. New York: Vintage, 1999.

Secord, Richard. *Honored and Betrayed: Irangate*. New York: Wiley, 1992.

Shemesh, Haim. *Soviet-Iraqi Relations, 1968–1988: In the Shadow of the Iraq-Iran Conflict*. Boulder, CO: Lynne Rienner Publishers, 1992.

Sick, Gary. *All Fall Down: America's Fateful Encounter with Iran*. New York: Random House, 1985.

icker, Martin. *The Bear and the Lion: Soviet Imperialism and Iran.* London: Praeger, 1988.

obhani, Sohrab. *The Pragmatic Entente: Israeli-Iranian Relations, 1948–1988.* London: Praeger, 1989.

Stubblefield, Gary. *Inside the US Navy SEALs.* Osceola, WI: MBI Publishing, 1995.

Tahir-Kheli, Shirim, and Shaheen Ayubi. *The Iran-Iraq War: New Weapons, Old Conflicts.* New York: Praeger, 1983.

Tarock, Adam. *The Superpowers' Involvement in the Iran-Iraq War.* New York: Nova Science Publishers, 1998.

Therme, Clément. *Les relations entre Téhéran et Moscou depuis 1979.* Paris: PUF, 2012.

Timmerman, Kenneth. *Le lobby de la mort: Comment l'Occident a armé l'Irak.* Paris: Calmann-Lévy, 1991.

Trab Zemzemi, Abdel-Majid. *La guerre Irak-Iran: Islam et nationalismes.* Paris: Albatros, 1985.

Tripp, Charles. *A History of Iraq.* 4th ed. Cambridge: Cambridge University Press, 2011.

Vaïsse, Maurice. *La puissance ou l'influence? La France dans le monde depuis 1958.* Paris: Fayard, 2009.

Vasset, Philippe. *Journal intime d'un marchand de canons.* Paris: Fayard, 2008.

Ward, Steven. *Immortal: A Military History of Iran and its Armed Forces.* Washington, DC: Georgetown University Press, 2009.

Wise, Harold Lee. *Inside the Danger Zone: The U.S. Military in the Persian Gulf 1987–1988.* Newport, RI: U.S. Naval Institute Press, 2007.

Woodward, Bob. *Veil: The Secret Wars of the CIA 1981–1987.* New York: Simon & Schuster, 2005.

Van Creveld, Martin. *Tsahal: Histoire critique de la force de défense israélienne.* Monaco: Éditions du Rocher, 1998.

Yodfat, Aryeh. *The Soviet Union and Revolutionary Iran.* London: Croom Helm, 1984.

Zabih, Sepehr. *The Iranian Military in Revolution and War.* New York: Routledge, 1988.

Biographies and Memoirs

Aburish, Said. *Saddam Hussein: The Politics of Revenge*. London: Blooms-
 bury, 2001.
Bakhtiar, Chapour. *Ma fidélité*. Paris: Albin Michel, 1982.
Balaghi, Shiva. *Saddam Hussein: A Biography*. London: Greenwood Press
 2008.
Bani-Sadr, Abol Hassan. *Le complot des ayatollahs*. Paris: Éditions La Dé-
 couverte, 1989.
———. *L'Espérance trahie*. Paris: Éditions Papyrus, 1982.
Bani-Sadr, Abol Hassan, and Jean-Charles Deniau. *My Turn to Speak:
 Iran, the Revolution and Secret Deals with the US*. New York: Brassey's,
 1991.
Bouvet, Béatrice, and Patrick Denaud. *Tarek Aziz: le diplomate de Saddam
 Hussein*. Paris: L'Harmattan, 2000.
Christopher, Warren. *Chances of a Lifetime*. New York: Scribner, 2001.
Hachtroudi, Fariba. *Ali Khamenei ou les larmes de Dieu*. Paris: Gallimard,
 2011.
Karsh, Efraim, and Inari Rautsi. *Saddam Hussein: A Political Biography*.
 London: Grove Press, 2002.
Khomeyni (Ayatollah). *Pour un gouvernement islamique*. Paris: Fayolle,
 1979.
La chute: interrogatoires de Saddam Hussein par le FBI. Preface and com-
 mentary by Pierre-Jean Luizard. Paris: Éditions Inculte/Actes Sud,
 Temps réel collection, 2010.
Moin, Baqer. *Khomeini: Life of the Ayatollah*. London: I. B. Tauris, 1999.
Saint-Prot, Charles. *Saddam Hussein, un gaullisme arabe?* Paris: Albin
 Michel, 1987.
Seale, Patrick. *Abu Nidal: A Gun for Hire*. New York: Random House,
 1992.
———. *Assad of Syria*. London: I. B. Tauris, 1988.

Fiction Films and Documentaries

Al-Qadisiya. Iraqi film directed by Salah Abouseif recreating the medi-
 eval Battle of al-Qadisiyyah between Arabs and Persians for control
 of Iraq. 1981. 120 minutes.

rgo. American film directed by Ben Affleck about the CIA's attempt to rescue American hostages in Tehran. 2012. 120 minutes.

Back to Babylon. French-Iraqi documentary directed by Abbas Fahdel showing the war's negative impact on Iraqi society. 2002. 52 minutes.

Bashu, Gharibeh-ye Kuchek ("Bashu, The Little Stranger"). Iranian film directed by Bahram Beizai telling the adventures of a boy trying to escape the war. 1986. 117 minutes.

Barzakhiha ("The Imperiled"). Iranian film directed by Iraj Ghaderi relating the adventures of several Iranian combatants who escape from prison and are forced to enroll on the front. 1982. 94 minutes.

Bassidji. French-Iranian film directed by Mehran Tamadon about the saga of the Basijis during the Iran-Iraq War and their lasting influence on Iranian society. 2010. 114 minutes.

Dar Koocheha-ye Eshgh ("In the Alleys of Love"). Iranian film directed by Khosrow Sinai about the battle of Khorramshahr. 1990. 83 minutes.

Ekhrajiha ("The Rejected"). Iranian film directed by Massoud Dehnamaki about war veterans' difficult return to civilian life. 2007. 90 minutes.

Enamoured of Love. Iranian documentary directed by Morteza Avini about the war's principal campaigns and the mystical connection between the Pasdaran and Imam Khomeini. 1988. 45 minutes.

The Flowers of Kirkuk. Italian-Iraqi film directed by Fariborz Kamkari about the repression of the Kurds during the Iran-Iraq War. 2010. 115 minutes.

Gilaneh. Iranian film directed by Rakhshan Bani-Etemad and Mohsen Abdolvahab following the life of a family disrupted by the Iran-Iraq War. 2005. 84 minutes.

House of Saddam. British television film directed by Alex Holmes and Stephen Butchard following the career of Saddam Hussein, notably in the period of the Iran-Iraq War. BBC Drama Production. 2008. 4 hours.

The Iran-Iraq War. British documentary directed by Terry Lloyd. ITN Production, VT Editor. 1991. 37 minutes. Available on YouTube.

Living in the Clouds. Iranian documentary directed by Azizolah Hamidnejad about combat in Iraqi Kurdistan. 1988. 45 minutes.

Persepolis. French animated film directed by Marjane Satrapi and Vincent Paronnaud relating the experiences of a teenage girl in

post-Revolutionary Iran, notably during the Iran-Iraq War. 200;
95 minutes.

Web sites

http://en.wikipedia.org/wiki/Iran%E2%80%93Iraq_War ("free" encyclo
   pedia rich with information about the Iran-Iraq War).
www.globalsecurity.org (site featuring a detailed synthesis of the Iran-Iraq
   War).
www.fas.org ("cult" Web site operated by the Federation of American
   Scientists and particularly useful for matters related to both belligerents' development of weapons of mass destruction).

ACKNOWLEDGMENTS

I must first acknowledge my Iraqi and Iranian friends, who will recognize themselves here, as well as those who participated in these epic events and were kind enough to provide me with their precious accounts. For obvious security reasons, many have chosen to remain anonymous: may these few lines express my sincere gratitude to them. My special thanks to the diplomats, industrialists, journalists, military personnel, and academics who enlightened me with their analyses. Thanks also to all those who made it possible for me to access the archives of the Service Historique de la Défense in Vincennes. I must specifically acknowledge Frédéric Guelton, whose advice, contacts, and friendship were most precious on this quest. Thanks also to Kevin Woods, David Palkki, Christian Ostermann, Lorry Fenner, and Pieter Biersteker, who helped me access the oral archives and "Saddam's tapes" in Washington. All my gratitude to Bernard Hourcade, who provided me with crucial keys to interpret power struggles in Iran; to Pesach Malovany, for his encyclopedic knowledge of the Iraqi army; to Farzin Nadimi, for his understanding of the energy stakes; to François Heisbourg, for his exceptional atlas; and to Tom Cooper and Farzad Bishop, for the extreme kindness with which they responded to unending questions. I am grateful to Jacques Frémeaux for agreeing to supervise my postdoctoral habilitation to carry out this research, which this volume allowed me to defend at Université Paris IV Sorbonne.

Thank you to the directors of the Institut de Recherche Stratégique de l'Ecole Militaire (IRSEM) [Institute for Strategic Research at the Military School] for their trust and support. I would also like to express my gratitude to Giuseppe Vitiello and the entire library team at the NATO Defense College, as well as to Florence Gaub and Michel Goya for their help with documentation. Finally, my heartfelt thanks to André Scialom, Jean Nicolas Gauthier, and Laurent Henninger for their careful rereading, their wise advice, and their friendly support. As ever, my closing thanks go to my wife and daughters, who showed extraordinary patience while I wrote this book.

INDEX

Cavallot, Guy, 175
Cave, George, 79
CEA (French Atomic Energy Commission), 93
Ceasefire/truce/peace: Iraqi proposals for, 43–44, 135, 136, 173, 203, 217–218, 243, 326–327, 395; Iranian refusals of, 44, 136, 173, 203, 218, 234, 243, 327, 357, 395; Khomeini's rejection of Resolution 514, 222; UN's proposal for, 234, 411–412; Soviet Union's offer to mediate, 339; UN's call for, 357; Iraqi conditions for peace, 464; Iranian acceptance of, 465; Iranian refusal to negotiate with Iraq, 466; acceptance of, 467–468; negotiations for, 474
Chaban-Delmas, Jacques, 89
Chamran, Mustafa, 21, 72
Chatty, Habib, 202
Chemical weapons, 234, 253, 267–268; Saddam's consideration of, 189; Iraq's acquisition of, 298–299; Iran's opposition to, 300; Soviets' use of, 300; defenses against, 301, 320, 451; Iraq's use of, 354, 355, 367, 399, 451; used at Basra, 396; Iran's use of, 398; in Halabja massacre, 438; in recapture of al-Faw peninsula, 441; banning of, 481; prohibition of, 587n14; deaths directly linked to, 589n9
Chernenko, Konstantin, 277
Chevallier, Guy, 297
Chevènement, Jean-Pierre, 94
Cheysson, Claude, 95, 275, 276
Child soldiers, 345. See also Basijis
Chile, 550
China: distrust of Soviet Union, 86; reaction to Iran-Iraq conflict, 86–87; military assistance to Iraq, 87, 190, 230, 242, 290, 547; change in position on Iran-Iraq conflict, 241; relations with Iran, 241, 579n31; military assistance to Iran, 241–242, 404, 551; willingness to supply arms to Iran, 291; ability to influence Iran, 395; agreement with Saudi Arabia, 405; support of peace plan proposal, 411; effects of war on, 480

Chirac, Jacques, 90, 91, 288, 415, 416, 418, 419
Christopher, Warren, 79
Chronology, 489–510
CIA: support for Iranian opposition, 6; work with SAVAK, 53; assistance to Kurds, 56; attempts to rekindle ties with Iranian leadership, 72; negotiations for hostages' freedom, 79; concerns about possible Iran-Iraq conflict, 80; attempts to recruit Bani-Sadr, 170; military assistance to Iraq, 206
CIEEMG (Commission interministérielle pour l'étude des exportations de matériel de guerre), 296
Civilians: bombing of, 247–248, 252, 302–303, 310, 325–327, 393, 435–436; Iran Air Flight 655, 457–459; Pan Am Flight 103, 460–461; death toll of, 471
Clergy, in Iran, 8, 63–64, 76, 123, 137, 151, 156, 483–484
Cogan, Charles, 280
Cold War, 48, 70, 83, 234, 239–240, 412
Combatant Clergy Association, 449
Comité de solidarité avec les prisonniers politiques arabes et du Moyen-Orient (CSPPA), 285, 288
Commission interministérielle pour l'étude des exportations de matériel de guerre (CIEEMG), 296
Committee of Solidarity with Arab and Middle East Political Prisoners, 285, 288
Communications: decoding, by Iraqi army, 255, 257, 269, 342; Iranian, 256, 257, 263, 352
Communists: Iraqi Communist Party, 54, 64; Tudeh Communist Party, 63, 76, 220, 240, 339, 342, 483; Iranian Communist Party, 83. See also Soviet Union
Congress of Vienna, 46
Constantinople Protocol, 47, 57
Convoy, 475
Cordes, Rudolph, 97
Cornéa, Aurel, 286
Cossiga, Francesco, 98

Raz, Ze'ev, 165, 167
Razak, Samir Abdul, 139, 371
RCC (Revolutionary Command Council),
   48, 58, 65–66, 219
Reagan, Ronald, 79, 81, 206, 277, 278, 279,
   381; plans to suffocate Soviet Union
   and Iran, 334; in Iran-Contra scandal,
   379, 386; reprisals against Iranian navy,
   429; summit with Gorbachev, 451;
   reaction to destruction of Flight 655,
   459–460
Realpolitik, 53
Red Sea, mines in, 310–311
Regier, Frank, 280
Reiss, Clotilde, 470
Religion: Shiite Islam, 4, 45; in conflict
   between Ottomans and Persians, 45;
   Islamic fundamentalist movement,
   63–64; Iraq's appearance of as victim
   of Iranian fundamentalism, 269, 290;
   and use of chemical weapons, 300;
   Saddam's avoidance of sectarianism,
   313; Iran's use of sectarianism, 314–315;
   Sunni Islam, 486. See also Islam;
   Islamic Revolution; Shiite Muslims
Reporters. See Journalists
Republican Guard, 322, 355, 356, 393, 434,
   441. See also Military, Iraqi
Reuter, Zvi, 116
Revolutionary Command Council (RCC),
   48, 58, 65–66, 219
Revolutionary Guards: after attempted
   coup, 5; accountability of, 16–17; rivalry
   with regular army, 19, 190, 200–201;
   command of, 19–20, 62, 179, 226; at
   Qasr-e-Shirin, 34; defense of Geilan
   Zarb, 35; in Sumer, 36; defense of
   Ahwaz, 42; creation of, 62; Martyrs'
   Foundation, 135, 178, 226, 315; power of,
   136; rivalry with air force, 139; after
   Operation Hoveyzeh, 156; structure of,
   156–157; Kazemi, 183–184; and liberation of Khorramshahr, 213, 215; lack of
   professionalism and training, 225;
   creation of Pasdaran ministry,
   225–226; equipment allocated to, 226;
   recruitment, 226; in Kurdistan, 248,

249, 253; communications, 256, 263,
   352; criticism of regular army, 269;
   operational doctrine, 300; naval
   branch, 324, 343, 421–422; plan for
   offensive by, 324; rotation of forces,
   360; given credit for regular army's
   achievements, 371; maritime raids by,
   377; at Basra, 396–397; request for end
   to hostilities, 401, 455; in politics,
   483–484; at outbreak of hostilities, 522;
   reinforcements, 535–537. See also Army,
   Iranian; Basijis; Military, Iranian
Rezaee, Mohsen, 122, 179, 200, 213, 215,
   221, 226, 235, 324, 350, 388, 396, 397,
   450
Reza Pahlavi, 47
Rochot, Philippe, 286, 287
Rogers, William, 456, 457, 460, 462
Romania, 548
Rondot, Philippe, 287
Rossignol, Hubert, 275
Rouhani, Hassan, 316, 433
Rouleau, Eric, 284, 286
RPR (Rassemblement pour la Répub-
   lique), 285–286
Ruhani, Hossein, 123
Rumsfeld, Donald, 279
Rushdie, Salman, 475
Russia, 46, 47. See also Soviet Union

Sabah, Ali, 371, 465
Sacrifice, children taught virtues of,
   345
Sadat, Anwar al-, 9, 58, 83, 105–106
Sadeq, Jafar, 437–438
Sadik, Ahmad, 409
Sadr, Mohammad al-, 3, 575n7
Sadr, Muqtada al-, 575n7
Sadr, Musa al-, 109–110
Safavi, Rahim, 122, 215
Saïda Agreement, 108
Sajid, Kamel, 437, 454
Saleh, Ali Abdullah, 110
Saleh, Fuad Ali, 415
Salim, Mohammed, 22, 33
Salimi, Mohammad, 220, 316
Samarra'i, Wafiq al-, 257, 259